Risk Management Essentials

The National Alliance Research Academy

THE NATIONAL ALLIANCE
RESEARCH ACADEMY

RISK AND INSURANCE STUDIES

Austin, Texas 2009

Risk Management Essentials
First Edition

Note:

While the information in this publication is accurate at time of printing, the risk management strategies and applications it offers may not be complete or absolute. It is sold with the understanding that the publisher is not engaged in rendering legal or other professional services. The explanations and examples may not be applicable in all situations and jurisdictions. There are many ways to evaluate risk and appropriate remedies, and some companies may have different opinions or interpretations that deviate from the perspectives contained in this work.

Although every reasonable effort has been made to verify the accuracy of the information in this book, readers are urged to check independently on matters of specific interest or concern. The National Alliance Research Academy makes no warranties or guarantees regarding the accuracy of the information contained in this publication.

ISBN 1-878204-35-1

The National Alliance Research Academy

P. O. Box 27027

Austin, TX 78755-2027

www.TheNationalAlliance.com

The National Alliance Research Academy

The Academy is a non-profit corporation, funded entirely through publication sales and affiliation dues. The Academy promotes and conducts practical research on all aspects of the risk management and insurance industry. As an extension of its robust research program, The Academy publishes monographs and studies aimed at serving the needs of those desiring to share in the growth and promote the professionalism of the insurance industry.

The Academy also serves as the research and development department of The National Alliance, which conducts educational programs for insurance and risk management professionals across the U.S., as well as in Mexico. Additionally, The Academy provides support to higher education through the University Associate Certified Risk Managers (UACRM) Program and assists educational institutions in their efforts to attract new people into the risk management and insurance industries.

Academy Membership

Research Associate: $1,000

For corporate entities or associations

With the support of our Research Associates we are able to enhance the profession we all serve. Contributions from Academy Research Associates help to support the research and publication activities of The Academy. They also assist The Academy in its efforts to attract students to the insurance industry through our career-oriented programs we have developed in partnership with various educational institutions. We invite you to become an Academy Research Associate. Benefits include:

- 10% off Academy publications

- Complimentary subscription to The National Alliance's Resources magazine, a great source of valuable technical information and schedules of all National Alliance programs

- Membership dues and contributions are tax deductible

- Complimentary copies of new publications

- Company name included in the Forward of all new publications

- Company name and logo included on the Academy website

- Complimentary copies of the research bulletin, Preliminary Findings, sent periodically with new discoveries and statistics based on Academy works in progress

- Opportunities to participate in upcoming studies and receive Executive Summaries of the results

Academy Associate: $35

Industry practitioners who are not designated, dues-paying CICs, CRMs, or CISRs. Annual Academy dues are $35.

- 10% discount on all Academy publications

- Complimentary subscription to The National Alliance's Resources magazine, a great source of valuable technical information and schedules of all National Alliance programs

- Complimentary copies of the research bulletin, Preliminary Findings, sent periodically with new discoveries and statistics based on Academy works in progress

- Opportunities to participate in upcoming studies and receive Executive Summaries of the results

Academy Fellowship: $15

Designated, dues-paying CICs, CRMs, or CISRs

- 10% discount on all Academy publications

- Complimentary subscription to The National Alliance's Resources magazine, a great source of valuable technical information and schedules of all National Alliance programs

- Complimentary copies of the research bulletin, Preliminary Findings, sent periodically with new discoveries and statistics based on Academy works in progress

- Opportunities to participate in upcoming studies and receive Executive Summaries of the results

Visit our website at www.TheNationalAlliance.com and click on "The Academy" to learn more about membership benefits and how to join. Or call 800-633-2165 for more information.

Research Associates

The Academy extends its gratitude to the current Research Associates who made publication of *Risk Management Essentials* possible through their support:

 Bancorp South

 Bowen, Miclette & Britt

 Brotherhood Mutual Insurance

 Gilbert's Insurance & Consulting

 ISU Insurance Services

MarketScout, Inc.

 The Omnia Group

 State Auto Insurance

Van Dyke Rankin Insurance

Alabama IIA

 IIAB of Arizona

 PIA of Connecticut

 PIA of Florida

 PIA of Georgia

 IIA of Houston

 PIIA of Illinois

 IIA of Indiana

 PIA of Indiana

 Kansas AIA

 PIA of Kentucky

 Massachusetts AIA

 Michigan AIA

 Minnesota IIAB

 Missouri AIA

 Nevada IIA

 PIA of New Jersey

 PIA of New York

 IIA of North Carolina

 PIA of Ohio

 IIA of Oklahoma

 Insurance Agents and Brokers (PA, MD, DE)

 IIAB of South Carolina

 Insurors of Tennessee

 IIA of Texas

 PIA of Wisconsin

 PIA of Virginia & District of Columbia

 PIA of Washington & Oregon

Foreword

The National Alliance Research Academy has designed *Risk Management Essentials* for those who are relatively new to the field of risk management and related topics. Experienced risk managers can still use this study as a ready reference source, and novice risk managers can learn more about the different theories and concepts.

Risk Management Essentials is a valuable study guide for professionals who are attending any of the Certified Risk Managers (CRM) programs. Insurance agency personnel can also use this study to learn the basics of risk management and apply these principles when assisting their clients. A study guide CD is included with this book to help readers check their knowledge and learn to apply the material.

The Academy would like to thank the many National Alliance faculty members who contributed to the writing and editing of this book. Special recognition goes out to Richard Rudolph, Ph.D., CPCU, ARM, APA, ARP, AIAF, CSP, who edited the entire book, enabling us to complete this important study. The authors' and editors' expertise and understanding of risk management issues have resulted in this comprehensive guide. A good understanding of the materials presented in this book should give each student a solid foundation on which to build the professional knowledge necessary to succeed in the risk management arena.

Those of us at The National Alliance want to be your partners in advanced education as you proceed with your professional insurance industry career. To obtain information on other Academy publications or National Alliance program schedules, please visit our website, www.TheNationalAlliance.com, or call 800-633-2165.

As always, we encourage your comments and recommendations for future editions of this study guide, and we solicit your ideas about research studies you would like to see us undertake in the future.

Sincerely,

William T. Hold, Ph.D., CIC, CPCU, CLU

President, The National Alliance Research Academy

Acknowledgements

The National Alliance Research Academy would like to thank the following individuals who contributed to the production of *Risk Management Essentials*:

Authors and Technical Editors

Bettye Buffington, CIC, CRM, CPCU, ARM, CPIA, AAI
Central Insurance Services, Inc.
Beltsville, Maryland

Richard Clarke, CIC, CPCU, RPLU
J. Smith Lanier & Company
Atlanta, Georgia

Don Donaldson, CIC, CRM, RPA, CHS-III
LA Group
Montgomery, Texas

John Earle, Ph.D., CIC, CLU, ChFC, CFP, ARM
University of Richmond
Richmond, Virginia

Dale Fenwick, ARM
Sovereign Insurance Services
Apopka, Florida

George Gladis, CIC, CRM, ARM
Huntleigh McGeHee
St. Louis, Missouri

Jim Green, CRM, ARM
Business Risk Solutions, LLC
Hernando, Florida

Michael Hay, CRM, CGFM, CPPM
The National Alliance for Insurance Education & Research
Austin, Texas

Steven Holland, CRM, ARM
University of Arizona
Tucson, Arizona

David McKinney, CIC, CRM, CSP, ALCM
IMA Financial Group
Wichita, Kansas

Margo Ramage, CIC, CRM, CPCU, ARM
Eisenstein Malanchuk
Washington, District of Columbia

W. L. Richard, CIC, ARM, AAI
Insight Consulting Group
Peoria, Arizona

Wayne Rogers, CRM, CPCU, CLU
Rogers Consulting, LLC
Brentwood, Tennessee

Richard Rudolph, Ph.D., CPCU, ARM, APA, ARP, AIAF, AAM
Seaver, Rudolph & Associates, Inc.
Georgetown, Indiana

Jerry Stevens, Ph.D., CCM
University of Richmond
Richmond, Virginia

Sarah Warhaftig, J.D.
Sigma Consulting Corp.
New Orleans, Louisiana

Gregory Wilson, CIC, CRM, ARM, CSP
USI Insurance Services
Houston, Texas

David Wood, Ph.D., CRM, CPCU
Appalachian State University
Boone, North Carolina

Kenneth Wood, CIC, CRM, CPCU, ARM, ARe,
AIC, AIS
Knowledge Learning Corporation
Portland, Oregon

Cory Zass, BSc, ASA, MAAA, FCA
Actuarial Risk Management
Austin, Texas

Production Editors and Graphic Designers

Jim Cuprisin, CIC, CRM, ARP
The National Alliance for Insurance Education &
Research
Austin, Texas

Becky Keeling
The National Alliance for Insurance Education &
Research
Austin, Texas

Carol Middlekauff, ARM
Freelance Writer/Editor
Austin, Texas

Priscilla Oehlert, CIC, CRM, ARM
The National Alliance for Insurance Education &
Research
Austin, Texas

Scott Williams
Think Ink Design
Austin, Texas

Brief Table of Contents

Table of Contents

SECTION ONE: PRINCIPLES OF RISK MANAGEMENT

Chapter 4: Ethics and Risk Management Policy **93**

SECTION TWO: ANALYSIS OF RISK

Chapter 5: Gathering Loss Data **103**

Chapter 6: Qualitative Analysis **113**

SECTION THREE: FINANCE OF RISK

SECTION FOUR: CONTROL OF RISK

SECTION FIVE: PRACTICE OF RISK MANAGEMENT

Chapter 20: Information Technology for Risk Managers 387

Chapter 21: Allocating the Cost of Risk 395

Introduction

A Unique Risk Perspective

Risks are all around us. We face them every day. In spite of actions we may take to avoid or control them, we will continue to face risks. After all, "The more things change, the more they remain the same." Think about the risks you faced by the time you arrived at work today:

You got out of bed, perhaps before dawn, and shuffled past bedposts and a dresser to the bathroom without turning on a light. You did turn on the light in the bathroom, probably barefoot on a bare floor in the vicinity of water pipes that may have burst during the night. You climbed into a plastic or ceramic booth, sprayed it with water, a natural lubricant, and covered yourself with soap, a very slippery substance. You stepped out onto a skidding mat, and still barefoot on that bare floor, perhaps still dripping wet, you may have turned on a radio or even a TV. Then you dried your hair, perhaps still barefoot and holding a hot electrical appliance just inches from your head over a sink full of water. You applied a variety of chemicals and volatile vapors to your skin, perhaps scraping some of it off with a sharp-edged tool.

During a morning thunderstorm, you fixed breakfast, using a coffee maker, toaster, refrigerator, and a microwave oven or stove. The milk, bacon, and eggs, nurtured by insecticides, pesticides, and growth hormones, could have been out of the refrigerator for several hours before you even bought them and the things that cause botulism, anthrax, and trichinosis were having a big party, just waiting to make you sick. Perhaps you then stuck your hands in hot dishwater bubbling with an unnatural slippery substance. You still may have been barefoot when you slopped water on that sheet-vinyl floor beside that high-voltage dishwasher. Under those bubbles in the sink were knives, forks, and the possibility of a broken glass or plate.

You drove to work, passing (or being passed by) speeding hulks of metal driven by strangers who may have been under the influence of drugs, alcohol, or anger, or even stupidity and carelessness. You may have been the one shaving, putting on makeup, reading the newspaper, tuning the radio, or answering the cell phone while maneuvering your car, with its bald tires, full tank of gas, and parts made of caustic chemicals.

Eventually, you rode the elevator, a steel cage, which was suspended on a thin metal wire, installed by the lowest bidder, inspected by a low-paid government employee, and maintained by a low-level employee of the lowest bidder, to the highest floor of a glass and steel building, built by the lowest bidder's brother-in-law.

Before sitting down, you poured yourself a cup of scalding coffee and then walked with it to the high-voltage printer, chatting with another half-asleep worker who likewise sipped hot sugary liquid, but over a desk full of sensitive electronic equipment.

And you didn't think you faced many risks, did you?

CRM Course Preparation

Because these personal risks only begin to reflect the risks businesses face every day, risk managers (who hold jobs at corporations, insurance companies, insurance agencies or brokerages, captives, and consulting firms) must confront the challenges of managing this risk with the best possible foundation of knowledge on the subject.

Risk Management Essentials attempts to anchor that foundation by presenting a well-rounded selection of subjects, for use as a reference tool or as a solid review of the materials before attending a Certified Risk Manager (CRM) program. Though there are differences, the topics included in this study are closely aligned with the CRM course materials.

Participants can read specific chapters from this study before attending a CRM program. Then the instruction from the teachers, and much serious review after class, will reinforce the material, making them much better prepared for their exams. For each of the five CRM Programs, the appropriate chapters to review are listed below:

CRM Principles of Risk Management

Chapter 1: Introduction to Risk Management

Chapter 2: Risk Identification

Chapter 3: Financial Statements

Chapter 4: Ethics and Risk Management Policy

CRM Analysis of Risk

Chapter 5: Gathering Loss Data

Chapter 6: Qualitative Analysis

Chapter 7: Cash Discounting

Chapter 8: Forecasting

CRM Financing of Risk

Chapter 9: Simple Risk Financing

Chapter 10: Loss Sensitive Financing

Chapter 11: Alternative Financing

Chapter 12: Actuarial, Auditing, and Accounting

CD Study Guide

The CD included with this book is intended for your use as a study aid and for knowledge reinforcement. On that CD, you will find two documents with 8 to 15 questions for each of the 24 chapters. One of the two documents contains the questions without the answers so you can use them to test your knowledge. The other document contains the questions with the answers so you can check your work.

Although some of the questions may be similar because they cover much of the same subject matter, the Q&A sections on the CD are not the same questions that will appear on your CRM exams.

SECTION 1

PRINCIPLES OF RISK MANAGEMENT

Chapter 1

Introduction to Risk Management

Introduction

Risk is present every day in everyone's life, and in some form, the attempt to manage that risk has been around for a long time. If you search the Internet for "risk management," you will find entries on project risk management, risk management for small and beginning farmers and ranchers, healthcare risk management, medical risk management, project risk management, army risk management, enterprise risk management, financial risk management, operational risk management, and many others. Risk management has come to mean different things to different people. In this book, we are attempting to provide the reader with some of the tools of operational risk management as taught in the Certified Risk Managers (CRM) program. It is meant to be a basic primer for insurance professionals interested in adding risk management to the services offered to clients and for others interested in pursuing a career in risk management, as well as serving as preparation for those planning to take any of the CRM courses offered by The National Alliance for Insurance Education & Research.

Origins of Civil Responsibility and Risk Sharing

The oldest known code of law is the Hammurabic Code. It was a written by Hammurabi, king of Babylonia (1792-1750 bc) and recorded in cuneiform writing on clay tablets. The code encompassed all aspects of life in Babylonia by codifying criminal, commercial, and personal activities. For example, some provisions cover the responsibilities of physicians to their patients and the responsibility of various tradesmen to their customers, while other provisions detail the financial responsibility of a son to his aged father. The code spells out responsibilities and imposed penalties, often very harsh in contemporary terms, for various injuries and compensation for injuries that depended upon station in life. It was the first example of written law that compensated victims and punished perpetrators.

Another early writing that spelled out the concept of liability and loss prevention can be found in the Hebrew scripture, known as the Old Testament. In Deuteronomy 22:8, we find, "When you build a new house, make a parapet around your roof so that you may not bring the guilt of bloodshed on your house if someone falls from the roof." – New International Version

In ancient China, merchants plying the Yangtze and other major rivers faced the loss of their vessels and cargos because of cataracts and rapids in the rivers. To minimize this risk of loss, the merchants came upon a simple but effective risk-sharing plan. Instead of each merchant facing the loss of his entire cargo and vessel, should he be unlucky enough to have the vessel break apart or capsize while attempting passage through the dangerous waters, the merchants divided their cargo among all the vessels present. Then, if one or two vessels were lost but the others emerged safe, each merchant lost only a small portion of his cargo. In this sharing mechanism, the merchants exchanged the uncertainty of risk for a smaller certain cost; the inconvenience of unloading and reloading their cargo.

Phoenician, Greek, and Roman shippers further refined this method of sharing risk by creating insurance-like contracts called bottomry and respondentia contracts. Bottomry contracts provided compensation for the loss of the "bottom", the vessel itself, while respondentia contracts focused on the cargo. The funds for repaying the shippers came from interested parties, shippers, ship owners, and investors, who took a payment for assuming the risk. These practices flourished until the Middle Ages and the rise of the Catholic Church as a political power. The charges for these contracts amounted to a higher interest rate on loans, usury. However, by papal bull (a particular type of charter issued by a pope), the charging of interest, or usury, was a sin. Originally, this sin was only of the venal variety, one that was often conveniently overlooked, but as the practice grew, the degree of sin was elevated to a mortal sin, one that imperiled the mortal soul of the Catholic who entered into the usurious agreement.

Eventually, this dilemma was resolved by a new contract that separated the risk of loss and the interest charge, with the interest contract being assumed by non-Catholics, notably Jewish merchants and bankers, and the Lombard merchants who were operating under a papal dispensation covering the sinful practice with insurance. (Lombard Street in London, a long-time center for insurance, was named for these merchants who left Italy for London during the growth of marine insurance in England during the 16th century.) The resulting risk-sharing contracts were called polizza, from which the word "policy" was derived.

As early as the late 15th century, ship owners and shippers collected in the ale houses that abounded around the docks in London to share news of voyages, perils of the sea, and to socialize. As England grew into a world economic power, the ship owners and shippers began to use risk-sharing ideas borrowed from those early Mediterranean merchants. The ship owners and shippers used bottomry and respondentia contracts to provide for indemnification for losses suffered by their fellow shippers. As the practice became more refined, and as coffee was introduced at Balliol College (thanks to a foreign student from Crete), the merchants moved away from the sometimes rough-and-tumble ale houses to the more staid coffee shops, one of which was owned by Edward Lloyd.

Lloyd's Coffee House on Lombard Street in London became well known as a meeting place for merchants and ship owners. To encourage the popularity of his coffee house as a spot for conducting maritime business transactions, Lloyd offered a variety of services to the merchants, one of the most useful being the publication Lloyd's News, a reliable source of business-related information. The business of shipping and insurance agreements continued after Lloyd's death in 1713, and eventually a formal organization evolved. By 1774 Lloyd's of London was out of the coffee business entirely and in the insurance business for good. Incorporated in 1871 by an act of Parliament, Lloyd's of London went on to become one of the most famous insurers in the world, expanding from maritime interests to all types of insurance by 1900.

From those earliest days of simply sharing the risk, then sharing information, ship owners and merchants would meet at Lloyd's to enter into agreements to offset the possibility of a large uncertain loss, with a small certain loss in the form of a premium, thereby decreasing their risk. This formal exchange of information and exchange of risk defined insurance as we know it today.

Types of Risk

There are two types of risk: pure and speculative. With <u>pure risk</u>, there is only a chance of loss. Common examples include a building burning down or an employee being injured in an accident. Insurance is usually concerned with pure risk.

With <u>speculative risk</u>, there is a chance of loss and a chance of gain. Speculative risk is usually associated with business or financial risk. The value of the company's stock may go up or it may go down; there may be a market for the company's goods, or its product may have become obsolete.

Sometimes, <u>gambling</u> is included as a separate type of risk, defined as chance of loss or gain, but the probabilities for a gambler favor a loss. For example, the patrons in a casino are gambling but the casino is not. The odds are always in the favor of the casino. The reason that the casinos are not gambling is that their chance for gain on an annual basis is 100%. The odds may favor the house in varying degrees, but the house always wins. However, we choose to ignore gambling as a distinct type of risk because it is speculative risk, and it is illegal except in narrowly defined circumstances.

Definition of Risk

Various definitions of risk appear in *The American Heritage Dictionary:* (1) the possibility of suffering harm or loss; danger; a factor, thing, element, or course involving uncertain danger; (2) a hazard: *"the usual risks of the desert: rattlesnakes, the heat, and lack of water"* (Frank Clancy); (3a) the danger or probability of loss to an insurer, or (3b) the amount that an insurance company stands to lose; (4a) the variability of returns from an investment, or (4b) the chance of nonpayment of a debt; and (5) one considered with respect to the possibility of loss: *a poor risk.*[1]

In the risk management arena (including the insurance world), we find another set of definitions of risk, usually depending upon the particular job function or area of expertise of the source. To an underwriter, the risk is the subject of the insurance, the person or entity being insured. To some agents or brokers, the risk may be the insured or the exposure, such as a building or a vehicle. To others, the risk may be the peril (like wind or fire) or the hazard (like poor housekeeping). Some of these terms have very specific meanings and will be explained in detail later. To the CEO or CFO of an organization, the risk may be the uncertainty or possibility of an event occurring.

In risk management, we use four definitions, each for a specific purpose. Risk is (1) chance or probability of loss; (2) uncertainty concerning a loss; (3) a possibility of a variation of outcomes from a given set of circumstances; and (4) the difference between expected losses and actual losses. While definitions (3) and (4) appear to be very similar, they are, in fact, importantly different.

Definition (3) applies to situations in which the outcomes are varied and uncertain, even though the circumstances may be nearly identical. Consider this scenario: Two buildings are located just 10 feet apart. Given the circumstance of a fire, the wooden building is more likely to be destroyed than the concrete block building. Given the circumstance of a tornado, both are likely to be destroyed. The risk from fire is greater than the risk from a tornado because the possibility of a variation of outcome. With a tornado, both are likely to be destroyed so there is a lesser possibility of variation of outcomes.

---

1 "risk" The American Heritage® Dictionary of the English Language, Fourth Edition. Houghton Mifflin Company, 2004. *Answers.com* 27 Jul. 2006. http://www.answers.com/topic/risk

Definition (4) suggests that one can forecast or predict losses (more about this later), so the risk is the variation between what is predicted and what actually occurs. This latter definition encompasses the first two definitions of risk (chance of loss and uncertainty concerning loss).

With respect to chance of loss, we often associate probabilities of occurrence. For instance, assume the probabilities of the following events happening are:

$P_{(A)} = 1\%$ $P_{(B)}) = 50\%$ $P_{(C)} = 99\%$

Which of the above probabilities is riskier? P(A) has little chance of occurring while P(C) has a high probability of occurring. However, neither of these events has great risk; the outcome is fairly certain on both. P(B) has the highest degree of uncertainty or risk because it has the greatest uncertainty in outcomes. It is far "riskier" than P(A) but far less certain than P(B) in terms of chance of loss.

General Classes of Risk

There are six general classes of risk that affect all organizations, regardless of the economic activity the organization. These classes of risk may involve pure risk or speculative risk.

Economic risk is the risk arising out what the organization does, or the risk from its operations, marketplace, financial, or entrepreneurial risk. For example, when financing a project, a company encounters economic risk that the project's output will not generate sufficient revenues to cover operating costs and repay debt obligations. **Legal risk** is uncertainty in the applicability or interpretation of contracts, laws, liability, or regulations. **Political risk** is the risk associated with legal changes by the government or governmental interpretations (or reinterpretations) of rules and regulations. For companies, **social risk** concerns public relations, image, and cultural problems. It is the risk of losing touch with the social direction of the country. **Physical risk** is familiar to most people because it encompasses the more "insurance-related" risks of damage or injury to property, persons, and other resources, such as information. **Juridical risk** is the risk of an adverse decision by a judge or jury, or adverse trends in the legal climate, such as the phenomena referred to as run-away juries or the litigation lottery.

Risk Management

Various definitions of risk management have been used over the years, but the basic theme of all of them is to protect the company's assets through identification and analysis of exposures, controlling the exposures, financing of losses with external and internal funds, and implementation and monitoring of the risk management process. While historically risk management has encompassed mostly operational risks, today it can also include enterprise-wide financial risks.

Few organizations operate successfully without a management plan. The old adage, "If you fail to plan, plan to fail," as trite as it may be, does have a kernel of truth. Without a plan, the organization may find itself operating without a purpose or moving toward a goal; it may not even have an idea of what its purpose or goal is, operating in a state of chaos or uncertainty. It may appear no one is in control, and no one may be in control because each thinks someone else is.

Benefits of a Risk Management Program

An organization can expect to gain benefits from having an effective risk management program. Some of these benefits can be measured quantitatively, often in terms of dollars, while others can only be measured qualitatively. Risk management, as defined above, needs a program to provide the greatest benefit to the organization through identification, control, financing, and implementation of the process.

An effective risk management program helps the organization identify its risks and exposures. Once the risks and exposures are identified, the organization can attempt to prevent and reduce costs associated with losses, and to spread the risk financially. Other benefits include determining the organization's risk appetite, integrating risk control and safety programs, and improving the organization's ability to budget and plan.

Recently publicized abuses of organizations, mostly in the corporate world, have increased attention to organizational governance and heightened awareness of an organization's responsibility and accountability to its constituents (e.g., owners, beneficiaries, customers, suppliers, vendors, and regulators). An effective risk management program also provides benefits to the organization because of the following dynamics: (1) increased corporate and individual accountability; (2) pressure on profitability and expense control; (3) competition and the need to grow market share; (4) increased regulatory and compliance requirements; (5) growth of litigation awareness; (6) the ability to increase defensibility through documentation; and (7) improved productivity.

Objectives of a Risk Management Program

The sources of risk to the organization can come from either internal or external sources. Internal sources of risk develop from the operations of the company. External sources of risk include suppliers and distributors, customers, government regulations, industry associations, and competitors. All companies operate in various environments, including our society, economy, the marketplace, and financial markets. These environments create risk for the organization.

Additionally, the risk manager must understand the company's culture and objectives and be able to address the issues that could affect the organization. Some of the issues the risk manager should be concerned with are whether the company wishes to be high or low profile, and the management style of the company (top-down; decentralized; learning organization; team leadership; or quality driven).

Organizations, like individuals, have personalities. Some organizations are daring, willing to venture into the uncertain, to take chances, and to risk what they have in an attempt to make more. Other organizations are more cautious, more careful of protecting what they have. In other words, some organizations are like skydivers, rock climbers and bungee jumpers; others pursue more sedate activities, like playing bridge, doing crossword puzzles, or bird watching.

Risk Appetite

The term risk appetite is frequently used in the risk management community to express the organization's personality in the risk arena. On an organizational level, risk appetite is the amount of risk exposure the organization is willing to accept or retain. Once the company reaches this risk appetite threshold, it implements risk management controls and treatments (such as external funding of the exposure) to bring the exposure level back within the accepted range.

In addition to the organizational personality, the appetite for risk can be affected by the organization's position in its life cycle or its development. A recently started organization may be more willing to assume risk (as if it hasn't already) because it has little to lose, while a mature or stable organization may be concerned about conservation of its assets and position. However, the start-up organization may not have the financial resources to assume much risk, particularly when it needs those resources for expansion and solidifying its position. It becomes clear that it isn't just the willingness to accept risk, but also the financial ability to accept risk that defines an organization's risk appetite.

Risk Terms and Definitions

A number of other terms and definitions are used frequently in risk management. We will consistently use these terms as common or universal language to facilitate communication and understanding. Other risk management and insurance terms can be found in the glossary at the end of this book.

Exposure – a situation, practice, or condition that may lead to an adverse financial consequence; an activity or asset

Hazard – a condition that may give rise to a loss from a given peril; physical, moral, or morale characteristics that make the likelihood of a loss from a given peril greater

Peril – the cause of a loss (e.g., fire, wind, hail, slip and fall)

Incident – an event that disrupts normal activities and may become a loss

Accident – an event definite as to time and place that results in injury or damage to a person or property

Occurrence – an accident with the limitation of time removed (an "accident" that is extended over a period of time rather than a single observable happening)

Loss – a reduction in value

Claim – a demand for payment or an obligation to pay as a result of a loss

Frequency – the number of losses occurring in a given time period

Severity – the dollar amount of a given loss or the aggregate dollar amount of all losses for a given period

Expected losses – projection of the frequency or severity of losses based on loss history, probability distributions, and statistics (This is often called the "loss pic" or "loss pick". "Pic" has been defined as "picture" or "predicted insurance cost", although these terms are really not descriptive of the process, and in a retention plan, certainly have little to do with the predicted insurance cost or premium.)

Cost of Risk

Chief Financial Officers, controllers, and cost accountants are quick to tell you what the cost of their goods and services are and why the price is set where it is. In a steel mill, the output is priced upon the cost of the raw materials and supplies consumed, the labor and benefits associated with labor, shipping and transportation, and a loading for overhead. This process is quantified rather precisely, as the people responsible for manufacturing the product must be able to keep their costs within line so as to competitively price the product yet still make a profit.

Similarly, to manage the risk management process effectively, the risk manager must know the cost of risk. The cost of risk is comprised of all the costs that fund losses or fund the implementation and monitoring of the risk management process. These costs include insurance premiums, retained losses (whether passively or actively retained), risk management departmental costs, costs for outside services, such as risk management consultants, third party administrators, and actuarial services, and finally other considerations which include the indirect costs of loss of productivity, cost of overtime, and lost opportunity costs. Costs generally associated with preventing and reducing losses may be included in the cost of risk if they represent period costs, such as a training session or a safety consultant. The loss prevention and reduction costs associated with physical measures such as a sprinkler system or installation of fire walls are usually included in capital budgeting costs of the company.

XYZ Corporation Cost of Risk

Insurance Costs (net of placement and other fees) $800,000

Retained Losses and Associate Loss Adjustment Expenses. 850,000

Risk Management – Internal (Administration) 100,000

Outside Services:

Consulting, Coverage Placement 50,000

Claims Administration (TPA) 85,000

Other Risk Control. 25,000

Total $1,910,000

Cost of Risk

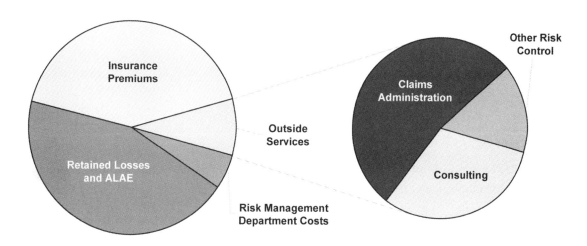

The Risk Management Process

There are five steps in the risk management process:

- Risk Identification

- Risk Analysis

- Risk Control

- Risk Financing

- Risk Administration

There will be more information presented about each of these five steps later in this book. For now, the steps will simply be defined.

The first step is **Risk Identification**, the process of identifying and examining the potential sources of losses faced by the company. The risk identification step is the most important because if exposures have not been identified, they cannot be analyzed, controlled, funded, or monitored. The risk identification step begins by categorizing loss exposures through the Four Logical Classifications of exposures, or the identification of property, human resources, liability and net income exposures. The Four Logical Classifications will be discussed more thoroughly later in this book.

There are various methods used to identify exposures. These will also be more thoroughly discussed later, but some of them are:

- Checklists / Survey Questionnaire

- Flowcharts

- Insurance Policy Analysis

- Physical Inspection

- Net Income / Financial Analysis

- Compliance Review

- Contract Identification and Analysis

- Policy and Procedures Review

- Loss History Review

- Consultation with Experts

Risk Analysis is the assessment of the potential impact that various exposures can have on the firm. There are two types of analysis associated with risk analysis: qualitative and quantitative. Qualitative analysis assesses three main areas:

- Risk assessment – To identify those loss exposures that cannot be easily measured by traditional statistical or financial methods and to understand their impact on the firm's ultimate risks and performance;

- Financial assessment – To identify and assess those broad loss exposures that have a financial impact on the firm but that may be difficult to quantify; and

- Loss data assessment – To identify, understand and apply various methods of assessing loss data and analyze the impact those losses may have on the firm's risk management policy and the ultimate cost of risk.

Quantitative analysis is the assessment of loss projections, cash discounting and net present value calculations, cost benefit analysis, and costs of risk calculations.

Risk analysis also is concerned with the impact of frequency versus severity of losses. Frequency (the number of times a loss occurs) is categorized as almost nil, slight, moderate, and definite. Severity (the dollar amount of each loss) is categorized as slight, significant, and severe.

However, there is no objective level for almost nil, slight, moderate, definite, significant, or severe. These are descriptive labels on a continuum and can be quite subjective. For those who do not like uncertainty and risk, a severity measure of slight is likely to be closer to a measure of severe for those who are not risk adverse.

Risk managers sometimes depict the relationship between frequency and severity on a chart or graph as a means to assist them in making decisions regarding how to handle the risk.

Relationship of Frequency and Severity

FREQUENCY:	Almost Nil (Low)	Slight	Moderate	Definite (High)
SEVERITY:				
Severe (High)	Transfer	Reduce or Prevent	Reduce or Prevent	Avoid
Significant	Retain	Transfer	Reduce or Prevent	Avoid
Slight (Low)	Retain	Transfer	Prevent	Prevent

Low Frequency/Low Severity: Retain

Low Frequency/High Severity: Transfer/Reduce

High Frequency/Low Severity: Prevent

High Frequency/High Severity: Avoid

Risk Control is an action to minimize, at the optimal cost, losses which strike the organization. There are both pre-loss and post-loss techniques that can be implemented. The six techniques for pre-loss risk control are avoidance, loss prevention, loss reduction, exposure segregation (separation or duplication), transfer (contractually or physically), and a combination of techniques. The post-loss techniques are all loss reduction techniques by definition as the loss obviously was not prevented. These techniques include claims management, litigation management, and disaster recovery.

There are also two theories to risk control. One was identified and explained in the early years of the 20th century and the other in the 1970s. The first is that people cause accidents (human approach), and the second is that things or energy cause accidents (engineering approach).

Risk Financing is the acquisition of funds at the least possible cost to pay for the losses that strike the organization. The acquisition of funds can either be from internal sources (retention) or external sources (transfer of financial responsibility). Additionally, retention can be either active or passive.

Active retention can be financed through current expenses, deductible, self-insured retention (SIR), funded or un-funded reserves, use of capital markets (bonds, hedging, lines of credit, etc.), group or single-parent captives, or risk retention and risk purchasing groups.

Passive retention, on the other hand, is the result of a failure to identify an exposure or source of loss, a failure to act on a known exposure or forgetting to act on a known exposure. Making the conscious decision to not act is not passive retention; that would still be active retention. Passive retention is not knowing or not acting on an exposure because it was forgotten or overlooked.

Transfer of risk is contractual in nature. In transfer of risk, the losses are financed from outside the organization. Transfers of risk can be accomplished in two forms: non-insurance transfer and insurance transfer. Non-insurance transfer is accomplished through the contractual use of indemnity agreements, additional insureds (even though the additional insured concept requires insurance, the transferor is not using his own insurance but facilitating the transfer by a contractual requirement with a non-insurance company), hold-harmless agreements, waivers of subrogation, and risk retention and risk purchasing groups. Insurance transfer is substituting, through an insurance contract with an insurance company, a relatively small (known) cost (the insurance premium) for a potentially (unknown) larger cost of a loss.

Risk handling axiom – Effective risk management programs utilize at least one risk control technique and one risk financing technique for each identified exposure!

Risk Administration is implementing and monitoring the risk management process. It encompasses the planning and risk management policy development for the company. Implementation includes commitment and participation, communication, design and structure, training, and accountability. Monitoring includes indicators and measures (benchmarking), continuous tracking, regular evaluation, adjustments and upgrades, and feedback.

Basic Risk Tenets

There are four basic risk tenets or "rules of thumb" commonly discussed and used in risk management.

1. Don't retain more than you can afford to lose.

2. Don't risk a lot for a little.

3. Consider the probabilities or likelihood of loss.

4. Don't treat insurance as a substitute for loss control.

The Risk Management Process

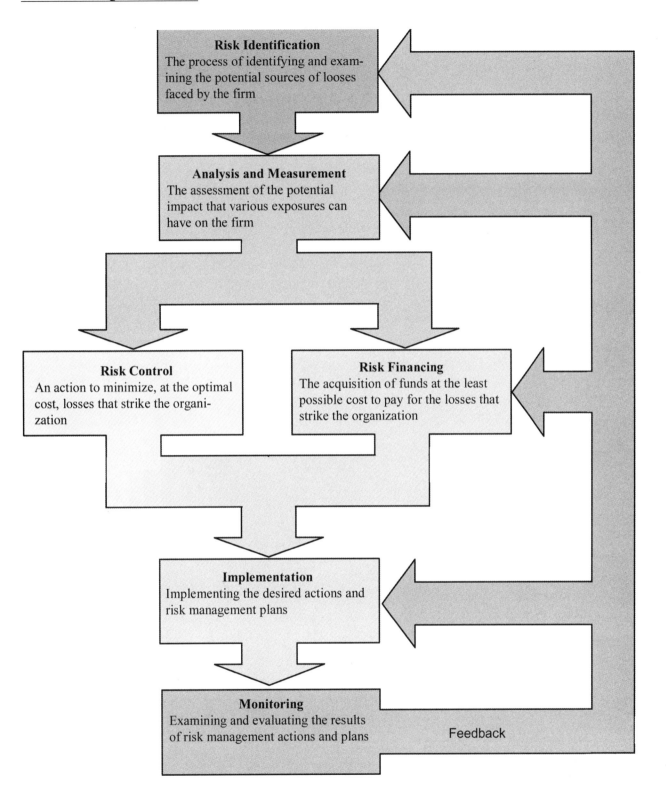

Risk Identification
The process of identifying and examining the potential sources of looses faced by the firm

Analysis and Measurement
The assessment of the potential impact that various exposures can have on the firm

Risk Control
An action to minimize, at the optimal cost, losses that strike the organization

Risk Financing
The acquisition of funds at the least possible cost to pay for the losses that strike the organization

Implementation
Implementing the desired actions and risk management plans

Monitoring
Examining and evaluating the results of risk management actions and plans

Feedback

Chapter 2

Risk Identification

Introduction

Exposures producing losses may interfere with the achievement of the organization's objectives, but these exposures cannot be successfully managed until they are identified, quantified, and treated.

Risk Identification – the First, and Most Important, Step in the Risk Management Process

The first step of managing risk is to identify the exposures that can cause loss and therefore interfere with the organization's objectives. This is the most important step of the risk management process, as an exposure must be identified before it can be analyzed or controlled or transferred or financed.

The risk manager must use a comprehensive and systematic approach in identifying risk exposures to minimize the possibility that an exposure will be overlooked. An exposure overlooked is an exposure left untreated. The use of logical classifications is a systematic way of identifying and categorizing exposures, perils, hazards, and losses so they can be analyzed, controlled, transferred, and financed.

Logical Classifications – Property, Human Resources, Liability, and Net Income

While the four logical classifications of property, human resources, liability, and net income are indeed separate categories, they are not necessarily mutually exclusive. A property exposure, peril, hazard, or loss may also involve (and is indeed likely to precipitate) a net income exposure or loss. Further, a human resource and liability exposure to loss may arise from that same property loss. Similarly, net income losses may develop from a human resource loss or a liability loss. As confusing as these logical classifications may seem, the structure provides a starting point for analyzing exposures, perils, hazards, and losses.

Property

Property exposures consist of real property, other tangible property, and intangible property, whether owned, rented, or controlled. Examples of real property are buildings, structures, and land. Buildings and structures are have traditionally been described by insurance rating authorities using the COPE methodology. COPE is an acronym that stands for Construction, Occupancy, Protection, and Exposures.

Construction describes the materials used and type of construction method of the building. Frame buildings are those whose walls and roofs are built with wood, even if the exterior walls are covered with brick or stone. Joisted masonry buildings have walls constructed of masonry, with roofs consisting of wooden joints and wood, tile, or metal roof covering material. Masonry non-combustible buildings have masonry, brick, or concrete block walls with unprotected steel joists or beams and a metal or non-combustible roof and a non-combustible floor. Fire-resistive buildings are masonry buildings with the steel beams or joists protected or covered with a fire-resistive coating or a completely non-combustible roof. Non-combustible buildings are constructed entirely from metal or glass.

Further, the building can be divided into smaller "buildings" through the use of approved fire divisions. A fire division is intended to limit the source of oxygen and fuel by creating a smaller area and to prevent migration of the fire from one part of the building to another. For example, a section of a building may be a fire division if there are parapets extending above the roof, automatically closing fire doors, or fire curtains made of non-combustible materials, and protected windows or bays that preclude the upward reach of flames into other openings.

Occupancy refers to the particular type of business or activity the building houses. Each type of occupancy has its own peculiar perils and hazards that may give rise to a loss. For example, an office occupancy typically has furniture that is metal, wood, or glass, carpeting, draperies, and supplies of combustible materials like paper, all fuel sources, but the occupancy does not typically have significant ignition sources like open flames or sparking. A restaurant, on the other hand, presents not only cooking surfaces with open flames and high heat, but also the hazards of grease-laden vapors that may accumulate in venting and support a fire. Welding shops, manufacturing facilities, or machine shops have the hazards of open flames, combustible supplies, and electrical arcing.

Protection includes two types of protection: public and private. Public protection is graded by insurance rating authorities using a Class System that considers the general level of fire protection provided by fire departments (location of fire houses, equipment, training, status of personnel, such as full-time or volunteer), and accessibility to and quality of the water supply at the rated location. Private protection consists of the protective measures provided at and for the exclusive use of the building, such as a sprinkler system, alarm system, fire extinguishing equipment and fire brigade, watchman, and water pressure and pipe size at the location.

Exposure is the occupancy of other buildings within specified distances from the rated location or within adjacent fire divisions.

Examples of other tangible property would be cash and securities, records and documents (e.g., accounts receivables, blueprints, corporate records, etc.), inventory, equipment, machinery, and furnishings and supplies. Intangible property would consist of licenses, trade secrets, copyrights or patents, trademarks or trade names, goodwill, and leases or leasehold interests.

Exposures and perils for property consist of loss exposures that have three criteria:

- A value exposed to loss
- A peril that causes a loss
- A financial consequence of the loss

A value exposed to loss and the financial consequences of the loss are closely related, the difference essentially being the pre-loss value and the value of the property post-loss, that is, the property that is damaged or destroyed.

Values exposed and financial consequences are measured by one of the following:

- Historical Cost – the price paid to acquire the property

- Book Value – the historical cost less accumulated accounting depreciation

- Market Value – what a willing buyer would give a willing seller for the property

- Replacement Cost – the cost to replace old or destroyed property with new material of like kind, quality, and construction

- Actual Cash Value – the replacement cost less a reduction for insurance depreciation or obsolescence

- Economic Value – the projected or future income stream assigned to the property

- Functional Replacement – the cost to repair or replace damaged property with materials that are functionally the equivalent of the damaged or destroyed property

- Other Valuation Methods – reproduction costs, assessed value, etc.)

Human Resources

Human resources exposures consist of relationships between the organization and its owners or constituents, board members, officers, employees (management and non-management), outside employees (leased, temporary), and independent contractors.

Employee perils and exposures include death and disability, (on or off the job), unemployment, retirement, resignation, termination, moral, and morale. Hazards consist of workplace conditions and characteristics, as well as personal characteristics such as honesty or dishonesty, activities such as smoking or drug and substance abuse, and avocations such as playing bridge, jogging, or skydiving.

Some auxiliary concerns include international employment, benefits programs, and employee contracts, including covenants and non-compete agreements, trade secrets, and incentive programs.

The Risk Manager may not have authority over Human Resources, but will likely have some responsibility, nonetheless. The scope of Human Resources is very broad and cross-functional.

Liability

Liability exposures are related to property, human resources, and activities (including activities conducted on the premises, away from the premises, and the products or services provided to customers and others). The exposure is essentially one arising out of harm to society in general and to individuals and property.

The interests of society are protected by criminal law and the interests of individuals are protected by civil law. In some instances, both criminal law and civil law will be involved in the event of harm or injury. The outcomes of either are likely to cause some degree of net income loss (income foregone or lost opportunity) or property loss (through fines, penalties, damage payments, or confiscation), and possibly human resources (through incarceration, perhaps).

Criminal liability is a breach of duty owed to society. The result of criminal liability may involve fines, penalties, or punishment in the form of probation, public service, or incarceration. Criminal liability ranges in extreme from simple matters such as speeding or causing an accident by improper lane use to serious or heinous crimes such as arson, robbery, or murder.

The risk manager is generally concerned only with civil law, particularly the Law of Torts, the Law of Contracts, and Statutory Law.

The Law of Torts: The Law of Torts defines a tort as a private or civil wrong, other than a breach of contract, for which the courts will provide a remedy in the form of an action for damages. A tort can arise from a negligent act or omission, an intentional act, or it can be imposed without negligence or intent by statute. Torts are usually defined by the common law, or body of law within a jurisdiction consisting of past court decisions, or by statute or ordinance. Another way of viewing common law is to consider the common law as a code of conduct applicable to nearly everyone based on prior precedents or rulings. In contrast, statutory laws are specific enactments of legislatures, executive bodies, and administrative delegations.

Through past decisions, some activities have been considered to be so potentially hazardous that anyone who engages in them will be subject to strict liability, or liability directed by common law without regard to the intent of the offender's actions. Fault is not considered, only the nature of the activity. Common examples of activities that give rise to strict liability or liability without fault are blasting, demolition, owning dangerous animals, and owning a public nuisance, such as a swimming pool.

Most torts are those associated with negligence: the failure to exercise a degree of care that a reasonably prudent person would exercise under the circumstances. Negligence is usually expressed in terms of these four elements: 1) a duty is owed, 2) there is a breach of that duty, 3) the breach of duty is the proximate cause of the injury, and 4) damages result from that injury. For example, a person has a duty to protect others from a flaming barbeque grill, but through carelessness, the flames, without any intervening cause, catch a neighbor's property on fire and destroy it. The destroyed property is the injury. The first three elements of a negligent tort are established. If the destroyed property is the neighbor's garage, there is damage resulting from the injury. However, if the property was the neighbor's trash bag, (yes, your trash is your property), there is no damage resulting from the injury as the trash is deemed to have no value when it is discarded.

Intentional acts are committed when an offender intends to commit an act that results in the private violation of another's rights. For example, if the neighbors from the above example get into an argument over the destroyed garage and one neighbor decides to strike the other neighbor, the striking would be an intentional act.

Products liability is an area where the manufacturer may be deemed negligent if their product is defective and causes injury to a person or damage to property. This is absolute liability. If in the previous example, the barbecue grill exploded due to a manufacturing defect and caused a fire and property damage to the grill owner's house, the manufacturer would be liable for the damages. There are many court cases and decisions regarding products liability to be considered in determining negligence and liability in more complex scenarios.

Remedies to torts, including negligence, strict liability, absolute, and statutory liability include compensatory damages, punitive or exemplary damages, and injunctive relief.

The Law of Contracts: The Law of Contracts controls the performance of a promise. There are four characteristics of an enforceable contract: competent parties, genuine agreement or assent (a willing buyer and a willing seller), exchange of legal consideration (payment), and a legal purpose. For a contract to be enforceable, the parties entering into the contract must be competent parties. The parties must be mentally competent (sane or not under the influence of drugs or alcohol) and cannot be a minor (the age of majority differs by jurisdiction and by the purpose of the contract). A thirteen year old cannot enter into a contract such as a lease of an apartment, but can probably enter into a contract to rent a movie at a video store or to buy the newest CD.

There must be genuine agreement or assent, sometimes called the meeting of the minds, without undue duress or pressure on behalf of either party. There must be an exchange of some legal consideration such as money or other valuable property or a valuable service. Lastly, there must be a legal purpose to the contract, or the activities contemplated must be legal. For example, a gambling debt is not enforceable in jurisdictions where gambling is illegal. A contract to "hit" someone or commit arson is also an illegal contract.

The remedies for breach of contract or failure to perform are damages (compensatory, punitive, and liquidated), reformation, injunctions, and specific performance. Compensatory damages are those intended to pay for the damages proved, such as the cost to repair property damaged by a contractor or to pay the medical bills of an injured party. Punitive or exemplary damages are those meant to punish the offender so as to preclude future activities of the same nature. Liquidated damages are those damages whose value is stipulated in the contract as the amount to be paid regardless of any provable damages if the contract is breached. Reformation of the contract is a legal concept that attempts to correct any error or mistake in the contract. Reformation is commonly sought in disagreements over insurance contract, such as inadvertently having a typographical error in description of a location or named insured.

The extent of liability exposures is very broad. The most prominent characteristic of liability risk is that it cannot be accurately measured in advance of a loss. The amount of the loss will depend on the circumstances of the event, the nature and severity of the damage or injury, the degree of negligence, the applicable law, and finally, the decision of the judge or jury.

Net Income

The cause of the net income exposure can be the company's problem or someone else's problem, but in either case, the result is the company's problem. Causes may be related to property (destruction of owned or leased property), human resources (personnel losses), or liability exposures (imposition of legal liability). Other causes may be speculative in nature, such as market risk, operational risk, business risk, fluctuations in financial markets, or weather (even without property damage, as when a flood prevents customers from accessing the company's business).

The causes that are someone else's problems are generally related to the organization's primary supplier or primary customer, or they can be environmental in nature, or they are related to local government, enticement businesses, or the economy. Factors that can affect the economic loss caused by a plant shutdown are length of shutdown, severity of shutdown/loss (e.g., the production line, a warehouse, the entire plant, the administrative offices, etc.), the frequency of shutdown/loss, and the timing of a shutdown/loss. The effect of a net income loss would be either decreased revenues or increased expenses. Decreased revenues would include business interruption, narrowing of a profit margin, weakening sales, or investment income reduction. Increased expenses would include the cost to repair or replace, expediting costs, incremental cost of normal operations, and or other expenses related to minimizing revenue reduction or expense increases.

Loss Identification Methods

The risk manager has several options available for identifying loss exposures. One option consists of organized, logical approaches to identifying loss exposures. A discussion of a number of specific methodologies will follow. Another option, while less organized and logical, is equally important: the risk manager must use common sense in seeking out loss exposures. The difference between a good risk manager and a great risk manager may lie in the subjective areas of instinct and intuition. A third option, also less structured, lies in education and networking. The risk manager must explore as many educational opportunities as possible, including formal training like Certified Risk Manager (CRM) or Associate in Risk Management (ARM) courses and designations, and the Risk and Insurance Management Society (RIMS) Fellow designation or a university degree in risk management and insurance, and informal learning through seminars and workshops such as those presented by RIMS. A very important part of all learning experiences is networking possibilities, where risk managers exchange information that is useful to others. Risk management is a profession where "competitors" do not really exist, even though the employers of the risk managers may be competing in the marketplace. In that sense, it is very much like the legal profession, where adversaries strive mightily in court but eat and drink as friends, to paraphrase William Shakespeare's view on lawyers in his play "The Taming of the Shrew." The risk manager must be willing to share and try experiences in handling loss because reducing risk, particularly in the form of injury to persons or damage to property, is simply the right thing to do.

Methodologies

Risk managers use various methods to identify loss exposures. The choice depends on the type of exposure to risk the risk manager is trying to identify. Some methods work better with some exposures and others work better with other exposures. The following section describes the various methods, their scopes, methods, benefits, and weaknesses.

The Checklist / Survey Questionnaire Method uses information-gathering documents (lists and surveys) to search systematically for as many loss exposures as possible. It is standardized, provides a history for the risk manager, is easily classified and tabulated, and, because very little training is required to use this method, can be utilized by non-risk management personnel.

Unfortunately, it cannot cover all areas or operations and provides limited financial effects. It also does not prioritize the greatest exposures.

There are five examples of checklists. The first is a <u>List of Assets</u>, a checklist best suited for property and physical assets. The benefits of this method are that it provides a list of all resources and capacities, stimulates staff to account for assets, and identifies assets that are often overlooked.

It does not ordinarily address liability risks, though, and it must be updated regularly, especially when new assets are acquired. It also provides varying costs estimates, depending upon when the survey was completed.

The second is an <u>Activity or Situation List</u>. This checklist is best suited for liability and human assets. The benefits of this method include instilling a thought process for loss prevention, evaluating equipment, personnel, and operations that function together, and, again, identifying activities that are often overlooked.

Unfortunately, it can become mired in minutia if too much detail is included, and the important exposures can get lost in those details. It does not focus on the financial aspect of identification, and operations and activities may vary by locale.

The third checklist is a <u>Perils Analysis</u>. Perils Analysis lists are commonly used to identify the potential cause of loss from human, economic, and natural perils. It provides a list of common or likely causes of loss, uses insurance nomenclatures, and can assist in identifying perils that occur infrequently and might otherwise be missed.

On the other hand, new perils are created daily, old perils are forgotten or overlooked, and the analysis may become obsolete. Upper management may be skeptical of this method as it may be perceived as a "Chicken Little," sky-is-falling mentality.

The fourth checklist is the <u>Insurance Checklist,</u> and it is used to determine the feasibility of contractual transfer. The Insurance checklist has the benefit of being a definitive list of available coverage and exclusions. Completing an Insurance checklist includes a process of evaluating exposures, and because insurance is the last resort for handling an exposure, it requires limited work by the risk manager.

An inherent problem with an Insurance Checklist is that it is, by definition, geared to exposures that are currently insured or are conventionally insurable. In addition, swings in the insurance market can cause the scope of insurable exposures to expand and contract.

The fifth list is somewhat an amalgamation of several other checklists. The <u>Industry List</u> is a checklist specific to a certain operation or industry and is generally tailored to specific assets, activities, perils, and insurable exposures commonly found in that industry or operation. Since anyone in a given industry can easily use the checklist, it facilitates comparisons with peers.

However, it can be too focused on the industry, overlooking assets and activities that are not common to all industry participants, or it can be too generic, capturing the obvious and not adequately addressing the unique issues facing industry participants. Also, if the checklist is not created or at least edited by others outside the industry, the users may continue to make the same mistakes other industry participants have made.

The Flowcharts Method graphically and sequentially depicts the activities of a particular operation or process. It is process-driven and follows a logical flow. It uses product analysis, dependency analysis, site analysis, decision analysis, and critical path analysis. The Flowchart Method illustrates the interdependency within the organization, can easily pinpoint bottlenecks, and can determine the critical path or activity.

However, the Flowchart Method does not indicate frequency or severity, show minor processes with major loss potential, and is too process-oriented. In addition, it has limited use for liability exposures and provides no information about financial impact.

Insurance Policy Analysis is used for reviewing an insurance contract or related documents to determine exposures and perils that are covered and those that are not covered, either because the insuring agreement does not extend to the asset or activity, or because terms, conditions, or exclusions are limiting. A common non-contractual document used in an Insurance Policy Analysis is a document, generally created by an insurance company, that explains the features of that carrier's insurance contract.

The risk manager can use internal or external resources in this analysis, but the focus usually is on what coverage is available in the insurance market rather than what coverage is desirable. In this method, many perils are given a precise definition, and its analysis will state what is specifically covered and not covered.

Unfortunately, it is difficult to analyze how an insurance policy will respond before a loss occurs. A judge or jury may even disregard or "change" the policy, lessening the reliability of the analysis and result. Last, not all policies are standardized, particularly for very large exposures or unusual situations.

Physical Inspections are conducted by informational visits to critical sites, both inside and outside the organization, to determine exposures to risk. They can be performed by internal personnel (e.g., risk manager, safety department, operating personnel, etc.) or outsourced to professional consultants, community services (fire department), and regulatory agencies (OSHA), or they can be provided by insurance company loss control professionals or agents. Physical inspections are usually personal, and provide a visualization of processes and locations that cannot be captured through using a checklist or examining a flowchart. One of the significant benefits is that a physical inspection may be able to find unreported hazards and assets. One of the CRM faculty members (by profession, a risk manager) reported the following conversation, which occurred during a physical inspection visit to one of his facilities:

"What's in that building over there?"

"That's where we keep the Rolls Royce and the Bentley."

"What Rolls Royce and Bentley????"

"Oh, didn't we tell you about those?"

"NO!!!"

Physical Inspections can also be time consuming, however, and situations may change often, so inspections must be repeated periodically, or whenever significant new properties are acquired or activities begun.

Some examples of a physical inspection checklist would be Monthly Safety Inspection Checklist, Bank Location Questionnaire, Physical Inspection Report, Floor Safety Evaluation Form, Property Survey Report, Swimming Pool Safety Checklist, Office of Risk Management Survey, and Worker's Compensation Program Analysis.

Net Income / Financial Statement Analysis is used to identify values that are subject to loss, the event that could cause the loss, and the fiscal impact after the loss. These types of reports analyze both growth in expenses and reduction in revenues. The person conducting the analysis must review the complete financial statements, including the balance sheet, income statement, statement of cash flow, statement of indebtedness and loans, and the notes to the financial statement, as well as the auditor's opinion statement. This analysis can assist in prognosticating the financial losses from a specific event, and it can demonstrate how the loss would affect other areas within the organization. It can be the basis for initial insight in developing crisis contingency plans.

On the negative side, Net Income/Financial Statement Analysis usually does not take into account business risks, and is difficult to predict the effect on the organization of losses suffered by key suppliers or customers. There also can be a tendency to manipulate the financial records, debts, or other reports, particularly when scrutiny may disclose underlying problems.

There are several types of **Compliance Reviews.** They can either be statutory (local, state, or federal) or professional (voluntary, involuntary, industry, or governmental insurance programs). Most compliance reviews are "free" and give you an outside look (whether you want it or not). Unfortunately, they can carry their own problems (e.g., insurance carrier declining or cancelling coverage because of an uncovered hazard) and the company has little or no control over the review, either from it occurring or in its aftermath.

Contract Identification and Analysis reviews contracts, leases, hold-harmless or indemnification agreements, purchase orders and sales contracts, bills of lading, warranties, advertising materials, mergers and acquisitions, joint ventures and alliances, employment contracts, and service contracts. This type of analysis helps identify gaps in the risk management plan revealing exposures the risk manager must address, but because the risk management department is often not involved in the drafting and negotiation of the contract, there may not be a chance for the risk manager to do much about the exposures revealed in the contract analysis.

Policy and Procedures Reviews evaluate corporate by-laws, board minutes, mission statements, organizational charts, employee manuals, procedures manuals, and risk management policy manuals. This type of review can uncover exposures that others in the organization create, but organizational politics and realities may prevent any effective treatment of the exposures.

A Loss Data Review can be performed on insurance company loss runs, internal loss runs, or accident and incident reports. Through collection, organization, and analysis, the loss data or loss history will reveal the effectiveness of the risk management program and will be useful for predicting and preventing future incidents, but since this information is historical and created after an accident or incident, it will not show a problem until there has already been at least one loss.

Expert reviews can either be internal (staff or operations) or external (industry or some specialty). The company can usually save time and obtain more immediate benefits from the expert's experience. On the other hand, a qualified expert may be difficult to find and services can be expensive.

General Rules

Six general rules apply to risk identification:

1. Exposure identification is the most important step in the Risk Management Process.

2. Risk is present in every phase of business.

3. Risk is not always self-evident.

4. Risk is subject to diagnosis and treatment.

5. More than one identification method should be used to diagnose and identify risks.

6. Often one method will reveal the greatest number of exposures.

Exposure identification is the most important step, as an unrecognized exposure cannot be intelligently managed. The risk manager's primary task is to identify the exposures, and once identified, the exposures must be quantified and analyzed. After quantification and analysis, the risk manager can create the matrix of avoidance, control, transfer, and financing to manage the risks. Until the exposure is identified, however, nothing else can happen.

Every business has risks, and every phase of business has risks. The risk manager can refer to these in their simplest form as being either pure risks (break-even or loss) or speculative (gain, loss, or break even). A more complex analysis of risks categorizes them into their underlying causation, such as social risks, compliance risks, juridical risks, legal risks, economic risks, and physical risks. Most of traditional risk management and nearly all of insurance coverages focus on physical risks, the loss of property, reduction in assets or income, and human resources. The broader scope of Enterprise-Wide Risk Management opens the range of risks to manage from the pure risks to include speculative risks.

Risk, once identified, can be diagnosed and then treated. Some risks are obvious, like those created by a looming hurricane, and some risks are not self-evident, for instance the possibility of a building sliding into a sinkhole cannot be observed simply by looking at the rather ordinary land. Publicity in 2007 and 2008 about the safety of children's toys changed from the obvious choking hazard for small parts on toys enjoyed by small children to the invisible presence of lead in the toy itself.

One of the first important textbooks on insurance and risk management told of ancient stone statuary weighing many tons stored far away from an earthquake zone in an isolated fire-resistive building with watchmen and alarms and waxed to prevent mold and mildew. The risk of loss from wind, flood, earthquake, theft, and fire appeared to be negligible due to the location and physical characteristics of the property. However, when the waxy rags at the base of the statuary caught fire, the heat melted the wax on the statuary and set it on fire, so when the firemen sprayed water on the flames, the statuary shattered. That risk was not self-evident to the firemen who were trained to put out fires.

This demonstrates why more than one method should be used to identify, diagnose, and analyze risks. The means of diagnosing are as varied as the identification process. While risks can be treated only by four methods (avoidance, control, transfer, and financing), the techniques for accomplishing these four methods also are wide and varied. One aspect that makes a risk manager's job particularly challenging is balancing the trade-offs between techniques. For example, an automatic sprinkler system is a commonly accepted technique for controlling the spread of fire, but it creates its own problem, such as water leakage from water-charged systems, system failure in dry-charged systems, and asphyxiation from inert gas-charged systems.

While more than one method for identification should commonly be used, generally one method will uncover the majority of the exposures. The key to exposure identification is to determine which method will accomplish the most. The other methods are then used to complete the exposure identification process and pick up the exposures that are not as obvious or are not as easily identified by the primary method. For example, an asset checklist may have identified the building used to store the Rolls Royce and Bentley discussed previously, but through a human error, these assets were not divulged on the asset list. Only a physical inspection prompted the question that led to their identification. Had that inspection not occurred, perhaps a loss history review would have disclosed the property, but only after its destruction (and even then, it might not have, if the two vehicles were not insured).

Chapter 3

Financial Statement Analysis

Introduction

What are financial statements and why are they important tools for the risk manager?

In this chapter, we will focus on four basic financial statements:

1. Income statement (also known as a profit and loss statement),

2. Balance sheet,

3. Statement of cash flows (SCF), and

4. Cash budget

Financial statements are prepared by internal accountants or by external accountants and auditors, usually certified public accountants (CPAs), to provide an overview of the organization's financial performance at a point in time, or over a period of time. Internally prepared statements are referred to as unaudited statements, even though staff may have audited the underlying accounts and statements. Externally prepared statements are generally audited statements, and if so, include an independent auditor's opinion as to the fairness and accuracy of the financial information. These statements are prepared using a set of accounting guidelines known as Generally Accepted Accounting Principles and are commonly called GAAP statements.

Another important differentiation is the way these statements are constructed. Most businesses use an accrual-based system, which attempts to match revenues to corresponding expenses. This differs from the cash-based accounting system individuals and many small businesses use, where revenues and expenses are recognized only when cash changes hands. For purposes of this discussion, we will assume that all statements are constructed on an accrual basis.

A third differentiation is the type of accounting system used. There are five major types of accounting systems: financial accounting, managerial accounting, government or fund accounting, tax accounting, and statutory or regulatory accounting. Each will use the same basic types of accounting reports.

Financial accounting is the body of accounting theory and practice used by all publicly owned companies and most other organizations. Financial accounting is also commonly referred to as GAAP accounting because of its use by public companies in filing public financial statements with governmental regulators and annual reports. The underlying purpose of using GAAP accounting is to provide financial information on a consistent basis for use by regulators and the general public for comparison and investment activities.

Managerial accounting is an internal accounting system created by its users for internal purposes only. As no public reporting is required, general public or regulatory agencies have no need for a common understanding.

Government or fund accounting is used by governmental bodies and many "non-profits" where public reporting may be required, but not for the purpose of investment activities. There are, however, protocols addressing how companies display such financial information.

Tax accounting is used by any tax-paying entity to determine its tax liability. The Internal Revenue Service and Internal Revenue Code provide the rules and regulations for this type of accounting system.

Statutory or regulatory accounting also has its own regulations and rules, generally referred to as Statutory Accounting Principles (SAP) or Regulatory Accounting Principles (RAP). The use of SAP or RAP is largely limited to financial institutions such as insurance companies, commercial banks, and investment bankers, where the emphasis is on solvency and protection of customers and depositors.

These types of accounting systems are not mutually exclusive (except in the case of governmental or fund accounting). Private sector entities, particularly large publicly owned entities, will use financial or GAAP accounting, managerial accounting, and tax accounting systems simultaneously. Insurance companies will use statutory accounting principles, managerial accounting, tax accounting, and, in the case of publicly owned insurance companies, GAAP.

The risk manager may examine financial statements generated under any of these accounting systems. Each statement will be discussed from the viewpoint of how a risk manager would use it to analyze a company or client rather than how an accountant would construct it.

Why are financial statements important? The following is a partial list of reasons the risk manager needs to be aware of the various financial statements and the information they impart.

Income Statement (Profit and Loss Statement)

The income statement provides information on revenues, expenses, and profit <u>over a period of time</u>. If an organization does not earn a profit over an extended period of time, it will not continue to exist. Organizations are established in order to earn a profit for the owners or provide a service to others. The survival of an organization depends on its ability to generate profits, and these profits are of paramount concern to investors, owners, and the risk manager.

Some people incorrectly believe the so-called "non-profit" organization cannot make a profit. This is an incorrect interpretation arising out of an incorrect reference to the status of the organization. The "non-profit" organization is formed under Section 501c of the Internal Revenue Code, a section that defines not "non-profit" organizations, but rather "tax-exempt" organizations. A 501c organization can and must earn a profit to continue to survive, even if the "profit" means an excess of contributions over expenses. The concern of a 501c organization regarding profit is to not earn too much profit or retain too much profit, as the Internal Revenue Service may then determine the organization does not qualify under Section 501c for tax-exempt status. The majority of such organizations are those formed to obtain a tax exemption as a 501c(3), or charitable organization. However, there are, in fact, over twenty-five other types of 501c organizations, including a category for small mutual insurance companies that are exempt from federal income tax.

Earning a profit is preferable to losing money, yet it is not enough for many corporations. Wall Street analysts estimate the earnings (often in terms of earnings per share or EPS) of publicly traded organizations on an annual and quarterly basis. If analysts expect an organization to earn $0.50 per share in the current quarter and the organization fails to meet those expectations the price of the organization's stock will generally decline in value, often precipitously. An EPS of $0.45, when "the market" expected $0.50 per share may lead to a significant decline in stock price. A lower stock price will make it more expensive for the organization to raise capital and limit the ability of the organization to expand the business, and in some cases it may lead to a change in ownership (e.g., a take-over) or a change in management (e.g., a stockholder revolt). A sharp decline in stock price often results in litigation by shareholders against the organization for reasons ranging from a breach of fiduciary duty to misleading them with overly optimistic information contained in the corporation's financial statements.

A popular approach to evaluating the performance of an organization and its management is shareholder value added or economic value added (EVA). Value added or economic value added distinguishes between accounting profit (often referred to as net operating profit after taxes) and economic profit (the amount an entity earns in excess of its cost of capital). The concept of economic value added states that in order to be viable, a business needs to earn a certain rate in excess of its cost of capital. The cost of capital is the organization's cost of obtaining money.

For example, assume an organization earned an <u>accounting profit</u> of $3 million, which might look good at first glance. However, the organization has a cost of capital of 6% and owners have invested $100 million in the business. The organization needs to earn $6 million (.06 x $100,000,000) in order to earn an <u>economic profit</u>, but this organization only earned $3,000,000. If the business operates under an economic value added framework, this operation would be a candidate for sale or, worse, simply closing down operations. On the other hand, if the firm had an accounting profit of $9 million, its economic profit would be $3 million ($9 million minus $6 million). Clearly, the risk manager needs to understand the importance of the income statement.

Typically, each organization has its own set of financial statements. Organizations that are more complex file consolidated financial statements that combine the financial statements of multiple operating units into one set of financial statements, although each operating unit will have its own set of statements, even if used only internally. Thus, an organization may have two or more operating units but only one income statement and balance sheet will appear in the annual report.

Balance Sheet

The balance sheet is a snapshot of the organization <u>at a given point in time</u>. There are two typical formats: assets and liabilities/owners' equity are displayed in side-by-side columns; or assets are shown on top and liabilities/owners' equity on the bottom. Each item is described by a heading and has a dollar value next to it. Thanks to a Franciscan friar named Luca Pacioli, who developed the concept of double-entry accounting in 1494, each entry has a matching entry such that the sum of the entries always equals zero (only accountants can truly understand this, but simply put, it makes finding entry errors immensely easier). This gives rise to the fundamental accounting equation: Total Assets equals Total Liabilities plus Owners' Equity. Since the total of all assets equals all claims against the assets (assets are used to discharge debts and to reward owners), the totals are in balance, hence, the term "balance sheet."

The balance sheet dollar values of assets are not particularly useful to the risk manager. Accounting is based upon historic value, or the value of an asset at the time ownership of the asset it is acquired, even though the actual assets may be received later. The value recorded in the books of account or accounting records is cleverly called "book value," and this value equals the historical cost. For assets that are subject to depreciation (an accounting recognition of the erosion of the asset value from use, wear and tear, and obsolescence), depreciation is an important concept in calculating income taxes and it theoretically exists to allow a build-up of capital to replace old assets. When an asset is depreciated, the accumulated depreciation is subtracted from the historical cost to create book value.

Book value bears little resemblance to current market value, as book value is historic while the current market value is contemporary. Also, book value bears no resemblance to the replacement value or insurable value, as these are insurance concepts, though these values are related to current market value. While the balance sheet values may have little applicability for the risk manager, the balance sheet does provide a list of assets and liabilities the risk manager needs to protect.

Statement of Cash Flow and Cash Budget

The statement of cash flow measures flows of funds in and out of the organization. It is divided into three sections to measure the flows of funds from operations, from financing, and from investing. The risk manager must keep in mind that the term "statement of cash flows" is somewhat of a misnomer in that the statement contains a number of non-cash entries, including accounts payable and accounts receivable, among others.

The cash budget is a pure, cash-based statement. Expenses and losses to the organization are paid with cash, not accounting profits. The risk manager needs to be able to assess the organization's ability to pay its bills in a timely basis (particularly when the organization has chosen to internally finance losses and related expenses) and its ability to absorb both expected and unexpected losses.

Notes to the Financial Statements

For the risk manager, the notes to the financial statements can be the most important part of the financial statement, even though they are usually read only as an afterthought. Notes are not found first, nor second, nor third, but as the last section of financial statements. In reality, the notes often explain why the values contained in the income statement, the balance sheet, the statement of cash flow, and the cash budget are what they are, thus the notes are best read first, before looking at the dollar amounts.

In addition to providing a broad understanding and appreciation for the dollar values, notes can assist the risk manager in a number of ways.

Hidden Assets and Liabilities

Often the organization has assets and liabilities that are not disclosed on its financial statements. Assets and liabilities are not hidden for nefarious purposes (although, unfortunately, assets and liabilities are hidden or misstated by less than scrupulous executives), but generally because the accounting guidelines do not require these "hidden" values to be disclosed. It is critical for the risk manager to be aware of these items, which are usually found by reading the footnotes to the financial statements.

One example of a hidden asset is the value of inventory that is "hidden" on the books because of the use of an inventory accounting system such as FIFO ("First In, First Out") or LIFO ("Last In, First Out"). In a period of rising prices, a LIFO system will result in the inventory value of the balance sheet being understated. The oldest and least expensive items of inventory are left "on the shelf" while the newest items, valued at the current, higher values, are used first. (Another financial statement, the income statement, is also affected by an inventory accounting system, and in the above case, profit, and therefore tax liability, also is understated.) In reality, it does not matter which nut or bolt leaves the bin first, but to an accountant, timing is everything. For a Fortune 500 organization, this can result in inventory being understated by hundreds of millions of dollars. These assets need to be identified and protected by the risk manager.

Conversely, if an organization has a defined benefit pension plan, there is a very high probability today that it is under-funded. The actuarial value of defined benefit pension plan obligations and the earmarked funds associated with this liability are examples of off-balance sheet transactions. Another common example occurs when leases involve off-balance sheet assets and liabilities. (While off-balance sheet entries are appropriate in financial statements prepared under GAAP rules, Enron is the poster child for misuse of off-balance sheet liabilities.)

Litigation

Pending lawsuits and possible environmental liabilities are disclosed in the notes, usually in notes titled "Contingent Liabilities." The opening sentence to these notes can generally be paraphrased as "Lots of people are suing us, but we don't worry because we have good attorneys who tell us we are not liable." The risk manager needs to worry about such wording, and other words, like asbestos, mercury contamination, lead paint, EPA, and Superfund Site, should raise red flags, as well. Often the organization's attorneys are not as good as management thinks they are. The value of the stock and the viability of tobacco companies and many other industries have been significantly affected by litigation issues, most of which were largely dismissed as "being without merit" by legal counsel.

Bonding Requirements and Ratios

Many organizations need to qualify for and obtain surety bonds in order to participate in certain endeavors (e.g., a completion bond for a construction contractor). The bond underwriter has a list of target financial ratios the organizations within a given industry must meet in order to qualify for a bond.

A common liquidity ratio used by a surety bond underwriter is the current ratio. The current ratio is calculated by dividing current assets by current liabilities. However, if the organization uses the LIFO inventory valuation system that understates the value of its ending inventory on the balance sheet, this will result in a low current ratio that does not correctly represent the organization's liquidity position. The resulting understated current ratio could result in a denial from a bond underwriter. The risk manager needs to understand this and provide adjusted data (and if necessary an accompanying finance tutorial) to the surety underwriter.

Ability and Willingness to Absorb Risk

A major task of the risk manager is to determine the willingness and ability of the organization to assume risk. The willingness to assume risk, also known as the risk appetite or risk tolerance, is management's psychological attitude on risk. Organizations vary in the degree of risk tolerance, with some being willing to take chances while others are very conservative. The simple exercise of purchasing an ordinary insurance policy provides an easy way to understand this. Since the premium should include expected losses plus administrative costs, plus a profit margin, insurance transfer is generally more expensive than risk retention.

However, the advantage of insurance is that it is a fixed cost for the term of the policy. Many organizations are willing to assume the certain cost of a premium because they are apprehensive about a large loss that probably will not, but could, happen. However, other organizations are willing to assume some or all of a loss exposure, even though the insurance premium that might be charged is much smaller than the potential loss. Clint Eastwood's character in the Dirty Harry movies illustrates this: "How lucky do you feel?"

Financial statements can help the risk manager assess an organization's willingness to assume risk. Ratio analysis evaluates performance in several key areas, one of which is leverage. A common leverage ratio is the debt ratio, or total debt by total assets. A high ratio indicates greater use of debt or leverage (other people's money), and higher risk.

For example, assume an industry average debt ratio is 50% (in the typical organization, half of the assets in this industry are financed with debt). If your organization's' debt ratio is 20%, your organization has taken a very conservative approach to leverage and a lack of willingness to take risk. If your organization's debt ratio is 65%, your organization appears to have a very high tolerance or appetite for risk.

Willingness to take risk needs to be combined with an ability to absorb the financial consequences of taking risk. The financial condition of the organization must be strong enough to pay for losses that occur. Contractors are often cited as organizations willing to take risks but lacking the financial strength to absorb losses that might occur. Banks are often financially able to take on risk, but may be psychologically unwilling to increase their risk exposure (though recent events show that their attitudes are changing). An organization that is able but unwilling to assume risk can change their risk profile after the risk manager analyzes and explains the costs and benefits to senior management.

Retention Levels

A crucial aspect of managing risk is determining the amount of risk to retain and finance internally and how much to finance externally.

Loss exposures fall into four logical classifications or categories: property, liability, net income, and human resources. For each exposure, the risk manager must determine two attachment points: where coverage starts and where coverage ends.

At the first attachment point or the lower end of the loss spectrum, the organization will retain losses in the form of deductibles, co-payments, and self-insured retentions (SIRs). These first-dollar losses are generally paid out of current income and cash flow and treated as an expense on the income statement. The organization with a stronger income statement and cash flow will be able to handle higher deductibles or retentions.

Regardless of the amount of retention and the limits of insurance layers purchased, if the risk is insured, there still will be a point where coverage ends. The organization retains the top-end exposure to risk beyond the point where the external risk financing ends, and any exposures to risk outside the scope of the insurance contract.

The balance sheet is used to finance a catastrophic loss. If the organization has a cash surplus or credit-worthiness, internal funds or borrowed funds will be used to pay the loss. There is a subtle difference between the internal financing described above in the discussion of the first-dollar losses and the internal financing of catastrophic losses. When balance sheet funds are used, the organization generally will rely on external financing in the form of borrowing to preserve liquidity for operations and opportunities.

The ability to raise large sums of money quickly will determine the ability of the entity to absorb top-end exposure to risk. Examples include lines of credit, unused debt capacity, and the ability to sell additional shares of equity.

Returning to the debt ratio, an organization with a 65% ratio compared to an industry average of 50% will face a difficult time obtaining additional financing. Lenders will either be unwilling to extend additional loans or will demand higher interest rates and/or fees to compensate for the risk level of the organization. The organization with the 20% debt ratio will be in a much stronger position when negotiating for additional financing, and can theoretically take on more top-end exposure to risk.

Increasing deductibles, co-payments, and SIR's allows the entity to save money on the cost of external financing, or to transfer additional amounts of risk beyond the retention. A risk manager analyzing retention levels is comparing exposure to the income statement against a potential impairment to the balance sheet. If the organization has a strong balance sheet and a weak income statement, the risk manager should decrease the bottom-end exposure by lowering first dollar retention and increasing the organization's top-end protection. This requires the organization to be willing to take on this risk. Many managers may be psychologically unwilling to do this. The risk manager needs to assess a company's willingness (appetite) and ability (financial strength) to be able to assess the costs and benefits of retention versus transfer of risk.

Income Statement

The income statement (also known as the statement of earnings, profit or loss statement, or, for many "non-profits," statement of revenues over expenses) presents revenues, expenses, net profit, and earnings per share (for publicly traded firms). Exhibit 3.1 is an income statement for XYZ Corporation.

Exhibit 3.1: Income Statement

	2008	2007	2006	2005	2004
Net sales	$1,070,000	$1,000,000	$950,000	$900,000	$850,000
Cost of goods sold	$888,100	$800,000	$750,000	$711,000	$663,000
Gross profit	$181,900	$200,000	$200,000	$189,000	$187,000
Selling, general, and administrative	$53,000	$50,000	$48,000	$45,000	$44,000
Depreciation/depletion/ amortization	$74,900	$70,000	$68,000	$65,000	$62,000
EBIT	$54,000	$80,000	$84,000	$79,000	$81,000
Interest expense	$22,500	$25,000	$24,000	$20,000	$20,000
EBT	$31,500	$55,000	$60,000	$59,000	$61,000
Income taxes	$11,025	$19,250	$21,000	$20,650	$21,350
Net income	$20,475	$35,750	$39,000	$38,350	$39,650

Exhibit 3.2: Common Size Income Statement

	2008	2007	2006	2005	2004
Net sales	100.0%	100.0%	100.0%	100.0%	100.0%
Cost of goods sold	83.0%	80.0%	78.9%	79.0%	78.0%
Gross profit	17.0%	20.0%	21.1%	21.0%	22.0%
Selling, general, and administrative	5.0%	5.0%	5.1%	5.0%	5.2%
Depreciation/depletion/ amortization	7.0%	7.0%	7.2%	7.2%	7.3%
EBIT	5.0%	8.0%	8.8%	8.8%	9.5%
Interest expense	2.1%	2.5%	2.5%	2.2%	2.4%
EBT	2.9%	5.5%	6.3%	6.6%	7.2%
Income taxes (35%)	1.0%	1.9%	2.2%	2.3%	2.5%
Net income	1.9%	3.6%	4.1%	4.3%	4.7%

The income statement is a function of a range of accounting options, estimates, and judgments by management and the auditor. Reported results are also affected by economic factors that may be beyond the control of the organization. In most cases, the income statement is developed using the accrual method, so the net profit indicated is not the same as the net cash flow. The income statement is a measure of flows of revenue and expenses over a period of time, usually quarterly or annually.

Sales or Revenue from Operations

The first line of an income statement is revenue or sales. The income statement in Exhibit 3.1 starts with net sales, or the gross or total sales revenue, minus an allowance for bad debts and returned merchandise. This allowance should be in line with the industry average and historical allowances for the organization being analyzed. This income statement does not include information on the size of the organization's allowance. Management would have to provide this information, compute the allowance as a percentage of sales, and then compare it to competitors and track it over time, usually for five years. When analyzing the organization's sales, several additional issues need to be addressed.

Price Times Quantity

Sales revenue is calculated by multiplying units sold times sales price per unit. Did the increase in sales come from an increase in the price per unit, an increase in units sold, or a combination of the two? For a publicly traded organization, this information is usually disclosed in management's letter to the shareholders or in the analysis section of the annual report. Because of a free market economy, most organizations are price takers. They must take the price the market creates through the forces of supply and demand, and cannot dictate their desired price to the market. Therefore, units sold should be the primary focus. The general price trend in most industries is downward due to economies of scale (as more units are produced and sold, the average cost per unit decreases because of efficiencies in the production and distribution process). In order to increase sales, these cost savings are passed on to consumers in the form of lower prices, and lower prices will attract consumers away from less efficient producers not having the economies of scale in their favor (e.g., Wal-Mart).

Computers, calculators, and televisions are examples of this phenomenon, as the cost to produce has plummeted in the years since these were first produced. A product to watch in the near future is the hybrid automobile. Currently (in 2009), these vehicles have a significantly higher cost than gas-powered vehicles because the storage batteries are expensive to produce. As economies of scale enter the marketplace, these component costs will decrease and the sticker price for a hybrid vehicle will drop accordingly.

For a manufacturer to maintain sales revenues as prices decline, it has to sell more units by attracting consumers away from other, less efficient producers or by creating new demand. In other industries, the product may be a commodity whose price is determined by the forces of supply and demand. Petroleum prices are an example of such a product. When petroleum prices increase, the revenue and profitability of companies like Exxon Mobil increase; as prices fall, so do revenues and profits. Volatile petroleum prices have led to erratic earnings due to forces outside the control of the organization's management.

The rises and falls of petroleum prices affect other industries. The financial health of the airline industry is inversely related to the cost of aviation fuel. As petroleum prices rise, fuel costs increase, costs of goods increase, and profits decrease, even to the point of eliminating industry profitability. However, this financial risk can be managed whenever senior management identifies such a potential. In 2004 and 2005, Southwest Airlines used derivatives (a security whose value is not intrinsic, but is "derived" from another security) to hedge their cost of aviation fuel. This allowed Southwest to earn a profit while the rest of the industry lost money. In this case, management was able to control some degree of costs imposed on the organization by external economic factors.

Cost of Goods Sold

Cost of Goods Sold (CGS) consists of three components: direct labor, direct materials, and an allocation of overhead. CGS is impacted by the organization's choice of inventory accounting methods. As stated previously, the primary methods of valuing inventory and therefore the cost of direct materials consumed in the production of goods are LIFO, "Last In, First Out," and FIFO, "First In, First Out," and the weighted average method. Once the valuation of inventory is determined, the corresponding value of the direct materials used in production is determined.

In Exhibit 3.1, CGS increased by $88,100 or 11% from $800,000 to $888,100 in year 2008. By itself, this information is of limited value to the analyst since sales increased as well. We would expect CGS to change proportionally with any change in revenue or sales. Exhibit 3.2 is a common-size or percent income statement. Exhibit 3.2 indicates that CGS as a percentage of sales increased from 80% to 83%. This is an area of concern the analyst needs to investigate.

Gross Profit

Gross profit is equal to net sales minus the cost of goods sold. XYZ's gross profit decreased from $200,000 in 2007 to $181,900 in 2008. The Gross Margin is equal to Net Sales minus CGS divided by Net Sales. In this example, the gross margin in 2007 was 20% ($1,000,000 –$ 800,000 or $ 200,000/$1,000,000). The Gross Margin declined to 17% in 2008, due to the increase in CGS as a percentage of Net Sales. While this is useful information, in order to make any trend-related conclusions, a minimum of five years of data is generally required.

Operating Expenses

Two categories of operating expenses are included on XYZ's income statement: Selling, General, and Administrative Expenses and the non-cash expenses of Depreciation, Depletion, and Amortization. Not all firms categorize expenses in the same manner. One firm might classify a sales related expense as part of CGS; another might include it in Selling, General, and Administrative. The analyst needs to be sure to compare apples to apples and to review at least five years of data.

Selling, General, and Administrative Expenses

Selling, General, and Administrative Expenses (SGA) include those expenses related to the marketing and sale of products or services in addition to other corporate management expenses. Those expenses can include rent, salaries (including benefits), utilities, insurance, advertising, and supplies, among others.

Lease payments may be included in SGA or listed as a separate line item. In the exhibit, SGA increased $3,000 from $50,000 to $53,000 from 2007 to 2008. This is a 6% increase. Exhibit 3.2 indicates that SGA decreased from 5% of sales in 2007 to 4.95% in year 2008. XYZ's SGA should also be compared to the industry average and specific competitors.

Depreciation

Depreciation is an accounting technique that allocates the cost of tangible fixed assets over their expected useful life. There are two reasons for calculating depreciation. First, the Internal Revenue Code recognizes depreciation as an expense, but because the source of the expense is a capital expenditure, only a portion of the capital expenditure can be deducted annually. Second, depreciation theoretically allows the organization to accumulate funds to replace the capital expenditure when it is no longer productive. Examples of capital expenditures commonly depreciated are buildings, machinery, fixtures, and automobiles. The organization has a choice between straight-line depreciation and Modified Accelerated Cost Recovery System (MACRS), a system of depreciation detailed in the Internal Revenue Code that accelerates the rate of deprecation and allows a greater tax deduction than would be generated by straight-line depreciation. However, the IRS establishes the parameters of the accelerated rates of depreciation with a schedule according to the type of asset.

Organizations tend to show investors straight-line depreciation in the annual report and utilize MACRS for tax purposes. Utilization of different depreciation methods results in deferred taxes. Deferred taxes are loosely defined as taxes you should have paid to the government based on the income shown to investors, but did not pay because the IRS was shown a different level of taxable income.

Depletion

Depletion allocates the cost of acquiring and developing natural resources, such as oil, gas, lumber, and mineral deposits, over the expected life of the resource. For example, if the organization believes there are 10,000,000 barrels of oil in a new field, the cost of production of those barrels, including the cost of acquiring, developing, and extracting, can be allocated on a per barrel basis, with the depletion allowance representing the costs associated with those barrels extracted during the accounting period.

Amortization

Amortization allocates the cost of intangible assets including goodwill, patents, trademarks, copyrights, and licenses, and others. The method of taking amortization on intangible assets is governed by Internal Revenue Code regulations as well as rulings by the American Institute of Certified Public Accountants (AICPA). An AICPA ruling, FAS 142, drastically altered how companies account for goodwill. Goodwill results whenever an organization acquires an asset or investment for an amount greater than the adjusted book value of the acquisition. The excess price is generally labeled as goodwill and amortized over a period not to exceed 40 years.

Assume an organization pays $200,000,000 for another organization with an adjusted book value of $160,000,000. The excess of $40,000,000 would be listed on the acquirer's balance sheet as goodwill. Over 40 years, the excess payment would be written off at the rate of $1,000,000 per year ($40,000,000/40). This amount would be shown as an expense on the income statement and the value in the goodwill account would be decreased by $1,000,000 each year, reducing the net book value of that asset.

Users of GAAP financial statements need to understand that this type of increase in net income and EPS is due to a change in accounting standards rather than an increase in operating earnings. Instead of an annual write-down of goodwill, organizations are required on a periodic basis (generally interpreted as once a year) to revalue the assets acquired. If the value of an acquired entity is determined to have declined, the acquirer is required to write down the value of those assets on the balance sheet. Instead of seeing a steady, predictable operating expense, investors will face the prospect of a large, unpredictable, asset write-down. Management must indicate these write-downs are "extraordinary" or "below-the-line." Financial analysts are trained to focus on operating on normal profits and to downplay extraordinary items since they are assumed to be non-recurring in nature.

Depreciation, depletion, and amortization expenses are categorized as non-cash expenses. They appear on the income statement as expenses, thus reducing taxable income and taxes paid, but they do not involve cash outlays to the organization in the period they are deducted from taxable earnings. They are added back to net income when estimating a firm's cash flow.

Operating Profit or Earnings Before Interest and Taxes

The flow of revenues starts with gross revenues and is decreased by reductions from revenues followed by the cost of goods sold and other selling, general, and administrative expenses. At this point, the remaining revenues are called Operating Profit, Operating Income, or Earnings Before Interest and Taxes (EBIT).

EBIT divided by sales is the operating profit margin, the percentage measurement of how much of sales revenue is available after paying for the operating expenses. In Exhibit 3.2, the 2008 operating margin is $54,000 divided by $1,070,000, or 5.946%. This operating profit margin would be compared to the industry average or to a competitor's margins (external benchmarking) or tracked over time in an attempt to identify a specific organization's trends (internal benchmarking).

Interest Expense

Interest on debt is tax deductible to the organization. Since the government subsidizes the use of debt, it tends to be the lowest cost source of capital for most organizations. The after-tax cost of debt is equal to the pre-tax cost times 1 minus the tax rate. The statutory tax rate for U.S. corporations is 35%. If a bank loan costs the organization 10% pre-tax, the after-tax cost to the organization is 10% (1-35%) or .10(.65) or 6.5%.

Corporate debt falls into two broad categories: bank loans and bonds. Bank loans are usually variable rates tied to a pricing index, either the prime rate or the London Interbank Offered Rate (LIBOR). The prime rate is the rate the large money center U.S. banks charge their best or most credit-worthy business customers to borrow money. Less credit-worthy customers pay prime plus basis points. One hundred basis points are equal to one percent. If the prime rate was 6% and the organization's loan rate was prime plus 150 basis points, the current interest rate charged would be 7.5%. When the prime moves up or down, the interest rate charged to borrow changes accordingly. This applies to new and existing loans.

Most loans made outside the U.S. (and a growing number within) are priced based on LIBOR rather than the prime rate since it is viewed as being more market rate sensitive.

Bonds pay a fixed coupon payment, usually semi-annually, for the life of the bond and then return the face value of the bond to the investor at maturity. The typical face value of a bond is $1,000.

Example

XYZ Corporation has issued a 10-year, 9% bond paying interest semiannually. The bond matures in 10 years. Each year the bond pays the holder $90 (9% of 1,000) in two semiannual payments of $45. At maturity, the investor receives the face value of the bond ($1,000).

Debts with maturities of less than a year are referred to as bills. Debts with maturities of one to ten years are called notes, and debts with maturities in excess of ten years are referred to as bonds.

When analyzing the debt position of an organization, it is necessary to understand the advantages and disadvantages of debt to the issuer.

Advantages

Interest is tax deductible to the organization, so the after-tax cost of debt is lower than other sources of capital. Holders of debt instruments do not have voting rights and ownership in the organization does not convey to the holder. Issuing equity or stock dilutes the ownership position of current owners. Also, interest is generally a fixed or predictable cost. If the organization can earn a rate of return on its investments greater than the cost of the debt (after-tax interest cost), positive leverage is generated. Leverage will be discussed when we cover the balance sheet.

Disadvantages

Interest payments are a fixed obligation and a fixed cost, so payment is not optional. An organization can reduce or eliminate dividend payments on its stock in periods of economic stress. This is not an option with interest payments on the debt. Failure to meet required debt repayments results in default. Many firms are confronting this situation in today's economic environment. In this case, the full amount of the debt becomes due immediately. Default usually results on the organization filing for bankruptcy protection.

Maturity Structure

The risk manager needs to ask questions relating to the maturity structure of the debt and whether the interest rate is fixed or variable.

The yield curve describes the relationship between maturity and the cost of money. The yield curve is generally upward sloping, meaning that long-term debt costs more than short-term debt. Economics describes interest as being an economic rent for capital, but there is an additional component added to the pure economic rent to compensate the lender for the additional risk of default. Since events are easier to predict in the short-run than in the long run, the risk premium is smaller for short-term loans than for long-term loans. Assume an organization can issue a two-year note at 6% or a 20-year bond at 9%. The organization can save 3% (ignoring taxes for a moment) by issuing the two-year note. The short-term borrowing has a lower cost, but has more risk in terms of the cost certainty. In two years, the debt must be either paid off or refinanced. If it is going to be paid off, the organization must make sure it has sufficient cash flow to meet the obligation. If the note is going to be refinanced and interest rates have increased, the organization's interest costs will increase. The bond's cost, while higher, is fixed for 20 years, bringing cost certainty to the issuer.

<u>Fixed Versus Variable Rate</u>

A bank loan at prime plus points is a variable rate loan. The cost of money to the borrower will rise or fall based on changes in the prime rate. This is a version of interest rate risk. The 9% 20-year bond is an example of a fixed-rate obligation. In an environment where interest rates are declining, organizations are willing to borrow on a variable rate basis. However, when rates begin to increase, the organization's cost of borrowing will increase. Short-term variable rate debt is typically the lowest cost source of borrowing. Long-term fixed rate costs more but is less risky in terms of the interest rate risk, or the possibility that the cost of borrowing is likely to increase.

Earnings Before Taxes

Earnings Before Taxes (EBT) is EBIT minus interest. This is also called the organizations' pre-tax income.

Taxes

The statutory tax rate for large U.S. corporations is 35%. State and local taxes may also be an issue in those states and localities that have corporate income taxes. The effective tax rate is the rate that the organization actually pays. Rarely is the effective rate equal to the statutory rate. The reasons for this difference include but are not limited to tax loss carry-forwards, tax credits, earnings in countries with tax rates other than 35%, dividends from one corporation to another, and the net income due on the tax return rather than the "tax" indicated on the publicly available financial statements (the annual report). In Exhibit 3.1, we assume the organization is paying the statutory rate.

Net Income

Net Income is the organization's after-tax profit. Net income divided by sales is equal to the net profit margin. In Exhibit 3.2, the net profit margin in the current period is $20,475/$1,070,000, or 1.913%. Net Income is often referred to as "the bottom line" since it is often the last line on the income statement. In the exhibit, this is the case, but it is not always so. If an organization has outstanding preferred stock, there is yet another reduction.

Preferred Stock

Preferred stock is a hybrid security having characteristics of debt and of equity. Preferred stock pays an after-tax dividend, as does common stock. The preferred stock dividend, however, is fixed much like the interest cost on a bond. Unlike a bond, preferred stock does not have a maturity date; it has an infinite life similar to common stock. A $100 par value preferred stock pays a fixed dividend per year forever; say 6% of the par, or $6 per year. This amount would be deducted from net income on the income statement. The value shown after the deduction of preferred stock dividends is generally called Earnings Available to Common shareholders. (EAC)

Disposition of Net Income

Net income (NI) or Earnings Available to Common shareholders (EAC), whichever is the last line on the income statement, is either paid out in the form of common stock dividends or retained by the organization. If it is retained by the organization, it shows up on the balance sheet as an increase in retained earnings. In Exhibit 3.1, in 2008 the organization had a net income of $20,475. There were 10,000 common shares outstanding and the organization declared and paid a $2 per share dividend, $20,000 is deducted from the net income (or EAC, if there had been preferred shares), and the balance of $475 is retained by the organization, with the value shown in Retained Earnings. Common stock dividends, when paid, are paid quarterly. In this case, the organization pays a dividend of $.50 per quarter per common share.

Payout Rate

The payout rate or ratio is the percentage of earnings paid out in dividends. In Exhibit 3.1, the 2008 payout rate was $20,000/$20,475, or 97.68%. In this case, the organization paid out almost all of its earnings in the form of dividends. This very high rate could be the result of an unexpected decrease in earnings, as some organizations are reluctant to cut their dividends. If earnings fluctuate and the dividend per share remains constant, the payout rate will fluctuate drastically. If the payout rate has been relatively steady at this level, it may indicate that the organization is in a mature industry with limited growth opportunities. A growing organization retains most if not all of its earnings to reinvest within the organization.

Retention Rate

The retention rate is the percentage of earnings retained or reinvested by the company. The retention rate is one minus the payout rate. 1 – 0.9768 = 0.0232 or 2.32%. Since the payout rate is very high, this retention rate is very low. The retention rate represents the extent of internal funding of the organization's operations. What the organization cannot fund internally, it must fund externally by issuing debt or equity. Evaluation of the organization's retention and payout levels provides insight into the organizations' growth potential, external funding needs, and the risk tolerance of management. Management of a growth-oriented organization tends to have a higher tolerance or appetite for risk than management in an organization with a lower growth rate or in a mature industry.

Earnings per Share (EPS)

Earnings per share (EPS) is equal to net income or earnings available to common shares divided by the number of shares of common stock outstanding. In the exhibit, in 2008, the net income of $20,475 is divided by the number of shares outstanding (10,000), giving an EPS of $2.05. Investors and analysts focus a great deal of attention (and probably too much attention) on the organization's EPS. If the organization meets or beats expected earnings the stock price will usually increase because the analysts view this as positive information related to the firm's current and future income. If the company fails to meet earnings expectations, the price of their stock usually declines, sometimes precipitously. In some organizations, maximizing EPS is a major goal.

Dividends per Share

Dividends per share are dividends paid divided by the number of shares of common stock outstanding. From the exhibit, $20,000/10,000 shares equals $2 per share paid in quarterly installments of $0.50 per share. Investors buy stock expecting a stream of dividends and/or the potential that the market price of the stock will increase (capital gains). Dividends provide a current stream of income to investors. If an organization cuts its dividends, investors seeking income or yield will sell the stock. The advantage of dividends to investors is that they provide current income. The disadvantage is that dividends are subject to income taxation to the recipient. The disadvantage of dividends to the issuer is that they are paid with after-tax dollars. Additionally, funds paid out in dividends often need to be replaced with external sources of funding.

Price to Earnings Multiple

The Price to Earnings (P/E) multiple is the stock price divided by the earnings per share. The market price for a share of the company's stock is $35. The P/E multiple is $35.00/$2.05, or 17.07. This logic is backwards to a degree. Investors determine the multiple of earnings they are willing to pay and multiply it by the estimated EPS to determine the price they are willing to pay for a share of stock. Investors are willing to pay a higher multiple for stocks that they feel will provide higher rates of growth in sales and earnings and therefore generate a higher price in the future or that will provide greater dividends. Growth companies (technology, biotech) sell at higher multiples than do mature companies (automobiles, insurance, home appliances) because of the possibility of capital gains and future dividends.

Dividend Yield

Dividend yield is equal to the annual dividend per share divided by the stock price, $2/$35 = 5.714%. Dividend yield represents the cash return on the investment's value, similar to the return on a bank account. A 5.714% yield is extremely high for a stock under most market scenarios. A 5% dividend yield is typical of utility stocks, real estate investment trusts (REIT's), and mature organizations/industries with limited ability to reinvest funds profitably. A dividend yield that is too high relative to the industry and market norms may be a red flag that the firm is in trouble (rapidly declining stock price) and that future dividends may be reduced or eliminated.

Common Size Income Statement

Common size income statements, or percent income statements, take the income statements from Exhibit 3.1 and convert them from a dollar basis to a percentage of sales basis. Sales each year represent one hundred percent. Each cost or revenue is converted from dollars to the percentage they represent of that year's sales revenue. The five years of common size income statements for XYZ Company are seen in Exhibit 3.2. In 2008, the cost of goods sold was $888,100 (Exhibit 3.1) and sales were $1,070,000. $888,100/$1,070,000 is equal to 83%, or the cost of goods sold was 83% of sales. This results in a gross profit margin of 17%. This profit margin needs to be compared to a benchmark in order to determine how well the organization is performing.

Possible benchmarks that can be used are:

1. Industry averages

2. Specific competitors

3. The overall economy

4. A time series analysis of XYZ company results

Note that benchmarks #1-3 are external benchmarks, and #4 is an internal benchmark.

With external benchmarks, we find that industry grouping often contains dissimilar organizations in terms of operations and size. When evaluating the performance of a local hardware store, the industry average gross margin would include results from Home Depot and Lowe's, two "hardware" stores whose economies of scale and diverse operations are significantly different from that small, locally owned store. If the data is available, it is better to compare the organization to specific competitors whose operations and size are the closest match to the organization being analyzed; Coca Cola versus Pepsi Cola, and Lowe's compared to Home Depot are examples of reasonably well matched competitors.

Exhibit 3.3: External Benchmarks for Profit Margins (2008)

ORGANIZATION	Gross Margin
XYZ	17%
Industry Average	21%
Competitor D	22%
Competitor E	22%

Looking at the external benchmarks for the year 2004 in Exhibit 3.3, the observer sees that XYZ's gross margin is significantly below the industry average as well as competitors D and E. Management and outside analysts need to determine why the organizations' gross margin is below the benchmarks. Going back to the discussion of the income statement, cost of goods sold (CGS) consists of direct labor, direct materials, and an allocation of overhead. This information is generally not disclosed in the annual report. The analyst needs to determine which of the three cost components increased as a percentage of sales. Assume that the only component that increased as a percentage was direct labor. The next question is why did labor increase? The answer might be that the company just signed a new labor contract with its major union that contained provisions increasing wage rates. Assuming that the new contract is binding, the organization has several options to restore or improve their profit margin. The options include raising the price of its product or service, increasing productivity, or cutting other costs. Cutting costs often is referred to as "rightsizing" and usually results in employees being terminated.

Internal benchmarking involves comparing an organization's margin over time to determine if a trend exists. Exhibit 3.2 indicates that XYZ's gross margin has declined from 22% in 2004 to 17% in 2008. Cost of goods sold has increased from 78% of sales to 83% of sales and the gross margin declined by 5%. A significant portion of this decline occurred between 2007 and 2008 when the margin declined by 3%. The trend is pronounced and negative. This should be a significant concern to management and analysts, especially when combined with the external benchmarks.

Operating Margin

Operating margin is defined as earnings before interest and taxes (EBIT) divided by sales. In XYZ's income statement, two categories of expenses occur between the gross margin and the operating margin. The categories are selling, general, and administrative costs and the non-cash expenses of depreciation, depletion and amortization.

Exhibit 3.4: Operating Expense Benchmarks (2008)

ORGANIZATION	SGA	Non Cash Item	Operating Margin
XYZ	5.0%	7.0%	5.0%
Industry Average	5.1%	7.1%	8.8%
Competitor D	5.1%	7.2%	9.7%
Competitor E	5.2%	7.1%	9.7%

Selling, General, and Administrative Expenses

In Exhibit 3.4, XYZ's selling, general and administrative (SGA) expense as a percentage of sales is lower than the industry average and competitors D and E. This generally is considered an indicator that XYZ is doing a good job of controlling this group of expenditures. An alternative view could be that the organization is not spending enough to promote and market the company and its products. Time series analysis (see Exhibit 3.2) indicates that XYZ had reduced its SGA expense as a percentage of sales from 5.2% to 5.0%, thus improving the operating margin by 0.2%.

Depreciation, Depletion, and Amortization

Depreciation, depletion, and amortization amounts shown on financial statements can tell an analyst, or a risk manager, a number of things about a company. In Exhibit 3.4, XYZ's non-cash expenses in 2008 are below those of the industry average and its major competitors. Additionally, Exhibit 3.2 shows that non-cash expenses have decreased from 7.3% of sales in 2008 to 7.0% in 2008, resulting in an improvement to the organization's operating margin. However, this is not necessary desirable. While the increased profit margin is viewed as a positive factor, non-cash expenses represent a tax shelter and a higher operating profit will result in higher taxes, assuming the same information is reported (highly unlikely) to the IRS. Second, the level of depreciation is related to the amount of money the organization invests in plant, property, and equipment. Investments in fixed assets such as plant and equipment represent potential future production and sales. A decrease in depreciation implies that the organization is not reinvesting capital to generate future growth. Generally, analysts will not view this as a positive outcome. Finally, under FAS 142, goodwill is no longer amortized; it will no longer appear on the income statement as an operating expense that will lower reported costs and increase the operating profits.

Net Profit Margin

The net profit margin is equal to net income divided by sales. Assuming that the organization pays the statutory tax rate (very low probability), the only controllable cost in XYZ's income statement (Exhibit 3.1) between EBIT and net income is interest expense.

Exhibit 3.5: Interest Expense and Net Margin (2008)

ORGANIZATION	Interest Expense	Net margin
XYZ	2.1%	1.9%
Industry Average	2.5%	4.1%
Competitor D	2.5%	4.8%
Competitor E	2.5%	4.8%

In Exhibit 3.2, XYZ's interest expense as a percentage of sales is below the industry average and competitors D and E. XYZ's interest expense was 2.4% of sales in 2004, peaked at 2.5% in 2006, and has declined to 2.1% in 2008. The lower interest expense can be attributed to XYZ having less debt, or a lower cost of borrowing than the industry and their competitors. XYZ's net margin has decreased from 4.7% to 1.9%, or 2.8% of sales from 2004 to 2008. Remember from Exhibit 3.3 that XYZ's gross margin was 4% below the industry average and 5% lower than competitors D and E. Based on XYZ's ability to control their SGA, non-cash and interest expenses have reduced the gap between the organization and its benchmarks at the operating and net margin levels.

As this case demonstrates, the common size income statement is a valuable tool for analysts, management and risk managers in understanding why profit margins increase or decrease over time.

Inventory Valuation Methods

The inventory valuation method chosen by the organization affects cost of goods sold, pre-tax profit, taxes, net income, and cash flow on the income statement in addition to the carrying value of inventory on the balance sheet. Inventory valuation methods assume no relationship exists between the actual order in which products are sold and the accounting for those units. If you produce 25,000 automobiles at a cost of $20,000 each and each is stamped with a vehicle identification number, it is possible to match the cost of producing that vehicle with the revenues generated from the sale of that vehicle. If you manufacture automobile tires that wholesale for $50 each, it is less practical to attempt to match unit costs and revenues to specific tires, even though each tire might be identified with a serial number.

Accountants attempt to match the cost of products sold during a period to the revenue generated from the sale of those products. If a manufacturer produces 50,000 tires and sells only 30,000 tires during the period, accountants use a cost flow assumption to match revenues to costs. If the cost of production and sales prices remained constant over the period, the choice of inventory valuation method is not an important issue. When the cost of product and or the sales price changes during the period, it is important for the risk manager to understand the impact of the choice of an inventory valuation method on the organization's financial statements.

The three major cost flow models used by U.S. companies are FIFO (First-In First-Out), LIFO (Last In First Out), and weighted average cost. Under FIFO, the first units produced or purchased are the first units sold. Using LIFO, the last units produced or purchased are the first units to be sold. The average cost method calculates an average purchase price or cost of production to determine the cost of goods sold.

Normally you must use the same inventory valuation method for shareholders and the IRS. You cannot show FIFO to the shareholders and LIFO to the IRS. However, if the organization owns multiple business units and files consolidated financial statements, each business unit can make its own selection of inventory valuation methods. If the organization owns or operates ten business units, six could choose LIFO, three FIFO, and one the weighted average method.

The following example will illustrate the importance of the choice of inventory valuation method by showing the impact on the balance sheet and income statement. This example assumes that inflation exists within the industry and the cost of producing or purchasing inventory is increasing during the period. This is not true in all industries. In a number of industries, such as computer hardware, economies of scale and market conditions result in declining prices over time, in which case the results will be the opposite of those outlined in this example.

Exhibit 3.6: Formula to Calculate Costs of Goods Sold

Beginning inventory
+ cost of items produced or purchased during the period
= available for sale
- ending inventory
= cost of goods sold

Exhibit 3.6 shows the accounting equation used to calculate costs of goods sold. Two organizations, Alpha and Beta, manufacture and sell the ubiquitous widgets found in all accounting textbooks. Both organizations have a beginning inventory of 10,000 widgets at a cost of $4 each for a beginning inventory of $40,000. During the accounting period, the organizations produce or purchase 30,000 additional widgets in three batches of 10,000 widgets each. The cost of the first 10,000 widgets is $4.50 each; the next 10,000 widgets cost $4.75 each, and the last group of 10,000 widgets cost $5.00 per widget. Both organizations have 40,000 widgets available for sale and both actually sell 30,000 widgets at a price of $6 per widget. Exhibit 3.7 outlines the revenue, cost of goods sold, profit, tax, cash flow, and balance sheet impact for Alpha (LIFO) and Beta (FIFO).

Exhibit 3.7: Comparing LIFO and FIFO

	Alpha (LIFO)	Beta (FIFO)
Beginning inventory	10,000 ($4) = $40,000	10,000 ($4) = $40,000
+ purchases	10,000 ($4.5) = $45,000	10,000 ($4.5) = $45,000
	10,000 ($4.75) = $47,500	10,000 ($4.75) = $47,500
	10,000 ($5) = $50,000	10,000 ($5) = $50,000
= available for sale	40,000 units = $182,500	40,000 units = $182,500
- ending inventory	10,000 units = $40,000	10,000 units = $50,000
Cost of goods sold	$142,500	$132,500
Sales	30,000 ($6) = $180,000	30,000 ($6) = $180,000
- cost of goods sold	$142,500	$132,500
= pretax profit	$37,500	$47,500
- taxes (35%)	$13,125	$16,625
= net income	$24,375	$30,875

In a period of increasing cost of production or purchasing inventory, FIFO (Beta) results in a lower cost of goods sold, a higher pre-tax profit, higher taxes paid, and lower cash flow resulting from the higher tax cost. The two organizations are operationally identical but their income statements are very different. A financial manager would choose LIFO since it reduces taxable income and taxes paid resulting in higher cash flow. FIFO results in higher profits that might impress potential investors if they are unaware that the higher income is simply the result of an accounting decision rather than operational factors.

LIFO results in understating the value of inventory on the balance sheet. Beta's ending inventory is $40,000 compared to $50,000 for Alpha. Since the most recent widgets produced cost $5 each, $50,000 is a more accurate reflection of the replacement cost of the widgets in inventory. An analyst or risk manager needs to be aware of the distortions caused by the inventory valuation choice. Many of the organization's key financial ratios (current ratio, net working capital, return on assets, and others) will be affected by this decision. The risk manager must be especially careful when considering the value of inventory and the cost of goods sold and net income for insurance purposes, as the values shown on the financial statements may not reflect the appropriate values for insurance.

The Balance Sheet

Assets

Assets are the positive side of a company's balance sheet and are made up of current and fixed assets.

Current Assets

Current assets, also known as Working Capital, are those assets that are cash or will be converted to cash within one operating cycle or have a maturity of one year or less. Current assets generate a low rate of return (if any), but provide the organization the liquidity to pay its short-term obligations. Despite the term "asset," which implies something of value, finance managers seek to minimize the level of current assets an organization maintains. The goal is to provide sufficient liquidity to enable the organization to pay its bills in a timely manner and keep its creditors happy while at the same time maximizing the return on total assets. Since the organization should earn a higher return on its fixed assets than its current assets, management will attempt to shift as many assets as possible to fixed assets if their goal is to maximize the organization's profitability. To a risk manager, current assets provide a cushion to pay for unexpected non-catastrophic losses. In this context, higher levels of current assets and liquidity are preferable. The risk manager will think about working capital issues along the same lines as a creditor: the more liquidity and working capital the better. This view conflicts with that of the chief financial officer, whose goal is to maximize returns on the organization's investment.

Cash

Cash on hand and balances in most corporate checking accounts earn a zero rate of return. Cash is an idle asset generating no income or yield. A standard formula in any corporate finance textbook calculates the minimum cash balance that the organization can maintain and still be able to pay its creditors on time. As mentioned above, to the risk manager, cash provides a cushion against unexpected losses. The CFO is extremely interested in generating cash flow, but wants to see that cash flow reinvested in projects that earn a rate of return in excess of the organization's cost of capital. Cash on the balance sheet is the money that the organization has been unable or unwilling to put to work. In Exhibit 3.8, at year-end 2008, XYZ held $70,000 in cash on their balance sheet or 8.62% of total assets ($70,000/$812,100), a significant increase from the 6.25% ($50,000/$800,000) of total assets in 2004. A risk manager may view this as a positive since cash would be available to pay for losses both expected and unexpected. The financial analyst would ask why management has allowed cash, with a zero rate of return, to reach this level.

Marketable Securities

Marketable securities are those short-term (less than one year, and usually less than 270 days) investments that are readily convertible into cash. Accountants refer to these securities as cash equivalents. These are low risk, low return investments. Examples are U.S. Treasury bills, certificates of deposit with a commercial bank, and commercial paper (high quality corporate debt). Assume that the current interest rate for a certificate of deposit is 3%. This return is clearly better than 0% on cash. However, the 3% is subject to taxation as income and has a low rate of return (unadjusted for inflation). Given a 35% tax rate and a 2.5% inflation rate, the after-tax real rate of return is negative. (3.0% x.65= 1.95% pre-inflation rate of return). Additionally, if a company needs to withdraw funds from a certificate of deposit prior to maturity, there will be an early withdrawal penalty. The bottom line financially is that while 3% is better than zero, it is not an attractive investment option for the organization. Again, the risk manager will view marketable securities the same way a creditor would: these are funds available to pay bills or losses. In Exhibit 3.8, the 2008 balance sheet marketable securities were valued at $25,000, the same level as 2004.

Exhibit 3.8: Balance Sheet

	2008	2007	2006	2005	2004
Assets					
Cash	$70,000	$60,000	$60,000	$55,000	$50,000
Marketable securities	$25,000	$20,000	$20,000	$25,000	$25,000
Accounts receivables	$130,000	$120,000	$115,000	$105,000	$100,000
Inventory	$145,000	$140,000	$135,000	$130,000	$125,000
Other current assets	--	--	--	--	--
Total current assets	$370,000	$340,000	$330,000	$315,000	$300,000
Property, plant, and equipment	$400,000	$400,000	$300,000	$300,000	$250,000
Land and buildings	$500,000	$500,000	$500,000	$500,000	$500,000
Machinery and equipment	$170,000	$150,000	$150,000	$134,900	$100,000
Gross PPE	$1,070,000	$1,050,000	$950,000	$934,900	$850,000
less accumulated depreciation	$627,900	$553,000	$483,000	$415,000	$350,000
Net PPE	$442,100	$497,000	$467,000	$519,900	$500,000
Other assets	--	--	--	--	--
Total Assets	$812,100	$837,000	$797,000	$834,900	$800,000

Liabilities and Stockholders Equity					
Accounts payable	$60,000	$55,000	$50,000	$46,400	$40,000
Accruals	$65,000	$65,000	$60,000	$65,000	$60,000
Other current liabilities	--	--	--	--	--
Notes payable (to balance)	$3,525	$33,900	$19,650	$100,150	$100,000
Total current liabilities	$128,525	$153,900	$129,650	$211,550	$200,000
Long-term debt	$300,000	$300,000	$300,000	$275,000	$275,000
Other liabilities	--	--	--	--	--
Total Liabilities	$428,525	$453,900	$429,650	$486,550	$475,000
Stockholders Equity					
Retained earnings	$183,575	$183,100	$167,350	$148,350	$125,000
Common stock	$10,000	$10,000	$10,000	$10,000	$10,000
Paid in excess	$190,000	$190,000	$190,000	$190,000	$190,000
Other stockholders equity	--	--	--	--	--
Total Stockholders Equity	$383,575	$383,100	$367,350	$348,350	$325,000
Total Liabilities and Stockholders Equity	$812,100	$837,000	$797,000	$834,900	$800,000
Dividends	$20,000	$20,000	$20,000	$15,000	$15,000
# Shares	10,000	10,000	10,000	10,000	$10,000
Stock price	$35	$40	$45	$40	$37

Accounts Receivable

Accounts receivable are balances outstanding on credit sales. Accounts receivable are recorded on the balance sheet on a net basis, with an allowance for doubtful accounts. Organizations extend credit to customers in order to increase sales. The benefit of increased sales and profit must be balanced against the delay in the receipt of cash and the potential for slow payment and customer default. Granting customer credit often requires the organization to borrow money to finance the receivables, which tie up funds that could otherwise be invested at a positive rate of return. There is an opportunity cost to the organization related to accounts receivable. The rate of return on receivables is negative due to the cost of financing them. The analyst needs to balance the benefits of increased sales versus the cost of carrying the accounts receivable to the organization. The goal of the finance function is to minimize the organization's investment in Accounts Receivable without adversely affecting sales. At year-end 2008 in Exhibit 3.8, XYZ's Accounts Receivables balance was $130,000, an increase of $30,000, or 30% from the level of $100,000 in 2004. In 2004 accounts receivable represented 11.76% ($100,000/$850,000) of sales, in 2008 they were equal to 12.15% ($130,000/$1,070,000). Accounts receivable should increase proportionally with sales and a slight increase as a percentage of sales should not be a major concern.

Credit Terms

Credit terms are the conditions under which a customer is expected to pay the accounts receivable. A common credit term for receivables is "net 30," meaning the full amount of the receivable is due in 30 days. Under these terms, the customer has no incentive to pay before day 30. (In fact, if they did, you would have to question their financial IQ.) Their goal is to keep their money as long as possible, just as yours is to get money owed you as soon as possible. One option to speed up the payment of receivables would be to offer 2/10 net 30 terms. If the customer pays by day 10, they take a 2% discount on the balance owed. If they do not pay by day 10, the full amount is due on the 30th day. The faster payment on day 10 needs to be balanced against the fact that the organization receives 2% less revenue. From the seller's perspective, this is an expensive inducement to pay early. A 2% discount to pay 20 days earlier equates to an annualized interest rate of 37.25% (2/98 times 365/20). Unless the organization can invest its funds at a rate in excess of 37.25%, it should not offer 2/10 net 30 terms. However, prompt payment reduces the risk of default. Also, some organizations may choose to increase their prices (when the marketplace allows this) to cover the discount on receivables. If creditors pay promptly, the seller is in the same position prior to the price increase, and if creditors do not take the discount, there is an additional 2% profit added on.

Inventory

There are three types of inventory: raw materials, work in progress, and finished goods. Similar to accounts receivable, some level of inventory is necessary to generate sales. The rate of return on inventory is negative due to the cost of carrying or financing them. The benefits of increased sales, longer production runs that may result in lower unit costs, and any potential discounts from purchasing raw materials in bulk must be balanced against the cost of carrying the inventory. Inventory is generally considered the least liquid of the current assets and is subtracted when calculating certain liquidity ratios.

The trend in recent years has been for organizations to reduce their inventory levels in order to lower the cost of carrying inventory. The just-in-time inventory method was introduced by the Japanese automobile industry in an effort to lower, if not eliminate, inventory carrying costs. Instead of holding an inventory of tires, engines, chassis, and other components, they subcontracted with suppliers to provide these materials to them on an as-needed basis. If a plant planned to produce 100 vehicles on a given day, suppliers would agree to deliver 100 engines, 400 tires, etc., on that day, thus keeping the value of inventory at a minimum and the inventory carrying costs at a minimum.

No system is perfect: just-in-time inventory leaves the producer vulnerable to a disruption in supply. Unless a substantial safety stock of inventory exists, the company has no protection if the supplier fails to deliver in a timely manner, a situation that could result in a possible shutdown of operations. Production-to-order is a variation on just-in-time inventory. In this case, the plant would only produce automobiles based on the number of orders from customers. Instead of producing 100 vehicles per day in the expectation that customers would eventually purchase them, a dealer would notify the manufacture when a customer placed an order and the plant would then build the automobile. This system eliminates inventory, but results in delays when delivering the vehicle to the customer.

Inventory is a tangible asset whose value must be protected by the risk manager. The list of possible perils to inventory includes physical damage, theft, and changes in technology that result in a loss of value due to obsolescence. In order to protect these assets, it is necessary to place a value on the inventory. The carrying value of inventory on the balance sheet is often not equal to replacement cost, market value, or insurable value; it represents the history cost or the arbitrary, and often tax-management-motivated, LIFO/FIFO valuations methods. Remember our discussion of the impact of the choice between LIFO and FIFO? LIFO resulted in the ending inventory value being understated on the balance sheet when prices are increasing.

Another challenge facing the risk manager is the treatment of work in process. In most manufacturers, raw materials do not instantly change into finished goods at the snap of some robotic fingers. Instead, the raw materials flow across the manufacturing floor and gradually are changed into finished goods when more raw materials and labor are added to them. The problem facing the risk manager is how to value work in process, both from a percentage of completion basis and the point at which general overhead charges are added. For example, the ubiquitous widget starts as a "wid", and then a worker adds the "get" to make a finished widget, but that process needs a factory floor, equipment, process materials, electricity, and all the other costs associated with producing a finished widget that are not raw materials and labor. But when does the overhead charge or burden get added – is it when the wid is first pulled out of the supply bin, or when the worker attaches the get, or when the finished widget leaves the assembly line and ends up in the bin awaiting sale? In the event of a loss to work in process, the valuation of the work in process will be challenging.

It is necessary to review the notes of the organization's financial statements (for publicly traded organizations) to estimate the amount of the understatement. If an organization is not publicly traded and does not disclose this information, the risk manager needs to ask management for an estimate of the replacement value of their inventory and work in progress. At year-end 2008, ABC's inventory value on the balance sheet in Exhibit 3.8 was $145,000, an increase of $20,000, or 16% from the 2004 level. However, inventory has decreased as a percentage of sales from 14.7% ($125,000/$850,000) in 2000 to 13.55% ($145,000/$1,070,000) in 2008. As sales increase, you would expect inventory to increase proportionally. The fact that inventory decreased as a percentage of sales would be viewed as a positive indicator by the CFO. Since the rate of return on inventory is negative, the reduction in inventory as a percentage of sales implies the organization has found a way to reallocate those funds to business opportunities that will generate a positive rate of return.

Fixed Assets

Fixed assets are those assets with an expected life in excess of one year. They are also referred to as tangible assets, capital assets, and long-lived assets. Most fixed assets consist of plant, property, and equipment (PPE). Specific fixed assets are often categorized as land, buildings and leasehold improvements, equipment, and construction in progress. The value assigned to fixed assets on an organization's balance sheet is based on the original acquisition cost or historical cost. These assets are carried at book value, the original cost minus accumulated depreciation.

The two basic depreciation methods available are straight-line depreciation and accelerated depreciation. Straight-line depreciation spreads out the expense evenly over the expected life of the asset. When using an accelerated method more of the expense is taken in the early years of the asset's life and less in the later years. The total depreciation over the life of the asset is the same regardless of the technique chosen. The carrying value of a fixed asset depends on estimates made by management related to the estimated useful life of the asset and the depreciation technique used by the organization.

If an asset has been held by the organization for an extended period of time, its book value may be substantially lower than its market value, replacement value, and/or its insurable value. For example, an organization purchases a warehouse for $1 million. The structure is estimated to have a useful life of 20 years with a salvage value of zero. If the organization uses straight-line depreciation, the annual expense or reduction in value will be $50,000. If the warehouse had been purchased 15 years ago, its book value would currently be $250,000. Book value is based on an accrual accounting system designed to make the balance sheet balance. Therefore, book value is not a reliable estimate of the value the risk manager needs to protect.

In Exhibit 3.8, XYZ's balance sheet lists values for gross plant, property and equipment, as well as net plant, property and equipment. At year-end 2008, gross PPE was $1,070,000, an increase of 25.9% from $850,000 in 2004. (It is a coincidence that these numbers are there same as the level of sales in each of those years.) Net PPE is equal to gross PPE minus accumulated depreciation. During 2008, XYZ's gross PPE increased by $20,000, depreciation on the 2008 income statement was $74,900 resulting in a decrease in net PPE of $54,900. Even though gross PPE increased during the period, net PPE decreased due to the ongoing accounting depreciation of assets. Net PPE represents the book value of the assets held by XYZ Company; it bears little if any resemblance to market value, replacement value, or insurable value.

Many organizations lease assets instead of purchasing them. Depending on the terms of the lease, the lease will be categorized as either a capitalized lease or an operating lease. If the lease is capitalized, the value of the asset and the liability incurred by the lease obligation will be shown on the organization's balance sheet. In the case of an operating lease, an off-balance sheet asset and liability will result. These values will not be included on the balance sheet, but will be disclosed in the notes to the financial statements. The lease payment will show up on the income statement as an expense. The risk manager must go to the notes in the financial statements in order to estimate the organization's exposure related to leased assets.

Liabilities and Equity

Current Liabilities

Current liabilities are claims against assets. Current liabilities are short-term obligations or bills owed by the organization with a maturity of one year or less or one operating cycle, whichever is less. Given the typically upward sloping yield curve, current liabilities will be less expensive than longer-term liabilities. Current liabilities represent low cost, or in some cases, free, financing to the organization. The CFO must balance the advantage of low cost against the fact that the organization must have sufficient cash or other current assets to pay these obligations in a timely manner.

Accounts Payable

Accounts Payable are the flip side of accounts receivable; they are the short-term obligations that result from credit extended by suppliers for the purchase of their goods and services. An example would be the purchase of raw materials from a supplier on net 30-day terms. In this case, the supplier is providing 30 days of financing at a 0% interest rate. This represents "free financing" to the organization. It is in the best interest of the organization to pay the supplier as late as possible without damaging their credit rating or their relationship with the supplier. It would make no sense to pay the supplier before the 30th day.

Organizations may attempt to stretch their accounts payable beyond 30 days in order to maximize this free source of financing. If a supplier offers 2/10 net 30 terms, this is no longer free financing. The cost of paying on the 30th day or beyond equates to a 37.25% cost of borrowing. In this case, the organization should pay promptly on day 10. In Exhibit 3.8, XYZ's Accounts Payable at year-end 2008 were $60,000. This figure represents a 50% increase from the $40,000 level in 2004. During the same five-year period, sales increased 25.9% from $850,000 to $1,070,000. The fact that Accounts Payable increased at twice the rate as sales may be something the analyst or risk manager needs to examine.

Notes Payable

Notes Payable are short-term promissory notes to financial institutions. Often notes payable are in the form of a line of credit. A $1 million line of credit means that the organization is pre-approved by the bank to owe up to $1 million at any point in time. On a non-guaranteed line of credit, the organization would not pay interest unless they utilize the line of credit. The interest rate on a line of credit and other notes payable from a financial institution are generally based on the prime rate or LIBOR. The prime rate is the rate the large money center banks charge their best business customers to borrow. Organizations typically pay the prime rate plus points based on their credit worthiness. The rate on the loan is typically variable, meaning that whenever the prime rate changes the rate on the loan will change as well. Remember, interest payments on business loans are tax-deductible to the organization so that the after-tax cost is equal to the stated rate times one minus the tax rate.

At year-end 2008 in Exhibit 3.8, XYZ's notes payable were $3,525, a substantial reduction from the $100,000 level at year-end 2004. XYZ has significantly reduced its reliance on short-term notes payable to finance the organization's continuing operations. The decrease in notes payable is the major reason that XYZ's total liabilities have decreased from $475,000 to $428,525 during a five-year period when total assets increased from $800,000 to $812,100. Creditors will consider the reduction in debt as a positive indicator. A financial analyst may be concerned that the reduction in debt and leverage may reduce the organization's return on equity.

Accrued Liabilities

Accrued liabilities arise out of accrual accounting, the basis used by nearly all businesses, as opposed to cash basis accounting. Revenue and expenses are recognized when earned or incurred regardless of when a cash payment is made. An accrued liability results when an expense is recognized prior to the actual cash payment. A less technical definition of an accrual is something you owe but have not yet paid. If you pay your employees once a week on Friday, during the week you create deferred wages and salaries. If you can arrange to pay your employees once a month instead of once a week, you will increase your accrued wages. Accrued wages would be a source of free financing to the organization. The two accrued liabilities for most firms will be wages (and salaries), and taxes. At year-end 2008 in Exhibit 3.8, XYZ had accruals of $65,000. Over the five-year period from 2004 to 2008, XYZ's accruals have remained relatively stable between $60,000 and $65,000 per year.

Commercial Paper

Commercial paper is a short-term unsecured debt obligation of a large corporation with very strong credit. The maturity of commercial paper is generally 270 days or less. Commercial paper is issued in large denominations, usually a $100,000 minimum. Commercial paper is only available to the largest, most creditworthy issuers; therefore, it will not be found on the balance sheet of most companies.

Long-Term Funds

Long-term debt and stockholders equity represent long-term sources of funds to the organization in the form of debt and equity. Debt with a maturity of one year or longer is considered to be long-term debt. Equity is considered to be long-term financing by definition since it does not have a maturity date. When a finance person uses the term "capital," they are referring to long-term funding sources. The cost of capital refers to the average cost of long-term funds to the organization.

Long-term Debt

Added Debentures, Bonds, Mortgages

Long-term debt instruments are obligations with a maturity date beyond one year, typically in the form of long-term notes, mortgages, and bonds. The portion of long-term debt that is due within one year will be classified on the balance sheet as a current liability. Long-term debt will typically be the least expensive source of capital to the organization because the interest on the debt is tax-deductible. In 2008 in Exhibit 3.8, XYZ Company had $300,000 in long-term debt outstanding, which represents a $25,000 or 9.09% increase from the $275,000 level in 2004.

Stockholders Equity

Stockholder equity represents the ownership interest in the organization. Owner's equity is equal to the value of the organization's assets minus its outstanding liabilities. Owners' claims are subordinated to the claims of creditors in the event of the liquidation of the organization. Owners bear the greatest risk in exchange for the potential rewards from a successful business operation.

Common Stock

Common stock represents the claims of stockholders, the residual owners of the organization.   Shareholders do not receive a fixed rate of return, but may benefit from dividends and a potential increase in the value of the shares. The amount listed on the balance sheet for common stock is equal to the par value of the stock times the number of shares of stock outstanding. For legal purposes, the par value is usually set substantially below the initial offering price of the stock to the public.

In Exhibit 3.8, XYZ has 10,000 shares of common stock outstanding issued to the public at a price of $20 per share. The par value of the stock is one dollar per share. The amount entered on the balance sheet for common stock is one dollar per share times 10,000 shares or $10,000. XYZ has not issued additional shares of stock during the five-year period for which we have financial information.

It is only advantageous to an organization to sell stock if the market price is greater than the book value per share of the stock on the balance sheet. If an organization sells common stock at a price less than book value, it will cause a dilution in earnings per share. When stock is sold at a price greater than book value, it will be accretive to earnings. Book value per share is equal to common stockholders equity divided by the number of shares outstanding.

XYZ's common stockholders equity is equal to their retained earnings plus common stock plus paid in excess: $183,750 + $10,000 + $190,000 = $383,575. $383,575 divided by 10,000 shares results in a book value per share of $38.36. At the end of 2008, XYZ's stock price was $35 per share. Since the stock price is less than the book value per share, ABC is unable at the current time to raise funds by selling additional shares of common stock without diluting their earnings per share.

<u>Paid in Excess Over Par</u>

Paid in excess over par is also often called additional paid-in capital. This is equal to the difference between the initial sales price of the stock and the par value per share. In the past, XYZ sold its stock to the public at $20 per share with a par value of one dollar per share. Paid in excess is $19 per share times 10,000 shares or $190,000.

<u>Retained Earnings</u>

Retained earnings are equal to the total earnings of the organization since inception minus dividend payments to shareholders. In 2008, XYZ's net income was $20,475 and the organization paid dividends of $20,000, resulting in $475 going to retained earnings. Retained earnings are often interpreted as the amount of internal funds the organization can spend without needing to raise additional capital. Retained earnings are not held by the organization in the form of cash. Retained earnings have been reinvested throughout the asset side of the balance sheet. Retained earnings represent undistributed profits.

<u>Other Stockholders Equity</u>

XYZ Company does not have an entry for this category on the balance sheet in Exhibit 3.8. Some organizations issue preferred stock. As mentioned earlier, preferred stock is a hybrid security having characteristics of debt and equity. Preferred stock pays a fixed dividend similar to debt and is similar to equity in that it has no maturity date. If a preferred stock with a par of $30 dollars has a dividend rate of 10%, it pays a $3 dividend each year forever; it is an example of perpetuity. A concern for the analyst when a company does have preferred stock is whether to classify preferred stock as debt or equity.

Statement of Cash Flows

The Statement of Cash Flows (SCF) is a statement required by Financial Accounting Standards 5, effective as of 1988. The SCF replaced the Sources and Uses of Funds Statement that was also referred to as the Statement of Changes in Financial Position. The SCF provides information about cash inflows and outflows during an accounting period. The cash flows are divided into operating activities, investing activities, and financing activities. One problem with the Statement of Cash Flows is the title. Even though it is called a statement of cash flows, it still refers to changes in non-cash items such as accounts receivable, accounts payable, and accruals. In reality, the SCF is a statement of the flow of funds, not just cash.

Exhibit 3.9: Statement of Cash Flow

	2008	2007	2006	2005
Net income	$20,475	$35,750	$39,000	$38,350
plus Depreciation	$74,900	$70,000	$68,000	$65,000
less increase/(decrease) in Accounts receivable	$(10,000)	$(5,000)	$(10,000)	$(5,000)
less increase/(decrease) in Inventory	$(5,000)	$(5,000)	$(5,000)	$(5,000)
less increase/(decrease) in Other current assets	--	--	--	--
plus increase/(decrease) in Accounts payable	$5,000	$5,000	$3,600	$6,400
plus increase/(decrease) in Accruals	--	$5,000	$(5,000)	$5,000
plus increase/(decrease) in Other current liabilities	--	--	--	--
Total cash flow from operating activities	$85,375	$105,750	$90,600	$104,750
Capital expenditures	$(20,000)	$(100,000)	$(15,100)	$(84,900)
less increase in Marketable securities	$(5,000)	--	$5,000	--
Total cash flows from investing activities	$(25,000)	$(100,000)	$(10,100)	$(84,900)
Dividends paid	$(20,000)	$(20,000)	$(20,000)	$(15,000)
plus Sale/(Purchase) of Stock	--	--	--	--
plus increase Other stockholders equity	--	--	--	--
Net borrowings	$(30,375)	$14,250	$(55,500)	$150
Total cash flows from financing activities	$(50,375)	$(5,750)	$(75,500)	$(14,850)
Change in cash	$10,000	--	$5,000	$5,000

This is not an accounting textbook and there is no intent to provide a detailed discussion of how to put an SCF together, but rather a discussion of how to use the statement. However, simply stated, in order to construct an SCF, it is necessary to have the current year's income statement and balance sheets for the last two years. From the income statement, we need to get information on net income or loss, depreciation and other non-cash expenses, and dividends paid. From the balance sheets, we will need to examine any changes in the level of the organization's assets and liabilities and categorize these changes as either cash inflows (sources) or outflows (uses). These cash flows are then divided into operating, investing, and financing activities.

Operating Activities

Operating activities are those activities that generally relate to producing goods for sale or providing services, and the cash impact of transactions related to the generation of income. Operating cash inflows essentially consist of the sale of goods and services, interest earned on assets, and dividends received on investments. Operating cash outflows include purchases of inventory, operating expenses (rent, salaries, insurance), purchases of supplies, interest payments to lenders, and tax payments. From the balance sheet, changes in short-term assets and liabilities linked to the generation of sales are considered spontaneous sources and/or uses of funds. Essentially, if the level of an asset class listed on the balance sheet increases over the period, this is considered a use or outflow of funds. If an asset level decreases, this is a source of funds or a cash inflow. The reverse is true for liabilities. Any increase in the liability is a source or inflow of funds, while a decrease in the liability is a use or outflow.

In Exhibit 3.8, XYZ's cash from operating activities was $85,375 in 2008. Obviously, positive cash from operations is preferable to negative cash flow and a higher cash flow is preferred to a lower cash flow. Cash from operating activities decreased significantly from 2005 when they were $104,750. To a financial analyst, cash from operations is generally considered the total of net income plus non-cash expenses. In 2008, this definition of cash from operations resulted in cash flow of $95,375, which is greater than the $85,375 shown on XYZ's SCF. In the 2008 SCF, accounts receivable increased $10,000 from 2007 to 2008 resulting in a cash outflow (use). Inventory increased $5,000 from $140,000 to $145,000, another use of funds. Accounts payable increased $5,000 during the period, but since this is a liability, the increase is categorized as a cash inflow.

Investing Activities

Investing activities include the acquisition (cash outflow) or disposition (cash inflow) of long-lived assets or long-term securities, and lending activities where the organization is the lender. For a business that is expanding, we normally would expect cash flows from investing activities to be negative. A negative flow implies the organization is investing funds to generate future growth. Occasionally cash flow from investing is positive which means the organization has disposed of more assets than it has acquired. While this may be expected on occasion, a consistent pattern of positive flows implies the organization is liquidating its productive assets. Investing inflows include sale of plant property and equipment, sale of securities and other entities, and principal payments on loans made by the organization to others. Outflows include the acquisition of assets, purchases of securities, and other entities. In Exhibit 3.9, XYZ's cash flow from investing was -$25,000 consisting primarily of a $20,000 increase in machinery and equipment.

Financing Activities

Financing activities generate cash inflows primarily from the proceeds from borrowing and the issuance of additional shares of stock. Cash outflows involve the repayment of debt, repurchase of the organization's stock, and the payment of dividends.

In Exhibit 3.9, XYZ's cash flow from financing in 2008 was negative ($50,375). The total consisted of $20,000 in dividend payments and a decrease in net borrowings of $30,375. Given the organization's above-average debt ratio, a reduction in outstanding liabilities would be viewed as a positive development. The fact that the organization's stock price is below book value combined with the high level of debt brings into question whether or not the organization should continue its current dividend payout strategy. Payment of a $20,000 dividend may not make sense given the organization's limited options to raise external funds.

Analyzing the SCF

The SCF can be constructed using either the direct method or the indirect method. The major concern of the analyst or risk manager is to determine how the organization raises funds (sources or cash inflows) and how they spend their money (uses or cash outflows). Internal sources of funds (operating activities) should provide the majority of funds the organization needs. If an organization is relying too heavily on debt as a source of funds, sustainability may be an issue, as there ultimately is a limit to how much funds can be borrowed to finance operations. In terms of cash outflows, most analysts prefer to see investment in plant, property, and equipment rather than increases in inventory or accounts receivable.

The last line of the SCF in Exhibit 3.9 indicates that XYZ's cash balance increased by $10,000 over the last year from $60,000 to $70,000. This increase would be viewed positively by the risk manager since it increases the ability of the organization to cover losses. The SCF can provide valuable insights to the risk manager who understands the strengths and limitations of the statement. It is always acceptable, for the purposes of internal analysis or reporting, to modify a statement if it improves your ability to evaluate the entity's financial condition.

Cash Budget

The cash budget may be the most important of the four financial statements. The cash budget is a forecast of the organization's cash inflows and outflows over a period of time. The cash budget differs from the SCF in that: 1) it is strictly a cash-based statement ("green pieces of paper" in and "green pieces of paper" out). No consideration is given to receivables, payables, or accruals unless they are accompanied by a cash payment; and 2) the cash budget is a forecast of future cash flows rather than historical flows. Unfortunately, the cash budget is an internal management statement that is not required to be included in the organization's publicly available disclosures. Interested outside analysts must attempt to create a cash budget for an organization based on available public information. However, the organization's risk manager will have access to this statement. Since the cash budget is a forecast, we need to recognize that at the end of the accounting period, it will be wrong. Virtually all forecasts are incorrect, and the further in the future we attempt to forecast the greater the error rate will be.

If everyone knows the forecast is going to be wrong, then why do organizations attempt to forecast? First, all organizations engage in strategic planning where they create a roadmap to the future of the organization. In the words of a Zen Master, "If you do not know where you came from and do not know where you are going, then you do not know where you are." In this context, the cash budget provides a set of standards from which to judge the performance of the organization's cash flows. Actual results will be compared to the standards, and the differences will be classified as the variances. Variances are investigated to find out why and how they occurred and this information is used to refine future forecast models. The second reason organizations forecast is that lenders and investors typically require pro forma (forecasted) financial statements before investing. Cash budgets are usually constructed on a monthly basis over a 12-month moving horizon. The cash budget is useful to identify periods of time when the organization has excess cash they can invest, and periods where cash flow is projected to be negative and the organization needs to borrow money.

Generally, it is not a good idea to go to a lender when you are in need of funds. Banks do not like to lend money to companies that "need" money. Organizations that are facing a financial crisis are a higher risk. In order to compensate for this increased risk, lenders usually charge increased fees or a higher interest rate. The way to avoid this situation is to approach the bank before the need arises or before a crisis develops and arrange in advance to have funds available. This is called establishing a line of credit. The organization will be able to obtain better terms from the lender when dealing from a position of financial strength.

There are two types of lines of credit: guaranteed and non-guaranteed. With a non-guaranteed line of credit, the organization is pre-approved by the financial institution to borrow up to a specified amount, provided funds are available. On a non-guaranteed line of credit, the organization will pay interest only if they access the line. Thus, non-guaranteed lines of credit are free unless the organization uses them. With a guaranteed line of credit, the borrower will pay interest on the average amount borrowed and a commitment fee on the unused portion of the line. Guaranteed lines of credit have a cost to the organization whether they are used or not and the organization should be careful when applying for these lines. The risk manager would view either of these lines of credit as a safety cushion against unexpected losses and more would be preferred to less.

The general format for a cash budget is as follows:

+ Monthly cash inflows

- monthly cash outflows

= cash from operations

+ beginning cash balance

= ending cash

- minimum cash balance

= funds to invest (or borrow, if negative)

Constructing a cash budget for an organization is a complicated endeavor. The following is an overly simplified example to illustrate the process.

Cash Budget Case Study

(All Numbers in thousands)

The Ubiquitous Widget Company (UWC), a producer of the famous Ubiquitous Widget, needs to develop a cash budget for the months of July, August, and September, as sales of widgets are somewhat seasonal, with peaks in August and September.

Experience shows that 20% of the sales are paid for in cash at time of purchase, 50% in the month following the sales (1 month lag), and the remaining 30% are paid in two months.

Purchases of raw materials (the wids and the gets) are equal to 50% of sales, and UWC pays 50% cash at time of purchase and 50% on the following month. Wages and salaries are 10% of sales plus $20 a month. Rent is $30 a month. The capital budget calls for the installation of a new packaging machine in September at a cost of $30. Taxes of $10 are due in July. The company wishes to maintain a cash balance of $10 at all times.

Sales are as follows:

May $150
June $200
July $250
August $300
September $300

Develop a cash budget. The organization's ending cash balance at the end of June is $20.

Cash Budget for UWC   **Monthly**

	July	August	September
Sales	250.00	300.00	300.00
.20 Cash payment	50.00	60.00	60.00
.5 one month lag payment	100.00	125.00	150.00
.3 two month lag payment	45.00	60.00	75.00
Monthly cash inflow	195.00	245.00	285.00
Purchases	125.00	150.00	150.00
.5 cash payment	62.50	75.00	75.00
.5 one-month lag payment.	50.00	62.50	75.00
Wages and salaries	45.00	50.00	50.00
Rent	30.00	30.00	30.00
Scoreboard installation			30.00
Taxes	10.00		
Monthly cash outflows	197.50	217.50	260.00
Cash Receipts	195.00	245.00	285.00
-Cash disbursements	197.50	217.50	260.00
Net Cash from operations	(2.50)	27.50	25.00
+ beginning cash balance	20.00	17.50	45.00
End Cash	17.5	45.00	70.00
-minimum cash balance	10.00	10.00	10.00
Funds to invest or borrow	7.50	35.00	60.00

Follow the numbers through the calculations for the month of July. The first entry at the top of the column is sales of $250. Sales do not necessarily result in immediate cash flow to the organization. The $250 is simply there to make the mathematics easier to follow; it is not part of the organization's cash budget. UWC customers pay 20% cash, 50% pay net 30 terms (credit cards), and 30% pay two months later. Cash receipts from sales in July are equal to sales of $250 times .2 or 50. In July, cash is collected on 50% of June sales or $200 times .5, or $100. 30% of sales from May pay in July. This is equal to $150 times .3 or $45. Total cash receipts in July are equal to $195.

Cash outflows for July follow. Purchases are listed at the top of the column similar to sales in order to make the calculations easier to follow. Purchases are equal to 50% of that month sales and do not necessarily involve cash payments. Cash purchases in July are equal to 50% of that month's purchases ($125) or $62.50. In July 50% of June's purchases are paid for in cash, or $100 times .5, or $50. Wages and salaries in July are equal to 10% of sales ($25) plus $20, equaling $45. July's rent is $30. Finally, taxes of $10 are paid in July. July's cash outflows are equal to $197.5. Cash from operations is equal to cash inflows of $195 minus cash outflows of $197.5 = ($2.5). Cash from operations for the month of July is negative. Adding in the beginning cash balance for July, which is equal to the ending cash balance for June of $20, results in July ending with cash of $17.5. Subtracting the minimum cash balance that the organization has decided to carry at all times, or $10, results in an amount of $7.5 in funds that the organization can invest in short-term marketable securities.

During August, cash inflows are $245 and cash outflows $217.5, resulting in positive cash from operations of $27.5. Adding in the ending cash balance from July of $17.5 results in ending cash for August of $45. Subtracting the minimum cash balance of $10 results in investable funds of $35.

September's cash from operations is a positive $25 that is then added to the beginning cash balance of $45 for an ending cash balance of $70 and investable funds of $60.

Cash from operations for the UWC is negative in July and positive in August and September. At all times during the three months, the organization has excess cash that can be invested in marketable securities.

Assume that cash balance at the end of October was $50. The fact that ending cash declined from $70 to $50 indicates that cash from operations during October was ($20). Now assume that there are no sales of widgets from November through January. In February, no cash is received, so ending cash would be negative, this indicates that aggregate cash flow between the beginning of the statement and February has turned negative. In this case, the organization needs to arrange in advance for financing to be available to the organization in February. If cash flow is negative for the months of February through April, financing must be available to bridge this period of time.

Assuming the maximum negative ending cash balance was ($75), what amount of lines of credit should the organization arrange for? Remember, there are two types of lines of credit: guaranteed and non-guaranteed. A guaranteed line of credit will have a cost associated with it simply for having the funds guaranteed to be available. Non-guaranteed lines of credit are free until actually used.

Very early in this chapter, we stated that the income statement pays for bottom end retentions such as deductibles, co payments, and self-insured retentions. Technically these retentions are paid for from the cash flow generated by the income statement. The risk manager needs to be able to forecast cash flows and determine if they are sufficient to pay for expected and unexpected losses. Several definitions and sources of cash flow have been identified in our discussions: 1) cash from operations, which a financial analyst would define as net income plus non-cash expenses, 2) cash from operating activities from the SCF, and 3) cash generated from the cash budget.

Ratio Analysis

A ratio is simply a number from the income statement or balance sheet divided by another number. We use ratios to remove size as a factor in the analysis. When we create a ratio, we can compare a small organization to a large organization without distortion. This is not an ideal situation; we would prefer to compare organizations that are comparable in size and operating activities, but sometimes this is difficult, so we resort to comparing an organization to the industry average. In this situation, we will be comparing organizations of different sizes, and ratio analysis assists us in making meaningful comparisons.

Exhibit 3.10: Ratios

	2008	**2007**	**2006**	**2005**	**2004**
Miscellaneous Ratios					
Earnings per share	$2.05	$3.58	$3.90	$3.84	$3.97
Dividends per share	$2.00	$2.00	$2.00	$1.50	$1.50
Payout rate	97.68%	55.94%	51.28%	39.11%	37.83%
Retention rate	2.32%	44.06%	48.72%	60.89%	62.17%
Dividend yield	5.71%	5.00%	4.44%	3.75%	4.05%
P/E multiple	17.09	11.19	11.54	10.43	9.33
Liquidity Ratios					
Current ratio	2.88	2.21	2.55	1.49	1.50
Quick ratio	1.75	1.30	1.50	0.87	0.88
Net working capital	$241,475	$186,100	$200,350	$103,450	$100,000
Debt Ratios					
Total debt to total assets	0.53	0.54	0.54	0.58	0.59
Long-term debt to stockholders equity	0.78	0.78	0.82	0.79	0.85

	2008	**2007**	**2006**	**2005**	**2004**
Coverage Ratio					
Times interest earned	0.91	1.43	1.63	1.92	1.98
Activity Ratios					
Inventory turnover (sales/inventory)	7.38	7.14	7.04	6.92	6.80
365 to inventory turnover	49.46	51.10	51.87	52.72	53.68
Accounts receivable turnover (sales/receivables)	8.23	8.33	8.26	8.57	8.50
365 to accounts receivable turnover	44.35	43.80	44.18	42.58	42.94
Accounts payable turnover (sales/payables)	17.83	18.18	19.00	19.40	21.25
365 to accounts payable turnover	20.47	20.08	19.21	18.82	17.18
Total asset turnover (sales/total assets)	1.32	1.19	1.19	1.08	1.06
Profit Ratios					
Gross profit margin	17.0%	20.0%	21.1%	21.0%	22.0%
Operating profit margin	5.0%	8.0%	8.8%	8.8%	9.5%
Net profit margin	1.9%	3.6%	4.1%	4.3%	4.7%
Return on assets	2.5%	4.3%	4.9%	4.6%	5.0%
Return on equity	5.3%	9.3%	10.6%	11.0%	12.2%

Benchmarks

Without a basis for comparison, a ratio has limited value. The ratios to which we compare our ratios are called benchmarks. These benchmarks can be internal or external. Time series analysis is an example of internal benchmarking. In this case, we would take a ratio for our organization and track it over a time period, perhaps five years or more, to identify trends. A common liquidity ratio is the current ratio, or current assets divided by current liabilities. For this ratio, a higher number is preferred. If we calculated the current ratio over a five-year period and it increased from 1.0 to 1.5, this trend would be considered to be positive.

External benchmarking compares the ratios of the organization to either the industry average or the ratios of a specifically identified competitor. If competitors of similar size and operations can be identified, the benchmark analysis will have more meaning than when industry averages are used. When using industry averages, we are comparing our organization to a group of organizations that may be dissimilar. If the entity is a locally owed, single location hardware store and we compare its ratios to the industry average for hardware stores, we are comparing them to Lowe's and Home Depot. This is not a valid comparison. Lowe's should be compared to Home Depot, and Fred's Hardware to Mabel's Hardware. If we do this, and if our current ratio is 1.5 in the current year and our competitor's current ratio is 1.3, then we are doing a "better job" than our competitor in terms of liquidity.

Key Financial Ratios

There is no universally agreed-upon set of "key financial ratios." A corporate finance book will include close to 100 ratios. Each analyst needs to devise a specific list of key ratios for the organizations and industries to identify. Once the key ratios are identified, they can be grouped into categories of ratios. There is no universal agreement as to the categories or the ratios within each category. For the purposes of our analysis, we will group ratios into five categories: (1) liquidity ratios, (2) debt ratios, (3) coverage ratios, (4) activity ratios, and (5) profitability ratios.

Liquidity Ratios

Liquidity ratios measure short-term solvency. Because, these ratios measure the ability of the organization's balance sheet to pay short-term obligations, creditors are especially interested in an organization's liquidity position. We will examine three measures of liquidity in this section, but keep in mind that many additional liquidity ratios exist.

Current Ratio

The current ratio is current assets divided by current liabilities. Current assets represent funds available to pay short-term bills and current liabilities represent short-term obligations. Clearly, an organization would like short-term funds to be greater than short-term obligations. The higher the current ratio is, the better.

For a manufacturing organization, if we do not know the industry average, we would prefer a current ratio of 2.0 or higher, meaning current assets are two times greater than current liabilities. Ratio analysis is an art, not a science. There are no exact or rigid rules as to what is a good ratio or a bad ratio. If we expected a current ratio of 2.0 and our ratio is 1.95, the slightly lower ratio would still be considered acceptable. If we expected a ratio of 2.0 and our ratio was 1.0, we would conclude that the organization did not have sufficient liquidity. If the industry standard is 2.0, and a higher ratio is better, a ratio of 7.5 is not necessarily "excellent." A current ratio of 7.5 times might be viewed by a risk manager as excellent since it implies the organization has a very large amount of current assets available to pay for losses. However, a financial analyst knows there is a trade-off between liquidity and profitability. The rate of return on current assets is significantly lower than the rate of return on fixed assets. The current ratio of 7.5 times implies the organization is sacrificing profitability for the sake of excess liquidity.

In Exhibit 3.10, XYZ's current ratio has increased from 1.5 in 2004 to 2.88 in 2008. The industry average current ratio is 2.0. XYZ's ratio has gone from significantly below the industry average to significantly above the benchmark over the five-year period. A current ratio of 2.88 compared to the industry benchmark of 2.0 is too high, implying XYZ may be sacrificing profitability. The organization's creditors and its risk manager may be happy with this ratio, but the financial analyst would like to see the ratio decrease in the future.

Quick Ratio or Acid Test Ratio

Most analysts consider inventory the least liquid current asset. The quick ratio is very similar to the current ratio, except it removes inventory from the current assets by taking current assets minus inventory divided by current liabilities.

Assume the industry average benchmark for the quick ratio is 1.0, and we see in Exhibit 3.10 that XYZ's quick ratio has increased from .88 in 2004 to 1.75 in 2008. The quick ratio has gone from slightly below the industry average to significantly above it over the five-year period. The same points mentioned when discussing XYZ's current ratio would apply to their quick ratio. The financial analyst would like to see this ratio lowered over the next several periods.

The interrelationship of two or more ratios can give an analyst valuable insights. Let us assume we are evaluating an organization's liquidity position using the current ratio and the quick ratio, and that the organization is an industry whose current ratio benchmark is 2.0 and quick ratio benchmark is 1.0. The organization's current ratio is 1.9 and its quick ratio is 1.5. What can we conclude from these two ratios? The obvious conclusion is that our organization has lower inventory than other organizations in our industry. The quick ratio (from which inventory is excluded) is well above the average liquidity. When we look at the current ratio (which includes inventory of the organization), we see that the current ratio is slightly below average. There are possible interpretations: first, our organization has too little inventory or, second, the other organizations in the industry are holding too much inventory. Answering this question requires additional analysis.

Net Working Capital

Net Working Capital is current assets minus current liabilities. Net working capital is not a ratio and is expressed in dollars. It represents the cushion of assets the organization has available to pay its short-term obligations. The greater the dollar cushion the more secure creditors will feel about their ability to be repaid in the short run. Since net working capital is not a ratio, it does not allow us to compare our organization to other organizations of dissimilar sizes or even to conduct time series analysis as the size of our organization will change over time.

In Exhibit 3.10, XYZ's net working capital in 2008 is $241,475 ($370,000 -$128,525). This represents a significant increase in net working capital from the year 2004 when it was $100,000 ($300,000 -$200,000).

Again, creditors and the organization's risk manager will view this as a positive since the cushion to pay bills and losses is greater. However, the rate of return on current assets is significantly lower than the rate of return on fixed assets, so the organization is sacrificing profitability in exchange for liquidity. If net working capital does not allow for comparisons over time or to the industry benchmark, why is it important? The reason is that minimum levels of net working capital are very commonly specified as covenants in loans or bonds. Loan and bond covenants represent items negotiated by lenders that either require the organization to maintain certain financial ratios or prohibit the organization from engaging in certain activities without the permission of the creditors. For example, with certain covenants, the organization cannot issue additional debt without the permission of existing creditors.

Loan covenants often require a minimum current ratio and a minimum level of net working capital. If a covenant specifies a minimum level of net working capital of $1 million and net working capital drops below that level, the organization has breached a covenant. Breaching a covenant, either intentionally or unintentionally, results in default on the organization's debt. Default means that the entire amount of the debt is immediately due in full. Breach of any covenant clearly has a significant negative impact on the viability of the organization, and indicates the need for ongoing monitoring of pertinent financial data.

Debt Ratios

Debt ratios measure the ability of the organization's balance sheet to pay bills over the long-term. Debt represents a fixed cost to the organization. As a fixed cost, debt has both advantages and disadvantages. The main advantage of debt is that the interest on the debt is fixed in that it does not increase as sales increase. If the organization can earn a rate of return on its assets greater than the cost of the debt, positive leverage will occur. The disadvantage of debt is that the interest on the debt is a fixed cost that must be repaid regardless of the financial health of the organization. Debt is a very popular source of long-term funding for most organizations since the interest on the debt is a tax-deductible expense. This results in a lower after-tax cost of debt compared to the cost of equity. Higher levels of debt represent increased leverage and risk.

Debt Ratio

The debt ratio is total debt divided by total assets. Total debt is equal to current liabilities plus long-term debt. When the debt ratio is high, the creditors face a greater risk of default. In the case of XYZ, assume the industry average debt ratio is 50%. In Exhibit 3.10, XYZ's total debt in 2008 is equal to current liabilities of $128,525 plus long-term debt of $300,000 for a total of $428,525. XYZ"S debt ratio is therefore $428,525 divided by total assets of $812,100 or 52.76%. XYZ's ratio is above the industry average, implying the organization has a slightly higher risk. However, the good news is the organization's ratio has decreased steadily from 59% in 2004. The fact that XYZ has a higher debt ratio may make it more difficult for the organization to obtain additional debt financing, but with a decreasing debt ratio, this favorable trend may lessen the difficulty. If a lender does decide to extend additional financing to the organization, they will probably charge a higher interest rate and/or additional fees to compensate for the increased level of risk.

Given what we have observed about XYZ, the organization clearly has significant restrictions on its ability to obtain additional long-term financing. First, the organization's stock price is below its book value, and this limits its ability to sell additional shares of stock. Combined with that is the fact that their debt ratio will make lenders reluctant to extend additional loans. These two facts do not leave the organization with many options. The risk manager must be concerned about the organization's ability to raise funds to pay for any uninsured catastrophic losses. The analyst must be concerned about the organization's ability to finance growth. At the moment, the financial picture looks uncertain for XYZ. On the positive side, the financial picture has improved significantly over the last five years, at least on the debt side.

Debt to Equity Ratio

The debt to equity ratio is long-term debt divided by stockholders equity. This ratio measures long-term funding sources by comparing long-term debt to long-term equity financing. A higher ratio implies a higher percentage of debt financing and a higher level of risk to the creditors. In the case of XYZ, assume the industry average debt to equity ratio is .75. XYZ's debt to equity ratio is currently 300,000/383,575 = .78, slightly above the industry average. The time series exhibits the same trend as the debt ratio with a significant improvement over the five-year period, decreasing from .85 to .78.

Coverage Ratios

Coverage ratios measure the ability of the organization's income statement to pay its short-term obligations. While liquidity ratios and debt ratios measure the ability of organization's balance sheet to pay its bills, coverage ratios focus on the income statement. There are several coverage ratios commonly used by financial analysts. For our purposes, we will focus only on the simplest of the coverage ratios, the times interest earned ratio (TIE).

As you move from the top of the income statement down, the first fixed financial cost is interest expense. Interest expense is a fixed cost that must be paid; otherwise, the organization will be in default. The line above interest on the income statement is earnings before interest and taxes (EBIT). EBIT represents the level of funds available to pay interest. The TIE ratio is EBIT divided by interest payments. If EBIT were $1 million and interest payments were $200,000, then the times interest earned ratio would be 5.0. The higher the coverage ratio, the more secure the creditors are. Assume XYZ's industry average TIE ratio is 4.0. In 2008, XYZ's times interest earned ratio was 2.40. Over the five-year period, XYZ's ratio decreased from 4.05 to 2.40. Clearly, this is an area of significant concern to creditors, financial analysts, and the risk manager, as it indicates the ability of XYZ's income statement to pay the interest on its obligations is significantly impaired.

Activity Ratios

Activity ratios measure management efficiency in utilizing assets. Activity ratios are output to input ratios, with output generally expressed in terms of sales.

Inventory Turnover

The inventory turnover ratio measures the relationship between sales (output) and inventory (input). Inventory turnover technically is equal to the cost of goods sold divided by inventory, but often sales are used instead of cost of goods sold. While cost of goods sold is the correct value to use, the information may not be as readily available as data on sales. Also, from a technical standpoint, the denominator in the ratio should be average inventory. Average inventory does not mean averaging the numbers on two consecutive balance sheets. Balance sheets are typically dated December 31. December 31 might be the highest or lowest level of inventory for a seasonal organization. Average inventory implies the average inventory over the entire period, not the average of inventory on December 31 for two different years.

For simplicity in our XYZ example, we will use the inventory listed for each year in calculating the inventory turnover ratio. For 2008, inventory turnover for XYZ is equal to $1,070,000 (sales) divided by $145,000 (inventory on balance sheet) or 7.38. A higher inventory turnover ratio is generally preferred to a lower ratio. The higher the turnover the more rapidly an organization turns over its inventory, and that results in a lower cost of carrying that inventory.

The average age of inventory is calculated by dividing 365 days by the inventory turnover. The average age of inventory for XYZ in 2008 is equal to 365 divided by 7.38 or 49.46 days. Average age of inventory is equal to the amount of time, on average, between the date raw materials arrive at the organization to the date finished goods leave. A lower average age of inventory is preferred. The industry average age of inventory is 50 days. XYZ's average age is slightly below the industry average; that is a positive sign. XYZ has reduced their average age of inventory from 53.68 days in 2004 to the current level of 49.46 days, also a positive trend.

Accounts Receivable Turnover

Similarly, an accounts receivable turnover ratio measures the relationship between sales and accounts receivable. Ideally, we would use credit sales rather than total sales but this data will be very difficult to obtain for most companies. When analyzing inventory, we probably could obtain data for cost of goods sold, but that would lead to inconsistency between our ratios if we use cost of goods sold for inventory and then sales for accounts receivable turnover. In 2008, XYZ's accounts receivable turnover was $1,070,000 divided by $130,000 or 8.23 times. Following the same rationale as inventory turnover, a higher accounts receivable turnover implies the organization is doing a better job collecting its receivables. XYZ gives its customers net 30 credit terms. Under these terms, the entire amount of the Accounts Receivable is due by the 30th day.

The average age of accounts receivable is equal to 365 days divided by the accounts receivable turnover. In 2008, XYZ's average age of inventory is equal to 365 divided by 8.23 or 44.35 days. The industry average age of accounts receivable is 36 days. XYZ's average age of accounts receivable is well above the industry average, and it has increased from 42.94 days in 2004. The level and trend for accounts receivable implies that XYZ is not doing a very good job collecting the money that is due them from their customers.

Accounts Payable Turnover

The accounts payable turnover ratio measures how promptly an organization pays its suppliers. Creditors will pay careful attention to the organization's past payment history before extending additional credit. Accounts payable turnover is equal to sales divided by accounts payable. Ideally, we would use credit purchases rather than sales, but this data will be difficult to obtain. In 2008, XYZ's accounts payable turnover is equal to $1,070,000 divided by $60,000 or 17.83. The average age of accounts payable is 365 days divided by 17.83 or 20.47 days. XYZ's suppliers extend the organization net 20 terms. The industry average age of accounts payable is 24 days. XYZ's average age is 3.53 days below the industry average, thus indicating the organization has a very good history of paying its suppliers on a timely basis. Since 2004, XYZ's average age has increased from 17.18 days to 20.47 days. XYZ has begun to do a better job of paying its bills a little bit later without damaging its credit rating or its relationship with its suppliers since they still pay their bills earlier than the industry average. Remember that accounts payable is a free source of financing, and extending the time period for paying to the maximum allowed without damaging credit ratings or relationships makes good financial sense.

Total Asset Turnover Ratio

The total asset turnover ratio is the most important of the activity ratios. Total asset turnover is equal to sales divided by total assets and measures the overall efficiency of the balance sheet (input) in generating sales (output). Total asset turnover is also one half of the DuPont ROA ratio that will be discussed in more detail in the next section on profitability ratios. The higher the total asset turnover ratio, the more efficient the organization is in utilizing its asset base to generate sales. Assume the industry average total asset turnover ratio is 1.25. XYZ's turnover ratio has increased from 1.06 to 1.32 times from 2004 to 2008. XYZ has gone from a ratio that was substantially below the industry average to one that is now above the average. At first glance, it appears XYZ has done a good job improving their efficiency in this area. However, an alternative explanation could be that the organization has stopped reinvesting in the assets necessary to generate future growth in sales. An analyst needs to ask management more detailed questions as to why this ratio has improved so dramatically over the five-year period

Profitability Ratios

Investors are extremely interested in how much money they can potentially make from their investment in XYZ stock. Higher profitability ratios are preferred to lower ratios.

Profit Margins

We discussed XYZ's gross, operating, and net profit margins in the common size income statement section of this chapter. To reiterate, all three of XYZ's profit margins are below the industry average and have declined significantly over the last five years. Investors would be less than pleased with the level and trend of the company's profitability. To the risk manager, these ratios indicate a deteriorating income statement that may not be able to provide the cash flow to pay unexpected losses in the forms of deductibles, co-payments, and self-insured retentions.

Return on Assets

The return on assets (ROA) ratio measures net income (output) divided by total assets (input).

ROA = Net Income / Total Assets

Investors and management closely monitor ROA. XYZ's ROA in 2008 was 2.5% (20,475/812,000) compared to the industry average of 5.13%. Since 2004, XYZ's ROA has decreased from 5% to 2.5%. The level and trend of XYZ's ROA would be of concern to investors and the organization's risk manager. A variation of ROA is the DuPont ROA. This measure breaks the ROA ratio into two components: net profit margin from the income statement and total asset turnover ratio from the balance sheet.

DuPont ROA = net profit margin times the total asset turnover ratio.

Thus, DuPont ROA = (Net Income / Total Sales) x (Total Sales / Total Assets)

XYZ's net profit margin of 1.9% times its total asset turnover of 1.32 is equal to a DuPont ROA of 2.5%. The industry average DuPont ratio is equal to the industry average for net profit margin of 4.1% times the industry average total asset turnover of 1.25, which equals 5.13. XYZ's total asset turnover is above the industry average but its profit margin is substantially below. The price investors are willing to pay for XYZ stock is adversely impacted by the organization's below average profit margins and ROA. These ratios, as well as the organization's ROE, help explain why the organization's stock price is below book value per share.

Return on Equity (ROE)

The return on equity ratio is equal to net income divided by stockholders equity.

ROE = Net Income / Stockholders Equity

ROE represents the return on the shareholder's investment in the organization. XYZ's ROE in 2008 is equal to $20,475 divided by $383,575 or 5.33%. XYZ's ROE has declined precipitously from 12.2% in 2004. Assume the industry average ROE is 10.25%. The trend and level of the organization's ROE is less than ideal, to say the least.

The DuPont ROE is equal to the net profit margin times the total asset turnover times a leverage multiplier. The leverage multiplier is equal to total assets divided by stockholders equity. The leverage multiplier measures the financial risk profile of the organization.

DuPont ROE =

(Net Income / Total Sales) x (Total Sales / Total Assets) x (Total Assets / Stockholders Equity)

In Exhibit 3.10, XYZ's leverage multiplier is equal to total assets of $812,100 divided by stockholders equity of $383,575 or 2.117 times. The organization's DuPont ROE is equal to 1.9% times 1.32 times 2.117 or 5.33%. DuPont ROE allows the analyst to decompose a change in ROE into an income statement, balance sheet, and leverage factor. XYZ has a weaker income statement, a stronger balance sheet in terms of total asset turnover, and higher leverage than the industry. The industry average ROE is 10.25%. The gap between ROA and ROE indicates the degree of leverage or risk present in the organization's balance sheet. For example, the industry average ROE of 10.25% is exactly double the industry average ROA of 5.125%. This is because the industry average total debt to total asset ratio is 50%. XYZ's DuPont ROA of 2.5% more than doubles to its DuPont ROE of 5.3% since the organization has a higher total debt to total asset ratio (53%) than the industry average.

XYZ's increased leverage and risk profile will make it more difficult and expensive for the organization to raise funds by issuing additional debt. The analyst or risk manager should view this situation negatively.

Summary of Ratio Analysis

Ratio analysis allows the analyst to evaluate the financial strengths and weaknesses of an organization by comparing that organization's ratios to internal and external benchmarks. The analyst or risk manager compares the organization's data to predetermined standards and then evaluates any variance from expected outcomes. Ratio analysis is an important tool, but it is only one of a number of evaluation techniques. As with any technique, there are limitations to the effectiveness of ratio analysis. These limitations include but are not limited to the following:

Many organizations operate in a number of different industries, a situation that makes it difficult to compare them to a particular industry or group of industries. It is difficult to find comparable organizations to conglomerates such as General Electric.

Many organizations have a goal to be the best in their industry and do not find it beneficial to be compared to the industry average. These organizations want to be compared to the best practices or leaders in their industry.

Inflation can distort an organization's financial statements. This situation is more of a concern during periods of high inflation in the economy. The analyst or risk manager will need good judgment to interpret the impact of inflation on the organization's data.

Accounting practices can distort the results. If our organization uses LIFO inventory accounting and our competitor uses FIFO, it will be difficult to compare results for the two organizations. Depreciation, leasing, and sales recognition are other areas where discretion exists within generally accepted accounting principles.

The use of ratios is an art, not science. The definition of a good versus bad ratio is often subjective. All ratios have an acceptable range and can be too high or too low. Again, the analyst or risk manager must employ sound judgment.

On occasion, organizations have been known to "cook the books." The financial press in recent years has contained numerous articles on organizations whose accounting practices went well beyond the scope allowed under GAAP. Examples include Enron, Adelphia, WorldCom, and Global Crossings, to name just a few. The quality of the data provided by the organization's accountants will affect the quality of the analysis.

Earnings Quality

The discussion about the limitations of ratio analysis is an excellent segue into the topic of the quality of reported earnings. Management has numerous opportunities to influence reported financial results through their choice of accounting methods, estimates, and assumptions involved in the process of constructing financial statements. Earnings management is a concept in disfavor with many investors today. Earnings management is a process by which management attempts to smooth out reported earnings in order to provide investors with a stream of steadily increasing reported profits and earnings per share. Some organizations can control the timing of revenue and expenses to a degree. For example, if an entertainment conglomerate were having a quarter where profits were not going to be sufficient to meet analyst expectations they could re-package and re-release a popular movie on DVD in order to boost revenue for that quarter. In the past, earnings management was viewed in a favorable light since investors could count on steadily increasing earnings per share. Today, earnings management is viewed as an attempt to manipulate reported earnings and share price.

When analyzing an organization's financial statements, the risk manager must understand the qualitative as well as quantitative components of earnings. Qualitative factors are defined as those situations or conditions that could adversely impact the organization, but it is difficult to place a monetary value on their impact. For example, the impact of a recession on the sales and profitability of the organization is difficult to value monetarily. In addition to broad qualitative factors, we need to consider the quality of the assumptions and judgments used by management and the accountants in constructing the financial statements.

There also are quantitative factors that do not appear in the organization's financial statements. Off-balance sheet liabilities and assets have become an area of increasing concern to regulators and investors. If an organization leases an asset rather than purchasing it, the value of that asset and the corresponding liability may or may not show up on the organization's balance sheet, depending on whether the lease is categorized as an operating or capitalized lease. A great deal of important information, both qualitative and quantitative, can be found outside of the financial statements. For a publicly traded organization, much of this information is found in the notes and management discussion sections of the annual report.

Earnings Management

Formerly, earnings management was concerned primarily with tax management, following the dictum that taxes cannot be avoided (at least legally) but taxation can be deferred or accelerated to a more convenient time. However, the practice of earnings management has been used to manipulate stock prices and customer confidence, as evidenced in recent corporate scandals. Consequently, the Securities Exchange Commission (SEC) has raised the issue regarding how publicly held firms manage earnings to show more consistent results.

The SEC defines improper earnings management in two ways: 1) actions taken without events or conditions occurring at the time to justify such actions; and 2) adjusting the organization's reported earnings to meet market expectations. In other words, the SEC permits legitimate earnings management, but there must be some event or condition to justify the action, and not just solely to meet market expectations.

Another concern for the SEC is "materiality." The SEC Staff Accounting Bulletin 99 defines a transaction as material if it:

1. Is capable of precise measurement;

2. Masks a change in earnings or other trends;

3. Hides a failure to meet to meet analysts' expectations;

4. Changes a loss into income or vice versa;

5. Attains compliance with regulatory requirements; and

6. Attains compliance with loan covenants.

Understanding earnings management is important to the risk manager as it is relevant to the risk financing structure. Earnings management assists in maintaining consistency in earnings, a boon in the cash budgeting process, and therefore aids in maintaining adequate cash flows to pay for losses and expenses.

Risk financing programs that utilize high retentions provide the risk manager with some flexibility in setting reserve liabilities. When discounted reserves are used, the level of discounted reserve liabilities can be managed through changes in the discount rate. This is not to suggest that unreasonable discount rates be used when a program is troubled, but a change in discount rates of 100 basis points or 1% over a ten year term changes the reserves by roughly 9%. Also, the range estimates have a degree of subjectivity, and can be expanded or contracted to manage loss reserves and earnings. Further, inflationary trends must be recognized, but these factors can be introduced into the reserve estimates gradually rather than slammed into the immediate accounting period where the impact on earnings would be the greatest.

However, because of the consequences of flagrant abuse, flexibility in earnings management is being eroded through increased regulation (e.g., Sarbanes-Oxley), senior management apprehension, SEC regulations, and IRS tax rules.

Sarbanes-Oxley Act of 2002

The Federal Corporate Accountability Act of 2002, more commonly known by the names of its two sponsors, Sarbanes-Oxley Act, was passed in 2002 with an effective date in May, 2003. This federal act was the direct result of the catastrophic collapse of Enron and other cases of corporate malfeasance. Its impact on corporations and their management is real and frightening. Not only are the corporation and managers subject to civil liability, fines, and damages (including forfeiture of earnings and bonuses), the managers are subject to criminal liability and face the possibility of lengthy prison sentences.

For corporations who must report to the SEC, management's required annual report on the financial status of the organization must also include a management report on internal control. The management report on internal control must state management's responsibility for establishing and maintaining an adequate internal control structure and procedures for financial reporting, and contain management's assessment, as of year-end, of the effectiveness of the internal control structure and procedures for financial reporting. The focus of Sarbanes-Oxley is to enhance the reliability of financial reporting beyond simply the numbers contained in the annual report and the financial statements.

With respect to the risk manager, a lack of controls in several insurance-related areas carries a risk of financial misstatement. Astute senior management will insist that the risk manager provide detailed information regarding the following activities:

- Insurance program structure (e.g., retentions, limits of coverage, breadth of coverage, solvency of insurance carriers) Note: One very important provision of Sarbanes-Oxley is Regulation S-K, dealing with impairments of intellectual property. Since intellectual property is rarely covered adequately in an insurance program (either because there is limited, expensive coverage available or because the exposure was not identified and treated), management has an obligation to disclose such impairments and their likely financial impact on the corporation.

- Risk management function (identification of exposures and treatment)

- Cost of risk allocation process (how cost of risk is identified and spread to operating units, and therefore how it affects the financial results of the organization)

- Vendor relationships (how vendors are selected and their performance monitored)

Sarbanes-Oxley requires a detailed documentation of the procedures management uses to provide controls and their assessment. An inquiry to the risk manager, "are we covered?" is not sufficient. Management must assess each risk area, asking the following questions:

- Are the controls complete?

- What are we missing?

- Is the information provided accurate?

- How can we establish provable accuracy?

- Are judgments appropriate?

- Have judgments been made based on reason and logic?

- Have any decisions been made for inappropriate considerations or influence?

Because many functions can be outsourced to independent service providers, the corporation's management must obtain representations from service provides with respect to financial reporting items and those representations must be subject to the same controls as if the corporation were performing the tasks internally. TPA firms and other claims administration functions will be subject to increased documentation requirements as part of this control and assessment process. Further, actuarial calculations of loss reserve estimates will likewise fall within the scope of these controls and assessments.

These representations may result in increased liability for service providers. Directors and Officers Liability and Errors and Omissions Liability coverages will be subject to additional exposures and the possibilities of reduced or restricted limits and more stringent exclusions.

Reading the Annual Report

We will examine (briefly in a non-technical accounting approach) the annual report of a Fortune 500 aluminum company whose identity may be apparent by the end of our analysis. We will focus on three areas of the report:

- Letter to the shareholders,

- Management's discussion of financial results, and

- Notes

The purpose is not to evaluate the financial condition of this particular organization, but to point out areas where the risk manager can find information to do the job more effectively.

Before we start, we will discuss two general "wives' tales" related to the analysis of annual reports. The first deals with the cover page of the report. There tends to be an inverse correlation between the ornate nature of the cover and the organization's profitability during the period. Generally, a boring one-color cover implies a successful year. The more decorative the cover the worse the financial results contained within tend to be. The second relates to the letter to shareholders and the calculation of a verbosity index for that letter. You can calculate the verbosity index by totaling the number of adjectives and adverbs and dividing by the total of the nouns and verbs. The higher index, the more likely management wants to talk about anything and everything other than the organization's financial results. While there have been no studies or statistics to back up these beliefs, their simple existence illustrates that financial analysis is an art rather than a science.

The aluminum company's annual report is one-color and relatively sedate, a good beginning to our analysis. Inside the front cover is a table titled "Financial Operating Highlights." The table compares two years for a number of key financial values. However, for this information to be useful to us, we would need a minimum of five years of data to evaluate any possible trends.

Next to the table is a discussion titled "The Organization at a Glance." A great deal of valuable information for the risk manager is contained in the four bullet points. The first paragraph states that the organization is the world's leading producer of primary aluminum, fabricated aluminum, and alumina and is active in all major aspects of the industry. The fact that the organization is the world's leading producer implies it is also the world's largest producer that should lead to economies of scale and a lower production cost for the organization. Further, the organization participates in all aspects of the industry leads, and that suggests that the organization is vertically integrated. A vertically integrated organization controls a product from raw material to the delivery of a finished good to the end consumer. The main advantage of vertical integration is that it allows the organization to control quality and cost throughout the process leading to a higher profit margin. The disadvantage is that it takes a great deal of assets to control a process from the beginning to the end.

Vertically integrated organizations are often referred to as capital-intensive. A capital-intensive organization or industry has a high ratio of fixed assets to total assets. Often these assets are financed with debt resulting in a higher debt ratio and higher levels of leverage. These organizations typically have high levels of fixed cost resulting in corresponding higher breakeven points. Using the DuPont ROA analysis, a capital-intensive organization would be expected to have a high profit margin and a low total asset turnover ratio.

The next bullet point states that the organization serves the aerospace, automotive, packaging, building and construction, commercial transportation, and industrial markets. A significant percentage of the organization's sales of aluminum are made to organizations that use the aluminum to produce products ultimately sold to consumers. For example, aluminum is sold to an automobile manufacturer that uses the aluminum to build vehicles that are then sold to an end consumer. In marketing, this is referred to as derived demand. In order for the organization to sell more aluminum, the automobile manufacturer's consumers must buy more automobiles. The risk manager needs to be aware of industry conditions not only in the aluminum industry but also in the industries that purchase aluminum from the organization.

Additionally, the majority of the industries listed in this bullet point are cyclical industries meaning that they are closely related to the strength of the economy. Aluminum is a cyclical industry, as are the majority of the industries they sell their product to. As we have seen, a recession in the United States or another major economic region will adversely impact the financial health of these industries.

The next bullet point (and information found elsewhere in the report) states that the organization is involved in markets in industries other than aluminum. These markets include consumer brands, vinyl siding, electrical distribution systems, and power plants. The organization's risk manager needs to be aware of how these operations impact the risk profile of the organization.

The final bullet point states that the organization operates in 43 countries, thus making it a true multinational organization. The risk manager should immediately begin to think about topics such as political risk, currency risk, regulation, taxation, cultural issues, limitations on the flow of capital and profits, terrorism risk, kidnap and ransom exposure, and a host of other issues related to operating in 43 different political, economic, social, and legal environments. The four bullet points contain a total of 109 words, but they provide the well-trained risk manager or analyst with valuable insight into the organization and the type of qualitative factors to be understood in order to protect the organization's assets.

Letter to the Shareholders

The first paragraph states the organization's vision to be the best company in the world. This statement has obvious ramifications for the risk manager if the company does not live up to this publicly stated vision. The second paragraph states that the organization encountered rising costs and currency challenges. The value of the dollar will have an ongoing impact on this U.S.-based, multinational organization's income. Despite these obstacles, the organization posted strong profits, cash flows, and reduced its debt by a substantial amount. This information should be viewed positively by investors, but a key question will be the ability of the organization to maintain similar results if these obstacles remain in place. The next paragraph states that the organization achieved a record low lost workday rate. This disclosure in such a prominent place in the annual report indicates management's commitment to safety and risk management.

A favorable external business environment contributed to the organization's financial performance. Strong global economic growth resulted in increased demand for aluminum. Additionally, key markets, including aerospace and commercial vehicles, rebounded due to an economic upturn. The favorable impact of these events was somewhat counterbalanced by increased costs related to energy and raw materials and the weakening of the U.S. dollar against other world currencies. To the risk manager, determining which of these trends will continue and whether or not the positive forces will continue to outweigh the negative trends is the key to predicting the future profitability of the organization. In spite of the organization's positive financial performance, the value of the organization's stock decreased during the period, illustrating the fact that the level of the overall stock market is a major factor in determining the return to investors of any company.

The company is restarting operations at a number of locations due to a strong economic climate. Two of the operations that are being restarted are being reopened after the resolution of an employee strike, one related to healthcare cost sharing. The possibility of labor unrest at the organization should be a major concern to the risk manager. The letter discusses developments at a number of the organizations' worldwide locations, including Canada, Iceland, Norway, Brazil, Trinidad and Tobago, Ghana, Jamaica, Guinea, Australia, Russia, Romania, Egypt, Honduras, China, and others. This list represents almost the entire spectrum of economic development among countries. Managing an organization and the organization's risk management department in such a diverse collection of environments is an extremely challenging, even daunting task.

Later in the letter, we encounter a subheading titled "Environment, Health, and Safety." In this section, the organization reiterates its commitment to the safety of its employees and sites specific improvements in their safety record. However, in a disclosure rarely seen in a corporate annual report, the company discloses that they suffered three fatalities. This disclosure represents unusual candor for an organization.

Management also acknowledges the existence of an ongoing portfolio realignment program. The organization continually evaluates the performance of its business units and requires these units to earn a return that exceeds the organization's cost of capital. Non-core businesses that fail to earn a rate of return that exceeds the cost of capital are candidates to be sold. Additionally, the organization is looking to "expand our footprint" through acquisitions. The sale or closure of business units affects many aspects of an organization, ranging from profitability to employee morale. Closure of a business unit results in layoffs, severance costs, a negative impact on the morale of the remaining employees, and can even lead to employee sabotage or violence. The risk manager needs to know in advance of any plant closings or sales and be able to implement programs in advance to mitigate the adverse impact of these events on the organization.

The sale of a business usually results in a gain or loss to the organization. If the business is sold at a price greater than its book value, a taxable gain results. Conversely, a loss results if the business is sold for less than its book value. These gains or losses are generally considered to be extraordinary in that they are nonrecurring in nature and are listed separately on the income statement as extraordinary, or "below the line" items. The sales, assets, and liabilities of these units will no longer be included in the organization's consolidated financial statements in the future.

The letter to the shareholders concludes with a brief discussion of the Sarbanes-Oxley Act of 2002 and its impact on the organization, including the conduct of over 140 financial reviews, and 300 process/location audits at a cost of approximately $10 million to the organization. The risk manager needs to keep close tabs on pending legislation, as well as accounting changes, in order to determine their impact on the organization's financial statements.

Even though the letter to shareholders contained very few specific dollar amounts, it provided valuable insights, hints, and clues about a wide range of qualitative issues that the risk manager must be aware of.

Management Discussion Section

After 17 pages of colorful pictures and news items, we arrive at the financial and corporate data section, followed by management's discussion and analysis of the financial condition of the organization.

Operations

Aluminum is a commodity traded on the London Metals Exchange (LME) and is priced daily based on supply and demand. Aluminum related products comprise approximately two thirds of the Company's revenues. The price of aluminum directly affects the profitability of the company. As a rule, the higher the price of aluminum, the higher the organization's profitability will be. Since aluminum is a commodity, the organization has limited control over the market price of its raw materials. Recently, the price of aluminum has increased significantly due to increased global demand, especially in China. As long as the Chinese economy remains strong, demand for aluminum should remain strong, leading to higher prices. The organization's risk manager needs to understand this relationship and be able to assess future prospects for the Chinese economy and its impact on aluminum pricing and company profitability. (This situation has changed dramatically since the report was published. Post Olympics demand from China has decreased substantially, as have commodity prices, including aluminum.)

Year in Review

The review of the year's results reiterates the organization's strong performance and focuses on improvements in income from continuing operations, record sales, strong cash flow, and significant reductions in debt. Once again, increases in energy costs, raw materials costs, and the weakening U.S. dollar are cited as impediments to continued improvements in profitability. The review also references the substantial completion of the organization's divestiture plan with the sales of a number of businesses during the period.

Forward-looking Statements

Forward-looking statements are paragraphs written by the organization's attorneys and or risk managers. Forward-looking statements include those containing words such as "anticipates," "believes," "estimates," "expects," "hopes," "targets," "should," etc. The bottom line for this section is, "Don't sue us if our forecasts of the future are not completely accurate."

Recent history has shown that an organization must be very careful when making forward-looking statements, either orally or in print, relating to the future financial prospects of the company. A major function of an annual report is to encourage potential investors to purchase the company's stock. As such, it should be expected, within reason, that the firm will put the best possible spin on the information contained in the report. Usually, good news is in the front of the report in a large font; bad news is in the back of the report in a smaller font. Given today's litigious environment, if management puts an overly optimistic spin on financial documents released to investors, and investors purchase the organization's stock based on his information, the organization is likely to face litigation if the forecasted results fail to materialize and the stock price drops dramatically.

Earnings Summary

The earnings summary contains reference to a number of extremely technical accounting situations which the risk manager needs to be aware of, but are well outside the scope of an introductory discussion of financial statement analysis. Items discussed include non-operating gains on the retirement of debt, interest rate swap settlements, the sale of a partial interest of the organization's investment in a bauxite project, and termination of an alumina tolling arrangement. Offsetting these gains were an increase in environmental and legal reserves and the absence of insurance settlements that occurred the previous year. Each of these items involves complicated legal, accounting, and financial issues that can impact the organization's current and future earnings.

Financial statements and the accompanying notes become more complicated each year. Whenever a risk manager or analyst does not fully understand a concept or activity encountered in the organization's financial documents, it is imperative to seek the advice and counsel of the qualified professional who specializes in that area. The risk manager must have access to accounting and finance professionals who can clearly explain these topics when necessary.

Income Statement

Management discusses the impact of price and units sold on sales. Since the price of aluminum is generally imposed on the organization externally, the analyst should focus on units produced and sold. The discussion involves a common size or percent income statement format analyzing cost of goods sold, selling, general and administrative, research and development, and depreciation, depletion, and amortization expenses as a percentage of sales. The section generally follows the approach laid out in our earlier discussion of common size income statements.

Restructuring and Other Charges

Restructuring charges generally relate to costs associated with the sale or disposition of business units. When a business is designated for sale, the organization must place a value on that entity. Significant judgments and assumptions are required to value a business. If the resulting value is less than the book value or carrying value of that business, the organization must reduce or write down the value of their assets, and the reduction in the asset has a corresponding reduction in owner's equity. For example, if a business unit has a book value of $400 million at the time of a proposed sale and the organization conducts a market value analysis of the business and determines its current value to be $350 million, the organization is required to write down assets by $50 million. This asset write-down will adversely impact the organization's stockholders equity and balance sheet.

An issue in the news recently discusses restructuring activities involving the level of reserves set aside to cover expenses connected to the sale or closure of a business. The closure of a business entails significant costs including, but not limited to, severance costs, demolition costs, and potential environmental remediation costs. Setting aside a reserve requires management to estimate the costs associated with closure of the unit, with the temptation to underestimate the costs, resulting in a lower reserve, especially since setting up an accounting reserve on the balance sheet also involves taking a charge on the organization's income statement.

An alternative temptation might be to overstate the reserve, especially if the organization's financial performance in the current year is less than stellar. For example, assume environmental remediation costs are forecasted to be $200 million but the organization sets up a $300 million reserve. The reserve will adversely impact the organization's profitability this year. However, next year, when the reserve turns out to have been set too high, the organization can reverse the reserve, allowing the extra $100 million to flow into profits. The organization can make a bad year look much worse, but releasing the reserves over time can potentially smooth out future reported earnings.

Cumulative Effect of Accounting Changes

The organization discusses the effects of three new accounting standards. Each of these standards will impact the income statement and balance sheet of the organization. The risk manager must have a working understanding of the existing accounting standards, as well as proposed standards that may be enacted in the future.

Market Risks and Derivative Activities

The organization has an exposure to the risks of changing commodity prices, exchange rates, and interest rates. The organization attempts to mitigate these risks by the use of forward contracts (swaps) and futures contracts. The futures market is a highly leveraged, high-risk market, dominated by sophisticated investors. The organization is attempting to mitigate its exposure to price changes in certain markets by creating financial hedges.

As an example, assume the organization has committed to deliver aluminum to a client at a fixed price 60 days from now. If the price of aluminum increases over the next 60 days, the organization still must deliver at the specified contract price that could reduce or eliminate the profit related to that contract.

In order to protect against an increase in the market price of aluminum, the organization needs to invest in a financial product that will increase in value as the market price of aluminum increases. The increase in value of this product or contract will hopefully offset any lost profitability on the aluminum delivery contract. By purchasing "long" aluminum contracts in the futures market, the organization will gain monetarily from an increase in the price of aluminum. This is called a hedge. If the hedge is constructed properly, any gain or loss on the derivative contract will offset the gain or loss on the commodity position being hedged. In our example, if the price of aluminum fell rather than increased, the organization would gain a higher profit on the contract to deliver aluminum but would lose money on the hedge. Constructing a hedge is a complicated process in which many things can and often do go wrong. An improperly constructed hedge can actually increase risk rather than decrease risk.

Let's attempt to understand the process of hedging through the following example:

The organization sells $15 million of aluminum to the London Aluminum Co. on net 60 terms. The current spot value of the British pound is $1.50 U.S. In order to obtain the contract, the organization was required to invoice the contract in pounds sterling rather than U.S. dollars. The contract will state that London Aluminum owes the organization £10 million in 60 days. The risk the organization runs is that in 60 days the value of the pound will change from its current spot price. If, in 60 days, the value of the pound is equal to $1.30 U.S., the £10 million the organization receives will be worth only $13 million U.S., resulting in a currency loss of $2 million U.S. to the organization.

In order to mitigate this risk, the organization enters into a contract today that specifies the organization will deliver £10 million in 60 days in exchange for a fixed number of U.S. dollars. This is an example of a futures or forward contract. Assume that today the 60-day futures rate for the British pound is $1.47 U.S. This means the organization can sign a contract today agreeing to deliver £10 million in 60 days in exchange for $14.7 million U.S. The organization has agreed to pay a $300,000 "insurance premium" in order to guarantee a fixed exchange rate in the future.

A forward contract is an over-the-counter agreement between two parties; a futures contract is an agreement that takes place on a securities market exchange. The main difference between the two contracts is that in a forward contract (swap) there is a risk that the entity on the other side of your contract (counterparty) may not perform its contractual responsibility. This is referred to as counterparty risk. For instance, in our example at the end of 60 days, the organization is ready to deliver the £10 million, but the counterparty is unable to deliver the $14.7 million U.S.

With a futures contract, the clearing corporation of the exchange absorbs the counterparty risk. Thus, a futures contract has less risk than the forward contract, but the futures contract is not risk free. The London Aluminum Co. could fall upon difficult financial times and be unable to pay the organization the £10 million in 60 days. Now the organization is obligated to deliver £10 million it does not have to honor the futures contract.

The purpose of this section of the chapter is not to provide an in-depth discussion of the derivative market, but to point out the complexities and risk involved in these markets.

The organization's derivative activities are subject to the oversight of a strategic risk management committee. All of their derivative positions exist for hedging rather than speculation. The organization states that they are not involved in energy trading derivatives (Enron), weather derivatives, or any non-exchange commodity trading activities. The organization purchases natural gas, fuel oil, and electricity to meet production requirements and hedges against increases in the price of these raw materials. The organization uses interest rate swaps to maintain a balance between fixed and floating rate debt. The organization hedges its currency exposure as well. The risk manager must understand the positions the organization is taking in these markets and the risks inherent in those positions.

Environmental Matters

Encountering a full-page section in your organization's annual report with this title is rarely a good thing. Generally, the risk manager or analyst would prefer not to see any of the following terms in their company's financial statements: pollution exposure, EPA, potentially responsible parties, or Superfund site(s).

However, this organization is exposed to numerous sites, including multiple Superfund sites. It is extremely difficult to estimate the cost of cleaning up a polluted site, never mind a Superfund site. The organization's exposure could easily run into the multi-million dollar level. The report cites the organization's exposure to a river contaminated with PCBs. The organization's estimate of the remediation cost is $2 million. The EPA's estimate of the remediation cost is $525 million. There is no guarantee the final cost will not exceed the EPA's estimate. The organization set a reserve for this site equal to $30 million. This section of the report alerts the risk manager to a host of high-profile, high-dollar exposures. It is imperative that the company's risk manager has developed a plan to manage these exposures.

Financing Activities

Management discusses the organization's debt rating from Standard & Poor's and Moody's. If either of these rating bureaus lowers the organization's debt rating, it will result in a higher cost of borrowing and make it more difficult for the organization to raise additional debt to meet future needs. It is crucial for an organization to take steps to maintain and improve its credit rating. The highest bond rating for corporate debt is AAA. Bonds rated triple-B or above are considered investment grade. Bonds rated below triple-B are termed high-yield or junk bonds.

ERISA prohibits organizations subject to the prudent person rule from owning junk bonds in any employee pension or welfare benefit plans. If an organization loses its investment grade rating on its bonds, employee pension and welfare benefit plans holding those securities will dump them in the market, and the market price will fall. It is vital for publicly traded corporations to maintain an investment grade rating on their debt.

Critical Accounting Policies and Estimates

In a number of sections of the report, management must make significant estimates, judgments, and assumptions. These areas include accounting for derivatives, environmental issues, values of business to be divested, postretirement benefits, asset impairment, and goodwill, among others. Management must be able to defend these assumptions and estimates to its external clientele, including investors, analysts, and regulators. The risk manager must understand the processes used and assumptions made in order to help ensure that they are reasonable and defendable, or at least to understand the rationale to recognize the effects these assumptions might have on the cost of risk.

Contractual Obligations and Off-balance-sheet Arrangements

As mentioned previously, this note usually starts with a statement that numerous individuals and/or entities are suing the organization and that the investor should not worry because the organization has good attorneys and all the suits are believed to spurious and without merit. It is important for the risk manager to understand the scope of litigation pending against the organization and the potential level of damages should the organization lose any of these cases.

Additional items contained in this note include a discussion of long-term purchase obligations, debt agreements, lease agreements, and take or pay contracts. The contents of this note are generally categorized as off-balance-sheet liabilities. Enron is the poster child for the off-balance-sheet liability notes. A key off-balance-sheet liability and asset for most organizations, regardless of size, is the lease of assets rather than their purchase.

Accountants have rules to determine whether a lease should be categorized as an operating lease or a capital lease. If the lease is categorized as an operating lease, the value of the asset and the accompanying liability will not show up on the organization's balance sheet. For capitalized leases, the accounts show the value of the asset and liability on the balance sheet. This note provides the risk manager or analyst with valuable information regarding the organization's exposure to off-balance-sheet liabilities. Regardless of the culpability of Enron's management and accountants in creating these off-balance-sheet transactions, potential investors would have been well served spending whatever time necessary to fully understand Enron's off-balance-sheet liability note.

Notes to Consolidated Financial Statements

Without a doubt, this is the most important section of any organization's annual report. The risk manager must seek the advice of accountants, attorneys, financial analysts, and whatever other professionals who may be required to fully understand the contents of the footnotes. Sarbanes-Oxley requires that the organization's top management personally sign and attest that they understand the organization's financial statements and that those statements accurately reflect the condition of the organization's financial position.

Notes contain a vast amount of qualitative and quantitative data that is of value to an analyst or risk manager. It is not the intent of this section to provide a detailed accounting-based explanation of the various notes, but rather to alert the risk manager to some key notes to be aware of.

Note A. Summary of Significant Accounting Policies

This note usually states that the financial statements of the organization are prepared in conformity with generally accepted accounting principles in the United States. However, not all organizations use GAAP: insurance companies adhere to statutory accounting (although the holding companies of insurance companies will use GAAP), and public utilities use regulatory accounting principles. Additionally, GAAP in the United States is not necessarily the same thing as GAAP in other countries, although international accounting standards are gradually converging toward a common system.

Principles of Consolidation

Large organizations file consolidated financial statements. If a large organization owns ten business units, the investor will see only one set of financial statements. The operations of the business units are combined into an aggregate set of financial statements. Consolidation does not necessarily mean that all the operations of the organization are incorporated within the common financial statements. If the organization owns more than 50% of the business unit, that unit must be included in the consolidated financial statements. If the organization owns 50% or less, the results of those entities may or may not be included within the consolidated statements.

Information on ownership interests not included in the consolidated statements can generally be found in a footnote usually titled Unconsolidated Joint Ventures and Associated Companies.

Goodwill and Other Intangible Assets

Effective January 1, 2002, goodwill is no longer amortized because of the provisions of FAS 142. Instead, the value of assets with indefinite useful lives is tested at least annually for impairment. If the carrying value of goodwill or an intangible asset exceeds its fair market value, an impairment loss will be recognized. FAS 142 exposes investors to the potential of unpredictable and potentially significant asset write-downs. If the organization does not do a good job preparing investors and analysts for the potential of asset write-downs, it could result in an adverse impact on the organization's stock price and potential shareholder litigation.

Derivatives and Hedging

This section expands on the coverage of this topic in the management's discussion of the financial results section. This very complex topic area has potential risk exposures that cannot be overstated.

Note B. Discontinued Operations and Assets Held for Sale

As discussed earlier, the sale of a business or closing of a business affects the organization's income statement and balance sheet as well as exposing the organization to potential employee morale issues.

Note C. Asset Retirement Obligations: FAS 143.

The organization has costs associated with residue disposal, mine reclamation, and landfills. These costs reflect legal obligations associated with mining, refining, and smelting operations. Organizations face a legal and ethical responsibility to return the environment to a condition similar to the one that existed before the organization's operations. This responsibility can result in significant cost to the organization. If the organization does not meet its responsibility, it can face sanctions from regulators and potential litigation.

Note D. Restructuring and Other Charges

Topics included in this note include layoff reserves related to terminated employees, reserves associated with the closure of business units, costs associated with the temporary shutdown of business units, and asset write-downs, among others.

Note E. Goodwill and Other Intangible Assets

The organization has approximately $6.5 billion of goodwill on its balance sheet. Under the provisions of FAS 142, this goodwill will no longer be amortized, resulting in higher than reported net income. The analyst and risk manager needs to understand that this increase in reported earnings is related to an accounting change rather than improved operating efficiency. A significant question is: What is the market value of a $6.5 billion intangible asset that you cannot touch, fund, use, or play with?

Note F. Acquisitions and Divestitures

Over the last several years, the organization has divested and acquired numerous businesses. A key component of the process of evaluating potential acquisitions is the due diligence procedure. The risk manager should be an integral component of the due diligence team. Proper evaluation and analysis before the acquisition can save the organization substantial costs later on. A number of the environmental exposures the organization faces were inherited from organizations that were acquired.

The organization states that all acquisitions are accounted for using the purchase accounting method. In the past, organizations were allowed to use the pooling accounting method for acquisitions. This method allowed organizations to manipulate post merger earnings per share to a significant degree. Because of these abuses, the term "dirty pooling" became part of the accounting vernacular. Substantial litigation resulted from abuses of pooling accounting. Organizations are no longer allowed to use pooling accounting for mergers and acquisitions.

Note G. Inventories

The organization uses LIFO and weighted average cost methods to value inventory. The use of LIFO understates the value of ending inventory. If the weighted average cost method had been used to value all inventory, the carrying value of inventory on the organization's balance sheet would increase by $700 million. This understatement represents a significant asset the risk manager needs to be aware of and protect.

Note H. Plant, Property, and Equipment

This is a brief but important note. The book value of the organization's plant, property, and equipment is approximately $11.4 billion. The initial purchase price of those assets was approximately $24.6 billion. Neither of those numbers represents the replacement value, market value, or insurable value of those assets. The risk manager is responsible for arranging to have these assets valued by professionals and to make sure that, in the event of a loss, sufficient funding is available for the organization to replace these assets.

Note I. Investments

Usually this note is titled "Unconsolidated Joint Ventures and Associated Companies." This note represents the organization's ownership interest in entities whose results are not incorporated in the organization's consolidated financial statements. Generally, this is a positive note in that it identifies assets that do not show up on the organization's balance sheet. The value of the organization's interest in these off-balance-sheet entities is approximately $2 billion. The risk manager needs to know the details about these entities to ensure the organization's interest in them is safeguarded.

Note J. Debt

This paragraph reiterates the importance of the organization's debt rating by Standard & Poor's as well as Moody's. The organization has revolving credit arrangements with a variable interest rate based on LIBOR. On one credit arrangement, the current rate is LIBOR plus 19 basis points. If the organization's credit rating is downgraded, the rate can increase to a maximum of LIBOR plus 86 basis points. The organization's debt rating has a significant impact on the organization's cost of borrowing. A rating downgrade also will adversely affect the organization's profitability and stock price. The risk manager needs to understand the rating process and the steps the organization must take to maintain and/or improve its credit rating.

Note K. Commitments and Contingencies

This note starts with a statement that various entities are suing the organization related to environmental, product liability, and safety and health issues. It goes on to say that although the amounts claimed may be substantial, the ultimate liability cannot be determined. Therefore, it is not possible to estimate the potential exposure of the organization to these lawsuits. The risk manager needs to be aware of and manage the organization's litigation risk exposure.

Note L. Preferred and Common Stock

The common stock section of this note deals with stock options granted to management. The use of stock options as an incentive component of management compensation recently has come under increased scrutiny. The accounting profession is rumored to be close to implementing and enforcing a FAS ruling requiring organizations to restate earnings to reflect the impact of stock options on earnings per share. The key issue for the risk manager to understand is how the organization plans to obtain the shares necessary to cover these options in the event they are exercised. One alternative is to issue shares from treasury stock. This approach results in additional shares of common stock outstanding, which will lead to a dilution in earnings per share, and which could adversely impact stock price. An alternative approach involves the organization purchasing shares on the open market to cover the exercise of management stock options. Since employees tend to exercise stock options when the price of the organization's stock is high, this approach results in a significant commitment of the organization's cash flow.

The preferred stock section of this note mentions a class B serial preferred stock with 10 million shares authorized and none issued. This preferred stock has a par value of one dollar per share. There is no discussion accompanying the disclosure that this preferred stock exists. Often class B preferred stock is used as a "poison pill." Poison pills are actions designed to make it difficult if not impossible for the organization to be taken over by another company. A great deal of controversy exists as to whether these provisions actually benefit shareholders or simply protect the jobs of management. The risk manager needs to understand the implications of a poison pill or other anti-takeover defenses for the organization's owners.

Note M. Lease Expense

This note discusses operating lease arrangements covering equipment, warehouse and office space, and oceangoing vessels. The value of these assets and liabilities are not included in the organization's consolidated income statement and balance sheet. The risk manager should be aware that the absence of these assets will influence a number of key ratios and valuation models, and the assets need to be protected and the liabilities repaid.

Note N. Pension Plans and Other Post-retirement Benefits

This note represents the ultimate off-balance-sheet liability for many large organizations in the United States today. The existence of a pension plan note indicates the existence of a defined benefit pension plan. Defined benefit pension plans are becoming an endangered species in this country and are being replaced with defined contribution plans. A pension note is a complicated but extremely important footnote for the risk manager to understand. The defined benefit pension plans of most U.S. corporations are significantly under-funded. A number of organizations, especially in the airline industry, have declared bankruptcy under Chapter 11 in order to turn control and responsibility for their defined benefit pension plans over to the Pension Benefits Guarantee Corporation (PBGC), a government agency that insures employee pension benefits.

A second component of this note deals with postretirement benefits other than pensions, most notably the promise to pay employee health care costs in retirement. FAS 106 requires organizations to account for health care retirement benefits in much the same manner as they account for defined benefit pensions. For many organizations, FAS 106 related benefits are significantly more under-funded than their defined benefit pension plans. Both of these situations would represent substantial off-balance sheet liabilities that investors and the risk manager need to be aware of.

When constructing this note, management makes three key assumptions related to the defined benefit pension plan: the discount rate used to calculate the present value of the organization's obligation; the expected long-term rate of return on plan assets; and the expected rate of salary increases over time. Manipulation of these assumptions can significantly alter the level of the organization's exposure and the funding status of the plan. The assumptions must be realistic and defendable in the light of current economic and financial market conditions. The risk manager must be involved or at least aware of how management makes these assumptions and estimates.

When calculating the organization's health care liability, it is necessary to estimate the health care cost trend rate for the next year as well as the long-term cost trend rate. A relatively small change in the estimate of these health-care cost rates can significantly alter the organization's projected liability. The inability of an organization to meet its contractual benefit obligations to employees can result in adverse publicity and potential litigation from employee groups.

Composition of the Board of Directors

The last several pages of most annual reports include pictures and a brief biography of the members of the organization's Board of Directors. The primary function of the Board of Directors is to ensure that management acts in the best interest of the shareholders. Additionally, the board is responsible for making sure that management acts in a legal and ethically responsible manner and complies with applicable laws, regulations, and accounting practices. A number of corporate boards have come under media scrutiny for abdicating their oversight responsibility and not adequately monitoring the actions of management. Numerous lawsuits have been filed against members of boards of directors for violating their fiduciary responsibility to the organization's constituencies.

The risk manager and analyst need to evaluate the ability of the board to conduct its oversight role. How many of the board members are true outsiders, having no financial ties to the organization? Do their backgrounds, educational experience, and professional expertise bring value to the board? Do their other responsibilities allow them sufficient time to fill their board responsibilities? Does the composition of the board reflect the cultural and ethnic diversity of the country? The key board committees to evaluate are the audit committee, compensation committee, executive committee, and governance committees. In addition to evaluating the competency of the organization's board, the risk manager needs to ensure that board members are protected with adequate directors and officers insurance.

Notes Conclusion

This concludes our brief tour of the footnotes of a large Fortune 500 organization. At this time, you are probably saying, "None of my clients is a Fortune 500 organization, and most of my clients do not have annual reports." While it is true that larger organizations generally have more complicated financial statements, many of the principles discussed in this section apply to organizations regardless of their size.

Almost all organizations lease assets, value inventory, own plant property and equipment, borrow money, buy and sell other businesses, and face litigation risk. Whether or not the organization publishes an annual report, a risk manager needs to develop a systematic process of understanding the organization's financial statements and the exposures related to the statements. The risk manager needs to know which questions to ask and whom to ask. When risk managers encounter a concept they are not familiar with, they need to have access to a team of professionals who can provide the necessary explanation and advice. The goal of this chapter is not to turn risk managers into accountants or financial analysts but to provide a brief overview of the language and thought processes of these professions.

Chapter 4

Ethics and Risk Management Policy

Introduction

The old joke, "If it weren't for people, the subject of the shortest book would be business ethics," has an element of truth. However, people are the subject, and business ethics could make a long book.

The business of risk management is grounded in ethics and honesty. From the earliest days of insurance history, the doctrine of uberrimae fidei, utmost good faith, guided marine underwriters who were unable to see the vessels and cargos they were insuring mid-voyage.

While the risk manager is not responsible for the ethics of the entire organization, anyone who fills that position can take a role in establishing or supporting an organization-wide climate of ethical conduct by establishing and maintaining a sound ethical behavior-management program in the risk management department.

What Would You Do?

Think about the following scenarios. Imagine yourself being involved in these situations, and ask yourself, "What do you do?"

Ethical Scenario #1: You are a producer in an insurance agency. It is the middle of December and you have validated your commission bonus for the month and the year, and no more bonus money is available. One of your prospective clients calls and tells you to stop by. When you do, the prospect gives you an order to bind the new coverage you proposed and wants to give you a check for the entire first year premium.

What would you do? Is there an ethical issue here?

Ethical Scenario #2: You are an independent risk management consultant retained by a large organization. You have conducted a comprehensive exposure survey, developed detailed specifications, and distributed the Request for Proposal package to several insurance brokers you and the risk manager have interviewed and qualified.

The organization's CFO, the risk manager's superior, calls you and instructs you to include another insurance broker you did not interview and qualify, and to give that broker the "last look" at the other proposals. You are aware the CFO's brother-in-law works for that brokerage firm.

What would you do? Is there an ethical issue here?

If you were the risk manager, what would you do? Is there an ethical issue here?

Ethical Scenario #3: You are a risk analyst in the risk management department of an organization with a strict organizational code of ethics. Over a period of time, you have observed a subordinate co-worker, a single parent with three school-aged children, taking pens, pencils, paper, and other office supplies that appear to have usefulness for school work.

What would you do? Is there an ethical issue here?

Ethical Scenario #4: You are the risk manager for a non-profit social services agency. Your insurance broker knows you and your children are actively involved in Little League baseball and softball. The broker has offered you a set of family season tickets to the games of the local professional baseball team.

What would you do? Is there an ethical issue here?

The answer to each of these scenarios is like the plain and simple truth: rarely plain and never simple. If you think the answer to any of these scenarios is plain and simple, then ask a few friends and relatives for their opinion of the scenario and see what they say.

What Are Ethics?

In the broad sense, ethics is a branch of moral philosophy that defines right conduct and good life, a life worth living. The term "ethics" is derived from the Latin ethica, a term borrowed from the ancient Greek ethos, meaning "custom, habit."

Many of the best-known early philosophers were Greek: Socrates, Aristotle, Aristippus, Epicurus, and Epictetus. They tried to bring meaning into man's life by explaining the role of knowledge, self-realization, gratification, moderation, and self-mastery. The Socratic dictum to seek self-knowledge and therefore do what is naturally good and the Aristotlean aim of self-realization of one's nature and development of one's talents established the basis of moral behavior that was modified over the following centuries. These schools of philosophical thought were contradictory in many respects, ranging from the attempt to maximize pleasure and minimize suffering (Epicureanism) and to obtain mastery over one's desires and emotions through abstinence (Stoicism).

Moral philosophers, such as the early Greeks, provide a number of ways that a system of ethics is created or defined, but these are theoretical discussions, existing only in the minds of the philosophers and their students.

Most of us seem to naturally know the difference between right and wrong (the exceptions being a sociopath and a three-year old brat), and we do not need philosophers standing by us to give us guidance. The difficulty comes, however, when situations confront us while cloaked in the minutia and nuance of everyday life, such as those described in the "What Would You Do?" scenarios. For that guidance, we look to applied ethics.

Applied ethics is a separate branch of philosophy that takes ethical theory and applies it (hence the name) to real-life situations. The concept of business ethics has naturally grown out of applied ethics as ethics theory was applied to the real-life situation found in business relationships and activities. It is based on the belief that people naturally want to do things right and they want to do the right thing, but sometimes the "right thing" is neither obvious nor universal.

Defining Ethics and Ethical as Used in Applied Ethics

The noun "ethics" is defined as the moral principles of a group or an individual as developed over time and with life experiences. "Ethical" is an adjective pertaining to standards of conduct or practice arising out of ethics.

"Business ethics", like "risk", has various meanings for many people. Three of the simplest and more straightforward definitions are as follows:

Knowing what is right or wrong in the workplace and then doing what is right.

The fundamental ground rules of our work lives.

The process of instilling into an organization's workforce a sense of how to responsibly conduct business.

These definitions focus on managing ethical behaviors in the workplace, not in establishing the underlying ethic or moral principles. We leave that daunting task to the philosophers.

The Sources of Ethical Problems

"Men at some times are masters of their fate. The fault, dear Brutus, is not in our stars, but in ourselves."

"The Tragedy of Julius Caesar"

Wm. Shakespeare

Most ethical problems stem from two common human failings: greed and ignorance.

Lapses in ethical behavior caused by greed are easily recognized and can be particularly egregious or harmful. A reading of the daily newspaper often provides examples of how greed directs human behavior into destructive or antisocial conduct. The obvious examples of ethical lapses of greed are clearly criminal in nature, such as embezzling funds from an employer, committing fraud in business transactions, or the taking or offering of kickbacks or bribes to direct business away from a fair and unbiased decision-making process.

Some common examples of ethical lapses arising out of greed may not make the evening news, but can be just as devastating to an organization and its workforce. Expense account padding hurts all honest employees and the organization, but is not likely to be criminally prosecuted. Similarly, stealing of time or materials from the employer increase expenses, decrease earnings, and destroy morale in the workforce. These actions can be as simple as calling in sick on the way to the golf course, playing games on the company computer during work, or use of the company's Internet access for non-business purposes.

Lapses in ethical behavior due to ignorance are more difficult to recognize and often appear with questions of conflicts of interest. Many of these arise out of commonly accepted business practices and that makes them particularly difficult to manage as "ethics" itself is defined as principles arising out of individuals and groups over time and life experience. When "everybody else does it," how can it be unethical?

Managing Ethical Behavior in the Workplace

The underlying intent of an ethics program is to instill and manage preferred ethical behaviors in the workplace. Ethical values and intentions are relatively meaningless unless they generate fair and just behaviors in the workplace. In more ordinary terms, it is "walking the walk," not just "talking the talk." The focus of applied ethics is to generate policies, procedures, and training that translate the ethical values or codes created by the philosophers into appropriate behaviors.

Managing ethical behavior in the workplace is a top-down process. The organization's ethical behavior begins inside the office of the organization's highest-ranking officer and flows down through every manager to every employee, regardless of that employee's hierarchal status or position.

"A fish rots from the head."

-- Old Italian folk proverb

In this sense, the managing of ethical behavior is no different that managing risk: if the higher-ranking officer does not support the risk management program, it will not produce the desired results.

Although ethical behavior is the responsibility of every individual in the organization, one person must ultimately be responsible for managing an ethics program. This is not the responsibility of the risk manager. However, the risk manager should be responsible for managing the ethics program of the risk management department.

This process of managing ethical behavior is never-ending. Unlike many management tasks, such as the completion of a new product creation and marketing roll out, ethics programs are more process-oriented than results-oriented, even though a positive result is desired. However, ethics programs do produce deliverables in the form of policies and procedures, budget expenditures, meetings, authorization forms, newsletters, questionnaires, and the like. The most important aspect of managing ethical behavior in the workplace is not the deliverables themselves, but the process of reflective and engaging dialogue that produces the deliverables: everyone doing the right thing because it's the right thing to do.

Specific Ways to Manage Ethical Behavior in the Workplace

Two of the techniques used to manage ethical behavior are similar to the techniques to manage risk: avoidance and control. The best way to handle ethical dilemmas is to prevent them in the first place. And like exposures to risk, the most important first step is to identify the possibility of an ethical dilemma, particularly conflicts of interest.

Once the possibilities for ethical dilemmas are identified, there are a number of control techniques that can be used to manage the ethical behavior and prevent adverse consequences arising out of ethical dilemmas in the workplace.

An important step is to integrate ethical management into other management practices. Just as a climate of risk management needs to be integrated into the organization from the top management down to the lowest echelon of workers, a climate of ethical behavior needs to become a part of all management, not a separate activity.

Because of divergent views and life experience, the strongest ethical decisions are made in groups. Ethics result from a collective belief, an expression of what society thinks is appropriate conduct and behavior. In the process of managing ethical behavior in the workplace, the workplace itself becomes the microcosm of society, and will form a core of ethics.

Similarly, using cross-functional teams when developing and implementing an ethics management program will strengthen the process, as varied life experiences and believes are integrated into the collective ethics.

In spite of the best intentions of management, ethical perfection may not be realistically achievable. Humans are prone to err, perceptions may not be clear, and emotions can cloud decisions. However, it is far better to attempt to create ethical perfection and make a few mistakes than to not try at all.

Creating a climate of ethical behavior requires ethical policies and procedures so as to give guidance to workers and managers. An underlying truth in these policies and procedures is that ethical dilemmas are a natural part of the workplace and must be addressed head-on. A common part of an ethics policy and procedure is a code of ethics or code of conduct.

Employee training will not make an employee more ethical; human behavior is largely determined at an early age. What does change over the years and with training, however, is the individual's ability to foresee ethical problems and to address them appropriately. In some instances, organizations may determine that providing rewards for ethical behavior and consequences for unethical behavior is appropriate. Philosophers may oppose this, arguing that the intrinsic reward of knowing one has done the right thing is sufficient, but behaviorists may counter by saying that punishment rarely produces the desired outcome. Nonetheless, the organization should consider imposing consequences for unethical behavior. While the threat of adverse consequences may not change the behavior of an individual who is teetering on an ethical brink, it may remove the individual from the organization and prevent further ethical problems.

Establishing a grievance policy to provide a forum for voicing concern over ethical dilemmas, including an anonymous hotline to report unethical behavior, recognizes that ethical dilemmas are a natural part of the workplace and provides a means to address these issues before they become problems. Morale in a workplace is closely related to the morals in a workplace, and when the collective groupthink is that management does not care about ethics and moral behavior, morale suffers.

Lastly, there are a few other specific ways to manage ethical behavior in the workplace. These include:

- Assign an employee to act as Ethics Manager.

- Establish a means to notify employees of new ethical situations and rules of conduct.

- Conduct annual conflict of interest surveys with all employees.

Code of Ethics or Code of Conduct

Most large organizations have a code of ethics or code of conduct that can be found on the organization's website. Several are included as exhibits to this chapter.

While these codes are as varied and diverse as their organizations, they typically address a number of common topics:

- Balanced and accurate reporting of all conditions and facts (this is tempered, quite naturally, by the need to preserve trade secrets, marketing strategies, and many planned activities)

- Presentation of information in a fair and unbiased manner so as to not unduly influence decisions

- Use of the organization's property and time for personal use

- Management of conflicts of interest, including the appearance of conflicts of interest

- Policy concerning entertainment and gifts from vendors and to customers

- Confidentiality procedures

- Procedures for reporting illegal or questionable activities

- Adherence to what is ethically sensitive to the organization beyond legal and regulatory compliance

The organization must recognize, however, that it is not always possible to include a preferred behavior for every ethical dilemma or to always foresee every possible ethical dilemma that might arise.

Conflict of Interest

The ethical dilemma created by a conflict of interest is one of the most common ethical issues to confront an organization and its workers. The situation in which an employee steals from the organization or one of its stakeholders to feed his family is truly rare in comparison to the subtle influences of gifts, entertainment, and camaraderie that are masqueraded as common business practices.

All employees, managers, officers, and directors (regardless of the exact title) have a common law duty to their employer to conduct their work with an undivided and unselfish loyalty to the organization. In many cases, the conflict of interest creeps in between the employee and the organization simply because the employee is attempting to fulfill the duty to the employer, but some benefit attaches to the employee in the process.

A conflict of interest is defined as a situation that places one between the duty to the employer and the employee's own self-interest. Further, the definition must be expanded to include the appearance of a conflict of interest, even though an actual conflict of interest does not exist. The old adage about the appearance, gait, and vocalization of an aquatic waterfowl describes the appearance of a conflict of interest adequately.

"If you lie down with dogs, you get fleas."

Anonymous Mom

Recall the "What Would You Do?" scenarios from the introduction. Reconsider those in light of a conflict of interest or appearance of a conflict of interest.

Managing Conflicts of Interest

Like ethical dilemmas in general, conflicts of interest can be managed systematically, with identification of the conflict of interest being the first and most important step. Conflicts of interest can be identified through periodic questionnaires or surveys, asking questions such as, "Do you or any member of your family have a financial interest in any vendor, supplier, or contractor with whom the organization conducts business?"

Also, frequent reminders about the possibility of creating a conflict of interest and education as to what constitutes a conflict of interest are importance parts of identification. The human failing of ignorance cited earlier as a common source of ethical problems gives rise to many conflicts of interest simply because individuals are not aware that there is a conflict of interest or how a seemingly innocent and common business practice may create an ethical dilemma.

Once a conflict of interest is identified, the best management response is to avoid the conflict of interest. In the common case of entertainment or gifts from vendors, a common business practice supported even by the Internal Revenue Service's allowance of a tax deduction for business entertainment (within reason, of course), avoidance would be practiced by a policy prohibiting all such gifts and entertainment completely, or restricting such gifts and entertainment to a nominal level. In other cases, an organizational policy might be to preclude any dealings with any party with whom a decision-maker has a familial or financial interest. Some conflicts of interest cannot be avoided, though, and another response is required.

A related problem arises here, when a customer and vendor become friends over an extended business relationship, an occurrence that is quite common. At this point, avoidance becomes impractical, and another response is required.

The third management step is to resolve unavoidable conflicts of interest. The first level of resolution is to disclose the conflict of interest to the appropriate parties. For example, if an employee responds in a survey that a family member has a financial interest in a vendor of the organization, that fact is disclosed. If the ownership is minimal, the disclosure is sufficient to resolve the conflict of interest. In other cases, an additional action would be warranted.

A second common method of resolving conflicts of interest is a recusal. This is commonly found in the legal profession, when a lawyer must refuse a case because of a conflict of interest or a judge must disqualify him or herself from hearing the case because of a conflict of interest.

In the business world, a recusal may take the form of a partial recusal, such as participating in a discussion of matters involving the conflicted party, but not taking part in the decision-making process. In other instances, the recusal may be complete, and the conflicted party does not participate in any part of the discussion or decision.

The last step in managing conflicts of interest is for the organization to include in its ethical policies and procedures a formulation of the appropriate responses to conflicts of interest, an organization-wide approach to identification, avoidance, and resolution through disclosure and recusal.

Benefits to an Organization

An organization that has an effective ethics program and a code of ethics can expect to derive benefits from their efforts. An ethics program and code of ethics are important because a reputation for ethical behavior, full and forthright disclosure, and integrity establish the level of trust that underlies all successful business dealings. What rational person wishes to do business with a scoundrel or a cheat?

An ethics program and code of ethics can have the following benefits within an organization:

- Promote a high standard of business practices

- Develop an awareness and sensitivity

- Define and communicate acceptable behaviors

- Integrate ethical guidelines into decision making

- Establish mechanisms for resolving ethical dilemmas

- Cultivate teamwork and employee productivity

- Provide a benchmark for employees to use for self-evaluation

- Promote a strong positive public image and adherence to good public practice

- Enhance conformity to the spirit and letter of all laws and regulations

- Help avoid accusations of criminal acts and lower possible fines and penalties under sentencing guidelines

Earnings and Management Fraud

There may be fraud with earnings management, as recent history has shown a number of prominent U.S. companies, such as Enron, with unethical management and presentation of their financial statements to stockholders and others. The statement on Auditing Standards (SAS) No. 82, Consideration of Fraud in a Financial Statement Audit, distinguishes fraud from error on the basis of whether the underlying action that results in a misstatement of the financial statements is intentional or unintentional.

Two types of intentional misstatements are relevant to the auditor's consideration of fraud (1) misstatements arising from fraudulent financial reporting and (2) misstatements arising from misappropriation of assets. Fraudulent financial reporting involves intentional misstatements or omissions of amount or disclosures in financial statements, perhaps as part of a scheme to manage earnings.

SAS No. 82 categorizes risk factors related to fraudulent financial reporting. Among the risk factors are those related to management's characteristics and influence over the control environment, some of which relate to the motivation for management to engage in fraudulent financial reporting and personal characteristics bearing on integrity and management style.

SECTION 2

ANALYSIS OF RISK

Chapter 5

Gathering Loss Data

Reasons to Gather, Review, and Analyze Loss Data

The risk manager can use the review of loss history or loss data as a loss exposure identification method in a variety of ways.

Evaluating Cost Effectiveness of Alternative Methods for Financing Losses

When evaluating potential costs/benefits of loss control alternatives, the risk manager can use loss data to assist in deciding which risks to avoid, which to control, which to transfer, and which to finance. Further, the risk manager can use loss data to assist in the risk financing decision between retention and insurance (internal versus external financing), and whether or not a loss-sensitive or cash flow financing plan is appropriate.

Establishing a Basis for Allocating Premiums and Loss Costs

When establishing a basis for allocating premiums and loss costs, the risk manager can create incentives or disincentives to help reduce and control losses by charging back losses to the departmental level, but the risk manager must always be careful not to erase the positive operations results of a location with the allocation of the costs of one loss. The risk manager should use an objective basis for sharing cost-of-risk. Consider a blend of exposure base and experience base, assigning cost of insurance and cost of losses to the cost center responsible. Many risk managers use a "minimum/maximum" model to prevent a single shock loss or one bad year from wiping out a cost center. Also, not all lines of insurance and categories of cost of risk are allocated to the various departments or locations.

Some risk managers allocate only those lines of insurance for which the cost center manager has the ability to impact premiums and losses. For example, allocate workers compensation, auto liability, general liability, employment practices liability, but not fiduciary liability or Directors and Officers liability. Do not allocate risk management department cost except through regular overhead cost because the cost center manager cannot impact the risk management department cost, but would get their share the old fashioned way through "corporate overhead."

Other Uses

The risk manager can also use loss data to identify the causes of the most frequent and serious accidents, to quickly and easily recognize trends in loss experience, to help focus management on the organization's overall cost of risk and to gain their support for loss control efforts, and to evaluate potential costs/benefits of loss control alternatives.

Gathering and analyzing loss data can also be used as a method for evaluating performance between operating units, vendors, and in-house adjusters, as well as benchmarking loss experience.

It is also used when considering product or service development and pricing. The cost of risk is included in the price of product or service, or the product or service may be redesigned based on expected losses.

The risk manager must have the ability to respond to litigation or regulatory actions by federal or state agencies, such as the federal or state Occupational Safety and Health Administration (OSHA) Injuries/Illnesses, Consumer Product Safety Commission (CPSC), Environmental Protection Agency (EPA), or Food and Drug Administration (FDA). By gathering and analyzing loss data, the risk manager has the ability to respond in a meaningful way.

The risk manager must also be able to satisfy insurance underwriting requirements when insurance is selected as a financing option. Working with an agent or broker (or sometimes directly with a carrier), the risk manager will use loss data to negotiate premiums and coverage restrictions or exclusions, to set equitable reserves for retrospectively rated programs, and to establish the amount of letters of credit or other required collateral.

Finally, the risk manager may gather and analyze loss data to use as a basis for establishing and monitoring vendor performance agreements, such as those used with a third-party administrator or loss control service.

Obtaining Loss Data

Internal Sources

Loss data can be obtained from several different places. The first most obvious source is the organization's own loss experience. The organization's loss experience must include accident, incident and near-miss reports. The old underwriting axiom of "frequency leads to severity" remains true: if an organization keeps having accidents, incidents, or near-miss events, eventually one of them will be severe. This is commonly expressed in the approach of risk control as actions to prevent a loss and actions to reduce the impact of a loss, or minimizing frequency through prevention and minimizing severity through reduction of a loss that was not prevented.

Also, the same accident cause (for example, leaking water from a refrigeration case in a supermarket) might produce far different results. For instance, a 17-year old male who slips and falls might get up, with only his coolness or pride injured, but a 75-year old woman who slips and falls might break her hip.

Loss data can also be obtained from first aid logs. First aid logs, while primarily capturing employee injuries, can also be used to document injuries to third-parties. Loss data can also be captured and recovered from Occupational Safety and Health Association (OSHA) logs, insurance company and third-party administrator (TPA) loss runs, litigation records (insurable and uninsurable lawsuits), from human resources and operations departments, and accounting entries (building and equipment repairs and replacements). The risk manager should be aware that non-claims people usually review loss runs, and many times, these people do not know what they are seeing.

Exhibit 5.1: Incidents and Accidents

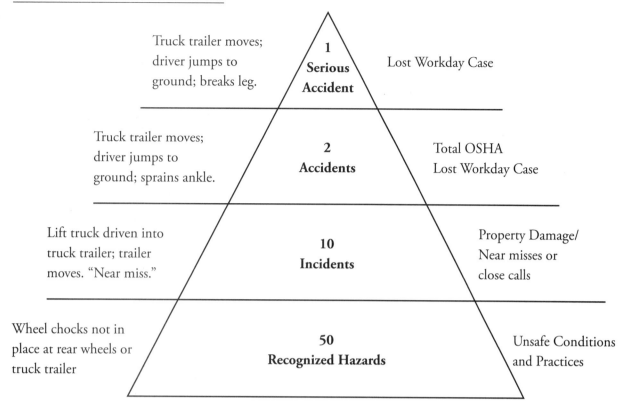

Truck trailer moves; driver jumps to ground; breaks leg. — **1 Serious Accident** — Lost Workday Case

Truck trailer moves; driver jumps to ground; sprains ankle. — **2 Accidents** — Total OSHA Lost Workday Case

Lift truck driven into truck trailer; trailer moves. "Near miss." — **10 Incidents** — Property Damage/ Near misses or close calls

Wheel chocks not in place at rear wheels or truck trailer — **50 Recognized Hazards** — Unsafe Conditions and Practices

External Sources

Loss data can also be obtained from external sources. While this loss data documents the experience of other organizations, the collective experience may be useful at several levels. First, it may indicate losses that others have had that have not yet affected the organization. Second, the accumulation of loss data may provide a degree of credibility that the organization's loss data does not have. However, no organization is exactly like another, and extrapolating information from collected data from many different organizations to apply to an individual organization may not always be appropriate.

Sources of external loss experience include industry associations. Insurance carrier loss records (on a company-wide basis) are another source, although the underwriting risk selection process may introduce unknown biases. Additionally, the risk manager can get incidence rates by NAICS (formerly SIC) Code from Bureau of Labor Statistics (BLS) and Bureau of Transportation Statistics (BTS). Loss data is also available from National Safety Council, Accident Facts, the Cost of Risk Survey prepared by Risk and Insurance Management Society (RIMS), the National Council on Compensation Insurance (NCCI), and the American Trucking Association (ATA), to name a few.

Specific Loss Data to be Collected

The risk manager must finely balance the volume of loss data that can be collected and its attendant costs against the anticipated benefits of having the data to analyze and use. The amount of loss data that can be collected is nearly unlimited, but much of it may be of little value. The risk manager, however, can establish protocols for the capturing of basic loss data that will certainly be needed. This data will form the basis for each loss record, and taken collectively, the entirety of the loss data that will be analyzed and used in decision-making.

The first determination the risk manager must make is the category of loss – whether it is property damage, auto accident, worker injury, injury from product, etc. While property and net income losses can be complex, the issues surrounding these losses are largely accounting in nature. The most challenging losses are those involving people: employees, customers, and the general public with no connection to the organization. Losses involving human resources or liability to third parties for personal injury, emotion, and the vagaries of human behavior become problematic, partially because recollection of "facts" is clouded by perceptions and emotions. A quasi-legal doctrine never taught in law schools, but one acknowledged by lawyers and judges, is "Memory is enhanced by the convenience of forgetfulness."

When the loss involves an injured employee, the level of data that should be collected is the claimant name, date of hire, and occupation at time of accident. The next level is the date and time of loss (for example, year, date, day of week, shift, time of day), as well as division, department or plant to determine if a "weekend" or off-duty accident has shown up as a workers' compensation claim. It is also important to know if one shift or department is having an abundance of accidents. A supervisor or manager's name should also be noted in the loss record. When the individual is not an employee, a customer or other third-party, similar information is needed: name, address, age, occupation, time and location of the incident, and particularly any witnesses' names.

The type of loss whether a sprain, strain, laceration, disease, water damage, or physical damage should be noted. When injury occurs to a person, the body part affected by the injury is required. Finally, the risk manager would want to know what hazards led to the accidents and what the actual cause of the accident was. The cause of loss should never be "employee was not working safely" or "pedestrian was not watching where he was going." The cause should be a specific cause such as fall from height, repetitive motion, inhaling fumes, electrical overload, or tank leak. A hazard should also be specific such as high noise level, slippery surface, unprotected combustible storage, or slippery walkway.

Exhibit 5.2: Loss Run

POL Term	DL/Type/ Clm#	Employee Name/ Department	Mos Emp	Cause of Injury/Injury/ Body Part	PdMed/PdIn- dem/PdTotal	ResMed/ResIn- dem/ResTotal	TotMed/ TotIndem/ Total	Status
6/06-07	06/05/06	Cohn. Deborah	6	Hit by object	378	0	378	Med Only
	MO	Housekeeping		Puncture				
	WC9834734			Thigh	378		378	
6/06-07	06/08/06	Display Xiomara	20	Fell from upper level	0	0	0	CMP
	MO	Recreation		Contusion				
	WC5218795			Mult Body	0	0	0	
6/06-07	06/08/06	Kane, Dean	58	Hit by Object	130	0	130	Med Only
	MO	Nursing						
	WC2358948				130	0	130	
6/06-07	06/09/06	Morales, Rosanne	33	Turned/ Wrenched Knee	2,004	5,946	7,500	Open
	LT	Maintenance		Strain	604	6,896	7,500	
	WC3251			Knee	2,608	12,392	15,000	

Following are a couple of sample claims reports that give the type of information that is normally included in loss analysis. In Exhibit 4.3, the first table lists the specific details for claims in a given time period (e.g. month, quarter, etc.). The second table summarizes claims activity over a certain period on an aggregate basis.

Exhibit 5.3: Detailed Claim Listings

Claims with Incurred Losses above $50,000

(1)	(2)	(3)	(4)	(5)	(6)	(7)	(8)	(9)
Claim Number	Claimant Name	Date of Injury	Type of Loss	Gross Loss and Expense Paid to Date	Open or Closed	Gross Case Reserves for Future Loss & Expense	Total Excess Recovery Received or Expected	Entity Handling Claim

Accident Period Aggregate Experience

(1)	(2)	(3)	(4)	(5)	(6)	(7)	(8)	(9)
Accident Year or Period	Number of Reported Indemnity Claims	Number of Reported Medical-Only Claims	Number of Open Indemnity Claims	Gross Loss & Expense Paid to Date	Gross Case Reserves for Future Loss & Expense	Gross IBNR Amount	Total Excess Recovery Received or Expected	Net IBNR Amount

Direct and Indirect Costs of Loss

Direct costs of loss are those costs that can be accurately identified and tabulated, such as medical/rehabilitation benefits, wage payments, disability settlements, legal expenses, claims administration, lost or restricted days, write off of net book value of damaged building, equipment replacement expenses, or increased construction costs to meet updated building codes.

Indirect costs of loss, also called **hidden costs**, are those costs that cannot be easily identified and tabulated with any degree of accuracy. These types of loss include things like disruption in production or sales, management time spent on loss related activities, cost of hiring and training replacement workers, lowered efficiency in production because of inexperienced replacement workers, and loss of goodwill or reputation.

Cost of Risk

In analyzing the loss data to determine the cost of risk, the risk manager must consider the costs for both direct and indirect losses. Because direct costs are objective in nature, they are readily quantifiable and can be proven through documents and will meet with less resistance from management or department heads. However, since indirect costs are subjective in nature and not easily quantified, they are not easy to prove through documentation. When cost of risk is used as part of an incentive/disincentive program, managers quickly complain of unfairness or bias in the establishment indirect loss costs, and frequently work to undermine the authority and effectiveness of the risk manager and the risk management program. Consequently, some risk managers do not include indirect loss costs in the organization's cost of risk, leaving uncovered or unconsidered exposures that can represent sizable amounts.

Motivating Change in the Organization through Cost of Risk

One effective use of cost of risk loss data is to motivate members of the organization to change behavior by showing the incremental sales or revenue that must be generated to pay for a loss. In this analysis, the risk manager puts on the hat of an economist and focuses on the gross profit margin. For an organization that has a profit margin of 1% (a grocery store, for example), an accident with a direct cost of $1,000 requires an additional $100,000 of sales to generate the $1,000 needed to pay for the loss.

The argument is that in a competitive environment, an organization will find it easier to reduce losses than to increase sales (sales can increase only by convincing some other organization's customers to change, by buying a competitor, or by creating new demand).

Exhibit 5.4: Sales/Revenue Required to "Pay" for Accidents

Accident Costs	Profit Margin				
	1%	2%	3%	4%	5%
$1,000	$100,000	$50,000	$33,000	$25,000	$20,000
$5,000	$500,000	$250,000	$167,000	$125,000	$100,000
$10,000	$1,000,000	$500,000	$333,000	$250,000	$200,000
$25,000	$2,500,000	$1,250,000	$833,000	$625,000	$500,000
$100,000	$10,000,000	$5,000,000	$3,333,000	$2,500,000	$2,000,000

Exposure Data

Loss data is often more valuable when losses are indexed against key units of measure for an organization; (e.g., indexed against an exposure basis that will allow accurate comparisons from one department or group to another, or from one time period to another). Without indexing against exposures, a doubling of loss frequency may appear to be a serious failure in a loss control program, but if the corresponding exposures have quadrupled, the analyst proves that the actual rate of occurrence has decreased significantly.

Depending upon the type of loss data, a number of exposure units can be used to index losses: revenue, gross receipts, net income, units of production, payroll by class code, headcount or hours worked, vehicles by type, vehicles by geographic area, annual mileage, square footage of building, and property values, which could include book value, actual cash value, or replacement cost. The risk manager must take care to connect an exposure basis to losses through an analysis of causation, not correlation. For example, in a retail store situation, slip and fall losses can be easily connected to square footage. A 100,000 square foot store should have twice as many slip and fall losses than a 50,000 square foot store, all other factors being equal. However, store area can be misleading, as a high-traffic location such as a fast-food restaurant of 10,000 square feet may have many more losses than an identical floor area housing a heavy equipment distributor's showroom. Gross receipts are frequently considered an acceptable alternative to area, but again in the case of the fast-food restaurant/heavy equipment showroom, the annual gross receipts may be identical for firms. In the case of the restaurant, there may be 50,000 customers each making a $10 purchase, while in the equipment showroom, there may be only a few customers perusing the $500,000 bulldozer that one finally purchases. Instead, for a fast-food restaurant, customer count may be the appropriate exposure unit instead of the more obvious square footage or gross receipts.

Evaluating and Ensuring the Quality and Credibility of Loss Data

To ensure the quality of loss data, the risk manager must be able to ensure statistical credibility and completeness and to identify changes in loss environment, as well as considering other variables.

A small number of highly variable losses over a short period of time have limited predictive value. In other words, to be statistically credible, there should be a substantial number of losses extended over a sufficient period of time. One year is never enough, and even five years may be suspect (in spite of the insurance underwriter's insistence on that time frame).

There should also be minimum variability in frequency and severity of losses and stable operations over time (consistent size and makeup of exposure base). A key way to improve the quality and format of data is to work closely with third-party administrators and insurance carrier claims departments. Even then, the formats and practices of outside organizations such as the third-party administrators and insurance carriers are primarily designed for their convenience and use, not for the risk manager's credibility.

Comparisons of data are invalid if comparisons are not made on an "apples to apples" basis. To ensure completeness, validity, and consistency of data, the data must have the same reporting format, the criteria for reporting data should be consistent and well understood, and the same definitions should be used for hazards, cause, and injury type. There should be a system in place for validity checks to limit duplicate reporting and incorrect coding. The loss runs should have consistent policy years, deductibles, and valuation dates. If they do not, interpolation should be used to make them consistent. Also, incurred but not reported reserves (IBNR) should be taken into account. (Some risk managers use a "comparison period" as opposed to a "policy year." Almost any good risk management information system will allow selection of any period for comparison (e.g., the policy may be on a July 1 renewal period, but the risk manager wants to do comparisons on a calendar year basis).

The quality of loss data can be affected by changes in the loss environment that may have influenced past losses and the predictability of future losses. This would include having a new product or service introduced; any changes in equipment, materials, or work process; any acquisitions, divestitures, or restructuring; legal and regulatory changes; changes in social and economic environment; any additional or resolved labor and management issues; changes in statutory benefits, inflation, or any other changes in wages; changes in incentive or safety awards programs; changes in deductible; changes in insurance carriers or third-party administrators; changes in insurance coverage that may affect loss reporting (exclusions or broadenings); or demographic changes (e.g., age, gender, education level, ethnic background, or turnover).

Another consideration regarding the quality of data is the organization of the data. The typical loss run or loss history prepared by an insurance carrier or many third-party administrators is grouped according to policy period, and within the policy period, losses are shown chronologically. While there is an important reason for grouping losses by year, the risk manager should consider other possible listing options, such as by size of loss, by date of reporting, by department or location, by day of week, or any other criteria that will address questions the risk manager is asking.

Other considerations that could affect the credibility and evaluation of data would be the cost of collecting data, any difficulty in collecting data, and the relevance and usefulness of data. There is a point of diminishing returns, when the cost to collect the last possible bit of detail does not add any value to the claims settlement and recording process. The data collected must be relevant to the problem the risk manager is attempting to solve and it must be useful in that exercise. Finally, the risk manager must be acutely aware of the need to adequately secure confidential data and protect it from improper disclosure or from improper accessing or use.

Types of Analyses to be Performed on Loss Data

When analyzing data, it is important to remember not to mistake data for information. Data is the input, but information is what becomes useful after the data has been analyzed. The risk manager should provide managers with a summary or analysis of the data so that it is useful and relevant, meeting with them periodically to ensure that the reports suit their needs and allow them to make decisions.

There are as many ways to analyze loss data as there are senior managers to accept the reports. A few of them will be discussed here.

Frequency and Severity Rankings

Loss data can be analyzed by frequency and severity rankings. The report could sort the number of losses by severity range (whether dollar cost or lost time days). Another way to look at frequency/severity is to study the number and cost of losses at each location, product line, or for each type of vehicle. The risk manager could also sort by hazards, causes of loss, or types of loss with the highest cost of injuries. Another report can show frequency and severity of injuries as they relate to length of service of the worker or some other demographic data: shift, time of day, or day of week.

Evaluating Time Intervals

The risk manager can also evaluate loss data by evaluating time intervals. This might involve looking at the time between loss occurrence and reporting of claim, the time between loss occurrence and closing of claim file, the average number of days of lost time or restricted duty, and the likelihood of return to work based on number of lost days.

Loss projections are determined from the expected annual losses, which can be calculated as:

Average number of losses × Average cost of a loss

Triangulation studies and analysis are used to determine loss development factors that can be used to determine ultimate paid losses, ultimate loss reserves, and payouts. Triangulation can calculate the development in cost of losses from time of initial reserve to final claim settlement.

Factors to be Considered for Financial Benchmarking

Benchmarking is "continually *comparing* an organization's performance against that of the *best in industry* (competitors) or *best in class* (those recognized in performing certain functions) to determine what should be *improved....*" Xerox was first to use the concept to improve its own performance. A company would want to benchmark when management is putting a baseline program into place, when internal trending and comparison are underway, and when improvement opportunities are sought.

The benefits to benchmarking are being able to keep track of continued improvement, being able to enhance "out-of-the-box" thinking and creativity, and being able to prioritize areas that need improvement.

It will be important to keep in mind that many risk management decisions will be based on the data collected. Senior management will want to know how the company compares with others in the industry and how the company is doing from one year to the next or one period to the next.

The smart risk manager also knows to be aware of the common pitfalls of benchmarking. Being lower is not always better. It depends upon what is being compared; some comparisons should be higher. Precision in results should not be implied where precision does not really exist.

Comparisons have to be made apples-to-apples for consistency. Comparing a manufacturing operation to a sales office will not be a meaningful comparison. Also, comparing data that varies from one group to another will not give meaningful results. For instance, comparing the profits of one group to the sales of another will not result in a meaningful comparison.

It also is important to have enough data to make a meaningful comparison. An insufficient comparison group population will not give results that the risk manager or senior management can use. The risk manager cannot conclude that only one factor is to blame for unfavorable results. Several factors usually combine to precipitate unfavorable results. One-time, point-in-time comparisons can give inaccurate assumptions; circumstances change over time, as will data. "Slightly" different comparison data can make the comparison "slightly" invalid.

Statistically invalid comparisons (e.g., comparing work injuries to car accidents) and statistically "massaged" data can lead to inaccurate, meaningless comparisons. Also, unknown data where the risk manager has no idea where it came from or what it is can lead to meaningless comparisons.

Chapter 6

Qualitative Analysis

Qualitative Risk Assessment

The purpose of qualitative risk assessment is to identify those loss exposures that cannot be easily measured by traditional statistical or financial methods and to understand their impact on the firm's ultimate risks and performance. There is a difference between qualitative analysis and quantitative analysis. Qualitative analysis can't be precisely measured and asks the question: "What?" With qualitative analysis we want to determine the implications and scope of the effect that risks have on firm. Quantitative analysis asks the question "How much?" and is precisely measured by acceptable traditional methodology.

We need both because each gives us different important information about losses. We use qualitative analysis to find out what losses are occurring. We use quantitative analysis to find out how much those losses cost.

We can make a qualitative assessment when we look at corporate objectives and risk management policy and ask: are they in conflict with each other, or are they consistent? Does risk management policy support the overall achievement of corporate objectives? There are ways that the risk management program can help senior management stay on track with objectives: by providing a means of handling unexpected drains in capital or interruption of operations and by providing management with loss activity data that may affect operations objectives.

Although not subject to specific financial measurements, qualitative risks can be assessed for potential harm to the firm. Some attempt should be made to assess the impact on the firm of all realistic qualitative exposures. For example, they can be categorized in to critical, important and unimportant risks. Critical risks are losses that could bankrupt the firm, threaten survival, or stop operations. Important risks are losses whose financial impact could result in the need to borrow funds from outside the firm in order to continue operations. Unimportant risks are losses with a low financial impact that would not harm operations or that can be paid from existing cash flows.

Qualitative Risk Assessment Areas

There are six main areas of qualitative risk assessment: management's appetite for risk; innovation, product development, and marketing; contractual analysis; compliance and regulatory analysis; human resources and employee safety issues; social responsibility and citizenship analysis; and internal policies.

To determine **management's appetite for risk** the risk manager should look at the company history, the company's long-term objectives, and its growth mode or location in growth cycle. Does the organization have a history of taking risks? Has it been a stable, continuous-growth company? Is the organization a start-up operation or is it established and has been around for years? Is the organization in a type of industry that historically takes risks, like construction, or one that doesn't, such as banks (at least in the old days)? Does the organization's public image support taking a risk? Does the organization have more appetite for risk than it has financial ability to retain the risk?

Innovation, product development, and marketing is the next main area of qualitative risk assessment. How critical are these activities to the organization? Does the survival of the organization hinge on creating new and better products (such as the high tech areas), or is it in a more sedate, stable industry? What is the market positioning and market share of the organization? Who is the competition? Are they risk takers? Is the organization subject to business interruption? What is the organization's production capacity? What is the nature of its operations? Are these operations inherently hazardous?

Contractual analysis means understanding the affects of contracts on the company. Is the company assuming or transferring risk to others through its contractual agreements? Is the legal department taking into account the risk factors included in each contract?

In the **compliance and regulatory analysis area**, is the organization subject to heavy regulation? Is management aware of regulatory governmental requirements? What are the possible industry and voluntary regulations? Has the organization been assessed any penalties or fines, and how did that affect the public image of the organization? What is the history of enforcement?

Human resources and employee safety issues are an important part of the qualitative risk assessment area. Does the organization have a union? Have ergonomic audits been performed? Has management been receptive to safety programs? Do safety programs exist and are they followed? Has the organization been able to recruit and retain a competent work force? Have safety issues impacted employee productivity? Is the organization subject to possible terrorist acts? Does the organization have a security plan?

Social responsibility and citizenship analysis include determing whether or not the organization has a high profile among the general public or within its industry segment. Is management concerned with such issues? What would be effect of negative press?

Internal policies also need to be reviewed as part of the qualitative risk assessment. Audit and oversight (internal, external, and board involvement), employment issues (leasing, contract, seasonal, and employment practices), product guarantees, and product recall should be evaluated. Are outside auditors used?

Financial Assessment

The purpose is to identify and assess those broad loss exposures that have a financial impact on the firm but may be difficult to quantify. These broad loss exposures include profitability, revenue growth, earnings per share, and financial capacity.

Profitability is concerned with adequacy of return in either total dollars, earnings per share, or profit margins. But rather than analyzing just the dollar amounts, the question to ask is, does it meet management's overall expectations? Does the organization have enough return on its investment to fund other opportunities? Where does the organization stand compared to the rest in the industry? Is it better than the rest of the industry and its competitors or is it worse? How critical is profitability to the organization? What is the organization's profit margin? What is the nature of the organization, and where is it in the growth cycle?

Revenue growth is concerned with the growth of revenue relative to growth in expenses and fixed costs. Is the organization improving market share as compared to overall growth in market? Is the organization improving market share as compared to competition either in industry or trade area?

Earnings per share is an important part of financial assessment. In addition to the actual amounts paid, the risk manager should be concerned with stockholder expectations and whether the organization pays senior management with stock options.

Financial capacity, or the ability to fund the activities and investments the organization wants to do or needs to do, is the final area of qualitative financial assessment. The risk manager should look at the current needs versus future opportunities, internal financing versus external financing or transfer options, liquidity and cash flow, long-term debt, and the cost of capital (credit rating, borrowing costs, and outstanding letters of credit).

Insurance Market Analysis

Insurance market analysis is concerned with the overview of the market, maximum probable loss versus maximum possible loss, how much insurance to buy, and insurance pricing and loss costs.

Market overview asks if the insurance market is hard or soft in both the primary and reinsurance markets and also if the insurance market is willing to take the organization's risk. Other areas of concern are alternative markets (non-admitted and foreign insurance carriers, pools, captives, etc.), "unbundling" opportunities, tailoring of insurance products and policies, and the financial positions of the organization's insurance carriers (solvency and company financial or claims-paying ratings).

Maximum probable loss versus maximum possible loss analyzes the values exposed to loss in both current and future projections. Probable maximum loss for a given peril under normal circumstances is the most likely loss to occur. Maximum possible loss is the greatest damage that could be done in a loss. Assessment of maximum possible loss is frequently forgotten, but this exposure is the most critical, as it absolutely will threaten the organization's survival. The risk manager must assess the organization's ability to procure adequate financing to cover the maximum possible loss and to manage what cannot be financed.

The risk manager is always concerned with **how much insurance to buy**. To determine this, he must determine the value of the exposure, the ability to absorb the maximum possible loss, the willingness to absorb the maximum possible loss, and the value and cost of available insurance.

The astute risk manager knows the cost of insuring predictable losses will nearly always be greater than the cost of retaining them. (If the risk manager can predict losses reasonably accurately, so can the underwriter, and the underwriter will add a "premium" for the possibly unfavorable variance in loss plus acquisition expenses such as underwriting costs, commissions, taxes, and profit.

The insurance premium will normally equal the expected losses divided by the complement of the insurance company's expense ratio.

Exhibit 6.1

10 doctors with 10 losses each of $10,000 and an insurance company expense ratio of 35%

Formula:

$$\text{Average Frequency} \times \text{Average Severity (Expected Losses)}$$

$$1 - \text{Expense Ratio}$$

$$\frac{10 \times \$10,000}{1 - .35} = \frac{\$100,000}{.65} = \$153,846$$

Therefore, Expected Premium = $153,846, and Expected Losses = $100,000.

On average it will cost $1.54 to transfer each $1.00 of loss to the insurance company or $153,846 ÷ $100,000.

Loss Data Analysis

The purpose of loss data analysis is to identify and apply various methods of assessing loss data and to understand the impact those losses may have on the firm's risk management policy and the ultimate cost of risk. The quality of the data is of major concern in loss data analysis. Without a degree of comfort in each of the following areas of data quality, it is not possible to make accurate projections of loss trends.

Completeness – There must be enough loss data to make an analysis meaningful. The number of years of data generally required varies by type of exposure or line of insurance. Generally, five years of data is considered appropriate, although more years are always preferred. In some types of exposures or lines, as many as 20 years are desired. However, the risk manager must be aware of possible events over the time period, such as implementation of a loss control measure (or removal of such a measure), technological change (e.g., robotics over manual operation of machinery), acquisition or divestiture of a division or product line, or any other change that would be likely to have an impact on the frequency and severity of losses.

There must be enough data included about each claim or accident to make an analysis meaningful, (e.g. date of loss, person causing loss or person injured, cause of loss, type of loss, dollar value of loss, etc.). It must be known what is included in paid and reserve amounts. Does the loss data include allocated loss adjustment expenses (ALAE), incurred but not reported losses (IBNR), and defense costs?

Consistency of data – The same types of data should be provided for each claim or accident (e.g., the type of loss, cause of loss, time of loss, claimant name, length of employment, etc.). There should be no change in policy year, accident year, or calendar year; a change might mean that the data would have to be interpolated to make it consistent. There should be no change in recording methodology (e.g., from one carrier or TPA to another). Once again, a change might mean that the data would have to be interpolated to make it consistent.

Integrity – The data should be reliable whether it is from an insurance company or third-party administrator (TPA), or generated in-house. The data should be checked for input accuracy. Data needs to be current, a characteristic enhanced by prompt reporting of claims. Loss reserving need to be accurate; it needs to be checked with whomever is reserving for losses, whether insurance company, TPA, or in-house claims department.

Relevance – The data that is collected should be data that will yield information on matters about which the organization is concerned. It is not necessary to continue including data from operations that no longer are a part of the organization, whether through divestiture, discontinued operations, or transferred exposure to a third party (e.g., leasing employees).

When the company has acquired an operation, it would not be necessary to include all loss data from the acquired company if the organization is only acquiring a portion or particular operation of the other operation. For example, if the organization is acquiring the restaurant operation of a diverse company, it would not be necessary to obtain the loss information on their meat processing operation. The risk manager must take care to not combine data from diverse operations when trying to analyze losses (e.g., as in above example, restaurants and meat processing plants). The data from one operation is not relevant to the other because the frequency, severity, types, and causes of losses will not be consistent. Data that is not relevant to the type of losses being analyzed should not be collected.

Useful Organization – A fifth aspect of quality data is its useful organization, but this aspect is not natural to the data; the risk manager adds this to the complete, consistent, reliable and relevant data. Data is always organized, but rarely in a useful manner. The loss run created by the insurance carrier (and many TPAs) is generally first organized by policy year and then within a policy year by the data of occurrence. This organization has limited use to the risk manager except in some manner for determining the age of a loss. More useful organization methods may include a listing by losses according to severity, by location, by shift, by employee demographics, or some other specific type of data that the risk manager believes is important in managing the exposures and losses.

Exhibit 6.2: Stanford University Hazard Identification Index

Action Guide

1-4	Institute corrective action if and when appropriate
5-9	Initiate corrective actions when practical
10-15	Institute all reasonable corrective action ASAP
16-25	Take immediate corrective action

Probability	5	5	10	15	20	25
	4	4	8	12	16	20
	3	3	6	9	12	15
	2	2	4	6	8	10
	1	1	2	3	4	5
		1	2	3	4	5
				Severity		

Probability (over life of condition)

1.	Remote	Extremely unlikely to occur
2.	Low	Possible but unlikely to occur
3.	Moderate	Moderate risk of occurrence
4.	High	Likely to occur
5.	Probable	Very likely to occur in immediate future

Severity

1.	Slight	Minor first aid injuries	Losses under $50
2.	Appreciable	Injuries requiring a physician's attention	Losses between $50 and $1,000
3.	Serious	1 or more serious injuries or illness	Losses between $1,000 and $100,000
4.	Severe	A death or disabling injury or illnesses	Losses between $100,000 and $1 million
5.	Catastrophic	Multiple deaths and/or disabling injuries	Losses in excess of $1 million

Classifying and Categorizing Loss Data

Losses can be **classified by type of loss** using <u>logical classifications</u>. The first logical classification is property, which includes real <u>property</u> and personal property. The report should include the locations of properties that have sustained loss and identify the perils causing loss: human perils (e.g., arson, pollution; economic perils like obsolescence, inflation, strikes); or natural perils (e.g., hail, earthquake, etc.). It should also include claim count and severity of loss information. <u>Human resources</u> is the second logical classification and is related to employee injuries, terminations, retirement, etc. The third logical classification is <u>liability</u>. This would include claim count and severity loss reports by type of liability coverage (auto liability, general liability, product liability, etc.). It should also include a report on litigation and large losses. <u>Net income</u> is the last logical classification. There are no loss reports for net income losses. Net income losses are a decrease of net income or an increase of expenses and will show up in the financial statements and notes.

Categorizing employee injuries is accomplished through qualitative methods. The categories to investigate are accident repeaters, length of employment when injured, cause of injury, type of injury, body part injured, evaluation of time intervals, location of accident (whether company location or at another location, etc.), or any other appropriate or meaningful (relevant) categorization. The injuries should also be categorized according to claim count and severity (the dollar value of the claims).

According to the Pareto Principal or 80/20 Rule, 80% of the problems are the result of 20% of the causes. Taking that into consideration, the risk manager can look at how frequency and severity can be evaluated, looking at the number of losses in each severity range, whether it is dollar cost or lost time days and looking at the number and cost of those losses (organizing the losses by location, by product line, or by type of vehicle). The hazards, causes of loss, or types of injuries with the highest costs should also be of concern to the risk manager, as well as frequency of injury as it relates to length of service of worker or other demographic variable.

Risk Mapping

Risk mapping is a visual analytical tool wherein all the risks of an organization can be identified and understood. Risk maps may be simple or complex, and can be a powerful representation of a firm's vulnerability to unforeseen loss exposures. Risk maps are useful tools for risk managers to convey important risk information to accompany the risk manager's recommended treatment plans to senior management. They are useful when making certain risk control decisions, when determining risk financing decisions, when modeling the effects of potential exposure scenarios that might develop in the future, when tracking risk reduction results, and monitoring changes in exposures over time.

A simple risk map consists of a graph divided into four (4) quadrants, each reflecting a different blending of frequency and severity characteristics for each risk.

Exhibit 6.3: A Simple Risk Map

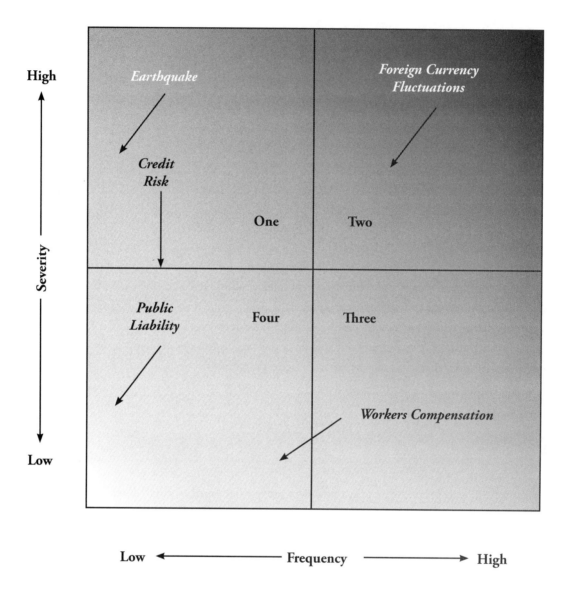

In the above exhibit, the arrows represent the desired movement of the risk exposures – from right to left. Risks that can be placed in quadrant four tend toward low frequency and low severity. Each quadrant relates to costs: the farther up and to the right, the more costly the risk. Ideally, organizations take precautions to avoid or transfer the effects of risks that represent extreme frequency and severity. Risks that inhabit Quadrant One can be dangerous to the company's resources in several ways. In this area, low frequency may mean that actuarial predictability is extremely low or nonexistent, yet the severity of potential losses is high.

Chapter 7

Cash Discounting Concepts

Introduction

"I would gladly pay you Tuesday for a hamburger today." – Wimpy

Wimpy values a current hamburger highly today, and presumably is willing to pay more for that current hamburger next Tuesday. However, the owner of the diner is likely to value the dollar received today more today than one next Tuesday. Why? For one, Wimpy may die or skip town or become bankrupt. Or perhaps the diner owner might have an opportunity to invest in a snappy fast-food franchise that must be concluded today. He can even deposit it into his savings account and earn interest. Both Wimpy and the diner owner are making financial decisions.

Financial decisions require the analysis of dollar cash flows occurring at specific points in time in the future. A dollar amount at one point in time has a different value than a dollar amount at another point in time. For example, a dollar received today is worth more than a dollar received next year simply because it can earn interest.

A common example that drives home the time value of money is the familiar story of the 1624 sale of Manhattan Island by the indigenous people to the Dutch for $24 or so in baubles, bangles, and beads and how that transaction was one of the first examples of the European-based society taking advantage of the so-called savages. However, if the indigenous people (or someone) had created a financial infrastructure and invested the $24 at 6% (assuming no taxes, as was the case until the mid-19th century), this paltry sum would have grown to nearly $135 billion in 2008. Had they managed to invest the $24 at 7.5%, the value of that investment in 2008 would have exceeded $21 trillion. Whether the $24 was invested (spent) wisely or not is another financial decision, beyond the scope of this discussion, but it appears that the value of the purchase price at the time was not such a paltry sum.

The Internet's Wikipedia explains cash discounting in the following way: "All future cash flows are estimated and discounted to give their present values. The discount rate used is generally the appropriate cost of capital and may incorporate judgments of the uncertainty (riskiness) of the future cash flows." In the above example, we can clearly see that the present value of the money in the early 1600s was entirely different from the future value.

Time Value of Money Concepts

The first important step toward learning financial decision-making concepts is to acquire an understanding of time value of money. The risk manager must be able to compare dollar amounts that occur in different time periods.

A well-known adage is "Time is money." While time cannot be spent in the same sense as a dollar, time can be quantified in terms of money. The interest rate provides a convenient and universal measure of the value of time. All financial decisions must balance the benefits versus the costs occurring through time, and that means calculating the value of the money at various points in time by using an interest rate.

The most common calculation is to find the present value of future cash flows and then make comparisons of different alternatives based on present values. There are times when the risk manager will want to consider future values, too. In all cases, the timing and sequence of cash flows is important. For example, cash flow may be a lump sum occurring in only one future period. In other cases, cash flows are annuities, a constant amount every period for a number of periods. The time value analysis is easily extended to a series of lump sums of different amounts occurring in different periods. All time value calculations have four key variables. If three of these variables are known, the fourth can be computed.

The first part of this chapter will be a complete review of the financial concepts involving the time value of money. The middle part of the chapter will illustrate applications of the most common decision-making tools, based on benefit and cost comparisons. The focus will be on net present value and benefit/cost ratios, the most useful financial decision-making tools to the risk manager. Other tools, both simpler and much more complex, payback, accounting rate of return, and internal rate of return procedures will also be addressed. The advantages and disadvantages of all these methods will be discussed in the last part of the chapter.

Once the time value of money concept is firmly in hand, the risk manager can apply this process to make dollar comparisons of financial decision alternatives. The language of management includes a heavy dose of techniques grounded in time value, since a good decision must ultimately add value to the organization. Thus, a good decision adds more in present value benefits than it adds in present value costs. Put another way, an investment must earn a higher rate of return than the rate paid to raise money to finance that investment.

All business activities, including risk management, must be justified in terms of value added. The basic method of justifying a business decision involves a calculation of its benefits and costs. Staffing, risk retention, risk transfer, safety programs, life safety initiatives, and all other related risk management activities require financing.

The minimum acceptable return on investment is also called the cost of capital, and it represents to the organization a percentage rate cost of raising money to fund assets and operations. To add value to the organization, the risk management program must generate cash flows through savings or enhanced revenues that represent a rate of return in excess of the cost of capital.

For example, if the organization has a 15% cost of capital, the risk management program must earn greater than a 15% rate of return to be viable.

The value of risk management activities can be compared in another way, still using time value of money. By using the organization's cost of capital, the risk manager can find the present value of all expected risk management costs and the present value of all risk management benefits. A viable risk management program must have a present value of benefits that exceeds the present value of costs (this is called a "positive net present value").

Because financial managers must use this logic to evaluate all expenditures of the organization, risk managers are better prepared to communicate with financial managers if they have a good understanding of the principles used to evaluate decisions of the organization.

Risk managers must also consider alternative approaches within the risk handling methods of risk avoidance, risk reduction, risk retention, and risk transfer. For example, common decisions involve changing retention levels, establishing captive insurers, increasing or decreasing expenditures on safety programs, expenditures on loss reduction technology, etc. These different types of decisions use time value calculations to determine the consequences of the alternative choices.

Time Value of Money and Valuation Applications

Any time value of money application involves four key variables:

1. The number of periods,

2. The interest rate,

3. The timing of the investment or payment,

4. The number of payments

These four factors are applied directly to a fifth variable:

5. The dollar amount of the investment or payment.

Alternatively, the four key variables may be used to calculate a factor that will be applied to the fifth variable.

Financial spreadsheet software programs offer the convenience of pre-programmed functions, such as PV for the present value of a single sum or an annuity, FV for the future value of a single sum or an annuity, and related values including the Net Present Value of an investment and the Internal Rate of Return, two financial decision-making tools to be explained later.

The number of periods means the length of time the investment or payment schedule is maintained. Generally, the time interval is assumed to be once a year, but the interval may be more frequent, such as every quarter, every month, or even every day. Financial institutions often advertise that "interest is compounded daily" in describing savings accounts, meaning that the investment interval or number of periods is literally 365 times per year.

The number of payments refers to the number of investments or payments made, such as a one-time investment (a single sum) or a series of investments or payments (each is an annuity) over the number of periods.

The interest rate is the rate at which the investment will be valued. This is sometimes called the "discount rate," in keeping with the concept mentioned above that cash discounting incorporates the time value of money that discounts a future dollar to today's present value. The "discount rate" is also used to calculate future value. Interest rate may be a more precise term, but custom and practice often blurs that technical distinction. The interest rates used are assumed to be annual; therefore, when interest is to be calculated more frequently (i.e., the number of periods is increased), the interest rate must be adjusted to reflect more frequent compounding or discounting.

The timing of the investment or payment refers to when the investment or payment is made, at the beginning of a period or at the end. The time value of money calculations also operate using the assumption that all single-sum investments (costs) are made immediately and all annuities are made at the end of the period. This may not actually be the case. Sometimes, the payment is received at the beginning of the period or the investment is made at the end. Adjustments must be made to handle this timing issue.

Lastly, payments are not always made on a regular or constant basis and the amounts are not always the same. Annuity calculations assume constantly reoccurring, regular amounts. For example, a project may return a benefit of $2000 for the first year, with an increasing benefit for each of the next four years. Another project might require an investment of $5000 in the first year and $2000 in the second year. A different project may require the decision-maker to recognize that the equipment purchased and used to generate a flow of funds for ten years will have the additional benefit of tax savings from depreciation, with the amount either changing every year or a salvage value in the 11th year. Fun and games in the decision-making arena, but the calculations can handle all of these permutations.

In the examples that follow, there will be a brief explanation along with a diagram for every relevant type of cash flow problem. Diagrams help the viewer identify the amount of the cash flow and the timing, including the convolutions when non-constant, intermittent amounts are involved.

Future Value of a Single Sum

(Table = Compound Sum of $)

The basic question being asked here is: What is the future value of a single sum of $1 invested today, or how much will the $1 be worth at the end of a specified time period?

The present value of a principal amount or single sum today (PV) can be invested at an interest rate (i%) per period for a number of periods (n) to earn a future value amount (FV). Compounding of interest earnings on the PV will create the FV. The PV is invested at the beginning of the period, and interest is earned and added to the principal. During the second period, interest is earned on the total of the principal and the first year's interest earnings. In the third period, interest is earned on the total of the principal and two year's interest earnings, and so on for each additional period. This accumulation of interest on interest is called compounding. The process is called the Future Value of a Single Sum of $1, or the Compound Sum of $1.

The mathematical formula looks like this:

$$FV = PV \, (1 + i\%)n$$

n = # periods

i = rate per period

A sketch of the cash flows looks like this:

```
        0     1     2     3       n
        |     |     |     |       |
        PV                        FV
```

n = number of periods

i = rate per period

Using the factor tables, the formula looks like this:

$$S = P*(If_{fv})$$

Where: S = the future value of a single sum

P = PV or principal or the single sum

If_{fv} is the interest factor for a future value or compound sum

For example, what if we had $1,000 today and we invested it for 5 years at an annual rate of 4% per year? The Compound Sum of $1 table with a column of 4% and a row of n = 5 give us a value of 1.217. So, $1,000*(1.217) = $1,217 of future value.

Note that if there were no compounding of interest, we would have only earned 4% x 5 = 20% so our future value would be $1,000 of principal return and $200 of interest for a future value of $1,200.

In the first example, the additional $17 of future value is due to the fact that we earn interest on interest in each of the five compounding periods. The equation PV (1 + i%)n takes compounding into account and the table values are calculated for compounded sums. For the calculation of future value, we only need to get our rate per period and number of periods to find the compound sum of $1 and then multiply the present value by the factor from the table.

A few time value concepts are in order here. Note that if everything else remains the same, a higher interest rate makes for a higher future value. Also, a higher number of compounding periods will make the future value higher, everything else remaining the same. To convince yourself of these relationships, review the values in the table to see what happens when you increase i% for any given value of n and then see what happens to the factor when you increase n for any given value of i%.

When you use time value tables, it is crucial for you to go to the correct table. You must make sure you are working with a future value single sum problem like our original example in order to use the Compound Sum of $1 table. As a self-check, be sure that all values in the table are greater than 1, since future values are higher than present values for all positive interest rates.

Present Value of a Single Sum

(Or Present Value of $1)

When we calculate a present value, we know the timing and the future value of a cash flow, the number of periods and the interest rate per period. When we calculate present values, we are "discounting" or reducing the future value to its present value. In effect, this is the reverse of computing the future value, where we start with a known present value and find what it increases to through investment. In present value calculations, we start with the known future value and determine what it is worth today, or the value that we could invest today at the same interest rate over the same time to arrive at that known future value.

For example, consider the mathematical formula we used for future values:

$$FV = PV (1 + i\%)n$$

For calculating present value, we simply solve for a different unknown, the PV, because we know the FV. Using basic algebra, the FV formula becomes:

$$PV = FV /(1 + i\%)n$$

All that we have done is to divide the future value by (1 + i%)n to get the present value.

The formula taken from the financial table for a present value of a future sum (or discounted value of a single sum is:

$$PV = FV*(IFpv)$$

The time line picture for a present value of a single sum appears below.

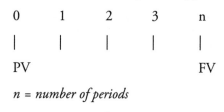

n = number of periods

i = rate per period

You can see that the results of these PV calculations, discounting the FV back to its PV, will be the same as the PV that you compounded to its FV in the earlier problems. Present value and future value are on the same time continuum; all that differs is your point of view, looking forward (compounding) or looking back (discounting).

Before we move into annuities, we will examine the relationship of changes in the interest rate to present values and future values. After all, not all interest rates stay the same, and assumptions on the appropriate rate to use may differ. In fact, we must ask the question, "What interest rate do we use?"

Determining the Minimum Rate of Return

One risk (or uncertainty) the organization faces is an interest rate risk, the changes in financial market interest rates that will affect the cost of borrowing for the organization. To gain a fuller understanding of what interest rate should be used to determine future value, we need to examine the financial structure of the organization, to delve into some basics of corporate finance (yes, not all organizations are corporations, but we'll deal with those later).

A corporation has four sources of funds to use for operations and growth. When the organization is formed, it sells common stock, the broadest form of ownership, to investors, an ownership claim that allows the investor to vote and one that may pay dividends according to the financial success of the organization. While the payment of dividends is not guaranteed, there is no fixed upper limit on the dividend, either. The amount to be paid is decided by the board of directors, and could be a fraction of the yearly earnings or a multiple of the yearly earnings.

The corporation may also sell preferred stock to other investors, ones who require a preferred claim on assets of the corporation, receiving their share of residual assets before the holders of common stock shares. While this type of stock has no voting privileges, these shares also have a preferred claim on earnings, or preferred stock dividends, if declared, must be paid before any dividends are paid on common stock. In exchange for these preferred claims, the amount of the dividend is fixed at a percentage of its par value. For this reduced risk (preferred claims on residual assets and earnings), however, the investor is assured of a fixed return that may be significantly less that the dividend paid on a common share.

The corporation may also borrow from commercial banks in the form of mortgages or other long-term loans, or from the financial markets in the form of corporate bonds and debentures. Bonds and debentures are similar, differing in technical terms as to priority over residual assets in the event of the dissolution of the corporation. All these instruments require the corporation to pay interest (and, eventually, pay back the principal amount borrowed).

The corporation may also elect to not distribute all of its earnings, instead keeping them within the corporation for future use. These earnings so retained are called, strangely enough, retained earnings.

Those are the only four sources of capital to the corporation, issuing common stock, issuing preferred stock, borrowing, and using past and retained earnings. Each has a cost associated with it and those costs can be calculated and totaled to represent the average cost of capital to the corporation.

The cost of each of these components of the capital structure of a corporation is well beyond the scope of what the risk manager does in a corporation, and the precise method by which the cost of each source of capital is calculated is something the risk manager will not have to do. For purposes of a general understanding, however, the risk manager should know the following:

The cost of debt is determined by calculating the yield to maturity adjusted for the effect of the corporation's tax deductibility of the interest expense.

The cost of preferred stock is determined by dividing the annual dividend by the price of a new share less the flotation costs of issuing that share. There is no tax adjustment because all dividends are paid out of after-tax earnings.

The cost of a share of common stock or retained earnings (the storehouse of earnings for the common shareholders, is determined by dividing the expected dividend payment by market price of a common share, with an adjustment for the anticipated growth in the dividend (and in the earnings and price of a share in the market).

The cost of a new common share is similar, with the divisor being the price of a new share less the flotation cost. Again, the quotient is modified by a growth factor anticipating the growth of dividends.

Given those components or elements of a corporation's capital structure, all that must be done is to measure the relative use of each element in the total capital structure and apply that percentage of the total capital structure to the cost of each element to determine the weighted average cost of capital throughout the corporation.

Once that is done, the corporation knows the cost of providing every dollar of capital in its structure, and any decision must be justified against that cost. If a prospective project cannot return at least the average cost of capital, then it should not be undertaken as the project will not increase the value of the corporation. Put another way, the corporation can earn at least its cost of capital by doing nothing but what it is already doing.

The cost of capital is known as the required rate of return or the minimum rate of return, the rate that all projects are required to return as a minimum. Another term for the cost of capital is the "hurdle rate," suggesting that each project must clear that financial hurdle if it is to be implemented.

That hurdle rate, or required rate of return, or weighted average cost of capital, is the "interest rate" to be used in time value of money calculations. Since the risk manager does not have the responsibility (and perhaps not the resources) to calculate it, the CFO will generally assign this cost as the minimum rate of return (hurdle rate, etc) and use it as the determining factor in financial decision-making.

The Relationship of the Interest Rate to Present and Future Values

Now that we have that out of the way, let's return to the relationship of the interest rate to present and future values.

As interest rates go up, present values go down, since the interest rate is in the denominator. More interest is earned, so a lesser sum is required to reach any future value. Also, as the number of periods of discounting goes up, the present value goes down, as there is a longer accumulation period. Combining increasing interest and additional periods generates an even more dramatic drop in present value.

Naturally, this is not all gloom and doom, for the future values (compound sums) rise with higher interest rates or more periods. A given present value generates more future value when invested at a higher rate or for longer periods or both.

Any of you who are skeptics can convince yourself of these relationships by looking at the Present Value of $1 table. For any value of n, an increase in the interest rate gives us a lower present value factor in the body of the table. For any given value of an interest rate, an increase in n gives us a lower present value factor. Also note that the discount factor for a single sum must be less than one. This makes sense when we are discounting a future value to a lesser amount. In the next sections we will look at future and present values of mixed stream and annuity cash flows.

Future Value of a Series of a Mixed Stream

We have started this explanation with the simple assumption that only one payment (a single sum) is involved. However, in risk management, we know from experience that an organization faces a different dollar amount of losses every year, and that those losses must be paid eventually, but certainly later.

We can extend the calculation of the future value of a single sum by considering a series of single sum cash flows of differing amounts (a "mixed stream"). This mixed stream of cash flows represents a series of separate calculations, one for each cash flow. The procedure is tedious, even when using a spreadsheet, when we have a lot of cash flows because there is a separate calculation for each cash flow's future value. At the end, we add up all the future values of the cash flows.

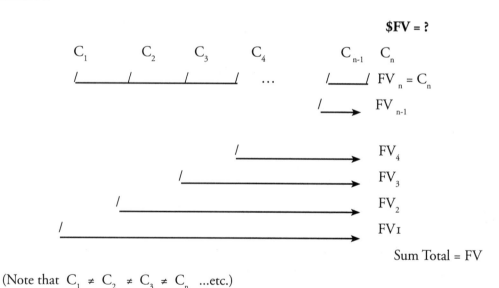

(Note that $C_1 \neq C_2 \neq C_3 \neq C_n$ ...etc.)

Consider the situation where we have reserves of $120,000, $131,600, and $137,800 at the end of each of the last three years, respectively. We have invested the reserve amount each year at 9%, hoping that we will have enough money to pay all the claims at the end of the third year. What is the future value of these sums at the end of three years if we assume an annual interest rate of 9%? First, it helps to make sure we understand the timing of these sums. A drawing appears below.

$120,000　　　$131,600　　　$137,800

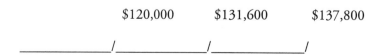

We can start with the last loss amount of $137,800. There is no time for it to earn interest (remember, the payment is made at the end of the year, so its future value at the end of three years is $137,800. The single sum of $131,600 has one period to earn at 9%, so its future value equals $131,600 (1.09) = $143,444. The single sum of $120,000 earns for two periods at 9% per period and its future value is $120,000 (1.188) = $142, 560.

The future value of the series of single sums equals $137,800 + $143,444 + $142,560 = $423, 804.

But what if we projected our losses and invested the funds at the beginning of the year, instead of the end. If the funds had been invested at the beginning of each year, each payment would have earned an additional 1.09. We can calculate this in two ways: First, we could "think" that the last year was really invested for 1 complete period, and use the factor for 9% for 1 period or 1.09. Similarly, we could think the second year was invested for 2 complete periods and use the factor for 9% for 2 periods, 1.188. The first year was then invested for 3 years, and we would use the factor for 9% for 3 periods, or 1.295.

$120,000*1.295 = $155,400

$131,600*1.188 = $156,341

$137,800*1.090 = $150,202

Total   = $461,943

Or, we could simply use the tables and the end-of-year assumption and then multiply the total of $423,804 by an additional 1.09, and arrive at $461,946, very close to the same answer.

Anytime you complete a future value calculation and want to see what happens if cash flows occur one period earlier, you can simply multiply by (1 + i%). The same logic tells us that a future value is less if payments occur at the end of a period rather than the start of a period. So, we divide by a future value by (1 + i%) if payments occur at the end rather than the beginning of a period.

It should be clear that future values are always less if payments occur later because there is less time to earn interest. By the same logic, a future value is higher if payments occur earlier.

Future Value of an Ordinary Annuity

In the above section, we examined the future value of a mixed stream of cash flows and saw how such a mixed stream could be analyzed to determine the time value of money. Sometimes, the mixed stream of cash flows is not mixed, but is actually a stream of cash flow in the form of an ordinary annuity. Cash flows in an ordinary annuity are of the same amount and occur at the end of each period for a number of periods. For example, when you retire, your Social Security "pension" will be in the form of an ordinary annuity, say $1867 per month.

We can calculate the future value of an ordinary annuity by using the amount of the cash flow, the number of annuity payments, and the interest rate per period (i%). The Compound Sum of an Annuity Table provides the factor that allows us to calculate the future value of the annuity.

The Compound Sum of an Ordinary Annuity table formula is:

$$FV_a = P*IF_{sa}$$

The cash flow time line for an ordinary annuity appears below.

$FVa

P P P P P P P P   P   P

/   /   /   /   /   /   /   / ...   /   /

(Note that P = P = P ....etc.)

An example should help reinforce the idea of calculating a future value of an annuity. Assume a self-insurer decides to put money into a funded retention plan. The self-insurer makes a contribution of $15,000 every six months. The fund earns an annual interest rate of 6%. How much will be in the retention plan at the end of five years?

We must go to the Compound Sum of an Annuity of $1 Table to find the future value annuity-factor. For a rate of 3% per period (6% annual rate on a six-month period basis) and 10 six-month periods (n) we find a future value annuity factor of 11.464. Our future value will be equal to $15,000 x 11.464 = $171,960.

Note that the values in the body of the table get bigger, especially as n gets bigger. This makes sense because we make or receive another payment for each added period, in addition to interest on a compound sum. So, for example, when n equals 10 we expect to get a factor of 10 even if interest is zero because we have 10 payments of future value. This concept should help you avoid getting nonsense answers by going to a wrong table.

A final consideration is the timing of the payments. An ordinary annuity has payments at the end of the period. If the payments occur at the beginning of the period, everything else equal, we call the series an annuity due. The table for future-value annuity factors is designed for ordinary annuities. But, the effect of having the payments occur one period earlier (at the beginning rather than end of a period) increases the future value by a factor of (1+i%), just like it did with a series of single sums. So, if we calculate the value of an ordinary annuity but want the value of an annuity due (at the beginning of a period), we just multiply by (1+i%).

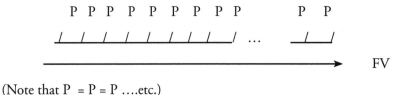

P P P P P P P P P   P   P

/   /   /   /   /   /   /   /   / ...   /   /

→ FV

(Note that P = P = P ....etc.)

Note: The Future Value of an annuity due = value of an ordinary annuity times (1 + i%)

Present Value of a Series of a Mixed Stream

We often make present value calculations for a series of future values, rather than just one. When the single sum amounts are not equal, we cannot treat the problem as an annuity, but as a mixed stream. For these cases, we treat each cash flow as a single sum and find the present value. After we do this for all cash flows, we add up all the present values. In all of our calculations, we continue to use rate per period and number of periods to find the present value of $1 using the Present Value of $1 Table.

The time value time line for these calculations appears below.

$$C_1 \quad C_2 \quad C_3 \quad C_4 \quad C_5 \quad C_6 \quad C_7 \qquad\qquad C_{n-1} \quad C_n$$

$$/ \quad / \quad / \quad / \quad / \quad / \quad / \quad \ldots\ldots \quad / \quad /$$

$PV = ?$ ⬅————————————————

(Note that $C_1 \neq C_2 \neq C_3 \neq C_n$ ...etc.)

Assume we have a safety program that we expect to generate after-tax savings of $13,000 in the first two years, followed by savings of $15,000 for the next two years. What is the present value of the cost savings of this program if we use a discount rate of 8%? We treat each cost saving as a future value problem as follows:

$$\$13,000 \quad \$13,000 \quad \$15,000 \quad \$15,000$$

$$/ \qquad\qquad / \qquad\qquad / \qquad\qquad /$$

($13,000) x (.926) = $12,038 = PV_____ $13,000 (FV)

($13,000) x (.857) = $11,141 = PV_____ $13,000 (FV)

($15,000) x (.794) = $11,910 = PV _____ $15,000 (FV)

($15,000) x (.735) = $11,025 = PV _____ $15,000 (FV)

PV = $46,114.00

Present Value of an Ordinary Annuity

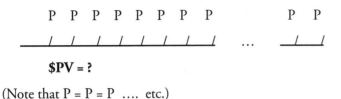

$PV = ?

(Note that P = P = P .... etc.)

Most finance decisions require present value calculations for a stream of expected future benefits and costs. When the stream of benefits or costs has equal cash flows, this is an annuity. Just like in our earlier work with future values, the cash flows of an ordinary annuity occur at the end of each period, while the cash flows of an annuity due occur at the beginning of each period. In both cases, we calculate the present value as if it is an ordinary annuity. If payments occur one period earlier (annuity due), we simply multiply the present value of an ordinary annuity by (1 + i%) to get the present value of an annuity due. The present value of an annuity due gives us our money one period earlier so it must be worth more than an ordinary annuity.

An example illustrates the calculation for the present value of an annuity. It is important to make sure you use the correct table. Use the rate per period (i%) and number of periods (n) to find the present value factor for an annuity in the Present Value of an Annuity of $1 table.

Assume we pay $2,500 at the end of every year for continuing education of our employees. Our cost of capital is 11%. How much would we need to put aside in a fund today to pay for these programs when they are due over the next ten years?

2,500   2,500   2,500   2,500   2,500   2,500   2,500   2,500   2,500   2,500
/   /   /   /   /   /   /   /   /   /

$PV

The formula for a Present Value of an Ordinary Annuity is:

$$PV_a = P * IF_{pva}$$

From the Present Value of an Annuity of $1 table using 11% as i and n = 10 for the number of periods, we get a factor of 5.889. The present value of this ordinary annuity is $2,500*5.889 = $14,722.50. If we fund an account with $14,722.50 today and earn 11% while the funds are in the account for 10 years, we will have just enough to fund the stream of payments. When the last payment is due, we will have exactly $2,500 left in the account.

How would our problem change if the payments were at the beginning of the period rather than at the end of the period? We would need more money in the account by a factor of (1.11), since everything is one period earlier. In this case we would need to deposit $14,722.50*1.11 = $16,341.97 today to fund the annuity due.

Financial Decision Making and Capital Budgeting

The objective of any investment is to earn a net positive rate of return in excess of the cost of funds. The investment analysis decision of an organization is also called capital budgeting, the process of deciding how to apply the various financial resources of the organization in order to increase value. The organization raises money at its cost of capital to finance investment outlays that add value to the organization. In this review, we will consider the most common capital budgeting techniques used to analyze potential investment outlays. We will continue to take the cost of capital as given for now and use it for our discount rate (i%). Eventually, we will specifically illustrate how the cost of capital is calculated.

Some of our capital budgeting techniques do not use time value of money, even though we know it is not correct to compare dollar amounts in different time periods without adjusting for the time value of money. Using time value of money concepts allows us to make sound financial decisions, but those decisions are based only on the capability of the investment to earn return greater than the cost of capital. Sometimes other factors must be considered. Thus, we should think of our financial decision "toolbox" as having several tools, some of which are precise in their financial benefit measurement and some that address other concerns. In this section, our key focus will be on net present value and benefit cost ratios even though we present a full range of capital budgeting techniques used in practice. This review presents the following concepts:

- **Payback** – the amount of time that passes until the cash flows break even with costs. The decision rule is simple: a shorter payback is better.

- **Net Present Value (NPV)** – the present value of benefits minus the present value of costs. A positive NPV represents an investment that adds value to the organization.

- **Benefit/Cost Ratio (BC)** – the ratio of the present value of benefits to the present value of costs. A benefit/cost ratio of 1 corresponds with a NPV of zero because the present value of benefits equals the present value of costs. This tool is useful in capital rationing, or selecting between mutually exclusive projects that have positive NPVs. It is also useful when comparing projects of different sizes because it measures the relative value of benefits to costs.

- **Internal Rate of Return (IRR)** – the IRR is the rate of return on an investment's cash flows that makes the net present value of the investment equal to zero. If a project's IRR is greater than its cost of capital, the project adds value.

For all our capital budgeting problems in this section, we will use the cash flows in the Data Example below. The cash flows are net of costs and taxes.

Payback

To calculate the payback, also known as the payback period, we add the cash flows for each period until we find the period where the sum of the cash flows equals the investment outlay for the project. Since the payback point seldom occurs at the beginning or end of a period, we take a simple interval average. An example will help illustrate how the technique works.

Exhibit 7.1: Payback

Year	After-Tax Net Cash Flow
X0	<7,000> Outlay
X1	2,000
X2	1,000
X3	3,000
X4	4,000
X5	3,000

The payback will be the number of years it takes to recover the $7,000.

Year	After-Tax Net Cash Flow	Cash Flow Sum
X0	<7,000> Outlay	
X1	2,000	2,000
X2	1,000	3,000
X3	3,000	6,000
X4	4,000	10,000
X5	3,000	13,000

Payback occurs between the third and fourth year. After the third year, we need an additional $1,000 from the fourth year to reach payback. Since we earn $4,000 in the fourth year and we only need an added $1,000, we take ¼ of that total. So, payback occurs in 3 ¼ years.

Payback is easy to calculate and easy to understand. The obvious drawback is the failure to recognize the time value of money. Cash flows per dollar in the fourth year are the same as cash flows per dollar in any other year with this technique. The payback technique also ignores all cash flows occurring after the payback point. Because many decision-makers require a quick return on their investment so the funds can be recycled into new investment opportunities, this technique favors projects with high cash flows in the first few years and penalizes projects that have high growth, but where large cash flows take longer to develop.

Net Present Value

The net present value requires a discount rate for the present value calculation. In practice, the discount rate should be the organization's cost of capital. Since we will illustrate the cost of capital calculation later, for now we will assume the cost of capital is 12%. The data in our example represents a series of unequal single sums that we bring back to a single present value. We can find the present value of each cash flow and add all present values to get the present value of benefits from the project. We get our present value factors from the Present Value of $1 table. The calculation using time value factors appears below.

Exhibit 7.2: Net Present Value

Year	After-Tax Net Cash Flow	Present Value Factor	$PV
X0	<7,000> Outlay		
X1	2,000	.893	$1,786
X2	1,000	.797	$797
X3	3,000	.712	$2,136
X4	4,000	.636	$2,544
X5	3,000	.567	$1,701
		PV =	**$8,964**

Net Present Value = $8,964 - $7,000 = $1,964

Since the NPV > 0, the project would be accepted.

Note: The mathematical form of the calculation would appear as follows: 2,000 /(1+.12)1 + 1,000 / (1+.12)2 + 3,000 /(1+.12)3 + 4,000 / (1+.12)4 + 3,000 / (1+.12)5 - 7,000 = $1,964

The net present value uses time value of money appropriately and holds projects to a standard based on the cost of capital discount rate. It is a preferred technique for making investment decisions in almost every case.

For most organizations, capital is a scarce resource and there are always competing uses. Net Present Value allows us to select projects that have a return greater than the cost of capital, but when there are two or more capital investment projects and insufficient capital to fund both, the decision-makers must ration out the scarce capital to those investment opportunities that promise the greatest return. This requires a new tool, the Benefit/Cost ratio. The Benefit/Cost ratio uses the same information as the NPV but it gives us a measure of dollar benefits per dollar spent. If a company is rationing capital, only those projects with the "biggest bang for the buck" receive funding. Any time we are evaluating mutually exclusive projects or face capital rationing we should consider using Benefit/Cost ratio procedure.

Benefit/Cost Ratio

When capital rationing occurs, the organization ranks projects by the ratio of the PV benefits to the PV of the costs. It allows the decision-maker to continue to select projects on the basis of Benefit/Cost ratio rankings, moving from the highest to lower rankings until the amount of money allocated to capital budgeting is spent.

For our example data, we calculate the Benefit/Cost ratio of Example 1 as follows:

PV Benefits / PV of Costs = $8,964 / $7,000 = **1.28**

By itself, this Benefit/Cost ratio means nothing (other than it is greater than 1, which always happens when the PV of the benefits is greater than the PV of the costs). However, when choosing between mutually exclusive projects, we should accept the project with the highest Benefit/Cost ratio.

Internal Rate of Return

The internal rate of return (IRR) is the discount rate that makes the present value of benefits equal to the present value of costs (NPV = 0). The calculation for the IRR is complicated, since the only way to find the IRR is a trial and error approach. This is laborious by hand, but a financial spreadsheet function or financial calculator makes the trial and error process easy. For example, the equation below illustrates the role of the IRR in the NPV equation.

$$2{,}000/(1+IRR)^1 + 1{,}000/(1+IRR)^2 + 3{,}000/(1+IRR)^3 + 4{,}000/(1+IRR)^4 + 3{,}000/(1+IRR)^5 - 7{,}000 = 0$$

Since the NPV was greater than zero when we used a discount rate of 12% we know the IRR must be greater than 12%. The logic is that it would take a discount rate higher than 12% (larger denominator) to make the NPV lower. A financial calculator or spreadsheet function can solve for the IRR by quickly using an internal trial and error process to hone in on the IRR answer.

For our purposes, it is most important to understand the logic of the IRR. Calculating the IRR requires a financial calculator, but we need to know how to use the IRR. Once we have an IRR value, we accept a project if the IRR is greater than the organization's cost of capital. The logic is that the IRR represents the anticipated return on the project and if the return on the project exceeds the cost of funding the project, the project adds value.

For our example, the IRR = 21.30% for the project (calculated with a financial calculator). Since the IRR > 12% we would accept the project from an IRR perspective.

The IRR is popular and normally appears in any investment project evaluation. In most cases, a good project meets all the other investment criteria, including payback, NPV, and Benefit/Cost ratio standards. Nevertheless, there are times when we might prefer to use the Benefit/Cost ratio or the NPV instead the IRR because of the following two problems inherent with the IRR.

> Multiple Roots for the IRR – When the net cash flows have a change in signs (positive inflow, negative outflow), we get more than one possible solution for the IRR. We have as many IRR values as we have roots to the solution to the zero NPV calculation, and we have a root for every change in signs of the cash flows. This is disturbing because we get more than one answer for our IRR calculation.

> Reinvestment Rate Assumption – For the NPV and Benefit/Cost calculations, we are assuming that cash flows are reinvested at the cost of capital when the cash flows come back to the organization. This is reasonable, since projects would already be taken if their rates of return exceed the cost of capital. The IRR calculations assume that the cash flows are reinvested at the IRR. Maintaining this high reinvestment rate is not likely since projects with such high returns were probably taken already, by the competition.

Investment Analysis Technique Summary

All capital budgeting investment analysis techniques covered in this section provide useful information to financial managers. The NPV, Benefit/Cost Ratio, and IRR use time value of money concepts. For the NPV and Benefit/ Cost Ratios the organization's cost of capital is the discount rate in the calculation. For the IRR, the organization's cost of capital is a benchmark that the IRR must exceed for a project to be acceptable.

When we must decide on mutually exclusive projects, where we can only take one of several alternative projects, it is possible that IRR decision rules will not lead to the same decision as NPV or Benefit/Cost ratio. In these cases, we suggest the use of the Benefit/Cost ratio technique.

An organization may be using capital rationing when it enters into a capital budgeting decision. In this case, the organization plans to invest a given amount and does not intend to raise enough money to fund all projects that have a positive NPV (benefit/cost > 1). When faced with capital rationing, the organization should use the Benefit/ Cost ratio and rank projects from high to low. The projects with the highest Benefit/Cost ratios should be taken first. Also, if an organization faces mutually exclusive projects that have different costs, the Benefit/Cost ratio is the preferred method for comparing projects.

Construction of Net Cash Flows for Capital Budgeting

In many cases the construction of the cash flows can be the crucial step in capital budgeting.

Net cash flows in a capital budgeting problem are not the same as net income. Normally, we do not assume anything about financing of a project, except that it is financed from a pool of funds like all other projects. There are no deductions of interest from operating income in our cash flow calculation. The use of the cost of capital as the discount rate is the only financing aspect of our calculations. In rare situations, a special financing arrangement may be tied to the project, such that we do not receive the special financing rate unless we take the project. In these cases, we would include the financing benefits and costs in our calculation. Finally, we are calculating cash flows rather than income so we must add depreciation and all non-cash charges back to our cash flow. If the project requires higher levels of inventory, account receivables, account payables, etc., we must also take changes in working capital into account. The following example of cash flow construction will help illustrate these points.

Exhibit 7.3: Cash Flow Construction

Assume we are investing in new machines that have better safety features. The old machines are sold for $50,000 and have a book value of $10,000 on the balance. The new machines cost $400,000 and will require additional inventory investment of $5,000. The life of the new machine is 10 years and will be depreciated using straight-line depreciation. The new machines will lower expenses due to better operating rates and fewer accidents. We estimate a net saving of $60,000 a year. The organization has a 34% tax rate (we assume the same rate on income and capital gains for the illustration).

We can set up three different sets of flows. First, we find the initial investment outlay to include all costs and taxes. Second, we find the cash flows for the ten years of operations. Finally, we find the terminal values that occur when the project ends.

Initial Outlay (CF0)

        <$400,000> = purchase of new machine

        $50,000 = sale of old machine

        <$14,000> = capital gain tax = .34($50,000 - $10,000)

        <$5,000> = added inventory investment .

        <$369,000>

Net Cash Flows for years 1 through 10 (CF1 = CF2 = …=CF10)

        $60,000 lower expenses

        <$40,000> = depreciation non-cash charge

        $20,000 = taxable operating income

        <$6,800> = taxes @ .34

        $11,200 = after-tax operating income

        $40,000 = add depreciation back to get cash flow

        $52,200 = annual net cash flow every year for 10 year

Terminal Year Adjustment

        $5,000 = reduce inventory when project ends

        $0 = book value of machine…if the machine is sold we get the selling price minus taxes on the capital gain… we assume no market value here.

        $5,000

Project time Line of Cash Inflows and Outflows

                                                                  $5k

$52.2k $52.2k $52.2k $52.2k $52.2k $52.2k $52.2k $52.2k $52.2k

<$369,000>

At this point, we use our capital budgeting tools:

- Payback = 7.07 years

- NPV = -46,303.28

- IRR = 7.01%

- Benefit/Cost Ratio = .875

You should be able to calculate the payback, net present value, and Benefit/Cost ratio. The IRR is given to provide a complete set of capital budgeting information. Note that the payback is 7.07 years, but for the 10-year period, the NPV is negative! This illustrates the distortion in the payback approach by not using time value of the cash flows. On paper, this project would not add value to the organization based on the cash flow estimates.

138

Cost of Capital

A brief review of the cost of capital calculation appears here to allow a more complete picture of capital budgeting.

The cost of capital is a weighted-average of the various costs of raising money to finance the organization's assets. For each of the component costs, market values of the organization's securities allow calculation of a % cost. Several alternatives are available for finding the weights for each of the component costs. The preferred approach is to use the organization's target capital structure, which is the mix of different types of financing that the organization thinks is optimal. The organization may not currently have this optimal mix, making the target weights different from existing book or market weights. Alternative weight systems appear below.

- Book Value

- Market Value

- Target (What would be the optimal combination? This is the preferred approach)

The alternative forms of raising money include the following:

- Long-Term Debt (LTD)…component after-tax cost = KATD

- Preferred Stock (PS)…component after-tax cost = KPS

- Common Stock (CS) (new)…component after-tax cost = KCS

- Retained Earnings (RE) (old CS)…component after-tax cost = KRE

- The calculation of the weighted average cost of capital looks like this where WT represents the weight

$$
\begin{array}{cccc}
 & K_{ATD} & x & WT \\
+ & K_{PS} & x & WT \\
+ & K_{CS} & x & WT \\
+ & K_{RE} & x & WT \\
\hline
= & WACC
\end{array}
$$

For example, assume it costs an organization 8% to issue debt and the tax rate is .34, and the after-tax cost of debt = 5.12%. Debt is cheaper than the other component costs, largely due to the tax treatment. We also assume the component cost of preferred stock is 9%. Common stock issued through an investment banker has an assumed component cost of 13.3%. Retained earnings of the organization represent equity financing and the assumed component cost is 13%. Given these component costs and target weights, we can calculate the WACC.

Assume the target mix is 40% debt, 5% preferred stock, 30% external equity, and 25% internal equity. Our cost of capital in this case would be:

$(5.12\%)(.40) + (9\%)(.05) + (13.3\%)(.30) + (13\%)(.25) = 9.73\% = WACC$

This is an abbreviated review of the cost of capital designed only to provide some perspective on how the organization comes up with a single interest rate cost of capital for financing projects. This rate becomes a benchmark for the organization's cost of funds.

Chapter 8

Loss Forecasting

Introduction

We considered various quantitative tools in the prior section and took all the data as given. In this chapter, we consider a variety of potential adjustments we can apply to the data <u>before</u> we employ our forecast tools. The key data questions addressed in this review appear below:

- Have the numbers been **adjusted for inflation**?

- Have the numbers been **fully developed** for incurred but not reported losses?

- Are industry development and inflation index **factors and values appropriate** for the firm's losses?

- How are development factors for loss **frequency**, **loss severity**, and **loss payouts** constructed?

- How would we forecast future total dollar losses if we made adjustments for changing exposures, developed frequency, developed $ severity, and inflation?

Before we go through each adjustment separately, it may help to see where we will wind up when it is all over. Total dollar losses can be broken down into components parts. The following definitions are useful as we define total dollar losses:

- (Fully Developed Number of Losses / exposures) = **Incidence Rate**

- (Fully Developed Incidence Rate) x (# Projected Exposures next Period) = **Projected Number of Developed Losses**

- (Projected Number of Developed Losses) x (Fully Developed & Inflation Adjusted $ Average Severity) = **Fully Developed Total Dollar Losses**

When we are comfortable with all data adjustments, we can use our quantitative tools to build confidence intervals (rather than estimating a parameter by a single value, we present an interval that is likely to include the parameter, a confidence interval that will indicate the reliability of an estimate) for estimates of Projected Number of Losses, Incidence Rates, or for Fully Developed Total Dollar Losses. It seems overwhelming to do all the steps at one time, so we will work with each adjustment separately. When we are finished with the review, you will be able to walk through all the necessary adjustments you may need to make before building your forecasts with confidence intervals. For now, be patient and concentrate on how each step works.

Inflation Adjustment

When we collect loss data, due to inflation, costs in each period of time are different. The purchasing power of a dollar today may not be the same as the value of a dollar when the loss report was created and will probably not be same as when the loss occurred. The data must be adjusted to reflect current prices. A price index provides an adjustment factor based on inflation rates for each year since a given year of losses.

In Exhibit 8.1, we will assume an inflation rate of 7% per year for the costs we are investigating. Our goal is to put everything in year X11 prices. For now, we assume the data are already fully adjusted for everything <u>other than inflation</u>.

Exhibit 8.1: (Assume Fully Developed $ Losses are given)

Year	Fully Developed $ Losses	Price Index*
X1	$500,560	$(1.07)^{10} = 1.967$
X2	$495,700	$(1.07)^{9} = 1.838$
X3	$547,800	$(1.07)^{8} = 1.718$
X4	$601,450	$(1.07)^{7} = 1.606$
X5	$650,300	$(1.07)^{6} = 1.501$
X6	$623,056	$(1.07)^{5} = 1.403$
X7	$700,680	$(1.07)^{4} = 1.311$
X8	$689,560	$(1.07)^{3} = 1.225$
X9	$756,111	$(1.07)^{2} = 1.145$
X10	$702,450	$(1.07) = 1.07$
X11	????????	

   * The index is based on a constant 7% rate of inflation per year.

The oldest data require the most adjustment, since prices have changed more over time. This index shows that it would take $1.967 today in X11 to buy what $1 would buy in X1. If we have inflation index numbers, we need to understand that the highest index factor applies to the oldest data.

The index is (1 plus the interest rate) taken to the power (or multiplied by the number of times) equal to the number of years back from X11. The calculation is based on the fact that there is compounding every year. For example, from X9 to X11 there was inflation of 7% per year for two years. This is not just 14% because after prices go up 1.07% for one year they go up 1.07% again. If something cost $1 in X9, it would cost $1.07 in X10 ($1 x 1.07). Prices go up 7% again, then it would cost $1.07 x 1.07 = $(1.07)^{2}$ = $1.145 in X11. Note that multiplying by 1 gives us the $1.07 and an increase of 7% on $1.07 adds another $.075 to equal $1.145.

Our inflation-adjusted data appear in Exhibit 8.2 below. Notice how much difference it makes when we put everything into X11 prices. The X1 losses of $500,560 become $984,601.52 when adjusted to the X11 price index, and so on down the list, clearly illustrating that the biggest changes occur over the longest time period.

Exhibit Data 8.2: Inflation Adjustment Illustration

Yr	Fully Developed $ Losses	Price Index	Fully Developed Inflation Adjusted $
X1	$500,560	$(1.07)^{10} =$ 1.967	$984,601.52
X2	$495,700	$(1.07)^9 =$ 1.838	$911,096.60
X3	$547,800	$(1.07)^8 =$ 1.718	$941,120.40
X4	$601,450	$(1.07)^7 =$ 1.606	$965,928.70
X5	$650,300	$(1.07)^6 =$ 1.501	$976,100.30
X6	$623,056	$(1.07)^5 =$ 1.403	$874,147.57
X7	$700,680	$(1.07)^4 =$ 1.311	$918,591.48
X8	$689,560	$(1.07)^3 =$ 1.225	$844,711.00
X9	$756,111	$(1.07)^2 =$ 1.145	$865,747.10
X10	$702,450	$(1.07) =$ 1.07	$751,621.50
X11	??		

The primary goal at this stage is to build an understanding of why we need inflation adjustments and how the index works. We will do more with adjustments later in the section.

While this is a relatively simple mathematic process, the risk manager has a challenge: using an appropriate index. The Consumer Price Index (CPI) is based upon the cost of a marketplace basket of common consumer goods and services. This may not be appropriate for some costs. For example, the cost of construction goods and services are not "consumer" costs found in the CPI. Similarly, many medical costs are not contained in the CPI marketplace basket. The risk manager must carefully consider and choose the index that most closely represents the nature of the losses and their costs.

Exposures

For insurers, losses are related to covered exposures. For example, for trucking, losses are highly related to the number of miles driven. If the miles driven in the past years are not constant, the dollar losses change from year to year due to differences in mileage exposures. We would not want to let changing exposures affect our forecast if next year's exposure is different from the past. Therefore, in addition to inflation factors, we must consider the number of exposures in the year we are trying to forecast, since that will affect our dollar losses.

Starting with our data in Exhibit 8.2, we can go back and find the number of exposures in each year and calculate a $ loss/exposure ratio. If we find the average of the $ loss/exposure ratio, we could use that to predict $ losses in X11 by multiplying the average ratio times the expected exposure in X11. We can use the historic data on exposures given in Exhibit 8.3 below to improve the forecast for X11.

Exhibit Data 8.3: $ Loss per Exposure Illustration

Yr	Inflation Adjusted $	Number of Exposures (miles)	$/mile
X1	$984,601.52	12,079,050	$0.0815
X2	$911,096.60	10,005,600	$0.0911
X3	$941,120.40	10,200,090	$0.0923
X4	$965,928.70	10,345,090	$0.0934
X5	$976,100.30	11,000,789	$0.0887
X6	$874,147.57	10,245,100	$0.0853
X7	$918,591.48	10,324,567	$0.0890
X8	$844,711.00	10,125,678	$0.0834
X9	$865,747.10	10,078,890	$0.0859
X10	$751,621.50	9,000,789	$0.0835
X11	??		average = $0.0874/mile

If we anticipate only 8,500,000 miles of exposure next year, we would adjust our X11 total $ loss estimate to be ($0.0874) x (8,500,000) = $742,900. This is still fully developed and inflation adjusted, but we revised it down from our earlier total of $903,366.62 based on our additional information about changing exposures. If there is no trend in the $/miles ratio we could build confidence intervals using the mean and standard deviation. There does not appear to be a trend in the $/mile ratio in this case, so we assume the regression R-square is very low. To build confidence intervals we would need to calculate the standard deviation of the $/exposure ratio and use it to get our interval.

You may need the following definitions as you read:

Mean: in these examples, the average of a series of numbers (the total amount divided by the number of numbers)

Standard Deviation: a measure of the variability or dispersion of a data set. A low standard deviation indicates that the data points tend to be very close to the same value (the mean), while high standard deviation indicates that the data are "spread out" over a large range of values.

Regression R-Square: provides a measure of how well future outcomes are likely to be predicted by the model.

Triangulation: the application and combination of several research methods in the study of the same data. It can be employed in both quantitative (validation) and qualitative (inquiry) studies as a method of determining credibility. By combining multiple observers, theories, methods, and empirical materials, researchers can hope to overcome the weakness or intrinsic biases and the problems that come from single method, single-observer, and single-theory studies.

We analyzed loss rates (sometimes-called loss ratios) in this section of the review. The rate will be different for different types of insurance products or intended uses. For example, it is common to use losses/revenues rather than losses/exposure to calculate a loss rate. The loss/revenue rate provides a link to profitability analysis.

Loss Frequency

In many cases our loss data may start with an analysis of the number of losses rather than dollars per loss. We will eventually put everything into total dollar losses, but the number of losses related to the number of exposures may allow for additional detail that can improve our forecasts. We will also introduce the idea of incurred but not reported losses (IBNR) to allow for development of the data before we go on to the total dollar loss forecast.

We can go back to our original data in Exhibit 8.1 and start over by considering the number of undeveloped claims, as well as the fully developed total dollar claims. The additional undeveloped number of losses are shown below.

Exhibit 8.4: Data for Undeveloped Number of Claims

Year	Undeveloped # Claims	Fully Developed Total $ Claims	Exposures (miles)
X1	98	$500,560	12,079,050
X2	95	$495,700	10,005,600
X3	108	$547,800	10,200,090
X4	115	$601,450	10,345,090
X5	117	$650,300	11,000,789
X6	110	$623,056	10,245,100
X7	120	$700,680	10,324,567
X8	101	$689,560	10,125,678
X9	80	$756,111	10,078,890
X10	76	$702,450	9,000,789
X11	?	?	?

When we examine the data in Exhibit 8.4, we notice that the number of claims is lower in the more recent years. Is this due to better loss control, or is something else going on with the data? In casualty coverage (e.g., automobile or general liability), it takes several years for all claims to be fully reported (this does not tend to be a problem with property coverage). The entity incurs a liability loss in a given year that takes more than one year to be fully reported. For years that are further back, however, there has been enough time for all claims to be reported. We would say these years are fully developed when there are no additional claims from these losses in subsequent years. But, for the more recent years, like X8, X9, and X10, it is likely that the number of claims is low because these years are not fully developed. Some types of losses have "long tails" because it takes a long time for all losses to be fully reported. For now, we will take the development factors as given to us, and we will see where they come from in a later section.

A third party, such as a rating bureau or consultant, often provides information about development factors for frequency of claims based on long loss histories in the industry for that type of exposure. We also could use firm-specific loss history to build the development factors if we have enough reliable data. Industry data should be closely related to the same types of exposures that the firm incurs or the development data will not be accurate. Thus, we want to make sure the provider of the factors has taken care to construct high quality development factors that match our firm's exposures.

Assume we are given the frequency development factors in Exhibit Data 8.5 below. We can then create fully developed data for the number of claims and build our forecasts.

Risk Management Essentials

Exhibit 8.5: Development of Frequency

Year	Frequency (# Claims)	Development* Factors	Developed Frequency	Exposures (miles)
X1	98	1.0	98	12,079,050
X2	95	1.0	95	10,005,600
X3	108	1.0	108	10,200,090
X4	115	1.0	115	10,345,090
X5	117	1.0	117	11,000,789
X6	110	1.0	110	10,245,100
X7	120	1.0	120	10,324,567
X8	101	1.1	111	10,125,678
X9	80	1.4	112	10,078,890
X10	76	1.5	114	9,000,789
X11	?	?	?	

* We assume a third party provides these factors. We will see how they are generated in a later section of this review.

If our goal is to predict the number of claims, we can take the average of the fourth column, calculate the standard deviation, and construct our interval around the mean. Of course, we would need at least 30 observations to do this in a real situation. We would also check for a trend by using regression analysis. In this case, there does not appear to be a trend, so we would expect a low R-square.

Our forecast of total dollar losses requires a calculation of an incident rate (# claims/Exposure) from our fully developed claims data and our exposure data. Our goal is to create the incidence rate data and construct our forecast of the X11 incidence rate. In many cases, we are interested in this incidence rate forecast alone, since it reveals how many accidents or claims the insured has per exposure unit, and loss control measures are aimed at lowering the incidence rate.

Exhibit 8.6: Fully Developed Incidence Rate Illustration

Year	Developed # of Claims (miles)	Exposures	Incidence Rate (Claims per 1,000 miles)
X1	98	12,079,050	.00811
X2	95	10,005,600	.00949
X3	108	10,200,090	.01059
X4	115	10,345,090	.01112
X5	117	11,000,789	.01064
X6	110	10,245,100	.01074
X7	120	10,324,567	.01162
X8	111	10,125,678	.01096
X9	112	10,078,890	.01111
X10	114	9,000,789	.01267
X11	?	?	?

From the data in the table, we can calculate statistics for our confidence interval. We would find the following statistics:

Mean Incidence Rate per 1,000 miles = .01071

Standard Deviation of the Incidence Rate per 1,000 miles = .00121

If there is a low R-square and we assume n>30, we can use the statistics to get a 95% confidence interval for the incidence rate:

95% Confidence Interval for the Incidence Rate per 1,000 miles = .00829 to .01313

Since we expect 8,500,000 miles of exposure for X11, we can now forecast the number of losses (frequency) to be equal to (.01071) x (8,500) = 91.035. We can build a 95% confidence interval for the number of losses as follows:

95% Confidence Interval for the Number of losses per 1,000 miles =

(.00829)(8,500) to (.01313)(8,500) =

70.465 to 111.605

Thus, the confidence intervals are fully developed, take into account our history of exposures, and use expectations for exposures in X11.

Frequency, Severity, and Payout Development

In this section, we review the triangulation process used to get development factors from past loss history. These factors allow adjustments of reported data to include incurred but not reported losses (IBNR) for a given year in our history. We start with loss history data to determine the normal lags that occur before full reporting of all losses. Our first goal in this review section is to illustrate how triangulation provides the frequency development, severity development, and payout development numbers we need. Our second, and more important goal, is to make sure that we can use development factors appropriately to improve our forecast of a Total Dollar loss pick (or pic, meaning expected losses or an actuary's estimation of future losses based on past losses) and loss pick interval.

It may help to start by identifying the measurements we want to see at the end of our adjustment process. Let's say we want an estimate of Developed, Exposure Adjusted, and Indexed Total Dollar Losses. Here are the steps we must complete to get to this final estimation phase:

Step 1: [(# Claims) x (Frequency Development)] = Developed # Claims per Year

Step 2: Average of [Developed # Claims per year / Exposures per Year] = Average Incidence Rate

Step 3: Average Incidence Rate x Expected Exposures Next Period = Fully Developed and Exposure Adjusted # of Losses

Step 4: (Total Dollar Losses per Year) x (Severity Development) = Developed Total Dollar Losses per Year

Step 5: Developed Total Dollar Losses per Year / Developed and Exposure Adjusted # losses per Year = Average $ Severity per Loss per Year

Step 6: (Average $ Severity per Year) x (Inflation Index per Year) = Inflation Adjusted Average Dollar Severity per Year

Step 7: Sum of Inflation Adjusted Average Severity per Year / # Years = Indexed Average Severity

Step 8: Indexed Average Severity x Developed and Exposure Adjusted Average # Losses = Indexed and Developed Total Dollar Loss Pick

Do not panic. The entire process looks overwhelming, but we will concentrate on one-step at a time. For now, we want to see where the development factors come from. We already looked at adjustments for losses if there are changing exposures and adjustments for the dollar value of losses for inflation. We were given development factors up to this point. Development tends to be more important for casualty losses because it generally takes longer for full reporting of all casualty claims. For example, asbestos claims may take many years to be fully reported for any one year of exposure. Our key objective is to show how development factors can be generated from the loss history data.

Frequency Development Factors

Our data in Exhibit 8.4 provides undeveloped claim data. We anticipate additional claims that have not yet been reported for the most recent years of X10, X9, X8, etc.

Data from Exhibit 8.4

Year	# Claims (Undeveloped)
X1	98
X2	95
X3	108
X4	115
X5	117
X6	110
X7	120
X8	101
X9	80
X10	76
X11	?

We now go back to our loss history and collect data to track the changes in the reported number of claims for each year of business. Note that the loss history data below is given to you at this point as an extension of Exhibit 8.4. We calculate the year-to-year development from the given loss history data by using triangulation.

Exhibit 8.7: Frequency (Number of Claims) Loss History

Incident to Date Loss History - Number of Claims

Months from Inception

Year	12	24	36	48	60	72
1995	67	73	93	98	98	98
1996	62	65	83	95	95	95
1997	73	79	100	108	108	108
1998	77	83	103	115	115	115
1999	79	82	107	117	117	**117**
2000	72	79	99	110	**110**	
2001	80	84	109	**120**		
2002	75	80	**101**			
2003	75	**80**				
2004	**76**					

Year-to-Year Development of Claims

Year	12-24	24-36	36-48	48-60	60-72
1995	1.09	1.27	1.05	1,00	1.00
1996	1.05	1.28	1.15	1.00	1.00
1997	1.08	1.26	1.08	1.00	1.00
1998	1.08	1.24	1.12	1.00	1.00
1999	1.04	1.30	1.09	1.00	1.00
2000	1.10	1.25	1.11	1.00	
2001	1.05	1.30	1.10		
2002	1.07	1.26			
2003	1.07				
2004					
Totals	9.63	10.16	7.7	6.0	5.0
Average	**1.07**	**1.27**	**1.10**	**1.0**	**1.0**

Age to Development – Development Factors

Year

1 to 5	1.07 x 1.27 x 1.1 x 1.0 x 1.0	= **1.5**
2 to 5	1.27 x 1.10 x 1.0 x 1.0	= **1.4**
3 to 5	1.10 x 1.0 x 1.0	= **1.1**
4 to 5	1.00 x 1.0	= **1.0**
5 and beyond		= **1.0**

The general approach is to calculate the factor of increase in claims when we move from the first 12 months to the 24-month point. We continue this until the claims become constant and fully developed. For example, in X1 our claims went from 67 to 73 as we moved from the first 12 months to the 24th month. This is a factor of increase equal to 73/67 = 1.09. When we went from the 24-month to 36-month period, X1 claims increased from 73 to 93. This is an increase by a factor of 93/73 = 1.27. We continue this process for all annual periods for every year of loss data.

If losses have just been recorded (X10), the total number of claims will be higher by a factor of 1.5 by the time everything is fully reported. Losses that were reported in the prior year (X9) will ultimately be higher by a factor of 1.4. We took these development factors as given in an earlier exercise and came up with the following fully developed frequency (# claims):

Exhibit 8.8: Illustration of Frequency Development

Year	Frequency (# Claims)	Development* Factors	Developed Frequency
1995	98	1.0	98
1996	95	1.0	95
1997	108	1.0	108
1998	115	1.0	115
1999	117	1.0	117
2000	110	1.0	110
2001	120	1.0	120
2002	101	1.1	111
2003	80	1.4	112
2004	76	1.5	114

As you would expect, the highest development factor goes to the most recent year of losses.

Severity Development – Based on Total Dollars Loss Data

In addition to loss frequency numbers, we also need to develop dollar losses. As the number of claims increases after the year of initial reporting, the dollar severity also tends to increase. We might expect the more expensive claims to take longer to be fully reported, especially if we are working with medical claims. We start with reported total dollar loss history (given in Exhibit 8.9) and again calculate development factors in much the same way we calculated frequency development factors.

Exhibit 8.9: Additional Data <u>Given</u> for Illustration of $ Loss Severity Development

Total Dollar Loss History (Units in $1,000s)

Months from Inception

Year	12	24	36	48	60	72
X1	428.75	461.00	489.60	500.56	500.56	500.56
X2	449.62	473.00	495.70	495.70	495.70	495.70
X3	476.22	511.46	536.01	547.80	547.80	547.80
X4	505.77	546.23	583.37	601.45	601.45	601.45
X5	560.41	599.08	630.75	650.30	650.30	650.30
X6	518.94	566.16	599.00	623.05	623.05	
X7	603.30	648.55	682.92	700.68		
X8	601.57	640.07	671.43			
X9	651.88	698.16				
X10	605.04					
X11	?????					

Year-to-Year Development

Year	12-24	24-36	36-48	48-60	60-72
X1	1.075	1.062	1.022	1.00	1.00
X2	1.052	1.048	1.000	1.00	1.00
X3	1.074	1.048	1.022	1.00	1.00
X4	1.080	1.068	1.046	1.00	1.00
X5	1.069	1.053	1.031	1.00	1.00
X6	1.091	1.058	1.040	1.00	
X7	1.075	1.053	1.026		
X8	1.064	1.049			
X9	1.071				
X10					
Totals	9.65	8.439	7.19	7.0	7.0
Average	**1.072**	**1.055**	**1.027**	**1.0**	**1.0**

Age to Development – $ Development Factors

Year

1 to 5	1.072 x 1.055 x 1.027 x 1.0 x 1.0	= **1.161**
2 to 5	1.055 x 1.027 x 1.0 x 1.0	= **1.083**
3 to 5	1.027 x 1.0 x 1.0	= **1.027**
4 to 5	1.00 x 1.0	= **1.0**
5 and beyond		= **1.0**

The interpretation of development factors is probably more important than the specific triangulation exercise, since we often take the development factors from a third party and use them for our losses. For total dollar losses reported in the most recent year, the dollar loss will be higher by a factor of 1.161 when losses are fully reported for that year of business. The development factors also show that full development occurs by the fourth year after the incident or accident is first reported.

Our dollar severity loss development factors allow adjustments for incurred but not reported dollar losses. Before we make a forecast for X11, we want to make sure that the number of claims and dollar losses are fully developed.

Forecast of X11 Total dollar Losses

All the ingredients are now in place to construct X11 total dollar losses that are fully developed for the number of claims, adjusted for exposures, fully developed for dollar severity of losses, and inflation adjusted. We did all the work in previous steps and we only need to put it together. The forecast boils down to the following calculation:

(Forecast Frequency) x (Forecast Inflation-Adjusted $ Average Severity per Claim)

= X11 Total Dollar Losses

In an earlier exercise (Exhibit 8.6), we constructed the 95% confidence interval for fully developed, and exposure adjusted number of losses. Our result appears below:

95% Confidence Interval for the Number of losses =

(.00000829)(8,500,000) to (.00001313)(8,500,000) =

70.465 to 111.605

We can complete the forecast if we have the Inflation adjusted Dollar Average Severity per Loss. We already have the following Developed data.

Exhibit 8.10: Comprehensive Example of Development

Year	Reported $ Losses	$ Severity Factors	Developed $ Loss	Frequency Reported # Claims	Development Factor	Developed Frequency
X1	$500,560	1.00	**$500,560**	98	1.00	**98**
X2	$495,700	1.00	**$495,700**	95	1.00	**95**
X3	$547,800	1.00	**$547,800**	108	1.00	**108**
X4	$601,450	1.00	**$601,450**	115	1.00	**115**
X5	$650,300	1.00	**$650,300**	117	1.00	**117**
X6	$623,056	1.00	**$623,056**	110	1.00	**110**
X7	$700,680	1.00	**$700,680**	120	1.00	**120**
X8	$671,431	1.027	**$689,560**	101	1.10	**111**
X9	$698,163	1.083	**$756,111**	80	1.40	**112**
X10	$671,431	1.161	**$702,450**	76	1.50	**114**
X11	???????					

Year	Developed $ Losses*	Developed # Claims	Severity Per Claim**	Inflation Index***	Inflation-Adjusted $ Severity per Claim
X1	**$500,560**	**98**	$5,107.76	1.967	10,046.96
X2	**$495,700**	**95**	$5,217.89	1.838	9,590.48
X3	**$547,800**	**108**	$5,072.22	1.718	8,714.07
X4	**$601,450**	**115**	$5,230.00	1.606	8,399.38
X5	**$650,300**	**117**	$5,558.12	1.501	8,342.74
X6	**$623,056**	**110**	$5,664.15	1.403	7,946.80
X7	**$700,680**	**120**	$5,839.00	1.311	7,654.93
X8	**$689,560**	**111**	$6,212.25	1.225	7,610.00
X9	**$756,111**	**112**	$6,750.99	1.145	7,729.88
X10	**$702,450**	**114**	$6,161.84	1.070	6,593.17

Sum = 82,628.41

Average Inflation-Adjusted Severity per Claim = **$8,262.84**

*We use the developed losses but not the inflation adjusted $ losses, so we can just adjust for inflation here.

** Severity per claim is the developed $ loss divided by developed number of claims.

***We use the same inflation index based on 7% inflation that we used in the Inflation Adjustment section.

We can now express our 95% confidence interval in total inflation adjusted dollars with fully developed frequency and severity. From our earlier work, the 95% confidence interval for fully developed number of losses is:

95% Confidence Interval for the Number of losses =

(.00000829)(8,500,000) to (.00001313)(8,500,000) =

70.465 to 111.605

We can now put our 95% confidence interval into total inflation-adjusted dollars with fully developed frequency and severity.

95% Confidence Interval for the Number of losses =

70.465($8,262.84) to 111.605 ($8,262.84) =

$582,241.02 to $922,174.26

These numbers represent a comprehensive analysis of loss history development, exposure changes, and dollar inflation adjustment. The overall example is very broad for a single question. Rather, you may need to deal with smaller questions about a given adjustment. Nevertheless, our comprehensive example illustrates how the X11 forecast uses all the various adjustments in an attempt to use more accurate estimates in the forecast process.

Triangulation to Achieve Payout Ratios

Now that we have a better understanding of the triangulation process, we can illustrate the use of triangulation to achieve another useful set of ratios for loss analysis. The payout ratio provides information about the percentage of ultimate loss payments completed for any given year. For example, we might want to know the percentage of ultimate losses paid out by the second year of the loss history. A payout ratio of 60% would mean that 60% of the ultimate losses are paid out by the end of the second year of the history.

To construct the payout ratio we use triangulation of actual loss payment data. In Exhibit 8.11, we assume that total dollar payouts ultimately equal total dollar losses. This need not be the case. Actual dollar payouts may be less than reported losses due to negotiated payments, subrogation, and settlements for less than reported full total dollar losses. Here we want loss history data that represents actual payments on losses for any given year.

Exhibit 8.11: Triangulation of Loss Payout Data (Take the $ Payout Data below as Given History for the entity.)

Dollar Payout History (Units in $1,000s)

	Months from Inception					
Year	12	24	36	48	60	72
X1	380.10	428.57	470.23	494.45	500.56	500.56
X2	401.57	449.56	475.56	489.37	495.70	495.70
X3	414.60	465.32	497.45	539.18	547.80	547.80
X4	505.77	546.23	583.37	601.45	601.45	601.45
X5	479.34	562.26	619.61	644.39	650.30	650.30
X6	467.47	530.58	577.80	602.65	623.05	
X7	587.32	645.47	682.26	700.68		
X8	562.69	624.59	671.43			
X9	611.88	698.16				
X10	605.04					
X11	?????					

Year-to-Year Development

Year	12-24	24-36	36-48	48-60	60-72
X1	1.127	1.097	1.056	1.012	1.00
X2	1.119	1.058	1.029	1.013	1.00
X3	1.122	1.069	1.022	1.016	1.00
X4	1.080	1.068	1.046	1.000	1.00
X5	1.173	1.102	1.040	1.001	1.00
X6	1.135	1.089	1.043	1.034	
X7	1.099	1.057	1.027		
X8	1.110	1.075			
X9	1.141				
X10					
Totals	10.419	8.615	7.263	6.076	5.00
Average	**01.158**	**1.077**	**1.038**	**1.012**	**1.00**

Age to Ultimate Payout		% Ultimate Payout Ratios
1 to 5	1.158 x 1.077 x 1.038 x 1.012 x 1.0 = 1.31	**1/1.31 = 76.33%**
2 to 5	1.077 x 1.038 x 1.012 x 1.0 = 1.131	**1/1.131 = 88.41%**
3 to 5	1.038 x 1.012 x 1.0 = 1.055	**1/1.055 = 94.78%**
4 to 5	1.012 x 1.0 = 1.012	**1/1.012 = 98.81%**
5 and beyond	= 1.0	**1/1 = 100%**

We interpret the payout ratios as the percent of ultimate payouts made within the given year. For example, in our data, 76.33% of total payouts occur in the first 12 months, on average. After three years, 94.78% of ultimate payouts occur, on average. You can go back to the payout data to help convince yourself that the procedure works. Take a first year loss and it will be approximately 76% of the ultimate payout (since 76.33% is an average). For example, in X1, the first year dollar payout is $380.10 and the ultimate payout is $500.56, representing a 75.9% payout in the first year.

Final Thoughts on Forecasting

In terms of all the techniques that are available, our review of forecasting was relatively basic. Actuaries and consultants often use simulations to analyze risk and uncertainty in loss data. Simulations make it possible to consider what happens to our loss picks and loss intervals for different distribution assumptions. Different scenarios resulting in different risk profiles provide additional sophistication to forecasting.

Third-Party Assistance

For certain, types of loss data, different types of distributions may be relevant. Professional forecasters, also known as actuaries, work with more complicated distributions than our bell shaped curve and can compare and contrast findings to see how sensitive results are to basic assumptions. Also, third-party consultants often maintain the development data and other benchmarks for types of loss exposures in a given industry. A key concern is to make sure the development data used by a third party is not too broad for the types of losses in question.

Because personal biases often creep into forecasts, outside opinions can be helpful because they start with someone who has a fresh perspective. A third party could review your work and give it more credibility. In many cases, a third party is necessary because there is not enough loss history for you to generate your own development factors and adjustments. In the final analysis, third-party help is expensive and the added accuracy may not justify the expenditure. This should be evaluated on a case-by-case basis.

Limitations of Statistics and Quantitative Forecasts

A final concern is the tendency to ask too much from quantitative statistics. The numbers do not make a decision for us. There are normally qualitative factors that make a big difference in the future relative to past data. Forecasts almost always require a consideration of the following factors:

- Legal changes

- Coverage changes

- Exposure changes

- Changes in risk control and safety programs

- Changes in risk handling procedures

SECTION 3

FINANCE OF RISK

Chapter 9

Simple Risk Financing Options

Introduction

While previous chapters have suggested that insurance should be the last resort of the risk manager, nonetheless, insurance remains an important part of most risk management programs. The insurance industry has its own special lingo. Below are some of the insurance terms we will be using in this chapter. Additional definitions can be found in the Glossary at the end of this book.

Written premium – The total of premiums on all policies written by an insurer during a specified period of time.

Earned premium – The amount of the premium that has been "used up" during the term of a policy. For example, if a one-year policy has been in effect six months, half of the total premium has been earned.

Unearned premium – The amount of premium remaining after deducting the earned premium; the portion of a premium representing the "unused" or unexpired portion of the policy period.

Incurred losses – The total amount of paid claims and loss reserves associated with a particular period of time, usually a policy year. Generally, incurred losses are the actual losses paid and outstanding, interest on judgments, expenses incurred in obtaining third-party recoveries, and allocated loss adjustment expenses.

Paid losses – The amount actually paid in losses during a specified period of time, not including estimates of amounts (i.e., reserves) that will be paid in the future for losses occurring in the specified period.

Incurred but not reported (IBNR) – Represents the liability for unpaid claims not reflected in the case reserve estimates for individual losses. The two components of this liability derive from the reporting of claims that have occurred but not yet been recorded as of the evaluation date (pure IBNR) and the additional development on known cases.

Loss reserve – An estimation of the liability for all unpaid claims that have occurred as of a given date, including those losses incurred but not yet reported (IBNR), losses due but not yet paid, and amounts not yet due.

Case reserve (claim reserve) – Amount the claims adjuster puts on an individual claim that has not yet been paid; there is no provision for development and IBNR (incurred but not reported).

Allocated loss adjustment expense (ALAE) – Includes all expense directly assigned to or arising out of a particular claim; any expense assigned and recorded directly to a particular claim (e.g., court fees and the expense of outside legal counsel). May also be noted as allocated loss expense.

Unallocated loss adjustment expense (ULAE) – Salaries, overhead, and other related adjustment costs not specifically allocated or charged to the expense incurred for a particular claim.

<u>Loss Ratios and Related Terms</u>

    1. Pure Loss Ratio

$$\frac{\underline{\text{Losses Incurred in the period (incurred, known, reserves, and IBNR)}}}{\text{Premiums Earned during the period}}$$

    2. Total Loss Ratio

$$\frac{\underline{\text{Losses Incurred in the period +Allocated Loss Adjustment Expenses}}}{\text{Premiums Earned during the period}}$$

    3. Expense Ratio

$$\frac{\underline{\text{Underwriting Expenses incurred during the period}}}{\text{Premiums Earned during the period}}$$

    4. Combined Ratio

        Total Loss Ratio PLUS Expense Ratio

Note: In some cases, the Expense Ratio is defined with the denominator as Premiums Written during the period instead of Premiums Earned.

Conventional Reinsurance

Reinsurance is used extensively throughout the entire spectrum of insurance coverages for several reasons, the most important being the ability to spread the risk or share the risk among many companies. Because reinsurance is such an intrinsic part of the insurance business, the risk manager needs to have an understanding of the basic types of conventional reinsurance and their characteristics.

Reinsurance is Not a Recent Development

"Musicologists know who put the "bop" in the "bop-she-bop" and the "ram" in the "ram-a-lam-a-ding-dong," but the practice of reinsurance developed naturally, and no one person or organization can really claim it as their own, although some have tried.

 "Of course, in modern terms, we now understand that reinsurance is nothing more than insurance that insurance companies purchase on the risks they have assumed. The unique language and mystique make it sound much more romantic and exciting than it really is." (adapted from "What's Past is Prologue: A Tedious Brief History of Insurance" by Richard G. Rudolph, Ph.D.)

Reinsurance Defined

Reinsurance is conventionally defined as a contractual agreement in which one insurer agrees to insure the assumed liabilities of another insurer, a self-insured firm, or another reinsurer. Reinsurance allows an insurance company to expand its capacity, obtain surplus relief, stabilize its underwriting results, finance its expanding volume, secure catastrophe protection against shock losses, and, lastly but most importantly, to share risks with other companies.

Reinsurance Glossary

Like insurance, reinsurance has its own specialized terminology.

Ceding company: The direct or primary insurer that contracts with a reinsurer to share all or a certain portion of its losses under insurance contracts it has issued in return for a stated premium.

Reinsurer: The insurer that accepts all or a portion of the liabilities of the ceding or primary company.

Ceding Commission: A commission paid by the reinsurer to the primary insurer for the placement of the reinsurance. It is analogous to the commission paid to the producer of primary insurance.

Cession: The transaction that transfers liability from the ceding company to the reinsurer.

Retention: The amount of insurance or ultimate responsibility for losses that is not transferred by the ceding company. It may be expressed as a percentage, a specific dollar amount, or a combination of both.

Retrocession: The transaction that transfers liability from the reinsurer to another insurer, perhaps even back to the primary insurer, in whole or in part.

Types of Reinsurance Arrangements

There are two major types of reinsurance arrangements:

1. Treaty reinsurance – The ceding company (the primary company or the company who wishes to be reinsured) agrees to cede certain classes of business to a reinsurer. The reinsurer agrees to accept all business qualifying under the agreement, known as the "treaty." Under the reinsurance treaty, the ceding company is assured that all of its risk falling within the terms of the treaty will be reinsured.

2. Facultative reinsurance – Each exposure that the primary company wishes to reinsure is offered to the reinsurer as a single transaction. The reinsurer underwrites every loss exposure individually upon its submission from a ceding company. The reinsurer is not obligated to accept every submission or any submission. Each transaction is individually negotiated with respect to terms, conditions, and pricing.

Forms of Reinsurance

Further, each of these two broad types of reinsurance contracts has variations. Each subtype is intended to accomplish a specific objective. These are typically used to manage the exposures in a treaty arrangement, but can be used with facultative agreements, as well.

Pro-rata reinsurance is also called proportional reinsurance. It is an agreement to share the insurance coverage. The reinsurer gets an agreed percentage of the original premium, less a ceding commission, and pays the same percentage of all losses covered by the reinsurance contract. Within pro-rata reinsurance contracts, there are two subtypes.

Quota Share – The primary insurer cedes a part of every exposure it insures within a class or classes subject to the treaty. Both premium and losses (from first claim dollar) are shared according to a stated percentage of the amount of insurance written.

Surplus Share – The primary insurer cedes to the reinsurer a pro-rata share of risks, but the reinsurer only pays its percentage of losses when the amount exceeds a net retention described in the treaty, thus falling into the "surplus" area.

Excess of loss reinsurance is also called Non-proportional reinsurance. Excess of loss reinsurance is an agreement to share specified losses. The reinsurer indemnifies the primary insurer for the amount of loss in excess of a specified retention. The retention amount can be stated as either a dollar amount or a percentage amount. The reinsurer does not participate in losses until a loss exceeds the amount retained by the primary insurer. Within excess of loss reinsurance arrangements, there are three subtypes:

Excess Per Risk – The reinsurer pays any loss on an individual risk in excess of a predetermined amount.

Excess Per Occurrence – The reinsurer pays only when the combined losses from any one occurrence exceed the predetermined retention of the ceding company. While this sounds similar to Excess of Risk, it is entirely different.

Aggregate Excess of Loss is also called stop loss or loss ratio reinsurance. The reinsurer pays all losses when the ceding company's aggregate net losses exceed a predetermined amount or proportion of premium income. For example, the reinsurance contract is triggered when losses exceed a 70% loss ratio.

These are basic examples of pro rata and excess. Actual reinsurance contracts could be different percentages and retentions as well as being a combination of these two approaches.

Application of the Types of Reinsurance

Now, let's look at some practical examples.

Exhibit 9.1: Pro rata Reinsurance (Proportional)

($1 M limit on each example)

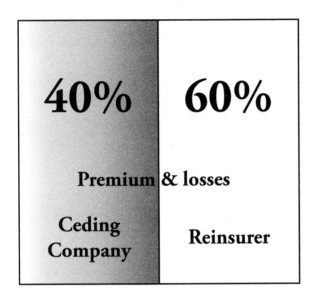

Quota Share

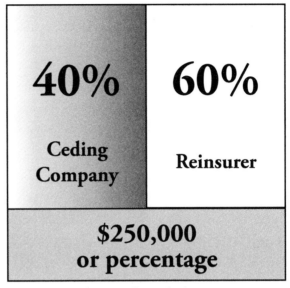

Surplus Share

Exhibit 9.2: Excess of Loss Reinsurance (Non-proportional)

Excess to limit of $1M

$250,000 or percentage

$750 in excess of $250 retention

Characteristics of Simple Financing Options

Program Mechanics

Simple financing insurance-based options are relatively simple and straightforward, for insurance policies, that is. Some of the issues are nothing more than the pure mechanics of the program: how and when the insurance policy is issued, and by whom; how the premium is paid, (e.g., one annual payment or installments); and how losses are paid and by whom. Since these simple financing options consist of ordinary insurance policies, the answers to these questions are likewise simple: the carrier does everything, paying any covered losses over deductibles or retentions and within policy limits, and is willing to negotiate premium payments. Annual payment is always acceptable, and if the premium is sizable, and the carrier is not a surplus lines (e.g., non-admitted or non-standard) carrier, installment payment plans of differing types can usually be obtained.

With insurance, the degree of retention or internal financing generally appears to be non-existent, except for the trivial degree of retention found in a "maintenance" deductible feature, or the use of a very small deductible to let the insuror eliminate small losses that would have an exorbitant cost of handling relative to the amount of the loss. While "small" is always a relative term, for any organization having a risk manager (in-house, hired, or gratuitous (e.g., an insurance agent or broker), anything up to $1,000 is certainly "small", and that threshold may even extend further. The key difference between a simple financing option and a loss-sensitive option will be the intent of the organization and carrier: "Small" deductibles are usually nothing more than a policy requirement with very limited alternatives, but can be increased somewhat, as discussed later in this chapter.

However, the degree of retention that is critical, and often overlooked, is the retention of losses outside the four corners of the insurance policy, or losses in excess of the purchased limits and losses subject to excluded perils, hazards, and property definitions, and losses limited by policy definitions, limitations, and conditions. For risk managers using the simple financing option and its "assurances" of insurance coverage, these extra-policy losses create the "worry factor" or the "what keeps you awake at night" scenarios.

Fixed versus Variable Costs

Simple financing options are rated prospectively, using rates that are determined prior to the policy date. These rates are generally based on rates taken from rating manuals for the applicable exposure classifications (types of building construction and location, ISO general liability codes, NCCI workers compensation class codes, etc.), modified by the underwriter, and applied to the units of the selected exposure base to create a "fixed" premium. In reality, only the rate is fixed, as the premiums may be adjusted based upon actual exposures determined after the policy expiration by premium audit. However, because the rates are determined prospectively or in advance of the policy term, the premium is considered "fixed" as it is predetermined according to the units of exposure the organization knows it is presenting throughout its operations during the policy term. In other words, it is "fixed" because it is highly predictable when considering the exposure units and is not dependent on losses during the policy period.

Services

Nearly all, if not all, required or necessary services (and a number of services that are not required) are provided by the insurance carrier. The quality of the services depends upon the philosophy of the insurance carrier and the professionalism of the employees the carrier has assigned to the particular insured. To some degree, this is negotiable, but only in terms of the personnel who will actually deliver the service. The insurance carrier provides all underwriting, loss control and engineering, claims adjusting and settling services, auditing, and reports to regulatory agencies and the insured. The important point to remember (and this is only a statement of fact, not an indictment against an insurance carrier) is that the providers of these services provide the services primarily for the benefit of the insurance carrier and not the insured. Loss control and claims management services, for example, may provide benefits to the insured, but they are primarily conducted to protect the insurance carrier's profitability.

Program Flexibility

Because the simple financing options are based on common insurance policies, there is little flexibility in program design except for limits of coverage, deductible options, and a rather small number of endorsements to tailor coverage to meet specific needs. In general, these programs are considered to be simply adaptable to specific needs, but not really flexible. Their customization possibilities are rather limited.

Accounting and Tax Impact

With these simple financing programs that use insurance policies, the accounting and tax issues are realtively straightforward. Premiums are deductible when the obligation is incurred for accrual basis accounting systems and when paid for cash basis accounting systems. Losses are deductible only to the extent the insurance policy does not pay, and thus are tax-deductible only when an uninsured loss is paid by the insured (e.g., under the deductible, excluded, etc.).

Premium Certainty and the Effects of Experience Modifiers

As discussed previously, though the rates are fixed, premiums are variable based upon audit; nonetheless, there is a high level of certainty as the insured should always have a good idea of the level of the variable exposure units upon which the premium is based.

However, there is an important aspect of premium uncertainty, and that arises out of the application of experience modifications, particularly the workers' compensation experience modification system. An understanding of the impact of workers' compensation experience modifiers on premium pricing is critical to risk managers for a number of reasons.

First, understanding how the experience modifier is calculated can help the risk manager generate fair treatment by rating bureaus. Second, the experience modifier is also a useful analytical tool, helping the risk manager track the progress of loss control initiatives, for both loss prevention and loss reduction. The risk manager can also interpret adverse developments in the cost of risk, assigning the portion of charges arising out of changes in exposures versus those charges arising out of changes in loss experience and its inevitable impact on future premiums. Thus, we recognize that loss experience has a "double whammy" on the cost of risk, as losses directly impact the cost of risk through retained losses and indirectly through changes in future premiums. Fourth, the risk manager can gain insights into the likely impact of losses on future modifiers and the potential effect of per-claim or per-occurrence deductible options.

However, there are some caveats associated with experience modifiers. The experience modifier is calculated on a three-year, weighted, rolling average with the most recent year excluded. Any significant changes in loss experience will not affect the experience modifier until after the end of the remaining portion of the current policy year and the end of the entire next year. This lag time may lull a risk manager into complacency, but there is work to do during this time.

Because of ongoing changes in claims development status and possible data-entry errors, the risk manager must coordinate with the claims manager to verify that the data reported by the insurance carrier on "unit statistical cards" (commonly called "stat cards") are accurate. In addition to the failure to accurately communicate changes, coding errors and loss data inputing errors can seriously affect the modifier. Related to that issue is the need to verify premium audit results, as these changes to total premium charges will similarly affect statistical reporting

Another concern for the risk manager is tracking subrogation recoveries. Adjusters may not automatically report subrogation results to the rating authority who promulgates the experience modifier. Also, organizations sometimes have exposures for operations conducted in the monopolistic states (although that number of states that insure workers through state compensation insurance funds is gradually shrinking), and those premiums and losses will not appear in the experience modifiers applicable to other states. Lastly, the inclusion of amounts for small claims will usually be restricted by law or the insurance contract; these small claims may or may not be reported or included by the rating authority. The rating authority also limits large losses so as not to over-penalize an insured for a shock loss.

Cash Flow

There are limited cash flow opportunities in simple financing programs. Cash flow arises only when premium deferral is possible through installments. Thus, the time frame for the organization to retain the use of cash is limited to a policy term of twelve months, and even then, installment plans rarely permit the premium to be spread over more than ten months. The only other cash flow possibility is also limited, that arising out of the retention of small deductibles. Here the limiting factor is the relatively low level of cash involved.

Loss Sensitivity

Because of the prospective nature of the premium computation, there is no real degree of loss sensitivity in the short run (e.g., during a policy year). However, that does not mean the program cannot be affected by losses, because experience modifiers and underwriter's judgments are affected at renewal time. These factors are sensitive to frequency (frequency leads to severity) as well as severity (large losses, while usually limited in their effect on experience modifiers, are still paid by insurance carriers, and underwriters know what the insured has cost the carrier at renewal time).

Fully Insured Programs

To reiterate some of the general characteristics described above, fully insured programs have the following characteristics:

There is a 100% transfer of the financial responsibility to the insurance carrier up to policy limits, and subject to policy terms and conditions.

There is no loss sensitivity in the current policy year for experience.

The premium is fixed, but can be endorsed for changes in exposures, and is often auditable when exposures are known to be variable.

The insurance carrier will provide all services; there is no "unbundling" of services.

Premiums are subject to discounts, credits and debits, and experience modifications (at the underwriter's discretion or according to manual rules), and the rating options can be customized to some extent (also at the underwriter's discretion and according to manual rules).

Advantages of a Fully Insured Program

There are several distinct advantages to a fully insured program, the first being budget certainty (even auditable premiums can be "certain" from a budgeting standpoint). Second, fully insured programs provide convenience, as the insurance carrier provides all services in "easy, one-stop shopping." Third, the insurance carrier or its agent/broker provides certificates of insurance required to support contractual compliance. In addition, poor experience may even go "unpunished" at renewal; tax deductibility is very clear and unlikely to trigger a tax audit; and sometimes there is flexibility in coverage options.

Disadvantages

Insurance policies are always the most expensive option for financing risk, as insurance carrier expenses are passed along in addition to the cost of losses and loss adjustment expense. Those insurance carrier costs, including their profit and contingency loadings, are rarely less than 30% of the premium. In addition, there is no cash flow advantage accruing to the insured organization; all cash flow advantages belong to the insurance carrier who collects the premium immediately (or in a few months) and then pays losses over the next several years. Good experience is not rewarded in the short run (unless the rewards come in the form of underwriting concessions). Services provided by the insurance carrier may not be appropriate or adequate, and any supplementary services required will be purchased at additional expense to the insured organization. Since fully insured programs are based on standardized policies, there is little flexibility in general, with few or no options for customization. Last, and most importantly, the lack of short-term incentives to reduce losses may affect the cost of risk in the long term.

Exhibit 9.3: Basic Premium Calculation for Guaranteed Cost or Fixed Rate Insurance Policies

Fixed Rate × Units of Exposure   =   Manual Premium

× Rate deviations

× <u>Experience Modification</u>

= Modified Premium

× Increased Limits Factor

× Scheduled Credit or Debit

× <u>Premium Discount</u>

= Modified Discounted Premium

+ Expense Constant

+ <u>State Assessments</u>

= Guaranteed Cost

Some types of coverage have the entire array of modifications applied; others have none or only a limited number. For example, a workers' compensation program may have state assessments, a premium discount, and an expense constant, but general liability programs rarely do.

Guaranteed Cost Programs with Dividends

Some types of coverage may use the basic guaranteed cost or prospective rating approach, and then provide an additional feature that may result in lower rates depending upon the insured's loss experience and the general loss experience of the insurance carrier. Typically, these programs are used only with workers' compensation coverage, but other dividend programs are technically possible, usually on larger accounts.

There are two variations to a guaranteed cost program with a dividend plan superimposed: a flat dividend program and a sliding scale or variable dividend program. Both of these programs require the insured to have a loss ratio under a specified threshold and the insurance carrier to have a minimum underwriting profit on its portfolio of similar policies AND the board of directors of the insurance carrier must vote to declare a dividend for that block of policies.

These programs are generally not considered to be cash flow programs for an organization or even particularly loss sensitive, although they are loss sensitive in the sense that costs can decrease based on loss experience, but never increase. This stems from the fact that, historically, the dividend represented a planned overcharge of premium that was a buffer or cushion against adverse loss experience, and when good loss experience resulted, the insured received a return of the excess charges. This arrangement was a common feature among mutual insurance companies, whose owners are its policyholders; in effect, the owners were charging themselves more premium "just in case" and giving themselves a reduction if losses were under the target. To compete with mutual insurance companies (and reciprocal insurers) many stock insurance companies began to offer dividend plans that were very similar to those offered by mutual insurance companies. To maintain profitability, the stock insurance companies made up for the return premium by reducing the commission paid to the agent.

The flat dividend plan is the least loss sensitive of plans that are not really loss sensitive, but whose effective premium can change according to losses. If the insured has a loss ratio under the threshold, and the insurance carrier also has an underwriting profit, the board can elect to pay a dividend of a flat or fixed amount, usually expressed as a percentage of premium.

The sliding scale or variable dividend program is much more loss sensitive (again, premiums can only be reduced by loss experience but never increased) in that the percentage of the premium reduction increases according to a schedule as the insured's losses decrease. An insured with losses in the lowest range or band will receive the maximum dividend or premium reduction scheduled, and as the losses rise, the percentage of reduction decreases. The schedule in Exhibit 9.4 depicts a possible sliding scale dividend plan on a workers' compensation policy having an audited premium of $270,000.

Exhibit 9.4: Sliding Scale Dividend

Losses	Credit (%)	Credit ($)
$0 - $24,999	50%	$ 135,000
$25,000 - $49,999	40%	$ 108,000
$50,000 - $74,999	30%	$ 81,000
$75,000 - $99,999	20%	$ 54,000
$100,000 - $135,000	10%	$ 27,000
Over $135,000	0%	$ 0

The characteristics of dividend plans are essentially the same as those of a guaranteed cost insurance plan, except for the limited or one-way loss sensitivity and the effect of the dividends. In these plans, the insured does have an interest in the loss results, at least to the point that the losses are under the upper limit stated on the dividend schedule. After the losses exceed that amount, the insured no longer has any real incentive to control losses. Like a guaranteed cost program, there is no cash flow advantage except premiums that are paid in installments. In fact, the dividend feature may have a negative cash flow if the dividends represent a refund of excess premiums.

The tax deductible feature of the guaranteed cost plan remains the same, premiums being deductible when the obligation is incurred for accrual accounting, and deductible when paid for cash accounting. Dividends are taxed as ordinary income (i.e., not as stock dividends or investment income).

The insurance carrier provides claims services. This leads to one common criticism or belief that the insurance carrier will bump up reserves and therefore the insured's loss experience prior to the date the dividends are calculated, intending to wipe out any dividend, even though the claims will probably settle for less. From a practical standpoint, this is unlikely. Some insurers are willing to have an independent claims consultant review their reserves prior to dividend computation.

Another feature of dividend plans that is not usually found on guaranteed cost programs is a loss limitation, an agreement that severe losses will be limited to a lesser amount, thus dampening the impact on the loss experience for dividend purposes. This is generally funded by a slightly lower dividend percentage.

Like most guaranteed cost plans, there is little flexibility in plan design. While there is a wide range of plans available, most of them are "shelf products" with little customization or flexibility possible.

Advantages

For qualifying insureds, dividend plans do have distinct advantages over non-dividend guaranteed cost plans. While the effective premium is subject to change because of the dividend, the maximum cost is known after audit. Another way of describing a dividend plan is to view it as a loss sensitive plan where there is no downside, although the potential upside benefit is also limited by the dividend schedule and the uncertainty if there will be a declaration of dividend by the insurance carrier.

Although the premium savings benefit can be dampened by the schedule, when the schedule has generous reductions for favorable loss experience, there is a real incentive to reduce losses, albeit less dramatic than true loss sensitive plans.

Disadvantages

Similarly, there are disadvantages, two of which are serious. Dividends are uncertain with respect to declaration, and nothing will disappoint managers more than working hard to reduce losses only to have the insurance carrier decide not to declare a dividend. Second, the insured is at the mercy of the insurance carrier with respect to the claims reserving process; while most insurance carriers operate honorably, it only takes one instance to cast aspersions on all. In addition, dividend programs can have much of the otherwise positive results of loss control wiped out by one severe claim. While loss limitations may be available, these features will come at a cost of a reduced schedule of premium credit.

Cash Flow under a Dividend Program

As mentioned previously, dividend programs are not really cash flow programs; it fact, it can be argued that the cash flow is negative, as the premium may be higher initially, only to be returned later, assuming a dividend is validated and declared.

That said, the flow of cash returns under a dividend program is as follows: There could be several adjustments under the dividend plan, more than under a guaranteed cost program. The first adjustment is the typical audit adjustment, and unearned premium will be returned or additional premium charged. In a hypothetical dividend plan, the remaining adjustments could occur at twelve months after the policy expiration and at twenty-four months. In the first dividend adjustment, 50% of the applicable dividend will be returned to the insured. In the second adjustment, 100% of the applicable dividend less the first adjustment amount will be returned. If the second adjustment is less than the first adjustment (because of adverse loss deterioration), the insured does not have to return any of the first adjustment to the insurance carrier. (If there is a case for conservatism in claims reserve calculation, this is a likely opportunity.)

For example, if the losses at twelve months after expiration are projected to be $90,000, with a $270,000 premium, the previously cited schedule would indicate a dividend adjustment of $54,000, or 20% of the premium. The insurance carrier will pay a dividend of $27,000, or 50% of the applicable dividend of $54,000.

If the losses deteriorate to $110,000, the applicable dividend indicated on the schedule is 10% of the premium, or $27,000, so no additional dividend would be paid. If the losses had deteriorated even more, exceeding $135,000, the applicable dividend would be 0%. In this case, no additional dividend would be paid, but neither would the insurance carrier seek reimbursement for the first $27,000 adjustment.

Exhibit 9.5: Net Present Value of Cash Flows, Guaranteed Cost Plan vs. Sliding Scale Dividend Plan

Assuming equal premiums of $270,000 for both a guaranteed cost plan and a sliding scale dividend plan, and assuming a 10% discount rate, the net present value of the cash flows would be as follows:

Outflow (current) is $270,000

Inflows: (measured from beginning of the policy to the second adjustment)

At end of 12 months from inception	$0
At end of 24 months from inception	$27,000
At end of 36 months from inception	$0

Calculating the discounted inflow:

$27,000(.826) = $22,302 discounted inflows

The Net Present Value of the dividend plan is $270,000 - $22,302 = $247,698.

Guaranteed Cost	$270,000
Dividend Cost	$247,698

If the premium for the dividend plan were higher, the net present value would be less.

Factors Affecting the Decision to Use a Dividend Plan

Dividend plans are generally designed for policies with premium levels that do not substantiate more aggressive loss sensitive plans. One factor is the level of confidence of the projected losses. Generally, insureds that use a dividend plan have not had an actuarial projection of losses, though the insurance carrier or broker may have provided some type of projection. While actuaries never guaranty the absolute accuracy of their predictions, their level of sophistication and the accompanying measures of confidence are generally better than those of the carrier or broker.

Another factor is the dividend history of the insurance carriers. Since dividends cannot be contractually guaranteed, insurance carriers often distinguish themselves by their consistency of dividend declaration, not unlike corporations who attempt to maintain stock dividend payments even when earnings are below those expected.

Additionally, since an insurance carrier's loss reserving practices play an important role in determining the applicable dividends, the risk manager needs to develop an understanding of their reserving practices, and, if possible, obtain some sort of input, even if it is in the form of a claims consultant reviewing reserves before the dividend calculation date.

Last, there are some tax considerations. The premium is tax-deductible either when paid or when the obligation to pay is incurred, depending upon cash or accrual accounting systems. Dividends are taxable as ordinary income when received.

Small Deductible Options

Much like a guaranteed cost program or a dividend program, a small deductible program is based on standard insurance policy options. Generally these are rated on a manual basis, with deductible options provided in a table of deductibles and their corresponding premium credits. These are usually called tabular plans, and the deductible options may range from a $1,000 to as much as $50,000. Further, the deductible might apply only to an occurrence or to each claim, only to an aggregate, or in combination, with an aggregate stop loss feature to cap or set a maximum amount of retention to the insured organization.

Mechanics

Small deductible options may be found in almost any line of coverage. While in many cases, the deductible is used by the insurer as an underwriting tool for acceptability, it can also be used by an insured to take a step toward more retention while obtaining a reasonable premium credit.

The amount of the total retention can range from very slight to very significant, particularly if the organization is subject to high-frequency loss issues and there is no aggregate deductible limitation.

The typical arrangement for applying a deductible option is for the insurance carrier to handle the claim as if it were fully insured, with a reimbursement to be made by the insured at a later date according to the deductible reimbursement agreement. With higher deductible amounts, this may entail a corollary contract to the insurance policy, one that may require some sort of collateral.

Characteristics

One characteristic is a fixed premium, as this is basically a guaranteed cost program that simply has a larger deductible than the standard policy deductible. However, the cost of risk is variable because of the inclusion of losses in its calculation. Such plans can be quite sensitive to losses, depending upon claim frequency, the size of the deductible, and whether or not an aggregate deductible limit is used.

There are two new cash flow opportunities: the first is on the fixed cost side – a reduced premium because of deductible credits; the second and more dramatic cash flow opportunity is tied to the payout lags inherent in the deductible reimbursement.

The insurance carrier provides all services, including claims services, although the insured may hire a claims consultant to review claim reserves to protect the insured's interests. The insurance carrier also provides loss control services, which may improve loss frequency or severity.

Small deductible programs have some flexibility with respect to deductible level options, including the use of aggregate deductibles, but the underlying forms and coverage tend to be standardized. Taxation issues are straightforward, with premiums being fully deductible as an ordinary business expense when paid or when the obligation is incurred (cash versus accrual accounting), but losses are only deductible when the deductible reimbursement is paid to the insurance carrier.

Advantages

Small deductible plans have several important advantages. Because of the fixed nature of the premium and with predictable losses, programs can be structured with reasonable budget certainty, particularly when aggregate deductible limits are used. The insurance programs underlying the small deductible options are commonly used policy forms that are easy to understand (for an insurance policy, that is), easy to establish, and deductible reimbursements are relatively easy to administer, depending upon the insurance carrier.

Certificates of insurance are standardized and issued by the agent/broker or insurance carrier. Because the insurance carrier pays the losses, there is no need to show any deductible on the certificate of insurance, as that is a private contractual matter between the insurance carrier and the insured (except in the case where the insured agrees to disclose any deductibles to a certificate holder).

The direct savings in premiums and cash flow savings can be substantial, particularly if loss frequency is low and the premium credits are large. A small deductible program can provide a real incentive for the insured to reduce frequency, and any reduction in frequency lessens the likelihood of a severe loss occurring (if no losses of any size occur, there can, by definition, be no severe losses).

Disadvantages

Small deductible plans, because they are based on standardized insurance policies that usually are class-rated or manually rated, often have little flexibility with respect to coverage and pricing. The rating schedules frequently do not offer credits that are adequate to justify the additional expenses of paying losses within the deductibles. This is particularly a problem for exposures where there is a real possibility of losses and where the premium credits are insignificant.

The services provided by the insurance carrier may be inadequate or inappropriate for a particular insured, but are included in the premium without the option of removal or unbundling. Additional services purchased to meet any inadequacies will increase the cost of risk.

The insured purchasing a small deductible plan may become more interested in claims handling, but in such a plan they have little or no control over the payments, as the insurance carrier provides the claims services and will reserve according to their own interests.

The cost of risk may also be increased, as the insurance carrier is likely to require some sort of security or collateral. When the security is provided in the form of an escrow account for claims payments, the insured loses the cash flow advantages. When the security is provided in the form of collateral, there may be fees or expenses (such as the fee for a letter of credit or premium on a surety bond) that increase the cost of risk. Further, a letter of credit or surety bond may reduce the ability of the insured to obtain other borrowing or increase the cost of other borrowing.

Last, another disadvantage arises for claims with a long development time (like products liability or medical malpractice), as the policy accounts may be held open for a long period of time before the final cost of risk is known. The length of development depends upon the type of program, the nature of the exposure, and the claims settlement philosophy and practices of the insurance carrier.

Exhibit 9.6: Deductible Plan

Guaranteed Cost × Deductible Factor = Deductible Premium

Deductible Premium + Converted Losses (or Losses × LCF) = Deductible Plan Cost

Deductible Premium	$141,000

Converted Losses

Losses × LCF = $110,000 × 1.10 = $121,000

Discounted for Timing of Ultimate Payout:

All claims paid at end of 2 years ($121,000 × .826)	$ 99,946
	$240,946

Note: Assumes $25,000 Deductible per Claim

Chapter 10

Loss Sensitive Financing Options

The risk manager has several options for selecting risk financing with a wider array of loss sensitivity. These options range from a program very similar to the simple financing options explained in the last chapter to a fully retained or "self-insured" option. It is nothing more than a matter of determining the mix of internal financing and external financing provided by insurance carriers.

Pricing Methodologies

Top-down Pricing

Guaranteed cost programs and their cousins, dividend plans and small deductible plans, are driven by manual or schedule rating. This approach is also known as top-down pricing, as it begins with a base rate that is established by a rating authority such as the Insurance Services Office (ISO) or National Council on Compensation Insurance (NCCI), two of the most common rating authorities. These rates are created on a state by state basis, further broken down into territories within those states, and still further by a rather precise definition of the exposure through the use of a classification code.

For workers compensation policies, the rating process established by the workers compensation rating authority generates a manual premium by multiplying the appropriate rate by the exposures for the class, with further modifications for an experience modifier (also determined by the rating authority) and scheduled credits or debits (experience modification factors), deductible credits, and premium discount factors (also created by the rating authority in the form of schedules).

There is some customization in this apparently rigid rating process, as insurance carriers can request specific changes to the rates and the process to reflect their particular expertise or competitive approach. These requests, when granted, are called filed rate deviations or filed rating plans. Even so, the process by which the final policy premium is calculated is formulistic and highly standardized with no flexibility beyond the filed structure and rates.

For other than workers compensation policies, insurance company underwriters may use a little more subjectivity in applying rating factors, but the outcome is still somewhat rigid.

Keep in mind that the rates developed by the rating authorities are based on a much larger statistical sample than a single insured. The rating authorities collect exposures by class code and losses associated with those class codes to promulgate or calculate rates that will apply to all insureds having exposures that fit those classifications. This process gives rise to the significant advantage of such an approach: the greater likelihood that the premium will represent an actuarially sound initial pricing. However, this advantage also has a parallel disadvantage: it is unlikely that the database of exposures and losses that give rise to the manual rates properly reflects the exposure of any specific insured and any specific loss control enhancements used by that insured. For example, an individual McDonald's restaurant franchisee store will have the same general liability class codes as an independently owned white tablecloth steakhouse, yet it is obvious that neither of these establishments would closely resemble the hypothetical "average" insured represented by the manual "restaurant" rate.

Bottom-up Pricing

Bottom-up pricing is the opposite of top-down pricing. It is commonly referred to as loss rating. Instead of using manual rates representing the hypothetical, "average" insured, it starts by generating a loss rate from the insured's own loss experience.

To find the loss rate, the person pricing the account must establish credible loss data for a pre-set number of years. These losses are trended and developed to their ultimate values. The unit of exposure (an independent variable, e.g., miles for a trucking company) for those same years is also trended, and the total ultimate loss is divided by the total number of exposures to create the rate of loss per exposure unit, the loss rate.

That loss rate is grossed up to include various expenses components, such as underwriting expenses, policy issuance expenses, policyholder service expenses, loss control, commission, premium taxes, and insurance carrier profit loadings. The policy premium is generated by multiplying the estimated exposure units for the policy period by the grossed up loss rate.

Advantages

The bottom-up approach has several advantages. First, the loss rate will accurately represent the insured's own experience and not that of the hypothetical "average" insured. If the insured's database is large enough and has sufficient credibility, the loss rate will accurately represent a loss projection and will be appropriate for the specific insured. Also, the number and nature of the claims are more specific to the insured, so variation from the expected claims can be more accurately assessed. Last, bottom-up pricing aids in developing loss control measures to address specific needs rather than being a generic, "average" approach.

Disadvantages

If the prediction of losses (the loss projection) is flawed (e.g., actuarially unsound, or the data is skewed by large, unpredictable, or severe losses) the process will probably result in an incorrect loss rate and therefore an inappropriate premium. The bottom-up approach also requires the underwriter have excellent skills, experience, and judgment. Last, since the loss rate is grossed up to include expenses, if the loss rate is wrong (too high or too low), the portion of the premium created by the inclusion of the expense components will be similarly inappropriate.

With this foundation of rating structures, we will continue with our discussion of loss sensitive financing options.

Large Deductible Plans

Mechanically, large deductible plans are like small deductible plans in a few areas: generally, an insurance carrier issues the policy; the insurance carrier retains the claims settlement function; and the insurance carrier or agent/broker issues certificates of insurance. Because the insurance carrier has a financial rating and may be an admitted carrier, this satisfies most requirements of certificate holders and regulators. However, the underlying difference is more pronounced: the insured has the opportunity to negotiate a much higher deductible (or retention) amount, and more than a minor premium reduction, while still maintaining the framework of a conventional insurance policy.

Specific Differences

"Large" deductible is a relative term, but in this context, it generally refers to a retention of $100,000 or more. The actual deductible amount is obviously negotiable, and can reach as high as $1,000,000, or in some special cases, it may even equal the policy limit.

Deductible equals the policy limit

In one case, an insured (a $3 billion-asset, privately held organization) purchased a $1,000,000 combined single limit commercial general liability (CGL) insurance policy with a general aggregate limit of $1,000,000, all subject to a $1,000,000 per occurrence deductible. Since the deductible is the responsibility of the insured, the carrier would pay a policy-limit loss and then seek reimbursement for the amount paid from the insured. In effect, this acted as a self-insured retention with no coverage available from the CGL policy. The insured used this approach to facilitate the purchase of high-limits umbrella coverage at a favorable premium and to satisfy certificate holder requirements without raising questions and concerns.

Since the large deductible is negotiable, the risk manager must be careful in selecting the appropriate attachment point. The size of the deductible means there is a great deal of loss sensitivity. The process of stratifying losses and calculating the estimated losses (the loss "projection") is critical for both the insured and the insurance carrier. Part of the attachment point selection process involves a determination if aggregate protection (maximum amount the insured will have to pay in a given time period) is needed. However, aggregate protection, when available in the marketplace, can be expensive.

Another characteristic that requires serious consideration is the tax impact. Premiums are deductible as paid or incurred, as discussed previously under cash or accrual systems, but losses are only deductible when paid, even by an accrual system taxpayer. This adds another layer of complexity to the analysis of the cash flow advantages of a large deductible plan.

Advantages

A large deductible plan has many more advantages than a small deductible plan. First, the potential for positive cash flow is much greater, and related to that is the opportunity for a big payback for loss control work. Since the carrier is farther removed from the financial responsibility of claims, the insured may be able to customize coverages, to specifically meet the organization's needs, as well as services, purchasing only the services desired, a process usually called "unbundling." The insured also may have some control over setting claims reserves and settlements, although the ultimate responsibility remains with the carrier. Finally, because of these abilities to negotiate and customize services, the insured should be able to receive lower expense components and loadings, further reducing the cost of risk.

Last, a large deductible may be a first step toward being fully self-insured, or retaining 100% of the risk internally. It allows the organization to gain experience as a self-insured entity without having 100% of the risk.

Disadvantages

The advantage of positive cash flow has its mirror image: a larger deductible has the disadvantage of a grander scale of negative cash flow if the plan's loss experience deteriorates. Consequently, an accurate determination of the attachment points (the level of the individual claim limit and the aggregate claims limit) is critical. A related disadvantage is that aggregate protection may be cost prohibitive or not available in the marketplace.

The third serious disadvantage is that the insurance carrier generally requires financial guarantees or collateral to protect their financial position. These guarantees can be expensive, in terms of the actual cost, and their effect on the insured's capability to borrow funds for operations or other uses. As long as claims remain open, a possibility that may run into years, the insured must maintain the collateral or security. As large deductible plans are used year after year, the collateral "stacks," with each year requiring its own collateral. Thus, the financial impact of tying up credit can increase dramatically over long periods of time.

The Collateral Conundrum

A simple definition of collateral is "property, usually in the form of funds or personal property, pledged to secure a debt or a loan." In the case of a high deductible plan, the insurance carrier is obligated to pay all losses and then seek reimbursement from the insured. The contractual arrangement that establishes this reimbursement creates a conditional debt (no debt is incurred unless a claim is paid). To secure this conditional debt, the insurance carrier nearly always requires some type of collateral. The organization wishing to be protected decides what type of collateral is acceptable for various obligations. Each type of collateral has its own characteristics, including a degree of risk and flexibility.

Security in the form of collateral is not a feature only of a large deductible plan, however. Other loss sensitive plans, such as retrospective rating programs, pools, and some captives may require the posting of collateral and security. The security agreement is not part of the insurance policy, but is a corollary agreement between the insurance carrier and the insured. We will define these terms within the confines of collateral agreements between insurance company and insured.

<u>Cash and Cash Equivalents</u> are the simplest form of collateral. The insured posts cash or cash equivalents (e.g., marketable securities of a high quality) into an escrow account controlled by the insurance company. Cash, the "poor man's credit," is the most certain type of collateral. Once deposited into the controlled account, cash has zero risk. The insured, however, may be reluctant to use cash, because the insurance company may spend the cash readily, and the insured loses the use of cash that might be needed for ordinary operations. Additionally, the insured may or may not earn interest on those funds, depending upon the outcome of negotiations.

<u>Certificates of Deposit</u> (CDs) are contractual deposits with a financial institution. When CDs are used as collateral, the financial institution receives instructions to not release the funds to the insured without the permission of the insurer. Generally, the insured continues to earn interest on those funds (but may not receive the interest). The funds are more secure from the standpoint of the insured, as well, because the financial institution also receives instructions not to release the funds without the permission of (or at least notice to) them. These are not used often.

A <u>Letter of Credit </u>(LOC) and <u>"Evergreen" Letter of Credit</u> are examples of pre-qualified loans an organization may obtain from a financial institution. In effect, the LOC states the insured has access to a guaranteed line of credit from the financial institution, and the insurer can access those funds according to the collateral documents. The "evergreen" LOC is simply an LOC that renews automatically and does not have to be replaced or renewed periodically.

However, this line of credit carries a small fee (usually less than 1%), and the commitment to supply these funds on demand reduces the amount the insured can borrow for security purposes or other operational and investing activities. Additionally, if the LOC is drawn down (the loan is made), the contractually stated interest rate on the loan applies. All this notwithstanding, letters of credit are the most used form of collateral in high deductible plans.

<u>Surety bonds</u> are three-party contracts, generally issued by the surety departments of disinterested insurance carriers (although private surety companies are also used). The surety agrees to pay the stated amount to the obligee (the one to whom the obligation is owed, in this case the insurance carrier desiring security or collateral) if the principal, or obligor (the insured owing the obligation), fails to perform the act stated in the surety agreement. For example, if the insured does not reimburse the insurance carrier for the amounts paid for claims under the deductible, the surety must pay the insurance carrier the amount the insured failed to reimburse. The surety then has a contractual right to seek reimbursement from the insured (the obligee or principal), and will have secured some type of collateral or security on its behalf. The premium on the surety bond is a cost of risk to the insured. These are not used often as collateral on high deductible plans.

<u>Accounts Receivable</u>, the trade credit collectible to the insured, can be factored or sold to another party to generate immediate cash flow rather than waiting for the slower receipt of funds from those vendors or other debtors. Because of this feature, Accounts Receivable can be pledged to the insurance carrier as collateral to secure reimbursement. If the insured fails to pay the reimbursement, the insurance carrier can factor the receivables. Since there is a credit risk and expense (and loss of cash flow) assumed by the purchaser of the receivables, the amount paid for the receivables is discounted from the full amount of the receivables. There is no cost associated with pledging the receivables unless the insured defaults. However, if there is a default, the insured losses the entire amount of receivables pledged and the cash flow that would have been generated, possibly leading to a liquidity crisis for the organization. This is not used often.

Retrospective Rating Plans

Insurance policies are rated in two different ways: prospective and retrospective. In a prospective rating plan, the effective policy rates are established prior to the inception date. This approach is commonly found in guaranteed cost and small dividend programs that are based on manual rates and subject to modification only prior to policy issuance. Once rated, the policy's only variation in the premium is for additional or reduced exposures changed by endorsements and for audit adjustment based on actual exposure units.

In a retrospective rating plan, the effective policy rates are a function of the insured's actual loss experience, with the effective policy rates to be determined after the policy inception date and usually changed on several occasions after the policy expiration. For the purposes of establishing the original policy rates, an estimate of the rates is computed using estimates of expected losses and exposure units and adding expense loadings and charges. Shortly after the policy expiration, an adjustment is made for actual exposure units. Then, using a predetermined interval after the policy expires, usually 6 months or 12 months, the insurer makes a series of periodic, usually annual, adjustments. These adjustments use the actual loss experience, <u>as determined at that point in time</u>, and the premium is adjusted according to the retrospective rating formula using losses as the independent variable. Premium is recalculated and a return premium or additional premium is recorded, and the appropriate amount of cash is exchanged.

These periodic adjustments continue until either all losses are closed or the insurance carrier and insured agree to a settlement value of all claims (even though some individual claims remain open) so a final adjustment can be made. With retrospective rating plans, each party bears its unique risk: the insured is transferring or externally financing the risk that the claims will be settled for more than agreed amount (its future retrospective premium adjustments would be greater) and the insurance carrier is risking that it can settle the claims for less than the estimate and make an additional underwriting profit on known and reported claims.

Types of Retrospective Rating Plans

Regardless of the type of retrospective rating plans, the retrospective rating formula is the same for all. The types are differentiated not by formula but by the source of the variables used in the formula or by the premium payment methods.

Loss Options

The type of loss is the primary independent variable used in the retrospective rating formula. Retrospectively rated plans can be based upon paid losses or incurred losses.

In a paid loss retrospective plan, only losses the insurer has paid are used in the periodic premium adjustments. Also, the initial outlay of premium is less, as only the expense components are included in the deposit premium. With respect to cash flow, this approach tends to defer the payment of funds until later on liability policies, as liability claims generally are not paid quickly. Thus, the insured retains the use of the funds longer. However, because claims are occurring, resulting in the obligation to pay claims in the future, the insurance carrier usually will require collateral, from which to pay claims, and the up-front payment of the full amount of anticipated premium taxes.

In an incurred loss retrospective plan, the projected or anticipated losses, calculated at their trended and developed ultimate value, are used to determine the estimated final retrospective premium, and the deposit premium is based on that ultimate value. The initial outlay of funds will be greater, but no escrow or collateral is required (generally, since the insurance carrier can cancel the program quickly if an adjustment is not paid on a prompt basis. Remember, the carrier has collected the projected ultimate value of claims up front).

Note: specific examples of both options will follow the explanation of the retrospective rating formula.

Premium Payment Option

Since the incurred loss retrospective rating plan has immediate cash flow disadvantages over a paid loss retrospective rating plan, some portion of the cash flow advantage can be recovered through a deposit premium payment option, a deferred premium.

In a deferred premium plan, the insurance carrier agrees that the premium payment will be made on an installment basis, with a deposit paid up front and installments payments continuing over the entire policy term, or perhaps even later. This provides another small cash flow benefit.

Tabular Plans

Retrospective rating tabular plans (using tables A, B, C, D, and strangely, J) are generally used, when available, for smaller retrospective programs. Instead of being negotiated between underwriters and an individual insured, the expense factors and limitation factors are fixed and applicable to all affected insureds. Since the premium is determined by a table (thus the name tabular plans) or schedule, these plans resemble guaranteed cost programs. Consequently, these plans are not very flexible. However, because the underlying rates will be modified retrospectively as losses develop, as under other retrospective plans, they do provide loss sensitivity.

Retrospective Rating Terminology

We include the following definitions here because retrospective rating plans have accumulated some peculiar terms, including the special application of common terms to retrospective rating programs.

Standard Premium – In a retrospective rating plan, the standard premium is the premium determined on the basis of authorized rates, any applicable experience rating modification, and loss constants and minimum premiums where applicable. However, premium discounts and expense constants are not included in the calculation of the policy rates. The standard premium is calculated in the usual manner, with the policy rate multiplied by the projected exposure base.

Basic Premium – The basic premium, commonly known as the "insurance charge," is usually a percentage of the standard premium, often determined by multiplying the standard premium by a basic premium factor. The basic premium factor is intended to provide for insurance carrier expenses, including loss control and commission, profit, contingencies, and an adjustment for limiting the retrospective premium to an amount between the minimum and the maximum retrospective premiums.

Loss Conversion Factor – The loss conversion factor is designed to modify the retrospective rating formula to allow for claim adjustment expenses and the cost of the insurer's (or third party administrator's) claim services. The loss conversion factor (LCF) is applied to any losses that are covered by the retrospective rating plan.

Tax Multiplier – The tax multiplier is a factor applied in the retrospective rating formula to cover licenses, fees, assessments, and premium taxes the insurance carrier must pay on the premium it collects. It may also include a charge whereby the insurance carrier helps to subsidize the applicable assigned risk or involuntary insurance market. As the last step in the retrospective rating formula, the tax multiplier is applied to all other charges and premium components.

Non-Subject or Excess Premium – The retrospective plan may include exposures that are not intended to be a part of a loss sensitive rating formula. There are two types of exposures that are not intended to be included in the retrospective rating plan. For example, in a retrospective rating plan, the non-subject premium may purchase excess insurance for losses over the intended loss limits (as opposed to insurance in excess of primary insurance or a self-insured retention).

Also, occasionally, the insured wants all coverages to be included on one policy, but state regulations or economics dictate that the exposure in one jurisdiction cannot be included in the retrospective rating plan. The "non-subject" premium would be charged to those exposures not intended to be included in the loss sensitive portion of the plan. For example, if state X does not permit retrospective rating for workers compensation and there is a single employee in state Y (the economics are against the loss sensitive rating), exposures for states X and Y could be included on the underlying insurance policy but not subject to retrospective rating.

The expression "non-subject" refers to the fact that the premium is a guaranteed cost and not adjustable based on losses. It will be included in the deposit premium, subject to premium audit and shown as a constant charge on all retrospective premium adjustment worksheets.

Maximum Premium and Minimum Premium – Maximum and minimum premiums are computed as a percentage of the standard premium using maximum and minimum factors negotiated with the underwriter. These premiums represent the greatest amount and least amount of premium to be paid by the insured, subject to the retrospective rating plan.

It has the effect of placing dollar limitations on the financial responsibility of the insured. Once the maximum retrospective premium has been paid, all additional losses are the responsibility of the insurer, subject to the limit of liability of the insurance policies.

The excess loss premium may be included in the maximum or in addition to the maximum, depending on the retrospective agreement. If the losses and other charges, when multiplied by the tax multiplier, do not reach the minimum premium, the insured does not receive any return premium, as the minimum premium is the floor.

Occasionally an insurer will compute the retrospective formula in reverse, using the maximum or minimum premium as the independent variable, and solve for the amount of losses that are contained within the minimum or maximum premiums. For example, the insurer might view the retrospective rating program as being effective between $250,000 of losses (the amount of losses included in the computation that exactly equals the minimum premium) and $1,250,000 of losses (the maximum amount of losses included in the computation before the maximum premium is reached and the financial responsibility for losses is transferred to the insurance carrier entirely). This range represents the greatest financial opportunity for the insured to prevent losses. Using this example, the insured, in theory, has no financial incentive to reduce losses below $250,000 or above $1,250,000. In practice, if it appears losses will not reach the minimum level or will exceed the maximum level, some insureds may decide to abandon further expensive loss control, as the policy in effect reverts to a guaranteed cost policy at either of those points.

The Retrospective Rating Formula

As complicated as the preceding explanations may seem, the retrospective rating formula consists of a series of simple algebraic steps:

1. Manual Premium × Applicable Experience Modifiers and Charges × Projected Exposure Units = Standard Premium

2. Standard Premium × Basic Factor = Basic Premium

3. [Basic Premium + (Losses × Loss Conversion Factor)] × Tax Multiplier + Non-Subject Premium = Indicated Retrospective Premium

4. Standard Premium × Minimum Factor = Minimum Premium

5. Standard Premium × Maximum Factor = Maximum Premium

The standard premium is subject to audit on actual exposure units at the end of the policy period, and all premiums are recomputed based on the audited standard premium (unless terms and conditions within the policy's retrospective rating endorsement state otherwise). Thus, the minimum and maximum premiums are generally recalculated at audit.

Because this is a loss-sensitive plan, the indicated retrospective premium is recalculated at the retrospective periods stated in the endorsement, based on the interim development of losses, with a return premium paid to the insured if losses are less than projected and an additional premium paid to the insurance carrier if losses are greater than projected.

In actual operation, because of lower than expected exposure units and the nature of developing losses, the insured might see a return premium from audit six months after expiration, a return premium twelve months after expiration for the first retro adjustment, followed by an additional premium for the second retro adjustment, with a third retro adjustment generating another return premium and a fourth requiring yet another additional premium.

This back-and-forth transfer of funds can create confusion and distrust among unsophisticated (and even among astute) insureds, particularly when one keeps in mind that these five transactions occur for only one policy term. The second year of the retrospective rating program would generate its own audit adjustment and subsequent annual adjustments, as would the third and fourth, and so on. In terms of the loss triangulation process, the audit and retro adjustment would similarly complete a triangulation pattern, with the oldest year having the most adjustments, followed by one fewer for each intervening year. After five continuing years, five retro policies would give rise to 6+5+4+3+2 adjustments, 20 in total. This process will continue as long as the retrospective rating plan is continued and as long as claims remain open.

In practice, most insurance carriers are willing to negotiate a final settlement after five or so years, when nearly all claims are reported and valued, but at least one major insurance carrier will not finalize any retrospectives until absolutely every claim is closed.

Examples of retrospective rating plans and their comparisons will follow at the end of the chapter.

Mechanics

In reality, there is no specific "retrospectively rated insurance policy." The underlying insurance policy is, for all practical purposes, a guaranteed cost policy that has been endorsed with a retrospective rating premium calculation endorsement. Thus, the retrospective rating plan is a typical or common insurance policy with all of the normal terms and conditions, perils and exclusions, limitations and restrictions, with one additional quirk: the Retrospective Rating Premium Calculation Endorsement.

The agreement to provide collateral or security is not attached to the insurance policy, but is a corollary document evidencing a contract between the insurance carrier and the insured with respect to reimbursement for losses. (This security arrangement is also found in a large deductible program.)

The retention can vary greatly from plan to plan, and both parties affect the amount of retention. The insured must select a retention that meets its risk taking attitude and ability; the insurance carrier will offer retentions according to the maximum and minimum premiums and per occurrence loss limits within its comfort zone (its risk taking attitude and ability).

Similarly, the range of ultimate premiums can vary greatly from plan to plan. First, the tabular plans are intended to address the smaller sized accounts that desire loss sensitivity, but cannot justify the risk of having a much greater exposure. Also, a narrow range of minimum and maximum premiums defines a relatively certain total premium for both insurance carrier and insured, while a wide range of minimum-maximum generates greater potential variance and uncertainty.

The degree of loss sensitivity can also vary greatly. If the maximum premium is high, there is a greater degree of loss sensitivity. Also, if there is no per occurrence loss limitation, loss sensitivity increases. If there is a low per occurrence loss limitation or the minimum-maximum range is narrow, there is less loss sensitivity.

While a retrospective rating plan is obviously intended to be a cash flow plan, the effect of the cash flows can actually be worse than many other financing mechanisms, including guaranteed cost. Options such as a paid loss plan and depressed or deferred premium pay-in privileges can ameliorate some of the adverse cash flow potential.

Last, the issue of tax deductibility is complex. Premiums that are paid and unrecoverable (e.g., the non-subject portion and the minimum premium) are tax deductible when paid or when the obligation to pay occurs under either cash or accrual accounting.

However, the deductibility of losses creates the challenge for the tax manager and risk manager. Generally, losses are tax deductible to the insured only when paid. Under an incurred loss retrospective plan, premiums are paid to the insurance carrier when the carrier bills the insured, but following the economic performance test, that portion of the premium related to the actual loss is not deductible until the loss is paid. The Internal Revenue Code has specific provisions to address such payments.

In a paid loss retrospective rating plan, the tax treatment is far simpler: the premium is not billed until the losses are paid, so the premium is deductible because the losses were paid.

Advice of tax counsel is critical with a retrospective rating plan, particularly if the plan is an incurred loss plan.

Advantages

A retrospective rating plan can be the least expensive option for an organization, as the premium is minimal if losses are below a certain level, only paying for insurance carrier-provided services of underwriting and other acquisition expenses, loss control, and general claims services, plus tax premium taxes and insurance carrier profit loadings.

Retrospective rating plans are widely available and offered by many insurance carriers. After all, with predictable losses, effective loss control and claims management programs, and properly set loss limits and maximum premiums, the insurance carrier is virtually guaranteed a profit, a challenge far harder to accomplish in a guaranteed cost plan.

Through the use of tabular plans for smaller organizations, and negotiable terms and conditions for larger retrospective rating plans, there is a great deal of plan flexibility available to insureds.

The high degree of loss sensitivity can easily create a strong incentive for loss control, and the results of effective loss control are quickly translated into excellent cash flow possibilities and reductions in the overall cost of risk. For an organization with a troubling past history of losses, the organization can take immediate advantage of a turn-around in that loss experience by proper timing of retrospective rating plan implementation.

Disadvantages

A retrospective rating plan can be the most expensive option if loss experience deteriorates during the retrospective rating period. Also, if the alternatives to other programs are limited or the insurance market limits the options available in a retrospective rating plan (such as high minimum premiums and low per occurrence limitations), the cost of risk can be higher than other options. Sometimes, an insurance carrier or agent/broker uses a retrospective rating plan as a pricing weapon. For example, if an organization is experiencing difficulties with a large deductible plan that requires a sizable escrow account, the initial appearance of an incurred loss retrospective rating plan looks like a significant improvement.

With a high degree of loss sensitivity comes the disadvantage of fluctuations in the cost of risk. Risk managers, financial managers, and executives like predictability, and fluctuations in a significant cost item can create budgeting difficulties.

When a retrospective rating plan requires collateral, the organization will incur additional costs to secure collateral as well as limit its options and pricing for other operational and investing/borrowing opportunities. Further, the amount of collateral may stack or increase as additional years of loss experience enter into the retrospective rating period. Committing credit and cash flow to an expensive retrospective rating plan may hamper other activities of the organization, resulting in less than desirable results.

Management of claims becomes critical, as losses quickly and directly impact premium payments. A common criticism of a retrospective rating plan is that the insurance carrier is indifferent to claims management, as the carrier knows it will recover its claim payouts in retrospective premium adjustments while still guaranteeing its profit margin. Insurance carriers may be reluctant to permit a third-party administrator to handle claims.

And last, and probably the most important practical disadvantage, is the general lack of understanding of how retrospective rating premium adjustments work. Many insurance and risk management professionals do not commonly encounter retrospective rating programs and are simply unfamiliar with their operation.

Consider this scenario where the insured opted to establish a retrospective rating plan in 1999 and eventually terminated it at the end of the 2006 policy term. Counting audits and retrospective adjustments (assuming all claims are settled in the fifth year), there have been 38 different adjustments. Over an eight-year period many things have changed: it is likely the original underwriter has left the insurance carrier; the account handler at the broker has changed (or the broker itself has changed hands); and the original risk manager may have even retired. No one remembers the reasons and objectives of the plan, and even if most of the documents were retained, no one remembers the details of how the plan was intended to work.

Self-Funding Approaches (SIR plans)

Self-funding approaches, or self-insured retention (SIR) plans, as they are commonly known, move the level of loss sensitivity to the highest level possible for an organization. There are several variations of the SIR approach, including the ultimate in complexity, a captive insurance company. There are two common types of SIR plans, qualified and non-qualified. These plans can be either fully self-funded or have excess insurance coverage in place, both per occurrence and aggregate, for catastrophic losses. Further, these plans can address a single exposure, such as workers compensation, or multiple lines (e.g., workers compensation, general liability, employer's liability, automobile liability, automobile physical damage, etc) covered within a single self-insured plan. These plans represent the ultimate in flexibility.

In all such plans, the term "self insurance" is somewhat of a misnomer from a technical standpoint. The term "insurance" implies a social mechanism for sharing risk through the collection of exposures into a pool with premium contributions from all participants and payment of losses from the collected premiums. Yet self-insurance is an action taken by an individual organization, hardly a collection of exposures from a number of participants, and the losses are paid (or internally financed) only by the organization suffering the losses. There is no risk sharing in self-insurance. The term, however imprecise, remains in common usage.

General Mechanics of Self-Insurance

For practical matters, self-insurance means an organization's management has decided to retain some layer of primary coverage or risk financing and to maintain some degree of control over the claims process. Also, the organization usually purchases some sort of excess coverage (although not necessarily). Services such as loss control or claims management may be provided by outside vendors or by the organization's staff members.

When frequency and severity of losses are predictable, self-insurance is always the most cost-effective manner of handing exposures, and reductions in the cost of risk will be significant. Remember, if losses are predictable to the insured, they are predictable to the insurance carrier. The premium charged by an underwriter will cover those losses, plus insurance carrier expenses, including premium taxes and assessments (on average, 5%) and profit loadings (another 5%) as well as the charge for services the organization does not need or desire.

Qualified Self-Insurance – Mechanics

Qualified self insurance is a mechanism for self-funding an exposure that is subject to state regulation, such as workers compensation or automobile liability. The state has an interest in regulating these lines of insurance as a means of protecting the general public, just as the state has taken on the responsibility to the general public for assuring that injured workers are provided for and minimum financial responsibility is maintained by motor vehicle operators. With state oversight of a self-insured organization, the victims of industrial accidents and illnesses and of motor vehicle accidents will receive the same benefits they would get from a traditional insurance carrier who is regulated by the state with respect to solvency and conduct.

For qualified self-insurance plans, regulators generally require three important filings. First, the plan must have a written actuarial opinion as to the expected losses and current valuation of open reserves. The self-insured organization must retain the services of a qualified actuary to perform this analysis. Second, the self-insured organization must complete and file audited financial reports establishing its financial viability and solvency on an annual basis, along with other informational applications and reports. Last, most regulatory bodies require each self-insured organization to file a surety bond as collateral, and do not permit other, less expensive forms of collateral or security that might be acceptable to an insurance carrier for a large deductible or retrospective plan.

Advantages

When losses are predictable with respect to both frequency and severity, self-insurance will be the lowest cost alternative to other treatment methods. At a minimum, the organization will save an amount equal to the profit and contingency loadings of an insurance carrier and premium taxes, generally at least a 10% savings, especially when taking into account the unbundling of other insurer services.

The self-insured organization maintains a high degree of control over claims management, subject to the constraints of the regulatory bodies and applicable statutes. Further, loss control efforts that result in a reduction in frequency and mitigation of severity can be pinpointed to address specific needs and are immediately recognized and rewarded.

Last, the self-insured organization is insulated from the adverse loss experience of other organizations that might be sharing their risk in any other traditional insurance program or pooling arrangement.

Disadvantages

If losses are not controlled through reductions in frequency or severity, the financial punishment is quick and direct. Hence, effective loss control efforts are critical to the successful operation of a self-insurance plan.

While regulators may be satisfied with a qualified self-insured organization, third parties wishing to have certificates of insurance or other proof of financial capabilities are generally apprehensive of any self-insured program, even if it is a qualified plan. Contracts between two entities, such as a construction contract, frequently address, restrict, or even prohibit the use of self-insurance programs to satisfy indemnification requirements.

As in any situation requiring collateral or security, the self-insured organization will incur the additional costs of a surety bond and will encounter restrictions of its cash flow and borrowing abilities. The principal sum of the surety bond is determined by the regulatory body.

An important drawback for privately held organizations is the disclosure of financial information required by regulatory bodies. Most jurisdictions have freedom of information acts, and thus the private financial information and ownership may become public knowledge.

Non-Qualified Self-Insurance

Non-qualified Self-Insurance plans, often referred to generically as SIR plans, are used whenever qualification by a regulatory body is not required. Common applications include general liability and products liability exposures, as well as professional liability lines such as medical malpractice. These plans are often used in lieu of deductible programs to retain higher levels of risk than the excess-of-deductible insurance market is willing to provide at an appropriate premium.

The mechanics of the SIR plan are the same as under a qualified self-insurance program, except there is no reporting requirement, actuarial opinion, or surety bond in favor of a regulatory body.

SIR plans can be structured to assume virtually all losses in the working layer (i.e., limit where losses are expected), particularly when the frequency and severity of losses are very predictable. Combinations of general liability, fronted automobile liability and workers compensation exposures (the self-insured organization acts as a reinsurer), employers liability, and other miscellaneous lines are possible with no per occurrence or aggregate stop- loss arrangement. However, the organization may choose to purchase aggregate stop-loss coverage for some or all lines, depending upon cost and availability in the insurance marketplace.

Advantages

Naturally, a non-qualified self-insurance plan preserves the same advantages as a qualified self-insurance plan, with a few additional advantages unique to SIR plans.

Collateral is a matter between an excess insurance carrier and the self-insured organization and is thus subject to negotiation, not statutory control. Collateral or security options are flexible and subject to negotiation.

Claims handling responsibilities in an SIR plan are vested solely with the self-insured organization or its designated third-party administrator. The self-insured organization can elect to use its own in-house staff to administer claims, and in doing so, maintains the ultimate level of control over claims.

Disadvantages

Any excess insurance carriers will provide few, if any, services, so loss prevention becomes the sole responsibility of the self-insured organization.

Unlike a deductible plan, the excess insurance carrier is not obligated to pay (in effect pre-fund) any claims beneath the SIR. The self-insured organization cannot generate any cash flow from having another party pay the initial expenses of a claim.

Probably the most serious disadvantage arises out of the potential for claims reporting and claim coordination issues.

Most excess insurance policies have terms and conditions that require prompt ("immediate") reporting of claims that fit within a described schedule of injuries (e.g., dismemberment, disfigurement, death), but at the initial report and even into the claim investigation, these kinds of facts may not be known. Also, a common condition under an excess policy requires prompt reporting of any claim likely to exceed a given threshold. At the initial report and investigation, however, a claim may appear to be routine, but later, a multi-million dollar legal demand is made and suit filed. This may result in a declination of coverage or reservation of rights (company "reserves" its right to deny coverage at a later date based on the terms of the policy) for late reporting of claims. The comprehensive understanding of policy terms and conditions and the coordination between excess carriers and third-party administrators is critical. If the self-insured organization has elected to handle claims internally, the organization must possess a high degree of sophisticated claims handling capabilities.

All-Lines Aggregate Program

With at least two lines of coverage, an all-lines aggregate program often combines a qualified workers compensation and/or automobile liability self-insured program with non-qualified self-insurance.

Mechanics

An all-lines aggregate program combines at least two lines of coverage into one program. Each line has its own retention, and those retentions may be different. Similarly, each line can have its own specific limit of excess insurance coverage applying to that line. In addition, higher excess insurance limits or umbrella coverage can be placed above the all-lines aggregate specific excess insurance. These limits provide protection from catastrophic per occurrence claims. To protect against a catastrophic aggregate claims scenario, aggregate excess insurance can be purchased with an attachment set at a multiple of the projected losses or loss pick.

Exhibit 10.1: All-Lines Aggregate Program

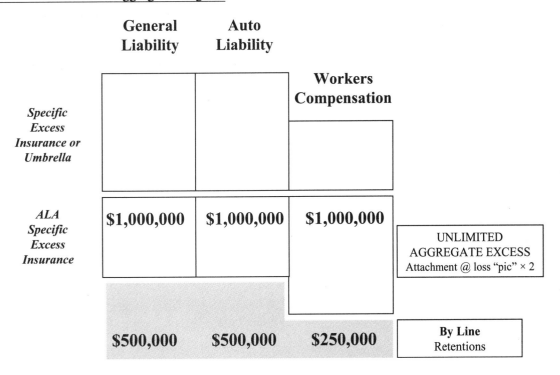

The advantages and disadvantages of an all-lines aggregate program are essentially the same as those of any self-insured retention program, qualified or non-qualified, with the additional advantage that frictional costs (the costs associated with maintaining separate programs) may be reduced. Further, there is some degree of internal risk sharing, because adverse loss experience in one line may be offset by improved loss experience in another line.

Multiple-Year Single-Limit Programs

A multiple-year single-limit program is described accurately by its name. It is a single insurance policy providing multiple years of coverage with a single policy aggregate limit. This type of program is most useful for organizations that have very low loss frequency with a potential severity exposure.

Mechanics

A multiple-year single-limit policy commonly has a term of at least three years, and generally five years or more, with one or more limits applying per occurrence and an aggregate limit of coverage applying to the entire policy term. The premium for the multiple years of coverage is calculated and spread over the policy term, generally by install-ment billings. Excess coverage can be purchased for part or all of the entire policy term, and because of the cash flow opportunities to the excess insurance carrier, the premium for that excess coverage is steeply discounted.

If there are no losses, the whole program usually can be renegotiated and rewritten annually, moving the availability of the aggregate policy limit further into the future time horizon. To provide additional protection from losses, a guaranteed reinstatement provision and reinstatement charge can be negotiated in the initial program.

Exhibit10.2: Multi-Year Single-Limit Policy

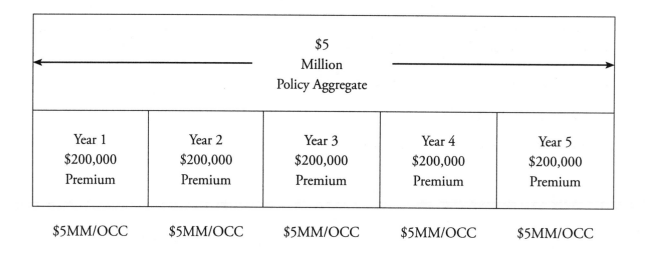

Advantages

The primary advantage of this type of financing arrangement is a cost savings. The frictional costs of purchasing and maintaining separate coverages, even those in an all-lines aggregate program, are further reduced. A corollary benefit is the advantage of improved budgeting capabilities, as "annual" premiums are fixed over an extended policy term. In addition, cash flow is enhanced because of the extension of the premium payment over multiple years.

Disadvantages

The program may not be available in the insurance marketplace, because of fear that expected loss frequencies do not materialize. Loss data will need to be long-term and extremely credible.

Comparison of Loss Sensitive Financing Options – A Case Study

The ACME Corporation wishes to fully examine the range of options available for their upcoming workers compensation renewal. ACME has received the following five loss-sensitive risk financing options. As risk manager for ACME, use the following calculations to compare the options based on using the net present value method, and select your desired program.

General Information:

1. Total Expected Losses: $750,000.

2. Standard Premium: $1,200,000. Assume all premiums are payable at inception.

3. Expected Losses will be limited or "capped" at $250,000/occurrence for a total of $680,000.

4. Allocated Loss Adjustment Expense and Unallocated Loss Adjustment Expense total 10%.

5. The CFO indicates ACME's weighted average cost of capital is 10%, so the risk manager decides to use a 10% discount rate, for a two-year factor of .826.

6. Assume all losses, on average, are paid out 100% by the end of two years.

7. Assume premium taxes are 10%.

8. Assume all insurance charges and factors are as given in the analysis.

Exhibit 10.3: Case Study – Large Deductible ($250,000)

Standard Premium	$ 1,200,000
(60%) Deductible Credit	$ 720,000
Net Premium	$ 480,000
Expected (capped) Losses	$ 680,000
ALAE and ULAE	$ 68,000
Total Outflow[1]	$ 1,228,000

(1) $480,000 + $680,000 + $68,000 = $1,228,000

Cash Flow

Initial Outflows	
Net Premium	$ 480,000
NPV of Losses[1]	$ 562,000
NPV of ALAE & ULAE[2]	$ 56,000
NPV of Total Outflows	$ 1,098,000

(1) $680,000 × .826 = $562,000

(2) $68,000 × .826 = $56,000

Exhibit 10.4: Case Study – Retrospective Rating Program (Comparing Incurred Loss Retrospective (ILR) with Paid Loss Retrospective (PLR))

	ILR		PLR
Deposit(1)	$ 1,200,000		$ 420,000
Excess Premium(2)	$ 50,000		$ 50,000
Basic	$ 240,000		$ 240,000
Losses(3)	$ 680,000		$ 680,000
LCF (10%)	$ 68,000		$ 68,000
Tax Estimate (10%)			$ 120,000
Ultimate (final) Retro Adjustment(4)	$ 1,087,000		$ 1,087,000
Letter of Credit			$ 20,000
Escrow (Losses)			$ 60,000
Cash Flows			
Initial Outflows			
Deposit (for ILR)	$ 1,200,000		
Basic + Taxes (for PLR)			$ 360,000
Letter of Credit			$ 20,000
Loss Escrow			$ 60,000
Excess Premium	$ 50,000		$ 50,000
Total Initial Outflows	$ 1,250,000		$ 490,000
(Inflow) Outflow at Retro Adjustment(5)	$ (113,000)		$ 667,000
Total Outflow	**$ 1,137,000**		**$ 1,157,000**
Total Initial Outflows (repeated from above)	$ 1,250,000		$ 490,000
NPV of Retro Adjustment(6)	$ (93,000)		$ 551,000
NPV of Total Outflows	**$ 1,157,000**		**$ 1,041,000**

Note: Min and max are the same for both ILR and PLR.

(1) ILR Deposit = Standard Premium = $1,200,000

PLR Deposit = Basic + Tax Estimate + Escrow = $240,000 + $120,000 + $60,000 = $420,000

(2) Excess premium for capping losses at $680,000

(3) Losses capped at $680,000

(4) Ult. Retro Adj. =   (Basic + (Losses × LCF)) × Tax Estimate =

($240,000 + ($680,000 × 1.10)) × 1.10 =

($240,000 + $748,000) × 1.10 =

$988,000 × 1.10 = $1,087,000

(5) Retro Adjustment less Deposit

ILR Retro Adjustment = $1,087,000- $1,200,000 = ($113,000)

PLR Retro Adjustment = $1,087,000- $420,000 = $667,000

(6) ILR = ($113,000) × .826 = ($93,000)

PLR = $667,000 × .826 = $551,000

Exhibit 10.5: Case Study – Qualified Self Insurance

Excess Premium	$ 250,000
(Loss limit $250,000/occurrence, $2,000,000 aggregate)	
Bond, Letters of Credit, etc.	$ 20,000
Administrative Costs* (See Note)	$ 40,000
Losses	$ 680,000
LAE (10%)	$ 68,000
Taxes & Loads (10% SIM Tax, GTY Fund)	$ 120,000
Outflows	$ 1,178,000

Cash Flows

Initial Outflows	
Excess Premium	$ 250,000
Bond, Letters of Credit, etc.	$ 20,000
Taxes & Loads	$ 120,000
NPV of Administrative Costs[1]	$ 36,000
NPV of Losses[2]	$ 562,000
NPV of LAE[3]	$ 56,000
NPV of Total Outflows	$ 1,044,000

Note: Underestimates start up costs.
$40,000 × .909 = $36,000
$680,000 × .826 = $562,000
$68,000 × .826 = $56,000

Exhibit 10.6: Case Study – Comparisons

	Gross Outflow	NPV	Comments
Large Deductibles	$ 1,228,000	$ 1,098,000	Very loss sensitive (if no aggregate)
ILR	$ 1,137,000	$ 1,157,000	Max & Min apply
PLR	$ 1,157,000	$ 1,041,000	Max & Min apply
Qualified Self Insurance	$ 1,178,000	$ 1,044,000	Very loss sensitive, if stop loss attachment point is high; watch for start up costs and administrative costs

Which Program would be Preferred?

With respect to the Net Present Value analysis, Qualified Self-Funding, followed by a Large Deductible plan, would have the lowest net present value. With respect to the "best" downside protection (when loss experience deteriorated severely), a retrospective plan would be preferred because of the maximum premium, and a large deductible plan would be the best if a stop loss or aggregate loss limitation is in place. With respect to the "best" upside opportunity (better than expected loss experience), Qualified Self-Funding or a retrospective plan, assuming the minimum equals the basic premium, would be preferred.

Other factors to be considered in the decision include the mechanics of the program, such as a requirement for collateral or security, the need for certificates of insurance, the availability of coverage in the insurance marketplace. Another concern is the mix of fixed and variable costs. Fixed costs provide certainty and an improved ability to budget, but are not responsive in the short run to loss control efforts. Variable costs offer the possibility of cost savings but are more challenging to budget. The organization's financial position and its position in the marketplace (e.g., start-up, emerging, mature, declining) will affect the desirability of the mix of fixed and variable costs.

A third factor becomes the source and quality of claims and loss control services and their related expenses. Yet another issue is the degree of program flexibility or possible customization. Organizations with unusual exposures or operations sometimes require unusual risk management program structures, and flexible, custom programs are highly desirable. Last, other factors are the related issues of accounting and tax management.

Exhibit 10.7: Transfer Options and Criteria for Comparison

	Type of Program	Degree of Retention	Cash Flow Advantages	Loss Sensitive
1.	Guaranteed Cost, Full Insurance	None	Generally No	No
2.	Dividends	None	No	Yes
3.	Small Deductibles	Low	Some	Some
4.	Large Deductibles	Moderate to High	Yes	Yes
5.	Incurred Loss Retrospectively Rated Plan	Varies	Some Possible	Yes
6.	Paid Loss Retrospectively Rated Plan	Varies	Yes	Yes
7.	Self-funding (SIR)	High	Yes	Yes
8.	Rent-a-Captive and Single-parent Captives	Varies	Varies	Yes
9.	Group Programs	Varies	Varies	Varies

The answer of which type of program is "best" for ACME is the universal risk management answer: it depends.

Chapter 11

Alternative Financing Options

This chapter focuses on some opportunities for handling risk in more creative ways. Besides the usual rational of organizations who desire autonomy in financing risk, as well as tax shelters, there is historic need and historic precedent for alternatives to traditional insurance or insurance products provided by traditional insurance carriers.

A Little History

The insurance industry has always been subject to hard-market and soft-market cycles of profitability and loss, of high and low premiums, of availability of coverage and a dearth of coverage, observed in the United States as early as the Civil War era. During the late 1970s and early 1980s, however, the traditional insurance carriers learned a harsh and expensive lesson. The wild market swings suddenly created a market crisis for products liability coverage availability, and many organizations were simply unable to purchase any coverage at any price, or they could only purchase pitiful amounts of coverage at exorbitant premiums.

In response to this market meltdown, Congress passed the Product Liability Risk Retention Act of 1981, permitting the creation of alternative risk financing mechanisms to correct the insurance market failure. In short, organizations could create their own insurance companies (captives) to offer the coverage that the broader, traditional insurance market could not or would not offer. A substantial portion of the casualty insurance market, as measured by premium volume, was forced into this alternative market mechanism. When the traditional insurance industry returned from its down cycle and began to pursue the products liability business they had disdained only a few years before, they learned a hard lesson: the product liability premiums did not return to the traditional market. The alternative market, a market controlled by its insureds and not by insurance companies, had proved its viability and sustainability.

Historically, this was not the first time this had happened, as years ago the same lack of availability and high premiums led to the creation of many mutual insurance companies. Nor was the 1981 crisis the last. Another liability crisis loomed in the middle of the decade, and in 1986 Congress amended the Product Liability Risk Retention Act to expand its provisions to include all lines of casualty insurance except workers compensation coverage. Again, premium fled the traditional market to newly formed alternatives, and once again, when the traditional insurance market sought to recover the premium, very little returned.

In the following sections we will examine the three major types of non-traditional risk financing techniques available to insureds who do not wish to operate in the traditional insurance market: pools, captive insurance companies, and finite risk contracts.

Risk Pooling

Conceptually, all insurance products are examples of pooling arrangements, as insurance is a risk financing arrangement designed to manage loss exposures of many by collecting those exposures into a pool of exposures so risk can be shared.

In a risk pooling arrangement, however, the loss exposures included are limited to those who have elected to join together to form a much smaller pool for the purpose of sharing their risks with others much like themselves. Though the concept of insurance is to gather a large group of homogenous exposure units, the typical insurance carrier pooling arrangement collects many insureds that are very dissimilar in operations, locations, size, financial ability, attitudes regarding loss prevention, and ownership, among other variables, for the purpose of making a profit for the owners of the insurance carrier.

Risk pooling is an option for an organization that is unable to legally or feasibly self-insure, but one that desires to gain more control over their loss exposures, their claims, and have an opportunity to gain financially by grouping together (pooling) with other similar businesses. For example, a group of small municipalities, counties or parishes, or other local governmental units may not be able to justify a large deductible plan or may be prohibited by statute from self-insuring, but the members of that group think their unique needs are not being adequately met by the traditional insurance market. As an alternative to that traditional coverage, those governmental bodies could form a pool to provide required or desired coverages.

A common line of coverage provided by pools is workers compensation coverage. Since this line of coverage is specifically excepted from the 1986 amendment to the Risk Retention Act, a manufacturer may join with similar manufacturers to "purchase" workers compensation coverage from a pool because that manufacturer cannot write the coverage in its captive insurance company and because statutes may bar specific treatments, such as a qualified self-insurance program. Many states have passed special legislation to permit pools and trusts (a similar device) to organize for the purpose of providing workers compensation coverage. Many times, a pool or trust will begin writing workers compensation, and if successful, expand the coverage to include other lines of insurance.

Mechanics

The mechanics of a pool are very dissimilar to the traditional insurance mechanism. The most striking difference is that the "insureds" collect themselves together to create the "insurance company" to protect and promote their own self-interests, rather than finding an insurance carrier created by someone else (for their self-interest), joining with others not of their choosing (and whom they do not know), and attempting to somehow protect their individual self-interests against everyone else.

A risk pool is not a separate legal entity, such as a corporation or partnership. Instead, it is an unincorporated association, a collective effort governed by a charter and by-laws, actually the collective alter ego of the members, and not a distinct organization.

Generally a pool is created by several similar organizations (e.g., county governments, small municipalities, machine products manufacturers, outfitters, sporting goods manufacturers, etc.) that feel the traditional insurance marketplace is not meeting their needs in terms of coverage, pricing, loss control, claims services, or other service areas. The organizations explore the possibility of joining together to create an alternative to the array of insurance mechanisms offered by the traditional insurance marketplace.

Once the feasibility of this is explored, the organizations may agree to "insure" or share in their loss exposures by combining contributions ("premiums") into a fund from which losses are paid. Exposures are underwritten, certificates of participation ("policies") are issued, equitable, fair, and adequate contributions are collected, required services are purchased, and losses are paid. Typically, the pool will purchase reinsurance or excess insurance, as well as third-party claims administration and loss control services.

Management of the pool commonly rests at two levels. The day-to-day management may be contracted out to others with expertise in underwriting, pricing, loss control, claims management, actuarial services, and accounting services. The participants form a board to provide strategic leadership and oversight management, which may also include entrance and exit rules for the pooling arrangement.

Pools generally rely upon a fixed-cost approach that resembles traditional guaranteed-cost insurance plans. Any excess "premiums" are retained for the future or refunded in the form of dividends to participants, as is done in an insurance dividend option. However, unlike insurance, the participants themselves can determine if a dividend is declared, and the size of the dividend, rather than waiting until a separate and distinct board of directors makes a dividend declaration.

The participants have greater control over selection of services and service vendors. Unlike the traditional approach, when an insured has little say over what loss control and claims management services are offered and even less control over who provides the services, the participants in a pool determine exactly what services they want, who provides the service, and how to maintain the quality of the services, including the right to terminate any vendors who are not meeting the participants' needs.

Similarly, the participants can create the type of "insurance" coverages they desire. Customization is not only possible; it is likely, as the participants formed themselves into a pool because the insurance marketplace was not meeting their needs. The only restraint upon the scope of coverage will be the limitation of reinsurance or excess insurance contracts; if those contracts will not provide similar coverage, the pool will have to bear the losses entirely on their own.

Participants face some accounting and tax issues in these programs. The pooling arrangement is not a true insurance transfer or external financing in the traditional sense, but rather more like a pre-funding of expected losses. As such, the IRS may not consider the "premium" to be tax-deductible when the obligation to pay is incurred or even when it is paid.

Advantages

There are several advantages to risk pooling, the first being cost stability and reduction. Insurance carrier loadings for profit, contingency, commission, and, in some cases, premium taxes, are eliminated. Since the pool managers either are the insureds or their designees, a pool with adequate excess funds can smooth out premium fluctuations, banking gains in good years to subsidize losses in bad years.

Because of the high degree of loss sensitivity, there is a heightened attention to loss control and claims management. Also, the ultimate control of underwriting by the participants gives the pool management the ability to design a rating plan that reflects the group's combined loss experience, insulating it from the loss experience of the broader insurance market. Related to that is the ability to design coverage forms to meet members' needs and to create loss control and claims management programs that are appropriate for the pool participants.

Last, as the pool matures and grows financially and experientially, the pool may increase the retention level under any purchased excess layers, eventually going to a fully self-insured format, or it may reduce or remove aggregate coverage, both of which increase the level of premium savings. Some successful risk pools convert to insurance companies, further increasing control and reducing costs.

Disadvantages

One of the most challenging disadvantages of a pool is inherent in the rational for its creation: risk sharing. The problems that pools face because of risk sharing can be monumental. For example, if one of the founding members develops a history of adverse loss experience because of inattention to loss control, the other participants may find it difficult to discipline or exclude the member from participation in the pool. If a key participant elects to withdraw, the financial or managerial viability of the pool may be threatened. If the industry of the participants becomes distressed and their economic position suffers, the pool may also suffer. In effect, the participants do not share only the pure risk that is the usual subject of insurance, but they also share economic risk, market risk, technological risk, social risk, legislative risk, and any other risks the participants in the industry face.

Another serious disadvantage of a pool is that the management of the "insurance company" typically is not composed of insurance professionals. For example, a pool of county governments has a management team consisting of elected public officials who may not be familiar with the unique operational characteristics of an insurance company and may not possess the necessary expertise to operate an insurance mechanism or to administer loss control and claims management. Related to the "amateur" status of the pool management is the failure to maintain adequate records.

Also, underwriting risk is a serious potential problem for a pool for two reasons. The first again hinges on the "amateur" status of management and its ability to select good pool members. The second is a subtle problem, for the pool usually exists because of dissatisfaction with the traditional insurance market. Potential participants will often seek out a pool as an option to reduce their costs when the traditional insurance market increases their premium because of their loss experience. Bad loss experience is cured by constant attention to loss control and good claims management, not by having a lower premium. Yet the pressure to expand membership and premium is always present. The age-old axiom of "the perfume of the premium overcomes the stench of the risk" applies to pools as much as it applies to traditional insurance.

An operational problem arises out of the nature of the participants. The board of directors of the pooling arrangement has the ultimate level of responsibility for the financial and operational success of the arrangement. This may require the board to take measures against a fellow participant or even a board member, if that organization is creating excessive losses or other financial and operational problems. In some cases, it may be the largest (and perhaps founding) participant; in others, it may be the most influential member. There is a great deal of social and political pressure on the pool management to keep the participants together while attempting to do what is in the best interest of the group. It is easy for the management group to lose its focus, particularly when operations are going well or going badly, and fail to maintain control over the operations, its finances, and its participants.

Normally, a traditional insured is concerned only about the financial status of the insurance carrier, and that is monitored by state insurance regulators and reported by financial rating agencies like A. M. Best and Standard & Poors. The traditional insured does not care about the financial status of fellow insureds (except the most extreme pessimist who might believe that their losses or failure to pay premiums will bankrupt his insurance carrier). However, in a pool, each participant has a vested interest in the financial health of the other participants.

The last, but absolutely most serious issue facing a risk pool is the legal concept of joint and several liability. Joint and several liability means that all members of the group are jointly liable (all are responsible for the obligations of any other member) and severally (or individually) liable (the so-called "last man standing" situation) for the total liabilities of the entire group. Put simply, if Thomas, Richard, and Henry form a pool, Thomas and Richard are responsible for Henry's obligations as well as their own, should Henry become unable to meet his obligations. Thomas is solely responsible for the entire obligations of Richard and Henry, as well as his own, if Richard and Henry are unable to meet their obligations.

Obviously, the most common source of joint and several liability problems arise out of the financial failure of the pool, when contributions are inadequate to fund losses that have occurred in the past and that continue to occur as participation declines. Like rats deserting a sinking ship, financially sound participants tend to withdraw from a financially troubled pool, and unless there is a clearly stated exit provision with penalties, the financial problems are exacerbated when financially sound participants leave, especially when those participants have better loss experience than the group in general. Also, it is difficult to attract new participants to replace departing ones or to bolster contributions when the pool is financially distressed.

Another source of joint and several liability problems is created by gaps in the structure of the pooling arrangement. For example, if total losses exceed the total of the maximum claim fund and the retained "profits" or "earnings" (technically, the excess of contributions over expenses), but are less than the attachment point of an aggregate excess insurance coverage, the participants must pay an assessment, or additional contribution of funds, to fund the gap. No participant ever wants to pay an assessment, as this indicates financial distress, a warning signal that is likely to drive current participants away (because the "premium" is no longer fixed, and may even increase more) and to keep new participants from entering into the pool. Many jurisdictions require pools to include an assessment feature; that is a critical consideration for the risk manager to investigate and ascertain.

The last source of joint and several liability exists because of the limits of the aggregate excess coverage. In a traditional insurance program, the insured is responsible for losses in excess of the limits of coverage that were purchased. In a pool, each participant is jointly and severally liable for every other insureds' losses that exceed the purchased aggregate excess coverage limits.

Captive Insurance Companies

Often regarded as the pinnacle of alternative financing options, a captive insurance company is an essentially simple concept. It is simply defined as a closely held insurance company whose insurance business is supplied by and controlled by its owners, and in which the insureds themselves are the beneficiaries. As such, and unlike a risk pool, a captive is a separate legal entity from its owners or insureds. The captive insurance company can fail financially, and the extent of the financial exposure to its owners is the loss of their investment. (Naturally, unpaid claims may become the responsibility of the insureds, but that is true even when the insolvent insurer is a traditional insurance company.)

A Brief History of Captives

The captive insurance company concept is not new and has been used in many different forms. For instance, during the late 1800s, a group of New England textile manufacturers formed an insurance company owned by the insureds themselves in response to the high fire insurance rates of the period. The company ultimately evolved into what is known as the Factory Mutual System, now the FM Global Insurance Company. Other notable captive insurers formed in the first half of the twentieth century included the Church Insurance Company (formed by the Episcopal Church in 1929) and Mahoning Insurance Company (established by Youngstown Sheet & Tube Company in 1935). Ocean marine insurers in the form of various clubs have used the captive concept for years. Protection and Indemnity (P&I) clubs such as the Steamship Mutual have been in existence in one form or another for centuries. A more recent example of a captive evolving into a global multi-line insurer is ACE. ACE was started in 1985 by several visionary investors responding to the lack of available insurer capacity for directors and officers liability and for higher limits of excess liability.

In spite of these early entries, captive insurers did not become prevalent until the 1950s. At the end of that decade, it is estimated that there were close to 100 in operation. The next 35 years witnessed explosive growth, and by 1999, about 4000 had been established. Annual written premiums are presently in the neighborhood of $23 billion, with an increase in written premiums of 150% occurring in fewer than the last 20 years. Currently, capital and surplus in captives are estimated at $45 billion.

Types of Captive Insurance Companies

The definition of captive shown above refers to the captive having "owners." As a separate legal entity, the captive must have owners of some sort, and the nature of the owner (or owners) is what determines the type of captive.

Single-Parent Captive

The single-parent captive is the simplest captive structure. Its owner is another business, generally a large corporation, and it exists solely to write the risks of its owner. While the captive will have its own board of directors, it is essentially under the complete control of the parent company as a wholly owned subsidiary.

Group Captive

A group captive is the opposite of the single-parent captive. It is owned by a group of non-related organizations that may be heterogeneous or homogeneous. The captive will write the risks of its owners.

Association Captive

An association captive is a type of group captive formed by an association to write the risks of its members. The captive could be owned by the association or by the member participants, but the distinction of the association captive is the required membership in the association.

Risk Retention Groups

A risk retention group is a formalized pool whose writings are limited to liability coverages for its owners/insureds and formed under the Risk Retention Act of 1986.

Agency Captive

An agency captive is a captive insurance company formed by an insurance agency or insurance brokerage firm to insure the risks of the agency's clients or to participant with an insurance company to provide coverage for a difficult risk.

Rent-a-Captive

A rent-a-captive is a captive insurance company, usually domiciled and licensed offshore, formed by an organization (insurance brokerage firm, reinsurer, insurance company, or other business enterprise) to write insurance for other organizations for a fee, which permits access to the underwriting facility (the "rent"). This is the most "non-captive" appearing captive, as traditional insurance companies are formed for the same reason. The primary point of differentiation is that the insureds typically consist of those large organizations that cannot quite justify the expense and effort of establishing their own captive(s), but desire to participate in this alternative marketplace.

Protected Cell Captive

A common feature found in some captives is the "protected cell" feature: separate, legally distinct portions or cells. Revenues, assets, and liabilities of each cell are segregated from all other cells. Thus, an organization can purchase or rent the cell but own only a small portion of the captive. This structure allows the organization to share the fixed costs of captive formation and management with others while protecting its underwriting activities to its own risks. It opens participation in the captive marketplace to organizations who could not otherwise justify the administrative expenses and effort.

Reasons to Form a Captive

Five important factors have encouraged organizations to seek risk funding alternatives, in the form of captives, to the traditional insurance marketplace.

Two factors are related, stemming from the natural business cycles in the insurance industry. First, captives provide solutions to coverage and limit availability problems, the lack of response by commercial insurers to meet the coverage needs of organizations. When losses mount in a particular class of risk or because of a particular peril, the insurance market tends to react in concert, canceling coverage or not accepting new applications for coverage, increasing retentions and deductibles, and reducing limits and the scope of coverage.

A second factor is pricing: premium inequity and the fluctuation and instability of premiums arising from the insurance market cycles. Since insurance carriers participate in a broad market (the essential sharing of risk that makes commercial insurance feasible), pricing decisions are made on a broad basis also, without much regard to the individual loss experience of an insured organization. The premium for a loss-free insured may increase as much as that of one with troubling losses. Conversely, when price competition returns, premiums plummet to levels to low to support expected losses. Extreme variation in pricing makes budgeting and planning challenging for organizations.

Third, a captive may improve insurance products and financing mechanisms for large organizations that require unique solutions. The insurance industry is based upon the coverage and service needs of the "average" insured. When the array of products and services provided by the commercial insurance carriers does not meet an organization's needs, a captive may be the answer.

The fourth reason is related to the above factor: a captive may provide flexibility in the breadth of coverage or limits required by an organization. Commercial insurance carriers are restrained by their regulatory filings and rating plans, and cannot economically justify the customization of their standardized policies and pricing methods for every twist and turn desired by a large organization. The unique regulation of captives, particularly Risk Retention Group captives and offshore captives, overcomes that inflexibility.

Fifth, some organizations view the conventional insurance transaction as lacking value. The concept of "added value" is generally misapplied or misunderstood, taken to mean added services or features that are unique or desired, when the true meaning is giving perception of a better value for the same price or the same value for a decrease in price. When an insurance carrier charges as much as 30% more than the premium necessary to pay highly predictable losses and fails to differentiate the value of its other services, the purchaser of the insurance is likely to feel the transaction lacked value. By forming a captive, the organization could have funded its highly predictable losses at a lower cost and purchased the services it desired while maintaining control.

A sixth, but "unofficial" reason that appears to influence captive formation is the cachet of having a captive, of being a financially sophisticated organization. Related to that is the appeal to some members of management of "vacationing" in exotic offshore locations on an expense account or being a "player" in the international world of reinsurance.

Mechanics of Captive Operation

Note: This section contains some comments meant as general guidelines for tax issues. Tax rules change and competent tax counsel should be obtained for legal opinions.

Many of the mechanical aspects of operating a captive are very similar to those of a commercial insurance carrier. However, a captive places the ultimate control over claims settlement philosophy and reserving practices in the hands of its owners (imagine what would happen if a traditional insurance carrier asked the stockholders to set claims settlement and reserving practices!). Similarly, the captive owners have control over investments made by the captive. In some jurisdictions, the regulations controlling acceptable investments for statutory reporting purposes are less restrictive for captives than for commercial insurance carriers.

Taxes

While a captive should never be formed for tax purposes (that benefit was eliminated nearly thirty years ago in a landmark case), there are nonetheless potential tax advantages available to a captive. Under stringent rules, the premiums paid to a captive might be tax-deductible to the owner/organization, but that is not the source of potential tax advantages.

A captive is technically an insurance company, and special tax regulations apply to insurance companies. First, small insurers (including captives) are tax-exempt under Section 501(c)15 of the Internal Revenue Code, if the stock company's gross receipts are less than $600,000 and more than 50% of their gross receipts is premium or if the mutual company's gross receipts are less than $150,000 and more than 35% is premium. For other "small" insurance companies, including captives, if net written premiums are less than $1,200,000, income tax is applied only to investment income, and not underwriting profit.

Second, under IRS regulations applicable to insurance companies, reserves are tax deductible when incurred as ordinary business expenses with respect to the captive, but only if the net written premium exceeds $1,200,000. Thus, the captive can manage its taxes (taxes can only be managed with respect to when they are paid, not avoided) by changing reserve amounts to affect its net underwriting profit and therefore net income. For example, if there is significant investment income, reserves could be increased to temporarily reduce underwriting profit to offset some of the investment gains, and vice versa.

Naturally, the above explanation is a simplification of very complex IRS rules and regulations, and should not be considered to be tax advice. Tax counsel must be consulted to determine taxability of captive insurance company issues and operations.

Profit Sharing

Another mechanic permits the owners of any insurance company (including the "owners" of a mutual insurance company, its policyholders) to share in the profits of the enterprise. The owners of a captive insurance company recapture investment income and underwriting profit arising from their premium contributions that would otherwise accrue to the owners (or stockholders) of a commercial insurance carrier. The captive owners share in the benefits of the cash flow that would normally be foregone when premiums are transferred to insurance carriers. However, a well-managed captive may be inclined to keep these excess funds to pay future losses.

Domicile

The last important mechanic is the domicile, or "home base" of the captive insurance company, the jurisdiction under whose laws the insurance company was originally formed and will be regulated.

To understand complex issues of domicile, the risk manager must be familiar with some arcane insurance language. The following definitions will help (adapted from What's Past is Prologue: A Tedious Brief History of Insurance, used with permission of the author, Richard G. Rudolph).

A domestic insurance company is one that is domiciled in a particular state. All domestic companies are admitted or permitted to operate in their state of domicile and are closely regulated in that state with respect to their financial condition and possibly with respect to what policy language or forms they use and what rates they charge, although there has been a trend in commercial consumerism that has loosened some of the traditional strictures on rates and forms in recent decades.

A foreign insurance company is not one domiciled in a foreign nation; it is another state's domiciled company, as an insurance company cannot be domiciled in more than one state.

An <u>alien insurer</u> is not one domiciled on Alpha Centari or Uranus, but only one domiciled in a foreign nation. Generally, alien insurers are not permitted to do business in the United States unless they provide a specified trust agreement and some sort of financial guarantee that they will not abscond with the premiums and leave unpaid losses. These financial guarantees often take the form of restricted deposits in banks that are part of the Federal Reserve System. Further, there may be federal excise taxes applied to the premiums of alien insurers. As if this were not confusing enough, it is possible for an alien insurer to be admitted or non-admitted and therefore permitted or authorized to operate as if it were a domestic insurer or a foreign insurer. The well-known Lloyd's of London organization is an alien insurer operating as a non-admitted carrier in most states and as an admitted insurer in Illinois.

An <u>admitted insurance company</u> is one that is licensed to operate in the state, and if that company is a foreign insurer, it is one licensed to operate as if it were a domestic insurer in exchange for agreeing to adhere to the state's statutes and administrative law governing insurance as if it were a domestic insurer.

A <u>non-admitted insurance company</u> is one that is not admitted to do business in a state, but instead can apply to be authorized to do business in the state. Non-admitted companies can be permitted to operate in states upon a filing to do business, but these companies are not as closely regulated with respect to financial state, policy language, and rates. The responsibility for financial scrutiny of these companies rests not with the regulators but the brokers who access these companies for their customers. In some states, the insurance market regulates what policy language is used and what rates are charged, and in others, the state insurance regulations require adherence to policy form filings and rate filings.

An <u>off-shore insurance company</u> is one that is domiciled outside the United States. By definition, all off-shore insurance companies are alien, in spite of ultimate ownership by a U.S. corporation.

On top of this fine kettle of financial fish is the so-called <u>alternative market</u> consisting largely of insurance subsidiaries of non-insurance corporations or insurance operations of cooperative associations loosely known as "captive" insurance companies. The key feature of a captive insurance company is that it is a corporation, a separate entity in the eyes of the law, created by its owners or sponsors to address coverage issues or pricing that was not handled by the conventional or traditional insurance market that consisted of all of those domestic, foreign, and alien, admitted and non-admitted, on-shore and off-shore companies.

Thus, a captive may be a domestic insurer, domiciled in Vermont, one of the popular states of captive domicile, or an alien insurer, domiciled in Bermuda or the Cayman Islands, two of the popular Caribbean domiciles. Because of the Risk Retention Act of 1986, an act passed to provide relief to large corporations who could not obtain adequate insurance at reasonable prices during one of the more severe economic contractions of the traditional insurance market, captive insurance companies gained a special regulatory privilege. To allow captives to avoid the rate and form issues that constrained the freedom of choice of corporate insurance buyers, federal law exempted a domestic captive from regulation except by its state of domicile. The Vermont captive could then operate in all other states but only be subject to Vermont regulation. In effect, the captive would operate on a non-authorized basis (under state law) in all states except its state of domicile because of the federal act.

Since that was not enough to solve all the problems faced by large corporate insurance buyers, off-shore, or non-U.S. domiciles, became more popular sites for captive organization and domicile, particularly if they were in nice places to visit for a mandatory board meeting during a cold snap in Vermont. These companies, domiciled in Bermuda, Cayman Islands, or some other foreign nation, became known as off-shore captives. Following the treatment of domestic captives under the Risk Retention Act, off-shore captives are regulated only by their country of domicile.

However, there are some particular tax implications for these captives, one being the imposition of a 10% federal excise tax on premiums paid to an off-shore captive, and the other a series of restrictions on repatriation of profits from off-shore insurance operations to the U.S. parent company. In addition, there are severe limitations on how business can be conducted, thus requiring those expensive vacation-like board meetings on a frequent basis to exotic locales outside the United States, or for the low-budget operation, to Toronto.

In summary, given this structure, it is possible for a domestic insurance company to be operating on an admitted basis in one state, as a foreign insurance company operating on a non-admitted basis in another state, and as a alien insurance company (through its off-shore captive operation) operating on a non-authorized basis in a third state.

More Aspects of Domicile

Given the choice of domicile (this is a chicken-egg question: does choice of domicile affect the aspects or do the aspects drive the selection?), there are a number of aspects for the risk manager to consider dealing with the regulatory environment as it applies to captives.

Some domiciles are very stringent with respect to the regulatory climate while others are very lenient. For example, the New York State insurance regulators have historically been very stringent. Illinois is relatively lenient with respect to regulation of investments. The Cayman Islands are relatively flexible and even lenient with respect to capitalization.

Part of the regulatory environment includes permitted business, the type of business the captive insurance company can write. Some captive domiciles limit the lines to one or a very few specifically defined lines of insurance, while others permit a wide variety of lines to be written.

All domiciles have requirements for annual meetings. Some domiciles might require more frequent meetings until certain benchmarks in operations are achieved.

Another issue for meetings is geographic convenience, as the most significant issue of having meetings is not when, but where the meetings must be held. For on-shore captives, the meeting must be held in the state (or in the District of Columbia) of domicile. For off-shore captives, the meeting (and all other insurance business) must be held outside the United States. This necessitates travel of all U.S. citizens who are board members of the captive to the country of domicile. International travel could be as simple as crossing the bridge between Detroit and Toronto or as exciting and expensive as traveling to the Grand Caymans, Isle of Man, Turks and Caicos, or Luxembourg.

The risk manager must recognize that wherever the captive is domiciled, there must be an adequate local service infrastructure. The captive needs accounting and audit, actuarial, banking, legal, and brokerage services at a minimum. For on-shore captives, these services only have to be convenient, not necessarily located in the state or district of domicile. However, because of a very stringent and restrictive IRS rule dealing with trade and business practice applying to off-shore captives, all such services for off-shore captives must be provided off-shore. Naturally, the domiciles that have invested heavily in providing captive domiciles to bolster or even dominate their local economies also have arranged for the required infrastructure. The only problem facing the captive is that their choice of service vendors is restricted to those available in the domicile. For example, if the parent organization uses national insurance brokerage firm M to handle their domestic business but only national insurance brokerage firms A and W have offices in the Isle of Oz, the off-shore domicile where they intend to establish their captive, the captive will have to use the services of A or W.

Domiciles also differ in their view of investment regulations. Investment regulations define the types of investments that are eligible to be included in the admitted assets of the insurance company. Admitted assets are those assets whose value is easily derived from a viable market for those assets (such as a stock or bond exchange) and can readily and quickly be converted to cash, thus enhancing solvency and liquidity. Some domiciles follow a conservative track, restricting investments owned by a captive to the same standards applicable to a domestic insurance company. Other domiciles, such as Illinois, permit practically any type of investment, while still others limit permitted investments to those securities on the U.S. Treasury list, the list of authorized investments the U.S. government accepts as collateral on surety bonds.

Capitalization refers to the original investment the captive founders must make in the newly-formed captive and the amount of capital that must be constantly maintained during operations. This amount is subject to domicile, and within a given domicile, by line of insurance written in the insurance company. The amount of capital can range from only $300,000 or less or as much as $2,000,000 or more. Also, the amount of capital required is a minimum; the captive formers may capitalize the insurance company at a greater amount, assuring the regulators of their commitment, both financial and operational. The initial capitalization includes the par value of the issued shares of stock plus paid-in-capital that takes the place of retained earnings in the early years and provides a surplus for unforeseen contingencies and initial operating expenses. Generally, the same amount of capital as required for formation must be maintained throughout operations, else the captive insurance company will come under regulatory scrutiny and perhaps have its operations restricted or its license revoked.

Captive insurance companies are subject to taxes of several types, as well as fees and licensing costs. Fees and licensing costs are commonly incurred at the time the captive is being formed as well as annually in the form of a license renewal. The fees and licensing costs, generally in the thousands of dollars, typically accompany the application for formation or renewal, and, particularly for an off-shore domicile, may be a major revenue source for the domicile's government.

More Tax and Regulation Issues

Again, this is a simplified description not intended to provide tax advice or counsel, but merely explain the general concepts the captive must address. For tax advice or counsel, consult an attorney or qualified CPA.

Captive insurance companies are subject to three major types of taxes: premium taxes and assessments levied by the domicile on written premiums; income taxes paid to the federal government or the state of domicile; and federal excise taxes. Premium taxes and assessments are charged by the local regulators to fund insurance departments and their services and residual market mechanisms and guaranty or insolvency funds, and, in a few states, to provide additional funds to the general budget. Income taxes, the complex issues alluded to earlier, may be incurred at both the state and federal level (and, in theory, at a more local level in some jurisdictions). Federal excise taxes are levied against off-shore insurance companies on the premiums written in the United States.

Another tax issue applicable to off-shore captives is more encompassing than simply paying taxes, U.S. trade and business practices restrictions. For an off-shore captive, the income earned is not taxable to the captive unless those monies are repatriated to the parent company. However, the IRS rules impose stringent requirements on how business must be conducted. For example, the most conservative view of avoiding problems with these trade and business practice restrictions holds that even ordinary certificates of insurance must be executed off-shore. Thus, the local domestic broker cannot issue or sign a simple proof of insurance as they do in thousands of routine transactions involving on-shore insurance companies. Certainly, all banking, legal, actuarial, and captive-management services, including retail insurance brokerage and reinsurance brokerage must be conducted with off-shore vendors. Any crossing of the line of U.S. trade and business transactions may result in the immediate and forced repatriation and federal taxation of income of the captive insurance company.

Political Climate

Last, the risk manager must consider the political climate. There are two separate aspects to the political climate issue: domestic or on-shore captives, and off-shore captives. With respect to domestic captives, jurisdictions may encourage captive formation as a means of bolstering the local economy and the prestige of the government. For example, Vermont and Hawaii are not likely to be the first states mentioned as domiciles for traditional insurance companies, unlike New York, Illinois, or California. However, Vermont chose to create and invent itself as an ideal captive domicile and has been rewarded for that effort. Politics could change, and Vermont could become less popular, or another state, say New York, could decide to compete as a captive domicile.

For the most part, the off-shore captive domiciles that have been used in the last thirty years are stable countries from a political standpoint. Most are relatively small in population and area, but do not appear in the media as hotspots of unrest. Among the largest are Sweden, Switzerland, Ireland, and Singapore; among the smallest is Vanuatu, of Survivor fame.

On a sub note, the risk manager must be cautious of unfamiliar domiciles. In the 1980s, a micronation was formed from several Pacific Islands and part of Antarctica by two individuals who have been convicted of and imprisoned for land and share-related frauds. The Dominion of Melchizedek has a website and promotes itself as a domicile for banking and insurance, even though its territory has previously been claimed by other sovereign nations and its population is less than 50.

Fronting for Captives

Because of restrictions on types of coverage that can be written, such as workers compensation and automobile liability, and the need for a rated, financially substantial insurance carrier for these coverages, some insurance coverage cannot be directly written in a captive. However, this does not mean that the organization that forms the captive is forced to use other alternatives. Rather, the organization's captive can function as a reinsurance company to reinsure another insurance company, which is authorized to write a restricted line of coverage, or a more financially substantial insurance company. This arrangement in which a rated, authorized insurance company issues a policy reinsured by a captive is called fronting.

The mechanics of a fronting arrangement are essentially the same arrangements as found in any other reinsurance arrangement. The insured (the captive owner) pays a premium to the fronting company (the primary company). The fronting company then cedes that portion of the premium designated to pay losses, a pre-determined amount based upon the sharing of risk, to the captive (the reinsurer). The captive functions as a reinsurer for the fronting company, with the insured retaining its own losses as intended. As in some reinsurance arrangements, the primary insurer may retain a share of the risk and premium; in most cases, the fronting company retains 0% of the risk and only a small amount of the premium (the fronting fee).

The fronting company issues a policy to the insured (captive owner) and pays insured losses to claimants. These claims payments are then recovered from the captive (through reinsurance). The fronting company provides services (e.g., underwriting, loss control, claims, accounting, etc., as defined in the reinsurance contract) and the use of its license and financial structure. The fronting fee is the compensation for those services and for the residual risk that the reinsuring company (the captive) may financially fail.

Fronting arrangements are necessary for two important reasons. First, for workers compensation and automobile liability, states require that insurers writing these lines be licensed and admitted to do business. This assures claimants of their benefits and payment of claims. Since captives and other forms of alternative risk funding structures generally cannot satisfy state capital and surplus requirements, a licensed, admitted fronting company must be used.

Second, several types of businesses (e.g., contractors) are required to provide evidence of insurance purchased from admitted insurers that hold acceptable claims-paying ratings from A.M. Best or other financial rating organizations. Captives usually do not qualify for a financial rating, although some of the larger captives have elected (and paid the fees) to be rated.

Advantages

In theory, a captive should have reduced operating costs. Since there is usually no profit motive behind captive formation, a captive can potentially reduce the cost of normal overhead items, which typically make up 30% of a traditional insurance premium. Normal insurer overhead generally includes the agent's commissions, insurer services (e.g., underwriting, claims, loss control), general overhead (e.g., rent, the G4 jet, golden parachutes), insurer profit and contingency loadings, and stockholder dividends. These savings alone can be expected to generate savings of 10 to 25% off conventional insurance expenses for the captive.

Captives provide the opportunity for their owners to earn investment income on loss reserves, to regain some cash flow advantage on premium payments. In conventional insurance plans, the insurance company is the primary beneficiary of investment earnings. Traditional loss-sensitive programs, such as an incurred loss retrospectively rated plan, provide for potential return premiums or delayed premium payments, but the formula does not include a provision for investment income. Also, the captive can earn an underwriting profit when loss reserves exceed the ultimate value of the losses at the end of the payout period.

Captive insurance companies can provide broader coverage. Unlike their commercial counterparts, most captive insurers (especially those domiciled off-shore) are often subject to fewer limitations in coverage format. This may not always be true, however, given the terms of some fronting arrangements.

Rating equity in a captive insurance company manifests itself in two forms. First, a captive can develop rates that accurately reflect the actual and expected losses of its insured(s) instead of relying upon the "average" rates developed by rating authorities. Second, traditional insurance arrangements often do not provide adequate credit when an organization assumes a high level of potential loss.

Captives also enhance coverage availability and stability because they mitigate the extent to which the underwriting cycle can cause radical short-term swings in premium levels and coverage breadth. Captives increase the probability that both the availability of coverage as well as the price stability of that coverage will track more closely with the risks inherent in its own exposures, rather than those built into the marketplace, over which the organization has no control.

Additionally, captives can directly access the reinsurance market. The ability to deal directly with reinsurers allows captives to eliminate or reduce the cost of commissions paid to reinsurance intermediaries. Direct access also allows the captive to obtain pricing that is driven by its own exposures and loss record rather than those of the marketplace. Also, the captive can access reinsurance pools that have been established by captive owners.

In a captive, the administration of underwriting, loss control, and claims adjusting services is oriented to its owner's special needs. This could entail greater accuracy in rating (underwriting), better safety engineering (loss control), and more input into and control over sensitive loss settlements (claims adjustment).

A number of states place onerous restrictions or do not allow self-insurance of workers compensation and automobile liability exposures. Additionally, for certain lines of coverage, some states have restrictions in the areas of policy forms, rates, and evidence of financial security. The use of a captive insurer as a reinsurer to a fronting company helps to overcome many such constraints.

There are a number of intangible but meaningful benefits accruing from establishing and operating a captive insurance company. These benefits include:

1. Increased visibility and enhanced appreciation of the risk management function within the organization;

2. The ability of the firm to select an "optimal" retention level, rather than one imposed on an insured by an insurer;

3. Facilitation of more equitable cost allocation between divisions of a company, and creation of a potential profit center; and

4. Attribution of the investment income generated by a captive to the risk management department rather than being absorbed in the general funds of the owner. Therefore, the investment income accrues to the risk management effort.

The bottom line is that the most important benefit and result of successful captive ownership is a reduction in the long-term cost of risk. Captives also provide a financial focus for the identification and management of risk.

Disadvantages

Participation in a captive may require more time of administrative, senior management, and risk management personnel than does a commercially insured program. This may strain available personnel resources, as well as costs.

Establishing a captive generally requires a substantial initial outlay of capital. Depending on the specifics of the company, this additional outlay could range from one-third to one-half of the insured's annual premium for the line of coverage the captive is insuring. The organization must commit these funds for at least 3 to 5 years. (However, the capital contribution is not an expense – it is an investment, but try explaining that to some senior managers when the bills come in.)

A captive is dependent upon a number of service providers, which must be selected, hired, and monitored by the captive owner, not an insurance company. The owner also must ultimately control and approve the recommendations, actions, and decisions of adjusters, tax attorneys, safety/loss control personnel, reinsurers, actuaries, accountants, and regulatory authorities, among others.

Unlike a traditional insurance arrangement, the captive owner must be prepared for the fact that the captive may suffer losses greater than originally expected. This situation could trigger the need for an additional infusion of capital and/or a sharply increased renewal premium rate. Similarly, the owner should be prepared for the possibility of having to increase inadequate reserves. This increases the importance of timely actuarial reviews. (Most captive domiciles require annual loss reserve certification by an actuary.)

Because of the complex federal tax issues, forming a captive opens up the possibility that the IRS will challenge the organization's tax and accounting treatment of losses, premiums, loss reserves, and investment income. Depending on individual circumstances, the captive itself is sometimes a taxable entity for federal and state income tax purposes. This factor places potential demands on the time of both administrative and senior management personnel, as well as possible tax liabilities.

Use of a captive insurer for a certain line of coverage may cause the premium for other lines that remain commercially insured to increase in cost because of the loss of account-basis credits. When the captive owner removes one line, particularly one that is profitable, an insurer may increase the price of other lines to offset the loss of premium or profit, or simply decide not to renew the policy.

Captive Development

The steps needed to form a captive are generally the same, regardless of the type of captive. For obvious reasons, the formation of a group captive or association captive that will involve multiple owners and policyholders requires a few more steps in the initial stages.

The success of many risk management initiatives requires the long-term support of top management of the organization, and this is never truer than in the formation of a captive. Forming and operating a captive insurance company means a long-term commitment of financial resources, both capital and human resources, and the ability and willingness to bear occasional severe losses.

At the early stage, the organization must invest significant funds into a review of the legal and tax issues of owning a captive, including the specific regulations for choice of structure and domicile. For a publicly owned company, this includes a careful analysis of SEC Compliance Registration and an evaluation of the impact of financial disclosure under laws such as the Sarbanes-Oxley Act of 2002.

For a single-owner/insured company, the organizers must identify potential directors and officers of the captive insurance company, keeping in mind that in addition to having directors and officers with skills and experience in the usual functional areas of management, this group of managers should also have insurance knowledge and experience. Once identified, the directors and officers must be formally elected and invested in their positions. The directors must draft the organizational charter and by-laws.

The organizers must identify prospective domiciles in light of the intended operations of the captive and the financial and operational goals of the captive and the parent organization. Regulators will require a business plan detailing the lines of coverage to be written, reinsurance to be secured, management to be retained, and financial and actuarial projections.

The organizers must identify prospective domiciles in light of the intended operations of the captive and the financial and operational goals of the captive and the parent organization. Top management and often times, regulators, will require a feasibility study. The feasibility study is based upon historic information and projections. In order to be effective and conclusive, the feasibility study will evaluate the captive opportunity based upon the potential captive premium, actuarially developed expected losses, and the development of the costs of services, such as claims administration, loss and safety control, premiums for excess insurance and reinsurance, and information needs.

The organization's in-house staff may be able to provide some services, depending upon its current risk management department operations. Alternatively, services can be purchased from outside providers. Claims handling, loss control, information systems, as well as other administrative services can be purchased on an unbundled basis from independent contractors or from individual insurers.

Regulators will require a business plan detailing the lines of coverage to be written, reinsurance to be secured, management to be retained, and financial and actuarial projections.

Based in part on the legal and tax analysis as well as other operational characteristics and likely domicile, the organizers must determine the type of captive to use. This includes the choice of a single-parent captive, formed independently or under the provisions of the Risk Retention Act of 1986, or participation in a collective effort such as a group or association captive, or use of an all-ready existing captive in a rent-a-captive or agency captive scenario.

Once the domicile is selected, the organizers must complete the required applications and supporting documentation for presentation to the domicile and pay the required fees.

If a fronting company is to be used for regulatory or contractual compliance, the captive management must identify and negotiate with fronting companies to find the mix of services and fees that are appropriate.

The captive managers must also identify and negotiate with reinsurance companies, again to find the mix of services, products, and fees that are appropriate for the captive insurance company's business. When the captive is intended to function as a reinsurer, the captive managers will seek out retrocessionairres, reinsurers who insure reinsurers.

For a single-owner/insured company, the organizers must identify potential directors and officers of the captive insurance company, keeping in mind that in addition to having directors and officers with skills and experience in the usual functional areas of management, this group of managers should also have insurance knowledge and experience. Once identified, the directors and officers must be formally elected and invested in their positions.

The directors must draft by-laws and establish the incorporation procedures, and complete the incorporation and registration necessary for the operation of the captive insurance company.

For a single-owner/insured company, the organizers must identify potential directors and officers of the captive insurance company, keeping in mind that in addition to having directors and officers with skills and experience in the usual functional areas of management, this group of managers should also have insurance knowledge and experience. Once identified, the directors and officers must be formally elected and invested in their positions.

The organizers must identify, negotiate with, and select service providers (domiciled-based, when required by the domicile) including legal counsel, auditor, actuary, and captive manager.

Group and Association Captive Formation

If the organization decides to participant in a group effort or association captive, the most significant step that is different is for the group/association to adopt membership eligibility guidelines and to create financial guidelines for initial and sustained membership.

For a group effort, qualifying under these guidelines often is the most difficult step, as it requires the disclosure of proprietary information to a group who might consist of competitors. Members of the potential group must provide individual data such as:

1. Historical premium and loss data, as well as loss projections;

2. Current and historical exposure information, such as payroll, receipts, etc;

3. Parameters of the current insurance coverage and risk management programs;

4. Outlines of services provided by insurance brokers and vendors, including pricing;

5. A commitment to participate in the captive if it is determined to be feasible; and

6. Financial information on each individual member.

Components of Projected Financial Statements (also known as Pro Forma Financial Statements)

The risk manager and others involved in a captive insurance company should have a basic understanding of the sometimes arcane and very specialized terms used in insurance company accounting or statutory accounting, as this accounting system is the one required by regulators.

Insurance regulation began in the United States as early as 1824, and four years later, New York first required the submission of financial information by insurers. Over the years, the type of information collected and the manner in which it was displayed was conventionalized, hence the creation of the term "convention statement," to describe the format of the insurance company's financial accounting report required by all jurisdictions. The following terms and definitions also are found in the convention statement of a captive.

Gross Written Premium (GWP) – the annual premium showing on the policies, collected on a gross basis. For a captive, GWP is the annual pay-in of premium by the organization(s).

Ceding Commission – the onshore expenses including fronting fees, premium taxes, loss control costs, excess insurance, brokerage commission, and unallocated loss adjustment expense

Net Ceded Premium – the premium that is actually deposited in the captive.

Underwriting Expenses – expected or projected losses at their ultimate value, allocated loss adjustment expense, domicile expenses, and any miscellaneous costs borne by the captive. (Note that the captive pays these expenses while the individual members pay the ceding commission)

Underwriting Profit or Loss – The difference between net ceded premium and total expenses.

Investment Income on Underwriting Results – investment returns on underwriting profit

Net Underwriting Income – the sum of underwriting profit and investment income from underwriting profit.

Investment Income on Cash and Short-Term Deposits – investment returns on cash and short-term deposits.

Income Tax Expense – federal and state income tax incurred on operating income.

Earned Surplus – cumulative net income (retained earnings, in financial accounting).

Admitted Assets – cash capital, letter of credit capital, invested assets, and investment income; the assets whose value is permitted by regulators to be included on the financial statements.

Liabilities – income taxes, outstanding loss reserves, and other financial obligations.

Capital – the sum of all cash, letters of credit assets, and earned surplus.

Exhibit 11.1 is an example of an insurance company's financial statement, based on these assumptions:

1. 35% loss ratio constant throughout the years

2. Annual gross premiums grow by $1 million each year

3. Capital equals 5:1 Net Ceded Premium to capital (solvency ratio)

4. Ceding commission equals 40% of Gross Written Premium

5. Outstanding loss reserves are based on 5-year loss payout: 30/25/20/15/10

6. Investment returns on underwriting profit at 7%

7. Federal income tax at 34% rate

Exhibit 11.1: Income Statement and Balance Sheet of a Stock Captive Reinsurance Company

Income Statement

Successful Casualty (Bermuda) Ltd.

A Stock Captive Reinsurance Company

35% Loss Ratio

Underwriting Expenses

	Year 1	Year 2	Year 3	Year 4	Year 5
Ultimate Incurred Losses and ALAE	1,050,000	1,400,000	1,750,000	2,100,000	2,450,000
Management & Acquisition Fee	120,000	160,000	200,000	240,000	280,000
Actuarial, LOC & Domicile	75,000	100,000	125,000	150,000	175,000
TOTAL EXPENSES	1,245,000	1,660,000	2,075,000	2,490,000	2,905,000
Underwriting Profit (Loss)	555,000	740,000	925,000	1,110,000	1,295,000
INV Income/ Underwriting	98,700	195,142	313,180	438,577	572,388
Net Underwriting Income	653,700	935,142	1,238,180	1,548,577	1,867,388
INV Income/ Cash & STD	17,500	18,725	18,811	18,817	18,817
Income Tax EXP (Benefit)	228,208	324,315	427,377	532,914	641,310
NET INCOME	442,992	629,552	829,614	1,034,480	1,244,895
EARNED SURPLUS	442,992	1,072,544	1,902,158	2,936,638	4,181,533

218

Balance Sheet

Successful Casualty (Bermuda) Ltd.

A Stock Captive Reinsurance Company

					35% Annual Loss Ration
ASSETS	**Year 1**	**Year 2**	**Year 3**	**Year 4**	**Year 5**
Cash Capital & STD	250,000	250,000	250,000	250,000	250,000
Capital (LOC)	110,000	110,000	110,000	0	0
Investments	1,290,000	2,635,492	4,115,044	5,724,658	7,469,138
Accrued Investments Income	116,200	213,867	331,991	457,394	591,205
Total Assets	1,766,200	3,209,359	4,807,035	6,432,052	8,310,343
LIABILITIES					
Income Taxes Payable	228,208	324,315	427,377	532,914	641,310
Outstanding Loss Reserves	735,000	1,452,500	2,117,500	2,712,500	3,237,500
TOTAL LIABILITIES	936,208	1,776,815	2,544,877	3,245,414	3,878,810
CAPITAL					
Cash	250,000	250,000	250,000	250,000	250,000
Letter of Credit	110,000	110,000	110,000	0	0
Retained Earnings (Earned Surplus)	442,992	1,072,544	1,902,158	2,936,638	4,181,533
TOTAL CAPITAL	802,992	1,432,544	2,262,158	3,186,638	4,431,533
TOTAL LIABILITES & CAPITAL	1,766,200	3,209,359	4,807,035	6,432,052	8,310,343

Tax Rules and Owners of Captive Insurance Companies

This is a simplified description not intended to provide tax advice or counsel, but merely explain the general concepts the owner of captive must address. For tax advice or counsel, consult an attorney or qualified CPA.

Since the captive is a real insurance company, it is subject to the special tax rules applicable to insurance companies. However, ordinary tax rules apply to the captive owner. The IRS considers a captive insurance company to be within the same economic family as its owner, and distinct rules apply in determining deductibility of premiums and losses with respect to the captive owner.

First, to attain tax deductibility for premium, there must be a transfer of the risk of loss to an independent third party. The policy must provide for a sufficient shift of risk. This rule applies to captive insurance companies as well as pooling arrangements, risk retention groups, and retrospectively rated programs.

The broad IRS position on captives is that premiums paid to captives, particularly single-parent captives, are not deductible as ordinary and necessary business expenses under Section 162 of the Internal Revenue Code. The premiums paid to a captive would be deductible to the captive owner only when loss payments by the captive are made on behalf of the captive owner. Also, the captive or any other alternative market must be used to, in the words of the IRS, "reduce the cost of risk." Last, a parent company cannot use a subsidiary such as a captive insurance company for a tax advantage not otherwise permitted to the parent.

There are several specific captive tax issues the risk manager must consider. These are in the form of IRS Revenue Rulings 2002-89, 90, and 91. These rules cover economic substance requirements, conformity with common insurance practices, and risk distribution characteristics.

The economic substance requirements address basic business issues in the parent-captive relationship. First, there can be no parental guarantees of any kind. The captive, once capitalized, must stand on its own. Further, the captive cannot loan funds to the captive owner or policyholder. Third, the capitalization must be adequate, not unreasonably high or low. Fourth, there must be a valid, non-tax reason for establishing the captive, such as unavailable or limited coverage in the conventional insurance marketplace. Last, the business operations and assets of the captive must be separate from those of the captive owner(s).

The conformity with common insurance practices assures that the captive is operating like an independent insurance company except in its acceptance of only its owner(s) exposures. Premiums must be priced at an arm's length, in accordance with customary rating formulas. The conduct between the captive and the policyholder(s) must be consistent with insurance arrangements between unrelated parties. Naturally, there is latitude in this, as the captive presumably will not cancel its owner(s) coverage for adverse loss experience, which a commercial insurance carrier might. The captive must establish validity of claims before paying them, just as a commercial insurance carrier would. Any administrative tasks or services performed by the captive using the captive's personnel or outside resources must be charged to the parent at commercial rates. The captive must hold all required licenses to conduct insurance business in the applicable jurisdictions, except for the limited jurisdiction provided for in the provisions of the Risk Retention Act of 1974. Lastly, the transactions conducted by the captive must be insurance transactions in the commonly accepted sense.

The multi-insured captive operations must meet certain risk distribution characteristics. Brother-sister arrangements must include at least 12 affiliated policyholders. An association captive must include at least 7 policyholders. Further, no single policyholder can account for more than 15% of the maximum aggregate exposure to loss.

With respect to loss events, there must be a significant number of potential events that could strike the captive, and those potential loss events must be independent of one another. There must be a real possibility of covered losses that exceed the premium paid into the captive. The pooled risk must be homogeneous in character. Premiums cannot be experience-rated, and a net underwriting loss by one policyholder is borne in substantial part by premiums paid by other policyholders. In short, these operational aspects mirror the exposure to loss and operations of a commercial insurance carrier.

Document Retention Program

Every risk management program needs a document retention program. When taxation issues are involved, the need for document retention is even more important. The policyholder and captive should all maintain copies of policies and declaration pages essentially forever (or at least 75 years) because of long-term exposures (e.g., occupational illnesses caused by asbestos and other hazardous materials and product liability related claims). Captive formation documents should be maintained for the duration of the captive plus six years beyond its dissolution. In keeping with the statute of limitations on tax matters, tax-related information should be maintained for seven years,. Actuarial standards require preservation of all loss documentation for at least seven years.

Finite Risk Reinsurance

Finite risk reinsurance, also known as financial reinsurance, is a risk financing term used by primary insurance companies and large self-insurers to describe the spectrum of nontraditional loss financing concepts. It is called "finite" because this reinsurance acts in a manner similar to a primary loss retention in, for example, a captive program (captives usually require that full annual aggregate expected losses be funded during the policy term). Subject to a potential penalty for worst-than-expected losses, the amount reinsured under a finite risk contract may be said to be finite (i.e., limited in time and amount).

Special Characteristics

Numbers versus Time

As is true of primary insurance, traditional reinsurance relies on the law of large numbers: a large number of homogeneous exposures facing the same perils. Reinsurers must write a diversified book of business to spread the risk among many insureds. However, finite risk reinsurance is not dependent upon a spread of risk across a number of exposures. Instead, finite risk reinsurance uses time to create the loss funding necessary to pay for losses, as the frequency of loss is very low. In traditional insurance, an annual insurance policy and a three-to-five-year experience period is generally considered appropriate, but in finite risk reinsurance, the time period may extend to five, ten, or more years. Further, whereas the time value of money plays a marginal role in traditional reinsurance, it is one of the central features in a finite risk reinsurance deal.

Annual versus Multi-year Policy Term

Traditional reinsurance contracts are typically set in an annual time frame. However, finite risk reinsurance would not work if it were constrained to a single annual policy term because of the low frequency of loss and the lack of traditional underlying primary annual insurance contracts. Another reason finite risk reinsurance is designed as a multi-year approach concerns the need for high limits of liability given the infrequent and unpredictable nature of excess losses. An annual policy term does a poor job of matching the demands of losses and coverage limits when the frequency of loss is low but potential severity is catastrophic. Finite risk reinsurance recognizes an event horizon of 5 to 10 years or more. Aggregate limits apply over the entire policy term, not one-year at a time, as it is easier to predict that a given loss scenario will occur within a span of 5 years than within one.

Insurable versus Uninsurable Exposures

Theoretically, a commercially insurable risk must have seven characteristics: 1) large number of homogeneous exposures; 2) a loss definite as to time, place, and value; 3) an accidental loss; 4) a loss whose change of loss is calculable; 5) an exposure that is unlikely to cause a loss to a large number of insureds at the same time; 6) an exposure that is unlikely to cause a large loss with respect to an individual insured; and 7) one that can be insured at an economically feasible cost.

Finite risk reinsurance has effectively rewritten the rules regarding what is considered commercially insurable and what is not. Barring exclusions imposed by reinsurers, risk managers can "insure" just about anything, as long as they are able to reasonably quantify its frequency and severity on a policy term basis. This requirement of predictability severely restricts the type of risk that may be self-insured. Another factor that determines insurability is the traditional reinsurance contract itself. It is usually written to cover only those exposures that are also covered within the primary retention.

Finite risk reinsurance contracts are theoretically funded to pay for all losses within the aggregate limit of liability. However, since it is reinsurance, it can be structured to include risks unanticipated within the primary layer, thus providing protection for the once-uninsurable risk.

Due to the nature of the finite risk reinsurance, the prototype finite risk reinsurance prospect is an organization with a high severity, low frequency exposure for which adequate coverage is either unavailable or prohibitively priced.

Examples of Subjects of Finite Risk Reinsurance:

1. Product-recall exposures

2. Warranty programs

3. Environmental impairment liability

4. Commodity price fluctuations

5. Credit risk

Common Features of Finite Risk Reinsurance Contracts

First, the finite risk reinsurance contract is a multiyear policy, extending for five or more years. The reinsurer establishes an "experience account" that is funded through an initial premium and subsequent premium contributions. In addition, the account grows through investment income that is earned and retained on behalf of the insured and not the insurance company. However, the rate of interest earned by the insured is a risk-free rate, such as the rate on a U.S. Treasury obligation or London Interbank Offered Rate (LIBOR). Investment earnings in excess of that amount are retained by the reinsurer.

Expenses of the plan, such as paid losses and the reinsurer's fee (guaranteed profit), and any return premiums, if available, are disbursed from the plan.

Due to the fact that finite risk reinsurance programs require annual funding of premiums, the insurer usually cannot cancel the contract for non-payment of premium as is done in traditional insurance programs, but there is an enforceable debt created by the contract. On the other hand, the insured may cancel at any time if the experience account is not showing a deficit.

Finite risk reinsurance programs are not guaranteed cost plans where the profit generated by underwriting and investment accrue to the insurance company. Instead, they utilize a commutation clause that disburses the residual in the experience account back to the insured as long as the expenses and paid losses do not exceed the balance in the experience account.

Reinsurers charge a predetermined fee, which can range from 5 to 25 percent of the premium. This fee is designed to cover transactional costs and provide a modest (and guaranteed) profit.

Deduction of premium payments depends upon risk transfer. If there is sufficient risk transfer, IRS rules permit the deduction of premium payments for tax purposes. The general rule is that risk transfer in finite risk reinsurance programs (that require tax deductibility) should equal or exceed the funded premium or experience account. In other words, the insured should face a loss greater that just the experience account.

Because of the smoothing out of catastrophic losses over a long time period, a finite risk reinsurance plan provides potential balance sheet protection. Variability in results and balance sheet values create budgeting issues for managers.

Organizations also face an interest rate risk because of the inevitable fluctuations in interest over the life of an investment or debt. When funds are invested to pay for losses, the interest rate assumption is critical in determining the amount of funds needed, and the premiums charged by insurance carriers and reinsurers will be based in part upon their expected investment income. Unlike traditional reinsurance, all finite risk reinsurance contracts explicitly rely on investment income. Since reinsurers usually stipulate that any excess interest income commutable back to the insured will be based on a "risk free" rate, this guarantee greatly reduces the insurer's or reinsurer's interest rate risk.

Similarly, organizations face a credit risk, and the longer the contract or debt, the more pronounced the credit risk. Finite risk reinsurers also face credit risk in that paid losses may exceed the premium payments made by the insured, either during the policy term or once the term has expired.

Types of Finite Risk Reinsurance Contracts

There are two types of finite risk reinsurance contracts: retrospective and prospective.

Retrospective finite contracts cover occurrences that have happened in the past and come in two forms: loss portfolio transfers and aggregate loss contracts. A loss portfolio transfer is a contractual transfer of a portfolio of losses which have already occurred and have established reserves. An aggregate loss contract covers a gap in coverage in prior policy periods for which there may be incurred but not reported (IBNR) claims. Examples of these two types of retrospective finite contracts are given on the following pages.

Prospective finite contracts cover occurrences which may happen in the future, as in the following Toxic Services example. Since finite contracts, by their nature, all happen to be aggregate limits instead of per occurrence limits, the prospective finite contract is also an aggregate loss contract, only forward looking.

Finite Risk Loss Portfolio Transfers

When a self-insurer or a captive (or an insurer) wishes to terminate or close out an existing retention program or an existing book of business, it must make a decision about handling the open losses (including the incurred but not reported loss (IBNR) estimates). The self-insurer, captive, or insurer may use a finite risk reinsurance contract to convert the unknown nature of these liabilities to a known quantity. The "unknown" nature of "known" losses arises out of the inevitable difference between the total of the individual actual losses and the predicted losses, as well as the ultimate amount of the estimated value of IBNR claims. The finite risk reinsurance contract is a finite, or definite, amount that reduces variance and uncertainty.

In addition to eliminating obligations for claims, the uncertainty of expenses can be reduced by an annual loss portfolio transfer (conversion from unknown to known), as well as eliminating the uncertainty of potential ultimate loss IBNR "time bombs."

Exhibit 11.2: Loss Portfolio Transfer Example

Angelic Children's Hospital operates 5 for-profit hospitals located in 3 states. Over the past 20 years it has accumulated a portfolio of self-insured general and professional liability losses. An actuary has determined that reserves on outstanding losses equal $8 million and IBNR reserves are $2 million, for a total of $10 million. It will be 10 years before all known and unknown losses from the 20-year period will be closed. The hospital wants to rid itself of all of its outstanding claim liabilities as it prepares to be sold to a nationwide healthcare corporation.

Finite Contract Details

- Contract limit of liability: $12 million
- Preset policy interest rate: 7 percent
- Payout (policy) period: 10 years
- Premium payment: Annual Installments

Premium Calculation

- Net present value (NPV) of expected losses
  (expected losses = $10 million): $4,970,000

- Premium for premature loss payout: $500,000

- Premium for interest rate risk
  (the reinsurer's exposure for losses between the contract's
  $10 million limit and the NPV of $4,970,000): $250,000

- Premium for $2 million coverage in
  excess of expected losses: $25,000

- $5,745,000

- Reinsurer's fee (10 percent): $574,500

- Total premium: $6,320,000

Commutation Provision The reinsurer establishes an experience account from which losses are paid. The insured will share in any profits under the contract in excess of the reinsurer's 10% fee, either at the end of the policy period or upon cancellation of the policy. If the insured cancels the policy midterm, the insured will receive 90% of the fund balance.

Benefits to Angelic Children's

- The hospital no longer must devote operational and administrative resources to handling self-insured claims.

- Angelic Children's may be successful in removing the outstanding claim liabilities from its balance sheet, which may improve its corporate debt rating and improve its borrowing capacity.

- Depending upon how aggressive Angelic Children's is regarding income tax deductions, the company may be successful in deducting the full amount of the annual premium from its corporate income taxes. (This tactic is questionable because of the relatively small amount of actual risk transfer involved in the program and the fact that the losses have already occurred.)

- Angelic Children's will share in the profitability of the program, as will its corporate purchaser.

Benefit to the Reinsurer Regardless of loss experience or interest rate fluctuations, the reinsurer is guaranteed its 10 percent fee, $574,500. This is the worst-case scenario. On the upside, if losses pay out longer than expected and interest rates average higher than the preset policy rate; the reinsurer stands to make a considerable amount of money.

Aggregate Loss Contracts

There are two variations of this type of finite risk reinsurance contract: prospective aggregate contracts and retrospective aggregate contracts. Prospective aggregate programs cover losses that have not yet occurred while retrospective aggregate contracts cover known losses. Retrospective aggregate contracts are similar to loss portfolio transfers in how they treat existing losses and the development of the premium. The major difference between a loss portfolio transfer and a retrospective aggregate contract is one of intent. A loss portfolio transfer is used to manage existing self-insured losses, and a retrospective aggregate contract is used to fill in holes in past insurance and reinsurance layers.

Exhibit 11.3: Prospective Aggregate Contract Example

Toxic Services, Inc. is a large asbestos removal contractor. Although it employs highly trained and experienced people, it cannot obtain environmental impairment liability (EIL) insurance coverage in either the standard or specialty markets due to poor loss experience, and the volatility of the exposure. In order to attract business, the company must show evidence of insurance to prospective general contractors. Toxic desires a policy with a $5 million limit.

Contract Details and Premium Computation

The contract will extend for 3 years and will offer a $5 million aggregate limit of liability coverage per year. The first year premium is $2 million with $1.5 million due in years 2 and 3. The experience account loss fund will accumulate and all funds not used to pay claims (less the reinsurer's 10 percent fee) will be returned to the insured at the termination of the policy.

Benefit to Insured

The contractor will obtain the needed $5 million annual aggregate limit of liability despite the unavailability of coverage elsewhere and will be able to provide evidence of insurance.

Benefit to Reinsurer

Unless interest rates plummet or the sky falls, the reinsurer will be able to lock in an almost risk-free profit on the transaction.

Chapter 12

Actuarial, Accounting, and Auditing Perspectives

Introduction

The risk manager needs to be able to manage risk management programs using accounting, actuarial, and audit support, but does not have to be the actuary, accountant, or auditor. The goal of using these professional support services is to be able to obtain appropriate reports and to understand the content of the reports made to management and to third parties, particularly the board of directors and officers, and to understand how the information contained in those reports relates to risk management programs.

The risk manager needs to understand the underlying concepts of these three disciplines and should have a working knowledge of how these professionals accomplish their tasks, particularly those tasks performed by an actuary.

How Actuarial, Accounting, and Audit Services fit with Risk Financing

Risk financing requires data on current and future payouts of uncertain estimates – an actuarial function. Financial statements provide documentation of risk financing results – an accounting function. These financial statements should be reviewed systematically to ascertain current and future abilities to provide risk financing – an audit function.

A Brief History of Actuarial Science

Actuarial work has been an integral part of the insurance industry since the 17th century, when John Graunt, an English shopkeeper, whose curiosity over the vagaries or life and death during the Black Death plague and Queen Elizabeth's death in 1603 drove him to the parish registries of births and deaths over the period from 1604 to 1661 for the entire city of London. Graunt, a religious zealot, was searching for proof of his belief that the more of the sinful, unwholesome life in London to which a person was exposed, the sooner he would die.

Graunt conveniently explained the deaths of infants and small children as the effect of the wages of original sin on their otherwise-innocent, frail constitutions, enhanced to no small degree by the contemporaneous sins of their parents. He attributed adult death to the accumulation of the deleterious effects of smoking, intemperance, gambling, carnality, associating with persons of ill repute, and walking about without clean underwear. Graunt published his conclusions and predictions regarding life expectancy and the likelihood of death from various sinful causes in "Natural and Political Observations Made Upon the Bills of Morality," a weighty tome published in 1662.

In spite of Graunt's attention to detail, he recognized the results were flawed, as medical diagnoses were uncertain or couched in euphemisms, and that only Church of England christenings and burials were recorded. However, in Breslau, Silesia (now Wrozlaw, Poland), more comprehensive records had been kept. Caspar Naumann, a local clergyman, reviewed these records while trying to disprove the common superstitious belief that the phases of the moon affected health and mortality.

Naumann compiled information on births, deaths, and causes of death, analyzed this data, but not knowing quite what to make of it, sent it to a more notable mathematician, Gottfried Wilhelm von Leibniz (or Leibnitz), who promptly forwarded the information to the Royal Society in London, where it attracted the attention of the mathematician and amateur astronomer Edmund Halley, discoverer of the famous comet. Halley had also studied Graunt's data, recognizing its weaknesses. Using the Breslau data, he wrote a paper for the Royal Society that included tables predicting the frequency of death at any age, the first example of actuarial tables.

While only the fledgling life insurance industry used these first actuarial tables, the concept of using historical information regarding the likelihood of loss was established, and eventually spread into other areas of insurance, giving the underwriters a better sense of the possibility of loss and therefore, a better idea of the premium necessary to provide funds for future losses.

The Importance of Actuarial Services

Regardless of the extent to which a risk management program uses commercial insurance, actuarial services are an important tool for the risk manager to understand and use. First, for any risk financing program using insurance products, actuaries can provide an assurance that the premium paid is reasonable (adequate and not excessive) and that any retentions included in the risk financing plan are appropriate. Second, if a captive insurance company is used for internally-provided financing and accessing reinsurance for externally-provided financing, the actuary can provide similar assurance of the appropriateness of premiums and retentions, as well as satisfy the common requirement of regulators to provide a statement of actuarial opinion as part of the captive formation and operation process. Last, actuaries are experts in trending and developing known losses and evaluating Incurred But Not Reported Reserves ("IBNR"), a key component of self-insured programs as well as self-insured retention and retrospective rating plans.

Common Examples of Actuarial Services

One common actuarial service is a loss reserve review. These reviews are used in conjunction with financial reporting, particularly when the organization is a public corporation. For example, the reserves associated with a fully retained workers' compensation program represent a liability and require funding to discharge the obligations. Investors and other stakeholders need to know this information, and the information must be as accurate as possible.

Operations managers and senior managers are constantly working with budgets, both in the current year and in future years. Managers often desire actuarial evaluations of the current year and projections for future years to assist them in budgeting.

Operations managers and the risk manager may be interested in allocating the cost of risk to influence behavior, sell risk control programs to workers, and to help in product pricing. Actuaries can perform an estimation of the cost of risk and assist in assigning costs of risk to appropriate business units.

Actuarial Issues

Business Profitability

In comparison to payroll and payroll-related expenses and raw material costs, typically the largest expenses for an organization, casualty losses (which can run as much as 5% of the revenue of an organization) generally are not that significant. However, the organization cannot function without the expenses of payroll and raw materials, and any attempt to reduce these expenses can only have a limited effect, as these expenses can be reduced but never eliminated. No organization requires casualty losses during its operation and any attempt to reduce the number of losses and the severity of those losses that cannot be prevented means an immediate boost to its profitability. In a perfect world, all casualty losses would be prevented, and the costs savings would drop to the bottom line.

Further, the balance sheet reserve (assuming there is an "on-balance sheet" reserve) is subject to more variability than most entries. Accounts payable are fixed in value based on credit purchases. Notes payable are determined by contracts. However, loss reserves are affected both by the rate of occurrence of the losses and by the effectiveness of attempts to settle those losses, neither of which is certain.

Criteria for Reserves

The risk manager must be able to understand loss reserves and related issues. Some business decisions that are affected by reserves include retention levels and limits of coverage, appropriate pricing for excess insurance and reinsurance, and implementation and monitoring of safety and loss control programs. Also, the organization may require forecasts of future results of managing claims and losses as part of the budgeting process and should use the cost of risk in pricing products and services.

One question is, "What amount of reserves should be carried?" A case reserve is the initial value of a claim set up by the adjuster when the claim is reported. Since these reserves are based only upon the first report, there are frequently many unanswered (and unasked) questions. Because of the freshness of this data and its natural incompleteness, case reserves are normally inadequate for setting estimates of ultimate liability to the organization, the value that will be entered into the financial statements.

Even if all of the information is available on the initial report for those claims, the total case reserves will still contain inadequate information. First, there is the problem that the set of case reserves existing at the end of an experience or valuation period may not include all of the claims that have occurred during the period. The claims that have occurred but not yet been reported are called pure IBNR (Incurred But Not Reported).

Additionally, industry experience shows that total claims reserves increase in value over time for several reasons beyond incompleteness and non-reporting. Existing claims may increase their value from inflationary pressures, and as more people become involved in claims (lawyers, medical professionals, rehab personnel, etc) the values of reserves may also increase. Also, claims that were closed may be reopened and additional values added to the loss reserve. These claim adjustments are also called IBNR, but purists will distinguish these from the pure IBNR by referring to them as broad IBNR or just plain IBNR (more technically, Incurred But Not Reserved).

While many risk management professionals may argue over the meaning of many risk management terms, there is a consensus over IBNR: IBNR as commonly used includes reserves for incurred, reported claims whose values can change over the evaluation period plus pure IBNR, and represents the difference between the claims values on the evaluation and the ultimate value of the claims. In theory, the value of IBNR decreases over time as the claims are settled, except for the possibility that an old, settled claim might be reopened.

For most self-insured entities and those having significant degrees of retention, a combination of case reserves and IBNR is the most common reserve amount.

Another question is, "When should reserves be reviewed?" Loss reserves should be reviewed whenever the risk manager wishes to evaluate (or reevaluate) retention levels and limits of coverage. In addition, loss reserves should be reviewed when the risk manager wants to estimate losses for budgeting purposes. Last, loss reserves should be reviewed when retained losses could be material to financial statements.

Materiality of Loss Reserves

The definition of materiality is akin to Supreme Court Justice Potter Stewart's definition of pornography: "I can't define it, but I know it when I see it."

Definitions of materiality vary according to the type of report and the nature of the actuarial engagement. Without delving into the types of reports and engagements, a broader definition of materiality is sufficient to the risk manager: an event is material if it would impact a decision.

Intuitively, a consideration is material if either of the following applies: 1) it is the subject of the study (e.g., loss reserves are material to a loss reserve study but might not be material to a financial statement); or 2) failure to include the consideration could produce a misleading conclusion, (e.g., failure to consider excess insurance or reinsurance could mislead people regarding the financial strength of cash reserves).

If a loss reserve is material to the overall cost of risk, then the loss reserve should be identified and quantified by a risk management professional, insurance professional, or actuary.

Reserve Stability

One definition of risk is "a possibility of a variation of outcomes from a given set of circumstances." With loss reserves, there is a possibility of variation of outcomes, many of which are caused by factors external to the organization. The risk manager, as part of the process of managing the risks, would desire to have no variation of outcomes from a given set of circumstances. All predictions and estimates would, in a perfect risk management world, occur just as predicted and estimated, and there would be no variability. Budgeting would be precise, and planning would be perfect.

Such is not the case in the real world because of a number of factors that assure instability of loss reserves. Some factors are economic, some social, some regulatory, and some operations.

First, inflation is a common economic phenomenon. If inflation were stable, loss reserves would change at a predictable rate, and, while changing in value, loss reserves would be stable with respect to predictions and estimates. Also, uncertain or declining economic conditions, both on an economy-wide basis and an individual organization basis, can introduce instability because claimants or claimants-to-be decide workers' compensation benefits are preferable to salary (and having to work) or unemployment benefits.

Social changes such as claimant and juror attitudes contribute to reserve instability. Phrases like "jurisdiction shopping," "litigation lottery," "runaway jury," and "It's not my fault" are demonstrated by increasing jury awards and an extension of liability based on only the thinnest degree of culpability and serve to increase reserves in an unpredictable manner.

Statutory activities also contribute to reserve instability. Tort reform, the action desired by activists to avoid unjust enrichment for spurious liability and exaggerated injury, is uncertain in itself. In jurisdictions that have instituted tort reform, legal challenges by plaintiff attorneys and creativeness in crafting lawsuits have dampened its promised benefits. When enacted, tort reform contributes to instability by reducing damages, but on an uncertain basis. Thus, exceptions to the tort reforms and the possibility of judicial reversal and statutory repeal reintroduce instability. In addition, changes to workers' compensation statutory benefits add to instability of workers' compensation loss reserves.

From an operational standpoint, reserve stability is hampered by organizations changing third-party administrator (TPA) firms or insurance carriers to those who have differing claims philosophies and capabilities, by changing management within a TPA or carrier, by differing capabilities of individual attorneys defending these lawsuits and negotiating settlements, and, in general, a lack of uniform procedures for claims adjustors.

Conversely, there are several factors that contribute to reserve stability. From an economic viewpoint, stable economic conditions within the economy or individual organization and a stable legal environment, including juridical attitudes and statutes enhance stability of reserves. Within the TPA or carrier, consistency of management, dedicated claims units, and reduced employee turnover make it more likely reserves will be more stable. Last, a large volume of similar claims increases the chance of reserve stability from two aspects: first, with a larger volume, economies of scale and effectiveness in handing similar claims should improve stability; and second, with more exposures, any projections of losses and their costs should be more statistically sound, lending to the stability that can be developed from improved statistical reliability.

Using Reserve Information

Loss reserves are used for several purposes besides case management, the process of settling claims. The income tax management function will need information contained in loss reserves to the extent the loss reserves are part of a retention plan or a captive insurer. Similarly, the chief financial officer of a public corporation will need loss reserve information for completion of any financial statements that will be made for compliance with the Securities and Exchange Commission or any stock exchange. Operations management and legal will need loss reserve information as part of the negotiation and pricing of deals in mergers, acquisitions, or divestitures. Last, the risk manager will need loss reserves to assist in negotiation of insurance renewals, as well as in establishing limits and deductible amounts on those renewals, and to establish and implement self-insurance programs or captives.

Types of Reserves and the Reserving Process

The types of reserves that are included in this process are the case reserves and IBNR, as well as reserves for allocated loss adjustment expense and unallocated loss adjustment expense.

Allocated loss adjustment expenses (ALAE) are the costs associated with managing a specific claim, such as the overhead charge made to each claim file, professional fees for attorneys, independent medical examinations, filing fees, photocopying costs, claims reconstruction costs, and any other charge that is specifically incurred for a particular claim. Unallocated loss adjustment expenses (ULAE) are not charged to individual files, but are borne by the overall claims management process. These include rent, utility expenses, insurance, management expenses, and other general and administrative costs necessarily incurred in the claims management process that would continue even if there were no claims. Adjustor salaries and benefits can be assigned to either category or both, depending upon the philosophy of the claims manger. The ALAE might include a basic charge for adjustor time, for example, to recognize the time required to collect the basic claim information and establish a claim file, or the entire adjustor salary and benefit might be included in ULAE as an overhead cost that is assigned to the home office function or the risk management office function.

Also, loss reserves will include an estimate of gross and net salvage, reinsurance, and other recoveries. Gross salvage is the total amount a company expects to recover from salvage, and net salvage is the gross amount less costs associated with the salvage process, such as vehicle towing and disposal costs. Reinsurance recoveries may be estimated and recorded in the loss reserves, either on a total or specific loss basis. Subrogation recoveries will be estimated and recorded. Each of these recoveries will reduce the amount of the claim reserve, the ultimate cost of the claim, and the cost of risk.

Last, reserves may be recorded as undiscounted or discounted. Undiscounted claims are those claims recorded at their full value, as trended and developed to ultimate or final settlement values. However, some risk managers (and some underwriters) recognize that many claims require an extended time to settle, such as workers' compensation indemnity claims, product and professional liability claims, and environmental claims. In keeping with the practice of insurance carriers, who invest earned premiums that will eventually be used to settle claims, the risk manager can invest funds set aside for eventual claims settlements and earn interest on those funds. By applying time value of money discounts, the risk manager can estimate how much must be set aside now to settle a particular claim, say $100,000, in five years. By discounting the reserve to its present value, the risk manager can justify a lower loss reserve, as the risk manager knows that these claims will not be paid out until some time in the future.

Approaches to Setting Reserves

There are several approaches to setting reserves, and the approaches vary primarily with the types of claims. In cases where there is a high frequency of small, self-limiting claims (such as glass or automobile physical damage), the adjustor can determine the average value per such claim from historical information. This average value is applied to every claim that is presented, and the total value of all such claims becomes the loss reserve. For example, if historical information indicates the average collision damage is $600 per accident, and the adjustor knows there are 30 accidents, each claim is initially reserved at $600, and the total reserves are set at $18,000. The $200 claim is offset by the $1000 claim, and at the end of the period, any differences are resolved.

Not all claims are that simple, however. If the risk manager is concerned about product liability claims or any other claim that does not occur frequently and whose severity can vary dramatically, predictive models such as those used by actuaries can be used to establish loss reserves based on exposures. For example, if historical information is introduced into a predictive model, the model may suggest that $67,000 in losses will occur for every $100,000 of payroll.

The most common approach uses adjuster established case reserves. The case reserve begins with initial information received and is created based on the adjuster's experience plus any loss development factors that the organization has created or elected to use. This approach is commonly used when there is some frequency and the possibility of severity, but where the claims generally do not vary a great deal, such as slips and falls in shopping centers or wind losses.

Who Sets Case Reserves?

In the instances when an initial case reserve is established, the question becomes, who sets the reserves? The obvious answer for insured losses is the adjuster, but the real question is, what is the relationship between the adjuster and the organization? Insurance carrier adjusters set individual case reserves whenever primary insurance is involved, but a risk manager may be the one to set individual case reserves for an outside organization. However, if the organization has opted to have a retention or high deductible, the organization could retain the insurance carrier's unbundled claim services or the claim services of an independent third-party administrator to perform the adjuster's function and set the initial reserves. Otherwise, if the organization has a competent risk manager or other in-house staff, the organization's employees will set the initial reserve.

Setting Case Reserves

Case reserves are established in several ways. The simplest method is stair-stepping. In stair-stepping, the adjuster sets the initial reserve by using a formula (such as the initial average) or claim processing experience, and changes to the reserve are made whenever additional loss expenses are incurred. Thus, the value of the case reserve, if graphed, resembles a staircase, where each change steps up (or down, on occasion), as the claim approaches settlement, forms the stair steps. The advantage of this method is its simplicity and minimizing of loss reserves in a manner similar to the inventory management method, the just-in-time system. The current loss reserves reflect only what is currently required to discharge the claims as currently known. The disadvantage is that only the current value is known, and future costs remain unknown. The cost of risk cannot be accurately computed using this approach.

A better alternative, but one that is more complicated, uses trending and development to build the initial reserve to its ultimate value. The development factors may be industry-wide or specific to the organization. (One methodology for establishing ultimate values will be discussed shortly.) Since these are projections, adjustments will be made as the claims are closed and a final ultimate value is determined. The accuracy of these predictions will depend upon the skill of the actuary or risk manager in selecting the appropriate trending and development factors. The advantage of reserve to ultimate is that an estimate of the ultimate liability is established early, and the actuary or risk manager can calculate an estimate of the cost of risk immediately for use in making decisions. The disadvantage is that this will result in the highest cost in the short run, and will impact the organization's financial position on a current basis.

An alternative to this "human" approach is the use of an automated reserving system. There are several types of automated reserving systems available. These systems are predictive models created by actuaries. The initial reserve is the input, and the output is the ultimate reserve. While this appears to be the same as the reserve to ultimate philosophy, the difference is the automatic nature. The claims management system incorporates the automated reserving system, so when the actuary or risk manager inputs the initial case reserve, the ultimate value is immediately recorded on the claims record. The advantage is that this is an automatic process.

Setting Individual Case Reserves

As discussed, there are several approaches to establishing initial reserves and building upon initial reserves as claims mature and develop. The actuary begins with the individual case reserves (however established) and adds paid losses to obtain the total reported losses. This amount may represent the anticipated ultimate cost of the claim if the actuary begins with a case reserve that is calculated or projected to its ultimate value, or it may simply represent an amount that will be stair-stepped as the claim is processed.

Historical losses are used in a loss triangulation (more on this in a moment) to trend and develop losses from their original value or current value (depending upon what losses are being triangulated), to their current value or their ultimate value, (again, depending upon what result is desired). This triangulation process should include an estimate of losses that have occurred but have not yet been reported (pure IBNR) to add to the development on reported losses. When this has been done, the loss reserves can be included in the financial statement, with paid losses being reflected on the income statement (at least for most organizations) and outstanding reserves being reflected on the balance sheet as a liability or in the notes to the financial statements as an off-balance sheet item. The risk manager may also use this information to project future losses as part of planning, budgeting, financing, or negotiating insurance coverage.

Data an Actuary Needs to Evaluate Loss Reserves

Generally speaking, an actuary will request five years of historical losses recorded by line of insurance. However, the number of years is a desired range, not an absolute. For some lines of coverage, ten to twenty years is preferred, but if too many years are included, factors that have changed (loss control, social trends, technology, to name a few) must be taken into account. Also, the most immediate time interval tends to be more predictive than past history. If too few, the "historical" aspect is limited.

With insured losses, the actuary must also know the retention levels in effect for the losses represented in the data. If retentions have changed, or are not reflected by loss data, details of these retentions must be included. Similarly, the types of insurance programs purchased are important, as the policy determines the scope of coverage and therefore the nature of the claims included in the data. Last, the actuary needs a detailed description of the underlying business operations being conducted by the organization and financed through insurance or retention programs.

The actuary must also determine if sufficient data is contained in the loss data to warrant computation and use of the organization's loss development factors. This process is somewhat related to the requirement to have five years of historical losses; the requirement is to have sufficient data to support actuarial credibility. A stated number of years of experience helps, but does not guarantee by itself, a sufficient volume of data. If the actuary determines there is insufficient data to warrant use of the organization's development factors, industry data will be used. The weakness of industry data is simple: each organization is unique, and industry data may not be reflective of the organization's uniqueness.

Loss Triangulation

Loss Triangulation has four purposes. First, loss triangulation will capture the growth of incurred losses from their initial value when reported. Second, it will reflect growth in loss data due to pure IBNR claims. While the organization's data may not be adequate to provide pure IBNR factors, the actuary has methodologies available to calculate a pure IBNR factor. Third, loss triangulation can be used to determine loss payment patterns over time. This permits budgeting of cash. Fourth, loss triangulation assists the actuary in capturing cost-increasing trends and ultimate values resulting from claim development over the life of claims.

Types of Loss Triangulation

There are three basic types of triangulation, each with a different purpose. Paid Loss Triangulation results in trended and developed paid losses. This triangulation focuses on the timing of claim payments. For example, a triangulation of property losses (commonly called first-party claims), would show that the rate of payout of claims is fairly quick, as the number of property claims and their values are known during, or very shortly after the end of, the policy period. However, liability losses or third party claims take longer to develop. In fact, these claims might not be known for extended periods, even into years. These so-called "long-tail claims" will often have a small amount paid out after a while, and then an additional amount, and eventually, the final amount. A Paid Loss Triangulation would show the pattern by which such claims are paid, and would reflect the funds required to finance the losses.

Incurred Loss Triangulation trends and develops losses from their initial value or an interim time period value to their ultimate value, recognizing the total liability that may exist for claims than have been incurred. Incurred Loss Triangulation is useful in predicting total claims for a time period and the potential liability that must be recorded on accounting records.

A third type of triangulation is Claim Count Triangulation. This triangulation is simply a development of the number of claims, with no indication of severity. Given the axiom of "frequency leads to severity," understanding the developed number of claims that have occurred during a period helps the risk manager in refine loss control programs aimed at managing the number of claims, and therefore, lowering the potential of having a severe claim. For losses that use an average value per loss, a claim count triangulation also provides information useful in establishing total loss reserves.

Mechanics of Loss Triangulation

At first glance, any loss triangulation appears to be a daunting task. The steps are, however, simple but repetitive; thus, a triangulation is a lot of work, but once the pattern is set, it is nothing more than simple arithmetic.

Step 1: Obtain loss data for each year period. If the triangulation is intended to cover five years of experience, the actual number of loss data sets is not five, but fifteen. For example, the risk manager needs loss data for year X1 valued as of the ends of X1, X2, X3, X4, and X5, then loss data for year X2 valued as of the ends of X2, X3, X4, and X5, and so on. If it is any consolation, the entire "loss run" or detailed display of every loss is not required, only the information from the year-end or summary page of the report.

Step 2: Display the loss data in the traditional triangulation format. (See example that follows)

Step 3: .Starting with the top row, calculate the "age-to-age" factors by dividing the earliest year into the next adjacent year, and so on across the row. The ratio produced represents the change from one period to the next. In the five-year example, this requires four divisions. Then drop to the second row and repeat the process, resulting in three divisions, and so on. These ratios are entered into an identical triangulation format.

Step 4: Calculate the arithmetic mean or average of the "age-to-age" factors for each evaluation period.

Step 5: Chain multiply (first column average multiplied by next column multiplied by next column, etc.) to obtain ultimate development factors.

Step 6: Multiply the ultimate development factor for each evaluation period by the last value of loss reserves for that year to obtain the ultimate value of that year's as-yet undeveloped losses.

Simplified Actuarial Analysis

Accident Year	Months of Development				
	12	24	36	48	60
X1	80	120	140	150	155
X2	90	130	145	160	
X3	100	145	170		
X4	120	170			
X5	110				

Steps 1 and 2: This exhibit shows the total incurred losses (case reserves + paid losses) for prior accident years evaluated as of the end of each year (All figures are in thousands)

Step 3: Calculate "age-to-age" factor by taking ratios of adjacent entries and enter on new exhibit (e.g. 120/80 = 1.5)

Step 4: Calculate the average of "age-to-age" factors.

Step 5: Chain multiply the average "age-to-age" factors (including, for now, a tail factor that the actuary will provide for IBNR).

Accident Year	Months of Development				Tail Factor
	12 to 24	24 to 36	36 to 48	48 to 60	
X1	1.500	1.167	1.071	1.033	XX
X2	1.444	1.115	1.103		XX
X3	1.450	1.172			XX
X4	1.417				XX
Average	1.453	1.151	1.087	1.033	XX
Ultimate	1.944(5)	1.338(4)	1.162(3)	1.069(2)	1.035(1)

1.035 is "given"

1.069 = 1.035 x 1.033

1.162 = 1.035 x 1.033 x 1.087

1.338 = 1.035 x 1.033 x 1.087 x 1.151

1.944 = 1.035 x 1.033 x 1.087 x 1.151 x 1.453

Step 6: Calculation of Estimated Ultimate Losses

Accident Year	Incurred Loss	Ultimate Factor	Estimated Ultimate
X1	155	1.035	160
X2	160	1.069	171
X3	170	1.162	198
X4	170	1.338	227
X5	110	1.944	214

The current balance of loss reserves is calculated by subtracting the accumulation of paid losses from the estimated ultimate losses. This result represents the outstanding liability for losses that would be reflected on the financial statements.

Calculation of Loss Reserves

Accident Year	Incurred Loss	Ultimate Factor	Estimated Ultimate	Paid Loss	Loss Reserve
X1	155	1.035	160	150	10
X2	160	1.069	171	152	19
X3	170	1.162	198	140	58
X4	170	1.338	227	110	117
X5	110	1.944	214	60	154

Earlier in the triangulation steps (Step 6), the IBNR factor was indicated as being given. At this point, we will explain a simple method for calculating the IBNR factor. While again appearing complex, the hard work has already been done (arriving at the estimated ultimate loss reserves). The rest is simple subtraction. There is only one step from the preceding exhibit: Subtract the total of the initial case reserves from the current outstanding loss reserve: this represents the pure IBNR. The portion of the broad IBNR has already been considered in the calculation of the estimated ultimate loss reserves from the known reserves as they have been developed.

Calculation of IBNR

Accident Year	Incurred Loss	Estimated Value	Paid Loss(1)	Loss Reserve(2)	Case Reserve	IBNR Reserve(3)
X1	155	160	150	10	5	5
X2	160	171	152	19	8	11
X3	170	198	140	58	30	28
X4	170	227	110	117	60	57
X5	110	214	60	154	50	104

[1]Paid Losses = Losses paid through most recent valuation

[2]Loss Reserve = Estimated Ultimate minus Paid Losses

[3]IBNR = Incurred but not reported (development of known losses and as yet unreported losses)

= Estimated Ultimate minus Incurred Losses

Trending

The previous triangulations and calculations do not recognize the impact of inflation (or deflation, whenever that occurs). The losses have been adjusted for their natural increases, or development, over time, but the initial claim reserves, from which all the ultimate loss reserves have been calculated, start with current dollars for the period in which the claim occurred. That means that over time, the developed losses are, in all likelihood, understated because of the effect of inflation. Thus, trending, or bringing past dollars up to current dollars, must be performed.

(Because of the commutative law of mathematics (i.e., a + b = b + a and ab = ba), we could perform this step first if we were not concerned about the IBNR factor.)

To create a simple example, assume that the rate of inflation has been a constant 12% a year. The estimated ultimate loss reserves in X4, or last year's results (assume it is X5), have only one year of inflation, so the reserve of 214 is multiplied by the inflation index factor of 1.12 for an indexed ultimate total loss of 240. Year X3 has two years of inflation, so the reserve of 227 is multiplied by 1.12 x 1.12, for a result of 285. (Yes, this could also be expressed as 1.12^2.) The next year is increased by 1.12 x 1.12 x 1.12 (or 1.12^3), and so on.

Naturally, there is never a constant rate of inflation each year. Also, another consideration is that there is no one absolute inflation rate that can be applied to any loss reserve. Workers' compensation losses require the use of medical or healthcare inflation rates, while household goods could use a consumer price index, but building materials would require a different index focusing on construction materials.

A number of inflation indices can be used, but these indices rarely have an index date from which the inflation is measured that coincides with the beginning year of the loss triangulation. For example, a price index may be based on X1, not X6. These inflators can be adjusted to a new base year with a simple arithmetic process.

Exhibit – Inflation Index (based on X1 prices)

X10	1.452
X9	1.390
X8	1.345
X7	1.278
X6	1.222
X5	1.174
X4	1.125
X3	1.085
X2	1.040
X1	1.000

What we wish to measure is the relative change from one year to the next, and since we have losses for X6 that need to be trended, we can create our own index as follows:

X6   1.452/1.222 = 1.188

X5   1.390/1.222 = 1.137

X4   1.345/1.222 = 1.100

X3   1.278/1.222 = 1.046

X2   1.222/1.222 = 1.000

The year X6 becomes the base year; all other index rates are based upon that first year by divided the index value by the base value.

Calculation of Indexed Ultimate Total Loss (Inflation)

Accident Year	Incurred Loss	Estimated Ultimate	Inflation Index Factor	Indexed Ultimate Total Loss*
X1	155	160	1.761	282
X2	160	171	1.572	269
X3	170	198	1.404	278
X4	170	227	1.254	285
X5	110	214	1.120	240

*Rounded

Note: This table uses a rate of medical cost inflation of 12%. Inflation rates would vary based on geographical location.

Total Loss Rate

Once the risk manager has calculated the indexed ultimate loss reserves for each year, this total loss reserve can then be divided by an appropriate exposure basis to create a total loss rate, or the relationship between the exposure and the expected indexed ultimate total loss. For example, for every dollar of $1,000 of payroll incurred in 2000, $0.0913 indexed ultimate total losses will occur for that year. An average of the indexed total loss rates can be used to predict losses for 2005; the risk manager would multiply the expected exposure by the average of the indexed total loss rate to obtain the predicted losses.

Calculation of Indexed Ultimate Total Loss Rate

Accident Year	Indexed Ultimate Total Loss*	Exposure (Payroll)	Indexed Total Loss Rate
X1	282	3,090	0.0913
X2	269	3,475	0.0774
X3	278	3,800	0.0732
X4	285	4,275	0.0667
X5	240	4,520	0.0531

*Rounded

Note: For ease of presentation, payroll has not been trended. However, if exposures are not trended, the loss rate will not be accurate, as only inflation in costs has been considered.

NCCI Workers Compensation Factors

NCCI 2005 Countrywide Workers Compensation Loss Development Factors to Determine Ultimate Losses

Valuation Month	Paid	Incurred
12	4.385	1.787
24	1.960	1.311
36	1.534	1.197
48	1.368	1.151
60	1.288	1.128
72	1.244	1.114
84	1.216	1.105
96	1.197	1.098

Assume that policy years begin January 1 and that the appropriate tail factor is 1.047.

Triangulation Exercise

Loss Development Factor Worksheets

Loss Information

X1 Policy Year			
Valuation Date	Paid Losses	Case Reserves	Total Incurred
12/31/X1	120	280	400
12/31/X2	230	270	500
12/31/X3	335	240	575
12/31/X4	425	208	633
12/31/X5	500	165	665

X2 Policy Year			
12/31/X2	110	311	421
12/31/X3	240	295	535
12/31/X4	340	270	610
12/31/X5	440	230	670

X3 Policy Year			
12/31/X3	130	309	439
12/31/X4	250	289	539
12/31/X5	355	270	625

X4 Policy Year			
12/31/X4	135	305	440
12/31/X5	270	280	550

X5 Policy Year			
12/31/X5	140	320	460

Loss Development Factor Worksheet

Total Incurred Losses					
Policy Year	Months of Development				
	12	24	36	48	60
2000					
2001					
2002					
2003					
2004					
Note: Months of development determined by valuation date.					
Total Incurred Loss Development Factors					
Policy Year	Months of Development				
	12 to 24	24 to 36	36 to 48	48 to 60	60 to Ult.
2000					
2001					
2002					
2003					
2004					
Average					
Ultimate					
Estimated Ultimate Losses					
Policy Year	Incurred Losses	Ultimate Factor	Estimated Ultimate	Paid Losses	Loss Reserve
2000					
2001					
2002					
2003					
2004					
Total					

Range of Estimates Predictions

From a practical standpoint, point estimates are nearly never correct. The concept of "loss pic" or "loss pick" (one number that is the predicted losses for a period, e.g., $375,000) is correct only when actual losses are exactly $375,000. This is not a matter of quibbling over semantics; as discussed in the chapter dealing with capturing and reviewing loss data, there is not a question of error, but only of how much error.

Actuaries overcome the inherent weakness of point estimates by using range of estimate predictions, (e.g., $300,000 to $450,000) as the estimated losses for a period. There are two main approaches to setting ranges. First, the actuary may use a variety of assumptions and a variety of actuarial methods to establish a range and then compare the results before deciding when range of estimates would be appropriate. Second, the actuary can use a probabilistic actuarial model in which confidence intervals can be logically deduced from underlying assumptions.

Regardless of the approach, a point estimate of reserve is inherently uncertain and some form of range assessment is necessary to communicate this uncertainty. Thus, the range is the key tool to determining whether reserve estimates are consistent from year to year or whether something has happened that requires further investigation.

Example of Range of Liabilities

Low	Point	High
90	100	110

Examples of the Spread of Ranges:

Property	± 5%
General Liability	± 10%
Workers Comp	± 15%

In the first example, the point estimate of losses is 100, but the range is 20, a band of predicted losses from a low of 90 to a high of 110. The actuary would assign a probability or degree of certainty to this range of estimates, such as 95% confidence that the actual losses would fall within the range. In the second example, the actuary had concluded that a property loss point estimate would have a range of ± 5% while a workers' compensation loss estimate would have a range of ± 15%

Discounting of Reserves

As previously discussed, loss reserves can be discounted for the time value of money to account for the lag time between the occurrence of an accident and payments made on the claim. This practice is neither mandated nor prohibited, but it is fiscally more conservative to use undiscounted reserves.

For purposes of preparing financial statements, the selected interest rate used for discounting is normally a risk-free rate of return as indicated by U.S. Treasury instruments or a risk-adjusted portfolio rate of return. For mergers and acquisitions, the chief financial officer will typically use the hurdle rate (the minimum or required rate of return).

Handling Reserve Liabilities in Mergers and Acquisitions

An important task for the actuary is the handling of reserve liabilities in mergers and acquisitions. The mergers and acquisitions team must accurately price the deal, and one of the variables that may factor into the deal is the value of reserve liabilities. Pricing the deal does not just mean denominating the price that will be paid for the acquisition or the transfer and sharing of stock in a merger; it also includes a determination of whether or not some or all of the liabilities will be purchased with the deal, the disposition of those liabilities, and the value of those liabilities.

There are three basic approaches to handling reserve liabilities in mergers and acquisitions: the acquiring organization assumes responsibility; the selling organization retains responsibility; or the parties agree to sell the responsibility for the liabilities to a third party.

When the acquiring organization agrees to acquire the reserve liabilities, the buyer must be confident that the purchase price properly reflects the cost of disposing of the outstanding claims. The buyer can then decide if they will pay the reserves off as if they were the acquired organization or they can sell this portfolio of liabilities to an insurance carrier.

If the seller retains the responsibility for reserve liabilities, the seller must set aside sufficient funds from the proceeds of the sale to dispose of the outstanding reserve liabilities.

If the parties agree that neither one wants the responsibility, as a part of the deal, they can agree that the responsibility for the reserve liabilities will be transferred to an insurance carrier in the form of a portfolio transfer.

Regardless of the approach taken, the actuary must provide an accurate valuation of reserve liabilities to support the decisions and pricing of the merger or acquisition deal.

Accounting Issues

In the opening paragraphs of this chapter, we summarized the tasks of the actuaries, accountants, and auditors. As a reminder, unlike the actuary, who makes an estimate of losses and reserves, the accountant is responsible for disclosing the liabilities associated with the reserves.

Public accounting is a self-regulating profession. The Financial Accounting Standards Board issues proclamations that detail how certain transactions will be treated and all Certified Public Accountants must follow the guidelines specified in these Accounting Standards. There are two major accounting standards that affect the risk manager: Statement of Financial Accounting Standards No. 5 (FAS 5) for corporations and Governmental Accounting Standards Board Statement No. 10 (GAS 10) for governmental entities.

As applicable to risk management, these two Accounting Standards have common elements that include the following details:

1. Objectives – Both establish accounting and financial reporting standards for risk financing and insurance-related activities of corporations and governmental entities.

2. Recording Losses on a Financial Statement – Two basic criteria for recording loss reserve estimates are established:

    a. There must be a reasonable probability that an asset has been impaired or a liability incurred as of the date of the financial statement; and

    b. The amount of loss can be reasonably estimated.

3. Range of Estimates

    a. Range of reasonable estimates – for financial statement purposes

        i. When some amount within the range appears at the time to be a better estimate than any other amount within the range, that amount should be accrued.

        ii. When no amount within the range is a better estimate than any other amount, the minimum amount in the range should be accrued.

    b. Range of possible outcomes – for retention analysis

        i. Confidence levels – for prospective funding requirements, financial scenario testing

        ii. By line of business and year – for mergers and acquisitions, loss portfolio transfers

4. Structured Settlements

Because large claims are sometimes settled through the use of an annuities (each of which make specified periodic payments for either a set period of time or for the life of the claimant), the accountant must record and disclose an appropriate amount for that liability. Generally, the funds for the annuity are provided by a life insurance carrier through an annuity contract. The cost of the annuity is less than the sum of the individual payments because of the time value of money and the insurance carrier's ability to invest the funds at a higher return than that guaranteed on the annuity contract.

There are three methods of accounting for a structured settlement:

    a. If the annuity is in the name of the organization, the loss reserve liability should be carried on the balance sheet;

    b. If the annuity is in the name of the claimant with no release, no balance sheet entry is required but a note disclosing the outstanding amount is necessary; and

    c. If the annuity is in the name of the claimant with a release, no entry or note on the balance sheet is necessary.

FAS 113 is another Accounting Standard that has relevance to the risk manager whenever the risk management program includes the use of a captive insurance company. It addresses the transfer of risk that is necessary to sustain tax-deductibility of insurance premiums. Under FAS 113, there must be a valid transfer of risk that is dependent upon the organization assuming significant insurance risk and the reasonable possibility that there may be a significant loss for the transaction. This standard is applicable to all insurance transactions.

When reinsurance is involved, FAS 113 provides guidance regarding accounting for reinsurance: there must be a 10% chance that a 10% loss can occur, testing the present values of cash flows for both premiums and losses while using reasonable interest rates. If this test fails, "premiums" must be treated as deposit accounting, (i.e., the organization cannot deduct the "premium" for tax purposes, but the organization can deduct losses as they are paid, such as reimbursing the reinsurer as the reinsurer pays losses).

From an accounting perspective, the questions under FAS 113 are, "when is risk transferred?" and "what is the probability of loss to an insurer or reinsurer?"

To illustrate how using the FAS 113 basic minimum criteria of 10% probability of a loss of at least 110% of premium works, consider the following exhibit:

	X1	X2	X3	X4	X5	X6	X7	X8	X9	X10
Premium	5	5	5	5	5	5	5	5	5	5
Losses	4	4	4	4	7	4	4	4	4	4

In this exhibit, the losses of 7 in year 5 of 10 satisfy the 10% probability of loss, and the value of 7 exceeds the 110% threshold for that year, so under FAS 113, the "premiums" would represent a transfer or risk with sufficient probability that tax-deductibility would be permitted.

Risk Management Tax Issues

While tax management is not the responsibility of the risk manager, the risk management program can be affected by income tax rules, and the risk manager must take the impact of taxes into account in making decisions regarding the risk management program. While the following discussion is not intended as tax advice (for income tax advice and counsel, speak to an attorney or certified public accountant), these are general guidelines to be considered in making risk management decisions.

Programs with Self-Insurance and Retained Losses – Losses are deductible as expenses only in the tax year the losses are paid. Loss reserve liabilities are not deductible when incurred. Premiums paid for insurance coverage, including excess coverage, are deductible in the year when paid, pro rata over the policy term, or as losses are paid, depending upon the structure of the program. For example, in a paid loss retrospective rating program, a substantial portion of the "premium" is based on paid losses. Any premiums paid on deposit that are not based on paid losses, such as the basic premium or any non-subject premiums included, are deductible when paid, but the variable portions based on the payment of losses are not deductible until the losses are paid and that portion of the premium is determined.

Special Tax Rules Applying to Insurance Companies

Since the captive is a separate economic entity, it is subject to income taxation on its insurance activities, even though the premiums paid by the policyholders to the captive are not generally deductible to the policyholder.

Under the IRS rules, insurance companies, including captives, are grouped into three size categories for purposes of taxation. For insurance companies writing less than $350,000 annual premium, the net underwriting income and net investment income is non-taxable under Section 501 c 15 of the Internal Revenue Code. (The reader will note that this is the same section that provides non-taxability of charitable organizations, the entities organized under Section 501 c 3, or the so-called "non-profit" organizations. These organizations are not "non-profit" but actually "non-taxable" or "tax-exempt.")

For insurance companies writing less than $1,200,000 in annual premium, net underwriting income is non-taxable, but net investment income is subject to income taxation. Because net underwriting income is non-taxable for all insurance companies writing less than $1,200,000 annual premium, there is no deductibility issue for loss reserves.

For insurance companies writing more than $1,200,000 in annual premium, all net income is taxable, and loss reserves are deductible as a business expense. For these insurance companies, loss reserves are deductible in the tax year in which the losses are incurred.

Organizations that have chosen to use captive insurance companies in their risk management program will pay particular attention to these specific taxation provisions for insurance companies. If the captive insurance company premium level approaches the $1,200,000 mark, the risk manager may determine, for tax purposes, that another captive insurance company should be formed, and the premiums split between the captives to keep the written annual premium of each below the $1,200,000 level.

Summary of Tax Deductibility of All Insurance Plans

Plan	Premium	Loss
Guaranteed Cost	Yes (deductible by insured)	No (losses paid by insurer and not deductible by insured)
Dividend Plan	Yes (deductible by insured, dividends are income)	No (losses paid by insurer and not deductible by insured)
Incurred Loss Retro	Yes (deductible by insured when paid to carrier)	No (losses generate adjustment to premium)
Paid Loss Retro	Yes (deductible by insured when paid to carrier)	No (losses generate adjustment to premium)
Large Deductible	Yes (insofar as premiums for excess insurance are deductible)	Yes (as losses within deductible are paid)
Self-insured Retention (SIR)	Yes (insofar as premiums for excess insurance are deductible)	Yes (as looses within retention are paid)
Pool	Depends on pool program (pool contributions treated as premium in above examples)	Depends on pool program
Captive	Depends on extent of transfer of risk to third party and other considerations	Depends on program and extent to which losses are retained by taxpayer, generally structured so losses are deductible as incurred

Fundamental Rule for Taxation

The risk manager, when reviewing risk financing options, including captive insurance companies, should always check with the organization's tax department to determine what they are doing and what makes sense in the risk management program. There are so many differences in individual organization tax situations that it is almost impossible to make sound decisions without relying directly on the respective tax department. The issues to consider include the basis of accounting, loss carry-forwards and carry-backs, interactions with tax treaties, and valuations of acquisitions and divestitures.

Audit Issues

As mentioned at the beginning of this chapter, company financial statements should be reviewed systematically to ascertain current and future abilities to provide risk financing. This is an audit function.

Another role of the auditor is to investigate statements and information that may trigger risk concerns in the following areas:

- Self-insurance program.

- Captive insurance company. Risk to consider: Infrequent actuarial review and low capital

- Past decision not to purchase insurance. Risk to consider: No historical losses, low frequency/high severity

- Past decision to purchase insurance for prior uninsured exposure. Risk to consider: Runoff of past uninsured exposures

- Cash flow advantages. Risk to consider: Paid loss retro - low first payments, higher later payments

- Deductible or retention increase/Liability limits reduced. Risk to consider: Retained Losses increase under both scenarios.

- Membership in risk pooling program. Risk to consider: Later assessments

- Property values unchanged from prior year. Risk to consider: Impact of inflation, new construction, or renovations

- Solvency of insurance carrier(s). Risk to consider: Increased liabilities if insurer becomes insolvent

SECTION 4

CONTROL OF RISK

Chapter 13

Risk Control Fundamentals

Risk control is "any *conscious* action or inaction to reduce the probability, frequency, severity, or *unpredictability* of loss." The focus of risk control is on finding and implementing solutions to prevent or reduce actual harm, and the cost of risk. The focus is not on providing for monies paid in compensation – that is the role of risk financing.

There are two theories to risk control, the human approach or Domino Theory, and the engineering approach or Energy-Release Theory. H.W. Heinrich, published his Domino Theory in 1931, connecting injuries to the hereditary and environmental factors of workers. Dr. William Haddon Jr. posited the Energy-Release Theory in 1970 by showing that accidents, caused by the transfer of energy in a sudden manner that leads to injury, could be classified and controlled.

Domino Theory

In the Domino Theory of H.W. Heinrich, there are five steps:

1. <u>Social Environment and Ancestry</u> affect worker personality traits (e.g., stubbornness and recklessness) that lead to faults of persons.

2. <u>Faults of Persons</u> (e.g., bad temper or ignorance) contribute to unsafe acts and/or unsafe conditions.

3. <u>Unsafe Acts and/or Unsafe Conditions</u> (e.g., starting machinery improperly or the absence of safety devices) cause accidents.

4. <u>Accidents</u> (e.g., falls or flying objects) cause injury.

5. <u>Injuries</u> (e.g., cuts or broken bones) result from accidents.

Under the Heinrich's Domino Theory, risk control programs focused on any one of these steps can interrupt the step and prevent the accident or injury, just as removing a domino from a standing line will stop the chain of falling dominos. For example, if a worker can be taught safety procedures, the environmental factor of a lack of knowledge of safe working procedures will be interrupted. If a personal shortcoming (unsafe actions) can be resolved by removing a decision, a negligent act by the worker will not occur. If a faulty machine can be identified and repaired or removed from service, an accident will not occur. If protective equipment can be used, an accident will not cause an injury.

From these steps, it is obvious that the focus of this theory is on human behavior, as heredity, environment, personal shortcomings, negligent acts or omissions, and permitting faulty equipment are all tied to behaviors. If the behaviors can be controlled in some manner, accidents and therefore injuries will be controlled.

Energy-Release Theory

In the Energy-Release Theory, the sudden transfer or release of energy from a source to an object causes injury. Therefore, strategies that interrupt or suppress the buildup of energy or the sudden release of energy will prevent or mitigate the accident. There are three steps to this theory:

1. The control and prevention of a buildup of energy that has the potential to cause injury.

2. Creation of an environment that is not conducive to permitting an excessive buildup of energy.

3. Producing measures to counter the excessive buildup of energy or to prevent the sudden release of energy.

Under the Energy-Release Theory, risk control programs are focused on interrupting the buildup or controlling the release. For example, a speed governor on a motor vehicle will prevent excess speed, and excess speed is a buildup of potentially injurious energy. Using vents to remove flammable vapors from a painting booth creates an environment that will not permit the buildup of explosive vapors. Installing a pressure relief value on a steam boiler will allow the excessive pressure to be released on a controlled manner.

From these steps, it appears that the focus of this theory is on machinery. However, the actions used to control and prevent the buildup and create the safe environment, including countermeasures, are engineering solutions. The theory is nonetheless an essentially human activity, as someone must recognize the potential for injurious buildup of energy and determine how to prevent this buildup or control its sudden injurious release. For example, the engineer designs the gauge on a pressure vessel, but to prevent the explosion, an operator has to see that the gauge is in the red zone and shut down the machine to avoid the explosion.

Regardless of which approach is favored or used, risk control remains a PEOPLE PROCESS. Without individuals to identify shortcomings, negligent acts, faulty machines, injurious buildup of energy, and to adopt measures to counter any of these potential problems, accidents will happen. Only when people are involved and engaged in the safety procedures will risks be controlled.

Risk Control and the Risk Management Process

In this chapter we will discuss seven risk identification methods used in successful risk control programs.

1. <u>Checklists</u> for safety hazards uncover the root or underlying cause of problems, but employee input and involvement are required!

2. <u>Checklists for insurance coverage</u> will help the risk manager discover what exposures are insured and not insured. Risk control must be applied to both insured, and, even more importantly, uninsured exposures. Insurance coverage checklists help an organization understand its philosophy of risk tolerance.

3. <u>Financial information</u> can reveal for the risk manager the sources of the organization's revenues, the activities that draw the organization's cash flow, and the entities who are its business and financial partners.

4. <u>Personal on-site inspection</u> provides a good opportunity to educate the organization's staff regarding risk control objectives. Also, it can demonstrate the organization's commitment to safety and loss control. Frequently, it is the only way to discover exposures, perils, and special hazards. It can also uncover problems requiring immediate attention. Sometimes this approach is referred to as MBWA (management by walking around).

5. <u>Flow chart analysis</u> can uncover a simple change in procedure that could reduce frequency/severity and eliminate some claims. It is especially useful in identifying operations in pre- or post-merger and acquisition situations.

6. <u>Loss data, incident reports, and claim data</u> can identify frequency and severity trends, but the accuracy and applicability of the data must be considered, particularly if insurance carriers produce the data, as those records will only identify insured exposures.

7. <u>Review of contracts</u> identifies risks assumed or transferred by entity in contracts. Common contracts and leases with risk transfer and/or assumption include construction contracts, rental contracts, vendor service agreements, building and equipment leases, bills of lading, purchase orders, employment contracts, and employee leasing agreements, as well as insurance contracts. Examples include such exposures as fire legal liability, hold harmless or indemnification clauses, safe workplace clauses, and financial responsibility clauses.

Other Risk Control Tools

Incident analysis, used as a risk control tool (see Exhibit 13.1), focuses on tracking all incidents without regard to any subsequent accidents or losses that result from the incident. An incident is a disruptive event that may result in a loss or claim (includes near misses), and an accident is an event that leads to an undesirable event or consequence. By tracking and analyzing incidents, the risk manager can apply risk control techniques that are more timely or proximate to the event, that are preemptory, and that may help avoid or lessen future events of a similar nature. Because it reviews all incidents, including those that do not result in injury or property or damage, it can reinforce risk control issues to specifically involved or related employees before a loss occurs. This technique also can be used to demonstrate "due diligence" or "reasonable investigation" in defense of subsequent claims or losses.

Using incident analysis, the risk manager must first define what an "incident" is for the organization and then set up forms, incident reporting procedures, tracking systems, and a method for review. The incidents can be categorized in several ways: by work unit, division, or department; by injury cause, injury type, or location; by cost (if any); or by outcome, such as whether there is injury or property damage, and whether the injury or property damage is slight, moderate, serious, or catastrophic.

Risk management information systems (RMIS) are essential to any successful risk control program to assist the risk manager in monitoring incidents, losses, and claims; however, RMIS are not standardized in their scope or tracking/data conversions (some systems may be Windows based, DOS based, mainframe, or a written in a highly proprietary program language and unique to a particular vendor. Pricing considerations and performance variations are very significant, so to ensure long term viability and value for the purchasing entity, careful consideration should be given to the purchase or licensing of any system.

Exhibit 13.1: Incident Analysis

Sample Incident Analysis

Operations Facts: Your organization has a fleet of 100 delivery vehicles operating in a metropolitan area Monday through Friday. Each calendar quarter, there are 50 separate times when a fleet vehicle is involved in an "intersection event" during the course of business operation. (An "event" might be a blown red-light or two vehicles in the intersection traveling perpendicular to each other – a near miss.)

- Of these 50 events, 40 events occurred in intersections where the possibility of a collision with another vehicle existed.

- Of these 40 events, 30 events required one of the drivers to take some sort of evasive action to avoid a collision or loss of control of their vehicle.

- Of these 30 events, 20 resulted in an accident or a citation by law enforcement officer.

- Of these 20 events, 10 resulted in contact with another vehicle or pedestrian or fixed object or involved damage to the fleet vehicle.

- Of these 10, 3 resulted in loss to a third party or injury to an employee of the fleet operator.

- Of these 3, 1 resulted in at least 1 day of lost time or serious injury

Use of the terms "event", "incident", "accident", "loss", "occurrence", or "claim" are highly individual for each organization, and the risk manager must take care in identifying and defining what constitutes each of these terms when implementing an incident analysis program.

(The numbers shown above are for illustration purposes only, and do not reflect any particular organization's experience or what constitutes appropriate relationships.)

Net cost benefit analysis is a tool used to help management choose between risk control alternatives. The risk manager can compare the present value costs (cash outflows) with present value benefits (reductions in losses and other cash inflows) over time to measure the best rate of return. The expected value of losses and probability of losses is based on past loss experience.

Net cost benefit analysis uses the concept of present value of money to determine the most cost-effective risk control method to use, but the solution with best rate of return may not be chosen unless it is compatible with the organization's management philosophy.

The Six Primary Risk Control Techniques

Avoidance

True risk avoidance is totally eliminating an activity and/or exposure to an activity. It is a self-sufficient risk control technique, and no further action is required so long as the activity is truly eliminated. It is often difficult for the risk manager to sell this technique to management for several reasons (e.g., avoidance may be in conflict with the goals and profit motives of the organization, the activity the risk manager wishes to avoid may be inherent to the overall corporate mission, or the activity may be significant to the organization's revenue stream). It is also a difficult technique to implement because the risk manager may lack the appropriate decision-making authority.

There are two other considerations arising out of reliance upon risk avoidance as a self-sufficient technique. First, the attempt to avoid the risk may not be successful. Second, this technique does not address the residual problems from activities that are avoided in the future, but were undertaken in the past.

Loss Prevention

Loss prevention endeavors to reduce the frequency of claims from activities that cannot be eliminated; unlike avoidance, it does not eliminate the chance of loss. The term "prevention" implies an action taken to break the sequence of events that lead to a loss, or at least to make it less likely; loss prevention interrupts the domino effect of accident causation or the release of energy. It also allows entities to conduct operations that might otherwise have to be avoided. For example, fire can cause a catastrophic loss. It affects business owners, employees, customers, and suppliers as well as public safety. In Exhibit 13.2, we see that there are three elements necessary to have fire: fuel, oxygen, and ignition.

Exhibit 13.2: Fire Triangle

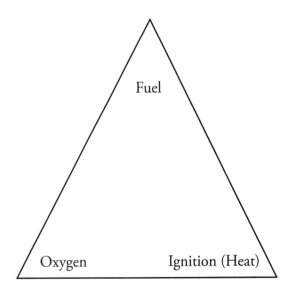

Eliminating all three is Avoidance.

Eliminating one is Prevention.

Note: It is interesting to note that in this example prevention achieves the same result as avoidance.

Loss Reduction

Loss Reduction is the reduction in severity or financial loss from losses and claims that are not prevented. It presumes a loss will occur but attempts to reduce the size or extent of the loss. There are both pre-loss and post-loss approaches. Using a fire as an example, a pre-loss approach would include installing firewalls in a building to prevent the spread of fire or installing fire suppression equipment such as sprinklers. A post-loss approach would be to implement emergency procedures, such as fire drills, escape ladders, and evacuation plans. Claims administration is also a post-loss approach to loss reduction.

Segregation, Separation, or Duplication

Segregation, Separation, or Duplication of Exposures is the fourth loss control technique. Segregation involves designating or designating a certain area within a building for high-risk exposure (e.g., segregating the computer room with security controlled access, or creating separate fire divisions within a building or structure).

Separation involves spreading property values and production activities over several geographical locations. When using separation, each single asset or operation is divided and kept in normal daily use. If one suffers a loss, the other must be sufficient to satisfy the needs of both. (e.g., warehouses in different locations and cross training of employees).

Duplication involves having a backup for critical systems or operations. The duplicate asset or activity is kept in reserve and unused; therefore, the duplicated unit is not exposed to the same loss (e.g., spare parts, duplicate accounting records and computer backups, or mutual aid pacts to use one another's facilities in case of a loss.)

Segregation, separation, and duplication do not attempt to avoid, prevent, or reduce loss to any single unit; they work primarily to reduce the severity of loss.

Transfer

Risk transfer is a technique that attempts to reduce risk to the organization or transfer a portion of the risk to another organization. Physical transfer shifts some or all of an operational function or exposure to an outside source (e.g., using a common carrier to distribute manufactured goods, employee leasing, or subcontracting). It also shifts the operational and, generally, at least some of the legal risk to another party or entity. Contractual Transfer is the assumption or limitation of certain liabilities relating to another. The four classifications of contractual transfers are hold harmless or indemnification agreements, exculpatory agreements, waivers of subrogation, and limit of liability clauses. A comparison of contractual transfers is shown in Exhibit 13.3, later in this chapter. We will discuss insurance transfers in another chapter.

Combination

Combination of one or more risk control techniques is another control technique. Avoidance is the only technique that works solely on its own. To be successful, all other attempts to control risk should apply a combination of techniques (e.g., the risk manager may decide to implement loss prevention and loss reduction techniques so that losses that are not preventable are at least capable of being reduced).

Using Contractual Transfer of Risk

Because contractual transfer is a much used and often misunderstood method of risk management, we will spend some time reviewing the details.

Hold Harmless Agreements

Is it an indemnification clause or a hold harmless clause, or is there really a difference? Hearing the words alone, one might expect an indemnification clause to work like an insurance policy written on an indemnification basis – to restore the insured to the financial position the insured was prior to the loss. Under the pure meaning of indemnification, the indemnitee would be made whole by the indemnitor, but only on a reimbursement basis. The term "hold harmless" appears to be broader in scope: that one party expects to be treated in such a way that any harm passes it by, suggesting that another party would have to stand in its place.

In practice, the terms are used jointly, as in "indemnify and hold harmless," and are, by custom and practice, used interchangeably, like many other terms in the insurance and risk management field. For purposes of this book, the term "hold harmless" will be used to mean either an indemnification clause or a hold harmless clause or an "indemnify and hold harmless" clause.

Hold Harmless Agreements are contractual arrangements whereby one party (the indemnitor) assumes the liability inherent in a situation, thereby relieving the other party (the indemnitee) of that liability. (To keep the terminology straight, remember that the employer is the one who hires the employee. Similarly, the indemnitor is the one who indemnifies the indemnitee.)

The hold harmless agreement may include the indemnitee's cost of settlements or judgments paid to a third party and the costs of defense. Hold harmless agreements may also require indemnification at the conclusion of claim or suit, or they may require the indemnitor to assume indemnitee's actual defense obligation during a claim or suit. This distinction is important because it addresses who is responsible for providing the indemnitee's defense and therefore who selects and controls the defense for the indemnitee. Beyond addressing the responsibilities of defense, there are three main classifications of hold harmless agreements: Limited, Intermediate, and Broad.

In a **limited form** hold harmless agreement, the indemnitor assumes responsibility for the indemnitee's liability for the indemnitor's own, sole negligence. This classification applies to agreements requiring indemnification for occurrences arising out of the indemnitor's operations.

> For example: Party A reaffirms responsibility for *his own negligent acts*. Party B is thus protected in cases where he is held vicariously responsible for Party A's negligence. Party B has acquired a *contractual* right to indemnity where the basic tort law of the jurisdiction may or may not entitle him to it absent such contractual transfer.

An **intermediate form** hold harmless agreement incorporates the responsibilities in the *limited* hold harmless agreement plus responsibility for the indemnitee's liability for the indemnitor's and indemnitee's joint negligence. This classification applies to agreements requiring indemnification for all occurrences arising out of the indemnitor's operations, excluding only the liability arising from the indemnitee's sole negligence.

> For example: Party A reaffirms responsibility for his own acts and agrees to assume full responsibility for *joint and/or concurrent negligence* of both parties. In many such contracts (especially construction contracts),

Party A will agree to assume responsibility for all events except those resulting from the *sole negligence* of Party B (i.e., 100% responsibility for all concurrent negligence situations). This does not apply to events arising from the sole negligence of Party B or the negligence of another subcontractor or entity beyond the indemnitor and the indemnitee.

A **broad form** hold harmless agreement incorporates the responsibility of both the *limited* and *intermediate* plus the indemnitor agrees to be responsible for the indemnitee's sole negligence. This classification applies to agreements requiring complete indemnification of the indemnitee for all occurrences without reference to negligence; it can even include those situations arising from the sole negligence of another entity. As an example: Party A assumes responsibility for *all liability without regard to fault* of himself and/or Party B. Here Party A assumes not only the responsibility for his acts, plus any acts arising from joint and/or concurrent negligence of Party A and Party B, but those situations which result from the sole negligence of Party B. This extreme variant may require Party A to assume responsibility for the negligent acts of some other entity (over whom Party A has no control), which result in a claim being made on Party B.

These broad form agreements would appear to be totally unreasonable, since they would include even losses that do not arise from the indemnitor's negligence and may involve situations in which the indemnitor has no control or involvement. These broad form agreements are sometimes referred to as being against public policy or unconscionable, in that a negligent party may avoid responsibility for injury by having made a contract with another party.

Nevertheless, the courts may enforce such agreements that do not violate a statute or public policy. Generally, the courts will require the intent of the parties to enter into such an agreement to be expressly reflected in the contract (absolutely clear and unequivocal) and may require specific consideration to be enforceable.

Many contracts that apply the risk control technique of transfer are used jointly with contractual transfers for risk financing purposes (more about that later). The common example is to join an indemnification or hold harmless agreement with the contractual requirement to provide additional insured status to the indemnitee. There are a number of insurance policy endorsements that have attempted to "clarify" the intent of the policy language regarding the broad form assumption of responsibility that have resulted in gaps in coverage which then leads to a breach of the contractual requirement of the indemnitor to provide coverage and indemnification to the indemnitee. The risk manager must be cautious when requiring indemnification and broad form hold harmless agreements or when assuming the indemnitee's liability under similar arrangements.

Real World Scenarios for Hold Harmless Agreements

Facts: A contractor (the indemnitor) is remodeling an entire supermarket while the supermarket (indemnitee) continues operations.

Limited Form – (Scenario 1) The contractor knocks over a display of eggs and walks away; a customer slips on the broken eggs and is injured. The contractor must indemnify the supermarket (contractor's own, sole negligence). (Scenario 2) The contractor knocks over a display of eggs and informs the supermarket manager, who does not clean up the mess promptly. A customer slips on the broken eggs and is injured. The failure of the supermarket to respond to a timely notification creates a shared liability situation; therefore, the contractor is only required to indemnify supermarket for its proportionate share of the total liability. The store may not seek payment for the supermarket's potential negligence, if any, in failing to timely clean up hazard from the indemnitor.

Intermediate Form – (Scenario 2 continued) Here the contractor is responsible for at least their proportionate share of fault, and the contractor must indemnify the supermarket for the supermarket's joint/comparative fault. (Scenario 3) A supermarket employee knocks over the eggs and a customer slips and is injured. The supermarket cannot obtain indemnity from the contractor for the loss as the loss arose from the sole negligence of the supermarket (failure to inspect, warn, and clean up); the contractor was not involved in the actions that produced the loss.

Broad Form – (Scenario 3 – continued) In this scenario, the contractor is responsible for all losses arising from the sole negligence of the supermarket as the contractor has willingly taken the responsibility for the premises generally. (Scenario 4) A supermarket customer or another unrelated contractor knocks over the eggs resulting in the slip/fall of a customer. The contractor is still liable, for the same reason as in scenario 3. (Scenario 5) A hurricane wipes out the building and kills a customer. The contractor may be contractually liable for the loss of the building and the death of the customer because of the broad assumption of liability.

Another Way of Looking at the Three Types of Hold Harmless Agreements

From the perspective of the indemnitor's liability, the limited form can be described as applying to "mine." The intermediate form can be characterized as applying to "mine and ours." The broad form can be labeled as applying to "mine, ours, and yours."

These types of wording commonly appear in construction agreements, services, purchase orders, waivers, hold harmless agreements, leases, and other contracts and instruments. When looking for hold harmless wording, the risk manager should look for references to insurance clauses, liability clauses, hold harmless and indemnification clauses, or other camouflaged language, such as mutual release or waivers of subrogation.

The risk manager should be aware of any anti-indemnity statutes (intended by the states to prevent parties from eliminating their incentive to exercise due care) that might affect the interpretation of a hold harmless agreement. Anti-indemnity statutes are laws limiting or prohibiting the use of hold harmless agreements in contractual transfers in certain circumstances. In many states, for certain types of contracts, broad form hold harmless agreements are restricted, even fully prohibited by state statutes as being against public policy. Since the determination of whether or not a statute applies is a legal opinion, the risk manager should always seek advice from legal counsel. The states with anti-indemnity statutes are listed in Exhibit 13.3.

Exhibit 13.3 – Anti-Indemnification Statute States - 2008

Anti-Indemnification Statute States - 2008

The states listed below have anti-indemnification statutes applicable to construction contracts, unless otherwise noted:

Alaska	Massachusetts	Oregon
Arizona	Michigan	Rhode Island
California	Minnesota	Pennsylvania[5]
Connecticut[1]	Mississippi	South Carolina
Delaware	Montana	South Dakota
Florida	Nebraska	Tennessee
Georgia	New Hampshire	Texas3
Hawaii	New Jersey	Utah
Idaho	New Mexico[3]	Virginia
Illinois	New York4	Washington
Indiana	North Carolina	West Virginia
Louisiana[2]	Ohio	Wyoming[3]
Maryland[1]	North Dakota	

1 Applies to construction contracts and leases
2 Applies to oil and gas contracts only
3 Applies to construction and oil and gas contracts
4 Applies to construction contracts, leases, and catering agreements
5 Applies to architects, engineers, and surveyors

Other Contractual Transfers

In addition to hold harmless agreements, there are other types of contractual transfers. These include exculpatory agreements, waivers of subrogation, and limit of liability clauses.

An exculpatory agreement is an arrangement whereby one party agrees to absolve a second party from any blame, even when damage or injury is caused by negligence of the second party. An exculpatory agreement is basically a waiver of liability.

For example, a health club member alleged that negligent design of a weightlifting bench caused weights to fall on him. The member had already signed a waiver of liability arising of use of the facilities and equipment. The court ruled that injuries from weightlifting were the responsibility of the member and upheld the exculpatory clause in favor of the health club.

Subrogation is the right of an insurer, after paying a loss to or for its insured, to sue the negligent party and reclaim the loss amount. In commercial agreements, parties often negotiate to waive the right of their insurer to claim against the wrongdoer after paying a loss. Thus, waiver of subrogation means that an insurer or other party entitled to subrogation waves that right in the particular context.

For example, a landlord buys a fire insurance policy from an insurer. The tenant's negligence causes a $1 million fire in the landlord's office building. The insurer pays the landlord $1 million. If the landlord's contract had a waiver of subrogation as to the tenant, that waiver would have barred the insurer from suing the tenant after the insurer paid the landlord $1 million.

A limitation of liability clause in a contract with a client typically limits the liability of the company to some proportion of its fee or a defined dollar value.

For example, a developer sued the consulting engineers who had designed a manmade lake for a housing project. The lakes liner failed, leading to a $5 million claim against the engineer. The engineer asserted that, as specified in a clause in its contract with the developer, liability was limited to the amount of its fee. A trial court agreed with the engineer.

Exhibit 13.4: Comparison of Contractual Transfers

	Hold Harmless Agreement	Exculpatory Agreement	Waiver of Subrogation	Limit of Liability Clause
Definition	Affirmative assumption of the financial consequences for liabilities of another by contract	Pre-event exoneration of the fault of one party that results in any loss or specified loss(es) to another (also called damage waiver)	Pre-event relinquishment of the right of one or both parties' insurers to seek recovery from culpable party for loss payments made to insured	Pre-event limitation of the amount, type or method of calculation of damages available by one or both parties to an agreement
Tort	Does not absolve the indemnitee from its tort liability to a third party	Absolves the tort liability between one or both parties to a contract – does not apply to 3rd parties	Does not absolve tort liability of the parties, but prevents insurers from any recovery of loss payments based on such tort liabilities	Does not absolve the tort liability of one or both parties, however, it limits recovery of the amount of damages between the parties
Funding	Requires Indemnitor to be able to provide funding/financing of assumed liabilities	No affirmative obligation to provide funding except that required to absorb loss	Same as exculpatory, except the loss is absorbed by insurer under insurance transfer	Requires funding or financing of amounts payable for amount of damages as defined in contract
Anti-indemnity Application	May be subject to anti-indemnity statutes	Not subject to most anti-indemnity statutes	Not subject to anti-indemnity statutes	Usually involves bills of lading, cargo, freight, or cartage and is not subject to anti-indemnity statutes
General Considerations	If too broad, may void entire indemnity obligation; may be effectively voided by additional insured endorsement wording	May be construed as a waiver of subrogation if claim is brought by a party's insurer	Typically, must be entered into prior to any loss payment by insurer to be binding on the insurer	May be the exclusive remedy of a party for any/all claims under contract without regard to amount of true loss

When creating a risk control program for contractual review, the risk manager or senior management must decide what contracts or agreements will be reviewed and determine a mechanism for completing the review. Ensuring access to and reviewing all appropriate contracts (both those the organization uses and those of others the organization enters into) will be a challenge. The risk manager must work with the legal department or legal consultants to monitor, evaluate, and continuously update contract language.

There are also some practical problems with the contractual review process, such as who is in the driver's seat to negotiating the contract – the risk manager, the operations manager, or the legal department. Sometimes the risk manager is the last to know about a contract, but coordination with attorneys is necessary to ensure the scope of assumed liabilities and the viability of contract language.

When negotiating a contract, it is wise to not ask for more than you can give. State-to-state contract interpretation will vary because governing laws are dynamic, and there are limitations, such as safety in workplace, sole negligence, and anti-indemnity statutes.

Some common practical issues concern contractual transfers:

The contract can shift the risk to another but the risk still exists.

Both parties are expected to perform or assume certain responsibilities; however, if either party fails to meet the responsibilities, those responsibilities may fall back on the other party.

There is little or no control of either party's performance by the other party, and sometimes the out-of-sight/out-of-mind or morale hazard comes into play.

A contract should not be substituted for normal business responsibility or more appropriate risk control techniques.

Approaches to Loss Control

There are three approaches to loss control: financial approach, systems approach, and practical approach.

The **financial approach** measures the net cost benefit and recovery of the investment in a loss control program.

The **systems approach** tracks risk exposures on a flowchart or hazard evaluation index.

The **practical approach** involves grass roots support (see Customer Satisfaction Survey), top management support, incentive and reward programs, effective safety committees, finding money for safety, and willingness of all to compromise and cooperate.

Administration of Risk Control Programs

Administration of the risk control program requires acquisition of resources and then allocation of those resources, both internally and externally. The risk manager should always try to consider alternative treatments. For example, when the risk manager is selecting a risk control technique to address the burglary exposure for an industrial warehouse in a high crime area, there are four alternatives:

1. Hire a night watchman – While this has the greatest potential to reduce burglary losses, it has a high, ongoing cash flow with a long payback period, as well as introducing a human resource exposure (e.g., the injury, disability, or death of the watchman) and a liability exposure (e.g., the watchman shoots an intruder).

2. Contract with a security firm – This should have a lower ongoing cash outflow, but there is less control over the third-party employees and therefore less potential to reduce losses

3. Install a central station burglar alarm system – Generally, this has the second highest potential to reduce losses; it has a high initial cash outflow with a shorter payback. Depending upon the response time of the local authorities, there may still be a residual risk of burglary

4. Buy two guard dogs – The alternative has the lowest initial cash outflow and a short payback, but may create an unacceptable level of liability and human resource risk (e.g., the dogs bite someone).

The key to successful risk control is **communication**. This includes communication between employees and third parties concerning post-claim/loss response (must demonstrate genuine care and concern) as well as communication between risk manager, organization management, and department heads. The risk manager can be an important information resource by sending copies of articles of interest to managers relating important changes in law and recent legal cases. The risk manager can arrange for some managers to attend quarterly loss or claim review meetings and invite other managers and executives to visit to see what goes on. Another form of communication is the stewardship report. This annual report to executive management and the board shows claim activity, new loss control activities, status of ongoing risk control programs, and the costs and benefits of these programs, etc.

Summary

Risk control is a people process! The true costs of loss to an organization go well beyond the obvious "hard" or quantitative costs. Successful risk control programs are based on careful risk identification and risk analysis. A successful risk control program will incorporate some or all of the risk control techniques, with contractual transfer of risk one of the most significant. With this in mind, a contract review program is a key component of loss control; in order to classify hold harmless provisions in contractual transfers and determine their impact, these provisions must be reviewed and analyzed. Administration of a risk control program requires prioritization, implementation, coordination, follow up, and communication throughout the organization.

Chapter 14

Risk Control and Mitigation

Introduction

Why should risk managers find it necessary to prevent injuries and accidents?

First and foremost, a responsible organization does not want to hurt anyone: employees, customers, or third parties. Also, accidents that are prevented do not involve any other part of the risk management process.

The cost of losses arising from damages and injuries are a key component of any organization's cost of risk, either directly, through retentions or deductibles, or indirectly, through future insurance premium increases due to adverse experience, not to mention adverse publicity and lost productivity. Further, the law, through OSHA, DOT, other federal and state laws governing the workplace, and state workers compensation statutes, require the implementation of safety programs.

What causes accidents?

There are two root or fundamental causes of accidents: unsafe acts or unsafe conditions. All accidents can be traced back to an individual committing an unsafe act, negligently or intentionally, or the existence of an unsafe condition.

Accident Prevention Basics

To help mitigate both of these conditions, the organization can use the six Accident Prevention Basics: eliminating the hazard, substituting a less hazardous substance or process, using engineering controls, administrative controls, personal protective equipment, and training.

Consider this "accident waiting to happen:" Humpty Dumpty is sitting on top of a wall so he can wave at the king and all his men when they parade by. What can be done, using the Accident Prevention Basics to attempt to prevent him falling and getting scrambled?

<u>Eliminating the hazard</u> – Eliminating the hazard is similar to the risk control technique of avoidance. If the wall is removed, Humpty will not be able to sit on it.

<u>Substituting a less hazardous substance or process</u> – Some substances or processes are less hazardous than others, such as a robotic punch press instead of a manually operated machine. If only low walls were used, if Humpty fell, he would not fall as far.

<u>Engineering controls</u> – Engineering controls are devices or equipment that will lessen the chance of an accident occurring. Instead of Humpty sitting on a wall, the king would provide a scaffold or perhaps an air cushion on the ground.

Administrative controls – Administrative controls consist of rules or activities that management undertakes, such as safety meetings, supervision, or safety procedures and manuals. The king might pass a law forbidding anyone from sitting on the walls and post a sign stating just that, or the king might send his men around to ask Humpty and others to climb down from the wall before they get hurt.

Personal protective equipment – Personal protective equipment are exactly what they sound like, safety goggles, steel-toed shoes, gloves, hard hats, respirators, and other similar gear worn or used by workers. Humpty might be carrying a parachute or bungee cord that will lessen the impact of his fall, or he might have a padded suit.

Training – Training is education. Humpty would be trained not to sit on the wall, or how to sit safely and how to use any personal protective equipment.

Safety and Health Standards and Enforcement

The Occupational Safety and Health Administration (OSHA), a part of the U.S. Department of Labor (www.osha.gov), was formed "to assure the safety and health of America's workers by setting and enforcing standards; providing training, outreach, and education; establishing partnerships; and encouraging continual improvement in workplace safety and health." The OSHA General Duty Clause states "each employer shall furnish to each of his employees employment and a place of employment which are free from recognized hazards that are causing or are likely to cause death or serious physical harm to his employees." OSHA also sees that the employee has a responsibility for working safely because according to OSHA "each employee shall comply with occupational safety and health standards and all rules, regulations, and orders issued pursuant to this Act which are applicable to his own actions and conduct." The General Industry Standards are listed in Title 29 of the Code of Federal Regulations Subpart B Part 1910 (29 CFR Part 1910). The Construction Safety Standards can be found in 29 CFR Part 1926. OSHA enforces these regulations through inspections and by citations or fines.

Many states have elected to establish their own agencies to administer federal OSHA standards through delegated authority. Authorized state OSHA programs are required to implement health and safety standards that are at least as stringent as federal requirements, and may be more extensive if authorized by state legislatures. The following states and territories have approved state plans:

Alaska	Michigan	South Carolina
Arizona	Minnesota	Tennessee
California	Nevada	Utah
Connecticut*	New Jersey*	Vermont
Hawaii	New Mexico	Virgin Islands*
Indiana	New York*	Virginia
Iowa	North Carolina	Washington
Kentucky	Oregon	Wyoming
Maryland	Puerto Rico	

*Note: The Connecticut, New Jersey, New York and Virgin Islands plans cover public sector employment only.

(www.osha.gov January 2009)

Despite extensive regulations and significant enforcement authority assigned to OSHA, some company executives and managers fail to take their compliance obligations seriously. The reasons are simple: First, they argue, it is the government, and the likelihood of an OSHA visit is almost non-existent since there are not enough inspectors. Also, OSHA fines may seem to be an insignificant portion of the total cost of risk. However, in addition to the usual fines and penalties OSHA can impose daily fines and even jail sentences on flagrant violators.

Thus, risk managers must continuously educate managers and supervisors of the importance of documenting all OSHA compliance activities. Not only is documentation in and of itself a compliance obligation, failure to maintain required records specified by regulation makes it difficult if not impossible to prove that required compliance measures have been implemented.

In addition to federal and state OSHA laws, there are other sources of legislation. The Mine Safety Health Administration (MSHA) is also a part of the U.S. Department of Labor, with jurisdiction over the mining industry. According to the MSHA website, their mission is "to administer the provisions of the Federal Mine Safety and Health Act of 1977 (Mine Act) and to enforce compliance with mandatory safety and health standards as a means to eliminate fatal accidents; to reduce the frequency and severity of nonfatal accidents; to minimize health hazards; and to promote improved safety and health conditions in the Nation's mines."

The U.S. Department of Transportation (DOT) oversees federal highway, air, railroad, maritime, and other transportation administration functions. The DOT's top priority is to keep the traveling public safe and secure, increase their mobility, and have the transportation system contribute to the nation's economic growth.

Statutes, including safety and workers compensation, differ by state. For that reason, employers must look to their own state's statutes to determine what the law requires for them to be in compliance. The Department of Labor maintains a website that outlines the list of benefits by state: www.dol.gov/esa.

The Office of Workers' Compensation Programs (part of U.S. Department of Labor, Employment Standards Administration) administers four major disability compensation programs that provide wage replacement benefits, medical treatment, vocational rehabilitation and other benefits to certain workers or their dependents who experience work-related injury or occupational disease. These programs, the Energy Employees Occupational Illness Compensation Program, the Federal Employees' Compensation Program, the Longshore and Harbor Workers' Compensation Program, and the Black Lung Benefits Program, serve the specific employee groups who are covered under the relevant statutes and regulations. They also serve taxpayers and employers by mitigating the financial burden resulting from workplace injury.

Other agencies and organizations also have significant involvement in employee health and safety:

The National Institute for Occupational Safety and Health (NIOSH) certifies respiratory protective devices and air sampling detector tubes, recommends occupational exposure limits for hazardous substances, and assists OSHA and MSHA in occupational safety and health research.

The American National Standards Institute and Safety Products (ANSI) tests and certifies other types of personal protective equipment, such as hard hats.

The National Fire Protection Association (NFPA) is an international organization that promotes fire protection and prevention.

The NFPA 101 Code, also known as the "Life Safety Code," addresses those construction, protection, and occupancy features necessary to minimize danger to life from fire, including smoke, fumes, or panic.

The American Conference of Governmental Industrial Hygienists (ACGIH) publishes a schedule of recommended biological and chemical exposure limits for the workplace. These limits are called Threshold Limit Values (TLVs), and typically include exposure limits based on short-term exposures and time-weighted averages for a full work shift. Although TLVs do not have the regulatory force of OSHA standards, they are based on the most current research from NIOSH and others, and can be updated much more rapidly than OSHA standards, which require extensive rulemaking and approval by Congress.

Safety and Health Program Elements

Good safety and health programs require the implementation of eight key elements: management leadership; accountability; responsibility and authority; employee participation; hazard assessment and control; employee information and training; accident reporting, investigation, and analysis; post injury management; and evaluation of program effectiveness. We will continue this review using only the term safety, but keep in mind that safety also advances health.

Element 1 – Management Leadership

Because it is foundational to the success of the risk management program, the safety policy should be included in the organization's overall mission statement. To demonstrate that management is fully committed to safety standards, it is critical that the CEO or organizational head include a signed statement that the organization expects cooperation and compliance with this policy.

The safety program must be in writing, and must identify safety policies, goals, and objectives. Responsibility and accountabilities should be defined for managers, supervisors, and employees. The written safety program should provide authority, information, training, and resources to fulfill these responsibilities. Management must "walk the walk" by integrating safety into the business process, with the intention of showing that safety is a matter of "do as I do," not just "do as I say."

For example, if the safety policy requires a hard hat and safety glasses at a job site, when the CEO visits the job site, that person and all accompanying persons must don the required gear.

Safety must be integrated into the business process, a part of the business, not in addition to the business.

Element 2 – Accountability, Responsibility and Authority

The safety goals and objectives should be included and properly weighed in performance reviews and employee compensation. They should be both activity-oriented and results-oriented. Safety responsibilities should be defined by position, whether organizational safety, risk management, purchasing, maintenance, operations, human resources, or any other area of the organization. There should be enforcement of safety responsibilities with authority assigned to appropriate individuals. The program must stress individual accountability to all employees, whether top management or front line employees.

Element 3 – Employee Participation

If the safety program is to succeed, every employee must participate. There are many opportunities for employees to participate in the safety program, from the establishment of the initial program to the implementation of the safety program, and even to the evaluation of the safety program. In some states, safety committees are mandated by law, but even if there are no state mandates, safety committees should be a vital part of the safety program. The safety committee should have a charter, or be recognized by the organization's top management as being important to the organization and its employees. It should have cross department representation with equal representation from management and front line employees. The designated safety coordinator should not be the chair of the committee. The chair should be another employee so that new ideas are implemented by the safety committee. There should be regular meetings, an agenda and minutes should be maintained for future reference, and action items should result from each meeting.

Employees should be involved in safety inspections because they probably know the operation better than either management, the risk management department, or even outside experts. There should be regular communication between management and employees covering workplace safety and health issues: access to relevant information; the ability to be involved in exposure assessment and control; the ability to report injuries, illnesses, and occupational exposures, and to recommend appropriate controls; as well as prompt response to reports and recommendations. Management should not act in any way to discourage participation by employees in the safety program. The safety program should allow reporting of unsafe conditions and actions, directly and anonymously.

Element 4 – Hazard Assessment and Control

Statistics show that most accidents are caused by unsafe behaviors or acts rather than unsafe conditions. Unsafe conditions account for 10% of the cases; uncontrolled events (such as a natural disaster) are the cause of only about 2% of accidents, but the root cause of 88% of all accidents is unsafe behavior. In other words, 98 percent of all accidents are caused by unsafe behaviors, unsafe conditions, or a combination of both, and all of these behaviors or conditions can be controlled!

Why do employees work unsafely? Often, they are unaware their behavior is unsafe because they have never been told it is unsafe, and they have not been properly trained in the safe methods of doing their jobs. When employees work unsafely, they are not getting regular reminders and feedback from their supervisors. Also, workplace conditions may encourage unsafe behavior. If management emphasis is on increasing production at any cost, rather than working safely and avoiding accidents, employees will develop slipshod behaviors that lead to accidents.

Why do employees take risks and get injured? The natural rewards usually favor unsafe behavior because it is nearly always faster, more convenient, and comfortable to work unsafely.

For instance, not using a machine guard can increase the number of widgets produced because the worker does not have to move the guard or reach around it to take the completed widget off the machine. The employee is rewarded for making more widgets.

Unsafe behavior rarely results in an injury on any single occasion, so when rewards are certain and risks are low, it is easy for a worker to take the risk. But regular unsafe behavior virtually ensures that injuries will occur, and there is no predictor that will pinpoint when unsafe behavior will result in an injury or to whom the injury will occur.

Why use reward rather than punishment to manage behavior? Both rewards and punishment influence behavior, but punishment produces minimal compliance and lower overall morale of employees while rewards result in extra effort from employees and high morale. Punishment should be used only as a last resort. Legitimate everyday praise is the best reward for safe employee behavior.

As shown above, unsafe behaviors and conditions cause accidents. There is usually time, however, to correct unsafe conditions before an accident occurs because someone observes unsafe behaviors and conditions at least once before an accident occurs. This is why systematic identification and assessment of workplace hazards lead to safer working conditions for all employees. They can be done in several ways: physical inspections uncover unsafe working conditions; audits determine management practices regarding safety; job safety analysis (JSA) is used to identify work methods and determine whether or not they are safe; behavior-based safety results help pinpoint unsafe acts; and accident investigations, incident investigations, and trending can identify unsafe acts and unsafe conditions, work methods, and management practices that led to losses.

Element 5 – Employee Information and Training

Employees need to know they are responsible for their own safety and health program and they need all the information necessary to fulfill their responsibilities to that program. Every employee should receive specific training for each exposure, which includes the nature of the exposure and how to recognize it, any control measures (such as machine guards) and any protective procedures the employee must follow, and any provisions of applicable standards or regulations.

Training should start when an employee is hired and before the initial work assignment. There should be periodic training to maintain competency. Additional training should take place when there is a change in a workplace exposure or procedure, or when there is a change in job assignment. An effective training method is to pair a new employee with a highly experienced, safety-minded coworker so the new person can become familiar with the workplace, learn the skills needed, and observe first-hand someone following proper safety procedures and using safety equipment correctly. This approach teaches the new employee that working safely is expected and routinely accomplished, and that shortcuts are not tolerated.

All general safety training does not have to take place in a formal classroom setting. Very effective training can be accomplished using outside vendors, specialized training videos, safety committee meetings, "tool box" meetings, paycheck stuffers, posters, newsletters, computer-based interactive multimedia, Internet/intranet based self-study, and regular reminders on the job.

Element 6 – Accident Reporting, Investigation, and Analysis

What is the difference between an incident and an accident? An incident is an event that disrupts normal activities and may become a loss or claim; it is "a near miss." An accident is an incident, resulting in injury or damage to person or property, which has or will become a loss or claim; it is an unplanned event definite as to time and place that causes bodily injury or property damage.

They say there are no new accidents. Everything has happened before. So why investigate accidents? Investigation is necessary to identify causal factors involved in the accident and any needed changes that need to be implemented, whether they are employee behavior or physical plant. Investigating accidents also leads to a reduction in employee and equipment downtime and expenses. All accidents that cause bodily injury or property damage, all OSHA recordable injuries, all first-aid cases, and all close calls or near misses should be investigated. However, management should make it clear to everyone that the purpose of investigating accidents is NOT to assign blame.

```
┌─────────────────────────────────────────────┐
│         ┌───────────────────────────────┐   │
│         │  AUTOMOBILE ACCIDENT REPORT   │   │
│         └───────────────────────────────┘   │
│                                              │
│  LOCATION NAME AND ADDRESS _____   │
│  DATE OF ACCIDENT _____ TIME OF ACCIDENT ____ │
│  LOCATION CODE _____ LOCATION PHONE _____ │
│  DESCRIPTION OF VEHICLE:                      │
│     YEAR _____ MAKE _____ MODEL _____  │
│  V.I.N. (VEHICLE IDENTIFICATION)_____  │
│  DESCRIPTION OF DAMAGE _____   │
│  NAME AND ADDRESS OF DRIVER _____   │
│                                              │
│  BIRTHDATE _____ HOME PHONE _____ BUSINESS PHONE ____ │
│  WHERE DID ACCIDENT OCCUR _____    │
│                       (STREET AND CITY)      │
│  NAME OF INVESTIGATING POLICE DEPARTMENT ___ │
└─────────────────────────────────────────────┘
```

A standardized reporting form should be used so that all investigations are conducted in a consistent manner. The best time to investigate an accident is as soon as possible after the accident, as the facts are clearer and include more details. Thus, accidents report should be completed within the first 24 hours. It also insures that the causes of the accident and any witnesses are still present and limits time for gossiping, creating excuses, and assigning blame. The best place to investigate is at the actual accident site, which should be secured as soon as possible after all necessary emergency actions have been taken, with someone assigned to take photographs to document the details.

Depending on the severity of an accident, there may be multiple individuals or groups involved in the investigation. The *Supervisor* has intimate knowledge of job conditions and procedures in the department and is responsible for promoting and enforcing safe behavior. The *employee or fellow employees* may have the best account of the accident, but those accounts might be misleading to avoid discipline. That is why management should make it clear to all employees that investigations are not done to place blame but to determine and correct the cause(s). The *Safety Committee or Accident Review Committee* has an unbiased perspective on the accident and can include multiple areas of expertise to determine the cause. The *supervisor* should follow-up to insure corrective action is taken. *Management* is responsible for appropriate, credible, and defensible investigation procedures. *Outside experts* with specialized knowledge may be called in for more complex situations. (e.g., OSHA will investigate if there is a fatality or serious accident, or if an employee files a complaint. In some jurisdictions, OSHA agencies have a consulting division that can assist employers with identification of compliance needs, provided the employer is committed to corrective action.)

All witnesses should be interviewed privately. Always begin accident/incident investigation interviews positively by emphasizing the purpose, which is not to find fault or assign blame but to identify ways to prevent the reoccurrence of situations where employees can be injured. The following witnesses should be interviewed: anyone who saw the events *leading up to the accident*, eyewitnesses who were actually *involved in the accident* or who actually saw it happen, those who *came to the scene immediately after the accident*, and those *who have information about the work habits* of an injured employee or *know about the equipment* involved in the accident.

It is important to remember the witnesses' perspective. A witness may intentionally give the wrong information to protect himself/herself or a fellow employee. Most witnesses are not trained observers. They may have observed only a few details and imagined the rest. The witness' own personality and perspective may distort his/her account of the accident. (Remember the story of the six blind men and the elephant: each person observed the elephant by holding a different part, leg, tail, ear, trunk, tusk, torso, and pictured an entirely different animal based on their limited perspective.) Every witness may make assumptions about what happened depending upon what they personally saw. It is only after the entire investigation has been conducted that a true picture of what happened can be ascertained.

To gather the most accurate information when interviewing witnesses, avoid asking "why" questions. These questions can lead to a defensive attitude. Additionally, it is better to ask open-ended questions that cannot be answered with a simple "yes" or "no," but it is also important not to lead or influence the witness. Consider the following story:

Exhibit 14.1: Credibility of Eyewitnesses

The Loftus Experiments

Elizabeth Loftus, a professor of social ecology, investigated the observation powers of eyewitnesses in the early 1970s. One test consisted of showing five groups the same pictures of an automobile accident. Members of each group were separately asked to describe how fast a car was going when it _____ (smashed, collided, bumped, hit, or contacted) the other vehicle. The estimates of speed at the time of impact ranged from 41 mph when the question used "smashed" as the verb down to 33 mph when "contacted" was used. In a follow-up question, the groups were asked if they observed broken glass at the impact site, with 32% saying they saw glass when "smashed" was the verb but only 14% when "hit" was used.

In another related experience, a group observed two cars approaching each other at an intersection. The vehicles then collided. In the questions concerning the accident, participants were asked several questions, such as, "Did the driver of vehicle B seem distracted before smashing into vehicle A?" or "How fast was vehicle B traveling when it passed the red barn?" A number of "observers" thought that the driver of B was adjusting the radio, the mirror, putting on makeup, or folding a map, when in reality the driver was doing nothing distracting. Many "observers" thought the vehicle was speeding past the red barn, but in fact there was no barn of any color.

The findings of the Loftus experiments and other researchers suggested that eyewitness recall is highly unreliable, and can be easily influenced by the descriptive language used the interviewer or can have false memories triggered by suggestion.

When interviewing eyewitnesses to accidents, the interviewer must be aware of the impact of word choice, language, gestures, or any suggestions, as those actions may result in interviewer-induced bias and inaccuracies.

Finally, ask the witness for suggestions to prevent future incidents, and conclude the interview positively by reemphasizing the need for prevention and not finding fault.

The final investigation report should be complete and thorough. Entries should make sense and provide insight as to the cause of the accident. Recommendations for prevention could include engineering controls, administrative controls, human resources' hiring and placement procedures, as well as training and discipline recommendations.

There should be a documented follow-up mechanism that provides for auditing by management or risk management, including the content of the report and the recommended remedies.

Element 7 – Post-Injury Management

Post-injury management is important to reduce health care and workers compensation costs, reduce lost work time, early evaluation, and improve employee morale. It is also important for addressing any legal issues that may develop from Americans with Disabilities Act (ADA), Family Medical Leave Act (FMLA), or any other governmental regulation dealing with employee injuries. Post-injury management enables the employer to maintain contact with the injured worker and assure the return of that worker to light or modified duty as soon as possible. It is an important tool for making sure the injured worker does not feel abandoned or neglected after having an injury.

A team that includes the supervisor, management, medical provider, claim adjuster, and injured employee should be involved in the post-injury management. There should be a written policy and procedure developed that includes chapters on return-to-work (coordinator or administrator and supervisor involvement) and ongoing employee training that includes instruction on workers compensation benefits, accident reporting procedures, established/approved medical providers (if any), and return-to-modified-duty procedures.

It is beneficial to direct care of injured employees to an established medical provider because the provider can develop a familiarity with the organization's operations, understands the treatment and return-to-work philosophy of the organization, and can assist the organization in disability management. Insurers sometimes require the use of their approved medical providers.

In most organizations, the insurance company, a third-party administrator or an in-house claims adjuster handles the claims. Regardless of who handles the claim, elements of successful claim handling include communication on claim status, physician referral, addressing the organization's return-to-work philosophy and availability of modified duty, medical cost containment activities, and recovery or subrogation from negligent third parties. There should be continuous communications among the employee, the medical provider, and the claim handler, particularly with respect to physical therapy, vocational counseling, and disability management.

Element 8 – Evaluation of Program Effectiveness

When determining whether a health and safety program has been effective, the risk manager must make sure the program is effective and appropriate for the workplace conditions. This should be a formal evaluation process with documented results. Either internal or external resources could be used. Financial and incidence rates from insurers and other sources such as OSHA (see Example 14.2) can serve as the statistical measurements used to evaluate the effectiveness of the program, including an examination of premium credits and debits, as well as workers compensation experience modifiers, and the analysis of insured losses per exposure unit and claim frequency and severity.

Exhibit 14.2: OSHA Incidence Rates

OSHA and the Bureau of Labor Statistics use incidence rates to track frequency and severity of losses. Three rates monitor frequency: incidence rate, loss workday rate, and cases without loss workday rate. Severity rates track lost workdays. Those OSHA formulas follow:

Incidence Rate:

$$\frac{\text{Number of Injuries \& Illnesses x 200,000*}}{\text{Total Hours Worked per Year**}}$$

Lost Workday Rate:

$$\frac{\text{Number of Lost Work Day Cases x 200,000*}}{\text{Total Hours Worked per Year**}}$$

Cases without Lost Workday Rate:

$$\frac{\text{Number of Cases with No lost days x 200,000*}}{\text{Total Hours Worked per Year**}}$$

Severity Rate or Number of Days Lost Rate:

$$\frac{\text{Number of Days Lost x 200,000*}}{\text{Total Hours Worked per Year**}}$$

* 100 full-time equivalent workers or 100 workers × 40 hrs/wk × 50 weeks (number of weeks usually worked in a year)

** Number of full-time equivalent workers × 40 hrs/wk × 50 weeks

Behavioral observations and statistics can also be used. Trends of overall totals of cause of loss, location, type of loss, etc. can be compared to previous indicators. It is possible to use regression analysis to compare these relative measures. The organization would want to look at how the organization or department is doing from one period or year to another, as well as how one location is doing compared to another. The organization can also compare itself to other companies in the same industry.

Ergonomics Issues

Ergonomics[1] is derived from the Greek words "ergon" or work and "nomy" or laws; thus, ergonomics is the "Laws of Work." The American Heritage Dictionary defines ergonomics as "Design factors, as for the workplace, intended to maximize productivity by minimizing operator fatigue and discomfort." In simpler terms, ergonomics involves studying human characteristics so that the design of the living and work environment will be the most appropriate. Stated another way, it is fitting the physical work environment to the person rather than expecting the person to adapt to the work environment. The cost to employers for inappropriate workplaces averages approximately $3,500 per injury with up to $30,000, or more, if surgery is required. The number of cases and resulting costs are increasing at an alarming rate.

Ergonomic Risk Factors

Ergonometric injuries usually result from long-term exposure to repetitive or forceful actions and generally cause injuries to muscles, nerves, and tendons. These types of injuries are also known as Musculoskeletal Disorders. The risk factors most likely to cause these ergonomic injuries are performing repetitive tasks, using excessive force, performing work in an awkward posture, static loading (maintaining a tense, still posture), working in a temperature extreme environment, and vibration. Other personal risk factors contributing to ergonometric injuries are the employee's physical condition, outside activities, proper work methods education, and stress.

Repetitive tasks are motions repeated throughout the work shift. The highest risk factors are in jobs where there are 2,000 or more repetitions per hour. This can be compounded in a job where there are few or no breaks because there is no recovery time for the muscles and tendons. Employees who work at least 50% of a work shift in this environment are at an increased risk to injury. Scheduling more frequent short breaks will reduce the number of repetitive task injuries.

Excessive force can affect small and large muscle groups as well as isolated tissues. Measures that reduce or spread the force provide relief for affected muscle groups.

Awkward posture arises when employees work while their bodies are deviated from neutral position in wrists, arm, trunk, neck, shoulders, legs, or feet. As the angle of deviation increases, discomfort and injury potential increases in the hand and wrist as well as overall posture. Two common sources of awkward posture are overhead and extended reaching and can be resolved by stepping stools, ladders, and raising or lowering surfaces.

Static loading is a sustained exertion of the muscles that causes decreased blood flow to the muscles and leads to general fatigue and discomfort. This can result from trying to use hands as a fixture or tool and poor posture. Applying pressure to certain points of the body, such as at the wrists, is a type of static load. The accompanying picture shows a design that alleviates static loading. Saloon keepers and pub operators learned long ago that patrons would stay longer and purchase more product if they could stand with one leg slightly elevated; hence, the bar rail.

Temperature extreme environments, both high and low extremes, can give rise to employee injury and illness. High extremes can give rise to dehydration, heat exhaustion, and heat stroke, as well as excessive perspiration that can cause grips to slip. Low extremes can cause muscles to contract and hypothermia or frostbite to occur.

Vibration, while enjoyable and relaxing under some circumstances, can add stress to muscles, tendons, and joints, particularly in coupling scenarios like operating an air hammer.

---

1 *The American Heritage® Dictionary of the English Language, Fourth Edition. Retrieved March 01, 2007, from Dictionary.com website: http:// dictionary.reference.com/browse/ergonomic*

Ergonomic Hazard Controls

The design and arrangement of furniture, fixtures, and equipment in the workplace can assist in controlling the ergonomic hazards.

Workstation Design – The workstation should be designed with the worker in mind to minimize the risk factors caused by the awkward postures that result in trauma to the muscles, nerves, and tendons. A well-designed workstation helps the worker maintain proper posture and reduces or eliminates the amount of bending and reaching.

Hazard control involves optimization of each workstation using anthropometric statistical data about the distribution of body dimensions in the population. Tools or fixtures, instead of hands, should be used for grasping objects. When feasible, the use of automation can decrease the number of repetitive tasks, and mechanical aids can lessen the force on muscles.

Administrative control in this area includes educating employees as to risk factors, proper work methods, and situation or incident reporting procedures; job rotation and job enlargement to reduce repetitive tasks; work breaks with stretching and strengthening exercises; monitoring the work environment (management by walking around); reducing stress factors; and implementing early injury intervention procedures.

Computer workstations – Because 45% of the workforce uses computer workstations, improperly designed areas can be a major source of loss costs. A poorly designed computer workstation can cause eyestrain, blurred vision, headaches, fatigue, and stress. The risk factors for a computer workstation are much the same as they are for other types of workstations: repetitive activity, awkward posture, static loading, pressure on tissues, and personal factors such as individual physiology and stress, as well as outside activities.

Exhibit 14.3: Ergonomic Computer Work Station

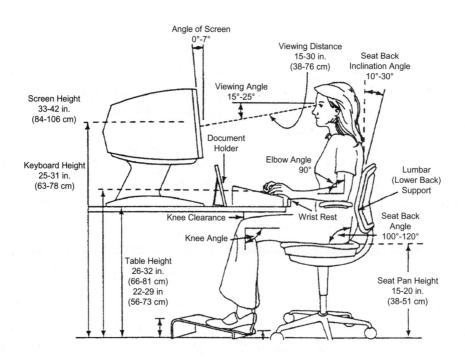

As shown in Exhibit 14.3, hazard controls for computer workstations would include adjustable table and monitor heights, footrests, ergonomic chairs, and wrist pads. They also include workspace organization, job enlargement (expanding the job to include activities that provide a break from repetitive activity, awkward posture, static loading, etc), frequent breaks, stretching and exercise, adequate lighting and glare control, and noise control.

Administrative controls include more frequent work breaks, job design factors, educating employees in proper work methods, monitoring the work environment, early intervention, exercise, and stress reduction measures.

Materials Handling

Manual material handling creates a multi-faceted ergonomic hazard, as some injuries arising out of a continued exposure to ergonomic forces, often called Cumulative Trauma Disorders, while other hazards result in a sudden occurrence. However, many of the "sudden occurrences" really are the result of continued exposure, but the worker does not realize the buildup of "mini-injuries" that are waiting for that one additional extra push or pull or stretch or strain to cross the line from unnoticeable to suddenly painful.

The respect to manual material handling exposures, these injuries typically are torso injuries, located in the lower back or shoulders, commonly being diagnosed as low back strains and sprains and shoulder strains, although sprains and strains to knees and wrists can occur. The differentiation between a strain and a sprain is a matter of degree; both involve the same type of causation and injury. A strain is a tearing or stretching of muscles or tendons (particularly at the point where the muscle becomes a tendon), some of which are instant while others are chronic, the result of long-term overuse or stress. A sprain is an injury to a ligament or to a joint capsule that involves tearing or stretching. Ligaments and joint capsules give a joint stability, so the weakening or tearing can create long-term instability. Sprains occur when a joint is forced beyond its usual range of motion.

Risk Factors

Frequency of lifts – There are two components of frequency of lifts, the number of lifts in a given time period and the duration of the lift at the vertical height of the lift. If there is insufficient time for recovery between lifts, stress and overuse can accumulate in the muscles and tendons. If the duration of the lift is excessive, the stress accumulates rapidly in the muscles and tendons involved in the lift.

> As a simple experiment to show how this works, extend your arms and lift a dining room chair from waist high to shoulder high repeatedly over a 30 second period. Observe how your muscles feel. Then hold the chair at arms' length, as if you were lifting it, and then hold it steady, simulating a long duration of one lift. You will notice your arm muscles beginning to tremble in a few seconds.

Excessive force or load weight – Manual material handling means more than lifting; it also includes moving materials by pushing or pulling. Weights that are excessive require more force to push or pull and to lift.

Awkward body posture – Awkward body position or posture arise from the load's shape and size. Lifting a box or crate 36 inches long and 18 inches wide with no handles is difficult as it is not easy to get a comfortable grip on a surface without using two or more the sharp edges that concentrate pressure on muscles and tendons. Asymmetrical objects are also challenging to lift.

<u>Improper lifting techniques</u> – Improper lifting techniques (twisting, reaching, and bending) are a risk factor in because of the location of the material being moved and the location to which the material will be moved.

> For example, lifting an item from the floor located on the worker's right and moving it to an overhead shelf on the left means the worker must bend far over or squat, lift the item off the floor and twist or move the feet from right to left, then lift the item overhead and finally stretch to put it into its intended position.

<u>Personal risk factors</u> – Personal risk factors usually arise from non-occupational causes. Workers are truly individuals, and differ in age, gender, and physical condition. Anyone looking around an office or factory will notice those differences. Younger workers are more resilient physically, as their bodies have not accumulated the normal stress and strain of the aging process, not to mention the increased stress and strain of work. However, they have less life experience, and may be more likely to take chances or engage in unsafe practices. Gender is also a factor, as most males are larger in stature, more muscular, and generally have more brute strength than females. Physical condition is also an important factor, as workers who are in poor physical condition tend to tire more quickly and have less strength and flexibility.

Lifting Techniques

The most important hazard control technique is planning before the lift! Planning before the lift is not just the <u>hazard control</u> of looking at the load and thinking about how to move it from one point to another. Planning before the lift, like all planning, also involves <u>administrative control</u>, and would also include planning how many lifts will be made in a specified time period, how much weight will be lifted, and what mechanical aids might be used to implement or supplement the lift.

To understand exactly how lifting techniques work to control accidents, the lifting components must be identified and evaluated. The National Institute of Occupational Safety and Health (NIOSH) has formulated a lifting equation that is composed of a load constant (the maximum recommended weight for lifting at the standard lifting location under optimal conditions, or 51 pounds, the weight that can be lifted by 75% of females and 90% of males. The formula then factors in several multipliers to arrive at a recommended weight limit.

The factors included the following:

1. The load constant

2. Frequency – how many times the load is lifted per minute and the duration of the lift at the vertical height of the lift from the floor

3. Horizontal distance from the body – a measure of the distance from the mid-point between the ankles (directly below the body's center of gravity) and a point projected on the floor directly below the mid-point of the hand grasps

4. Vertical distance from the floor – the distance from the floor to the mid-point between the hand grasps

5. Distance the load travels – the distance of travel of the hands between the origin and the destination of the lift

6. Asymmetry – the degree of trunk rotation (twisting)

7. Coupling strength – the quality of the grasp and vertical position of the load

In addition to the lifting equation computing the recommended weight limit, understanding the factors included in the lifting equation gives insight into effective lifting hazard control methods.

1. The load – limiting the load reduces the hazard.
   Consider this: Given the same time period which scenario would be more likely to cause an accident – lifting one 50-pound weight or two 25-pound weights?

2. Frequency – reducing the number and the duration of lifts of a given weight permits recovery between lifts and reduces the stress during the lift.
   Consider this: which scenario would be more likely to cause an accident – lifting a 25-pound weight every ten seconds and holding it for ten seconds or lifting the same weight every 20 seconds and holding it for 5 seconds?

3. Horizontal distance – holding the load closer to the torso reduces stress on the arms and shoulders.
   Consider this: which scenario would be more likely to cause an accident: holding a 25-pound weight extended at arms' length (perhaps because of the shape of the object) or holding the same weight close to the torso?

4. Vertical distance – reducing the vertical distance of the lift reduces stress.
   Consider this: which scenario would be more likely to cause an accident – lifting a 25-pound weight from the floor to a shoulder-high shelf or lifting the same weight from a table waist-high to a shoulder-high shelf?

5. Distance the load travels – reducing the distance the load travels reduces the stress.
   Consider this: which scenario would be more likely to cause an accident – moving a 25-pound weight 24 inches or 12 inches?

6. Asymmetry – reducing twisting or rotation of the legs, knees, hips, torso, shoulders, etc. reduces the stress on muscles, tendons, and joints.
   Consider this: which scenario would be more likely to cause an accident – lifting a 25-pound weight and turning 180 degrees to place it on a shelf or turning 18 degrees?

7. Coupling strength – increasing the coupling strength or quality of the grasp reduces stress on the hands and lessens the likelihood of the load slipping or shifting.
   Consider this: which scenario would be more likely to cause an accident – lifting a 25-pound weight with slick sides or the same weight with handles?

While NIOSH has reduced these factors to a mathematical formula, common sense tells the risk manager that taking any steps to reduce weight, frequency, distance, and asymmetry or any steps to increase coupling strength will serve to reduce the likelihood of accidents arising out of manual material handling.

Mechanical Aids

The last component of material handling involves the use of mechanical aids. Conveyors that move materials from a loading area to an assembly area eliminate much of the manual lifting hazard (weight, frequency, distance, asymmetry are zero). Hand trucks and pallet trucks eliminate much of the distance traveled while carrying the weight. Using hand tools that are suspended above the work area require less effort to pull into place than repeatedly picking up the same tool, and having the tool within ready reach of the work surface reduces asymmetry.

One mechanical aid deserves special attention – the back belt. There is considerable controversy over the efficacy of back belts. According to a NIOSH study, there is no physiological value to these devices. However, various industry studies suggest that back belts, even when not worn correctly, reduce back injury frequency. Back belt programs are most effective when accompanied by a material handling education program, and not just passing the belts out with an admonition to wear it. The design of the belt, when property worn, makes an individual think before the lift, thus planning the lift. However, even when a belt is worn improperly, there is anecdotal evidence suggesting a reduction in frequency because of the thinking and planning factors.

Walking Surfaces – Slips, Trips, and Falls

Slips, trips, and falls are the leading source of injuries to employees and to the public. Physical inspections (management by walking around) and accident investigations can help prevent these types of accidents. Controlling slip/trip/fall hazards involves using suitable surface materials, spill control, surface continuity, illumination, stair design, maintenance and inspection, and other engineering controls.

Risk Factors and Hazard Control

Surface materials – can pose high, moderate, or slight hazards, depending upon composition. Hazard controls would be avoiding the use of slick surfaces or replacing them with rougher textures to reduce slips, trips, and falls. Other hazard controls would be increasing surface coefficient of friction[2] by cleaning the floor, installing non-slip strips, or using entrance runners for areas slick from rain and snow.

Spills – even small spills can pose high hazards. Hazard control would include the use of warning signs and immediate clean up.

Lack of surface continuity – slip/trip/fall hazards. When people are walking, they expect a continuous walking surface. When the walking surface is not continuous, slips, trips, and falls can occur. Repairing holes and cracks, eliminating raised edges, and good housekeeping can help keep the surface continuous.

Inadequate illumination – trip/fall hazards. Illumination should be at one foot-candle[3] at surface level so that a person is able to see the contour of the walkway.

Faulty stair design – is another hazard for slips, trips, and falls. Stairways that deviate from the expected or normal height or width should be avoided. Falling while descending is the most common stair accident; therefore, stairways should have handrails and the incline should be at an angle of less than 40° from vertical.

Other engineering controls include using slip-resistant surfaces, marking the floor as to walkways and work areas, using floor gutters and drains, repairing leaking equipment, repairing building leaks in roofs, etc., and encouraging the use of slip-resistant footwear.

2 According to The American Heritage Dictionary "friction" is "a force that resists the relative motion or tendency to such motion of two bodies in contact." "Coefficient of friction" is "the ratio of the force that maintains contact between an object and a surface and the frictional force that resists the motion of the object." The American Heritage® Dictionary of the English Language, Fourth Edition. Houghton Mifflin Company, 2004. http://dictionary.reference.com/browse/coefficient of friction (accessed: February 15, 2007).

3 "Foot-candle" is defined as "The amount of illumination produced by a standard candle at a distance of one foot." Webster's Revised Unabridged Dictionary. MICRA, Inc. http://dictionary.reference.com/browse/foot candle.

Administrative Control

Maintenance and inspections should be planned, documented, and performed by properly trained staff. Maintenance should include planned replacement when necessary and repair of surfaces, and should be a part of capital budgeting.

Fleet Exposures

Fleet safety is an exposure that requires specific hazard control techniques. It is worth noting that fleet exposures can represent risk to all four major areas of risk exposure – property (the vehicles), liability (injury to third parties), human resources (worker injuries), and net income (loss of revenue).

The first step is to determine the type of fleet being used. Each type of vehicle has unique exposures and control. Long-distance cargo transportation uses large vehicles, and while the trips are longer, they tend to be primarily on highways with flows of traffic that are parallel, not perpendicular with the route of the vehicle. Service and delivery fleets are smaller vehicles used for intermediate and scheduled routes. They tend to operate in more urban areas with concentrations of other vehicles traveling parallel and perpendicular, as well as having pedestrians, bicyclists, parked vehicles, and other obstructions. Private passenger vehicles are not used to transport goods or services, but may be used by sales forces or to transport passengers (e.g. taxi cabs). They tend to be used in more urban areas and are operated generally by non-professional drivers, those who do not have any special training in driving beyond simply having a driver's license. Buses may operate in a small or large radius, and have the high-exposure cargo of high numbers of passengers. Finally, non-owned vehicles of any type used at any time on a rental basis must be addressed in a fleet safety program.

In addition to authority over other types of transportation, including air, rail, and pipeline, the Department of Transportation (DOT) issues Federal Motor Carrier Safety Regulations, as well as education and assistance, for large commercial vehicles and buses, including special regulations for those that transport hazardous goods, and for port security. DOT also has rules and regulations covering drivers pertaining to license requirements, hours of service, and drug and alcohol use. The vehicle requirements include roadside inspections and keeping maintenance records. DOT has the authority to fine companies that do not follow the rules and regulations and remove from service any vehicle that is not in compliance.

Fleet Hazards

Fleet exposures include property damage to the fleet vehicles, the cargo, and liability for injury, harm, or property damage to third parties. Large vehicles can cause big accidents and damage to the cargo and the vehicle itself. Smaller vehicles have more frequent accidents, but the property damage is not as great. Private passenger vehicles can have expensive accidents. Liability can arise from a negligent operation of an owned vehicle, resulting in third-party injury or property damage, or from negligent entrustment of a vehicle, or from hired or borrowed vehicles.

Any or all types of accidents can occur with any of these vehicles. Rear-end collisions, accidents at intersections, accidents while backing, and hitting stationary objects are collisions where someone is at fault, creating liability for owner and driver alike. In addition, natural perils may also cause property damage even when the vehicle is parked and the driver is not present.

Hazard and Administrative Controls

There are several hazard and administrative controls that can be used to prevent or lessen fleet accidents. Because the physical condition of the fleet (e.g., tires, engine performance, brakes, etc.), can be as much a factor in accident prevention as safe operation of the vehicles, hazard control mingles with administrative control in controlling risk.

The first line of defense is the fleet safety policy. This would include a management policy statement, driver responsibility and accountability (which includes authority to drive and rules and regulations), drug and alcohol policy, and vehicle responsibility. Along with the driving responsibility, the vehicle inspection and maintenance program is a part of vehicle responsibility. Pre-trip and post trip inspections should be made, along with scheduled preventive maintenance. All corrective action should be documented in case of vehicle malfunction or failure.

The second line of defense would be making sure the driver is qualified and has been properly trained. Obviously, each driver should have a valid driver's license for the class of vehicles driven. Before a driver can be accepted as qualified, there must be some criteria by which he/she is gauged as qualified. The criteria for an acceptable driving record should be in written form and a part of the policies and procedures. The employment application should have information regarding the driver's qualifications and experience and should be in accordance with the written criteria for an acceptable driving record. Drivers who are transferred from another division should also have some type of record that shows their qualifications and experience, even if it is not in employment application format. Driver disciplinary procedures also should be incorporated into the policy and procedures. The U.S. Department of Transportation Federal Motor Carrier Safety Administration sets forth general qualifications of drivers in their regulations. In Subpart B §391.11 General Qualifications of Drivers, it states, in part, that a driver must:

- Be least 21 years old,

- Be able to read and speak English sufficiently to converse with general public and understand highway traffic signs,

- Be capable of safely operating the type of commercial motor vehicles he/she drives, and be physically qualified to drive a commercial motor vehicle,

- Have a currently valid commercial motor vehicle operator's license issued by only one state or jurisdiction

- Have prepared and furnished the motor carrier that employs him/her a list of violations (motor vehicle record or MVR),

- Not be disqualified to drive a commercial motor vehicle according to the rules outlined in §391.15, and

- Have successfully completed a driver's road test or hold an operator's license or a certificate of road test that the motor carrier that employs him/her has accepted as equivalent to a road test.[4]

Beyond careful selection, training of drivers should include written procedures concerning orientation to the vehicle, instruction in defensive driving, and in specific areas of awareness or exposure (e.g., backing). It should also include instruction on responding to accidents, such as rules for reporting, as well as investigation forms and procedures. An Accident Review Committee should play a more active role than simply determining if a driver is "at fault," thoroughly investigating accidents and determining what can be done to prevent similar accidents in the future.

---

4 See http://www.fmcsa.dot.gov/rules-regulations/administration/fmcsr/ for verbiage from Subpart B §391.11. Federal Motor Carrier Safety Administration, 400 7th Street SW, Washington, DC 20590 • 1-800-832-5660 • TTY: 1-800-877-8339.

The last element of a fleet accident hazard control program involves the vehicles themselves. There should be a procedure that includes pre-trip and post-trip inspections to identify potentially hazardous conditions of the vehicle. One need only watch the pilot of a commercial aircraft do a "walk around" of the aircraft before it departs the gate to understand how important pre-trip inspections are. (This author was on an aircraft waiting for departure as last-minute luggage was being loaded. The ground crew observed a sizable hole in the fuselage skin near the cargo door that the pilot would not have been able to easily observe. Obviously, the aircraft was taken out of service. Safety is EVERYONE's business!) In addition, vehicles should be scheduled for preventative maintenance. All corrective action must be documented.

Property Exposures

An important category of the property assets of most businesses includes the buildings occupied as offices, manufacturing, storage, sales, residential, etc. The continued availability of building space for conducting operations is critical to the survival of most businesses, and for this reason the risk manager must develop the knowledge and skills to protect these assets.

Property exposures fall under four general classifications: Construction, Occupancy, Protection and Environment, commonly referred to as COPE.

Construction types are frame (wood construction), joisted masonry (masonry with wood joists), masonry non-combustible (masonry with steel or concrete floors and roofs), non-combustible metal (entirely metal structure) and fire resistive or modified fire resistive (metal beams and concrete coated with protective coatings such as gunite). (See Exhibit 14.3)

Occupancy means who and what is in the building. For example, the occupancy of a McDonalds is "restaurant" and for the headquarters of an insurance group, the occupancy is "office."

Protection refers to the local, on-site protective safeguards, such as sprinkler systems or firewalls that are in place to minimize the impact of perils and hazards, as well as external protection, such as fire departments.

Environment looks at the sources of potential damage, for instance, whether or not the building is next to another building used to store flammable liquids.

Exhibit 14.3: Construction Types

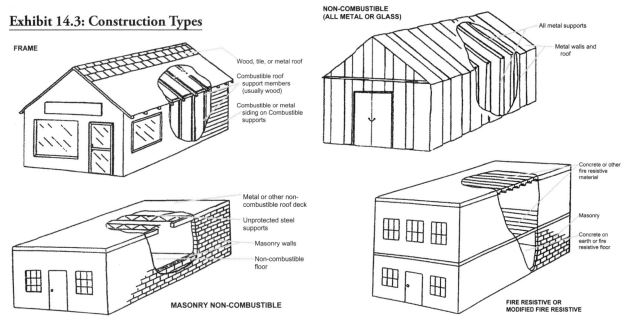

The risk manager must be concerned about two measurements of loss potential when considering COPE: Maximum Possible Loss and Probable Maximum Loss.

Maximum Possible Loss

First, and most important, the risk manager must be concerned about the Maximum Possible Loss (MPL) or amount subject to loss. This is the measure of the greatest loss potential arising from the property, regardless of protective measures. The risk manager must assume the absolute worse combination of events, (e.g., a fire is accompanied by high winds, a sprinkler system fails, automatic doors fail to close, and (not or) a host of other possible systems fail). What this entails is looking at the entire amount subject to destruction from the same chain of concurrent events.

The MPL is limited only by adequate separation between structures or locations. For example, if an organization has all of its operations conducted at one location, even though there are several buildings, the entire location would be considered to be subject to one loss. If the organization breaks up its operations, (one building located in Texas, one in building in California, and one building in North Dakota), the original MPL would be broken into three lesser MPLs, one for each location.

Further, a single location may have several MPL values depending upon the nature of the peril. If an organization has three buildings at one location, all the three buildings would be subject to the peril of a tornado, hurricane, or earthquake, but if the separation between buildings were great and there was no source of fuel (such as tall grass or brush between the buildings), the MPL from fire might be less. If one building had been built into the side of a hill and was primarily underground, the MPL from tornado would be diminished.

Probable Maximum Loss

The Probable Maximum Loss (PML) is the amount of loss expected, given some level of impairment or delay in fire protection (the definition varies by insurance carrier and by risk manager). Fire protective devices that serve to reduce the PML are automatically closing fire doors, parapets, protected openings such as windows, sprinkler systems, the protection class of the building, the water supply, the capabilities of the local fire department, and the like.

Property Hazards

Hazards that can contribute to the loss of property exposures are human, economic, and natural in origin. While a hazard is a factor that increases the chance of a loss, a peril is the cause of the loss. These terms often blur together as we look at the ways losses occur. Human perils are such perils as electrical fire caused by negligence or poor maintenance, theft, and vandalism. Economic perils would be property damage to a supplier or customer that causes another organization an economic loss, and natural perils would be wind, hail, lightning, flood, etc.

Other factors affecting exposure to loss are geographic location (having a building where windstorm or earthquake might be more prevalent), maintenance, particularly of plumbing, electrical, heating/ventilation/air conditioning (HVAC) and the roof, storage practices (especially storing flammable materials), and any special hazards, such as cutting, welding or cooking activities.

Administrative Control

To control these hazards, *management programs* can be implemented. Management programs consist of inspection programs, good housekeeping, proper facility maintenance, and policies for especially hazardous activities such as welding or cooking.

Hazard Control

Fire protection services can also be used to control hazards. The amount of protection would depend upon whether the source is an internal fire brigade or an external municipal fire department. The amount of loss would be further affected by the protection class of the building. The protection class is a classification insurance underwriters use to measure the proximity of the fire department and availability and distance of the water supply and the capabilities of the external fire department, such as its status as a volunteer or full time department, its training, and its equipment.

Even the best fire protection services are of little use if there is no fire alarm system, usually in the form of smoke detection or heat detection, but sometimes a 24 hour watchman system.

Sprinkler systems are also a hazard control measure for property. The purpose of a sprinkler system is to contain the fire in a small area to reduce the severity of the loss, not to prevent a fire from starting. The effectiveness of a sprinkler system is determined by design density (whether it is specific to occupancy) water supply (pressure and flow rate), maintenance procedures, and impairment procedures.

Security protection involves the use of physical barriers (safe, locks, bars, etc.), lighting, and either local or central station alarm systems.

Summary

Though we have used the terms administrative controls and hazard controls, it is clear that most of the reduction methods will come into play in almost every area: eliminating the hazard, substituting a less hazardous substance or process, engineering controls, administrative controls, personal protective equipment, and training.

Chapter 15

Workers Compensation Experience Modification

Introduction

Virtually all employers have a responsibility to provide benefits for their employees who are injured or become ill because of their employment. If an organization is large enough or complex enough to have a risk manager, chances are good that the workers compensation exposure is one of the largest, if not the largest, elements of the overall risk management program, and the risk manager must be knowledgeable about anything that affects the risk financing of this exposure. For all organizations whose workers compensation premium is subject to a state or national workers compensation rating authority, the risk manager needs a thorough understanding of the experience rating modification system.

In previous chapters, we discussed the effects of experience modifiers on premium certainty and loss sensitivity and the application of the final experience modifier to premiums. Because this factor can have an enormous impact on the cost of risk, in this chapter, we will delve into the rationale for the factor and the actual development of an experience rating modification (ERM).

For most organizations, the National Council on Compensation Insurance (NCCI) provides the individual state rates that apply to all classifications of workers compensation exposures, and it promulgates the experience rating modifiers that apply to an individual company's premiums. For the few states that promulgate their own rates, the state-specific method for developing an experience rating modification is similar.

The experience rating modification system will affect the financing of workers compensation exposures whether fully insured, insured under a dividend plan, partially retained through a large deductible, subject to a retrospectively rated program, or invested in a fully self-insured program (with or without excess insurance, a workers compensation pool, or a fronted captive insurance company program.

The Rationale

The underlying rationale of any rating system is to promulgate (create and publish) a rate that is fair, adequate, and equitable. Insureds should pay rates that are fair to both the insured and the insurance carrier; otherwise, insureds will attempt to avoid paying the premium and insurance carriers will be punished or rewarded unjustly. The rates must be adequate or the insurance carrier will refuse to write the coverage or run the risk of financial ruin. There must be equity in rates between insureds that are indifferent to loss control and those insureds who expend the time, effort, and money to minimize their losses; otherwise the attentive organizations will unfairly subsidize the indifferent organizations.

The experience rating modification system supports that overall general rationale by modifying the generalized class rates that apply to all organizations whose workers perform specifically defined tasks in their employment, to more accurately reflect the specific organization's historic loss experience arising out of those specifically defined classifications of tasks.

In theory, the rates assume that all employers in a particular class of business are identical, and the tasks for each classification are defined in the NCCI Scopes Manual or Scopes of Basic Manual Classifications (for NCCI states, gives descriptions of class codes, as well as cross-references and state-specific classification and is available with many other valuable resources on the NCCI Website, www.NCCI.com). Those basic rates will apply in exactly the same way to all employees so classed. The development of these rates also assumes that these identical employers have the same aversion to loss and practice appropriate loss control, that all injuries will affect the employees in exactly the same way, and that all claims will be settled in exactly the same manner. Obviously, this assumption will not hold in the real world of businesses and claims.

To apply this real-world problem to the across-the-board rates, the experience rating modification system is in place to adjust those rates according to the historic loss experience of each employer, according to the organization's actual losses and actual exposure (in terms of payroll only) falling within the applicable job classifications as defined in the Scopes Manual.

The experience rating modification (commonly called the ERM) is a moving average. It is generally computed on three full years of experience, starting one year prior to the effective date of the experience modifier and counting back three years. In some cases, the experience period may be less than three years (as little as one year) or more (as much as three years and nine months). These variations commonly arise because the insured has been in business for less than four years, has two or more policies with different expiration dates, or has had a change in its anniversary rating date.

Simply put, a company's payroll and loss figures, by classification code, are collected for the year, and the total of Expected Losses is determined. This amount equates to an experience modification of 1.0. Once a company's specific Actual Losses are determined, they are compared to the Expected Losses. If Actual Losses are higher than Expected Losses, the experience modifier will be greater than 1.0 such as 1.10 (in this case the company's premium would increase by 10%). If Actual Losses are less than Expected Losses, the experience modifier will be less than 1.0 such as .90 (in this case the company's premium would be 10% less).

The ERM is adjusted annually by dropping off the oldest year and adding the newest eligible year. Consequently, the effect of any one year's experience (good or bad) is dampened by the moving average. The internal workings of the ERM system also dampen the effect of individual severe losses. Because smaller losses are fully included in the development of the ERM, the system quickly punishes an increase in loss frequency and rewards improvement slowly. Thus, it reacts more to changes in average frequency than it recognizes changes in average severity. However, this is consistent with the general rule that loss control activities are more effective in managing frequency than severity. The loss that is prevented can never be severe.

Reporting Process

Every insurance carrier subscribing to the NCCI is assigned a unique identification number to facilitate reporting. Using this ID number, the carrier reports payroll exposures and losses on a form called the Unit Statistical Card, more informally known as the "unit stat card."

The unit stat cards are used to report audited exposure (payroll) and premium data within 20 months following the inception month of the policy, and losses, which are valued at 18 months after inception. This first loss report is then modified at 12-month intervals when there is an open claim on a previous report (updating open reserves), when there are reopened claims (new reserves on old claims), when there are claims previously reported (but no values), and when there are changes in valuation (changes in reserves). The resulting reports track the natural development of claims over time, as well as capturing incurred but not reported developments.

Correction reports are used to remedy errors in loss data or exposure and premium data. Exposure or premium data may change because of a re-audit or readjustment of premium, classifications, or exposures, or a final audit completed after the first unit stat report. Similarly, errors in losses are reported on a correction report, but only when there are clerical (not judgmental) errors in reported loss values or when there is a declaration of a non-compensable claim (official ruling, statute of limitations tolls, or failure to prosecute the claim). Corrections are not permitted when there is a change in reserve due to normal claim development, a change in a departmental or judicial decision, or a change in the injury type due to development. The limitations on correcting a unit stat card are more restrictive for losses than for exposures, classifications, and premiums.

After the premium audit is completed and finalized, the insurance carrier reports the payroll exposure for each standard classification code identified by the auditor during the audit. While audits on smaller premiums usually involve the insured reporting the actual exposures at the end of the policy term, larger accounts usually require physical audits, where an insurance company adjuster visits the insured's office and looks at the books. The auditor will audit payroll, as well as classifications of work, using the definitions of standard classification codes from the Scopes Manual, and subject to the listed exceptions and limitations.

As losses occur and are reported, an initial case reserve is posted and that value is reported. With each non-judgmental change in reserves, an updated value is reported.

Terminology

To understand the experience rating modification methodology and the ERM worksheet that communicates the ERM to the insured and the underwriter, the risk manager must be familiar with the distinctive terminology used by the rating authorities.

Primary Actual Losses – For each loss equal to or less than $5,000, the actual loss amount is the primary loss value. (Each loss over $5,000 is limited to a primary loss value of $5,000.)

Expected Loss Rate – The factor taken from actuarial tables used to calculate "total expected losses" for the specific classification.

Discount Ratio (D-ratio) – The factor taken from actuarial tables and used in conjunction with the payroll and Expected Loss Rate to determine "Expected Primary Losses." The D-ratio is the portion of the Expected Loss Rate that represents the Primary Actual Losses.

Ballast Value (B Value) – A specific value taken from actuarial tables and used to limit the effect of any single severe accident on the modification factor. This is one of the dampening factors to smooth the effect of severity. The B Value is a percentage of the state's multiple claim accident limitation, generally stated as a percentage of the "self-rating point," the level of expected losses where the experience is deemed to be statistically credible. As the expected losses amount approaches the self-rating point, the B Value decreases to zero.

Weighting Value (W Value) – A percentage value taken from the same actuarial tables used above and used to determine the percentage of excess losses to be used in the calculations. The Weighting Value recognizes that some portion of excess losses will be included, but not all excess losses, as that would add too much volatility into the ERM. The Weighting Value increases as the dollar amount of expected losses increases; again this continues until it reaches the "self-rating point."

Exhibit 15.1 is an example of the NCCI experience modification worksheet or Experience Rate Modification (ERM) Calculation. (For convenience, all but the first column has been identified with alpha characters at the top of the column. As is true with every NCCI worksheet, the actual column identification is in very small type in the last few rows.) This worksheet includes the following abbreviations:

- MOD - Modification

- CODE – the applicable classification codes

- ELR – Expected Loss Rate

- EXP PRIM LOSSES – Expected Primary Losses

- ACT INC LOSSES – Actual Incurred Losses

- ACT PRIM LOSSES – Actual Primary Losses

Exhibit 15.1: 1999 Experience Rate Modification Calculation

	A	B	C	D	E	F	G	H	I
				MOD CALCULATION WORKSHEET					
		D-		EXPECTED	EXP PRIM	CLAIM	O	ACT INC	ACT PRIM
CODE	ELR	RATIO	PAYROLL	LOSSES	LOSSES	DATA	IJ F	LOSSES	LOSSES
CARRIER	_____	POL NO.	_____	EFF-DATE	09/01/94	EXP DATE	09/01/95		
4250	1.22	0.29	486504	5935	1721			6589	5000
8742	0.33	0.28	38900	128	36			679	679
8810	0.17	0.31	960574	1633	506			750	750
POLICY-TOTAL			1485978	(SUBJECT	PREMIUM)	23083)		8018	
CARRIER	_____	POL NO.	_____	EFF-DATE	09/01/95	EXP DATE	09/01/96		
4250	1.22	0.29	365108	4454	1292			15500	5000
8742	0.33	0.28	30581	101	28			1489	1489
8810	0.17	0.31	1023354	1740	539				
POLICY-TOTAL			1419043	(SUBJECT	PREMIUM)	20539)		16989	
CARRIER	_____	POL NO.	_____	EFF-DATE	09/01/96	EXP DATE	09/01/97		
4250	1.22	0.29	302634	3692	1071				
8742	0.33	0.28	94992	313	88				
8810	0.17	0.31	813069	1382	428				
POLICY-TOTAL			1210695	(SUBJECT	PREMIUM)	17237		0	
	[A]*	[D]	[C] EXPECTED EXCESS [D-E]	[D]	[E]	[F] ACTUAL EXCESS [W-I]	[G]**	{W}	{I}
	0.07		13669	19378	5709	12089	9250	25007	12918
				[11] PRIMARY LOSSES	[12] STABILIZ-ING VALUE	[13] RATABLE EXCESS	[14] TOTALS		
				[I]	[C] X [1-W] - [G]	[A] X [P]	[J]		
			ACTUAL	12918	21962	846	35726		
				[E]		[A] X [C]	[K]	[15] EXP. MOD.	
			EXPECTED	5709	21962	957	28628	1.25	
*	(A) IS THE "W VALUE"								
**	(G) IS THE "B VALUE"								

The worksheet is organized into three specific divisions, one for data (the large top section), one for totals (highlighted by darker borders near the bottom forth of the page), and the actual calculation of the modification (just below the totals). The data is further divided into three segments, one for each of the three years included in the calculation of the moving average.

The following is an example of the application of the moving average:

- The current policy year is the year for which the experience modifier is being calculated (the upcoming policy year).

- The previous policy year is not included in the calculation of the modifier, as the exposure data is incomplete until the audit is finalized, and the losses are still being reported in the early months of the current year and initial reserves are being set.

- The second previous policy year is the most recent set of data entered on the modification worksheet in the last of the three data segments and considered in the calculation. It will rotate through for the full three years of the experience rating period.

- The third previous policy year is the second set of data considered in the calculation. It will be considered for two years in the moving average.

- The fourth previous policy year is the last set of data considered in the calculation. It is the oldest set of data and will rotate out of the modification formula for the next calculation.

For example, for a policy with an effective date of January 1, 2009, the 2008 data is excluded, and 2007 data will be used to compute the modifiers for the 2009, 2010 and 2011 policies. The 2006 data will be used to compute the modifiers for the 2009 and 2010 policies. The 2005 data will be used to compute the modifier for the 2009 policy only. In 2010, the 2008 data enters the calculation, and the 2005 data is dropped. The Exhibit 15.2 explains this same concept in a different way:

Exhibit 15.2: Data used for Experience Modifiers

	Eff. Date: Jan. 1, 2009	Data used:	2005	2006	2007		
	Eff. Date: Jan. 1, 2010	Data used:		2006	2007	2008	
	Eff. Date: Jan. 1, 2011	Data used:			2007	2008	2009

Since insureds can and do change insurance carriers during the experience rating period, each carrier is identified by its assigned NCCI number. This permits continuity of the modifier and may provide some insights on why the modifier changes, given the unique claims adjustment and settlement processes/attitudes of individual carriers or third-party administrators. The policy number is provided to verify that the data reflects the right insured's experience.

Code: This column identifies the specific standard classification codes (defined in the Scopes Manual) determined at audit, which are used to categorize the insured's exposures and losses.

Column A: The Expected Loss Rate (ELR) applicable to each standard classification code. The ELR is the statistically determined loss rate per $100 of payroll by code. For code 8810, the loss rate is $0.17 per $100 dollars of payroll.

Column B: The D-ratio, the portion of the ELR that represents the Expected Primary Losses contained in the Total Expected Losses.

Column C: The audited payroll by standard classification for each of the three years in the experience rating period.

Column D: The expected losses by standard classification code for each of the three years in the experience rating period. It is obtained by multiplying the ELR factor (Column A) by the payroll (Column C). This represents the total expected losses based on the exposures and usually matches the audited premium for that classification.

Column E: The expected primary losses by standard classification code for each of the three years in the experience rating period. It is obtained by multiplying the expected losses (Column D) by the D-ratio factor (Column B). This represents the total primary losses, or the actual totals of those losses under $5,000, and the first $5,000 of all losses over $5,000 based on the exposures.

Column F: Lists the claim number for each claim over $2000 and the total number of claims that are under $2000 each.

Column G: Identifies the number of claims resulting in indemnity payments (IJ) and the status of each individual claim as "O" (open) or "F" (closed or final).

Column H: Gives the actual amount of the loss for each individual loss, identified by a claim number, and the total amount of all smaller losses (those losses under $2000 threshold).

Column I: Gives the actual primary amount of each individually identified loss (losses over $2000) up to a maximum of $5000. For example, if claim number 7845309 has a recorded value of $2,734, the entire $2,734 would be reported in Column I and considered in the computation of the modifier. However, if the recorded value of that claim were $7,234, the amount in Column I would be $5,000, the maximum primary amount considered in the experience modification calculation.

Following the three years of data segments is a segregated line of entries of additional factors or totals of certain columns. Column A contains the Weighted Value or "W" value. The "W" value is an actuarial credibility factor that increases as the size of the exposures, and therefore the losses, increases.

Column C is the amount of expected excess losses, computed by subtracting the sum of Column E, expected primary losses, from the sum of Column D, total expected losses.

Column F is the amount of actual excess losses, computed by subtracting the sum of Column I, actual primary losses, from the sum of Column H, actual incurred losses.

Column G is the Ballast Value, or B Value, a specific value taken from actuarial tables and used to limit the effect of any single severe accident on the modification factor.

The last element of the experience modification worksheet is the actual computation of the experience modifier. The experience modifier is computed by dividing the actual loss total, 35,726 (H33), by the **expected** loss total 28,628 (H35).

The formula for the numerator (H33) is:

Actual Loss Total = Actual Primary Losses + Stabilizing Value + Ratable Actual Excess Losses

$$35,726 = 12,918 + 21,962 + 846$$

The actual primary losses value (I29) is taken from the sum of Column I.

Actual primary losses = 12,918

The stabilizing value is the expected excess (which is D29 – E29) multiplied by 1-W, and then the Ballast is added to this product.

The stabilizing value = [C29 x (1 – A29)] + G29

$$[13,669 (1 - .07)] - 9250 = 21,962$$

The ratable actual excess value is F29 (which is H29 – I29) multiplied by the weighting or credibility factor W (A29).

$$12,089 \text{ x } .07 = 846$$

These three values are summed to generate the numerator.

The denominator is calculated in the same manner, using expected losses instead of actual losses.

Expected Loss Total = Expected Primary Losses + Stabilizing Value + Ratable Expected Excess Losses

$$28,628 = 5,709 + 21,962 + 957$$

The expected excess losses value (E29) is taken from the sum of Column E.

Expected Primary Losses = 5,709

The stabilizing value = 21,962

The ratable expected excess value is C29 (which is D29 – E29) multiplied by the weighting or credibility factor W (A29).

$$13,669 \text{ x } .07 = 957$$

These three values are summed to generate the denominator.

Simple division completes the process, and the experience modification factor indicates the relationship between the actual loss history and the expected losses. A factor in excess of 1.00 indicates the actual losses are worse than statistically expected for the exposures; a factor less than 1.00 indicates the actual losses are better than statistically expected. The modified premium (reflecting a debit or credit experience modifier) rewards or punishes the insured for the result.

Problems and Concerns Affecting Experience Rating Modifications

Since the experience rating modification system is a critical factor in pricing workers compensation insurance and can be a valuable tool for the risk manager in managing loss prevention and control measures, the risk manager needs to verify the accuracy and integrity of the modifier. There are several important matters for the risk manager to consider.

Errors in Payrolls and Premiums

Payroll is the employer's variable factor in determining expected losses, the key component in the denominator of the experience rating modification formula. Errors in the payroll recorded will affect the modifier.

One major source of error is the premium audit. Premium audits may be incorrect because of decisions by the auditor in determining classifications (which then determine the ELR and D-Ratio), by including incorrect compensation amounts (overtime wage premiums are not included), or by simple clerical errors. The audit information may be corrupted when the unit statistical card is completed because of clerical errors made by insurance carrier personnel. Similarly, clerical errors can occur at the rating authority when the data from the unit statistical card is entered into the employer's account.

In addition to clerical errors involving payrolls and classification codes, errors can be made in recording the unique employer identification number assigned to every insured, with the result that the payroll (and loss history) of one employer is recorded to the account of another. Similarly, clerical errors in the recording of the insurance carrier's number could corrupt the employer's account.

The integrity of the experience modifier relies upon correctness of payroll entries: understated payrolls reduce the denominator and increase the modifier while overstated payrolls do the opposite. If the modifier is incorrect in either direction, the true effectiveness of loss control activities is masked, and the pricing of the insurance policy is inaccurate.

To minimize the chance that the payroll and premium are incorrectly recorded, the risk manager should check the payrolls indicated on the experience rating modification worksheet against the premium audits. Discrepancies must be promptly reported to the rating authority to correct the modifier and the employer's account for the calculation of future modifiers (the rolling average).

Loss Reserves and Closed Claims

Reserves change constantly, and the reserve that is entered in the modification system (and applies to the premium for a year) reflects the case reserve only at a given point in time. If the insurance carrier has a track record of establishing inaccurate case reserves (too high or too low), the chance that an inappropriate reserve will be entered into the modification system is increased. Also, there is a common belief that insurance carriers deliberately establish excessive reserves prior to reporting the reserves on the unit statistical card, only to reduce them to their appropriate level after reporting, and thereby try to increase the premium to better assure them of a profit. Regardless of the type of inaccuracy or its reason, inaccurate reserves affect the numerator of the experience rating modification formula and result in an inappropriate modifier.

Also, some claims may be omitted, thereby understating the actual losses and the numerator, and understating the modifier, or some claims belonging to another employer may be included with the opposite effect.

Frequently, claims are closed for less than the last posted reserve. For claims that are closed close to the date the unit statistical card is prepared and filed, the higher reserve may be the value included in the calculation of the modifier. This may tend to overstate the modifier, but only for the current period, as the data entry will eventually be made.

Some closed claims may never be reported as closed, however, so the higher reserve stays on the account and overstates the modifier. Both types of closed claims, those individually recorded and those included in the "basket" of claims under $2,000 that are reported in a lump sum, may overstate the modifier in this manner.

Thus, it is imperative for the risk manager to monitor reserves on an ongoing basis to verify that reserves are always at appropriate levels to lessen the chance that excessive reserves will be reported. Insurance carriers tend to err on the side of conservatism in their reserves, so this can be a constant battle between insured and insurance carrier.

To minimize the chance that the reserves are incorrect, the risk manager should check the open loss reserves indicated on the experience rating modification worksheet against the current loss runs. Discrepancies must be reported to the rating authority promptly to correct the modifier and the employer's account for the calculation of future modifiers.

The rating authorities closely control the challenging of errors in payroll and losses, and the time frames for making these corrections are rather narrow, so diligence and timeliness in monitoring loss runs and audits is critical.

Multi-state Operations

The risk management program for workers compensation exposures may include NCCI states, non-NCCI states, and four remaining monopolistic states (North Dakota, Ohio, Washington, and Wyoming). The experience rating modification system may differ between these states, and the risk manager with operations in more than one state may have to deal with having two or more experience modifiers.

Also, a few states have their own workers compensation boards, bureaus, or experience rating plans, and do not permit the use of the NCCI plan. The operation of these plans are similar to that of the NCCI, but the rules, rates, and factors used are determined by the state workers compensation authorities, not the NCCI.

As of 2009, the non-NCCI states are California, Delaware, Indiana, Massachusetts, Michigan, Minnesota, New Jersey, New York, North Carolina, Pennsylvania, Texas, and Wisconsin.

Independent Contractors

Since compensation paid to independent contractors will be considered as compensation to employees by a premium auditor unless the insured can prove the independent contractors were covered by their own workers compensation coverage, the risk manager must make sure that current certificates of insurance are available for review by the carrier's premium auditor, indicating workers compensation coverage in effect for the term of the employment contract.

Further, the risk manager must understand whether a person is functioning as an independent contractor or as an employee. The risk manager can use the common test for employee status used by the Internal Revenue Service, and the risk management policies and procedures manual can specify what managers and human resources departments must do when there is a question of status as independent contractor or employee.

The tests can be grouped into three areas: behavioral control, financial control, and the type of relationship. Behavior control refers to actions dealing with instruction, training, integration into the work force, hiring, supervising, setting work time, location of work, ordering the sequence of work, and providing tools and materials. Financial control addresses actions such as payment methodology (hour, day, week or month), payment for business or travel expenses, or having the potential for profit from work. The type of relationship deals with such factors as the rights of discharge, termination, or discipline, if reports are required, the continuation of the relationship over an extended time, and whether the service is rendered personally.

Beyond the potential for insurance premium charges for subcontractor payroll, a whole range of liabilities can result from subcontractors when certificate tracking procedures are not in place.

Changes in Ownership

Because the organization's management can greatly affect loss experience, any change in ownership may change the modifier. The majority ownership position determines whether or not the organization will have an experience modifier based on its own loss and exposure history or if it will be combined with other organization's experience. Combinations can have a dramatic effect on the experience modifier based upon the relative differences between the losses and exposures of the entities to be combined.

The specific rules for determining ownership are found in the NCCI reference materials, but the basic guidelines are as follows:

1. Who owns the majority of the issued voting stock?

2. Who are the majority of members if no voting stock is issued?

3. Who are the majority of the board of directors (or other governing body) if (a) or (b) above do not apply?

4. What is the participation of general partners in the profits of a partnership?

For combination, there must be common majority ownership interest in the potential entities to be combined. When a simple majority of ownership occurs in the same person, group of persons, or an organization such as a corporation, a common majority ownership exists, and the entities are combinable.

> For example, assume Sam Pepys owns 51% of Parmesan Cheese Wheels, Inc, and Alex Pope owns 49%. Sam also owns 75% of Locks Corporation, and Henry Percy owns 25%. Parmesan and Locks are combinable for experience modification because Sam owns a majority of both corporations

> Assume instead that Pepys and Pope own 75% and 25% of Parmesan, respectively, and 75% and 25% of Locks, respectively, but Pepys and Pope each own exactly 50% of Whitehall Explosives, Inc. Parmesan, Locks, and Whitehall are combinable because the same owners as a group own the three corporations, and, as a group, they hold 50% or more ownership in each corporation.

> Assume now that Pepys owns 100% of Parmesan and 75% of Locks, with the balance of Locks owned by Pope. Pepys and Pope together own 60% of Plague Noir, Ltd., and Percy owns 40%. Parmesan and Locks are combinable because Pepys owns more than 50% of both. Plague Noir is combinable with Parmesan and Locks because Pepys and Pope as a group own more than 50%.

The owners will submit an ownership change form to apply for the combination of experience modification. If one organization has a debit modification, and the other has a credit modification, the risk manager may or may not want to request combination.

Similarly, changes in the relationship of ownership interests may affect the experience modifier. The NCCI rules differentiate between "nominal change" and "material change." A change in ownership may arise from any of the following events:

1. Sale or other disposal of all or part of an entity's ownership interest

2. Sale or other disposal of an entity's physical assets to a successor entity

3. Merger of combination of two or more organizations

4. Creation of a new entity after dissolution of another entity

5. Creation, voluntary or involuntary, of a trustee or receiver (except not a debtor in possession or a trustee under a revocable trust)

Most changes in ownership are nominal; a material change occurs only when a new owner acquires a majority ownership from other previous owners or when a minority owner (defined as less than 33⅓%) acquires all of the majority owner's interest.

Whenever there is an acquisition, merger, or other change in ownership, the risk manager must be alert to the possibility that the experience modifier will be changed because of the combination and ownership change rules.

From the seller's perspective, the experience modifier will be calculated without the experience of the entity sold when the entire entity is sold. If a part of the operations is sold but operations continue, the experience of the sold portion will continue to be included unless the organization provides adequate information to NCCI for the transfer of the experience to the acquiring entity. If the organization simply discontinues part of their operations, the experience will continue to be included. Similarly, if the organization decides to self-insure any part of the operations, the experience will continue to be included.

From the buyer's perspective, the experience modifier will be calculated to include the experience of the acquired organization. If the change in ownership results in the previous experience being excluded, the new modifier will be 1.00 unless the acquiring organization already had an experience modifier. This modifier will continue without recalculation until the losses and exposures are reported in the usual manner.

The risk manager must also be alert when the organization contemplates entering into a joint venture. If the joint venture partners are not combinable, and there is a separate contract in the joint venture's name, the joint venture will have its own modifier calculated. The joint venture's modifier is computed by averaging the modifiers of the joint venture partners until the joint venture has been operating long enough to be eligible for its own experience modifier (a minimum of four years).

Controlling the Experience Rating Modifier

In summary, the risk manager must pay close attention to any experience rating factor, whether it applies to workers compensation or any other line of coverage. The following basic steps for controlling the modifier apply to any type of coverage:

1. Practice loss control, focusing on loss frequency. Experience rating plans punish high frequency more than severity.

2. Review loss reserves and meet with claims representatives regularly. The time to change loss reserves is before the losses are filed with a rating authority (or the underwriter).

3. Verify the calculation of modifiers by comparing loss and exposure data to loss reports and audits.

4. Track subrogation recoveries. Subrogation reduces the value of losses and improves experience.

5. If an auditor or underwriter reclassifies operations, review the current and past modifiers and request a recalculation when it is beneficial.

6. Ensure that the classification codes are accurate and, if there are choices, that the most appropriate and favorable standard classification codes are used.

For workers compensation rating modifiers:

1. Request and review the unit stat cards before they are submitted to the rating authority.

2. Prepare a "test mod" in advance of the rating anniversary. Proprietary programs that compute modifiers are available for calculating renewal modifications and premiums. By test-altering the loss information (on the assumption that loss control will improve experience), the cost of NOT following loss control can be readily calculated and used to elicit change in the behavior of managers and supervisors.

Note: Some states are "net reporting" states. In net reporting states, amounts paid by insuring companies for deductibles and collected from the insured are removed from the losses reported, thereby reducing an insured's Actual Loss total. In net reporting states, deductible programs can have a positive impact on lowering the experience modifier, and it behooves the risk manager to carefully monitor what the insurer is reporting, confirming that the deductible amounts have been removed.

Chapter 16:

Claims Management

Introduction

Risk control is one of the five steps in the risk management process. A key step, it includes all actions that attempt to minimize, at the optimal cost, losses that strike the organization. Virtually all risk management procedures are developed and implemented prior to loss. Risk control techniques, however, can be implemented before or after a loss, making this step even more important in the risk management process. The post-loss risk control techniques include claims management, litigation management, and disaster recovery.

Claims Management

Claims management is defined as "The prompt resolution of an organization's losses subject to insurance or an active retention program, including claims by other persons or entities to which it may be legally or ethically bound."

There are several key points in this definition that need to be discussed in greater detail.

Prompt – The goal of claims management is to resolve claims matters promptly. Unlike fine wines and cheese, claims do not get better with age. Like fine wines and cheese, however, they do increase in value with age.

Resolution – Resolution is the process of bringing claims to their conclusion through the use of denial of responsibility, negotiation, alternative dispute resolution techniques, litigation, subrogation, or salvage disposition.

Losses – Losses result in a reduction in asset values and, ultimately, shareholder value. Losses can occur on a first-party basis, affecting or affected by only the organization itself, or out of the organization's legal or moral liability to an employee or third-party.

Subject to insurance or an active retention program – Except in the case of non-insurance contractual transfers where the responsibility for an exposure is transferred to a third party outside the direct control of the organization, all losses or claims of an organization will be financed externally (through insurance) or internally (preferably through an active retention program).

While an insurance company is responsible for managing insured claims, its goal will always be to protect the assets of the insurance company before those of the insured entity. Because of the impact on future premiums, deductibles and retentions, limits, and underwriting acceptability, the risk manager must still monitor the management of insured claims.

Actively retained losses must be handled by the organization or by outsiders. In either case, the risk manager must manage these losses, even if the actual processing is outsourced to an insurance carrier, law firm, or third-party claims administrator.

Passively retained losses must still be brought to their conclusion, using the same resolution techniques as other claims, and will be managed in the same manner as actively retained losses.

Claims – Just as a distinction is made between incidents, accidents, and losses, there is a difference between a loss and a claim. A claim is a demand from or obligation for payment or performance to another party (an employee or a third party) who is alleging a breach of a common law or a statutory or contractual duty. A claim against the insured does not become a loss to the insured unless and until the insured's assets are reduced by payment or legal expense.

Other persons or entities -- The "other person" may be an employee working in the course and scope of employment, or a "third party," an outside or unrelated person or organization (such as a corporation, limited liability company, partnership, or governmental/regulatory entity).

Legally or ethically bound – The entity may be legally obligated to another party because of common law (usually a negligent act), statutory liability, or contractual liability. An organization may also feel morally or ethically obligated to make a voluntary payment, usually called an ex gratia payment to compensate the injured party without legal fault or responsibility. Ex gratia payments can be used to resolve issues where there may be a question of liability, to maintain customer relations, or the organization's reputation.

The Role of Claims Management

In the broader risk management process, the first key step is to identify loss exposures or risks. Once identified, a risk or exposure is analyzed, controlled, financed, and administered. As an essential part of risk control, claims management follows this same format: the claims manager identifies claims and the related facts of the claim, conducts an analysis of the potential liability, undertakes actions to minimize or reduce the financial impact (the loss was not avoided or prevented, so the only remaining option is to reduce it), identify financial obligations and resources, and then resolve the claim and report the results.

The role of the risk manager in claims management is to gather data, enforce contractual obligations, mitigate damages, promote an equitable resolution, reduce fraud, forecast loss values, and advise and consult with other departments within the organization.

Gathering Data – Claims management serves a data gathering function, in which the claims manager will collect incident/accident reports, identify and analyze contractual obligations, verify loss or claim amounts, and conduct appropriate investigations to determine liability.

Enforcing Contractual Obligations – Related to the data gathering aspect of identifying and analyzing contractual obligations is the enforcement of those contractual obligations. A hold harmless or indemnification provision or additional insured status is meaningless if no one requires the responsible party to perform.

Mitigating Damages – During a claim and after a loss, the claims management process serves to reduce or mitigate damages. Some mitigation actions reduce the dollar amount of damages paid out, while others attempt to restore asset value by recovering amounts from responsible parties through subrogation or from salvage.

Reducing Fraud – Claims fraud can exist internally, externally or systemically. Internal fraud is that perpetrated by persons inside the organization (e.g., embezzlement). External fraud is conducted by individuals outside the organization (e.g., a claimant who exaggerates an injury or damages, or someone who makes away with a company's assets by trick or device). Systemic fraud arises out of organizational failures or inadequate or lacking organizational governance (e.g., Enron).

Forecasting – Claims management is involved with setting reserves based upon the initial report of the incident and the flow of information that follows. Losses may be trended to account for the effect of inflation and developed to account for the natural increase in the dollar value (or the number of losses) that occurs over time. This information may be used to predict or forecast losses into future periods.

Advising and Consulting – Claims management may advise or consult with other departments within the organization. Legal, operations, administration, sales, product development, and human resources may benefit from information provided by the claims management function.

To Bundle or Not to Bundle, That is the Question

During the risk financing decision-making process, one consideration in evaluating risk financing plans involves the use of internal department resources or the use of outside services, a component in the cost of risk, to handle claims management. Organizations may feel that they can handle claims or losses on their own or through an independent third party at a lower administrative cost than when claims services are included as part of an insurance premium. Further, with an inside or independent claims manager, the focus of the claims settlement process (or other services) is on the organization's best interests, not the insurance carrier's profit and stakeholder value.

The process of an organization providing claims administrative services on its own is familiarly known as "unbundling," the separation of insurance (the external financing of risk by an insurance carrier), from loss control and/or claims administration.

In a typical unbundled insurance arrangement, the insurance carrier provides all other policy management services, including filing proof of coverage with state agencies when required, reporting claim and loss data to insurance rate-making authorities such as the National Council on Compensation Insurance and other state and federal agencies. When proof of coverage is required by others, the insurance carrier may provide certificates of insurance or evidence of insurance coverage, or may delegate that authority to the agent or broker.

Not every organization is a candidate for unbundling of the claims handling function. Generally, unbundling requires the organization to assume a much larger portion of the risk (compared with organizations using a loss sensitive program in which the insurance carrier plays a greater part in claims handling). Also, the annual insurance premium (for the traditional insurance product lines such as general liability, product and completed operations liability, workers compensation, automobile physical damage) must be large enough to justify the insured's assumption of risk and administrative services and still be attractive to target insurance markets (some markets prefer to keep the control they have in handling claims).

Further, the organization must have a greater risk tolerance for higher self-insured retentions, frictional costs, and management costs, as well as being prepared to accept a potentially different array of services under an unbundled program compared to traditional insurance placements.

Last, the organization's financials must support the anticipated cost of risk associated with claims administration. The risk manager must consider the nature of the traditional insurance product line (e.g., property, workers compensation, etc.) because of factors such as the development of claims in future years, the impact of inflationary trends on claims costs, market risk, interest rate risk, general economic patterns, and the increase in the level of uncertainty over time.

If an organization decides to unbundle claims services, it may still participate in an insurance program, even though the retention level is high, and thereby reduce its risk from catastrophic claims or aggregation of losses. The organization controls, to a greater degree, its own destiny when it assumes the claims administration function through unbundling without assuming the administrative burden associated with compliance with state self-insurance applications and reporting requirements.

Occasionally, an organization using self-insurance in some areas of exposure operates or expands into a state that does not permit self-insurance in another area of exposure, or its operations in a state do not meet the minimum requirements for self-insurance, including small operations that cannot be economically self-insured. An unbundled insured program provides a good alternative in those instances.

Perhaps most importantly, unbundling may avoid problems associated with a "run-off" situation created when the organization changes insurance carriers. If the organization provides its own claims management or purchases the services from a third party administrator, continuity of dedicated claims handling is maintained despite the change in carriers.

Types of Claims Management Plans

As hinted at earlier, there are three approaches to claims management: insurer-administered plan, third-party administrator, and self-administration. One very blurry distinction between these three types of plans is the amount of the retention.

Nearly all insured plans have deductible options, but the deductible is "small." Small in this context is a relative term used to describe what is essentially a maintenance deductible, one designed to avoid insurance carrier involvement on claims of a trivial size relative to the organization, the most expensive kind of claim to handle because of the high fixed cost as compared with the amount of the settlement. These deductibles can reach several thousands of dollars, and in some cases, tens of thousands of dollars, where the insured is willing to assume more of the smaller sized (and probably highly predictable losses) in exchange for premium savings. Common examples might include a $500 or $1,000 deductible on automobile physical damage, $5,000 on property coverages, or $25,000 per occurrence on general liability or products liability coverage.

Third-party administered plans might have a deductible that starts at $500 or $1,000 when there are a large number of claims (also highly predictable) that the insured organization wishes to outsource, or where an independent claims adjuster brings objectivity and distance into the settlement process, such as under workers' compensation coverage.

Self-administered plans usually have still higher deductibles and retentions, even to the point where a deductible might equal the policy limit.

Consider this example of a very high deductible program:

> The insured organization was not risk adverse, and had a dedicated claims management function. It wished to have high excess liability limits, but the organization's clients, and the umbrella insurance carrier desired by the organization, required underlying primary insurers with a minimum rating and size. A Best's rated A+/XV primary carrier issued a $1,000,000 occurrence and aggregate general liability insurance policy subject to a $1,000,000 deductible and a $1,000,000 automobile liability policy, also with a $1,000,000 deductible. In effect, the maximum potential exposure of the insurance carrier was $0 plus the cost of issuing the "fronting" policies. The premium charge represented the residual risk that the insured organization would not pay the deductible reimbursement, in spite of the guarantee of an irrevocable letter of credit of $1,000,000 and the fact that the insured would be paying and handling claims. This plan was technically an insured plan where the insured covered the losses and provided all claims services, and the insured organization retained nearly 100% of the risk through the policy limit deductible.

This is an extreme example; however, it demonstrates the variability and application of deductibles.

Insured Plan

In the insured plan approach, the insurer provides both insurance and claims management services. The types of plans where the risk manager must pay more attention to claims management are those that are immediately sensitive to losses, or those that have deductibles, small self-insured retentions, and retrospectively rated plans.

Keep in mind that there is a subtle but essential technical difference between deductibles and retentions, even though many in the risk management and insurance industry use these terms interchangeably.

From a purely technical viewpoint, in a deductible plan, the insurance carrier provides all policy services from the first dollar of loss. The insurance carrier then bills the insured organization after payment of the loss, seeking reimbursement for the costs falling within the definition of the deductible. Thus, the insured organization's cost of risk is sensitive to loss, but delayed, and the claims services are the responsibility of the insurance carrier.

In a self-insured retention, commonly called an SIR, the insurance carrier has no obligation to provide any services, including payment of losses and defense costs, until the SIR assumed by the insured organization has been satisfied. In other words, there is a dual or double trigger in the insuring agreement: for a loss to be covered by an SIR insurance policy, the event must be covered (peril, location, policy term, no exclusion or limitation, etc.) and the amount of the loss paid by the insured organization must exceed (or be reasonably expected to exceed) the SIR before the insuring agreement is triggered.

Other features of an insured plan include the insurance carrier providing at least an annual "loss run" or a listing of all losses ("all" is defined by the reporting guidelines), either in print or through online access. A valuable expansion of this service is ad hoc reporting, or the ability of the insured organization to acquire loss runs on demand rather than periodically, such as ongoing online access or a printout once a month or once a quarter.

In an insured plan, the insured organization has little or no input regarding reserving philosophy or case reserves. The insurance carrier establishes reserves with the presumption that these are set to protect the interests of the insurance carrier, even in a loss sensitive plan.

Additionally, the insurance carrier determines and controls the staffing of its claims department. Some insurance adjusters are competent, some are mediocre, and a few are just plain bad. Within some limits, an insured organization can work with the insurance carrier to reassign staff, but the direct control is always the prerogative of the insurance carrier. Another problem with insurance carrier staff is that the insured organization's geographic operations and sources of loss may not coincide with the insurance carrier's claims presence. It is generally preferential to have claims resources in close proximity to the insured's exposures to loss.

Last, the feature that often creates the most dissatisfaction with insured plans is the process of resolution and settlement. Resolution and settlement is directed by the insurance carrier, and the goal is to protect the insurance carrier's profit and stakeholder value. Insured organizations frequently accuse insurance carriers of wasting the organization's premium or funds by paying non-meritorious claims or by freely paying "nuisance value" claims to avoid the expense of litigation. The reality is that even a fully self-insured organization must consider these options to minimize its total cost of risk. Fighting a righteous battle may result in losing the economic war when the costs of litigation exceed the settlement value of the claims, not considering the risk of losing a case in a court of law. The exception to this feature is the SIR plan, where the insured organization has much more control, unless the SIR is clearly breached by a large claim or the insurance carrier assumes the defense and resolution.

Third-Party Administered Plan

A third-party administered (TPA) plan usually entails a combination plan, using a deductible or sizable retention and an excess insurance policy issued by an insurance carrier that does not provide claims services. The insured organization hires an independent third party to provide claims services (and possibly other services that insurance carriers traditionally provide). The size of the deductible or retention is normally larger than those found on traditional insurance plans, although there is no specific retention amount that is needed to qualify a program for third-party administration.

Loss information can be provided on a regular schedule, as with an insured plan, or on an ad hoc basis. As can be true with insured plans, the ability to access loss information in real time via the Internet allows the organization to obtain information on an inquiry basis.

Reserves reflect the third party administrator's reserving practices and may vary widely from office to office. However, since the TPA is chosen through a selection and negotiation process (and the interests of the insured organization are ostensibly paramount), the insured organization has more input into the process than in a traditional insured plan. The organization must plan for resources to regularly monitor and audit the TPA reserves as necessary.

One critically important aspect of the reserving process is notifying the excess carrier when stipulated claims thresholds are met. The TPA service agreement must clearly state who is responsible for notice to the insurance carrier when claims reach or are expected to reach the amounts stated in the excess policy.

Choice of TPA staffing is under greater control of the insured organization during the TPA selection process. During TPA selection it may be possible to designate specific adjusters to handle the insured's account. If designated staffing is not negotiated during the selection process, the TPA staffing issues are similar to those under insured plans. Also, geographic issues and concerns are similar to insured plans.

For the fees charged, the TPA can take loss reports, investigate all claims, establish reserves, hire defense attorneys, monitor claims development, and enter the data into boilerplate or tailor-made loss reports.

The process of settling claims is more flexible under a TPA plan than under an insured plan. Since claims that are within the retention amount are the complete responsibility of the insured organization, the input of its risk manager carries more weight than under an insured plan. The loss payment procedure is determined by both the primary layer of insurance and the insured organization's retention policy. Payments within the retention amount are administered by the TPA, although consultation with the client organization for approval prior to settlement is customary.

Many excess insurance policies have requirements for reporting claims of a defined nature (e.g., loss of a limb, sight, hearing, or disfigurement) or of a stated amount that is within the retention amount but less than the attachment point of the excess coverage. Approval or authorization of the excess insurance carrier is typically required prior to settlement activity on these types of claims as there is a chance that, if settlement efforts are unsuccessful, the claim may end up being more costly and in excess of the attachment point. Also, many excess insurance policies have so-called "hammer clauses," which stipulate that if the insured organization refuses to approve a settlement recommended by the carrier and acceptable to the injured party, the insurance carrier's liability is limited to the amount for which the claim could have been settled.

Self-Administered Plans

The deductible or retention in a self-administered plan normally is very large, perhaps even reaching the policy limits. In some instances, there may be no excess insurance coverage purchased, the entire exposure being retained.

Loss runs have the greatest flexibility of options in a self-administered plan. Generally, a self-administered plan will feature the organization assuming responsibility for data management through a Risk Management Information System (RMIS). This includes the costs of system acquisition, set-up, maintenance, and operation. Thus, the self-insured organization can obtain loss runs regularly or on an ad hoc basis, with the ability to customize reports or search and monitor for specific problems or issues on a virtually instantaneous basis.

Reserving is the total responsibility of the organization. There is a significant incentive to be accurate and to maintain appropriate internal funding and/or credibility, especially when reinsurance carriers are involved. Unfortunately, there can be a tendency of upper management to keep reserves low and reduce the apparent cost of risk, thus freeing available financial resources for other uses. Self-administration requires careful monitoring of claims and reserves as part of the financial auditing process.

The self-administered organization has the ultimate control over the entire claims staff. However, there are restraints, as the staff must satisfy reinsurance carriers and state regulatory authorities where applicable through licensing, administrative, and continuing education requirements.

Similarly, the self-administered organization has ultimate control over settlements. Cases that have catastrophic potential may still require coordination with reinsurance carriers. Cash flow and cash management issues require the risk manager's proactive attention to the settlement process.

Claims Audits

Claims audits are an important part of any claims management plan, whether that of an insured plan, a third-party administered plan (TPA), or a self-administered plan.

With an insured plan, the home office of the insurance carrier assumes the primary responsibility for claims audits to maintain adequacy of premium, equity among insureds, and compliance with insurance regulations and legislation. Home office auditors will visit claims offices and scrutinize randomly selected files. The results of home office claims audits are rarely, if ever, shared with an insured organization. The risk manager should consider conducting an independent claims audit to the extent possible, for the purpose of justifying premium charges in loss sensitive rating programs.

In TPA plans, excess insurance carriers will infrequently audit claims. The TPA should audit itself (as does the insurance carrier), but with less regulatory oversight and financial auditing, there is less frequency of audit within most TPA organizations. The results of internal audits conducted by TPAs are rarely shared with a client organization unless the results are very good. Because of their independent nature, the risk manager has a greater responsibility for claims audit and oversight of TPA plans.

Internal audits by the risk manager are vital to the success of self-administered plans. Outside independent claims audits are very desirable, and may be required for financial reporting reasons, because of the objectivity inherent in the process. When they are involved, excess insurance carriers or reinsurers also will audit a self-administered plan regularly.

From the perspective of an insurer, the intent of a claims audit might be to reduce errors and check for any possible dishonesty or fraud, as well as to determine compliance with regulators and the IRS. From the perspective of an organization, the audit should perform the following functions:

- Assuring appropriate loss data for experience rate modification unit stat cards

- Improving overall loss history picture, thus offering better renewal options for insured and reinsured plans

- Providing accurate claims and loss reserve information for a company being considered for merger or acquisition

- Reducing collateral requirements

- Reducing the number of open claims, thus lowering existing reserves on the balance sheet and protecting earnings

Claims audits bring the risk manager a number of advantages: eliminating surprises, discovering whether or not best practices are being used by the insurer, TPA, or in-house claims administrator. In addition, the review helps identify problem claims, areas of frequency or severity concerns, and potential cost of loss issues while avoiding difficulties arising out of claimant complaints, settlement costs that exceed case reserves, unexpected increases in reserves, and claims going to trial without adequate preparation.

The Risk Management Function of Claims Audits

Claims audits are a proper and necessary risk management function. The claims audit process requires a regular and ongoing verification of the status of all outstanding claims. Regardless of the type of claims administration, claims audits must be regularly conducted by the risk manager or risk management audit team. The only difference between the audits of each type of claims management approach is the degree of involvement and responsibility of the risk manager.

When preparing to conduct a claims audit, the risk manager must consider the composition of the audit team. The expertise of risk management and claims professionals is important, but cross-functional participation increases the credibility and acceptance of the claims management process. Another decision to be made is the frequency of the audits and the degree of depth of the audits. Naturally, due to the types of claims administration approaches, there will be variations in the audit process.

Control of Litigation

Control of litigation is also an important part of any claims management plan, whether an insured plan, a TPA plan, or a self-administered plan.

In an insured plan, the insurance carrier controls litigation, motivated in large part by the internal interests of reducing attorneys fees and related costs that will impact their profits and shareholder value. In most cases, the carrier, which often has a legal team on its staff, is insensitive to requests from the insured for a particular law firm. In a small number of cases, especially with larger organizations, the insured may have the right to choose claims counsel from a list of attorneys approved by the insurance carrier.

Some carriers choose to retain only outside counsel, while other carriers elect to use in-house or staff counsel for routine litigation, but in other instances, will retain specialists to handle certain types of litigation.

Insured organizations have almost no ability to prevent an insurer from settling litigation to minimize the insurance carrier's exposure when liability might be questionable but the cost of defense will be high. Unhappily, settlement may cause adverse publicity for the insured. On the other hand, an insurer keeping a high-profile case open also can cause damage to the company's image, but the insured organization will have only limited ability to compel the insurance carrier to settle any given case. The risk manager must be mindful of the financial influence the insurance carrier can have over the appointed counsel, a situation that may even create a conflict of interest.

As very few TPAs use inside counsel, their legal representatives will be more likely to be responsive to the insured organization's settlement and litigation philosophy. Selection of the outside counsel is based on experience and knowledge with respect to the subject of the litigation, with the potential for input on that selection from the organization.

Self-administered plans tend to be more willing to litigate to promote a "tough" image or reputation, even if there may be a risk of encouraging more litigation or the risk of larger jury awards. Self-administrators very seldom use inside counsel, generally retaining outside counsel based on experience and knowledge.

Selecting a Third Party Administrator

When an insured organization decides that hiring a third party administrator is the appropriate choice for claims management, the organization must consider a number of important factors in making this selection.

Accessibility

First, the administrator must be readily accessible. Accessibility means not just the number and location of claims offices, but the risk manager's ability to communicate with each claims office. Ease of claims reporting and communication, particularly through Electronic Data Interchange (EDI), which is the transfer of data between different companies and state agencies using networks, reduces delays in reporting and monitoring claims activity. Another important aspect of accessibility is willingness and ability to conduct file reviews and have meetings with clients to discuss claims.

Usefulness of Information Systems

Second, the information system and other proprietary claims management software used by the third party administrator can support meaningful risk management analysis through revenue codes, divisions, departments and locations, special client-specific coding, and statutory reporting required fields such as NCCI codes, NAICS (formerly SIC) codes, and OSHA codes.

Also, the information system must have the ability to convert existing claims data to the administrator's system. The administrator should have experience with the current format and timelines. Ease of extracting data and Internet access aids in ad hoc reporting and drive-down capabilities, entering claims notes and financial information, reporting packages online or by email, exporting to excess carriers, and downloading and reporting formats. For security, the information system must include firewall levels, both internal and external. It is desirable to have the access in a Windows format because of the popularity and universality of that platform.

Accessing data in real time means that financial information can be and must be accurate, that overall financial exposures are quantifiable, and that funding needs and requirements are handled on a timely basis.

The extent of inquiry capabilities should include the use of claim notes, claim financials, rollbacks, and "as of" values. The system should be loss-detail driven, with data accessible for analysis in multiple formats and criteria. Optical character reading (OCR) and scanning capabilities, online training and tutorials, and vendor interface should also be available.

Account Handling Flexibility

Third, the administrator must provide flexibility in account handling. The cookie cutter approach belongs in a kitchen, not a claims office, because claims, as routine as they might seem to be, are never exactly the same. There should be a set of customized claims-handling instructions, particularly for claims within the retention or deductible. Claims handling instructions encompass notice of large losses to the risk manager, reserve and payment authority limitations, settlement authority limitations, selection of counsel procedures, preferred vendors, quarterly (or more frequent when indicated) claims reviews, an assigned account manager and dedicated claims team, regular claims audits, banking assistance, monthly reporting packages, the ability to design a program to match needs and objectives, a negotiable fee structure, and the ability to continue handling a claim if it exceeds the attachment point and penetrates the excess coverage.

In case of a necessary move from TPA to insurance or excess carrier, or to another TPA, there should also be a detailed transition plan for the orderly takeover of claims with minimal disruption of services to claimants.

Flexibility in Service Team Selection

Fourth, the administrator provides the staff, but through the selection process, the risk manager needs to have the capability of shaping the service team by selection of the vendor and within the selected vendor to find the optimal match of personnel. Thus, the risk manager should have the opportunity to request and review professional bios of all candidates for the claims team, including conducting interviews. The turnover rate for the vendor and the involved branches of that vendor need to be examined, as a high turnover rate suggests a possibility of inconsistency of staffing in the assigned team or in overall management.

Experience is an important consideration, both in terms of the longevity of the vendor, its assigned staff, and the specific experience handling the lines of business the risk manager has chosen to entrust to the third party administrator, as well as handling claims for the organization's industry type. A list of carrier references and client references, both past and present clients, facilitates the verification of TPA expertise and performance on service commitments.

A review of licensing of staff, regular professional development, and internal training provides an indication of the vendor's commitment to quality service. Related to this is the general area of professional demeanor and appearance. An office area that is cluttered beyond the normal organized chaos of a claims office or personal workspaces that hint at non-professionalism are warning signs that the glossy proposal and sharp appearance of the presenters are facades. However, appearances can be misleading, and a review of writing samples or claims reports can help to ascertain that the work product is professional, even if the staff appears to be less so.

Quality Control

Fifth, and related to the professionalism of the vendor, is the existence and use of a "best practices" and quality control procedure. If there is a written best practices policy or a minimum claim standards policy, it must reflect current industry standards, technical and system competencies, compliance review, and the vendor must be willing to incorporate a best practices or quality control commitment into the service agreement as a material element of performance.

The service agreement should also indicate how performance and quality control are measured. The measurement parameters may include an internal audit process, the identification of the auditors, how well the audit worksheet and criteria reflect best practices, the frequency of audits, the sufficiency of the sampling of claims files, results and an action plan to correct deficiencies, compliance and improvement elements, and the willingness to provide the audit reports to the client.

Further, the risk manager should determine the administrator's position on independent or outside claims audits and establish the expectation that the client or its representative also will be allowed to perform audits.

Industry Experience and Reputation

Sixth, industry experience and an excellent reputation are needed to secure the optimal settlements. If the closest or most practical TPA is unknown to the risk manager, colleagues and industry resources may know the vendor. The risk manager should view websites and promotional materials, keeping in mind that these represent "best foot" practices and puffery. No vendor's website begins with "We are leaders in mediocrity" or "For the best in incompetence, call…."

As in the case of hiring internal staff, contacting references is critical, and when calling them the risk manager must be prepared with specific questions framed to determine capabilities and experience in the needed areas. Additionally, it is appropriate to ask the vendor for its benchmarking statistics so the risk manager can measure how the results of the vendor's work compare nationally, state-wide, across industry groups, and by type of insured organization. If the vendor does not produce its own benchmark data, the risk manager must ask how the vendor measures financial performance and results against the administrative services marketplace.

When the search comes to the point of directly interviewing the TPA, part of the interview process should also be directed to inquiries about lost clients and cancelled contracts, financial status, longevity, and professional liability insurance limits, as well as the existence of any pending litigation against the firm itself. While details may not be provided, a check with counsel to search on legal databases for filed suits will verify the accuracy of responses.

Also, it is important to ask about ownership involvement in the day-to-day operations of a third party administrator. While vendor size does matter, the corporate administrator with thousands of distant owners may not have the same feelings of urgency in handling client affairs as the smaller vendor whose ownership is present and involved.

Ability to Unbundle Services

Seventh, one of the underlying reasons for selecting third party administration as a claims management approach is the ability to unbundle services, moving from a prix-fixe insurance carrier-dictated service menu to the ability to select needed services ala carte. Thus, the administrator must be willing to allow the client organization to select only the services the organization wants and to work with existing service providers on other matters. The risk manager should determine whether the TPA can provide services beyond the current program, perhaps expanding into loss control and medical case management with preferred provider organizations (PPO) or managed care organization (MCO). Another important issue is one of transparency, in which the administrator will disclose any ownership interests in recommended services, such as when a bill review company is a subsidiary of the vendor or owned by the vendor's principals.

The risk manager should confirm pricing for bundled and unbundled services, particularly allocated loss adjustment expense (ALAE), an important component in the cost of risk. The risk manager should also know if any subcontractors will be providing work for the administrator, with the necessity of approving those subcontractors, as well as obtaining proof of insurance coverage, including additional insured status in favor of both the TPA and the client organization.

Appropriateness of Pricing for Services

Lastly, the risk manager must be satisfied that the pricing and value added services are appropriate. "There ain't no such thing as a free lunch," the well-known phrase (a favorite of Nobel Laureate and former University of Chicago economics professor Milton Friedman), applies to pricing and value added services. Everything, even "free" services, have a cost buried somewhere.

The risk manager must be careful in evaluating proposals, as the "cheapest" is not always best. Services and selection criteria must be evaluated along with the indicated pricing. Whenever possible, the pricing of competing vendors must be compared on the proverbial "apples to apples" basis.

Flexibility and transparency in pricing is a major factor to consider. Options for close evaluation will include fees per claim, annual flat fees, quarterly payments and reconciliations, or virtually any combinations the parties can imagine. The service agreement must precisely define what the services agreement covers, as well as the amount of the annual administration fee or annual management fee. Related to this is a definition of the allocated expense categories. It is imperative that the parties confirm their agreement on this particular matter.

Specific to claims management administration services is the need to compare how per-claim pricing is developed, as it might be based on a two or three year planned life of a claim or "cradle to grave." "Cradle to grave" must be further defined in terms of continuation of the administrative services contract. Some "grave" definitions refer to the end of the claim regardless of the administrative service contract, while others have the caveat that the services contract must be in force.

Other services that will be provided or can be offered must be described with their associated pricing. For example, the administrator may offer consulting services for the development of specific risk management or claims management programs for the organization (e.g., a drug-free workplace program or transitional duty program) or training programs for pertinent issues (e.g., employment discrimination, harassment, or lockout and tag-out programs). The vendor may also offer to design safety programs or assistance with safety initiatives specific to locations, operations, or loss types.

Another optional service is the design of internal forms and processes to streamline the claims reporting and claims management processes, particularly in the areas of data capture, recording, and reporting. Related to the reporting service would be analysis of claims by type, loss causes, frequency, or severity, as well as consulting to improve results.

Two last considerations in selecting a TPA are the availability of the third party administrator to attend industry meetings and seminars or other educational events, and the providing of refresher systems training for the internal staff of the client organization.

As mentioned at the beginning of this section, this multitude of optional services may be presented as "free lunch" or as value added services, but the astute risk manager knows that everything has a cost, even if it is not clearly indicated, and will ask specific questions.

The Claims Management Process

Now that we have considered the reasons for claims management, the types of claims management, and who might do the claims management, we will discuss the process of claims management. The claims management process has three key steps: investigation, evaluation, and resolution.

Investigation

The claims management process begins with a report of an event, whether an incident, accident, occurrence, claim, or loss.

Investigation – Reporting

While every person in the organization is responsible for reporting the events that come to their knowledge, every report should be directed to one person in the organization who will be the point of contact for reporting. Considering the organization's defined claims management philosophy, this person will make the determination whether the event is "reportable." This person may be the risk manager or a designated person (DP) in the organization.

Note: As a refresher, an event being reported falls into one of these definitions:

Incident – an event that disrupts normal activities and may become a loss

Accident – an event definite as to time and place that results in injury or damage to a person or property

Occurrence – an accident with the limitation of time removed (an "accident" that is extended over a period of time rather than a single observable happening)

Claim – a demand for payment or an obligation to pay as a result of a loss to a second or third party.

Loss – a reduction in value of the insured's (or organization's) assets

In an organization that is highly proactive on loss prevention will be far more interested in <u>incidents</u> than accidents, knowing the definition of accident prevention: the prevention of an incident that could lead to an accident prevents the accident. Thus, employees would be trained to report every single incident to the DP. The DP then forwards incident information to the risk manager, safety manager, or loss control manager for further action.

Information about <u>accidents</u> reported to the DP must be forwarded to the insurance adjuster, third party administrator, or internal claims administrator immediately, and, if required, to the appropriate regulatory body (e.g., workers' compensation authority, OSHA) within the reporting timeframe.

If the DP's first notice of an accident is the service of a summons and/or complaint, the DP must deliver that notice to the risk manager, insurance adjuster, administrator, or defense counsel without delay.

If the DP learns of a catastrophe or crisis, or a potential catastrophe or crisis (e.g., flood or storm warnings, fire), the crisis management team leader must be notified immediately, in addition to the risk manager, insurance adjuster, or third party administrator.

Response and Investigation

The next activity is a proper <u>response</u>, which will differ according to the nature of the event. Since catastrophes and crises are addressed in other chapters, and litigation will be discussed later in this chapter, this subsection includes only the activities in terms of an injury to an employee or third party (e.g., a workers' compensation loss or a simple slip-and-fall on premises).

The most important step in responding is to establish and maintain prompt and effective contact with the injured party. Prompt and effective contact is the single most outcome determinative element in the entire claims process. As mentioned earlier, unlike wine and cheese, a claim does not get better sitting undisturbed on a shelf. Ideally, the adjuster (insurance carrier, TPA, or in-house administrator) contacts the claimant in person or by telephone within a set time frame, typically 24 hours. Lack of prompt, effective communication with injured parties promotes attorney involvement and litigation. Attorney involvement inhibits the ability to deal directly with the injured party and typically delays the resolution of the claim. Litigation increases total loss costs to the insured and/or its insurer and seldom improves the monetary outcome for the injured party.

In the initial contact, the adjuster should acknowledge the claim, provide a name, address, and other contact information, assign a claim number, take a recorded statement or obtain a completed claimant questionnaire, and obtain consent forms that are HIPAA (Health Insurance Portability and Accountability Act of 1996) approved. All written requests to claimants for additional information or documentation should be accompanied by self-addressed, stamped return envelopes.

Once contact has been established, maintaining the triangle of communication is critical. The adjuster should make sure the lines of communication with the claimant and any medical providers remain open, and if the injured party is an employee, with the employer or supervisor. Similarly, the employer or supervisor should strive to keep an open line of communication with the claimant. Showing concern for the claimant, even when denying responsibility, aids in keeping the ultimate costs of claims, and their defense, at lower levels than when a fortress mentality is displayed.

When appropriate, initial medical case management also becomes part of the response and investigation process. Many claims become "worse" when non-productive treatment is started and allowed to proceed without review.

In some instances, a response of an outright denial of the claim is appropriate early in the investigation, even though denial is usually considered as an option during the last step of the process, resolution.

Prompt and thorough <u>investigation</u> is critical, including such factors as weather, physical conditions, official reports, and even media reports. Witnesses must be identified, contacted, and statements taken quickly, as memories fade with the passage of time or are altered by subsequent exposure to the "facts" as reported by others. Additionally, investigators must promptly and carefully collect and preserve any physical evidence.

Outside support may be used to aid in the investigation. Appraisers, engineers, accountants, and other experts provide a specialized focus and an independent eye for the investigation. A claims history or record of previous claims involving the same individual(s) or circumstances should be procured. The principle goal of any investigation is to uncover the facts that bear on liability and damages. However, an investigation that collects only outcome-oriented details undermines the goals of insurance and retention programs. As Sergeant Joe Friday used to say on the TV show, Dragnet, "All we want are the facts, ma'am." They will fall where they may.

The specific questions the investigators must ask are deceptively simple: What happened? Who was involved? Where did it happen? When? How? Simple questions, but getting complete and accurate answers can sometimes be more difficult.

Another question should be asked: the "what else" or "what else could have happened" question. The answers may give rise to possible defenses to litigation, such as the assumption of risk, contributory or comparative negligence, the existence of a hold harmless or indemnification agreement, or defective work or product of another potentially responsible party.

In the investigation, the examiners must attempt to determine if the organization is potentially responsible for the claimant or injured party's damages. Related to that is the question of damages, or what amount of money will justly compensate the claimant for injury or loss. The investigator must also identify potential issues that will influence resolution, such as the presence of a claimant's attorney or advocate, public opinion, likely publicity, and jurisdictional issues. Last, the investigator must identify if any insurance policy, including any policies purchased by other potentially responsible parties, provides coverage for defense or damages. The last phase of the investigation leads naturally to the evaluation step.

Evaluation

Evaluation of first party claims is relatively simple, as there is no adversarial investigation and evaluation. The organization simply attempts to determine the value of the loss, preparatory to funding the loss payment, internally or externally. However, understanding the liability issues inherent in third party claims is also important in first party losses, as the organization may, in the investigation, find that a third party is responsible for paying the damages or for reimbursing the organization or the insurer for the damages. This latter source of repayment is referred to as subrogation and is treated at greater length later in this section. Thus, in all losses and claims, it is important to think about theories of liability that may be used, for or against the organization.

Three General Theories of Liability

There are three general theories of liability. These theories explain how liability is determined and the potential remedies for liability.

Contractual liability is the theory of liability that is established by the body of contract law. The potential remedies include the payment of actual damages (the most common remedy) as well as liquidated or limited damages, reformation of the contract, rescission or avoidance of the contract, and rarely, specific performance.

Regulatory or statutory liability is that theory of liability that is established by legislation or regulation. Common examples are consumer protection statutes, financial responsibility laws, and environmental protection acts. Remedies include payment of actual damages, statutorily determined damages, fines, penalties, and injunctions.

Torts are civil wrongs, or harm committed by one party against another. Some torts arise out of **strict or absolute liability**, (i.e., situations in which one party is responsible without regard to fault). Common examples of strict liability are some types of products liability and absolute liability imposed for certain activities, such as those of inherently dangerous activities (blasting, excavation, demolition, etc.) or by statute (e.g. product liability or dram shop laws covering dispensing of alcoholic beverages).

Some torts are **intentional** torts, or acts that intended to result in harm. Common examples are assault and battery, libel (written), and slander (spoken). The tortfeasor (the person who commits the wrong) intends harm through an assault, a battery, libel, or slander.

Negligence is the last type of tort, and is the one that occurs most frequently. Negligence is based upon the failure to act according to the reasonable person principle. There are three tests that establish a cause of action based on negligence. First, one party owed a duty to another party. Second, there was a breach of that duty. Third, injury resulted as a proximate result of the breach of duty. This concept is often described in terms of a three legged stool, with one leg representing duty, one the breach, and the third the resulting damages. If any leg or test is missing, no cause of action is established.

For example, a motorist owes a duty to others to drive safely. Assume that the motorist is distracted by a cell phone call and drives through a stop light. If there is no collision, there is a breach of duty, (i.e., negligence), but the negligence did not cause any damage. However, if the motorist crashes into another vehicle and causes damage to that vehicle and its occupants, the breach of duty (carelessness in driving) is the proximate cause of the injury and damages, and cause of action attaches.

Negligent Entrustment and Negligent Supervision

In many business activities and some personal activities, the concept of negligence may be extended from the primary tortfeasor (wrongdoer) to include other parties. This result of ever-growing and evolving theories of negligence has given rise to the concept of negligent entrustment and negligent supervision.

Negligent entrustment is the entrustment of a dangerous instrumentality, usually a vehicle, boat, or piece of mobile equipment, to anyone the owner of that instrumentality knew or should have known was not sufficiently capable of operating that instrumentality in a safe manner without causing injury to himself or herself, to some third party, or to the property of another. For example, a business owner entrusts the company car to someone who is obviously intoxicated (or someone the owner knows might be intoxicated) by giving the intoxicated person the keys. If the intoxicated person causes injury, they will be negligent, either by strict liability if a dram shop law applies or in common law (a tort), but the business owner may be held liable for negligent entrustment.

Negligent supervision arises out of an employment situation, and is the failure to supervise or regulate the behavior of a person whom the supervisor knows or should have known was a danger to him/herself or a danger to a third party (e.g., hiring a known violent felon to work in the complaint department of a retail store). Another common situation that does not involve a high degree of danger, but nonetheless creates a scenario of negligent supervision, is tolerating the behavior of a person who continues to sexually harass fellow employees.

Compensatory (or Actual) Damages, Statutory Damages, and Punitive or Exemplary Damages

The types of damages available in tort liability are compensatory (or actual) damages, statutory damages, and punitive or exemplary damages. Compensatory damages (or actual damages) include past and future economic damages called special damages, or damages that can be clearly established through bills or paystubs for lost wages. Compensatory damages also include past and future non-economic damages known as general damages, or payments for pain and suffering, loss of companionship, consortium, or affection, or inconvenience.

Statutory damages under tort are those damages defined by statute, such as payment of attorneys' fees or civil penalties paid under consumer protection statutes.

Punitive or exemplary damages are imposed by the courts to punish a negligent party for their egregious, willful, or wanton conduct. Some statutes impose double or treble damages, or a formulaic calculation of punitive damages based on specific damages. These damages are intended to discourage such behavior by the negligent party or others in the future.

Setting Reserves

Also a part of evaluation, setting reserves will have an ongoing impact on many facets of the organization. After the potential liability we just discussed has been established, the anticipated values of the damages and related expenses will be captured as reserves in the claims file. The reserves for liability claims reflect the future funds needed to resolve those claims. Accurate reserving ensures that the organization will have sufficient funds to pay its contractual obligations and liabilities imposed by statute or tort in the present and in the future.

Reserves must include both anticipated loss payments and loss adjusting expenses. Accurate reserving is critical to the organization's "bottom line" or financial results and long-term financial solvency. With respect to an insurance carrier, accurate reserving is important in determining the insurer's financial rating in the insurance industry. Also, for insurers and self-insurers, accurate reserving is a factor in avoiding excessive scrutiny by regulators (e.g., the IRS and others).

There are two methods of establishing reserves: individual case method and formula methods.

The individual case method is the preferable method because the reserve is more likely to represent the actual liability of the organization. This method works best where there are no coverage issues and the extent of the loss is readily calculable. However, it requires a high level of expertise and experience on the part of the claims adjuster. This method is most commonly used for property claims and some third party liability claims.

Formula methods are those based upon a mathematical approach.

The **Average Value Method** relies on past experience for specific categories of claims to project reserves. For example, an organization may reserve its automobile physical damage claims (claims that are limited with respect to their ultimate value by the value of the vehicle) by calculating the average value of physical damage and multiplying that value by the number of accidents.

The **Tabular Value Method** is useful in workers' compensation and bodily injury claims where a disability percentage, mortality, morbidity, and remarriage rates are established. The adjuster establishes the reserve by multiplying the tabular factors for each category times the average wage for that person. (e.g., if the person is determined to be 50% permanently disabled, has a life expectancy of 20 years, and has an average annual wage of $50,000, the adjuster will calculate the reserve for the claim to be $25,000 times 20 years.

The **Loss Ratio or Formula Reserve Method** is used in workers' compensation and bodily injury claims where a statute or regulation provides a formula for reserving. For example, if a state insurance regulation sets the loss ratio for workers' compensation claims as 65%, the "standard premium" (the state-mandated rate times the exposure units) is multiplied by 65% to establish the initial reserves in the aggregate.

Accurate reserving is important for several reasons. If reserves are set too low, the organization's assets will be overstated, the risk of future insolvency or bankruptcy is increased, problems with industry ratings may be created, and regulators may focus attention on the organization. If reserves are set too high, the organization's assets are understated, tax reporting problems and stockholder problems may be created, and the organization may mistakenly believe it does not have the financial resources to pursue profitable ventures or underwrite additional business.

A very important aspect of accurate reserving and reserve adequacy is the proper inclusion of reserves for Incurred But Not Reported (IBNR) claims. There are two types of IBNR claims; "pure" and "broad."

Pure IBNR claims are those that have occurred but have not yet been reported or recorded as reserves. Pure IBNR claims arise out of the reporting and recording process through naturally-occurring delays between the event and the discovery and/or report. For example, a product manufactured by the insured fails and causes injury to a third party on January 2nd. Although the third party pursues a workers' compensation claim against his or her employer almost immediately, it takes several months – perhaps a year – for the product defects claim to be reported to the manufacturer. Finally, on December 10th of the same year, the manufacturer learns of the alleged product failure and resulting injury to the third party. The claim against the insured manufacturer, although incurred, was not reported or recorded for a long period after the injury-producing event.

Broad IBNR claims represent the natural change in the value of claims over time. The claims represented by broad IBNR values have been incurred and have been reported and recorded, but the value has changed, and that difference in value has not yet been reported and recorded. In the early life of a claim, the broad IBNR portion of the claim tends to increase. Near the end of the life of the claim, the board IBNR portion tends to decrease.

IBNR reserves, both pure and broad, are a component of loss development factors. Loss development factors represent the relationship between the value of a claim at one time period and its value another time period, and show the rate of change between periods. Casualty exposures have greater IBNR reserves than first-party property losses and have more fluctuation in value.

Regardless of who calculates the IBNR reserves (actuary, risk manager, broker, underwriter, or consultant), the basic factors that compose the IBNR reserve estimates are the same: the relationship of previously reported and unreported claims, the number of reported claims weighted by average severity, and the organization's exposures, an indicator of activity.

IBNR reserves are subject to statutory accounting regulations for insurance carriers, captive insurance companies, and qualified self-insurers. Reserve inadequacy, particularly because of IBNR claims, will submit the organization to heighten regulatory scrutiny.

Coverage Issues

Early in the investigation, especially if there is any doubt whether an insurance policy provides coverage, the insurance carrier's adjuster or a claims representative will undertake an analysis of the insurance policies to make a coverage determination. This evaluation or analysis is familiarly known as a "DICE" analysis, an acronym taking from the first letters of the four sections that will be analyzed in depth:

- Declarations (the who, when, where, and how much) of the policy,

- The Insuring agreement (the how),

- The Conditions (requirements for coverage to be made available)

- And the Exclusions (the "small print" that modifies the insuring agreement).

From this investigation, coverage issues may arise, and those issues must be resolved. There are two initial activities that the adjuster or claims representative will consider: a reservation of rights letter or a non-waiver agreement. Both are used when the investigation indicates there may be a question of coverage.

To fully understand how these documents are used, it is important to understand two legal concepts: waivers and estoppels. Many times, these two words are used together as if they are a necessary pair. However, they are two separate concepts.

A <u>waiver</u> is a voluntary relinquishment of a known right. In a claims context, the insurance carrier may accept the claim without having fully investigated it, only to find out that coverage is lacking. Since the carrier accepted the claim, they can be said to have voluntarily surrendered their right to deny the claim.

<u>Estoppel</u> is a legal concept that keeps someone from asserting or denying something in court that contradicts what has already been established as the truth for one of several reasons, or it is a legal doctrine that prevents re-litigation of facts or issues that were previously resolved in court. There are several types of <u>estoppels</u>. Generally, only equitable estoppels arise in insurance situations.

Equitable estoppel bars one party from being harmed because of another party's voluntary action. (Note the only similarity between waiver and estoppels – a voluntary action.) There are two specific types of equitable estoppels, promissory and by laches. A promissory estoppel arises out of the situation when one party relies upon the actions or promise of another party and because of the reliance, suffers damage or harm. An estoppel by laches bars a party from bringing a legal action after the party knowingly failed to claim or enforce a legal right at the appropriate time. Estoppel by laches is similar to a statute of limitations, except the courts do not impose a "proper" time to bring the action, while a statute of limitations is very precise in the time limit.

As a tool used to avoid the repercussions of estoppel or waiver arguments, a <u>reservation of rights letter</u> states that the insurance carrier believes there are issues as to whether the insurance policy provides coverage for the type of claim made against the insured or submitted by the insured. The letter specially identifies and states all policy provisions that are at issue in determining whether coverage for the claim exists. It also specifically states that the insurance carrier does not waive its right to deny the claim following its subsequent investigation. By stating this up front, the reservation letter attempts to avoid arguments that may force the insurance carrier to be responsible for an otherwise uncovered claim.

Reservation of Rights Letter

For example, a policyholder submits a claim for an automobile accident. The adjuster reviews the declarations and finds that the vehicle involved in the accident was not listed on the policy. The adjuster will issue a reservation of rights letter that states the reason for the coverage issue, all applicable policy provisions, and "we reserve the right to deny coverage pending the results of our investigation." If the letter were not sent, an insured might argue that the actions of the insurance carrier to accept and investigate the claim report were a voluntary relinquishment of their rights under the policy (waiver) or that their actions constituted a promise to pay the claim, and the subsequent denial caused injury or harm to the insured (estoppel).

In most claims, the insurance company sends a reservation of rights letter automatically, as a way of permitting investigation and preserving policy defenses. Because it is unilateral, (one-sided, only protecting the interests of the carrier) created by the insurance carrier and sent without any discussion with the insured party, a reservation of rights letter tends to irritate insureds or to be seen only as an automatic response.

A <u>non-waiver agreement</u> is a better alternative to a reservation of rights letter. It is bilateral (two-sided, protecting the rights of both the insurance carrier and the insured), the result of both the insurance carrier and insured organization discussing the case and recognizing that there may be coverage issues. It permits the adjuster to continue processing the claim while preserving the rights of the insurance carrier to deny the claim if development of facts and establishment of the law warrant such a declination.

In both instances, there are important timing issues in resolving coverage issues. The insurance carrier must respond promptly after the claim is submitted, either by use of the reservation of rights letter or the non-waiver agreement. Failing to respond promptly might be considered a waiver of rights (voluntary action to not respond) or an estoppel (action inconsistent with a position taken). The insured organization must act promptly for the same reasons.

When all coverage issues are resolved, the insurance carrier must promptly notify the insured organization, particularly if the coverage is disclaimed, to avoid allegations of unfair claims settlement practices or bad faith claims practices and suits for extra-contractual damages. Another timing issue arises because of the insurance policy language "duty to defend" (pay first) versus "duty to indemnify" (pay back).

When remaining coverage issues cannot be resolved by the parties through negotiation, the parties have three methods for resolving the open issues. Either party may file a <u>declaratory judgment action</u>, a legal proceeding asking the court to resolve the issue based on the law rather than the facts. <u>Arbitration or mediation</u> involves a meeting of the parties in a forum that encourages a resolution or that forces a resolution without entering into litigation. In an <u>assignment</u>, the insured organization that has a cause of action against another party can assign the cause of action to its insurance carrier. The insured organization receives whatever benefits are available under its insurance policy and the insurance carrier assumes the responsibility for resolving the matter through whatever means are at its disposal.

Whenever coverage issues arise, two additional factors must be considered. A dispute may harm the continued relationship of the parties, particularly if the disagreement is divisive, extended, or expensive. Another concern is how the resolution will be funded. Litigation is the most expensive method of resolving a coverage dispute, and while arbitration is often part of the insurance contract wording, litigation costs of resolving the coverage issue will not be covered by the insurance policy.

Reporting

Once the coverage issue is resolved, the claim is documented. The claims management administrator should have a protocol in place for determining what gets reported, by whom, and when. There are cost-benefit issues in the reporting process. Ideally, every iota of information will be reported, as each detail might have predictive or defensive value later, but the cost of capturing, reporting, recording, and maintaining minutia is high. The value of more specific data must be balanced against its cost of capture and maintenance.

Related to this issue is the question of who benefits from the reported information. Some information that is captured may be used against the organization or the insurance carrier, and its cost would be increased beyond the obvious. Often this issue is humorously illustrated with the following observations:

1. The documents contained in the claim file have a title "Dear Ladies and Gentlemen of the Jury" emblazoned with a rubber stamp on every page. Whatever is in a claim file is discoverable in a court of law, and documents placed before a jury are often enlarged to be the size of a poster, with the damaging comment, typed or a hand-written note, prominently highlighted.

2. Another person observed that the "e" in e-mail and electronic data stands for "evidence" or "eternal."

Resolution

There are four mutually exclusive possibilities for arriving at claim resolution when settlement is disputed: negotiation, denial, alternative dispute resolution (ADR), and subrogation. (Astute readers may be thinking, "What about litigation?" Litigation is actually a part of the denial process, as negotiation and ADR attempt to resolve the claim without litigation, but if there is a denial, the only remaining avenue is litigation.)

Negotiation

Negotiation is the process of preparing the facts and law, exploring the positions of the parties, exchanging offers and counteroffers, and eventually reaching closure or agreement, followed by the settlement or resolution.

Denial

Denial, an unpleasant action for both adjuster and claimant, requires a higher standard of investigation and evaluation to avoid allegations of bad faith or deceptive claims practices. The timing and method of the denial is critical as part of the defensive nature of the denial (waiver or estoppel issues). Even when the claim is denied, it is important to maintain good communications, as subsequent information may arise that might alter the original decision to deny the claim. Related to that is the need for the adjuster or claims representative to keep an open mind.

Note: As mentioned above, because of the adversarial nature of a denial of a claim, litigation is a common result.

Alternative Dispute Resolution (ADR)

There are three broad types of alternative dispute resolution approaches: mediation, arbitration, and mini-trials (or summary jury trials).

<u>Mediation</u> is the least formal of the three approaches. No evidence (in the legal sense of "evidence") is presented. A neutral third party acts as a facilitator to explore settlement between the disputing parties (much like Henry Kissinger's famous "shuttle diplomacy" between the Palestinians and the Israelis), and the mediator has no power to impose a decision. In the usual mediation setting, the parties will meet together to voice their positions and then retire to separate rooms. The mediator will start with one party, attempting to determine points that are obdurate and those that are flexible or negotiable then meet with the other party for the same purpose. During the second round of meetings, the mediator suggests areas that might be investigated with the intent of bringing the parties closer together. During the entire process, the mediator has the ethical obligation to not disclose specific positions or matters that either party advances, but only to facilitate discussion and movement to a common ground.

Arbitration is a semi-formal process. Summary or documentary evidence is provided, as opposed to testimony. Each party selects an arbitrator to negotiate on their behalf (presumably with their interests foremost in the arbitrator's mind) and the arbitrators select a neutral third arbitrator, sometimes called an umpire. When arbitration of this type is written as a part of resolution in an insurance policy, often agreement between any two of the parties will be binding. In more complex issues, a panel of arbitrators may be used in lieu of a single individual. If the parties agree, the arbitrators' decision may be final and binding, but in some instances, the decision is advisory only, with the parties reserving the right to litigate. In practice, arbitrations often appear to end with the arbitrators taking each party's position and finding the middle value or position.

Occasionally, the dispute may be resolved by a <u>mini-trial or a summary jury trial</u>. This is the most formal of the alternative dispute resolution types, as they are conducted in a quasi-judicial format. Evidence and testimony is presented, but in an abbreviated (summary) format. In a traditional courtroom, the fact finder is the jury (or, if a bench trial, the judge), but in a mini-trial or summary jury trial, the fact finder is a mini-jury or a magistrate. A mini-jury is composed of a smaller number of jurors. A magistrate is a lower-ranked judicial officer, elected or appointed (depending upon state statute), with jurisdiction limited to the county or parish over which the magistrate presides. A magistrate is also commonly known as a justice of the peace.

Generally, the finding of a mini-trial is final, but finding in a summary jury trial is not, unless agreed to by the parties prior to the summary jury trial. Summary jury trials are sometimes referred to as mock trials, where the parties try out their theories and evidence to determine what might happen if the dispute were traditionally litigated, as an aid to reaching a mutual settlement without the delay, expense, and risk of a traditional jury trial.

Subrogation

The legal concept of subrogation is related to salvage, as it is the attempt to recover damages after a claim or loss has been settled, just as sale of salvage is undertaken to lessen the cost of the loss payment.

There are two broad types of subrogation, equitable and contractual. <u>Equitable subrogation</u> arises out of the common law right to recover damages from another party who caused the loss. <u>Contractual subrogation</u> arises out of a contract provision that authorizes a right of subrogation. In risk management, both types of subrogation are considered, although contractual subrogation is the most familiar as most insurance policies contain right of subrogation provisions and many non-insurance contracts include waiver of subrogation provisions.

The broad definition of subrogation is "the legal right of one who has paid another's obligation to collect from the party originally owing the obligation." The insurance definition of subrogation is "the insurer's right to recover from another party the amount that the insurer paid to (or for) its insured for a covered loss."

Subrogation has the effect of minimizing the cost of risk for an organization by recovering from negligent third parties the amounts paid out for losses, including the portion of an insured loss that falls under the deductible or retention.

Simple Subrogation

For example, an organization has a $1,000 deductible on its automobile physical damage coverage and one covered vehicle suffers $5,000 collision damage because of a negligent third party. The insurance company will pay the insured organization $4,000 as payment of the claim and pursue recovery of the whole amount from the third party. In most instances, if the subrogation attempt is successful, the insurance carrier must repay the recovered $1,000 deductible to the insured organization, thus reducing the cost of risk to the organization, while also reducing the cost of risk to the insurance company, which gets to keep the recovered $4,000.

Subrogation possibilities create a special consideration for an organization whenever there is a legal relationship between the parties involved in a claim. Another example will illustrate this consideration.

Subrogation Gets More Complicated

Assume that Beaver Builders has entered into a construction contract with Water Works. The contract includes a hold harmless agreement wherein Beaver agrees to hold Water Works harmless from any and all loss arising out of the work contemplated by the contract. Beaver also agrees to be fully insured for general liability. During the work, Daphne Duck is stuck in the mouth and injured when a Water Works employee accidentally hits her with a shovel. Daphne sues Water Works who tenders the claim to Beaver under the hold harmless agreement, and Beaver's insurance carrier pays for Daphne's bill under its policy's contractual liability wording. However, Beaver's insurance carrier now attempts to recover from Water Works (the negligent entity) through subrogation. However, Water Works says Beaver agreed to hold it harmless in the construction contract and that a subrogation action would violate the spirit and letter of the hold harmless agreement.

This becomes more complicated if Water Works is an additional insured under Beaver's general liability contract, as Water Works is a party insured under the contract and it has long been understood that an insurance carrier cannot attempt to recover from an insured entity. Now Beaver's insurance carrier would have to argue that this interpretation applies only to an insured under the definition of the insurance policy, not an additionally insured party, by delineating the responsibilities and duties of an insured person (right to benefits, notice of termination, change or cancel the policy, and receive a return premium) vis-a-vis solely the right to benefits held by the named insured. (According to policy provisions, additional insureds cannot cancel the policy, change the policy, receive return premiums, or, by the wording of the notice of termination provisions, receive notice of termination or material change.)

In either case, the hold harmless agreement between Beaver and Water Works appears to be breached, opening the possibility of breach of contract damages or subsequent litigation.

Special Concerns of Resolution

Regardless of the means of resolution, there are two important special concerns to be addressed. First, when a resolution has been established, the essential elements of the agreement must be reduced to writing immediately. Once the agreement is signed, it is binding on the parties. A common element of any resolution is a release, a legally binding agreement between the parties in which one party typically agrees to pay the other party for specified damages and the other party promises to forgo further claims or litigation arising out of the event.

Second, the means by which the payment is effected is critical. For the responsible organization, a lump sum settlement has the highest effective cost as it loses the investment income on the settlement sum over future years. For the claimant, it may have the highest effective cost as most large awards are squandered away within five years. Inexperience in money management, victimization by "advisors," and poor financial discipline take their toll on lump sum awards. While the settlement amount is tax-exempt, the interest income on the amount invested (until it is squandered, that is) is taxable, thus adding to the financial drain.

Structured settlements can provide substantial advantages to both the claimant and the responsible party. First, for the responsible party, periodic payment settlements cost less than lump sum payments as the responsible party has the opportunity to invest the funds not paid out immediately and earn income from those assets.

For the claimant (and family), periodic payments are not taxable as income, unlike the interest earned on an invested lump sum settlement. There is less possibility that the entire proceeds will be squandered early, as only small amounts are available at any one time. However, this advantage can be destroyed if the claimant succumbs to advertisements targeting recipients of lump sum settlements (usually broadcast during late-night television programming), as organizations state they are willing to purchase structured settlements "so you can get what you deserve now." Naturally, the purchase amount will be a lesser amount because of the time value of money, so at least the claimant has a smaller sum to squander.

For both claimant and responsible party, a structured settlement schedule of payments can be tailored to meet the claimant's personal and family needs. For example, if a claimant has young children, the settlement payments can be structured to provide additional funds for college years.

For the claimant's counsel, a structured settlement helps the attorney meet his fiduciary (and moral or ethical) obligation to his claimant, to secure funds for future years to meet future needs. Some attorneys prefer the entire legal fee to be paid immediately and the residual settlement amount to be paid out in a structured schedule while others will take a structured payment themselves, easing their tax burden. Again, these choices will affect the organization's cost of loss.

Litigation Management

Managing litigation does not mean managing claims. Rather, it refers to the broader concept of specifically managing the litigation aspects of claims, particularly the selection of legal counsel and monitoring the litigation process. Keep in mind as you read these paragraphs that the legal team may be suing, as well as defending suits.

Considerations in Selecting Counsel

Legal practice, like medicine, has become more specialized over the years. The general legal practitioner still has a place in providing legal services, but the plethora and complexity of laws, regulations, and industry practices has led to narrow and specific legal practitioners with specialty training and experience.

In selecting a lawyer, reviewing the management profile of the law firm is an important first step. A wide base of expertise, experience, and training in the firm provides a solid support team for any individual lawyer retained. The risk manager should also inquire about and consider the workload of the lawyer or legal team, particularly in contrast to the size of the firm. Small, boutique firms may have a high level of expertise, but only in a narrow range of practice with a very limited number of practitioners. Large case loads may spread the capabilities of these firms too thin.

The risk manager should consider the experience level, education, and training of the individuals who will be assigned to the organization's claims. The risk manager must also be comfortable that the legal team and the risk management or claims management staff can relate effectively with one another.

Further, the risk manager should ascertain the law practices' and individual team members' reputation in the insurance and/or business community, especially among the attorney's or law firm's current and past client base.

Last, the risk manager must consider the fee structure and how billing will occur.

Potential Billing Problems or Issues

Most law firms have differentiated fees or rates for senior partners, junior partners, associates, counsel lawyers, investigators, paralegals, secretaries, and any other function so enumerated. The concern is not the absolute value of the rate, as that is a function of experience, education, training, specialty, and geography. The real issue is understanding who will do what activity, or what levels of activities will be performed by each fee strata. It is very costly (and probably not very effective or efficient) to have a senior partner billing at $500 an hour for legal research that a paralegal could do at $75 an hour.

The risk manager must also identify the minimum charge increments. Some firms charge by .10 hour or .15 hour blocks, so a one-minute telephone call costs the same as a five-minute call. But the differences between these two schedules can make a big difference in the total billable with frequent short-duration projects.

In addition, the risk manager must identify other possible charges. Some firms charge for time spent with a client at lunch or dinner, perhaps for the full length of time at dinner, even though some portion of the time is spent in eating (and may even expect the client to pay for the meal). Other litigation costs that may appear on an invoice for legal services are court reporter fees, photocopying costs, overnight mailing fees, courier fees, travel time and expenses, and usage charges for the law firm's computer hardware, software, telephone lines, and facsimile lines or

Internet email lines, as well as actual connection time. Some of these charges may be billed as incurred; others may be marked up, or increased, by some factor over their actual cost to the law firm.

Because of the multiple opportunities for charges to be created, any good litigation management plan will have an activity review function. An activity review function will match billings to activity reports, and provide information to the risk manager or claims manager regarding those findings.

Billing Agreements

Billing agreements delineate in advance how the legal services invoices will be generated. These agreements can be grouped into three broad approaches, hourly rates, flat fees, and contingent fees.

Hourly rate invoices are generated by multiplying the number of billing units (e.g., .10 hour, .15 hour, 1.5 hours) per staff member times the specified unit rate for that staff member. The hourly charges are added, and the total is the amount shown on the invoice for legal services. Other options under the hourly rate approach are the use of a negotiated discounted rate, wherein the rates charged to a particular client are discounted to reflect a volume of legal work from that client, or a negotiated hourly limit, where the maximum time to be spent on a particular activity is limited.

The flat fee approach may consist of a flat fee per claim or a flat fee for all claims. When a flat fee for all claims approach is used, the law firm becomes virtually the in-house counsel.

The last fee is a contingent fee base. This is a common approach for billing by plaintiff's counsel, where the attorney's fee is stated as a percentage (30%, 33%, 40%, etc.) of the damages recovered. If the plaintiff receives nothing, the lawyer earns nothing. This approach does not work well for defendant's counsel (although it could, theoretically, if the lawyer received 33% of the amount that would have been paid had he lost and nothing if he actually does lose).

In the words of a well-known insurance defense counsel, "Everyone complains about the 33% the plaintiff's lawyer gets when he wins, but no one talks about the 100% of the billed fees we defense lawyers get whether we win or not."

Summary

It is clear that a risk manager's tasks in claims management (or assignment of claims management) and follow-up are varied and costly in terms of cash and/or personnel and will greatly affect the organization's overall cost of risk.

Chapter 17

Crisis Management

Introduction

"What's in a name? That which we call a rose by any other word would smell as sweet."

-- Wm. Shakespeare

This well-known line uttered by Juliet about Romeo's surname applies to the process of managing a crisis also, except a crisis, disaster, critical incident, catastrophe, or emergency rarely smells sweet. Regardless of what the calamitous event is called, the risk manager must be prepared to respond. For ease in this discussion, our "rose" will be called a crisis.

The standard dictionary definition of "crisis" is "a turning point, as in a sequence of events, for better or worse." In traditional Chinese, "crisis" and "opportunity" are closely related, both sharing a common character. Disasters, critical incidents, catastrophes, or emergencies may differ in degrees, but each represents a turning point in a sequence of events, the time when it either gets better or gets worse.

The definition of "crisis" used in the Certified Risk Management program is "any critical incident that involves death, serious injury, or threat to people; damage to environment, animals, property and/or data; disruption of operations; threat to the ability to carry out organizational mission and goals; and/or, threat to the financial welfare and image of the organization."

A crisis is an event that can have one or more common characteristics. In some cases, a crisis may have the potential to cause significant damage to the organization's reputation, yet in others, the crisis is entirely self-contained. A crisis may be damaging to consumer, shareholder, and employee confidence in the organization or its brands, but in other cases, the crisis may serve to strengthen confidence. It may directly involve multiple audiences and stakeholders, or it may affect only a few. A crisis may be newsworthy and attract the attention of the media or it may be simply noted and forgotten almost as soon as it becomes known. It may be unique to an organization or it may affect many. It may be entirely unpredictable or largely anticipated. A crisis does not have to be "big" in dollar terms to qualify as a crisis; what constitutes a crisis for Apu at Springfield's Kwik-E-Mart is not the same for the risk manager at Bentonville's Wal-Mart.

The impact of a crisis may take many forms. The crisis may affect operations, ranging from a disruption in activity to a total shutdown, and from increased expenses or reduced income to bankruptcy. Without a question, Hurricane Katrina created a multitude of crises in August 2005. However, for some businesses in the French Quarter, the storm was a temporary disruption (except for the lack of new customers), while it meant a total cessation of business for many other organizations, large and small, in other parts of the area. Organizations went out of business because of this crisis, while others suffered or prospered. As the following example demonstrates, as a result of the organization's operations, the crisis may cause serious personal injury to customers, employees, and other persons, even including members of the public who are responding to incorrect reporting.

Mining disaster affects thousands

On January 2, 2006, an explosion in the Sago Mine in Sago, West Virginia, trapped 13 miners over 9,000 feet inside the coal mine. Malfunctioning emergency breathing apparatus on some rescue workers added to the woes of the trapped miners. Only one of the thirteen survived. Complicating this crisis was the initial report by mine officials that 12 had survived and only one had perished. Journalists then reported that the mine reopened on March 11, 2007, with a loss of production for over 12 months that affected the entire community of Sago and users of coal from that mine. On March 19, 2007, the mine was closed permanently, with the loss of a source of coal for customers and employment for the local community.

The crisis may create potentially damaging media attention, public opinion, or regulatory action.

Cans of contaminated soup bankrupts soup company

On July 2, 1971, following the death of a man and the serious illness of his wife, the FDA issued a warning that vichyssoise canned by the Bon Vivant Soup Company might be contaminated by deadly botulism. Bon Vivant recalled over 6,000 cans made in the same batch, a small portion of the 4 million cans of soup the company made in the typical year. After testing a sample of 324 cans, five were found to contain the poison. More cans showed the tell-tale bulging ends of contaminated cans. Five days later, the FDA closed the Newark, New Jersey plant. This action destroyed the public confidence in Bon Vivant foods and the brand, and Bon Vivant filed for bankruptcy within 30 days. It made an attempt to reenter the food market under a different name, but the lack of public confidence in the new brand ultimately led to its failure.

Crisis management is so important and interesting because effective crisis management transforms the "crisis" into an "opportunity" to excel and perform. When the "crisis" is managed effectively, the severity of other crisis-related disruption is reduced, whether a disruption of name, reputation, branding, operations, stakeholder relations, or public image.

Sources of Disasters

A crisis may be created by many sources. Some of the hardest to avoid and the most expensive to mitigate are those caused by <u>human hazards</u>. These hazards may be accidental in nature, or arise from simple negligence, or be organized and deliberate. For example, in Louisville, Kentucky, an amusement park ride that was not maintained properly and was operated by a relatively untrained worker caused a catastrophic injury to a young patron. However, the bombing of the Alfred P. Murrah Federal Building in Oklahoma City in April 1995 was an organized, deliberate attempt to harm persons and property. Both could have been avoided, but the costs, both economic and social, for mitigating organized, intentional acts are even higher than the unintentional catastrophe.

Occurrences of <u>environmental and natural hazards</u> also are difficult to mitigate. Science and engineering have developed ways to prevent or reduce the damage to structures from hurricanes and earthquakes, but not to prevent the hurricane or earthquake.

<u>Industrial or technological disasters</u> run the gamut from a loose connection on a wire that causes a serious fire to the failure of an entire system.

System-wide failures kill more than 10,000 in India

The 1984 release of pesticides that killed more than 10,000 people from the Union Carbide plant in Bhopal, India, was not the result of a loose connection, but rather the failure of an entire system, including the use of hazardous chemicals instead of less dangerous ones, storage of the chemicals in large tanks instead of several smaller tanks, improper maintenance, the failure of multiple safety systems, the location of the plant near a population area, and post-loss failure to respond quickly and appropriately.

Industrial hazards can be mitigated, reduced, or avoided by redundancy and the far less expensive use of preventative maintenance, but as the Bhopal disaster shows, even redundancy and maintenance plans are not a guarantee of a good result.

Disasters may also take the form of a <u>biological event or a pandemic</u>. These may be natural in origin, such as the Spanish influenza outbreak in 1918 that spread throughout the world and killed as many as 100 million people, or intentional, as is feared if terrorists use biological agents.

Last, some disasters may arise from breakdowns of <u>infrastructure and transportation</u>. The mortgage crisis of 2008 was a breakdown of a financial infrastructure that led to severe financial consequences for many who had over-extended themselves with debt. A bridge collapse in Minneapolis caused 13 deaths and 145 injuries, as well as a significant disaster for the local economy and has led to increased attention on other potentially dangerous bridges that are vital to local areas.

Crisis Management

Like claims management, crisis management is a subset of risk control in that some actions are preventative, undertaken prior to the occurrence (pre-loss activities), and some mitigate damages, undertaken after losses have occurred (post-loss). Following that risk control model, crisis management is the act or process of managing a crisis to prevent the occurrence of a catastrophic loss, if possible, and reduce the impact of catastrophic losses to the organization.

To be effective, a crisis management program must adhere to a number of principles. A crisis management program must be:

1. **Comprehensive**: Considering and taking into account all hazards, all phases, all stakeholders, and all impacts relevant to disasters;

2. **Progressive**: Anticipating future disasters and formulating preventive and preparatory measures to build disaster-resistant and disaster-resilient plans and operations;

3. **Risk-driven**: Using sound risk management principles (hazard identification, risk analysis, and impact analysis) in assigning priorities and resources;

4. **Integrated**: Ensuring a unity of effort among all levels of the enterprise and all elements of customers, suppliers, government, and community;

5. **Collaborative**: Creating and sustaining broad and sincere relationships among individuals and organizations to encourage trust, advocate a team atmosphere, build consensus, and facilitate communication;

6. **Coordinated**: Synchronizing the activities of all relevant stakeholders to achieve a common purpose;

7. Flexible: Using creative and innovative approaches in solving disaster challenges;

8. Professional: Valuing a science- and knowledge-based approach based on education, training, experience, ethical practice, and continuous improvement.

Just as a risk management program or risk control program has goals or objectives, a crisis management plan must have goals. Some goals are pre-loss objectives, some are post-loss objectives. Both types are generally established by the organization's management or by governmental bodies.

General pre-loss goals address economy of operations, legality of operations, and humanitarian activities. One important pre-loss goal for the risk management function is to obtain top management's full support and commitment to the crisis management program, just as top management has completely endorsed the risk management goals or objectives.

Post-loss goals address restoring and/or maintaining operations, sustaining profits and stable earnings, working towards growth, and maintaining a good public image. Goals will have different weights or priorities with management, and will compete for scarce organizational resources along with all other investment opportunities.

The Major Phases of a Crisis

Effective crisis management requires a comprehensive analysis of actions to be done during the three major phases of crisis management: pre-crisis (before the crisis occurs), crisis response (during the occurrence of the crisis), and post-crisis (after the crisis).

The three major stages leading up to a crisis are 1) threat, 2) warning, and 3) impact. The threat is simply a likely probability of occurrence, but the event has not yet occurred. For example, a tropical storm brewing in the mid-Atlantic is not a threat to the American coast as its landfall is not likely. However, if tropical storm Hillary increases to hurricane strength and curls toward the Caribbean, and then heads for the Florida coast, it becomes a threat. The second phase is the warning, when the occurrence is imminent as the outer bands of Hurricane Hillary are just beginning to be felt. At this moment, the storm could still lose strength or turn out to sea. The final phase is the impact, when the event actually occurs, the hurricane starts tearing up the coastline, and its people and properties.

Recognition of these phases helps the risk manager time specific pre-loss, response, and post-loss activities. Continuing the hurricane example, as the threat forms, the crisis management program would be triggered, and such activities as preparing for board-up by purchasing materials, testing generators and emergency radios, and collecting blankets, cots, water, and food supplies would be undertaken. At the warning, boarding up and removing signs or awnings would begin, and evacuation of non-essential personnel would occur. With impact, essential emergency measures would be conducted as needed to finalize the measures to protect persons and property.

Following the impact, post-loss activities would begin. These are divided into two broad categories: recovery actions and media relations. Common activities undertaken after a hurricane loss would be clean-up, restoration of operations, filing insurance claims, securing funding for recovery, and generating press releases.

Four Essential Steps in the Crisis Management Process

The actual crisis management process consists of four essential steps: planning, preparation, response, and recovery.

Planning – the First and Most Important Step

"Failure to plan on your part does not constitute a crisis on my part."

-- Anonymous

"There is no "I" in "team."

-- Anonymous

Crisis management is too monumental a process to be successfully handled by any one individual. First, a one-person "team" likely lacks the cross-organization, multiple-level vision to truly comprehend what happens when the proverbial stuff hits the fan. Second, the individual is not likely to secure the cross-organization and multiple-level buy-in to coordinate activities in a climate of uncertainty, chaos, and disruption. Third, few individuals have detailed knowledge of all the important activities an organization undertakes on a day-to-day basis. A crisis management team is essential to establishing an effective crisis management program.

Establishing the Crisis Management Planning Team

The Crisis Management Planning Team must have an effective coordinator or team leader. While expertise is always desirable, leadership and communication skills are more important, along with the appropriate level of authority to generate actions and create buy-in. The team will develop the plan as a committee composed of representatives from across the organization's various operational and managerial levels. This multi-level structuring engenders upper management support and garners the details of operations from line managers, supervisors, and employees. Participation by line employees is important, as these employees are the potential members of an immediate response team, the ones who know how to shut down equipment and secure property, and who must implement evacuation and the myriad other details needed to protect persons and property.

The members of the planning team need to have expertise in operations and how operations can be protected or recovered. They need the individual authority to obtain missing information required to formulate a plan, as well as the requisite level of group authority to represent their organizational interests. Depending upon the situation, a crisis will require other special skills, such as knowing how to effectively communicate with the media or public authorities and officials. Lastly, all of the team members must have leadership skills to inspire others to cooperate with the plan creation effort and the plan execution.

The planning team must determine the structure of the crisis management team. The structure of the team can be flexible, depending upon the structure of the organization, except with respect to the crisis communication system. The crisis communication system is best served by a wheel structure, where information flows between a single person (or single position) to and from all others in the network. There are no structural connections between the various members in the network. There must be one, and only one, officially designated spokesperson to receive and disseminate information from the team to authorities, media, and stakeholders.

The planning team must also define authority within the group. One key authority is that of the designated spokesperson, the only authority for official communications. Similarly, there must be one person who has the authority to initiate the crisis management plan. A defined chain of command and commensurate authorities at appropriate levels is critical to having an effective crisis management plan. Imagine the chaos on a cruise ship if a dining room steward had the authority to issue an "Abandon ship!" order.

The planning team must also establish a schedule and a budget to track their progress and justify the costs and benefits to upper management. The schedule and budget include the training requirements and exercises (test runs) of the crisis management plan.

Vulnerability and Impact Assessment

Once the team is established, its first order of business is to determine the organization's vulnerability to disasters of all types reasonably foreseeable by conducting a vulnerability and impact assessment. This is best accomplished by a brainstorming activity, an exercise in which there are no "wrong" responses. The team must be encouraged to consider all possible disasters or crises, regardless of likelihood of occurrence. An attack by alien elves armed with ray guns is as valid a concern as a hurricane at this stage of planning. Once the team has identified a large number of possible disasters, the team ranks the disasters. Though it was important to bring up all of the possibilities, the alien elves might not make the list.

The elements of a disaster or crisis to be included by the team are the sources of perils (natural, human, or economic), the timing (length of warning, seasonality, business peaks, etc.), the impact (human, property, operations, public image, customers, etc.), the probability of occurrence, and the likely effectiveness of pre-loss and post-loss controls.

The team should also consider types and effects of disasters or crises previously experienced in the organization, the industry, in organizations with similar operations, or geographic area. The possibility of new technological factors, human error, intentional acts, and physical issues such as facility, plant, or process design must also be considered.

One possible method of ranking disasters is the use of a flow chart that lists the type of disaster or crisis, its areas of impact, probability of occurrence, the expected effect of controls, and the anticipated dollar value of the impact.

While considering the listed disasters or crises, the team should identify critical products, services, and operations. Aspects of these include equipment and personnel issues, utilities (including telecommunication capabilities), products and services provided internally or by others, and employee, vendor, and customer contact lists.

Similarly, the team must review any applicable codes: building codes, zoning codes, hurricane and earthquake codes, fire codes, life safety codes, and any other regulations, laws, or ordinances that apply to the organization, both with respect to pre-loss plans and conditions and post-loss recovery activities.

As the disasters or crises are ranked, the team must assess the organization's current situation and capabilities. This sub-step would require a review of internal resources in the form of the risk management plan, insurance programs, employee handbooks, hazardous materials ("hazmat") plans, safety manuals, security procedures, environmental policies, fire protection plans, and evacuation plans. The insurance review must include identification of coverage, conditions, and exclusions and applicable limits and deductibles/retentions.

Also, the team must identify contracts and vendors that may provide <u>pre-loss and post-loss resources</u>. Included in the internal resource review is the identification of key personnel from each operational unit, backup personnel and services, and the availability of warning, response and recovery equipment such as fire suppression, communication, and transportation.

The team must also assess <u>external resources</u>. Some services are provided by governmental agencies such as the Federal Emergency Management Agency (FEMA), state and local government disaster planning and response organizations, law enforcement agencies, and fire departments. Others are provided by vendors like utility companies, information technology service suppliers, insurance brokers or carriers, particularly engineering resources for pre-loss actions and claims handling resources for post-loss actions, and other types of vendors. Customers, clients, and even competitors may also provide external resources (e.g., reciprocal arrangements for office or manufacturing space). Lastly, the team must assess the capabilities of hospitals and emergency clinics, first responders like paramedic and EMT services, and the American Red Cross and Salvation Army.

Part of the resource assessment process requires the team to identify the <u>amount of funds</u> (and their potential sources) needed when the crisis management plan is triggered. Also, the team must identify <u>necessary supplies</u>, such as water, food, first-aid and first response, generators and fuel, and protective equipment, as mundane as ordinary gloves, boots, goggles, hard-hats, and coats or as exotic as hazmat suits. Further, the team must determine if emergency materials such as sandbags, braces, plywood, pumps, and blocks are required, and if so, the amount needed. Related to the material resources is the issue of <u>where the physical resources are stored</u>, on-site or remotely, and how such resources will be collected when needed. The team should also consider the availability of alternative premises from which the crisis management team, or the entire business, can operate.

After the team accumulates this vast array of information, it must <u>prioritize activities,</u> initiating those that are considered essential, moving to enact those that are important, and, if funds and personnel are available, arranging for those activities that are desirable.

As a final step before the plan is fully developed, the team must entertain three additional considerations. First, the team needs to consider the <u>proximity of the organization's facilities to risk factors and infrastructure resources</u> such as highways, railways, rivers, power plants, military bases, earthquake zones, tornado zones, flood plains, and hazardous activities such as nuclear power generators and chemical plants. Second, the team needs to review the <u>vulnerability of the organization's key vendors and clients,</u> asking the questions, "What happens if a disaster strikes their operations?" and "How does their disaster affect our operations?" Third, the team must consider <u>contingency plan options</u> for the crisis management plan, using variations of the apocryphal "Murphy's Law," "If anything can go wrong, it will" or "Anything that can go wrong will go wrong."

Developing the Plan

Once the planning team has completed the vulnerability and impact assessment, the next step is to develop the crisis management plan. For each identified impact, the team must determine the strategic plan for that impact, the emergency response procedures specific to that impact, the mitigation plan, the recovery plan, and all necessary support documentation.

During this process of creating the impact-related elements of the plan, the team needs to consider the likely obstacles, such as the following:

- financial constraints,

- organizational resistance,

- informational gaps,

- communication snarls, and

- the "fog of war" factor, the natural haziness caused by uncertainty,

- communication difficulties, and an

- unexpected event that can cloud a crisis during its impact and shortly after its occurrence.

The team must prioritize the impacts of the contemplated activities (e.g., the scarce or limited resources needed by ordinary operations may become even more scarce or limited during the crisis period), and must allocate them according to their priority in the pursuit of the pre-loss and post-loss goals.

After the activities have been prioritized, the team must write the plan, including an executive summary for those (primarily stakeholders who are outsiders) who are not expected to read the entire crisis management plan. The written plan is then distributed to a wider audience within the organization to seek feedback and organizational buy-in, following which revisions and addenda are included.

Testing the Plan

After a review and revision process, the plan is ready to be tested. Testing can occur at several levels, the least disruptive to the organization being a tabletop exercise. A crisis is introduced in a conference room setting, and the plan is implemented as a talk-through exercise. Obvious flaws and weaknesses are noted for future consideration and revision. A more intense level of testing can be performed using simulations in which the mock disaster is staged in a more realistic setting than a conference room, and the crisis management plan is executed.

The testing can occur with respect to specific functions rather than on an organization-wide basis, and may include evacuation drills, either specific to a function, department, facility, or on a wider scope.

The last step in testing should be a full-scale drill. Full-scale drills will involve the entire organization in a more realistic simulation. These simulations may also include external resources who participate in the testing with respect to their necessary response, such as having a fire department, local, state or federal disaster agencies, the American Red Cross or Salvation Army, or other outside organizations respond in a training exercise. In some cases, a mock media session may also be conducted.

Once the plan has been thoroughly tested and appropriately modified, the crisis management plan is integrated into company operations. Like any risk management plan, integration is facilitated through upper management endorsement and encouragement, proper communication, effective orientation and training, and emphasis on the benefits to the organization and its personnel, vendors, and customers.

Evaluating and Updating the Plan

Since organizations do change over time, any crisis management plan must be continuously evaluated and updated, with at least a semi-annual review and a formal annual audit. Also, if a catastrophic event occurs, a post-event review is essential, as that event has provided an opportunity to observe the successes and weaknesses of how the plan actually worked.

The importance of a post-event review can be illustrated by the Sago Mine disaster (a moot point now since the mine is closed permanently). The mine had a disaster plan that included warning devices to detect explosive gases, blast curtains, emergency rations and oxygen, and evacuation plans. The investigation after the accident indicated that rescue equipment was inadequate and faulty, communication in the mine was impossible, and perhaps most tragic, the initial press conference inadvertently leaked information, indicated that 12 of the 13 missing miners were safe and being rescued, when in reality all twelve reported as alive were already dead and the one reportedly dead miner was alive. In a post-event review, these issues would be analyzed and corrective actions implemented to strengthen the plan.

Crisis management plans must also be evaluated and updated whenever there are major changes in operations, personnel, customers, or vendors.

Building the Crisis Management Kit

Building the crisis management kit really is a planning exercise, as it consists of pre-loss planning for a number of activities that must be done at the warning stage and impact stage.

A crisis management "kit" is not just an accumulation of equipment or gear. Rather it is an eclectic assembly of information, instructions, and plans, as well as physical materials.

There are two important "compartments" in the crisis management kit: the actual contents and the communication system.

Contents of the kit:

- Lists of team members, structured organizationally, and their back-up members, as well as a list of non-employees (e.g., authorities, customers or clients, and vendors, and designated providers of emergency supplies and services) to be notified. The list should include telephone numbers (both landline and cell phone numbers), and e-mail addresses to accommodate communication via PDAs.

- Lists of emergency contact information: landline and cell phone numbers and e-mail addresses of emergency services, such as police, fire, medical, and disaster agencies.

- Aerial photograph of each site and the geocode for its location, using latitude and longitude in a geographic information system (GIS). Although one would think emergency responders could find a street address, the confusion and chaos of a disaster can change everything (e.g., a tornado or hurricane obliterates street signs and landmarks). Use of technology reduces the potential for error. Further, the emergency responders would be aware of impediments on routes to a disaster location and can use the GIS data to calculate response times.

- Maps and directions for travel to and between locations and evacuation routes and alternative routes, including locations of assembly areas for those at the facilities and the location of on-site and off-site shelters. Information regarding the communications outpost must be provided in the event telecommunication systems are disabled.

- Detailed emergency procedures, including essential shutdown procedures for employees not familiar with the normal operations (in the event the trained employees are unable to safely close down and secure systems).

- Master keys and access codes to secured locations in case the employees having access keys and codes are unable to get to the sites or are incapacitated.

- Physical equipment, ranging from the extreme of hazmat gear to more mundane gear like radios, walkie-talkies, flashlights, cameras, and money.

Communications systems and procedures (internal and external):

- Internal communication systems revolve around notification and training. The natural changes in seasons (or quarterly) can be appropriate times to remind employees of evacuation procedures and to set dates for training drills. Employees need to know the method of notification, when they will be notified, and who will notify them. The notification plan must accommodate employees with physical disabilities, as well as those who work in environments where the normal notification devices will not be adequate (e.g., using a horn or siren in a noisy work setting where employees must wear protective gear like headphones). Further, if visitors are permitted on the premises, the notification plan must address knowing what non-employees are present, where they are located, and how they will be notified and accounted for. The notification process also provides an opportunity to show the organization cares about the safety and well-being of the employees by addressing home disaster safety tips.

- External communication systems can be divided into two types, communication with the general public and communication with the media. Pro-active crisis management involves informing the public as to what they can and cannot expect from the organization at the time of a disaster. This includes giving information on alternative premises that would be occupied in the event of a disaster. Communication with the media begins well in advance of any disaster by establishing positive media relations. A positive relationship with the media is an invaluable asset during times of crisis for organizations facing strikes, terrorist threats, or allegations of sexual harassment or age, race, and sex discrimination. Further, service organizations may use the media to disseminate general disaster safety advice, as a public service.

Preparation – the Second Step

The crisis management team should have identified each peril or crisis during the planning stage. During preparation the preparation state, the team must generate countermeasures for both loss prevention and loss reduction. A series of questions will aid in this process. For instance:

338

1. Are emergency response and evacuation procedures in place?

2. What prevention and control measures have been implemented for expected events such as fire, bomb threats, snow or ice loading, and flood or earthquake?

3. Is a backup power source needed and available? If so, what type is it? What areas, facilities, functions, or operations does it cover? Is the backup source maintained and serviced on a regular basis? Who provides fuel supplies, service, repairs, and maintenance? Has the backup power source been tested and evaluated for adequacy, and reassessed as new operations and equipment are added?

4. Do emergency response employees and outside emergency service providers know where all shut-off values and equipment are within facilities and on any public access?

5. Have pre-loss and post-loss control measures been organized?

6. Are control measures specific to each peril?

7. Is there a maintenance or safety program designed to prevent or mitigate potential perils and hazards?

8. Are contracts or agreements in place for backup equipment, facilities, and personnel?

9. Have emergency funding needs been evaluated and established?

10. Are pre-approved purchase requisitions needed/available for emergency supplies?

11. Does the response team recognize, understand, and have a plan for each of the perils and hazards? (e.g., Does the response team know about hazardous materials, and has it considered how these materials may precipitate or exacerbate a peril? Are specific teams members educated about unlikely perils such as kidnap and ransom, terrorist acts, products recall, etc?)

12. Are all employees trained on situation reporting, evacuation of personnel and visitors, and use of emergency equipment, supplies, shut down procedures, etc?

13. Has a crisis management plan review procedure been developed and assessed?

14. Is an emergency communication system for personnel and others in place? Does it consider special needs, such as visitors or physically disabled persons?

15. Is production and support equipment regularly inspected and maintained?

16. Have emergency supplies been purchased, inspected, and tested where necessary?

17. Have evacuation routes been established? If so, have they been reviewed to address alterations or new construction? Do the emergency response team leaders have the most current evacuation routes? Have employees been trained and drilled to use the most current evacuation routes?

18. Have important records been safeguarded? Are there backups of critical information and records? If so, where are the backups?

In summary, the preparation step includes these essential components: communication, education, evacuation, identification, inspections, procedures, purchasing, safeguarding, and training. Every organization needs its own dynamic list of questions and checklists.

Response – the Third Step

Life safety comes first in any response. Protecting the lives of employees and non-employees takes precedent over all other activities. Besides the moral issue inherent in protecting human life, no organization could survive the aftermath of public outrage and media condemnation following any response that protected property before life, even if no lives were actually lost.

- Once the crisis management plan is triggered, the type of response is determined. However, all response plans have common steps (listed in no particular order):

- The appropriate number of communication outposts and the control centers must be established with personnel staffing. Basic access must be considered, as well as backup sites.

- Outposts must be well stocked with all necessary supplies. Restocking must also be considered.

- The communication plans must be well practiced and in place to be effective.

- Damage assessment must be conducted. The assessment includes documentation of details, site access, and status of utilities, the taking of photos and videos, and documentation of damages and losses.

- Coordination efforts must be initiated with first responders and local, state, and federal agencies.

- Communication efforts must be initiated.

- Financial expenditures must be made as needed and documented, with the need for additional resources evaluated.

- Employee and family considerations such as notification and assistance must be initiated.

- Media time must be scheduled.

- Insurance partners (carriers, agents/brokers, and claims staff) should be utilized.

Recovery – the Fourth Step

Recovery is a combination of policies, procedures, and restoring operations that will be critical to the organization's resumption of ordinary business activities after a disaster occurs (after "impact").

An organization can take any of a number of sub-steps in the recovery process for a given disaster or crisis, but the five overall steps should be undertaken first, as these will apply in almost every situation.

1. Follow the hierarchy of priorities developed during the planning process.

2. Coordinate all activities as stated in the plan.

3. Identify and provide for essential personnel.

4. Assure that those personnel and the chains of command are in place.

5. Establish communications with insurance and/or recovery partners, customers and clients, vendors, and employees.

Depending upon the crisis or disaster, the crisis management team will take other specific sub-steps as appropriate. Some possible sub-steps follow:

1. Initiate any mutual aid agreements with vendors, customers or clients, and competitors.

2. Secure the site, control access, and prevent looting or subsequent damage or injury.

3. Protect the site and property from further damage.

4. Document damages.

5. If operations are to resume at existing premises, ensure the safety of returning persons.

6. Initiate salvage efforts.

7. Review recovery needs and timelines for each affected department, facility, or location.

8. Resume limited operations to meet customer and client needs.

9. Implement special accounting procedures.

10. Initiate employee support programs.

11. Initiate communications with the public to preserve reputation, image, and brand.

12. Review and revise the plan for the future.

Reputation Management

"If you lose money for the firm by a bad decision, I will be understanding. If you lose reputation for the firm, I will be ruthless."

-- Warren Buffet, the "Oracle of Omaha,"

Buffet views the reputation of the organization as its most valuable asset, even though its worth is not reflected on the balance sheet.

Reputation management is strategic, proactive, and ongoing. The organization should not attempt to rescue its reputation after a crisis or disaster; it should take all necessary steps to protect the reputation before it is impugned. Following a loss, the task is to manage the public and media perception of the organization, as perception is the real hazard in reputation risk. Just as sloppy housekeeping and poor maintenance can lead to a fire or worsen the impact of a fire, an unfavorable perception of the organization can lead to financial problems or bankruptcy.

A crisis can take any form, and not always the flood or earthquake scenario. The following Tylenol product tampering case provides a textbook case of how to manage public perception in a crisis, an action that the Bon Vivant Soup Company did not undertake.

The Tylenol case

In 1982, an unknown person poisoned several bottles of Tylenol with potassium cyanide. These bottles found their way into the homes of unsuspecting consumers in the Chicago area where seven people, three from one family, ingested the capsules and died before investigators discovered the Tylenol link. Johnson & Johnson, the ultimate owner of the Tylenol brand, distributed warnings to hospitals and distributors. Johnson & Johnson stopped production and advertising of all Tylenol products, not just the capsules. Within a week, all Tylenol products were recalled, involving roughly 31 million bottles worth an estimated $100 million. The organization also immediately started a nationwide media campaign warning individuals not to use any Tylenol products or any other products containing Tylenol. Once authorities learned that only the capsule form of Tylenol was involved, Johnson & Johnson offered to replace capsules with solid tablets.

Johnson & Johnson's market share for over-the-counter analgesics plummeted from 35% to 8%, but because of the quick and aggressive reaction, they recovered their former market share within a year. By November, 1982, Tylenol capsules were back on the shelves, packed in the now-familiar triple-sealed packaging. Unlike Bon Vivant, Johnson & Johnson continued to thrive and even prosper.

An organization must know how the public perceives it if it is to manage that perception and its reputation. Market research activities are useful in assessing public perception of the organization and its brands and image. Even among organizations enjoying a strongly favorable public perception and a high level of public trust, astute management will take pre-crisis actions to bolster the "trust piggy bank" to prepare for that rainy day of adverse circumstances that might tarnish an otherwise spotless perception.

Post-loss crisis communication is a critical crisis management tool for managing public perception and protecting the organization's reputation. Four important goals of crisis communication are to:

1. Quickly and accurately address any issue that has the potential to threaten the organization's reputation.

2. Establish a network of advocates, both internal and external, that will work on its behalf in managing perception and reputation.

3. Prevent an issue from escalating into a crisis.

4. Minimize the long-term adverse impact of a crisis.

There is cautionary advice, however, with respect to these goals. Accuracy trumps quickness in addressing issues. Consider the damage done by the speed in which Sago Mine officials announced the survival of the twelve missing miners against the accuracy of only one survivor

A network of advocates must have credibility to be effective. Public relations firms and publicists are often referred to as "flaks," a military term derived from a World War II German air defense weapon, the "Flugabwehrkanone, "flak" for short. These weapons fired at a high rate, indiscriminately sending up a dense cloud of explosive projectiles into the vicinity of Allied aircraft rather than acquiring one specific target. Debris from detonated shells and dud shells showered down on the populace they were intended to defend. Organizations must be certain that their "flaks" aim with precision and do not simply shower the public with multiple messages that may not hit their mark and may do more harm than good.

Mishandling the crisis communication may turn an otherwise non-newsworthy event into a full-blown crisis of its own rather than preventing the escalation of a crisis. Again, consider Sago Mine.

Poor crisis communication can exacerbate the long-term adverse impact of a crisis (Bon Vivant) and effective crisis communication can build long-term public perception and trust (Johnson & Johnson).

342

A Day in the Life of a Crisis: The First 24 Hours

How the organization acts and responds in the first 24 hours of a crisis situation sets the tone for the narrative that follows. An organization under the dark cloud of a crisis must show true leadership, letting actions speak louder than words. Bluster, evasion, denial, and empty reassurance ring hollow when the truth becomes known, and the "truth," real or otherwise, will become known, thanks to a chaotic media circus and the reliance many "truth seekers" have upon blogs and other media-sharing mechanisms such as YouTube.

Communication in the first 24 hours of a crisis should focus on the organization's crisis story. This consists of telling the facts as they are and become known, the truth without exaggeration or speculation.

After that first 24 hours, the second day is the time for communicating the response. By the second day, more of the facts will be known and the initial "fog of war" or confusion in the midst of rapidly breaking news and shattered or disrupted systems will have cleared enough for the organization to see and report the full extent of the crisis.

The second day will be the time to monitor the news media, including the informal news network that many use to disseminate the facts, real or otherwise, via blogs, Internet-shared video, and audio messages. It is the time to communicate widely and consistently, telling the official story.

Crisis Communication - Art, not Science

Communication, as an art, has its own set of five Muses to inspire and guide its practitioners.

1. The organization and the speaker must establish, before the crisis, sound relationships with the media, to create the underlying element of trust and reliability. Truthfulness, frankness, and an appropriate level of openness help build those relationships.

2. The speaker must maintain credibility. If the speaker cannot create an aura of trust and credibility, the listeners, particularly the media searching for the "real" story, something to sensationalize, will scrutinize every aspect of the message.

3. The speaker must control the dialogue. Press conferences can disintegrate into media feeding frenzies, but a strong communicator can and must maintain control to tell the story, not create the story the media wants.

4. Employees and customers are important advocates in the communication process, but those individuals must be guided (and possibly coached) to tell the truth and to follow the same rules all speakers must follow.

5. Last, communication exists to tell the story, not to speculate or discuss blame and shift responsibility.

Telling the Story

How the story is told is as important as the facts of the story itself. As a witness swears in court, it is important to tell "The Truth, the Whole Truth, and Nothing but the Truth."

"All we want are the facts, ma'am."

-- Sgt. Joe Friday of Dragnet fame

The speaker must tell the plain and unvarnished truth. In the chaos and uncertainty of a crisis, some facts may be forgotten or a misspeaking may occur. The public, consisting of ordinary people who have forgotten important things in their everyday lives, will be forgiving of forgetfulness or an accidental misstatement, especially when it is corrected right away. However, a lie requires intent, and most people will be more reluctant to forgive a deliberate act such as a lie. The media initially will not parse the difference, but there is no real story behind a truthful and convincing, "I forgot" after the initial flurry of accusations claiming cover-ups and obfuscation. Once a lie is revealed, the search intensifies for what else was untruthful, and inventions about intent proliferate.

The speaker must demonstrate empathy toward others affected by the organization's crisis. These affected parties might be employees, customers, clients, vendors, or the general public. A "let them eat cake" attitude does not endear the speaker or the organization to the listeners.

The focus of the truth-telling should be first on the facts, but with emphasis on the organization's measures that are being taken to protect lives and mitigate damage. The Ford Explorer/Firestone Tire product crisis reactions illustrate how one organization created a more favorable public perception than the other. Ford disclosed only a few facts, with an emphasis on what Ford was doing to protect the public, while Firestone pointed an accusatory finger at Ford and only at Ford, without an expression of empathy to families hurt by the product failure or to the general public.

However, as mentioned elsewhere in this book, and which bears repeating here, one cynical, expert witness has repeatedly referred to a little-known and never-taught legal doctrine: "Memory is enhanced by the convenience of forgetfulness."

Get the Details Right and Fast

The organization only has 24 critical hours to quickly gather the information, confirm its accuracy, and tell the story. Letting issues linger without being addressed, even when the facts are unknown or uncertain, appears to be an attempt to cloud the issue, conceal facts, or shift blame. Regular communication, even if no additional information is confirmed or available, is better than permitting one-sided speculation.

Be Prepared!

The speaker must have the available confirmed facts on hand at the time of the press conference or press release. In a press conference setting, the organization's crisis communication team should prepare responses to anticipated questions. Planning and preparation are essential for controlling the dialogue.

There are two phrases that should never be uttered at a press conference. "No comment" is evasive and is naturally interpreted as being the same as a confession of guilt, just like taking the 5th Amendment on the grounds of self-incrimination in a criminal trial. "No comment" has no factual basis and inspires speculation as to what the speaker is hiding.

"Off the record" is an attempt to control what the media releases to the general public. In the era of strong journalistic integrity, no ethical reporter would use "off the record" information, but in the current environment of sensationalistic journalism and blogging by the informal network of reporters via the internet, any "off the record" comment is likely to be prominently displayed for the record. Further, it suggests the speaker does not know the facts or wishes to hide the facts.

Answering the Tough Question

Truth and facts are not nearly as interesting as lies and fiction. Answering the tough question is always easier when the speaker focuses on the truth and known facts.

The following comment, attributed to Donald Rumsfeld, received more attention than his real answer to the question (which, of course have been forgotten):

"There are known knowns. These are the things we know we know. There are known unknowns. That is to say, there are things that we know we don't know. But there are also unknown unknowns, the ones we don't know we don't know."

Was the speaker being evasive or telling the truth? This is a good example of a quote from the devious lexicon, "Eschew obfuscation and prolixity with verbosity and sesquipedalianism."

There are four critical elements of answering a tough question.

1. Acknowledge responsibility. This is not the same as blaming ones' self or organization; rather, it might take the form of saying, "There was an explosion in our plant today and employees were severely injured. This is all we know at this time."

2. Control the agenda. It is always easier to do this in a press release than in a press conference, but since it does not give the media a chance to ask questions (even if the questions will not be answered in detail), a press release tends to increase speculation.

3. Enforce message discipline. The most important factor in message discipline is restricting communication to one and only one individual. The organization's crisis management and crisis communication system must make it clear to all individuals that they are not authorized to speak on behalf of the organization, and that all questions must be directed to the designated official. Even "off the record" remarks will reappear in print, "according to an unidentified source within…."

4. The response must be proportionate to the crisis. A complete media lockdown is not appropriate for a largely internal crisis, just as a one-line press statement regarding the complete destruction of a major facility is not appropriate. The authorized speaker must address media speculation appropriately, with "those are the facts as we know at this time," or "we do not have that information available right now," and not with abusive remarks, threats, or worse, "no comment."

Reputation Lost, Reputation Regained

Because proactive reputation management is strategic and ongoing, there is really no distinction between building a reputation with customers and stakeholders before or after a crisis. Trust is an essential part of a successful business relationship and continuing to act sincerely and substantively, even in the midst of uncertainty, chaos, and confusion, is the primary path to maintaining a positive reputation, as well as recovering one that has been adversely affected by events.

Within the context of a crisis communication plan, there are a number of specific steps management must take to recover a damaged or imperiled reputation, the most important one being the organization must accept responsibility for its role in the crisis.

Management must also <u>help those immediately impacted</u> because it is humanitarian, the right thing to do. Then, management must <u>take long-term corrective action</u> to assist in their recovery and to prevent future harm. The organization must <u>address any systemic problems</u> and resolve those promptly to start rebuilding the relationship with all stakeholders.

These actions are most effective when the organization communicates its intentions and actions, openly and transparently. When confidence is shaken, a public relations campaign may be warranted to help restore the level of confidence in the organization, its management, and its brand. Public relations initiatives can solicit support from other organizations within the same industry or region. As a way to maintain relations with the general community, individuals from the organization can participate in forums, such as speaker's bureaus.

To prepare for the future while recovering from a tarnished reputation or a catastrophic event, the organization can establish a media outreach program to create a positive image with the existing media and new media contacts. Educating the customer aids in developing and maintaining a positive reputation, as does an advertising or marketing campaign that focuses on organizational responsibility and capabilities. Lastly, the organization should implement a government affairs program to establish a positive relationship with applicable levels of government, particularly those who assist during a crisis.

Summary

All the varied aspects of a crisis or disaster management program can be summarized into a concise list of key activities. The organization, through its crisis management team must:

- Identify its points of vulnerability.

- Develop a strategic planning matrix to guide its response.

- Create a cross-functional team and define roles, responsibilities, and authority for managing a crisis or disaster.

- Develop a crisis management process that includes the drafting of likely scenario plans, which are tested, implemented, and revised as needed.

- Have and execute a communication plan and system (internal and external and before and after the event) with an identified spokesperson and a backup spokesperson.

- Monitor issues proactively.

- Provide and support annual training and disaster or crisis simulations.

- After a crisis or disaster, debrief participants, learn from its actions, and update the crisis management plans using that knowledge.

SECTION 5

PRACTICE OF RISK MANAGEMENT

Chapter 18

The Risk Manager

Introduction

Being an effective risk manager should be the goal of every risk manager. However, being an effective risk manager does not simply mean having technical expertise in identifying, analyzing, controlling, and financing risk, and administering the risk management process. Those are definitely necessary skills, but one of the most important aspects of being an effective risk manager is understanding how to develop and maintain relationships within the corporate structure and knowing how to create allies and advocates who will further the corporate risk management goals and functions.

In reality, no organization has just one risk manager. There may be an individual with the title "risk manager" or something similar, but effective risk management requires the efforts of many different individuals within the organization.

> A well-known story in management circles is the story of the "supreme leader." The chief executive officer (and founder) of a very progressively managed company was engaged in managing by walking about (MBWA) one day and he asked a worker on the assembly line her name and what her job title was. She gave him her name but replied she didn't have a job title. He told her that she should have a job title and that she should pick whatever she felt was appropriate. She thought for a moment and then suggested that if she had a job title, she should have business cards. He told her to have cards printed and give him the bill. When he got the bill, he also got a copy of her business card, Helen Smith, Supreme Commander. He was amused at first, a little at her audacity, but then he realized she really was the supreme commander of her task on the assembly line, working only on a tiny aspect of the final product, but nonetheless one that was critical.

So it is in risk management: Everyone manages risk within his or her assigned job responsibilities, even without the official title of risk manager. Everyone manages risk, from the CEO to the janitor or mail clerk. Thus, the effective risk manager needs to build a risk management team from all available human resources.

To become an effective risk manager, the person holding that title must take four key steps:

- A first step is to demonstrate the positive financial impact good risk management can have on the organization. In most organizations, the sales or production departments get the attention and credit for the bottom-line results, good or bad, while management often views other staff functions as being a drag on profits. However, an effective risk manager is as important as any other financial manager or production manager or sales manager – the reductions in costs associated with successfully managed losses (avoided, minimized, or transferred) go directly to the bottom-line results. The effect amounts to having additional sales without the costs of sales.

- Another step is to work with the formal and informal networks inside the organization to ensure that the risk manager is "plugged in" as a team player. Being "plugged in" means the risk manager has formed alliances and entered into relationships within the organization. The risk manager knows who makes a difference in the organization and can create and use relationships with those individuals to further the risk management process and contribute to the bottom-line results.

- The risk manager must also communicate risk management results to appropriate levels of management, employees, and stakeholders. Getting the right message to the right people is part of the process of being "plugged in." The effective risk manager knows who needs to know, and what they need to know, to accomplish the organization's goals.

- Being effective also means understanding that a risk manager cannot rest on the merits of pass successes. It means that the risk manager realizes that being brilliant or an expert at any one or even all areas of risk management is simply not enough. The effective risk manager is, first and foremost, a manager, and that implies the ability to plan, lead, organize, and control, as well as communicate – risk management is more than being able to read an insurance contract, negotiate a claim, or conduct a safety audit.

Demands on a Risk Manager

The risk manager wears many hats to meet the many different demands of the job:

Technical – The risk manager uses technical expertise to purchase insurance programs or retentions, select insurance carriers, intermediaries, or administrators, negotiate bids, supervise inspections, analyze losses, evaluate and interpret coverages, manage claims, conduct cost benefit analysis, and the like.

Managerial – The risk manager uses the managerial skills of leading, organizing, and controlling others to accomplish risk management objectives. In addition, risk managers are typically "staff authority" and are considered to be advisory. Therefore, they must implement their programs and plans through other managers. For this reason, solid people skills, particularly in communication, coupled with strong senior management support will be essential to success.

By definition, risk management is a managerial process. By planning, organizing, leading, and controlling the resources of people, money, materials, and time, the risk manager is able to establish and attain the desired level of risk to help the organization achieve its goals.

Ability to Plan – The work a risk manager performs to predetermine a course of action, involves establishing a risk management policy, publishing loss control procedures, determining an insurance or self-insurance budget, and forecasting losses.

Organizational – The way a risk manager arranges and relates the work to be done allows the human resources to perform the work in the most effective way. The components of organization are building the risk management team, organizing safety committees, assigning claims management tasks, and developing the organizational structure.

Leading – A risk manager uses leadership skills to cause people to take appropriate actions. In this function, the risk manager hires risk management personnel, selects a third party administrator (TPA) to handle claims, and motivates the safety committee. Effective leadership behavior encompasses the following:

- Providing clear direction and goals

- Using sound judgment

- Fostering open communications; keeping others informed

- Listening attentively to suggestions and complaints

- Managing disagreements and conflicts fairly

- Promoting teamwork and cooperation

- Removing obstacles to employee performance

- Rewarding, inspiring, and helping to develop potential

- Being a positive role model

Controlling – The risk manager assesses and regulates work in progress and completed work. To accomplish this, the risk manager must determine cost of risk and establish an allocation system, submit reports to senior management, and establish performance standards.

Coordination – The function of risk management is to treat risks in the most beneficial, economical, feasible, and sensible methods on behalf of management, boards of directors, shareholders, employees, and the general public. The function carries great responsibility, as the risk manager has to communicate so much information to so many different individuals inside and outside the organization. And all those individuals, from senior executive management down to new hires need to understand the risk management function and authority. Success rests entirely with all of those others, who have the ability to make it all happen.

The Influence of the Risk Manager

To be effective, the risk manager has to have an influence on the activities of the organization. To do this, the risk manager should make sure all levels of management understand and accept risk management policies and procedures. This means elevating the importance of risk management within the organization by getting senior management's proactive support of the risk management goals and policies. This can be done by demonstrating that effective risk management will accomplish the following:

- Enhancing profits by reducing costs or increasing revenues (in the form of reduced cost of risk and protecting assets and cash flow)

- Allowing management to plan and budget more accurately

- Reducing frequency and severity of losses

- Allowing more effective analysis of losses for projection of future losses

- Providing increased awareness of indirect losses

- Reducing exposures in new operations, mergers, and acquisitions

- Increasing productivity and morale in the work force

- Improving product quality, processes, and technology

It is the risk manager's job to show a direct tie-in between these benefits and risk management issues.

The Risk Management Program

The risk management program includes the risk management mission statement, the risk management policy statement, and the standard operating procedures manual or the risk management policy and procedures manual.

The Risk Management Mission Statement

A risk management mission statement broadly states what the risk management department is about and what it stands for. It should tie into the organizational mission. It should be stated as concisely and clearly as possible, and it should include a few of the highest priorities of the risk management program.

Participation is the key to creating a successful risk management mission statement. To ensure participation in the various steps of its creation, the risk manager should form a mission statement task force of the main people involved in risk management. The steps in creating a risk management mission statement are brainstorming, prioritizing, refining, and implementation.

Brainstorming consists of reviewing the organization's overall mission statement and picking out symbols (e.g., the products and services, customers, risk tolerance) that make the organization unique. The task force should create a condensed list that states each idea as concisely as possible, and then express those ideas in terms of risk management objectives.

The task force can then prioritize the statements, ranking them according to appropriateness. They will then refine the statements and create a rough draft to determine if it is consistent with the organization's overall mission and understandable to others outside the risk management department. They can then circulate the rough draft for feedback and make revisions until all of the task force members accept the final version.

The last step is implementation of the risk management mission statement. After the appropriate supervisors, executives, and directors have approved the risk management mission statement, it is important to make sure all employees, as well as third-party service providers, are aware of the statement. The mission statement should be continually evaluated and modified whenever necessary.

Like all mission statements, the risk management mission statement should be succinct, a modest paragraph in length. Think of Lincoln's Gettysburg Address as a model mission statement. At only 184 words, it is one of the most powerful statements ever made.

The Risk Management Policy Statement

The risk management policy statement deals more specifically with the various areas of risk management. It defines the organization's policy for managing risk and its relevance to its overall strategic plan, goals, and objectives, including its risk management philosophy and ethical considerations.

The risk management policy statement should be in writing. It will clarify the risk management goals and direction, outline fundamental guidelines, focus on essentials, and address ideas that might not otherwise be expressed. Developing a written policy statement also forces the organization's senior management to think about the subject of risk management, a process that develops ideas and increases management's appreciation for risk management as a business tool. A well-written policy statement clearly specifies responsibility and authority, open up lines of communication, and minimizes duplicate efforts.

Preparing the policy statement starts with the risk management mission statement. Insurance policies, contracts, and leases should be reviewed so that all contractual duties and responsibilities of the organization can be part of risk management policy. As is true in all phases of risk management, the support and approval of senior management is vital. Once approved, the policy statement should be distributed with the mission statement to all employees under the CEO or president's signature, as a part of the risk management standard operating procedures manual.

The Risk Management Standard Operating Procedures Manual

The risk management standard operating procedures manual (also known as the risk management policy and procedures manual) is a "How to" book for accomplishing the risk management policy statement. As such, it describes the procedures for implementing the policies. The purpose of the risk management standard operating procedures manual is to:

- Affirm and communicate senior management's support for the risk management program to all employees;

- Define the scope and authority of the risk manager and others involved with managing risk;

- Establish levels of performance and cooperation expected;

- Familiarize personnel with procedures for dealing with exposures, hazards, and perils;

- Provide a convenient reference or "How to" guide for operating machines and doing jobs safely, and reporting injuries and losses, (explaining reporting processes in accordance with insurance policy and/or risk management department terms}.

The risk management standard operating procedures manual should contain a letter from the chairman/president, the risk management mission statement, and the risk management policy statement, any ethical and regulatory considerations, an overview of the risk financing program, and the risk management procedures (e.g., safety and loss control, incident/accident reporting and investigation, supervisor accountability, return to work program, crisis/emergency management procedures, etc.). The overview of the risk financing program is meant to be a summary tool for management. It should include the risk financing philosophy and process, retention levels, standards for selecting insurance carriers (or TPA), philosophy of renewal dates, and insurance (or TPA) bidding and placement process.

The same guidelines that apply to writing a standard operating procedures manual apply to the risk management manual. The risk manager should know the audience by interviewing key personnel within the company and obtaining input from brokers and consultants. The manual should be written in user-friendly style, avoiding insurance and risk management jargon, and it should be as clear and concise as possible. It should use a clean and consistent format, and include a glossary of terms. Most importantly, it should be distributed to all personnel and updated regularly.

Implementing the Risk Management Program

To effectively implement the risk management program and integrate it into the organization, the risk manager must communicate frequently, using all available communication tools (e.g., illustrating interactions with other departments on an organizational chart or flow chart). Top management should regularly refer to the program and reinforce organization-wide commitment to it. All employees, as well as third party service providers, should be made aware of it.

Communicating the risk management program to the risk management team will be critical. They must have a complete understanding of the risk management function (e.g., how it handles insurance policy provisions, loss control, claims reporting, and the general treatments of risk). Cooperation is vital and must be solicited from all levels of management and as many people as possible. To accomplish this, the risk management function should mirror the concerns of executive management and vice versa.

Though the support of upper management is critical, the support of middle management is almost as important because they will put the goals of the risk management program into practice. Middle management contains the "doers" for carrying out loss control techniques, claims information gathering, observations, ideas, and feedback. The risk manager wants the members of middle management to be his close confidants and friends, because he needs their help!

All other employees are the ones most affected by risk and loss control measures, and the risk manager needs their cooperation, input, and insight. Their cooperation and help makes or breaks the risk management policies and loss control procedures.

Monitoring Effectiveness of a Risk Management Program

After the risk management program has been implemented, the risk management mission statement, policy statement, and standard operating procedures manual all should be subject to periodic review and updating. The risk manager should evaluate and report on the effectiveness of all procedures, meaning monitoring all statistics, with reports going to various managers, departments, etc. This will give more credibility to the risk management process.

A stewardship report will reassure management about the protection of the company's assets and resources. The report should be distributed to the board of directors, executive management, departments and operating divisions, insurers (as required), and third party service providers. The reports can be time-driven (monthly, quarterly, etc.), event-driven (at insurance renewals, etc.), or issue-driven (when employee injuries reach an all-time high or low). The reports can cover a multitude of issues including incidents and accidents, open and closed claims, litigated claims or large loss claim reports, analysis of deductible/SIR levels, limits, risk financing options, cost of risk and allocation, loss trend analysis, reports to third party service providers, and contractual issues.

To Whom Should the Risk Manager Report?

The risk manager should interface with, and report directly to, senior leadership within the organization. Risk managers can report:

- Directly to the chief financial officer

- Directly to the president or chief operating officer

- To human resource director

- To legal counsel

- To head of administration/operations

- To a risk management committee

As shown in Exhibits 18.1-3, the risk manager's relationship with others will vary with the type and size of the company.

Exhibit 18.1: Risk Manager Reporting – Small Risk Management Department

Exhibit 18.2: Risk Manager Reporting – Medium Risk Management Department

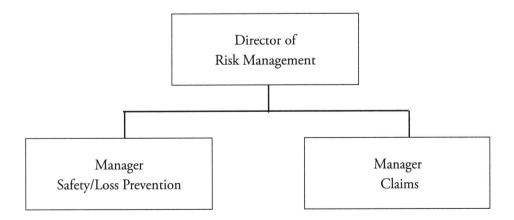

Exhibit 18.3: Risk Manager Reporting – Large Risk Management Department

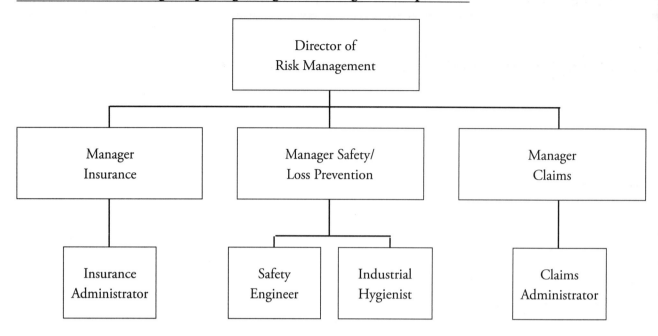

Summary

Risk management continues to evolve as a profession when those who hold the title, and others around them, learn that risk management is about managing risks, not avoiding risks, that it is about managerial skills as well as technical skills, that risk managers need to be active participants in the organization's leadership team, and that all management is essentially risk management.

Chapter 19

Building Your Risk Management Team

Introduction

A risk manager cannot perform every risk management function alone. Besides the ideal of having everyone in the organization practicing risk management, the risk manager may need information or expertise from others within the organization as well as expertise from outside the organization. In other words, the risk manager needs a team. The risk management team comes from two areas: the internal team and the external team. While the two teams can perform different functions, both are important to the risk manager.

The **internal team** comes from within the organization, (e.g., the staff in the risk management, human resources, accounting , operations, and manufacturing departments), with the risk manager taking special care not to overlook or underutilize these excellent sources due to political and jurisdictional issues.

The **external team** comes from outside the organization (e.g., insurance agents and brokers, risk management, financial, legal, and safety consultants, as well as captive managers, and even private investigators). The range of outside service providers is broad and can be tapped according to the issues requiring support.

Regardless of the source, selecting appropriate team members requires that the risk manager not only understand the organization's needs but also know the capabilities of the inside personnel, as well as the expertise offered by other providers and how to contract and manage the provider in order to obtain the desired risk management objective.

Who can be on the Team?

One of the most important members of the team can be the insurance agent or broker. In some cases, it is difficult, if not impossible, for the risk manager to assess or access the insurance market without an agent or broker, although that appears to be changing in some markets. As an external team member, the insurance agent or broker brings knowledge and expertise about the broader insurance market the risk manager may not have. We will go into more detail about agents and brokers later in this chapter.

Other members of the risk management team can include legal consultants, who can handle the organization's usual legal matters, as well as other things like statutory filings, claims management, claims litigation, general litigation, and litigation management.

Claims administrators or third party administrators (TPAs) can handle claims from third parties and employees as well as first-party property claims. Safety inspections, site security, and setting up safety committees can be organized and administered by safety or loss control personnel, security personnel, or engineering and environmental safety personnel. Private investigators usually perform work for claims adjusters on claims, but they could also fall within this security category. Emergency medical providers perform first aid and provide employee injury care.

Other medical providers can provide long-term and disability care.

Human resource professionals often handle payroll, benefits, hiring, and terminations. Accountants, CPAs, and financial consultants perform tax filings, auditing, and keeping the organization's financial records.

Actuaries can be called upon to audit the organization's insurance program, determine the adequacy of loss reserves, and calculate development factors.

Other team members could include risk management information system consultants or providers (covered later in this book), operations and department managers, captive insurance company managers, risk management consultants, structured benefits and settlements consultants, providers of certificates of insurance and bonds, providers of motor vehicle records (MVRs) and workers compensation history, and other risk managers.

Outside Service Providers as Team Members

It is impossible for a risk manager to have expert knowledge or experience in everything. It is imperative for the risk manager to recognize when outside assistance may be needed. For example, in confirming a conclusion already reached by the risk manager on an important risk management program, the opinion of an outside company furthers the credibility of the decision with the organization's senior management.

The risk manager also can be more efficient and effective by using outside experts to supplement the risk management team. A risk manager calls on outside service providers for assistance when:

- Internal skill or talent is not available for a particular project,

- An outside or objective viewpoint is required,

- Time is of the essence,

- Use of outside experts is more cost effective,

- Trying to substantiate an existing position,

- Starting new projects,

- An expert is needed on a single project or on a piece-meal basis or a specified ongoing project,

- Upper management requests it,

- Outsourcing is the standard operating procedure.

Expectations and Questions

Before hiring an external service provider, the risk manager needs to know if senior management will agree to spend the money for an outside service provider. In some cases, management may expect the work to be done internally. However, if the decision is to outsource the work to a provider, the risk manager should know some details before approaching the provider:

- The specific service or work product to be provided or performed.

- How long the service provider will be needed (e.g., whether for one project or over a period of time).

- When the work is to be completed.

- How to communicate the details of project to the service provider.

The Selection Process

The risk manager needs to determine whether the selection will be by a direct hire or a request for proposal (RFP). If an RFP is used, the number of providers who will compete, and, depending on the type of organization, whether that list of bidders must include a minority.

During the interviewing process, the risk manager will need to:

- Determine the provider's experience or skill in this specialty,

- Request information about the last major project the provider worked on that was similar to what is needed for this one,

- Get information on the most difficult project and/or client the provider had to deal with,

- Obtain samples of provider's previous work,

- Ask for specific references of past clients and follow up on those references,

- Find out if provider can meet the goals, expectations, budget and time frame,

- Find out whether the provider been involved in any recent litigation,

- Find out whether the provider will sub-contract any work and to whom,

- Determine whether the service provider is a good fit for style and comfort level

- Determine what support the organization will have to provide to the service provider.

Once the array of services has been selected, the contract should spell out all the risk manager's requirements for completing the work. This would include time frame and length of the project, as well as how the work is to be performed and how accomplishments and deadlines will be reported. There should be sections on how change orders will be handled, how compensation will be handled, including timing of payment and payment methods, and whether the contract includes any incentive or disincentive clauses. Additional items that should be included in the contract are:

- Performance and failure to perform clauses,

- Confidentiality and disclosure clauses,

- Liability and indemnification clauses,

- Requirements to carry insurance (e.g., workers compensation, general and automobile liability, and professional liability) and additional insured status, and to provide certificates of insurance evidencing the required coverages,

- Contract cancellation and re-negotiation terms.

- Dispute resolution clause, including arbitration, mediation, lawsuits, and jurisdiction.

At the conclusion of the contract period, the service provider should submit the final presentation and plan for follow up, maintenance, and continuation if there is any.

The Agent or Broker as a Team Member

Insurance agents and/or brokers can play very important roles in the overall risk management program. Both are valuable members of the risk management team since they often provide insurance expertise, loss control, international business advice, training, and access to coverage. The risk manager will work more often with the agent or broker than any other service provider. In addition, all effective risk management programs will incorporate some form of insurance either at the primary, excess, or reinsurance level. While in practice there is very little distinction between the capabilities of an agent or broker, some differences should be noted.

Agent versus Broker

An Agent is considered to be a representative of an insurance company. In this capacity, the agent has the legal authority to act on behalf of the carriers the agent represents, as well as acting on behalf of the agent's own agency. The scope of authority varies, but normally an agent is allowed to collect premiums, bind coverage, and in some cases, issue policies. In other words, the agent is the insurance company and the insurer is legally responsible for commitments the agent makes on its behalf. The agency agreement signed with the carrier spells out the extent of the agent's authority.

A broker, however, is not considered to be a representative of an insurance company. The broker is instead the representative of the insured, and the broker may place coverage with an insurer directly or through an intermediary agency. The insurance company is not responsible for acts or omissions of the broker.

There are several types of agents and brokers. Direct writers are insurance companies that market their products directly to the consumer organization through an employee sales force. Direct writing sales personnel only represent their company's products and often have little flexibility with respect to underwriting. Also, if their company does not write the insurance, they cannot sell it.

Exclusive agents are independent contractors who write business primarily for one insurance company. That insurance company will usually have "first right of refusal" for any business that agent writes.

Independent agents are independent contractors who write business for any insurance companies with whom they are contracted, and as such, they usually represent several companies and can write business through any of them. Generally, this arrangement is referred to as the American Independent Agency system. The agency contracts detail the scope of authority of the agent (e.g., binding authority, draft authority, and policy issuance authority).

An excess and surplus lines broker (commonly called an E&S broker) is specifically licensed to do business with insurers who are not admitted in the particular state. An E&S broker acts as an intermediary for the agent or broker with the E&S (or specialty) insurer. Each state's licensing laws determine how these relationships will be established. E&S brokers are often not able to bind coverage for the insurers they represent and are held to a different standard of care than a non-E&S agent or broker. E&S brokers usually represent insurers that provide tailored coverages and difficult to find coverages, coverages for difficult risks.

Another way of categorizing the agent and broker system is by the customers. Those agents or brokers who deal directly with insureds are called retail agents or retail brokers, or retailers for short. Other agents and brokers, who deal with retailers only and not with insureds (except in very unusual circumstances), are called wholesale brokers or wholesalers.

Selection of Agents and Brokers

Any agent or broker selection process should strive to be fair and realistic for competitors and should allow the organization to be comfortable with any choice made. This process usually includes the use of formal requests for proposals, also known as bid specifications.

In order for all parties to devote an adequate amount of time to the selection process, much of this preparation for insurance should begin six months before the renewal date of the existing insurance policies (using the same date for all coverages avoids coverage gaps caused by non-concurrency among the policies).

Bid specifications should have an introduction that includes the organization's name and address and the contact person with phone number, and email address. They should also include and general instructions, a description of the loss exposures to be covered, instructions regarding specification variations, and additional information requested outside of bid specifications.

The bid specifications must include a time line. The time line addresses such items as the date and time responses are due; if a public bid, the date and time of any open meetings, and the time period for review of bids received and the decision making process.

The bid specifications should also indicate the bid selection or rejection criteria. The common assumption is that the "low bidder" wins the bid process. However, this is not always the case, even in public bidding conducted by municipalities or other governmental agencies. State statutes may require public bidding and stipulate that the lowest bid must be taken, but it is just as common that the statutes state something like "the lowest responsible bidder," with a flexible definition of "responsible," or one of the lowest three bidders. A common rule of thumb or practice in the insurance industry is that incumbent carrier or agent/broker is given a 10% margin; any alternative program proposed must be 10% lower than the current program or broker to justify the time and effort in changing programs.

During the time the bid specifications are being prepared, the risk manager will have decided who will be involved in the bidding process. The agent/broker selection process is critical to the risk management program, as the agent/broker is a key member of the risk management team. As much time and care should be put into "hiring" the prospective agents and brokers as is in interviewing and hiring any other member of the risk management department. However, custom and practice in the insurance industry and within the organization may dictate how the agents and brokers are selected.

Open Bidding

The simplest agent/broker selection process is not to make a selection until the bids are in. This is usually called "open bidding" and is most commonly used by public entities that treat buying insurance and risk management services the same way they buy toilet paper and road salt. Unfortunately, professional service is not a commodity, and the lowest premium is rarely ever the lowest cost. In open bidding, a widespread invitation is made, (e.g., published in a newspaper) advertising that the organization will entertain bids on specified coverages and services. Any member of the public who qualifies according to bid specifications can submit a bid. The open bidding process is problematic because agents and brokers can submit applications to any insurance companies with whom they have a contract or relationship, the first agent or broker to get the specifications can flood the market and effectively block all others from accessing many insurance carriers, thereby giving himself the advantage of controlling the bidding process. Also, these agents and brokers, sometimes known as intermediaries, may go into the insurance market before they are qualified by the organization, and intermediaries who are not qualified according to the specifications may block markets, even though those intermediaries may think they are qualified. Last, many insurers will refuse to offer quotes on open bidding submissions because they know they are committing to a large amount of work when their chance of getting the business will be very small.

Agent/Broker Assignment

The opposite of this approach is the Agent/Broker Assignment, where one agent or broker is designated through a letter of authority as being THE agent or broker for the organization. This assignment can be made on a broad or limited basis. In the broad basis, the agent or broker is designated as the agent of record, or broker of record, for the organization and is free to approach all insurance markets or other service vendors to negotiate on behalf of the organization. In the limited basis, the same assignment process works, but the scope of the authority is limited to specific markets, a specific purpose, a specific line of coverage, or a specific time, (e.g., "for the purpose of negotiating Directors and Officers coverage only," or "for the purpose of reviewing loss data." There are various industry protocols or customs and practices regarding letters of authority, such as granting the holding intermediary (incumbent) an opportunity to obtain a rescinding letter of authority, or at least notifying the holding intermediary that the vendor has received a letter of authority designating another intermediary.

Request for Proposal

A more formal process is called the Request for Proposal (RFP). This process takes some features from the Open Bidding process and the Agent/Broker Assignment process. A RFP letter, or invitation, is sent to a number of prospective agents and brokers, but not to the general public as in Open Bidding. The RFP contains general information on the organization and a general statement of coverages and services desired. The recipients of the RFP are asked to submit a statement of their qualifications and a list of insurance markets and other vendors, including wholesale or excess/surplus lines brokers they would intend to contact to secure a quotation or proposal for coverages and services in their order of preference, given the nature of the organization. The organization then makes a preliminary qualification of the agent, broker, or vendor, and for those selected, assigns the markets the intermediary requested according to the multiple preference lists.

While this sounds confusing, it is actually relatively simple, as custom and practice holds that the current markets are reserved for the holding intermediary (assuming it is not "fired", in which case a letter of authority (agent of record letter) would transfer the assignment to another intermediary), and the other markets are sorted according to preference, with the inevitable ties being decided on the basis of providing a fair spread of markets to the several qualified intermediaries. This process can only reasonably accommodate two or three, or perhaps four intermediaries. Those selected intermediaries will receive the bid specifications detailing coverages and services desired and all necessary exposure and operational information needed by underwriters and service providers to provide proposals.

While this is a fair, controlled, and, more importantly, organized approach generally accepted by insurance carriers and vendors, there are a few issues. First, the holding intermediary and carriers have the advantage as they have absolutely all the information regarding premium history, exposures, and claims. Even the best and most detailed claims runs do not have all the information that can be useful in pricing and setting terms and conditions. Second, most agents and brokers and insurance carriers want to know who else is involved in the proposal process. The organization can determine its own response to these issues, ranging from providing no information to any of the selected agents/brokers/vendors to providing ranges of premiums (e.g., general liability premiums in the range of $400,000 to $500,000, instead of $476,429) to complete disclosure of all information to all involved intermediaries.

Conceptual Bidding

The last agent/broker selection process, Conceptual Bidding, is generally considered to be the best and most difficult. In the Agent/Broker Assignment, Open Bidding, and RFP methods, the providing of insurance coverages and services is dependent upon an intermediary (in most cases, as most insurers do not deal directly with their insureds). Direct writers, however, such as Liberty Mutual and FM Global, often will deal directly with their insureds. There is a risk that the insurance carrier or vendor that provides the most attractive proposal may be represented by an agent or broker who is not the most qualified or appropriate for the organization. While this mismatch can be corrected with properly drawn specification provisions that reserve the right to assign any market to any intermediary with a letter of authority AFTER the proposals have been evaluated, intermediaries do not like this provision for obvious reasons. In Conceptual Bidding, the evaluation of the professional capabilities and services of the intermediary are examined without considering any insurance coverage or service proposals, and are based solely upon the intermediary's qualifications and conceptual approach to handling the needs of the organization. This process is frequently called a "beauty contest" as the evaluation process is largely qualitative (even though some attempt may be made to assign quantitative values to specific attributes). The "prettiest", "most talented," and "most inspiring" intermediary wins the sash and the right to receive a broad letter of authority, giving them complete and exclusive access to the insurance and services market.

Qualification Process

Regardless of how the agents and brokers are selected, all should be subjected to a qualification process. The prospective insured needs to identify the following items as part of the qualification process:

- In what jurisdiction or jurisdictions are they licensed?

- How long has the organization been in business?

- Who will be on the team? What are their qualifications (experience, professional designations, education, tenure, position in the company)?

- What draft authority does the company have?

- Does the agency or brokerage firm have errors and omissions (professional liability) insurance? What are the limits?

- Has the agency or brokerage firm had professional liability losses?

- Summary of services the agency or brokerage firm intends to provide.

- Listing of carriers represented, direct or through other intermediaries.

- Carrier compensation arrangement, including contingent commissions or profit sharing.

- References, (e.g., insurance company underwriters, and at least one former client).

Contracting For Agent and Broker Services and Vendor Services

Once the agent or broker or other vendor is selected, the organization should enter into a contract with that service provider.

As mentioned in previous chapters, a contract must have four elements to be a legally enforceable contract:

1. Competent parties (of legal age, no undue influence, sane, etc.),

2. An agreement,

3. An exchange of consideration (usually dollars for services),

4. A legal purpose.

Once those elements are identified and in place, the rest of the contract consists of details. The 12 essential elements or parts to a professional services contract follow:

1. Introduction – Provides details on the contracting parties and where they are located.

2. Objective of Work – States the desired outcome of the work.

3. Scope of Work – Outlines the extent of the work and provides limits of how far the work will go.

4. Methods – Provides specifics as to how the objectives will be accomplished.

5. <u>Time</u> – Establishes the start time (which may be different from the date the contract is signed) and when the contract will end, (e.g., the termination time may be stated in terms of a calendar date, a specific length of time, or at the conclusion of the work).

6. <u>Output/Product/Expectations</u> – Provides details that establish when the work is completed, and complements the Time section.

7. <u>Fees and Billing</u> – States the required legal consideration element of an enforceable contract, but more importantly, memorializes the fees that will be used, how billings will be produced (e.g., monthly, quarterly, completion of work), and when payment is expected.

8. <u>Time and Expense Reconciliation</u> – Provides the structure for the contracting parties to reconcile fees and billings, hours spent, work performed, and expenses incurred during the contract.

9. <u>Disclaimers and Indemnification/Hold Harmless Clauses</u> – Provides any disclaimers the parties wish to incorporate and how any contractual transfer of responsibility or liability will be made.

10. <u>Reporting and Status Reports</u> – Provides the method and timing of interim reports and the final report of the contracted work.

11. <u>Confidentiality and Non-disclosure Agreements</u> – Provides any confidentiality and non-disclosure provisions the parties wish to incorporate.

12. <u>Termination and Renewal</u> – Establishes how either party may terminate the contract prior to its natural end and how a renewal of the contract will be accomplished, with provisions for renegotiation and changes in the essential elements or other details.

In addition to these provisions, the service contract may also contain additional details:

- <u>Change Orders</u> – Establishes how such modifications will be negotiated and incorporated into the existing contract, since the objectives, scope, and methods may change during the project.

- <u>Incentive/disincentive Clauses</u> – Permits the parties to include an incentive or disincentive provision to modify the planned compensation. This provision is usually tied to the time period, methods, objectives, or reporting provisions.

- <u>Failure to Perform Clause</u> – Establishes the procedures the parties will follow in the event of a failure to perform by either contracting party.

- <u>Liquidated or Limited Damages Clause</u> – Sometimes the parties will agree to a provision that states in the event of a failure to perform, a stated amount of damages will be paid.

- <u>Additional Insured/Certificate of Insurance</u> – Establishes whether additional insured status must be provided to any party, how coverage and additional insured status is documented (usually through a certificate of insurance), and provides for notice of cancellation of coverage.

- <u>Dispute Resolution</u> – Details how the parties will resolve disputes. Generally, this section establishes an escalating protocol of "Meet and Agree" (an informal meeting between the contracting parties), Mediation, Arbitration, or Litigation.

- <u>Jurisdiction</u> – States the jurisdiction whose laws will be used in enforcing any part of the agreement, including dispute resolution, and where such resolution will be held.

Common Agent and Broker Services Specified in the Agreement

In addition to the obvious service of submitting the applications and exposure details to insurance company underwriters, the agent or broker service agreement commonly includes the following services:

- <u>Claims Reporting</u> – Details how claims reports from the insurance carriers will be communicated to the insured, for example, open or closed claims, timing, and format.

- <u>Loss Control and Safety Inspections</u> – Specifies if the agency or brokerage firm is responsible solely for loss control and safety inspections, if the agency or brokerage firm will supplement services provided by insurance carriers, or if loss control and safety work is solely the responsibility of the insurance carriers; also addresses who prepares any reports and communicates action items.

- <u>Audit Assistance</u> – Contains any audit assistance the agency or brokerage firm will provide.

- <u>Claims Analysis and Trending</u> – Addresses who is responsible for claims analysis and any trending and development of claims data.

- <u>Documentation of Coverage</u> – Details the responsibility for issuing documents providing evidence of coverage (certificates of insurance, etc), including time frames. Also, if the agency or brokerage firm intends to assist the insured in monitoring incoming documents proving coverage, the agreement will specify that responsibility.

- <u>Issuance of Bonds</u> – Addresses any responsibility for procuring bonds.

- <u>Contract Review</u> – Should stipulate who is responsible for reviewing contracts the insured enters into and uses for risk transfer implications (e.g., hold harmless agreements, indemnification clauses, and requirements to provide certain types and limits of coverage, including documentation and cancellation notices).

- <u>Due Diligence</u> – If the agency or brokerage firm is involved in any due diligence analysis on behalf of the insured, the agreement should address what the agency or brokerage firm will do and how results will be reported.

Agent and Broker Compensation

There are two fundamental methods of compensation available for agents and brokers: commission and fee-for-services. Commission compensation is the traditional method and the most common method. Fee-for-service compensation is not common across the broad market of insureds, but becomes increasingly common as the size of the insured and its premium volume and service requirements grow.

Commission compensation is usually included in the premium and is based upon the commission percentage granted by the insurer to the agent or broker. While agency and brokerage contracts with insurers frequently state the commissions applicable by line of coverage or type of policy, most insurers are willing to negotiate commissions downward to increase competitiveness. In theory, those carriers should be willing to increase commissions to the agent or broker upward when a competitive premium is not needed, but the practice is generally held in disrepute as being unethical.

Fee-for-service compensation is based upon several factors. In its purest form, the fee is similar to the fees charged for legal services and based upon the number of hours of work required to provide the contracted service times an agreed rate per hour of each person performing the work. The hourly rate per person is determined by the experience, education and training, reputation, and position of the individual, as well as a loading for the general operating expenses of the agency or brokerage firm. A common "quick and dirty" method of determining the hourly rate is to divide the annual salary of the individual by 2,000, the assumed number of working hours in a year (50 weeks at 40 hours a week, with adjustments possible for longer vacations and differing work weeks). This raw rate is grossed up by a multiplier of 2, 3, or even more for employee benefits provided to the individual as well as the general overhead of the office. Some intermediaries, particularly those not experienced in the practice of fee-for-service or not wanting to be involved in detailed record-keeping activities, hours, and personnel, will set the fee based on an average percentage, such as 10%, of the premium.

State insurance regulations also control how agents and brokers are compensated. Many states forbid the practice of collecting of premium and charging of a fee-for-service, while other states permit the practice. In these states, problems arise when insurance carriers will not issue "net of commission" policies, forcing the intermediary to collect a premium that includes the commission and making it impossible to charge on a fee basis. Also, some direct writers issue all of their policies net of commission because their employees handle the sale, and the compensation for the sales personnel is not separately reported in the acquisition expense analysis that is included in the Annual Convention Statement (the financial report all admitted insurance carriers make to their respective state insurance departments). This creates a problem for the agent or broker who collects commission on all of the policies included in the risk management program, except a non-commissioned policy, for which it is illegal to charge a fee. The agent or broker is forced to forgo a specific fee for services involving those directly written policies.

Advantages and Disadvantages

Fee-for-service Compensation

Fee-for-service compensation has several distinct advantages for both the intermediary and the insured.

From the perspective of the intermediary, a fee-for-service guarantees compensation for work performed and should promote objectivity. The natural pressure to sell a policy and collect a commission is removed and the intermediary can recommend lower-premium or lower/non-commission alternatives (e.g., excess over retention programs or non-insurance programs) and still be fairly and adequately compensated. In addition, fee-for-service protects the intermediary from the vagaries of the insurance markets, providing a steady, more predictable income than reliance on the hard market with its high premiums (and insureds' tendency to shop other intermediaries for premium relief) to balance out the low-premium soft markets.

From the perspective of the insured, the value of the service provided can be more objectively judged against its cost, as a fee-for-service arrangement clearly spells out the intermediary's compensation far better than commissions included within the premium, which generally are unknown and often overestimated by the management of the insured organization. The fee-for-service arrangement raises the perception of the quality and level of insurance provider's services to that of other professional services, such as those of accountants, lawyers, actuaries, and management consultants. In addition, a capped fee, also commonly referred to as a "not to exceed" fee, assists the risk manager in computing the cost of risk for the organization and should lead to a stronger relationship, one in which the providing of insurance protection and risk management advice is elevated from the process by which the organization purchases commodities such as office equipment. (These advantages also accrue to the intermediary.)

There are several disadvantages with this compensation method, however. When the fee-for-service approach is teamed with the "beauty contest" selection, intermediaries who do not use the fee-for-service approach and rely on the traditional commission structure will be precluded from participating in the bidding process and will not provide their experience and expertise to the insured. The quoted fee may be increased if additional services are required, thus eliminating the advantage of having a predictable cost of risk. Added services might include special research projects, conferences, legal research or opinions, or other activities not contemplated originally. Also, some intermediaries charge separately for faxes, mail, travel, and telephone usage, much like attorneys and other consultants frequently do, sometimes marking these costs up above their underlying cost to the intermediary.

In addition, the intermediary may not be able to provide all value-added services required, thus forcing the insured to contract separately for these services. Related to this is the option of having the intermediary procure these services and mark up those fees beyond their cost to the intermediary.

Lastly, some believe that a fee-for-service stifles creativity as the compensation is fixed and predictable, and therefore performance need only meet the minimum requirement to keep the contract in force and the fees being paid. With a fee-for-service contract, there is no pressing need to attempt to sell more insurance for inadequately covered exposures.

Commission Compensation

Some believe that the disadvantages of fee-for-service compensation are the advantages of commission compensation and vice versa. While there is some validity to this view, there are distinct advantages and disadvantages of commission compensation.

With commission, there is every incentive for the intermediary to attempt to sell more insurance. Since nearly all intermediaries will take compensation in the form of commission, using a commission compensation structure should create a more competitive environment for all, with nearly all the intermediaries being willing to work on the account. There are no additional fees because all requested services are included as part of the process of placing the insurance coverage. Also, the "all-or-nothing" nature of commission compensation, being totally dependent on gaining the award of the bid, makes it likely that the intermediaries will try their very best to win the bid. There is no prize for being second best. Lastly, commission compensation is the traditional method, well understood by all intermediaries, and easily calculated, at least with respect to the intermediary's accounting system.

The disadvantages are also several. The most glaring deficiency is that, being included within the premium, the compensation cost is not readily discernible to the buyer. However, the cost of risk computation uses premium as a component, so it does not matter if the premium is net of commission or gross – one way or the other, the compensation to the intermediary is included in the cost of risk. However, it is much harder for an insured to evaluate the value of service received when the insured does not know what he is paying for the service component of an insurance policy or any other service included in the commission amount. When the intermediary is assured of getting an order (e.g., a letter of authority is used or a sole representative is selected in a beauty contest), there is no incentive for the selected intermediary to find the lowest reasonable cost. In a few instances, the premium might be overstated due to the non-disclosure of commission earned by the intermediary and not reported to the insured.

Summary

One disadvantage accrues to both methodologies, and this problem should be addressed regardless of which approach is taken. The fee-for-service amount and commission amount may actually be understated by overriding commissions, profit-sharing commissions, production incentive commissions, and investment income on premiums held for a period before being tendered to the insurance companies. In themselves, these forms of additional compensation are not inappropriate. These are the same types of income sources that create additional value for the low-cost retailers, volume sellers, and many of the insureds from whom these revenues are generated. What is inappropriate is the failure to disclose these sources of income, although they are uniformly difficult to quantify with respect to any particular insured. A properly drawn service agreement will specify how such additional compensation that might be generated will be identified, and to the extent possible, quantified or prohibited. For example, an insured may insist upon holding the premium until the very last day before the premiums must be tendered to the insurance company.

Coverage Specifications

Insurance companies require (or should require) applications for coverage every year. The underwriter uses the information on the application and supporting documents to set the premium and determine policy terms and conditions. Coverage specifications are not applications for insurance, although they often contain most, if not all, of the information needed to complete an application and submission to an insurance carrier. The risk manager should prepare coverage specifications for three reasons:

1. They detail what the risk manager is seeking in the insurance program, including optional treatments;

2. Since coverages and terms and conditions can vary between insurance companies, they serve to help equate differing coverages, terms, and conditions;

3. If the coverage specifications are written in such a manner as "confirm that coverage applies…" and the agent or broker or underwriter sign off on the confirmation, they easily serve as a post-policy issuance checklist to verify that coverage was provided as requested, ordered, and bound.

Coverage specifications should contain the following features:

1. Delineate lines of coverage.

2. State required limits and deductible/retention levels, including optional limits and deductibles/retentions.

3. Define breadth of coverages with respect to terms and conditions.

4. Provide schedules of property values, a statement of values, appraisals, and/or lists of fine arts and valuable papers, a list of vehicles, a list of drivers, a business income worksheet, and other pertinent information, useful to the underwriter.

5. Include a five-year loss history – for each line of coverage.

6. Include historic premiums and exposures to provide a benchmark for the underwriter.

7. Provide requirements for minimum-financial-strength and policyholder-service ratings for all insurance carriers offering coverage proposals.

8. Provide a "coverage summary" form for completion by agent/broker.

Occasionally, the risk manager may need to make changes in the original specifications after their distribution, and will do so by submitting the necessary changes or clarifications to all bidders in writing.

After receiving the coverage specifications and proposals, the risk manager must then evaluate the proposals. Depending upon the number of proposals received, the risk manager must consider whether the proposals were received according to the required time line. The risk manager can then confirm adherence to the mechanics of the bid specifications with respect to financial qualifications and minimum coverage provisions. The risk manager must review the proposals for accuracy and complete responses to the coverage specifications, and that the coverage proposed meets the bid requirements. Last, the risk manager must analyze the cost-vs.-coverage aspects of the proposals.

In addition, if the proposal contains additional recommendations proposed by the agent/broker outside the bid requirements or any options requested in the specifications, the risk manager must analyze those recommendations and evaluate their cost-vs.-coverage aspects. If there are any deviations from the original specifications, the risk manager must seek clarification from the agent/broker or underwriter.

Finalizing the Decision

Once the proposals have been evaluated, it is time to make the decision regarding the insurance program. In some organizations, the final decision is that of the risk manager; in others, the risk manager will make recommendations to a committee or to another officer, often the Chief Financial Officer. Each vendor not selected receives notification with a disclosure of the reasons why the vendor was not selected.

The selected vendor is notified and given instructions for implementation of the selected program. Together, the selected vendor and the risk manager will establish an implementation plan and a time schedule for reviewing progress toward implementation. As time unfolds, the risk manager must monitor the implementation of the risk management program and evaluate the performance of the selected vendors and service providers.

Insurance agents/brokers are not the only external service providers to be selected. The risk manager will undertake a similar dissemination of information, vetting, and selection for each provider.

Communicating with Internal and External Team Members

Communication is not just talking or writing a letter or sending an email. Communication is a complex process involving several senses and social conventions, and is one of many characteristics that separates humans from most other animal species.

Communication is a critically important part of successfully managing an organization, as the very survival of that organization may depend upon how well the managers communicate with others. Research has shown that managers spend approximately 80% of a typical workday in some form of verbal communication, and the remaining 20% reading or writing some type of communication. This means that a manager's overall effectiveness is 100% dependent on the ability to communicate with others effectively.

For the risk manager, those all-important communication skills improve cooperation with risk management team members (internal and external), better identify changes in the company's environment, and allow the organization to readily adapt to external influences related to organizational goals, stakeholder expectations, and organizational performance.

The Communication Process

One definition of communication is "the exchange of information using a shared set of symbols."

The communication process consists of five steps, each of which is vital to the effectiveness of the communication encounter. While these steps may appear to be simplistic, the process is harder than it seems. Three simple examples will illustrate this point.

Miscommunication

Example A: Does ERA have a place in major league baseball?

Baseball enthusiasts will quickly identify "ERA" as a symbol for "earned run average" while ERM feminists will remark that women should play major league baseball if qualified and receive the same multi-million dollar pay as men because of the Equal Rights Amendment. Others will refer to the ERA real estate company that sells homes to baseball players, and still others will be thinking about all those dirty uniforms being washed in ERA brand detergent. The symbol "ERA" has several possible meanings.

Example B: An American visitor is traveling abroad and meets an Englishman, an Italian, and an Egyptian. During the course of a conversation, the American makes the "peace" sign with his palm facing him, makes the "okay" gesture by forming a circle with his forefinger and thumb, the other three fingers extended, and, apparently getting some dust in his eye, rubs the corner of his eye with his forefinger. The three "foreigners" stomp off, leaving the American bewildered.

In America, waving the peace sign or Churchill's signature "V" for victory is a positive sign, but in England, with the palm facing toward the giver of the sign, this "friendly" gesture is hardly friendly at all. Similarly, the familiar "okay" is a vulgar non-verbal euphemism for a sexual act in many parts of Europe. Lastly, rubbing one's eye is an unspeakable insult in the Arab-speaking world. Common "American" gestures may be perceived as vulgar insults in other cultures and societies.

Example C: Tom told Fred that he would drive.

Who is going to drive? Tom? Or Fred? Did Tom tell Fred to drive or that he, Tom, would drive? Without some feedback or confirmation, Tom and Fred might be fighting for the keys or the passenger seat.

In these unclear examples, we clearly see that communication is not always as clear as we think it is.

The Five Steps of the Communication Process

1. The sender decides what idea or information to transmit.

2. The sender creates a message by encoding the idea or information into symbols. These symbols may consist of written or spoken words, gestures, or pictographs.

3. The sender selects a medium for transmission and sends the message. This medium may be a letter or email, a telephonic device, a line of sight, or any other means by which messages are sent.

4. The receiver receives the message and decodes the symbols or interprets the symbols to extract the idea or meaning of the symbols.

5. The receiver provides a response or feedback, both to confirm receipt of the message (the transmission was successful) and understanding of the message (the encoding and decoding was parallel and successful).

Noise

Noise can adversely affect the communication process. Noise is not just a racket or din or any other auditory perception. Noise is anything that distorts a message by interfering with the communication process. It can affect the process at any stage, take many forms, and is often unrecognizable. Common examples of noise are ambiguous wordings or symbols, multiple-meaning symbols, jargon or unfamiliar terms, external or internal distractions of receiver and/or sender, misunderstood gestures due to misinterpretation or diversity of experience, and even diversity between personalities of sender and receiver.

Communication within an Organization

Within an organization, communication takes two forms: informal and formal.

Much of an organization's communication is informal and interpersonal, the communication between individuals. The nature of informal and interpersonal communication is that part of it generally focuses on the exchange of purely personal information, a part of our social nature when we gather in a group setting, and part of it focuses on the exchange of information pertaining to doing our jobs.

In addition, there is formal communication, the exchange of information that flows through established channels understood by the organization and its personnel as being purely a function of accomplishing the organization's goals and activities. This formal information flows in three directions: upward, downward, and laterally.

Upward communications flow from lower to higher organizational levels, from the functional levels to the decision-focused levels. Common examples are progress reports, safety reports, potential litigation circumstances, cost of risk analysis, and the like.

Downward communications flow from higher to lower organizational levels, from the decision-focused levels to the functional levels. Common examples are directions to subordinates, performance feedback, compliments and criticisms, and organizational plans and changes.

Lateral communications flow between equal organizational levels, or peers. Common examples are advice sessions, problem-solving discussions, and activity coordination.

These directional communication flows can further be described in terms of the network through which information is exchanged.

Communication Networks

While the direction of communications flows can be described in the general directions of upward, downward, and lateral, the pattern of these directional flows consists of five specific patterns or networks: chain, Y, wheel, circle, and all-channel. The nature of the information to be communicated, the purpose of the communication, and the structure of the organization and its management style heavily influence the actual pattern each communication flow takes. Most organizations also have a combination of patterns within the organization that will be influenced by the internal relationships within the organization.

The chain network is simple, linear, and sequential:

> Example: communication that flows from the Chief Financial Officer to the risk manager who then communicates the informational content to the risk management staff.

The Y network resembles an inverted letter "y."

> Example: communication that flows from the risk manager to two or more risk management department staff members.

The wheel network is circular. Information flows between a single person or a single position to and from all others in the network. There are no network connections between the various members in the network.

> Example: In a crisis communication system, a designated spokesperson receives and disseminates information.

The circle network is similar to the wheel network, but there is no axle or pivot point that serves as the spokesperson.

> Example: Communication only with peers in other departments or functions, but in a sequential manner.

The all-channel network is a combination of other patterns. A portion of the network might be a chain that leads into a circle with a branch from one individual into a Y. Communication flows in all directions and among members of all groups.

> Example: Common in many organizations is the informal network or channel called the "rumor mill" or the "water cooler" network, not as useful or effective as all-channel network that allows for easy give-and-take communications among all risk management team members.

Informal Communication Networks

Informal communication occurs outside of the organization's formal channels and may prove to be the most effective and reliable form of communication within the organization. There are two main types of informal communication.

The grapevine is one of the most recognized means of informal communication. It supplements formal channels of communication, especially if employees believe the organization's information is inaccurate or incomplete. It may be the strongest, most active form of communication during undefined or ambiguous times. The quality of information flowing through the grapevine is generally good despite its informal structure, and it is a strong indicator of issues of genuine concern to employees. Managers should encourage open communication and stay informed and "in the loop" as much as possible.

The "good-old-boy" network is an exclusive group or clique that wields power within an organization through an informal structure. Members share information and resources only among other members of this select group. The group encourages advancement in the formal organization by helping each other via favorable reports, promotions, and similar acts of preferential treatment, but this help is unavailable to non-members. On a positive side, it assures rapid and consistent promotion of group members and keeps the network members informed about the organization's plans, vision, and strategies. Conversely, it prevents the organization from accessing talent from throughout the organization and prevents the remainder of the organization from actively participating in creating a competitive advantage.

Why is an understanding of these communications systems important to a risk manager? The communication networks and directional flows are a required component of the communication process. The flow of information must go somewhere, and these networks and directional flows explain how information travels throughout the organization. The risk manager who understands what communication is, how it is done, what disrupts communication, and how information flows within and without the organization by following directions and patterns can make the best use of the communication process, and that leads to effective risk management.

Exhibit 19.1: Communication Networks

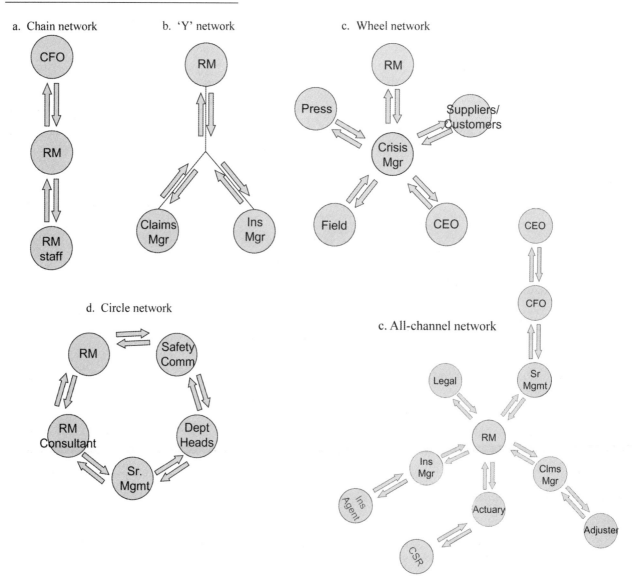

Personality Types

In addition to understanding the mechanics of the communication process, the risk manager also needs to understand personality types. Personality types of the two communicators are an aspect of noise. Psychologists have identified four major personality types, and these personality types are so common in the American workplace that television shows, movies, and cartoons are created, "communicated," and laughed at (or cried over) across the country on this very subject.

The Director/Driver

The Director/Driver type is the commander. This person has a strong personality and generally seeks out a leadership role, focusing on results, directness, and getting the job done, sometimes by trampling on or running roughshod over other personality types. Typically, the Director/Driver is an expert in all areas (or so they sometimes think) and always has an opinion that is correct. They tend to be very entrepreneurial in nature and are frequently found in boardrooms, sitting in the chair at the head of the table. Often, others see this personality type as cold and calculating, rather standoffish, and slow to give compliments. Their watchwords are "Ready, Aim, Fire!"

Well-known personages generally considered to be director/driver personality types include Donald "You're Fired" Trump and General George S. Patton.

The Relater/Amiable

The Relater/Amiable person is the facilitator. Relater/Amiable personality types excel in the team atmosphere, where they work to build a team and seek a consensus. They are driven to prompt cooperation, to do the job right, to be customer oriented, and tend to listen carefully before taking action. Unlike the Director/Driver, they rarely seek the limelight and are not self-promoting.

In some cases, Relater/Amiable types tend to be wishy-washy and afraid to make decisions, as decisions may leave someone outside the consensus. Relater/Amiable types may also be easily offended or hurt, particularly because this behavior is outside the team atmosphere, but are reluctant to show offense. However, like the sadistic coach who makes his team run after a loss, they will try to get even later. Their watchwords are "Are all of you ready? Have all of you aimed?"

Two well-known personages generally considered to be Relater/Amiable types (without the negative tendencies) are Mahatmas Gandhi and Dr. Martin Luther King.

The Thinker/Analytical

The Thinker/Analytical type often poses like the Rodin sculpture, chin on hand, elbow on knee, deep in contemplation. Thinker/Analytical types thrive on detail and data. They have a strong analytical skill set and are natural systematizers, planners, and perfectionists. An individual of this type tends to be impersonal, or not a "people person" and can be long-winded on non-consequential issues, overestimating the listeners' interest. Their watchwords are "Ready? If you have enough information, you can aim. Fire, but keep your eyes open so you can track the bullet and adjust."

Two well-known personages generally considered to be Thinker/Analytical types are Bill Gates and Albert Einstein.

The Socializer/Expressive

The Socializer/Expressive is the charmer, the life of the party, the center of attention. Socializer/Expressive types are charismatic and opportunity seekers and live for attention, but unlike Director/Drivers, they are unprepared, vague, and change their minds frequently. They work best with an audience, freely express themselves with gestures, and detest agendas and other structures. They are natural salespersons and are emotional, often wearing their hearts on their sleeves. Their watchwords are "Ready, Fire, Aim."

A well-known personage generally considered to be a Socializer/Expressive type is Bill Clinton.

Observations and Limitations

While the above structure implies there are four distinct types of personalities, in reality, no one is always one personality type. Also, some people can have the traits of more than one personality type. For example, Dr. Martin Luther King, while generally a Relater/Amiable type, was very purpose-driven and focused on results, seeking the limelight not for personal glory, but to advance his cause. Bill Gates, clearly a Thinker/Analytical is very personable and a natural salesperson, traits of a Socializer/Expressive and Relater/Amiable, and is not the typical computer nerd.

Also, stress can cause a person to move from the usual personality type to another personality type, sometimes for a short period, sometimes a long period, and sometimes, even for years. Further, a strength overdone can become a weakness (e.g., being too decisive can lead to excessive control).

The risk manager must understand personality types to be able to tailor communication methods and symbols to the audience, a daunting task since the audience probably consists of many different personality types. Failing to understand the traits can easily lead to noise, interference with the understanding of the content of the message.

Business Communication Media

Business communication takes the form of written and verbal, as well as non-verbal, messages. Written messages appear in letters, memos, emails, reports, recommendations, data analysis, procedure manuals, press releases, and other common documented methods by which business communicates within its internal environment and its external environment. However, the overwhelming volume of business communication is verbal, accompanied by non-verbal symbols or clues (e.g., rolling eyes when the other person looks away). Even in the organization that seems to flood the office and exterior environment with paper, the vast majority of all the communication remains verbal in nature.

Written Communication

Written communication is intended to create a more permanent means of communication, which also allows the writer to more carefully consider the content and tone of the communication. Because it takes longer to create, and sometimes to transmit, there tends to be less emotion. A written message is void of gestures, intonation, pitch, and volume.

The effective use of written communication has three important advantages. First, a permanent record of the communication will exist (sometimes this is a distinct disadvantage, particularly in the case of litigation). Also, the slow nature of this media allows the writer to think deliberately and thoroughly before reducing the thoughts to the written word and transmitting the message. Last, written communication is particularly useful in circumstances where a record of the communication is important or complex, but non-controversial.

Risk managers frequently use written communication for the following types of messages:

1. Risk Management mission statement – written evidence of the organization's support of the risk management process and how that ties in to the organization's overall mission

2. Risk Management policy statement – written evidence of the organization's policy for managing risk and its relevance to the organization's strategic plan, goals, and objectives

3. Risk Management Policy and Procedures Manual (also known as the Standard Operating Procedures Manual) – written evidence of the organization's procedures relative to risk management issues, a "how to" book for accomplishing the policy statement by describing the procedures for implementing organizational policies

4. Internal memos – written directives and communication within the organization to share information and direct organizational and risk management activities

5. External letters and memos – written communication with suppliers, customers, media, and other stakeholders relative to products, services, and issues affecting the organization

6. Email – written (in the sense that it looks like a letter or memo, even though it may exist only in an electronic format) communication that is rapidly becoming a replacement for the traditional written document

7. Reports – written communication reporting finding and delivering recommendations internally or externally. (e.g., the Annual Risk Management Report, a report that details the results of the risk management program to upper management)

Verbal Communication

Verbal communication is the most frequent means of communication. It requires little effort, is spontaneous, and can convey meaning beyond the words through accompanying gestures and variations in pitch, tone, and volume. Imagine the difficulty and impracticality of circulating an information notice informing the audience that the theater is on fire and that all should evacuate immediately. One the other hand, imagine the problems of delivering a verbal insurance policy to a customer. Verbal communication consists of four distinct types.

Transactional communication is a direct transfer of information used in one-on-one and group presentations. Its advantages are that it is efficient because it is direct and focused on content, and effective according to the perception of the speaker. It maintains the superior position of the leader. Its disadvantages are that there is no exchange of ideas, values, or beliefs, that it may be superficial relative to meaning, that it is not as effective as perceived by the sender, and it eliminates the opportunity for input from the collective intelligence of the group.

Transformational communication is an open exchange of ideas, beliefs, and values. This form is commonly used in small gatherings of individuals, such as families, teams, workgroups, and community groups when seeking collaborative agreements. The advantages are that it elicits the collective intelligence of the organization or group, exposing new ideas, beliefs, and values, that it provides opportunity for everyone to be heard, that it asks the bigger questions and eposes genuine beliefs and values, that it increases the potential for broad support of initiatives, and it determines if an individual's values are aligned with the organization's values. Conversely, the disadvantages are that it may take more time than the sender perceives is necessary, and the sender/leadership may not be willing to hear or use what emerges from the collective intelligence of the group or organization.

Social communication is composed of informal, often impromptu, conversations in informal settings where there is no stakeholder interest in the outcome. Some examples would be in coffee houses, pubs, around the water cooler, and on an airplane. The advantages are obvious: there is a relaxed atmosphere that may allow for more open exchange of ideas, and true beliefs and values are more likely to emerge. On the other hand, the communication may not include the thoughts of the collective intelligence or carry the emerging thoughts and ideas back to the collective intelligence. Also, the conversation may become petty and mean, and be destructive, or it may be genuine and caring and supporting, all depending upon the personalities of the individuals and their motivations.

Reflective communication is defined as personal time to reflect on or assess issues that matter, and time to reflect on beliefs, values, and meaning of ideals. In effect, it is a verbal conversation, albeit perhaps unspoken, with one's self. It provides an opportunity to reflect on personal beliefs and values without external interference and may allow better understanding of the beliefs and values of others. Conversely, it may allow personal beliefs and values to overshadow opportunity to consider others' contributions and become cynical and rigid without consistent input from others.

Non-verbal Communication

Listening is an essential part of the communication process – this is exactly what the receiver of a verbal message does that enables the receiver to understand what is being said more fully than may be superficially evident.

Active listening consists of listening to others with an attentive, professional attitude. The listener is present in the fullest sense of the word, not distracted by one's own desire or agenda (noise). The listener seeks to understand the inner world of the sender. By hearing, the listener observes the inner person of the sender, and by seeing, the listener observes the outer person. Both hearing and seeing help the receiver color in the message through consideration of the sender's gestures, body language, appearance, pitch, tone, and volume.

Passive listening consists of listening to others in a disconnected, distracted, or disinterested manner, with no concern over the content and context of the conversation.

The sender must seek clues through body language, gestures, and verbal comments to determine what type of listening the receiver is using. While it is possible to deliberately send incorrect or confusing feedback, most listeners are not that devious, and the sender can distinguish between nodding assent and nodding off, and between the enthusiastic "Yes" and a lackluster "Uh-huh."

The advantages of listening, particularly active listening, is that the sender may reveal the content the sender is really trying to convey, and the receiver may actually understand. Conversely, the receiver may misinterpret the sender's message and read more into the message or process than really exists.

Body language consists of the mostly static posture of the sender and receiver's bodies. It is a pose. It provides a physical, visual means of communication and of coloring the verbal message. For example, standing with arms crossed generally suggests antagonism or disbelief, and standing with hands on hips implies impatience.

<u>Gestures</u> consist of the movements a person makes with their face, hands, legs, feet, and general body position and attitude. These gestures have many and varied meanings, depending on the communication outcome desired. For example, raised eyebrows and an o-shaped mouth can connote surprise at a brilliant thought or incredulity over an outrageous comment. Gestures are particularly susceptible to differing cultural interpretations.

<u>Appearance</u> consists of the general demeanor of the individual, including grooming, clothing, and social behavior, such as being friendly and outgoing versus reticent and reserved. A well-dressed, well-groomed person is generally perceived to be more intelligent, honest, straightforward, or moral than a disheveled, dirty-looking person. Of course, these perceptions are also particularly susceptible to varying interpretations. One only has to look at the Academy, Golden Globe, or Country Music Awards or stroll through a college campus to understand how ambiguous or incorrect these perceptions can be.

Setting Up and Controlling the Communication Environment

Good communication can be managed by establishing a hospitable communication environment. The purpose of creating a hospitable environment is to create a safe space where everyone feels free to offer quality thinking and active participation. The members of the group can address issues that are important, avoiding personal agendas, and keeping the discussion focused on the general topics of importance to the group. Participants can ask meaningful questions about the issues, powerful, open-ended questions that provide focus and coherence to networks of conversation that might spin off in random directions.

A positive communication environment allows everyone to participate. Each person has a contribution that adds to the collective intelligence of the whole. Each person respects the views of others, as social development requires different points of view, different ideas, and different experiences to combine into larger, more complex wholes.

It also considers the audience or stakeholders, engaging multiple stakeholders, including employees from all levels of the organization, customers, and suppliers. The organization may use checklists in each venue, creating the master checklist not as an agenda, but to assure that all issues are addressed by the conversations.

Another aspect of establishing and controlling the communication environment is recognizing and working with communication styles. Communicators differ in the degree to which they want to provide or receive information by the amount of information they expose about themselves or the way they elicit information from others.

The Johari Window[1] is a technique for describing tendencies for either enhancing or discouraging interpersonal communication. A combination of behaviors towards these two tendencies represents the relative size of the following information categories:

Unknown information – information is unknown to presenter and to others and arises from lack of communication. It may cause reluctance to act, or it may cause autocratic tendencies to emerge. Group members may have difficulty determining what the manager wants or is requesting. The manager can facilitate communication by identifying missing or incomplete information and providing that information to the group.

Hidden information – information is known to the presenter but is unknown to others. The leader shares little of what is known and creates suspicion by others who believe information is being withheld. The manager can alleviate feelings of suspicion by disclosing more information and being more open.

1 Developed by Joseph Luft and Harry Ingham

Blind spots – information is known to others but not to the presenter. Blind spots are usually found when someone seeks to provide information to others and does not solicit feedback. The presenter may spend energy and time committing mistakes arising out of this lack of information and attempting to cover them up. The manager should attempt to clarify or avoid any blind spots by encouraging feedback and response, and providing any missing or incorrect information.

Arena – information is known to presenter and to others. It occurs when communication is open and feedback is encouraged. A large arena can enhance understanding and cooperation; however, it may open opportunities for those with selfish agendas to exploit their motives at the expense of others.

Communicating Content versus Communicating Context

Traditional business communication is content-based. It is driven by details, the details of an organization's products or services, or a crisis), or by an inquiry. Content-based communication has several advantages: it is direct and to the point; quick; without extraneous information that creates noise; and highly factual (e.g., Dragnet's Sgt. Joe Friday's comment, "Just the facts, ma'am."

It also has several disadvantages: there may be a lack of awareness of real issues and needs; a lack of understanding (the sender never knows if the receiver really understood the message); a lack of willingness to own the process or outcome; and it creates an opportunity for objections to be raised.

Common examples of content-based communication are newspaper news items or news and weather reports broadcast over the radio. In business, common examples of content-based communication are found in the risk management plan (once it is implemented), a safety video, an insurer-prepared loss run, or communication during a crisis.

Context-based communication is that type of communication that fills in the gaps around the facts and details. It is the color inside the lines. The context provides a structure for the content portion of the message and helps shape the complete message. Context-based communication has several advantages: it generally addresses deeper, more meaningful issues than is possible through content-based communication; it allows the communication process to unfold naturally, rather than creating an artificial process; it provides the opportunity for all participants to leave the encounter with a clear understanding of the outcomes; and it leads to long-term collaboration, understanding and agreement.

Conversely, context-based communication takes more time to process initially than the participants may wish to allow; the participants must be aware of any personal agendas that can distort the process and outcomes; and participants are often unaware of the bigger picture, and tend to focus only on the specifics of content.

Common examples of context-based communication are newspaper op-ed pieces and editorials, letters to the editor, and televised weather and news reports, particularly those promoted as "an inside" look or "in depth" reporting. In the business world, context-based communication examples are found in board meetings, planning sessions, discussions to create the risk management plan, and in crisis team meetings.

Content-based Communication during a Crisis

What constitutes content-based crisis communication, and why is this important to the risk manager? We will start with an example.

Content-based Communication during a Crisis

Consider this scenario: you are the risk manager for a national-wide meat processing organization operating a number of facilities across the U.S. A tornado strikes several of your facilities, destroying them in a matter of minutes. Employees are injured and possibly dead. Thousands of pounds of frozen meat, once safely stored in your immense freezers, are now strewn about the grounds and beginning to thaw; power is out with no estimate of when it will be restored; your vehicles are destroyed; roads are blocked with debris. The only thing moving is a news helicopter, and it is about to land. You know the cameras will be headed right towards you. What do you say to the nation?

Whatever you decide to say, it must be content-based communication with no embellishment.

A crisis in an organization may arise from a wide variety of scenarios and may take on many shapes and forms. Thus, communication responding to the crisis must also be flexible and take on many forms. Effective advance preparation for crisis communication can make the difference between a swift return to normal after a crisis or a significant loss event that may jeopardize the organization for years to come.

The old management adage, "If you fail to plan, plan to fail," rings true in a crisis.

Who is the Audience?

In a crisis, timely communication, accurate information, and appropriate delivery methods are all critical to get the right message to the right people at the right time. The audience can range from the employees at or near the crisis location to customers and suppliers, and from investors to the general public. Each audience sector has unique needs and the communication must be appropriate to each. For example, for employees at a single location, rapid, informal communications may be appropriate, but for investors, customers, and the general public, the communication might consist of carefully crafted public information releases that may even be distributed throughout the U.S. and internationally

To this end, it is useful to divide the recipients of crisis communications between internal and external groups, and to recognize the unique needs of each.

Internal Recipients

Internal recipients generally consist of employees. They may be the directly affected employees at or near the crisis location, or throughout the organization. Customers or visitors at or near the crisis location may be internal recipients, as they may be directly affected by the crisis. Family members of the affected persons are also internal recipients. The needs of the internal recipients are the most immediate and pressing, with informal distribution of critical information a key element in handling the crisis.

External Recipients

External recipients consist of the customers not at or near the crisis location but who will be affected by the event nonetheless. Also, neighboring businesses and residential areas near the crisis location are external recipients. Partnering companies and suppliers, industry sector contacts (such as competitors), local government officials ("local" could expand to state or national government, depending upon the size and influence of the organization in crisis), regulatory agencies, and law enforcement or emergency services agencies are external recipients. The last important set of external recipients will be the press or media who will be responsible for communicating the details of the crisis to the general public and investors.

These organizations need details, but there is a trade-off between immediacy and the extensive nature of the details. More formal types of communication (e.g., press releases and staged press conferences) are appropriate for the external recipients.

What types of messages are communicated in a crisis? The types of messages depend upon the types of recipients. The most basic internal message is the command to evacuate and other safety instructions.

> (Author's note: One of my customers called to say his business was on fire and ask what he should do. I asked him if he had called the fire department. He hadn't. He thought it was more important to call the insurance agency to get the claim started!)

Beyond the initial information disseminated in training and planning, internal recipients should receive current information on the situation to aid in rumor control. Without any official communication, rumors will flourish and people will begin to act on their own. In addition, the internal recipients need to know the expected duration of the crisis (e.g., when to return to their work posts), the actions being taken to address the crisis and by whom, how future communications will be done (type and frequency), and how to reach assistance if needed.

Internal communications during a crisis must be swift, concise, and as accurate as possible. In the absence of complete information, uncertainty can be acknowledged, but some form of official communication should still be distributed. It should be assumed that internal communications may be provided to the media or other external entity by an affected person and will likely be distributed to a larger audience, whether intended or not by the organization.

External recipients should receive a concise description of what happened and the status of the crisis. This statement should include the extent of damage and injury if known, as well as steps being taken to provide treatment or other assistance to those impacted by the incident. The communication should indicate the steps being taken to mitigate further loss or damage and danger to others. Also, it is appropriate to describe the preparations made in advance for this crisis (assuming that it had actually been foreseen) and how those preparations are being implemented. There should be an indication of when operations are expected to return to normal. Lastly, the communication should clearly designate the official spokesperson and indicate how further information will be distributed (type and frequency).

External recipients should receive messages that are similar to internal messages, but they serve a different purpose for an external audience, principally the media. The contents of internal and external messages will be compared, so it is critical that they are consistent with each other.

Crisis Communication Tools – Methods of Transmitting the Information

The risk manager has a number of transmission methods available, and will select the method depending upon the situation and the tools and infrastructure available after the crisis, keeping in mind that some tools and infrastructure may have been destroyed or damaged during the crisis. To maximize the delivery and understanding, the astute risk manager will utilize multiple methods and tools to communicate the message.

Some of the common tools or methods used to communicate during a crisis are as follows:

1. Telephone tree – One person calls another person, and that person calls someone else (an old idea, but it still works, and cell phones have made this method even more effective, particularly when the landline system has been compromised).

2. Broadcast voicemail – A spoken message is recorded and updated regularly into a voicemail system. Instructions for accessing the system can be distributed to the media, by email, posted to a website, or in public information releases.

3. Email listservs – This method requires recipients to be "subscribed" in advance, but a single message can be distributed at once to a large population of recipients. Email should never be used to send sensitive or confidential information in a crisis, and sender should assume that email will be forwarded to others, whether intended or not.

4. Website – Summary information can be posted on a website for access via the Internet. Information must be updated regularly, and there must be sufficient capacity for the expected traffic level. If the web address is designated in advance for this purpose, make the URL as short, simple, and memorable as possible.

5. Press Release – A professional, public information message should be crafted, if possible. Press releases should be used for broad messages about status and actions being taken. Avoid technical information and industry jargon.

6. Press Conference or other public appearance – These tools are very effective with the right person (e.g., the actions of New York Mayor Rudy Giuliani on 9/11/01). A skilled individual can deliver a message during a crisis that demonstrates confidence, competence, comfort, action, credibility, and elicits appropriate actions and responses from the audience, while still acknowledging their own grief, uncertainty, and humanity.

Dealing with the Media

If the crisis is significant enough, it will attract the attention of the news media. The spokesperson is the only one who should be in contact with the media so that all information that is to flow out can be controlled and managed.

There are two statements the spokesperson should absolutely NOT make to the media: anything that is untruthful and "No comment." The spokesperson must remember that the media has a job to do – reporting the news. To report the news, they need quotes, and as soon as they get the quote, they will leave.

However, the spokesperson does not have to answer every question that is asked. Questions not relating to the incident should be answered honestly and accurately, but only if the spokesperson has direct and complete knowledge of the facts. If the spokesperson does not know the facts, it is appropriate to simply say, "I don't know," or "I don't have that information at this time."

Other appropriate remarks are:

"We acknowledge there has been an incident involving…."

"We do not have all the details available at this time."

"We will continue to cooperate with the proper authorities throughout the process."

Members of the organization who are not the designated spokesperson must be very careful when they are contacted by the media to follow the same two admonitions about lying and saying, "No comment." Their appropriate response is "Please direct your questions to our designated spokesperson, _____."

Essential Content of Effective Crisis and Risk Communication

The overriding element of all effective crisis and risk communication is acknowledgment. The spokesperson must make a sincere and convincing acknowledgement of the crisis. The specific acknowledgement elements are as follows:

1. Acknowledge uncertainty – Be willing to recognize that not every possible contingency is known and that actions being taken are based on the best information available at the time.

2. Acknowledge tension and emotions as legitimate – Help people bear their feelings, and respect those feelings, even if it creates discomfort.

3. Acknowledge obvious mistakes and apologize – This should be done in consultation with legal counsel, as this approach generally goes against the grain of typical legal advice, but if the mistake is clearly known, the public is much more forgiving of an organization that accepts responsibility than one that is perceived as hiding information or trying to duck responsibility.

4. Acknowledge the hazard and avoid over-reassuring – The audience will process their perception of the crisis or risk based on their own outrage level. By presenting a message that leans slightly towards alarming versus over-reassuring, the audience will better allow itself to accept a conclusion of a lesser, more realistic risk level (things are not as bad as they seem).

Summary

Risk Managers will need to use the services of others inside and outside of the organization in order to achieve their risk management objectives. The risk manager is often likened to an orchestra leader: one who carefully directs the members in achieving the outcome as the leader visualizes it.

Selecting outside providers requires a knowledge of who, what, when, and how to work with them. A risk manager should know which service providers are integral to the risk management needs of the organization.

For most risk managers, the agent/broker relationship is the most critical of all outside provider relationships. Every effective risk management program has some element of insurance included in the program.

Internal departments and services are not unlike outside service providers. They should be treated with the same care and courtesy as outside service providers.

Knowledge and skill in communicating will often mean the difference between successful implementation and an ineffective risk management program.

Chapter 20

Information Technology for Risk Managers

Introduction

An organization's most valuable information resides on servers, in separate databases, on employees' PCs, in employee minds, in file cabinets, and in its legacy systems. A legacy system is a predecessor application to a newer information collection and storage system. Though they may be obsolete, legacy systems are still important because they contain data artifacts that may not be transferable to the newer system due to software or hardware compatibility issues.

This is a problem faced by all risk managers, and indeed, all managers: there is rarely one place all the information needed is stored. Some of the storage media are paper files while others are electronic, including the most elusive form of electronic storage, the human brain. The effective risk manager must understand how to collect all of this information, store it efficiently, and be able to retrieve it quickly and use it in decision-making.

The ongoing development of powerful computers, private and public networks, and the Internet has made this process easier, and the effective risk manager will master the use of the Internet and information technology to publish information, share knowledge, and access remote databases. We will begin with a discussion of the Internet.

The Internet – Basic Concepts

The Internet is accessed using browser-based applications, such as Netscape®, Windows Internet Explorer®, Mozilla Firefox®, and Opera®.

Groupware is also used. Groupware is any type of software designed for groups and for communication. There are two types: asynchronous groupware and synchronous or real-time groupware.

Asynchronous Groupware

Email is the most common asynchronous groupware application. Software designers developed the basic technology of email to pass simple messages between two people, but even relatively basic email systems today include features for forwarding messages, filing messages, creating mailing groups, and attaching files to messages.

- Newsgroups are similar to email systems except that they are intended for messages among large groups of people instead of one-to-one communication.

- Workflow systems allow documents to be routed through organizations with a relatively fixed process.

- Hypertext is a system for linking text documents to each other, with the Web being an obvious example.

- Group calendars allow scheduling, project management, and coordination among many people.

Synchronous or Real-time Groupware

- <u>Shared whiteboards</u> allow two or more people to view and draw on a shared drawing surface

- <u>Video communications</u> allow two-way or multi-way calling with live video (a telephone system with video)

- <u>Chat systems</u> or rooms allow many people to write messages in real-time in a public place

- <u>Decision support systems</u> provide tools for brainstorming, and critiquing ideas to help groups in decision-making activities.

Open architecture is software whose specifications are public, and which allows anyone to design add-on product for it. The downside is that by being open or public, it also allows others to duplicate its product. The opposite to open architecture is closed or proprietary architecture.

An example of open architecture is Linux, as opposed to DOS, Windows, and Macintosh, all examples of closed architecture.

The Internet is a worldwide network of computers accessible to anyone who has a computer and an Internet Protocol (IP) address. The IP address is a set of unique numbers that defines the computer's location.

The Intranet is a network belonging to an organization (e.g., a company, school, or public entity), which is only accessible by the organization's members, employees, or others with authorization. If the Intranet is connected to the Internet, then it will reside behind a firewall to control access to the Intranet by outsiders on the Internet.

An Extranet is basically an Intranet that is partially accessible to authorized outsiders on the Internet.

Uses of the Internet in Risk Management

The main reasons people use the Internet is to communicate with others, to find information on any subject (research), and to access information that is not easy to find elsewhere. Risk managers can use the Internet for the same reasons: research on risk management subjects, communicating with others on the risk management team, and gathering information that is not easily accessible in any other way.

Using the Internet can improve workflow in the risk management department by:

- Allowing remote access to the company's risk management information system

- Creating online reports that can be more easily accessed by others on the team and upper management

- Data interchange with other databases

- Collaboration and interaction with colleagues

- Enhanced technology images

- One-to-one marketing

- Customer feedback

- Recruiting

Risk Management Information Systems

A risk management information system (RMIS) is a relational database that supports the risk manager in identifying, measuring, and managing risk in the organization or, in the case of a risk management consultant, other's organizations, as well as a customer satisfaction tool. This multi-functional tool can include such applications as claims administration, tracking, and analysis; automated check processing; interfacing of claims data with insurance carriers and third-party administrators; and maintenance of insurance policy records. Most RMIS have reporting tools that can generate an array of reports in both data and graphical formats.

History

The term "database" was first used in the 1960s to describe a system that could organize and categorize data so that it would be useful. The earliest database applications were used primarily by the military. Commercial users quickly adopted them, however. The "relational database" also has its roots in the 1960s and 1970s, but the function was not refined and used commercially to any extent until the 1980s. But even the "relational database" was not adequate for all types of data because commercial users needed database applications that allowed them to customize how they accessed and manipulated their data. By the 1990s, the first Object Oriented Database Management Systems were being used.

During the 1970s the first computer systems emerged for risk management applications. These systems ran on mainframe computers and were primarily used to organize and keep track of claims data. Even with those first primitive systems, having the claims on a computer made it possible to keep track of more data concerning each claim and, more importantly, sort claims according to varying criteria, which lead to being able to identify trends and patterns of losses. This improved accuracy in budgeting and facilitated reduced claim frequency and the severity of losses.

In the 1980s, organizations began retaining more of their risk, even creating captives, and risk managers needed a way to analyze this data. It became even more important to generate loss reports with the information in a format risk managers could use. Improved software applications for electronically stored data have allowed risk managers to manipulate and sort the data in ways that are more meaningful for the job they have to do. This is leading to the decline in the reliance on printed (or paper) loss runs and to the rise of computer terminals connected directly to insurance companies and third-party administrators, meaning that risk managers can access the claims data on the insurance company or third-party administrator's host computer.

In the 1990s, risk managers developed the capability of downloading their information to personal computers, thus accessing and manipulating the data to create reports that were meaningful to their own departments, to the company's department managers, and upper management. The 21st century has brought even more advances in RMIS. Risk managers now use it, not only to track claims and losses, but also insured and uninsured exposures, insurance policies, and any other data that a risk manager needs to have tracked on a continuous basis.[1,2]

1 © 2000 CERN (http://wwwdb.web.cern.ch/wwwdb/aboutdbs/history/industry.html)
2 "Data Day" by Allen Monroe, Founder of RiskINFO, Larkspur, California, 1996 (http://www.riskinfo.com/tech/apr_96.htm)

Why do I Need to Know about RMIS?

We will start with risk managers. Organizations face a myriad of risks, and management holds the risk manager accountable for all of it. A RMIS is an extraordinary tool for keeping track of exposures (both insured and uninsured), claims, loss development, loss trending, insurance policies, cost of risk allocation calculations, and all the other pieces of data a risk manager needs to analyze to do the job effectively.

Insurance agents/brokers are held to higher and higher standards of professional service to their clients; they are assuming more of a risk management consultative role rather than the strictly insurance seller role they played in the past. Those large agent/brokers consulting with larger organizations that do not have in-house risk managers may need a RMIS in their own offices. Otherwise, they should be able to advise clients on how to research leading RMIS providers and applications, possibly even participating in the selection process, so those clients can make intelligent RMIS choices.

Insurance companies are providing and using more outsourced services and may be connecting their systems to vendors' or larger insureds' RMIS. They need to understand their vendors' and clients' needs and the compatibility issues between insurer data and other RMIS.

Using a RMIS

Originally, a RMIS was used only to track claims and claims data. Since its inception, it has been expanded to include many other valuable functions. For instance, it is used to track organizational structure information, from past to present to future. This includes tracking of acquisitions and divestitures, and the claims and exposures related to such entities. It is also used to consolidate risk data from diverse sources, such as insured and self insured workers' compensation programs, and in support of cost containment, risk analysis, safety and loss control, financial reporting, cost allocation, loss allocation, loss forecasting, and vendor performance benchmarking. It can be used to allocate loss and insurance costs to profit centers, keep track of certificates of insurance issuance (including incoming and outgoing certificates), and to track surety bonds or other collateral.

Additionally, it can be used to generate forms such as the Workers' Compensation First Report of Injury form. It can then submit the form and manage the claim data, including medical cost containment and management of legal costs.

By tracking and measuring exposures to risk, the risk manager can analyze loss trends per exposure for loss control and budgeting purposes, create models for analyzing risk financing alternatives, generate risk management departmental reports, letters, and graphical presentations, and create an executive information system for upper management. RMIS also facilitate communication with other departments and subsidiaries within the organization, as well as with other organizations, such as insurers and brokers.[3]

The basic uses fall into several categories.

---

3 *"Data Day" by Allen Monroe, Founder of RiskINFO, Larkspur, California, 1996 (http://www.riskinfo.com/tech/apr_96.htm)*

Collecting Data to Further Risk Control Activities

The RMIS allows access to sources of text-based information, archives, and libraries for risk managers. It can be used to:

1. Monitor, take action, and make improvements.
   a. Who got hurt and how much will it cost?
   b. What was the cause of the accident?
   c. How can this accident be prevented in the future?

2. Track claims and losses necessary for trending and forecasting losses.

3. Track exposure bases (revenues, vehicles, miles driven, units produced, payroll, number of employees, etc.) used for indexing losses to an exposure basis (e.g., automobile liability accidents per miles driven, employee injuries per unit produced, etc.).

4. Track any other data for which the risk manager is responsible.

Creating an Insurance Program Summary

The RMIS can create lists of insurance policies with type of coverage, coverage dates, deductibles/retentions, limits of loss, etc. and the issuance, receiving and organizing of certificates of insurance and other proof of coverage documents.

Creating Charts and Diagrams

The risk manager can use the RMIS to create charts and diagrams for reports to management. These could include loss trending reports, litigation reports, and OSHA log reports. An important function is to calculate, forecast, and allocate the cost of risk.

Tracking Improvements (Benchmarking)

A RMIS can be used to track improvement in the risk management program by setting standards using benchmarking. Many risk management decisions will be based on data collected and the comparisons made with it. There are two types of benchmarking: external and internal. External benchmarking is a continuous comparison of an organization's performance against that of the others in the industry (usually competitors) or best in class (those recognized in performing certain functions) to determine what should be improved. Internal benchmarking is a comparison in performance from one year to another or from one department to another; this is also called trend analysis.

There are several points at which benchmarking will be appropriate. It is important to benchmark when the organization or risk manager puts a new program in place so a baseline can be established. Additionally, a company should benchmark when internal trending and comparisons are underway, when seeking improvement opportunities, when using a follower strategy, and even when environments are stable.

The benefits or advantages of benchmarking are to record continuous improvement (or so see deterioration), to promote "out of the box" thinking and creativity, and to prioritize areas that need improvement.

The <u>disadvantages</u> are that management places too much emphasis on benchmarking as a result, not as a process. Benchmarking is just a tool, but it is not the only tool a risk manager can use; it must be combined with judgment. It is a mistake to think being lower (or higher) is always better; it depends upon the criteria of the comparison. Risk managers should also beware of implying more precision than really exists in benchmarking. There also can be some data problems. If there is insufficient data, unknown data, or statistically massaged data, the results will probably be skewed.

If comparisons are made between inappropriate comparison groups (dissimilar operations, for instance), if there is an insufficient group or population for the comparison, or if there is inconsistent comparison data, the comparisons will be statistically invalid. When making comparisons, the risk manager cannot conclude that only one factor is to blame.

Determining the Need for a RMIS

When determining the need for a RMIS, the risk manager must look at several areas. First, a critical mass of data must be reached before a RMIS system is feasible. Each risk manager must make this determination in conjunction with those in the information technology (IT) department.

Does the organization or risk management department have the resources to commit to a RMIS? Beyond the cost of the system, initial data entry will be costly in terms of time and personal resources. It is also likely the volume of data and information stored after purchasing a RMIS will become more complex because it is capable of being more complex. More data can be added to each record since the RMIS has the capability of handling and applying more data. More records can be stored since most RMIS have virtually unlimited storage capabilities. The types of reports that can be generated (or rather the functionality of the RMIS) can be customized and expanded to meet the needs of the risk management program.

Is management committed to the need? Management must recognize that, by computerizing the risk management data, the workflow will be more streamlined, communication will be more efficient within the department and with outside team members, and information can be more easily shared between two or among thousands. When determining whether to purchase a system, and in deciding which system to purchase, the risk manager must consider the potential for integration with other internal and external systems.

Finally, is the organization at a position where it needs a system that, while chosen for internal use, also has compatibility with an insurance company or a third-party administrator system?

Elements of a RMIS

The elements of the RMIS system are:

Hardware – the actual physical components of the computer, which would include, but not be limited to, the internal circuitry, monitor, keyboard, mouse, memory, and hard drive.

Software – the set of computer programs in place to execute the commands within the hardware. It is "soft" because it can be easily changed or deleted whereas the hardware is not frequently changed.

Data – an important element of the RMIS. The risk manager must determine how data will be captured, exported and imported, managed, and analyzed and reported.

Communication method (network) – Another element of the RMIS is its method of communication with other systems through a local-area network (LAN). This communication is usually on an Intranet that has access behind a limited-access firewall to the Internet.

Maintenance – Hardware must be serviced and maintained like any other physical asset. Software must be updated regularly, and glitches, bugs, and other imperfections identified and corrected. Data must be continuously updated and stored, with errors removed as found. Communication networks must be updated and protected against security breaches and natural and infra-system perils (e.g., power fluctuations).

Data Integrity

The issue is not whether a data integrity problem exists, but rather when it is caught and how high the error rate will be. There are several causes of data integrity problems. One is an absence of standards, including a lack of data requirements and a lack of consistency in collecting and maintaining data. Another data integrity problem is in the data itself because of input errors, system errors, and data transfer and conversion glitches from old systems, third-party administrators, and/or insurance carriers. The risk manager must take appropriate measures to address the data integrity problem. The old computer mantra of the 1960s and 1970s, GIGO (Garbage In, Garbage Out) still applies. Data entry training should focus first on accuracy, then on speed. Regular system maintenance should be a part of every budget.

Data integrity is a particular problem with data conversions as the previous system may have been outside the direct control of the risk manager and may have used different codes and formats. To address the data integrity problems of data conversion, the risk manager should be an integral part of the data conversion process and the mapping of data fields. The risk manager should provide the layout of the data requirements, audit the requirements (using a different vendor than the one converting the data), and insist on non-proprietary programming language and database formatting. However, if the programming language is proprietary (as it often is), he must make sure that the data is readily exportable, and obtain documentation (data mapping) for future programmers and acquire code access or ownership, or make sure a third party has it in trust.

But the most important step in the protection of data integrity is to back up the data on a regular basis, and to store the backup of the database and the software in a remote site with its own adequate security. All too often, operators back up data and software on a regular basis, and then they store the backup copy in the same room as the hardware, exposing both sets to the same crisis.

RMIS Resources

Risk managers can find multiple resources for locating RMIS providers and vendors on the Internet. The site www.rmisweb.com displays multiple articles, press releases, columns, and RMIS reviews from risk management and insurance publications. Some industry periodicals publish an annual listing of RMIS providers. *Business Insurance, Risk and Insurance*, and *National Underwriter* regularly publish articles about RMIS and other technology products and services available to risk managers.

Off-the-shelf Software

Many risk managers use modern off-the-shelf software for the development of basic risk management information system components. Microsoft Word™, Word Perfect™ and other word processing software can be used to prepare policy narratives, claims summaries and litigation reports. Excel™, Lotus™ and other electronic spreadsheet programs are available for statistical analysis, graphics and arraying selected claims information. Relational database programs like Access™ and dBase™ are powerful enough to manage basic claims record keeping and reporting needs. They can even be used to track and manage certificates of insurance.

Insurer Systems

Many major property and casualty insurance carriers use claims reporting and management systems and may make them available to their policyholder clients. In the best carrier-provided systems, the risk manager can download selected data fields from the carrier's system to their own off-the-shelf software for enhanced analysis, graphics, and report preparation. Some carrier-provided systems can import claims data from a policyholder's former provider, permitting continuity of data following a change in carriers. The availability and quality of a carrier's RMIS is another facet for an insurance buyer to consider when weighing proposals from competing carriers.

Commercial RMIS

Commercial RMIS are currently available from over 30 vendors. Most are listed at www.rmisweb.com or in Business Insurance Magazine's Directory of RMIS Vendors. These systems take two different approaches:

Server-based systems – require a greater initial hardware commitment by the client company, a higher degree of information technology sophistication, but a lower ongoing cost than web-based systems.

Web-based systems – permit secure access by the risk manager to their claims information. These systems require a lesser degree of IT sophistication and can normally be accessed through any web-enabled computer. Because the software and data is stored on the vendors' computers, the ongoing costs for these systems tend to be higher than server-based systems.

The breadth of information depends on the system, but usually includes virtually every data element relating to a claim. These systems usually permit preparation of reports based upon multiple selections and limiting criteria. The better systems offer not only a menu of common report formats, but also include the ability to generate ad hoc report formats.

Chapter 21

Allocating the Cost of Risk

Introduction to Allocation Systems

Why do we allocate cost of risk? In order to remain competitive, an organization must be able to track and properly provide for all types of organizational costs, including the cost of risk. An allocation system is the process that identifies and attributes the cost of risk among various business, operating, or accounting units. Allocating the cost of risk is simply an extension of the broader accounting system of the organization, like cost accounting, where the various costs of production are tied back to the revenue generated from the production process.

A risk management allocation system has several key objectives. The primary objectives are to understand the true costs of the risk management program and to create accountability in each department cost center, division, store, etc., so that they can be evaluated and budgeted accordingly. Bonuses, salary increases, and performance evaluations can be tied to the cost of risk allocation system so that employees are directly aware of the costs associated with losses and exposures. Another objective is to identify those locations, managers, employees, and environments that need risk management attention.

Related to these objectives are the objectives of enhancing loss control by motivating personnel to reduce frequency and severity, building risk control into projects, products, and business acumen, providing managers with site-specific loss and exposure information, and making the investment in safety, loss prevention, and risk control equipment more cost appealing and effective.

A further objective is that the allocation system allows the company to stay competitive by tracking and providing for all types of costs and holding fluctuating costs to a minimum, but the system must be easily understood and not easily manipulated by department heads or upper management.

Lastly, an objective of the risk management allocation system is to alter behavior by expanding the risk management influence beyond the core team and encouraging managers to accept responsibility for their departmental losses.

We will discuss the process, and at the end of the chapter, a case study illustrates a simple allocation.

Steps in the Allocation Process

Step 1: Define Your Costs

Which of those costs will the company allocate, and which will they not allocate? There is no rule that says a company must allocate its entire cost of risk. That depends upon the objectives of the allocation system and the costs involved. So, the first step in the allocation process is to define the costs the organization wishes to allocate. We will start by defining the cost of risk.

Several items make up the cost of risk:

- Insurance premiums, fees, and premium taxes

- Retained losses, which could include deductibles, self-insured retentions (SIRs), self-funded costs (e.g., accruals, bonds, etc.)

- Risk management departmental costs (e.g., internal risk management information systems -- RMIS, payroll, travel, seminars, conferences)

- Outside services (e.g., agent/broker and service fees, external RMIS, actuaries, legal fees, third-party administrators -- TPAs, etc.)

- Indirect costs such as training costs for new employees and loss of productivity after an accident

Where can we find these costs? We can get some of them internally or from insurance agents/brokers, insurers, and industry groups. Some of the indirect costs we can estimate from benchmarks or standards from the RIMS Benchmark Survey: created by the Risk and Insurance Management Society, Tillinghast-Towers Perrin, and articles in *Business Insurance, National Underwriter, Wall Street Journal*, etc.

Step 2: Carefully Review Company's Allocation Variables.

The organizational structure and ownership will determine the allocation system to be used. If the organization is privately owned, the structure of the allocation system will probably be different than if it is a public entity or governmental body, such as a city or school district. It might also be a government-regulated tax structure such as a hospital district, airport, or joint powers authority (JPA), such as a port authority.

Geographic locations will also make a difference in the allocation system used, prompting the following types of questions:

- How many locations are there?

- Where are they located?

- Are they permanent or temporary locations?

- Are there any restrictions or regulations regarding the type of insurance permitted in the jurisdiction where the organization is located?

The company may find it advantageous to allocate various costs differently, depending upon how certain states treat some types of insurance.

Other considerations would be strategic in nature, such as where the organization is in its business cycle, political environment (both internal and external), and tax structure.

Step 3: Define Desired Result.

In order to develop an effective allocation system, the organization must determine the goals and objectives of the allocation system and have defined procedures to measure progress. If the objective of the allocation system is to alter behavior, the company must have in place a method of determining whether the behavior of the employees has been altered. In other words, are fewer accidents happening or are the losses that do occur less severe?

The risk manager will have more questions:

- Will retrospective or prospective, or a combination of both, influence the allocated program?

- Will costs be allocated before they are actually incurred, as they are incurred, or at the end of the year?

- Will costs be allocated in advance and then adjusted at the end of the year?

All of these things must be determined and explained fully before implementing the allocation program so that everyone understands the process.

The intended results will help define which costs will be allocated to operating units. Some organizations allocate all costs, but others allocate some of the costs and retain other costs at corporate. For example, some organizations may allocate costs associated with employee injuries, but not Directors and Officers liability insurance. Some companies do not allocate risk management departmental costs, as they feel that this should be a corporate overhead cost.

Additionally, for each allocation, the organization needs to determine what value method or factoring will be used. This would include exposure method, historical method (experience), minimums and caps, and aggregates. The company also needs to determine how the allocation system will affect the accounting system, company culture, international issues, existing budgets, motivation and incentives, and loss control.

And last but not least, for the risk management allocation system to be successful, the risk manager must have upper management's input and "buy-in," and the system must be consistent and equitable throughout the organization and easily communicated to all departments.

Step 4: Create It.

The last step is to create the allocation formula and start allocating costs. However, there is a major caveat: Because of organizational diversity, there is no "right way" to allocate costs. The "right way" is whatever works and is accepted by the organization.

To the greatest extent possible, the cost of risk should be captured by, and be discreetly identifiable within, the accounting system, often made possible by adding to (or amending the current account code structure so it captures such transactions.

Bases of the Allocation System for Cost of Risk

Commonly, risk managers can use two broad approaches allocate the cost of risk: exposure and experience.

Exposure

When using the exposure basis, the group shares the costs associated with the programs on an equitable proportionate basis, based on their respective exposures. Here, exposure units are defined as those things that could have a loss (e.g., buildings or square footage of buildings, number of vehicles, miles driven, number of employees, payroll, sales, units produced, value of assets, or revenues).

Two variables can affect the outcome of this method: change in exposure values (e.g. appreciation of an asset such as a building) and change in the number of exposure units (e.g., increase or decrease in the number of vehicles or employees). When period-to-period exposures are consistent, this is an easy method.

The advantages to this method are obvious: it is easy to administer, simple to understand, and easy to adjust in real time. The weakness is also obvious: it is not linked to experience, and therefore, produces no incentive to reduce losses.

Experience

When a company uses an experience basis for their allocations, each unit bears 100% of the costs it creates due to its loss experience. The costs are borne solely by the unit that has the loss(es), so the only variable is each unit's own loss experience. Experience-based allocations can be based on number of losses, cost of losses, or percent of losses compared to other units (e.g., loss per number of units, payroll, revenue, etc.).

The advantages to the experienced-based allocation system are obvious: it encourages loss control, is explainable to department heads, and, depending upon the method used, can be easy to adjust.

The weaknesses are also obvious: it does not allow for strategic allocation, it creates many details to be tracked to keep the allocation fair and accurate, and, depending upon the method used, it can be complex to adjust. It also may obliterate the department's budget.

Balanced Mix of Exposure and Experience

To most risk managers, the ideal allocation is a balanced mix of an exposure- and an experience-based allocation system. This type of allocation system can take many forms, which range from simple to complex.

Consider the following example of a balanced mix allocation system:

- A portion of the insurance premiums (from 1% to 100%) is allocated to operating units on the basis of exposures, though, as mentioned above, some insurance premium costs may be allocated to an administrative department.

- A portion of risk management department costs (from 1% to 100%) is allocated to operating units on the basis of exposure, but this exposure base may not be the same as that used for allocating insurance premiums.

- A portion of outside consultant costs (from 1% to 100%) is allocated to each operating unit that uses services.

- A portion of retained losses (from 1% to 100%) is allocated to operating units based on their historical loss experience. The cost of retained losses is either derived from a loss forecast or from actual experience. These costs may be valued on an incurred basis or a paid basis for the current period or an ultimate incurred value.

- Any portion of expenses or losses not allocated to operating units based on exposure or experience may be spread equally among all operating units or to non-operating units (e.g., the organizational offices) on an exposure basis of some type.

Case Study – Springfield Meat Packing and Processing Plant

The plant and number of employees has grown over the years, now organized into three separate divisions: Beef, Chicken, and Hog.

Even though all the divisions are located on the same property, they are housed in separate buildings. Beef Division has 30% of the employees, generates 40% of the revenues, and occupies 15% of the building space. Chicken Division has 40% of the employees, generates 15% of the revenues, and occupies 25% of the building space. Hog Division has 25% of the employees, generates 45% of the revenues, and occupies 40% of the building space. Corporate has 5% of the employees, generates no revenues, and occupies 20% of the building space. Only corporate has employees who are executives (see the following table).

Exposure	Beef Division	Chicken Division	Hog Division	Corporate	Total
Employees	30%	40%	25%	5%	100%
Revenues	40%	15%	45%	0%	100%
Occupancy	15%	25%	40%	20%	100%
Executives	0%	0%	0%	100%	100%

To keep costs in check and make all the division managers accountable for losses in their divisions, the CEO, Wendy McDonald, has decided there is a need to allocate the cost of risk. She directs her risk manager, Jack Bell, to come up with a plan that is fair, equitable, and easy to understand and administer. The first thing Jack has to do is figure out what he wants to allocate. After investigating insurance premium, retained losses, risk management departmental costs, and outside costs, he comes up with the amount he thinks is fair to allocate. According to his calculations, the total cost of risk is $600,000 per year. It is broken down this way:

Cost Category	Amount
Insurance	$430,000
RM Department	$100,000
Outside Consultants	$58,000
Actuary	$12,000
Total Cost of Risk	$600,000

First, Ms. McDonald notifies all department heads that Jack has been authorized to speak for corporate regarding a cost of risk allocation system. She explains to them that Jack will be working with them to establish a fair and equitable system for allocating the costs associated with risk.

At a meeting with all department heads, Jack explains that up until this time, all of these costs have been absorbed at the corporate level. He also explains that the allocation system he is proposing is based on exposures as well as historical losses. To make it more fair, he is only going to take into account the previous four years of losses, but not the most recent year. They understand this because they know that their workers compensation experience modifier is calculated using the same method. For the present, they are cooperative, but he entertains a few fears that they will not be as cooperative when the allocations actually hit their bottom lines.

He then confers with the accounting department to see if the allocation system he wants to use would be feasible. He is able to work out some of the coding glitches with them.

Upon closer investigation, Jack determines some patterns in the loss history. First, he finds that the Beef Division has had most of the workers' compensation losses even though they did not have the most employees. He also found that the Chicken Division has had most of the general liability losses, mostly products liability, and the Hog Division has had the most property losses. Since there have never been any D&O losses and all the executives are employees of corporate, he decided that corporate should pick up this entire cost of the D&O insurance. He put the percentages of losses by types on a spreadsheet to make the data easier to work with.

Experience	Beef Division	Chicken Division	Hog Division	Corporate	Total
WC losses	55%	25%	18%	2%	100%
GL losses (including product liability losses)	20%	59%	19%	2%	100%
Property losses	25%	30%	35%	10%	100%
D&O losses	0%	0%	0%	100%	100%

Since all the departments have the potential to have losses (since they all have exposures), he thinks that they should all share in some of the costs (except the D&O premium and/or losses). But he recognizes that it should not be a majority of the cost of risk, since all the divisions have the ability to control their losses. With the agreement of Ms. McDonald, the CEO, they decide that 25% of all the insurance costs should be allocated on an exposure basis, and the remaining 75% should be allocated according to experience. In addition, each division as well as corporate, should pick up its own losses as they are paid in retained losses or deductibles. Additionally, they decide that the risk management departmental costs and the costs for outside consultants should be allocated according to use.

The averages for workers' compensation, general liability (including products liability), and property losses are given below:

Experience	Beef Division	Chicken Division	Hog Division	Corporate	Total
Average Losses	33%	38%	24%	5%	100%

Since the use of outside consultants usually follows losses, they have decided to use these percentages to allocate risk management departmental costs and outside consultant costs, except for the actuarial consultant. The cost of the actuarial consultant, they feel, should be allocated mostly to corporate since it is essentially a corporate function. They have decided to allocate to each division 10% of the cost. The remaining 70% of the cost will be picked up by corporate. Now all he needs to do is work out some of the details and present the plan to the division managers.

The first step in the calculations is to figure 25% versus 75% of the insurance premiums. Jack has determined this to be $107,500 and $322,500, respectively. He then allocates 25% of the premium based on the exposure percentages shown previously:

25% of the insurance premium costs:

	Beef Division	Chicken Division	Hog Division	Corporate	Total
WC	$ 20,250	$ 27,000	$ 16,875	$ 3,375	$ 67,500
GL	10,000	3,750	11,250	0	25,000
Prop	1,875	3,125	5,000	2,500	12,500
D&O	0	0	0	2,500	2,500
25% Insurance Costs	$ 32,125	$ 33,875	$ 33,125	$ 8,375	$ 107,500

The second step is to calculate the other 75% of the premium based on historical losses.

75% of the insurance premium costs:

	Beef Division	Chicken Division	Hog Division	Corporate	Total
WC	$ 111,375	$ 50,625	$ 36,450	$ 4,050	$ 202,500
GL	15,000	44,250	14,250	1,500	75,000
Prop	9,375	11,250	13,125	3,750	37,500
D&O	0	0	0	7,500	7,500
75% Insurance Costs	$ 135,750	$ 106,125	$ 63,825	$ 16,800	$ 322,500

The third step is to allocate the risk management departmental costs of $100,000. These are also being allocated according to average losses.

	Beef Division	Chicken Division	Hog Division	Corporate	Total
RM Department	$ 33,000	$ 38,000	$ 24,000	$ 5,000	$ 100,000

The next group to allocate is the outside consultants' fees. The safety consultant will cost $23,000; the risk management consultant will cost $20,000, and the TPA costs will be $15,000. Like the risk management departmental costs, theses costs will be allocated according to average losses (see previous tables).

	Beef Division	Chicken Division	Hog Division	Corporate	Total
Safety	$ 7,590	$ 8,740	$ 5,520	$ 1,150	$ 23,000
RM consultant	$ 6,600	$ 7,600	$ 4,800	$ 1,000	$ 20,000
TPA	$ 4,950	$ 5,700	$ 3,600	$ 750	$ 15,000
Total	**$ 19,140**	**$ 22,040**	**$ 13,920**	**$ 2,900**	**$ 58,000**

The final cost to allocate is the actuarial consultant costs. The actuary charges $12,000 to determine the most appropriate loss reserves. Jack and Ms. McDonald have decided to charge the divisions only 10% of the cost each, so that corporate will pick up the remaining 70%.

	Beef Division	Chicken Division	Hog Division	Corporate	Total
Actuary	$ 1,200	$ 1,200	$ 1,200	$ 8,400	$ 12,000

If we add all these amounts together for each division, we will have that division's allocation for cost of risk.

Experience	Beef Division	Chicken Division	Hog Division	Corporate	Total
25% insurance costs	$ 32,125	$ 33,875	$ 33,125	$ 8,375	$ 107,500
75% insurance costs	$ 135,750	$ 106,125	$ 63,825	$ 16,800	$ 322,500
RM Department	$ 33,000	$ 38,000	$ 24,000	$ 5,000	$ 100,000
Outside consultants	$ 19,140	$ 22,040	$ 13,920	$ 2,900	$ 58,000
Actuary	$ 1,200	$ 1,200	$ 1,200	$ 8,400	$ 12,000
Total Allocation	$ 221,215	$ 201,240	$ 136,070	$ 41,475	$ 600,000

There is no one best way to allocate costs, but a system that uses allocation based on both exposures and experience is a popular and logical way to do the allocation.

Reality Check for the Allocation System

To make any allocation system work, the risk manager must get agreement from the finance and accounting departments. Though senior management's acquiescence is critical, the finance and accounting people are the ones who actually make the system work on the organization's books.

Also, international cost allocation will never be equal because of fluctuating monetary exchange rates. Business politics are always a factor because some managers will not like any allocation system that makes them accountable for their department's losses.

Decentralization and dilution of claims handling could also occur, and loss reserves are never as accurate as the risk manager needs them to be.

As is true with legal settlements, mediations, negotiations, and the like, the best reality check for any allocation system is to measure the level of dissatisfaction of the participants: if all are dissatisfied in some degree, it is probably a good allocation system. Any time one party is particularly happy, it is probably due to an advantage in the system that will lead to difficulties later.

Chapter 22

Executive Risk

Introduction

Risk, as defined in the first chapter, has four definitions, each for a specific purpose. Risk is:

1. Chance or probability of loss;

2. Uncertainty concerning a loss;

3. A possibility of a variation of outcomes from a given set of circumstances; and

4. The difference between expected losses and actual losses.

Risk can further be viewed as being pure risk (chance of loss only) or speculative risk (chance of gain or loss). Further, the concept of enterprise-wide risk management captures still another view: that an organization can consider its risks as consisting of strategic risk, operational risk, financial risk, and hazard risk.

Many of these risks, regardless of how defined, occur away from the boardroom or manager's offices. They are the risks that arise out of uncertainty in weather, accidents, product marketplaces, environments, financial marketplaces, customers' facilities, suppliers' and vendors' operations, and the like. However, some of the aspects of strategic risk (mergers and acquisitions, for example) and operational risk (management issues) do originate in the boardroom.

The risks that arise out of the decision-making function of management are referred to as executive risks, even though not every decision emanates from the corporate boardroom. Executive risks include directors and officers liability exposures, fiduciary liability exposures, and employment-related exposures other than workers compensation. Employment-related exposures consist of employment practices, an extremely broad issue in itself (e.g., wrongful termination, discrimination, and sexual harassment, as well as substance abuse and violence in the workplace).

The roles of the risk manager vary significantly in the area of executive risk. Certainly, the role is not to be the organizational arbiter of executive behavior. The more likely roles are to suggest risk treatment exposures and negotiate insurance coverage, and that includes casting the organization in the best possible light to the underwriters. In between these extremes, the risk manager may work with other functional areas to identify potential problems and to work to resolve those issues and lessen the likelihood of loss.

Directors and Officers Exposures

The usual connotations of Directors and Officers liability exposures are those of large public corporations, and corporate scandals in recent years have called public attention to the role and responsibility of corporate governance. Legislation and enhanced political careers have followed widespread public outcry against arrogant and intentional abuse of managerial authority.

However, the Directors and Officers liability exposure is not only a creature of large public corporations. Privately held corporations have directors and officers who perform many of the same functions of their Wall Street brethren. Limited Liability Companies have members who provide managerial oversight and direction of those organizations. Partnerships have managerial partners who do the same. And last, but not least, many more "non-profit" organizations (e.g., churches, youth athletic teams, parent/teacher organizations, charities, social service agencies, clubs, and a host of similar, volunteer-run organizations) draw on governance from directors, officers, board members, trustees, deacons, or however referred.

For the most part, these various types of organizations face exactly the same issues, and the methods of handling their exposures are remarkably similar in structure and design.

While these different types of organizations use precise terminology for the individuals providing governance, for convenience, we will refer to all such individuals as "directors and officers," even though their actual titles may differ.

For purposes of this book, the liability facing Directors and Officers is:

"The liability resulting from a director or officer of an organization committing an intentional or negligent act or omission or making a misstatement or misleading statement".

Similarly, all directors and officers, regardless of the type of organization, share the same fundamental responsibility: to prudently represent the interests of the organization's owners or beneficiaries and other organizational constituencies while directing the business and affairs of the organization within the law.

Corporations, limited liability companies, and partnerships generally exist to benefit their owners. "Non-profit" organizations and social service organizations exist to serve others. The "other organizational constituencies" are the employees, vendors and suppliers, customers, and governmental agencies.

Risks facing Directors and Officers

In most business activities, the common law master-servant rule (also known as respondeat superior) holds that an act conducted by an agent of the organization is vicariously imposed upon the organization, and unless certain conduct is present (e.g., willful and wanton disregard or gross negligence), the individual will not be held personally liable. However, in directors and officers liability, the acts of those individuals are not vicariously transferred to the organization. Each director and officer is personally liable for his/her organizational misbehavior, and without limit. Further, each director and officer is liable for the organizational behavior of every other director or officer. This total responsibility for organizational behavior is called "joint and several liability."

The organization may, if the charter permits (and no laws prohibit), agree to indemnify the directors and officers for their wrongful acts. The contemporary directors and officers liability insurance policy provides coverage for both the personal liability of directors and officers as well as for reimbursement to the organization after it has indemnified directors and officers in accordance with the corporate bylaws, and in some instances, for any organizational liability imposed upon the organization specifically (the so-called "entity" coverage).

406

Business Judgment Rule – the Backbone of a Directors and Officers Defense

Understanding the Business Judgment Rule (BJR) and following it is the single most effective defense against directors and officers liability claims. By following its precepts, many claims can be avoided, and those that are not avoided can be mitigated by establishing that the directors and officers acted appropriately.

The underlying concept in the BJR is the recognition that not all decisions and actions of directors and officers will benefit the organization and its constituents.

> As an example, think of last year's Major League Baseball home run leader. Real baseball fans and some others will know the name of the player, his team, and the number of home runs. However, very few will know how many times he "failed" to hit a homer (e.g., the number of at-bats, strikeouts, walks, hits, errors, fielder's choices, and hit batters for that home run leader). Regardless of the number of "failures," the home run leader is still the king of the diamond.

Similarly, the management of an organization does not have to be a success every time a decision is made; all that is necessary is to be successful enough to make up for the mistakes.

Some of the critical aspects of the BJR include:

Business decision – The directors and officers must take action. Failing to act is not excused. However, the conscious decision not to act is a business decision, as it is an action to be inactive. For example, if the directors and officers fail to identify a problem and therefore take no action, they have not followed the BJR; but if they defer making a decision until more information can be gathered, they have followed the BJR.

Disinterestedness – The directors and officers must act in a disinterested and independent manner, making decisions without an expectation of personal financial benefit, unless that financial benefit also inures to the organization or other constituents in general. Directors and officers who earn high levels of executive compensation or are given "golden parachutes" when the organization is struggling financially may not be acting in a disinterested manner. This cognizance of avoiding "conflicts of interest" is very important.

Due care – The directors and officers must make studied, informed decisions after due consideration of relevant information that is reasonably available. The so-called "rubber stamp" of the board on a key executive's pet project is a common example of not acting with due care. The directors and officers do not have to extract every possible bit of information, but only relevant information that is reasonably available.

Good faith – The directors and officers must have the belief that the action taken was in best interest of the organization and its constituents, and not simply taken to preserve their own positions or provide other benefits. The same example of excessive executive salaries and financially rewarding exit packages in financially struggling organizations can easily raise doubts about whether such actions were taken in good faith. Another common example of a failure of good faith is the use of insider information, such as purchasing land personally so it can be sold to the organization in a planned expansion.

No abuse of discretion – The directors and officers have protection against honest errors in judgment that can be supported by a rationale or that are not egregious on the surface. Remembering the baseball example, not every decision must be a home run, as long as every decision has a supportable rationale or is not blatantly abusive of the director's or officer's position.

The Business Judgment Rule is an "all-or-nothing" rule. Satisfying four of the five criteria does not mitigate responsibility. All five must be present to preserve the protection of directors and officers. The BJR is probably the strongest defense available to directors and officers who are legally challenged for their actions.

Directors and Officers and Applicable Law

Implicit in the part of the Business Judgment Rule dealing with Due Care, the directors and officers must know the applicable laws governing organizations and decisions. While directors and officers do not have to be lawyers, the applicable laws are certainly relevant information and if the information is reasonably available. Therefore, a basic understanding of the sources of applicable law and the broad types of behavior governed by those laws is important to the directors and officers.

Common Law

Common law is the body of law consisting of past legal decisions rendered by judges and juries, as contrasted to laws promulgated by legislative or executive branches of government. Historically, the U.S. legal system is based upon the English legal tradition and its reliance on common law for the last 1,000 years or so. Thus, the legal doctrine of stare decisis, or past opinions, creates and modifies the laws that govern social behaviors.

Under common law, directors and officers have three principal duties to their organization and its constituents: to be loyal, obedient, and diligent.

The <u>duty of loyalty</u> means the directors and officers must act with undivided and unselfish loyalty or faithfulness with no conflict between the organization and self-interests. Common examples of loyalty issues arise out of the personal use of organizational assets, having a conflict of interest in personally owning property that will be sold to the organization, or nepotistic hiring of staff or vendors. This duty is at the core of the BJR elements of disinterest-edness, good faith, and no abuse of discretion.

The <u>duty of obedience</u> essentially means the actions of the directors and officers must conform to applicable legal standards and requirements, including the organization's established operating procedures, code of conduct, or other internal definitions of behavior. This duty is at the core of the BJR elements of due care, good faith, and no abuse of discretion.

The <u>duty of diligence</u> means the directors and officers must conduct competent oversight of the organization in an expedient, knowledgeable manner using the standard of care of a reasonably prudent person in a similar position in similar circumstances. This duty is at the core of the BJR elements of business decision, good faith, and due care.

Private Law

Private "law" is the collection of voluntarily assumed controls on behaviors found in an organization's written and verbal doctrine. These "laws" are expressed in corporate charters or by-laws, operating procedures manuals, codes of ethics or codes of conduct, or any other writing that attempts to establish the standard of conduct and behavior within the organization.

A basic legal concept the directors and officers must understand is the ultra vires act, an action outside the permissible boundaries of the organization's charter and by-laws.

> In the earliest example of litigation against directors and officers (England, 1823), the stock prospectus of Alliance British & Foreign Fire & Life Assurance Company stated the company would underwrite fire and life insurance, and a Royal Charter was granted to Alliance, keeping it within the boundaries of the underwriting monopoly created by the Bubble Act of 1720. However, as soon as the company was formed, it began underwriting marine insurance in direct competition to Underwriters at Lloyd's of London. A Lloyd's underwriter who had purchased 15 shares of Alliance then successfully sued the directors for breaching the corporate charter.

Federal Law

Federal law refers to laws and statutes created by legislative action by the U.S. Congress or administrative law created by the Executive Branch of the federal government or regulatory agencies established by empowering legislation.

A number of specific statutes directly affect directors and officers and their organizations. Some of the provisions in these laws address both criminal acts and civil acts, and some establish set penalties and punishments.

Some of the federal laws that affect operational, investing, and financing decisions of directors and officers are the Securities Act of 1933, Securities Exchange Act of 1934, Private Securities Litigation Reform Act of 1955, Sherman Antitrust Act of 1890, Clayton Antitrust Act of 1914, Robinson-Patman Act of 1936, and Federal Trade Commission Act of 1914, and more recently, the Sarbanes-Oxley Act of 2002. These laws address public financing through the sale of securities and disclosure of financial information, antitrust and restrictive trade activities, price-fixing, and anti-competitive strategies.

A number of other federal laws, though they address operations that are conducted at a lower managerial level than the boardroom or executive offices, still affect directors and officers. Many of these are addressed in the chapters covering employment practices, such as Americans with Disabilities Act, Age Discrimination Act, Equal Pay Act, and the like.

In addition to the laws specifically identified here, general topics of laws cover nearly all business practices. These include intellectual property rights (e.g., patent infringement, copyright, and trademark), racketeering, political contributions, environmental pollution, fraudulent dealings in connection with government contracts, and tax withholding.

State Laws

Most states have "mirror" laws that reflect the protections and prohibitions contained in federal laws. In addition, states have their own business corporation acts and other laws that directly govern business activities within their boundaries (and sometimes outside their boundaries, as in the case of New York State insurance regulations).

Local Laws

In a few instances, cities have passed ordinances or laws that further modify (and in at least one instance, conflicts with) federal or state laws in governing business activities.

Claims

Directors and officers need to understand the sources of claims as part of their efforts to protect themselves and their organizations. Many boardroom issues can give rise to claims, but two of the activities most likely to be sources of claims are investing and financing activities. Mergers and acquisition/divestitures are common causes of claims, as stockholders of the acquiring company or the acquired company may feel that the value they received was too little. Similarly, in a merger, either set of stockholders may feel they received too little value or that the deal was inappropriate or inadvisable. A common practice in either merger or acquisition involves the golden parachutes (severance agreements) for exiting management, even when that management has underperformed. Stockholders tend to take exception to rewarding those executives for past, less-than-adequate service.

Related to the merger and acquisition issue is the growth of initial public offerings (IPO) and repurchase activities. The process of issuing new stock to financing new growth and opportunities tends to create excitement and the promise of future gains in shareholder value and growth in the market price of the stock. If the gains are less than those suggested (every savvy financier knows better than guaranteeing results) in the IPO materials, stockholders tend to point the finger at everyone in the deal. Similarly, repurchase activities are often viewed negatively, either as a means of consolidating control by executives who own stock or improving the value of the shares for those who do not sell.

Also, some lawyers and "professional" stockholder gadflies look at large corporations as nothing more than pots of money to be raided in every search for deep and deeper pockets.

Wider stock ownership, while ostensibly a desirable characteristic, creates an additional source of litigation and claims, as there simply is a larger pool of potential claimants. In recent years, stockholders have brought about 35% of claims against Directors and Officers, according to governance claim statistics.

Decentralization of management and autonomy of operations also can give rise to an increase in claims, as local employees may feel disenfranchised by the "home office" or threatened by the whims of local managers. Nearly 40% of all directors and officers claims involve employees.

The size of each claim varies widely by claimant and the nature of the claim. Multiple million-dollar verdicts make headline news, and while relatively rare, have no practical upper limit. It is not uncommon for defense costs to exceed $250,000 even before the matter is brought to an initial hearing, either in court or in an administrative process. Regardless of who brings the complaint or why, directors and officers liability claims are expensive to manage, even if related lawsuits do not ultimately arrive in court. While insurance products are common and high limits are available, insurance should be used only as the last resort, the fail-safe measure in an ideal application of the risk management function. Avoiding the claims in the first place is always the preferred treatment. That brings us to risk control techniques.

Risk Control Techniques for Directors and Officers

One of the biggest challenges faced by a risk manager is managing the directors and officers risk. Nearly every risk manager was hired by an existing organization that had been successful in its organizational mission for a number of years, and the old adage, "don't fix what ain't broken," comes into play. The organization's board and management, its executive officers, its organizational charter and by-laws, all existed prior to the hiring of the risk manager, the young upstart who dares to tell the "old guard" how to manage risk. However, the exposure looms as a real threat to the organization.

Some risk managers (and executive management) may believe that this risk control feat cannot be accomplished. The reality is that nothing can be done until some action is initiated. As the risk manager goes forward in initiating that change to the old guard, there are four primary risk control techniques to be used in managing directors and officers exposures: board composition, procedural actions, delegation, and managing conflicts of interest.

Board Composition

Recent corporate governance scandals have brought board composition into the limelight, and subsequent laws have established minimum standards to guide boards of directors.

<u>Independence</u>

First, the board must have independence from management. The primary task of management in an organization is to accomplish tasks and move the organization forward in meeting its goals. The primary task of the board of directors is to provide strategic management, oversight, and evaluation of management. Boards that have too many insiders, representatives of management, may lack the independence to perform this task, free from conflicts and bias. The outside directors should also have independence from operations of the organization, freedom from potential conflicts of interest because of association with competitors, major suppliers, major customers, or any other organization with which their organization has significant relationships.

There is no magic ratio, except that the board should have more outsider directors than insider directors (or directors who are also employed officers of the organization). The composition should be such that a sufficient number of outsiders permits only outsiders on the three key committees:

- The audit committee

- The compensation committee

- The nominating committee

In other words, the board should have non-employed officers and managers making the following decisions:

- Who should become a fellow director

- How the senior officers should be compensated

- Reviewing the financial dealings of the senior management

Beyond the effectiveness of this board composition as a risk control mechanism, it is an absolute must since the enactment of the Sarbanes-Oxley Act of 2002, which mandated the importance of effective governance in the wake of several corporate governance scandals in the U.S., beginning in 2001.

<u>Size</u>

In the world of organizational governance, bigger is not necessarily better, and size does really matter. Some U.S. corporations and other organizations have large boards, perhaps 40 or more "representatives" of various constituencies the organization serves.

Management and corporate governance experts are reluctant to proclaim the "right" number, except most agree that more than 15 directors makes the operations of the board unwieldy, if for no other reason than maximizing director attendance.

There is no "magic" number of directors or board members: only the answer to the question, "How many is "enough?" There should be enough board members to provide diversification and expertise in important organizational functions, as well as a balance between insiders and outsiders. At a minimum, there should be a director for each of the major functional areas:

- Finance

- Law

- Human Resources

- Marketing

- Management

For an organization that manufactures and distributes products, the board should include expertise in Production and Distribution. If the organization is involved in international trade or business, there should be an international relations expert. If there is a union, a labor relations expert might be helpful.

There is no need to have several CEOs of other organizations on the board if the organization has a competent CEO of its own. Similarly, there is no need for three lawyers, three accountants, or three of anything.

Additionally, there is a tendency to have "movers" and "shakers," individuals who can create business opportunities solely by their affiliation, or personal friends serve on boards. In one actual situation, a prominent lawyer who was a close friend of the President of the United States, and consequently recognized as a "Beltway Insider" who could open doors that presumably would remain closed, served on a well-known board as well as ten other boards. In another notable example, the CEO insisted his personal attorney, personal architect, and child's elementary school principal, as well as the president of a university who had received a huge endowment from that CEO serve on his board. If these individuals can provide needed expertise and experience, their service may be of value; if they serve only as a reward or as a "door opener," the interests of the organization are not likely to be served.

Also, the simple mechanics of conducting a meeting are more challenging with a large number of directors. From the basics of attendance to distributing information, and from conducting discussions to voting, a smaller number is easier to manage.

Self-Evaluation

The board must be willing to analyze its own performance as a group as well as the performance of its individual members. When a number of the directors are officers and fellow employees, individual criticism and group criticism is less likely to be frank.

Education

Board members must know and understand the organization. Further, to meet the common law obligations of diligence and obedience, the directors must know the applicable laws and regulations that control the organization's activities and operations. New members must be educated about the past activities and decisions of the organization's board of directors, and all directors must be educated about applicable laws and regulations.

Procedural Actions

Procedural actions of directors and officers range from mundane actions like scheduling a meeting to the challenging role of a director or officer in making decisions that may affect the financial viability of the organization. As mentioned previously, each member is responsible and liable, as an individual and as a part of the group, for each action, and must take that accountability seriously.

Meetings

The board members must decide upon the frequency of meetings beyond the required annual meeting. There is no set number of meetings that is appropriate, other than enough meetings to properly represent the interests of the organization's constituents. An organization that is running smoothly with no planned changes in the future likely requires fewer meetings than those organizations that are facing challenges or instituting significant changes in products or services or financial structure.

Even with the luxury of having a well-qualified and properly balanced board and a good mix of outsider and insider directors and officers, scheduling the meetings is always a challenge. The board should schedule the required meetings well in advance to provide adequate notice to each director to maximize the number of directors in attendance.

Also related to scheduling meetings is the need to provide notice of the likely length of the meeting and the content of the meeting. There is no standard meeting length, but the time allocated should be adequate to completely analyze and discuss items on the agenda and to make a decision when appropriate. As the meeting approaches, the directors must receive in advance the agenda and any support documents so they can prepare for the meeting and effectively participate in any discussions and decisions.

The attendees must also decide how information will be presented prior to the meeting and during the meeting. Individuals have different learning and communication styles, and the presentation methods, such as written documents, charts, PowerPoint, verbal exchanges, and teleconference attendance must all be considered.

In some instances, the board must decide if persons who are not directors or senior officers should attend the meeting for purposes of adding to the discussion and analysis. Non-directors might include key management, outside advisors, and employees.

Conduct at Meetings

In many organizations, the Chief Executive Officer or the Chairman of the Board chairs the meeting. This is not necessary, as anyone can be appointed to act as the chair of the meeting, the person whose job is primarily to call the meeting to order, run the agenda, resolve administrative issues, call for discussions and votes, and adjourn the meeting.

Regardless of who chairs the meeting, the chairperson should remain neutral on issues and encourage others to engage in open discussion and debate on the issues before the board. For the board to make the optimal decisions, there must be active questions and a challenging of issues. When the chairperson "runs" the discussion, there is less likely to be a meaningful challenge of issues, and the "rubber stamp" syndrome takes over. Scott Adams, creator of the cartoon strip "Dilbert," has made a successful career of lampooning organizational conduct that occurs when the chair is not functioning in a neutral manner. For example, in one strip the CEO visits, stating, "My meetings go faster when I set the tone" and "Opinions are treason."

In the decision-making process, each director makes (or at least should make) an individual choice based upon a studied consideration of the issues and facts. The board should record every vote by name and vote, not simply the number of "yeas" and "nays." When a director is against a proposal before the board, the dissent must be expressly presented as an affirmative vote against the issue. If the decisions are challenged in a lawsuit, the director who was affirmatively against the proposal has the defense of saying, "I was against this proposal and was outvoted. Don't hold me responsible."

In the real organizational world, it is not always easy to vote affirmatively against a proposal, as the board members are a group who must work together on future proposals, and the inevitable organizational politics may temper any individual's decision. Another consideration arises out of the sequences of the individual's votes: a dissenting director voting early, before the outcome is formally known, is more likely to vote against a proposal than when the dissenting director is voting late, after the measure has already received enough votes to pass. Dissenting directors voting for a lost cause may be tempted to change their vote for the sake of unity or politics, or may choose to abstain; however, an abstention is often viewed as the same as a tacit approval, as abstention should be reserved to avoid a conflict of interest.

Documentation

The board must document its activities accurately and completely in the meeting minutes. The minutes provide a precise record of all matters considered and discussed, as well as a precise record of any vote taken, including the identification of dissenting directors. The minutes must also identify documents incorporated by reference, or those documents must be attached to the minutes, as these documents formed the basis for discussion and decision-making.

The minutes should also avoid any ambiguous language, imprecise wording, or any inflammatory or defamatory comments.

Last, the minutes should have a pre-finalization review by the directors to ascertain accuracy and completeness and by legal counsel for conformity to legal standards and the avoidance of problematic language. Further, the minutes must be made available to any absent directors for their review of the business conducted, and, in the event they disagree with any decisions, their written dissent can be attached to the minutes.

Delegation

The board is responsible for the oversight of the organization's activities and management, but it does not have to act in isolation. Boards can delegate certain tasks to others (e.g., to the internal members through board committees, or to outsiders such as management or consultants). Board committees, management, and outside consultants can facilitate an in-depth study of issues and bring special talents, expertise, and experience to bear on problems. Management delegation or outside delegation must have clear documentation of the delegated authority when an assignment of responsibility passes between the board and management or outsiders.

Reliance Defense

Directors who have used experts, officers, committees, or other agents of the organization, including outsiders, have the reliance defense available. Directors can rely in good faith upon the recommendations and observations of these parties if the directors themselves have acted in good faith and with due care in the selection of competent experts. The nature of the advice must be within the scope of the expert's proficiency and the directors must have made a full disclosure of all relevant facts to those experts.

The problem facing the directors must be unambiguous and the advice provided by the experts must not be unreasonable or repugnant on its face. The directors have oversight responsibility to be reasonably familiar with the advice. For example, if the directors are faced with litigation over stock values and outside consultants are hired for advice, if the consultants (apparently students of William Shakespeare) suggest killing all the lawyers, that advice is repugnant on its face and clearly unreasonable. The directors could not rely upon that delegation, even if the source is highly credible.

There are some special considerations when the directors use delegation to obtain legal counsel. This is one of the most important issues in loss prevention for directors, as legal counsel can provide guidance to legally acceptable conduct as required by the common law duties of obedience and diligence and the business judgment rule (BJR) elements of business decision, due care, and no abuse of discretion. The reliance defense requires the directors to choose qualified counsel with experience and expertise in the subject matter, and not just any attorney. Further, if any one director meets resistance from other directors in seeking legal advice, the director must persist in the effort to obtain that advice.

Managing Conflict of Interest

One last area of risk control for directors and officers is the managing of conflicts of interest. A conflict of interest also includes the appearance of or a potential conflict of interest. Avoiding conflicts of interest is central to the common law duty of loyalty and the BJR element of no abuse of discretion.

Conflicts of interest are ethical dilemmas, and like most ethical dilemmas, arise out of two common human failings: greed or ignorance. A greed-based conflict of interest is intentional (e.g., the individual attempting to profit (benefiting personal interest) because of an interest or position in the organization). An ignorance-based conflict of interest is more benign, generally arising out of a failure to identify the conflict or simply not realizing there is a conflict as opposed to intentionally taking advantage of a conflict of interest.

Identification

The first step in handling conflicts of interest is to identify the existence of conflicts or potential conflicts. Uncovering conflicts of interest begins with an increased sensitivity to conflicts or the awareness of how conflicts of interest arise, generally from surveys or questionnaires undertaken on a regular basis. For example, every three years, a school board sends a questionnaire to each of its employees, teachers, administrators, maintenance staff, etc. asking them to disclose if they or any member of their family or any organization in which they have an ownership interest does business in any manner with the school district. In addition, the board needs to formulate appropriate responses to conflicts of interest and ways those conflicts can be addressed.

Avoidance

The preferred method of handling conflicts of interest is to avoid conflicts of interest whenever possible. For example, an insurance broker who has provided years of brokerage service to a non-profit organization and is asked to serve on the board while continuing to provide brokerage service (or one who attempts to get on the board to control the insurance) has a conflict of interest. The director/broker is earning a commission on the decision to purchase insurance from the brokerage firm. To avoid the conflict, the broker should refuse the directorship or, as a director, transfer the insurance business to another brokerage firm.

Recusal

Sometimes when conflicts of interest are identified, the avoidance alternative may not be practical or may be deemed to be too severe. This often is seen in the legal system, when a sitting judge has a case before the bench in which the judge has an interest in either party. In 2008, this exact scenario existed in the United States Supreme Court, when a suit arrived at the Court and one of the Justices owned shares of stock in one of the parties. It was be too late for the Justice to sell the stock to avoid the conflict, and there was no alternative to the court of highest resort.

In this case, the Justice recused himself from hearing the case or participating in the formation of the opinions. The opinions were written with only eight Justices commenting.

Similarly, a director facing an unavoidable conflict can seek to resolve the conflict of interest by first disclosing the conflict. All other directors, management, and owners are then formally aware of the conflict. If the conflict of interest is technical in nature and not financially significant, the directors, managers, and owners can indicate the director can continue to function normally. If there is a more serious conflict or a continuing concern, the director can be removed from a vote or removed completely from a discussion of the matter, so that the remainder of the board can make the decision. Recusals such as a recusal from voting or discussion may not completely exonerate a director, as other constituencies may feel that the remaining directors acted on behalf of the *in absentia* director.

Fiduciary Exposures

There are two broad types of fiduciary exposures. The more serious type of fiduciary exposure is the fiduciary liability exposure, the legal or statutory (or even criminal) liability arising out of the breach of duty to the organization's benefit plans. The simpler type of fiduciary exposure is the dishonesty exposure, the possibility that a fiduciary may abscond with plan assets through theft or embezzlement. Since a reasonably prudent person could comply with applicable laws, the failure to maintain the required dishonesty bond becomes a fiduciary liability issue, as well as exposing the assets of the plan.

Fiduciary liability exposures present two separate but related issues to the risk manager. First, the legal definition of a fiduciary is someone who has the power and obligation to act on behalf of another under circumstances that require complete trust, good faith, and honest dealing. Second, the Employee Retirement Income Security Act of 1974 (ERISA) defines a fiduciary as "any person who exercises any discretionary authority or control with respect to the management or administration of the plan or its assets." ERISA is clear in its depiction of the personal liability of persons who are fiduciaries, as defined.

The risk manager needs to realize that fiduciary responsibility and liability imposed by ERISA applies only to benefit plans that fall within the scope of ERISA. However, that does not mean that non-ERISA plans do not create liability for the employer, plan sponsor, or fiduciaries. It means that non-ERISA plans can give rise to liability under common law, not statutory law.

Thus, the risk manager must be concerned about both the common law liability arising out of a fiduciary relationship and the statutory liability under ERISA provisions that impose criminal penalties, civil penalties, and fines. Further, the definition of "fiduciary" under ERISA is sufficiently broad to include the obvious fiduciaries such as an employee benefit plan sponsor, administrator, trustee, or investment manager. However, the phrase "discretionary authority or control with respect to management or administration" could be construed as applying to an individual in the company mailroom who has the capability and opportunity to divert a benefit check from the rightful recipient to his or her own pocket.

Under common law, a fiduciary has the same general duties as a director or officer, namely, loyalty, diligence, and obedience. In addition, ERISA imposes particular standards, defined by statute, upon a fiduciary. According to ERISA, all actions on behalf of the plan must be solely for the benefit of the plan participants. Further, plan investments must be sufficiently diversified to minimize risk. Fiduciaries must follow ERISA standards and the "private law" as defined by the plan document, the benefit plan "organizational charter and by-laws," unless the provisions of the plan document conflict with provisions of ERISA. All fiduciaries, where under ERISA standards or common law, must act as a prudent person in a similar circumstance using the same level of care, skill, prudence, and diligence.

Further, ERISA defines certain transactions as "prohibited transactions." One type of prohibited transaction is self-dealing, the use of plan assets for personal gain of the fiduciary, undertaking transactions on behalf of persons whose interests are adverse to the plan, and any personal gain inuring to a fiduciary in connection with any transaction with the plan.

For example, a plan may have a policy of making investments in the form of loans to plan participants. However, if the loans are made only to trustees or highly compensated officers, this may be self-dealing and would be prohibited.

Another type of prohibited transaction is a party-at-interest transaction. A party-at-interest is fiduciary, counsel, plan employee, or vendor providing services to a plan, or anyone with a stated interest in or relationship with a party-at-interest.

For example, if the spouse or significant other of a plan trustee provides professional services to the plan, that transaction involves a party-at-interest and is prohibited.

Common Causes of Claims Involving a Fiduciary

The common causes of claims involving a fiduciary can be categorized into two broad groups: administrative errors and managerial decisions.

Administrative errors may take one of the following forms:

- A denial or change of benefits for a participant or beneficiary

- Simple clerical errors (e.g., typographical or data entry mistakes)

- Incorrect benefit calculations

- Incorrect or inappropriate advice or counsel with respect to participation of an individual in a plan

- Misrepresentation as to benefits or features of a plan

- Wrongful termination of an individual's participation

- Civil rights denial

- Discrimination as to an individual

Managerial decisions may take one of the following forms:

- Wrongful termination of a plan

- Civil rights denial or unfair discrimination systemic to the plan

- Inadequate funding of a benefit plan

- Imprudent investment decisions

- Conflicts of interest

The financial consequences of managerial decisions are generally more severe than for administrative errors – and are not as easily corrected.

Sources of Claims

Fiduciary claims arise out of relationships between the fiduciaries and other constituents. Unlike director and officer scenarios, there are only three constituencies. Most claims come from past and present employees, the <u>participants</u> in the benefit plans. The families of past or present employees, the <u>indirect beneficiaries</u> of the plan, bring some claims. Last, a few claims are brought by the <u>federal government</u>, generally the Department of Labor or the Internal Revenue Service. These claims usually result in injunctions or fines and penalties for criminal activities or breaches of fiduciary duty. With the decline in most 401(k) plans resulting from the investment market upheaval beginning in 2008, increases in fiduciary liability allegations can be expected.

Risk Control Techniques for Fiduciary Liability

There are four primary risk control techniques used in managing fiduciary liability exposures: selection of fiduciaries, procedural actions, delegation, and managing conflicts of interest or prohibited transactions.

Selection of Fiduciaries

Both common law and ERISA impose requirements on fiduciary selection. The standard of care under common law is the reasonably prudent person rule. Under ERISA, the selection requirements are specifically defined by statute as follows.

Eligibility Requirements

Fiduciaries cannot have been convicted of certain criminal offenses. Generally, these are offenses involving money such as embezzlement and fraud. Under a Taft-Hartley plan, more commonly known as a union plan, there must be an equal number of management- and employee-representative trustees. Other than that provision, there is no "magic" number of fiduciaries.

Fiduciary Attributes

Fiduciaries should be persons who are independent in thought and action. They should have good character, with inquiring minds, wisdom, and sound judgment. Further, fiduciaries must have adequate time to devote to the oversight management of the benefit plan. Since an organization, such as a bank, investment company, or third-party vendor could be a fiduciary, the fiduciary organization must have adequate staff size and experience, including legal, accounting, and other professional advisors. Responsibility for selection of banks or other third parties to perform functions associated with employee benefit plans rests with the fiduciaries of the organization.

Evaluation of Fiduciaries

Fiduciaries, like directors and officers, must be evaluated. This evaluation can be performed by the plan sponsor (typically the employer is also the plan sponsor, but in a Taft-Hartley plan, the union is the plan sponsor because there is no single "employer."), by co-fiduciaries, or by outside consultants. Independent evaluation (e.g., that performed by outside consultants), is preferred over internal evaluation. The fiduciaries should be evaluated individually as well as in the group.

Evaluation of fiduciaries should include the identification of complaints by participants, beneficiaries, and regulators. Further, fiduciaries, particularly outside fiduciaries or other fiduciaries compensated on a time basis, should be evaluated on administrative time and cost efficiencies. Lastly, the investment performance should be evaluated.

Procedural Actions

Procedural actions of fiduciaries range from the ordinary actions like scheduling meetings of the trustees and fiduciaries to the challenging role of making decisions that may affect the financial status of the plan and its assets.

The decision-making process requires a review of reasonably available and adequate information on a timely basis. Meetings must be scheduled with sufficient advance notice to maximize trustee attendance. The agenda and proposed items for discussion and action should be provided in advance for review and preparation. The trustees must decide if outside counsel or management attendance is required.

There must be sufficient time at a fiduciary meeting for review and discussion of pending matters. A deferral of action to a later meeting is acceptable if the delay is needed to allow for proper review and discussion. All discussions should be conducted in an open manner, with healthy skepticism and challenging of issues.

All votes should be recorded in writing, and any dissenting vote must be made in an affirmative manner. Abstention is viewed as a tacit approval.

The trustees have an oversight responsibility to establish routine operating procedures, evaluation procedures covering various reports, compensation records, outside benefit records, and rules for participant entry to and exit from the employee benefit plans.

Proper documentation is required, and the normal formalities of a meeting must be maintained. Minutes of all meetings must be complete and accurate, detailing actions and limitations imposed by the trustees. A conscious decision not to act must be recorded with reasons. The minutes should incorporate, by reference or attachment, any authorities or documents used in the decision-making process. The minutes should also reflect all investment decisions made and the reasons for all investment decisions, with supporting documentation.

Prior to approval, all attending fiduciaries should review the minutes to check for accuracy and completeness, and legal counsel should likewise review them to avoid ambiguous or imprecise wording as well as any inflammatory or defaming language. A written record of the votes and any dissent by name of trustee must be documented.

If a fiduciary is unable to attend, the absent fiduciary should review the minutes of the meeting and record any dissent or disagreement in writing for distribution to other fiduciaries and for filing with the official minutes of the meeting.

Delegation

Fiduciaries may delegate virtually all responsibilities to other parties who specialize in management assets and employee benefit plans to transfer fiduciary liability. The one aspect of being a fiduciary they cannot delegate is the oversight responsibility, the duty to hire competent and honest administrative and investment firms and to monitor their performance and the performance of all other fiduciaries. However, the fiduciaries cannot delegate administrative and investment responsibility if the "private law" (the plan document) does not permit delegation. Further, all delegates must meet ERISA requirements with respect to the committing of certain crimes.

When the fiduciaries wish to delegate responsibility for management or control of plan assets to avoid fiduciary liability, the delegate must be a registered investment advisor (such as a stock brokerage firm), a bank, or a qualified insurance company. Also, the fiduciary must acknowledge the delegate's fiduciary status in writing.

A delegation of responsibility cannot be made and forgotten; the fiduciary must continuously monitor and evaluate the program through a formal periodic review and day-to-day review. When the delegate fails to perform adequately, the fiduciary must be willing to revoke the delegation.

Support Services

Since the fiduciaries can retain management and investment support service organizations, as part of the oversight responsibility, the fiduciaries must ascertain that the service team is competent and trained for the administrative tasks to be performed. The service team must have clear instructions and responsibilities, detailed in writing. In addition, the fiduciaries should review the longevity and turnover rate of the service team with the goal of avoiding errors and omissions in handling administrative matters.

Fiduciaries should also use legal counsel. Counsel must be experienced in the area of employee benefits and ERISA, as the legal advice should define legally acceptable conduct, under both common law and statutory law.

Conflicts of Interest

Fiduciaries must take appropriate steps to avoid conflicts of interest, using most of the same techniques used for directors and officers. However, there are two specific issues involving conflicts of interest for fiduciaries: special problems and prohibited transactions.

Special Problems

Employed by the Plan Sponsor

First, many fiduciaries are employed by the plan sponsor, often the employer. This common situation creates a real conflict of interest between the common law duty of loyalty to the employer, the common law and statutory fiduciary duty to the plan and its participants and beneficiaries, and the individual fiduciary's self-interest in plan benefits as an employee. This is particularly acute when the employed fiduciary is a highly compensated senior manager, owner, or officer of the employer.

When there is a built-in conflict of interest, the decision-making process requires extraordinary caution, not the usual standard of care of reasonable prudence, to make certain decisions are fair to all participants and to the plan itself. The fiduciaries must make decisions on the basis of provable fairness and that provable fairness must be documented.

In addition to the elevated standard of care, special problems for the employed fiduciary occur when the plan sponsor (employer) fails to contribute to the plan or when an over-funded plan is terminated.

The Greater Duty to the Plan

Consider this: You are the CEO of a corporation and a fiduciary of the employee benefit plan. Sales and therefore cash flow have dramatically decreased. The employee benefit plan contribution of $1,000,000 is due tomorrow. So is the payroll of $750,000. The balance in the checking account is $1,000,000. What gets paid?

If the plan contribution is paid (as legally required by ERISA), the employees will not be paid and are likely to quit, go on strike, sue, and other bad things will happen. If the payroll is covered, the employees will be happy until they learn their employee benefit plan is suddenly under-funded, at which time they will quit, go on strike, sue, report you to the Department of Labor, and call the media. As the CEO and one of the fiduciaries of the employee benefit plan, which obligation (duty of loyalty, obedience, and diligence to the corporation or statutory duty of a fiduciary to the plan and its participants) is greater?

The answer is the duty to the plan. You may have to tap that line of credit to pay the employees.

Plan Termination

Over funding of an employee benefit plan usually occurs when a defined benefit retirement plan exists. The financial obligation owed by the plan to the participants can be precisely determined actuarially by knowing the age, retirement date, marital status, gender, scheduled benefit, and interest or investment return guaranteed. The organization has made contributions to the plan based upon these factors for every employee when they become eligible to participate in the plan. However, some employees leave before their account becomes fully vested, and their retirement benefits are forfeited, with the assets remaining in the plan. Also, the actual investment income may exceed the guaranteed return, with the "profit" accruing to the plan.

Sometimes, the organization decides to terminate the defined benefit plan, and must make a decision on distribution and closing out the plan. Other times, a corporate raider sees the excess assets accumulated in the plan and can decide to purchase the company in a takeover, terminate the plan, distribute the guaranteed benefits, and use the excess funds to pay off some or all of the debt used to purchase the company.

Regardless of the reason, the fiduciaries, some of who may also be employees of the plan sponsor, must make termination decisions, and such decisions are likely to give rise to complaints and claims from employees and plan beneficiaries.

Prohibited Transactions

Conflicts of interest arise out of transactions of self-dealing or transactions with a party-at-interest.

Self-dealing Transactions

Self-dealing transactions mean the fiduciary is immediately involved in both sides of a transaction or the fiduciary has a close relationship with a person dealing with the plan. The conflict of interest is between the self-interest of the fiduciary and the fiduciary obligation to the plan.

Party-at-interest Transactions

The party-at-interest transactions are more indirect. In these transactions, the fiduciary is not directly involved as a potential recipient of benefit from both sides of the transaction; rather, the plan deals with a person or party who has a relationship to the plan, but the person or party is not a fiduciary.

Regardless of the source of the conflict of interest, the conflict of interest must be addressed through identification, then avoidance or resolution through disclosure or recusal.

Employment-Related Exposures

A plaintiffs' lawyer once pronounced, "In the 1980s and 1990s, environmental claims paid my children's tuition. Employment practices claims will fund my grandchildren's Harvard Law School tuition."

For the risk manager, employment-related claims represent the single greatest threat to a company's existence and profitability in the new millennium. Every sizable business needs employees to perform its functions and generate its revenue, but with employees comes a myriad host of employment-related problems: discrimination on age, length of employment, gender, race, ethnic heritage, or creed; the use of substances; a hostile work environment; violence in the workplace; absenteeism; aging workforce; and the like.

Like all exposures, identification is the first and most important step to take in managing the risks. Part of the identification process for employment practices requires "knowing the players" who provide the system of administrative opportunities for resolving employment practices issues before they reach the litigation level and are tried in court. Employers should take every effort to win disputes at this level. Facts inserted or omitted at this level may be the very elements that make or break the case in a courtroom. Three notable federal "players" are the Equal Employment Opportunity Commission (EEOC), the Department of Labor (DOL), and the Federal Employment Practices Agency (FEPA). States, and even some cities, have their own versions of these key federal agencies. These players have promulgated the rules everyone must play by.

Sources of Statutory Liability Governing Employment Practices

While the sources of statutory liability include a number and scope of federal state and local laws protecting the rights of individuals, which have grown to nearly incomprehensible and complex levels, three are three key pieces of legislation that are of a general concern to all risk managers.

The Civil Rights Act of 1964 prohibits unfair discrimination on a number of broad and common bases, such as race, ethnic heritage, and gender. Title VII of the Act created the Equal Employment Opportunity Commission to enforce the laws, and those laws were expanded thirty years later to prohibit employment discrimination based on race, color, religion, sex, national origin, disability, or age. Discrimination based upon these factors is prohibited in hiring, promoting, firing, setting wages, testing, training, apprenticeship, and all other terms and conditions of employment.

The Americans with Disabilities Act of 1990 requires employers to fully understand the definitions of "disabled individual," "reasonable accommodation," and "disparate impact."

- A **"disabled individual"** is any individual who has a physical or mental impairment that substantially limits one or more major life activities (such "routine" activities as walking, seeing, hearing, bathing, feeding oneself, or using the restroom), has a record of such an impairment, or is regarded as having such an impairment.

- A **"reasonable accommodation"** is any modification or adjustment to an employment, an employment practice, or the work environment such that a qualified individual with a disability has an equal opportunity to obtain and hold that employment.

- **"Disparate impact"** refers to a practice that appears to be a facially neutral employment practice but has an otherwise unjustified adverse impact on individuals within a protected class. Common examples of a disparate impact practice include a written test, height and weight requirements, educational requirements, and subjective practices such as interviews.

The Occupational Safety and Health Act, more commonly known as OSHA (and its state versions) requires the risk manager to understand occupational safety and health issues as well as "exclusive remedy" and how the Americans with Disabilities Act affects OSHA.

Sources of Employment Practices Complaints

While the specific allegations of unfair employment practices can be wide and varied, generally, three categories will incorporate the vast majority of these issues and therefore focus the risk manager's approach and treatment. The challenge the risk manager always faces is to manage (and sometimes counter) common human behaviors that naturally emerge when two or more people are put into close proximity to each other.

Sexual Harassment

One of the most common sources of complaints arises out of sexual harassment. Regardless of societal norms and legislation regarding sexual conduct, sex remains a powerful human motivator of behavior (generally misbehavior), and in the workplace it is most commonly exhibited as sexual harassment.

Sexual harassment is not a new phenomenon. What has changed is society's collective view of proper and improper conduct. The Old Testament, when balanced against today's legislative climate, chronicles countless examples of sexual harassment and discrimination.

Nor is sexual harassment confined to the proverbial "dirty old man in the office." According to the U.S. Equal Employment Opportunity Commission, "sexual harassment can occur in a variety of circumstances, including but not limited to the following:

- The victim as well as the harasser may be a woman or a man. The victim does not have to be of the opposite sex.

- The harasser can be the victim's supervisor, an agent or client of the employer, a supervisor in another area, a co-worker, or a non-employee.

- The victim does not have to be the person harassed, but could be anyone affected by the offensive conduct.

- Unlawful sexual harassment may occur without economic injury to or discharge of the victim."

Regardless of the nature of the sexual harassment, there are several common characteristics of sexual harassment.

Overt harassment, usually called "crossing the line," consists of those overt, visible behaviors that frequently involve unwanted physical contact. This may include "quid pro quo," or the promise or hint of something, such as a promotion or appointment, in exchange for sexual favors.

Another characteristic is a pattern of inappropriate conduct that creates a hostile or uncomfortable working environment. This behavior generally does not result in physical contact, but rather consists of an atmosphere, such as being subjected to off-color stories or language, gestures, whistles, or other suggestive signals. The concept of "hostile work environment" is not solely within the province of sexual harassment, however. Three specific federal acts address the concept of hostile work environment: the Civil Rights Act of 1964, the Age Discrimination in Employment Act of 1967 (ADEA), and the Americans with Disabilities Act of 1990 (ADA).

A third characteristic, and one that creates many of the challenges, is that the definition of "the line" that is crossed can be blurred, and that some unacceptable, inappropriate, or questionable remarks and behaviors are simply a matter of extremely poor taste rather than blatant misconduct. The distinction, like Justice Potter Stewart's definition of pornography, cannot be defined but is known when observed. Management must understand the concepts of acceptable and unacceptable behaviors and determine what is "normal conduct" for the work environment. As an example, admittedly extreme, consider the expectation of "normal conduct" in an office environment versus an exotic dance revue venue.

Wrongful Discharge

Another common source of employment practices issues comes out of allegations of wrongful discharge. Any termination process, even including voluntary termination by the employee, can give rise to a wrongful discharge allegation. The risk manager faces an unusual challenge in managing this risk, as two other functional areas within the organization are likely to stake their claims to this exposure: human resources and legal. Both of these functional areas have their own motivations; legal relies upon the letter and spirit of the law, and human resources attempts to keep employees happy. The risk manager, of course, is focusing attention on minimizing the adverse financial impact of allegations of wrongful discharge and must recruit both of these areas as part of the risk management team.

A common belief is that jurisdictions that have "employment-at-will" legislation protect employers by permitting termination "at will," but this is not true if the terminated employee can establish a motive for discharge that is unfairly discriminatory.

For example, an employer, attempting to reduce its cost structure, decides to terminate all employees earning more than $75,000 per year. If the only employees earning such a level are over 60, the discharge appears to be based more on age, but if there were some employees of all ages and genders earning over $75,000, the discharge would appear to be based more on pay than age.

 Another important issue for the risk manager to consider is the quality of the written employment policy and how it is implemented. Actions speak louder than words; precedent outweighs written policy. The risk manager must be concerned that the employment policy is consistently enforced. Once an employment practices claim has been established, the risk manager must understand the concept and value of settling the claim without an admission of fault and with a nondisclosure agreement. Wrongful discharge claims, like many ergonomic claims, are highly communicable: if one person is successful in pursuit of damages, the "contagion" spreads like wildfire throughout the organization, particularly if the organization is undergoing dramatic change.

Discrimination

Though many claims arise out of employment discrimination based on race, color, religion, sex, national origin, disability, age in hiring, promoting, firing, setting wages, testing, training, apprenticeship, and all other terms and conditions of employment, the third major source of employment practices matters is the result of the Americans with Disabilities Act (ADA). The risk manager must be concerned with what constitutes a "disabled employee" and when an employee falls into that protected class (or is excluded from it), particularly when the issue is one of substance abuse. Also, the risk manager must be aware of the types of measures that provide a "reasonable accommodation" to the disabled employee, and by extension, to a disabled customer or vendor. In addition, the risk manager needs to understand "disparate impact" as it is defined under the ADA. The last critical piece for the risk manager is the most current information concerning the applicable state's opinions on the interaction of their workers' compensation statutes and the ADA.

Risk Control for Employment Practices Exposures

Employment practices claims are expensive to defend and to pay. Conversely, prevention techniques are generally inexpensive in comparison to the cost of suits and damages, and, when diligently applied, highly effective in preventing and mitigating claims.

1. The risk manager, in working with human resources and legal, must ensure that management has established sound policies and procedures.

2. Equally important, the risk manager must ensure that the policies and procedures are communicated to all personnel throughout the organization, are clearly understood, and are universally applied at all levels within the organization. Not adhering to a policy is far worse than not having a policy!

3. The policies and procedures must be regularly reviewed for content, legal conformity, and intent. As organizations change, policies and procedures must adapt to the "new" organization and its personnel.

4. Management must continuously express their support of established policies and procedures through written statements, in meetings, and by its own conduct. The old Italian folk saying, "A fish rots from the head," accurately describes the peril of having upper management adhere to their own set of rules while expecting all other personnel to follow the organization's established policies and procedures. Upper management must take the lead in identifying individual situations and patterns of behavior that are acceptable and unacceptable. To borrow a military term, upper management defines "conduct unbecoming" of an officer, a gentleman, and any other employee.

5. The risk manager must assist the organization in taking reasonable care that the established policies and procedures are being followed. Common methods of verifying adherence include:

   - Employee questionnaires, even the so-called "blind" surveys that do not identify specific individuals

   - Supporting an open-door policy by executives to discuss employment practices concerns

   - Managing by walking around

   - Retaining objective and confidential written records on all personnel, with a periodic review of those records

6. The risk manager must ensure that the organization conducts a prompt, complete, and documented response to all allegations or grievances. The risk manager is not the judge, jury, or defense counsel on these matters; instead, the risk manager is more like the court reporter, being sure that the facts are documented in and unbiased manner and retained.

7. The risk manager must ensure that the appropriate functional area that conducts any disciplinary action does so in a manner appropriate to the individual situation and in a manner consistent with actions taken on any previous situation involving substantially the same set of facts.

8. Last, and simplest, the risk manager must be sure the organization is consistent in its employment practices dealings and must document appropriately.

Summary

Claims under the directors and officers, fiduciary, and employment practices liability exposures can undermine or destroy organizational goals if the risk manager fails to identify and address the areas discussed in this chapter. It behooves the person wearing the risk management hat to carefully explore these huge exposures and then to consistently apply suitable solutions.

Chapter 23

Due Diligence

Introduction

> In the words of the late U.S. Senator Everett McKinley Dirksen of Illinois, "A billion here, a billion there, and pretty soon you're talking about real money."

In its purest form, due diligence is part of the risk identification process, a methodology by which the exposures of the organization are diligently considered to identify sources of risk, exposures to loss, perils to which assets are exposed, and hazards affecting those perils. It also means diligently evaluating the underlying assumptions and data used in making those identifications and resulting conclusions.

In its most common application, due diligence is part of the merger and acquisition process. It is a method by which an organization gathers information then decides to merge with another organization, acquire all or part of another organization, or to dispose of all or part of an owned organization. This application is the one that gets much of the attention, as the dollar value of these transactions can be staggering and the potential impact on markets, investors, customers, vendors, and employees can be dramatic.

Most risk managers are never involved in a merger, acquisition, or divestiture; their time is generally consumed with more mundane matters, in terms of dollars, complexity, and breadth of impact. However, each decision to acquire a new location, build a new facility, launch a new product line, hire a new safety manager, contract with a new vendor or insurance broker, select a new insurance carrier, or even begin a relationship with a new client should be the subject of a due diligence examination.

In examining these two ways of viewing due diligence, for the purposes of this text, we will refer to the general due diligence process, the process engaged when acquiring assets, products, personnel, or third-party vendors or customers as due diligence, and the more complex process engaged when an organization is merging, acquiring, or divesting another organization or part of an organization as M&A due diligence. Regardless of the subject of the examination, due diligence involves much the same underlying process and the same basic activities.

The Due Diligence Process

The due diligence process begins, as should all types of analysis, with a thoughtful analysis of the data and assumptions, a four-step process.

Step 1: Identify and Qualify Material Issues

First, the examiner must confirm that all material issues have been identified or disclosed. Material information that is unidentified, misidentified, or undisclosed is bad information. The due diligence examiner then must ascertain that information to be used in the examination is complete and accurate. Only by accident are good decisions made with bad information.

Material Misinformation

During the planning for a toll road in the western Chicago suburbs, some investors, operating on information that they had gleaned from a "knowledgeable insider," purchased land and built a high-rise hotel adjacent to the planned intersection of the toll road with a major U.S. highway. However, the decision to connect the toll road with the highway was overturned, and the up-scale hotel had no convenient access and therefore, no guests. After several decades of vacancy, it is now a residence for senior citizens. The original investors assumed their information was complete and accurate, and that the "insider" had material information when he, in fact, did not.

Step 2: Review All Key Assumptions

The second step is to review all key assumptions to be used in the due diligence process. Many decisions will involve assumptions. This can be true when a decision must be made before verifiable information is available.

For example, if an organization is planning to install an automatic sprinkler system in a new facility in a new industrial development, one key assumption is the availability of water at a minimum pressure. Another is whether the installation of the automatic sprinkler system will generate a property insurance rate reduction.

Step 3: Identify Any Critical Transition Issues

The third step is to identify any critical transition issues.

For example, if an organization decides to change its insurance carriers or insurance agents/brokers, there will be transition issues in the change because of the need to provide continued claims service, issuance of certificates of insurance, and loss control.

One decision may precipitate many transition issues while another triggers none.

Step 4: Identify Personnel Requirements

Due diligence personnel requirements vary with the nature of the examination. In some due diligence decisions, particularly those that are complex or involve a significant investment, a team conducts the examination. The team includes employees who have expertise in different functional areas. The team approach may avoid the possibilities of overlooking a material issue in an unfamiliar area or not considering a key assumption or potential impact.

If the internal team lacks expertise in a particular area, or wishes to have a second opinion or validation, the risk manager may call upon outside experts. In many applications of due diligence in the risk management arena, the insurance agent or broker, insurance company personnel (e.g., underwriter, claims adjuster, loss control representative, etc.), and other third parties may be valuable additions to the internal due diligence team.

In less complex or financially involved due diligence decisions, the individual approach works well. However, that individual must have expertise in the critical areas or be willing to call upon other internal and external resources, as above, to supplement expertise.

The examiner(s) must allocate adequate time to the due diligence process. This process can take very little time, perhaps only several days, to several weeks or months, depending upon the size and complexity of the tasks.

One general activity of a due diligence team (or individual) is to collect necessary information for the decision-making process. In most organizations, the examiner or team members should request information well in advance of the scheduled time for the due diligence results and decision to allow other personnel and departments sufficient time to respond. Given time for review, any additional information can be requested and available within the decision-making timeline. If the team approach is used or supplemental expertise is needed, each functional area will be assigned specific tasks. Each area will complete a brief, written summary addressing the specific tasks undertaken. These summaries may be shared across the team, or compiled by one central team member. At the conclusion of the examination, the team or examiner will complete a brief overall summary of key due diligence findings. In the end, the examiner has the obligation to carefully read the due diligence material and relevant documents.

The Four Phases of Action

There are four phases of action in due diligence: identification, analysis, reporting, and transition (post-acquisition, post-hire, post-purchase, post-acceptance, etc.).

Identification

The identification phase begins by establishing the goals, assumptions, and facts. The examiner must then gather available information and identify the risks inherent in the proposal. These may be viewed in the traditional manner, focusing on risks that expose the organization to pure loss, or on an enterprise-wide manner, considering strategic, operations, financial, and hazard risks. Any information found that could alter or refute the assumptions must be identified and considered in the decision-making process.

Regardless of the approach, the information gathering and risk identification process uses some or all of the following:

- At least ten identification methods (checklists/survey questionnaire, flowcharts, insurance policy analysis, physical inspection, net income, financial analysis, compliance review, contract identification and analysis, policy and procedures review, loss history review, consultation with experts)

- The four logical classifications of exposures (property, liability, human resources, and net income)

- Six general classes of risk (economic, physical, political, juridical, social, regulatory, and legal)

When appropriate, the risk management department conducts interviews in addition to the more mechanical aspects of collecting information.

Analysis

The analysis phase begins with an overall evaluation of the assembled data. Data, whether financial, pertaining to losses, or historical, must be of quality, be complete, be consistent, be relevant, and have integrity.

Then the team or individual must identify any pending litigation, as well as specific concerns, such as environmental conditions for real estate, past employment for new hires, financial qualifications for new clients or vendors, references, product testing, or the like. The process should also include a review of insurance policies and risk management initiatives.

Reporting

The reporting phase begins with a summary of exposures, key assumptions, statement of material issues and analysis process, and it ends with recommendations, conclusions, or findings. The executive summary is important, as many managers will not read the minutia of a report, perhaps delegating this to a subordinate or analyst, and instead will read only a summary with recommendations.

The report should identify the "worst case" scenario (or scenarios) in any given situation to make estimates of what might possibly happen, as well as incorporating the anticipated "likely" events.

Transition

The last phase of action is the transition phase, which outlines the steps to be taken after the decision is made to go forward with the proposed activity. The specific transition phase actions depend upon the activities to be undertaken. The transition can include integrating assets or human resources into the organization or eliminating assets or human resources in a divestiture or consolidating merger. Also, an organization should expect a number of administrative issues, ranging from the relatively mundane (e.g., changing addresses, telephone numbers, obtaining new certificates of insurance, etc.,) to the traumatic (e.g., terminating employees, shuttering facilities, and severing long-standing relationships).

Specific Due Diligence Applications and Associated Activities

As management assigns the necessary action items, other personnel who are tasked with performing specific activities may call upon the risk management team for assistance in the following areas:

Purchasing new assets, particularly real estate

1. Identifying environmental concerns

2. Obtaining appropriate valuations

Bringing a new product or service on line

1. Verifying advertising and marketing issues

2. Obtaining testing opinions for safety, reliability, and warranty agreements

Entering into a new joint venture or contract

1. Verifying credentials of a venture partner or contracting party

2. Verifying the financial status of a venture partner or contracting party.

Entering into a relationship with a new customer, supplier, or vendor

1. Verifying the credentials of the customer, supplier, or vendor

2. Verifying the financial status of the customer, supplier, and vendor

Hiring a consultant, agent, or third-party administrator (TPA) for risk management, insurance, claims, or safety

1. Verifying credentials, education, training

2. Verifying capabilities

3. Verifying references

Mergers and Acquisitions (including Divestitures)

The basic purpose of M&A due diligence is not significantly different from that of "ordinary" acquisitions or divestures of assets or personnel. However, because the financial stakes are greater, the due diligence team must pay more attention to the process of identifying and analyzing all the potential liabilities and risk management strategies necessary to help the involved parties understand and manage the business and financial impacts of risk.

Purchasing a building or constructing a new facility or hiring a new manager is an important decision, but the immediate scope of most of these transactions is relatively limited. In the merger and acquisition world, potential liabilities and issues discovered through due diligence are more likely to significantly impact the terms of the deal (e.g., price, indemnification for past liabilities (legacy), the maintenance of past activities, and personnel of the acquired or merged organization).

Some common examples of information that may affect the terms of the deal follow:

- Adjustment of balance sheet asset or liability values (e.g., an overstated or understated building value)

- Adjustment of liability values for overstated or understated values of claims reserves

- Adjustment of historic cost of risk to future cost of risk of new owners

- Severance terms of a new manager, employee, vendor, or customer

Risk Manager Plays a Key Role

The risk manager always should play a key role in the merger and acquisition process, beyond the simple task of managing the risk. Attorneys who structure merger and acquisition deals are not always familiar with risk-related language in insurance contracts and other agreements. While insurance contracts are clearly within the scope of contract law, a subject addressed in all law school curricula, many practicing attorneys admit that the time spent on the mysterious language of insurance, as practiced by insurance professionals, is only a tiny fraction of the entire contract law curriculum.

Similarly, the merger and acquisition team, generally composed of a number of financial experts, rarely have an understanding of how insurance protects, or does not protect, the organization from liabilities. The comment, "Well, it's insured, isn't it?" may bring comfort to financial wizards, but risk managers and insurance professionals understand that recovery from loss depends upon far more than insurance.

Also, the accounting and financial experts who create financial reports, pro forma modeling, and filings rarely have much experience in risk management and insurance issues.

M&A Due Diligence – A Multi-Disciplinary Approach

In the earlier discussion, we addressed the concept of a due diligence team with various functional areas as needed. For the ordinary transactions, the functional areas are largely those common to the organization. In a merger or acquisition, however, the M&A due diligence team takes on a more complex nature.

By custom and practice, the merger and acquisition team refers to the group of legal professionals (many legal professionals) and other specialized professionals whose collective responsibility is to ensure and complete a comprehensive due diligence investigation, one that goes well beyond the scope of traditional risk management and may even test the boundaries of enterprise-wide risk management.

An attorney usually heads the team, as the legal aspects of a merger or acquisition often control nearly every activity. Additional attorneys (with specialized expertise in the field of mergers and acquisitions, a particularly daunting field when publicly owned entities are involved), may be needed to keep the transaction in compliance with the vagaries of securities laws and reporting.

The functional areas of a due diligence team in a merger or acquisition may include:

- Financial reporting and accounting

- Taxation

- Management information systems or information technology

- Human resources

- Environmental

- Actuarial

- Operational

- Sales and marketing

Ideally, a risk management professional will also be a part of the team to assist in identifying, analyzing, and measuring the financial and operational impact of risk management issues and activities, as well as analyzing any risk management information systems (RMIS).

Basic Types of Deal Structures

Mergers and acquisitions are not a new phenomenon. Since the Civil War, observers have seen at least five major spikes in mergers and acquisitions.

The basic types of deal structures, entity deals and asset deals, are not indicative of all deal structures, but present the basic extremes. Most deals fall somewhere in between.

Entity Deal – "the Whole Enchilada"

In the classic entity deal, the buyer purchases the entire entity, acquiring all the assets and all the liabilities. Typically, the acquiring entity handles this by purchasing a controlling interest in the outstanding shares of stock of a corporation (or other measurement of ownership interest an entity other than a corporation).

In an early (1866) example of an acquisition, Cornelius Vanderbilt wished to purchase controlling interest in Michigan Southern Railroad, but he soon learned that Erie Railroad was also attempting to purchase Michigan Southern. Vanderbilt took a new tack: if he could control Erie, he reasoned, he would control Michigan Southern, as well as eliminate a potential competitor in his desire to connect his steamship and railroad lines, headed by the New York Central Railroad, to the growing industrial center in Chicago.

This indirect acquisition (there were very few federal restraints on such actions at this time) would have allowed Vanderbilt to acquire the entire railroad assets and liabilities, except for the efforts of three large Erie stockholders who had different ideas. They launched an effective initiative to thwart Vanderbilt with a process now known as "greenmail." (Greenmailing is the practice of purchasing enough shares in a firm to threaten a takeover and thereby forcing the target firm to buy these shares back at a premium in order to suspend the takeover.)

Analyzing Liabilities from Past Losses

Since, along with the purchased assets, the acquiring organization (the buyer) now owns all the liabilities, the buyer is responsible for all future and current liabilities, including financial responsibilities for past losses that have not been closed.

Moving from the extreme position of acquiring all the assets and liabilities, the buyer might insist on indemnification for some or all of the past liabilities (or even for future liabilities arising out of activities conducted prior to the acquisition). These liabilities and their indemnification must be detailed in the deal structure and legal agreements.

As in any scenario regarding indemnification, the due diligence team must consider some issues:

1. Does the seller have the financial capacity to indemnify the buyer? Should funds be reserved from the purchase payment in an escrow or trust account to satisfy any indemnification, and if so, for how long?

2. What is the process of indemnification? Is there a notice of indemnification made to the seller? Is there a billing and collection process?

3. Are the legal documents sufficiently detailed to facilitate such indemnification? What are the legal options available to the buyer when the seller refuses or delays in providing indemnification?

The Asset Deal

The other extreme is an asset deal. In an asset deal, the buyer purchases the assets and/or liabilities as if ordering ala carte from a menu (tuna salad with mayo on toast, hold the tuna and mayo). The seller offers specific assets and liabilities, not the entire entity. For example, the buyer may acquire any combination of the following:

Assets	Liabilities
<u>All</u> <u>All except</u> those listed on an attached schedule <u>Only</u> those listed on attached schedule <u>None</u>	<u>All</u> <u>All except</u> those listed on attached schedule <u>Only</u> those listed on attached schedule <u>None</u>

In a more complex organization, the buyer might purchase all of the organization except a certain division, location, or product line.

Thus, the buyer may purchase all the assets but no liabilities, or all the assets except certain specified assets and only the liabilities associated with the acquired assets.

For example, if an organization had two divisions, farm machinery and football helmets, the buyer could purchase all the assets of the organization, including production equipment associated with football helmets, and the liabilities associated with the farm machinery division, but none of the liabilities associated with the football helmet division.

Risk Managing the Deal

The flexible nature of the deal structure in a merger or acquisition requires thoughtful consideration in the application of M&A due diligence. The risk manager must engage with the due diligence team for the answers to many questions, some of which might try the patience of the "masters of the universe" (a common phrase used to describe M&A experts), but which are critical to the risk manager's objectives.

To effectively coordinate insurance and risk management programs and procedures, the risk manager must know if the transaction is an entity deal or an asset deal. If the organization chooses not to purchase a portion of the liabilities, the team must recognize and account for those outstanding liabilities. If assets are involved, the risk manager must adjust the program to include them.

The risk manager must know and understand the organization's business purpose in doing the deal. If the purpose is to acquire or divest a product line, or to consolidate the industry, the risk manager must adjust the program, considering the impact of each facet, including Directors and Officers liability coverage.

If the M&A team has any uncertainty regarding expectations of the risk management team, the risk manager may need to explain the expected scope and reasoning of the risk management aspects of due diligence. Furthermore, the risk manager must understand any M&A issues related to risk management.

Lastly, in an ideal situation, the risk manager will obtain a copy of the acquisition (or merger or divestiture) documents, such as the letter of intent and the acquisition agreement. In reality, the risk manager will rarely be given that information because of the extreme confidentiality issues. However, the risk manager should receive, at the very least, sections of the acquisition agreement that pertain to risk management, such as any section referring to insurance and retention programs, outstanding liabilities, and indemnification agreements. The objective of this review is to make sure the risk manager's findings from the due diligence process are consistent with the legal documents. Some pertinent questions are as follows:

1. Are all of the assets properly valued, identified, and defined in the acquisition agreements? Should any assets be added to or removed from the schedule?

2. Are all of the liabilities properly valued, identified, and addressed?

3. Are any assets or liabilities to be acquired (or not acquired) difficult or impossible to separate from the other types of assets or liabilities?

4. How are intellectual properties addressed?

Information Gathering and Risk Identification

Risk management information gathering for M&A due diligence follows the same basic format as the risk and exposure identification process used in other situations. The tools for identification are essentially the same, subject to the natural constraints raised by the confidentiality and secrecy that often surrounds M&A activity. For example, the risk manager will not be able to conduct a physical inspection of properties of a target firm unless the M&A activity is public and friendly. Gathering such information for an unfriendly or non-disclosed M&A attempt would likely be considered industrial espionage.

The broad categories of information include company, financial, and insurance and risk management information.

Company Information

Some company and financial information will be available publicly (e.g., annual reports, web sites, periodicals and other publications, etc.) particularly when the organization is a publicly owned company. However presented, any financial information needs to be that controlled by generally accepted accounting principles, and not the "real" numbers used by the organization in its daily business operations.

If possible, the risk manager must gain an understanding past and current investment and capital outlay programs, particularly if the organization to be acquired has been involved in joint ventures. An investigation of capital outlay programs and joint venture relationships might uncover asbestos abatement projects, removal of underground storage tanks and other environmental impairment issues, lead paint removal, or the addition of new facilities or closing of existing facilities.

Insurance and Risk Management Information

In order to make a thorough due diligence investigation, the risk manager must examine the insurance and risk management aspects of any merger, acquisition, or divestiture.

The risk manager must ascertain if the acquired organization has a formal risk management <u>department</u>, and if so, where it is located and how it is staffed. Related to that, the risk manager must know if risk management decisions are decentralized (distributed to divisions or subsidiaries) or centralized. If there is no formal risk management department, the risk manager must identify the person responsible for insurance and risk management.

Similarly, the risk manager must determine whether the organization to be acquired has a formal risk management policy, including a <u>policy</u> statement and procedures manual. If so, the risk manager should (whenever possible) review any manuals and statements, including the details of any safety program, employee health and well-being program, the crisis management program, the crisis management communication program, and disaster recovery plans and activities.

The key areas of <u>insurance exposure </u>for examination will differ by organization, but the common areas are property, surety bonds, automobile, products liability and general liability, environmental liability, workers compensation, employment related, any claims-made policies or "tail coverages" included in other liability coverages, such as professional or directors and officers. The due diligence team will be seeking information about coverage and/or retentions in place, as well as loss histories and outstanding claims.

The risk manager must also know how all insurance policies and records, loss control inspection documents and recommendations, and claims records are maintained. Related to claims, the risk manager must establish whether the reserves are current, their valuations appropriate (including IBNR), and the availability of any actuarial forecasts.

The need for insurance and risk management information and the availability of the information will differ according to the activity. A merger or acquisition will bring together two different insurance and risk management programs, as well as two different sets of existing exposures, personnel, suppliers, vendors, and customers. A merger or acquisition will bring new exposures into the existing insurance and risk management program of the successor organization. Similarly, the divestiture of a division, location, product, supplier, vendor, customer, or even personnel will alter the insurance and risk management program of the divesting organization.

Furthermore, since the merger or acquisition creates a new mix of partners, contracts, customers, suppliers, vendors, and personnel, the credentials, capabilities, financial capacity, and references of the newcomers to the successor organization must be reviewed. Failure to vet the newcomers brought into the organization by merger or acquisition can be construed as negligence as much as if the organization sought out the newcomers.

Similarly, the risk manager must review the details of any joint ventures to which the merged or acquired organization was a party, as well as the insurance and risk management program that provided the coverage for those joint ventures.

Special exposures or situations, such as environmental exposure recommendations, OSHA citations and requirements, and citations and actions of the EPA, EEOC, ADA, or other governmental regulatory agencies must be examined and evaluated.

Lastly, the due diligence team must examine the total cost of risk report for the merged or acquired organization. If the organization does not have a total cost of risk report, the team must determine whether developing such a report would be of value to the successor organization.

In that same vein, the risk manager will assemble and review loss runs by lines of coverage. The analysis of loss runs will capture the loss history in total, including information on open claims and claims in litigation. In addition, the loss information should include an actuarial review of the adequacy of current reserves and an estimate of IBNR claims, along with loss trending and indexing to exposures, and measuring the potential for adverse development.

When the risk management and insurance program includes retention, an evaluation of retained losses must be performed, with current and prior levels of retention. If any insurance or risk management program has been terminated, the disposition of open losses under that program must be addressed. This may involve loss portfolio transfers, or selling off the open liabilities to an insurance carrier, or a financial reinsurance product.

Property exposures must be identified and reviewed, with special attention to HPR (highly protected risk) status and standards of the acquired property. Also, attention must be focused on prior inspections to identify direct physical damage and time element exposures, as well as maintenance records to support equipment breakdown (boiler and machinery) exposures. In addition to the organization's property, the risk manager must attempt to identify and quantify contingent exposures created by off-site power issues or key customers or suppliers that might give rise to direct property damage or indirect property damage.

Since many risk management programs have a significant insurance component, the risk manager should conduct a detailed insurance coverage review. This review should address the scope of coverage, insurance carrier contracts, specific property and liability issues, and, if a captive insurance company is present, a detailed report on the operations and financial state of the captive.

The risk manager can easily determine the scope of coverage by creating a comprehensive schedule of insurance coverage, defining each area by line of coverage, type of policy (e.g., occurrence, claims-made), exclusions and restrictions, limits of liability, terms and dates, premiums, policy numbers and insurance carriers, and agents/brokers placing the coverage. Any gaps in coverage, either because of an excluded peril, restricted property or activity, conscious decision to not purchase coverage, or an inconsistency between primary and excess policies should be clearly stated.

Insurance carrier contracts include the obvious insurance policies, but also the peripheral contracts that support the insurance policies. These agreements are commonly found in conjunction with loss-sensitive plans like retrospectively rated plans, self-insured plans, and large deductible plans, and generally involve the use of security or collateral in the form of collateral trusts, letters of credit, and escrow accounts to the insurance carrier that advances funds or evidences of coverage on behalf of the organization.

The risk manager must also consider the projection of claims costs for any losses assumed in the acquisition or merger, premium calculations, including short-rate calculations, cash flow analysis for loss sensitive plans, increasing (or decreasing) collateral, service costs, and transfer costs.

Summary Report to Management

At the conclusion of the M&A due diligence examination, the due diligence team must prepare and present a report to management.

The management report must state its purpose, the scope of the examination, and the assumptions and data used in the analysis.

Some aspects of the analysis are <u>qualitative</u> in nature, best described in words rather than numbers. Some examples of qualitative analysis subjects are:

- Insurance carrier ratings (e.g., A.M. Best financial ratings, Standard and Poors, Duff & Phelps, etc.)

- Existing insurance carrier insolvencies affecting any outstanding claims

- Safety engineering recommendations that are already funded and under way

- Any discontinued products, services, locations, or activities

- Successor liabilities from previous acquisitions or consolidations

- Contractual obligations, particularly those that involve indemnification or a contractual transfer of risk financing

- The need for environmental impact studies, appraisals and estimates

- Expert and professional reports

- Interviews with key personnel

- References

Other aspects of the analysis are <u>quantitative</u> in nature, expressed in numbers. An example would be any risk financing arrangement that has significant elements of loss sensitivity (e.g., retrospectively rated programs, deductible programs, self-insured retentions, captives, collateral requirements, cash flow funding mechanisms, and experiences modifiers).

Post-Merger/Acquisition Activities

The previous activities should be performed, to the extent possible, prior to the merger or acquisition (or divestiture). The exact activities to be performed after the change depend upon the nature of the merger, acquisition, or divestiture. In general, the following actions should be considered, and, if appropriate, undertaken.

The risk manager should arrange to visit as many of the new locations as possible, since a personal inspection is one of the best ways to identify many exposures, and is similarly one of the best ways to begin to build bridges between personnel.

Furthermore, the risk manager should conduct a review (or interview) of the acquired organization's risk management department and its personnel.

In the event of a merger or acquisition, the risk manager should obtain the original insurance policies. Since the "other" organization's exposures have now become part of the successor organization, the successor organization can have the original insurance coverages assigned to it as the new, and surviving, entity. As such, the successor organization needs the original policies (as it will soon become the assignee of those contracts, upon acceptance by the insurance carrier).

For assimilating existing exposures into a comprehensive program, the risk manager should begin with a schedule or spreadsheet of insurance policies (which may be a part of the prior due diligence report), complete with their important terms and conditions, such as limits, exclusions, and premiums. Upon examining, the risk manager may even conclude that the acquired program is superior to the existing program (or vice versa).

Either way, when the new exposures come into the organization, the risk manager must project expected incidents and claims as well as the total cost of risk for the new exposures and consider how the new exposures will affect the existing insurance and risk management program. As these effects (if any) become clear, the risk manager must decide whether to consolidate the two insurance programs.

Thus, the risk manager must decide how to procure insurance brokerage services for the new organization. In some instances, the risk manager might determine that maintaining separate insurance and risk management programs with both sets of original agents/brokers makes sense; in other cases, the risk manager must decide which of several agents/brokers will continue with the new organization.

Related to that is the issue of fee versus commission. If the risk manager chooses to maintain two (or more) insurance brokers and one is a commission broker and one a fee broker, the risk manager must decide how broker compensation should be provided.

As part of this process, the risk manager should also obtain a summary of loss information (usually a part of the due diligence reports) that identifies and examines open claims, litigation, unusual reserves. It is important to detect any activities that may affect the valuation of the open claims, such as reservation of rights letters, waivers of subrogation (the rights to recover), and potential salvage.

With respect to property, the risk manager must see that assets are properly valued and addressed appropriately in the successor insurance and risk management program.

The risk manager must decide whether to consolidate the insurance programs into a master program (one extreme) or to maintain separate programs for the "other" organization and the successor information (the other extreme). (These are the extremes; in some cases, the risk manager may decide to maintain separate programs except for specific exposures, such as executive risk, employment practices, or the like.)

The risk manager must also begin to assess the impact of the new exposures on the successor organization's insurance and risk management program, as well as adjust property limits and liability aggregate limits levels to accommodate the increase in exposures.

In other cases, such as integrating an organization that has a three-line retrospectively rated workers compensation, automobile, and general liability plan with an organization that has only a self-insured workers compensation plan, the organization must change the fundamental characteristics of one of the programs.

Even if the programs are not as complex, the risk manager will also have to consider the effect of the merger or acquisition on experience modifications, particularly that for workers' compensation. The NCCI rules are specific as to combinability, and the risk manager must determine if the organizations' respective experience will be combined or if it can be maintained separately.

The risk manager must pay particular attention to any claims-made policies to examine whether to elect the "tail coverage" option when and if those policies are cancelled, and, if not, how any claims that have occurred but cannot be reported under claims-made policies will be funded.

Related to that issue is the question of the ultimate cost of known claims and the ultimate cost of incurred but not reported (IBNR) claims. The risk manager must consider if such claims should be assumed by the organization or financed externally through a loss portfolio transfer or finite risk contract.

What if the Risk Management Department is Redundant?

When the organization that is the successful target of a merger or acquisition and the organization it joins both have risk management programs and/or risk management departments, the acquiring organization must decide how to integrate the two programs and/or departments. Are two heads better than one? The old folk wisdom may not be applicable in risk management. Which risk manger or risk management department stays and which goes? What staff stays or goes? These are not always easy choices.

In one merger scenario between two very large and complex organizations, each of the organizations had a very complex and involved insurance and risk management program with multiple insurance brokers and insurance carriers and a risk management department staffed with talented personnel. In the post-merger integration, the new organization decided to maintain separate insurance plans (each managed by the original brokers and using the same insurance carriers) for most of the insurance program, except for the consolidation of executive risk coverages.

Most of the risk management personnel were maintained in a decentralized structure to accommodate the geographic spread of the organization, but of the two very capable and competent risk managers, only one survived. The new organization believed this separation preserved options, presented healthy competition between insurance carriers and brokers, and maintained the necessary level of risk management support, but with only one risk manager to direct the entire operation.

In some cases, the organization will decide to consolidate programs and departments, with a resulting elimination of duplications of staff, insurance carriers, and insurance programs.

With the new exposures, the risk manager, working with the chief financial officer, must consider how the addition of the "other" company will affect cash inflows and outflows.

Lastly, the risk manager must determine if any other administrative costs from operating the "other" insurance and risk management program can be eliminated, and if not, the impact of those additional costs on the successor program.

Other Post-Merger Issues

As discussed in earlier chapters, the risk management department does not exist in its own world, but rather is part of the corporate structure. The risk manager may be responsible for coordinating internal procedures between the "other" organization and the successor. Those risk management decisions affect all other parts of the organization, and the decisions of any other part of the organization affects risk management. Consequently, the risk manager must consider the after-merger/acquisition impact on other functions within the organization, particularly human resources, the "other" risk management department, and all other functions in the "other" organization.

The risk manager must attend to some specific administrative issues. Some of these arise out of features of the insurance program; others arise out of regulatory concerns. Specific attention must be paid to certificates of insurance and other proof or documentation of coverage. Workers' compensation issues arise because of state filings, self-insurance plans and required bonds (to guarantee payment to claimants), and claims administration services.

The risk manager must work with other functional areas to be sure that the "other" organization's obligations under OSHA, ADA, "right-to-know" statutes, and other federal, state, and local regulations are being satisfied.

One particularly sensitive issue is claims procedures. It is a commonly observed phenomenon that claims tend to increase when the "other" organization is merged or acquired. Employees seem to assume there will be lay-offs, and some start to believe workers' compensation benefits are always preferable to unemployment benefits. Thus, the risk manager must be diligent, taking extreme care in disseminating information (where possible) on the lay-off process while monitoring claims to prevent non-meritorious claims. Consolidation of the claims processing is as important as the consolidation of any insurance coverage providing benefits for claims.

Lastly, the risk manager must consider the consolidation of third-party vendors and suppliers. Generally, the co-ordination and consolidation of claims services suggest that the consolidation of third-party claims administrators also would be warranted, but sometimes this consolidation is not possible because of geographic or regulatory constraints. When consolidation is not possible, an alignment of claims philosophy becomes critical.

Similarly, it is generally advisable to consolidate all consultants, whether claims, safety, environmental, or risk management.

Summary

Whether the organization implements due diligence exercises to explore changes to current activities or to investigate the ramifications of a merger, acquisition, or divestiture, the risk manager's role in the process becomes critical to the success of the venture, and possibly to the ongoing life of the organization.

Chapter 24

Enterprise Risk Management

Introduction

Plus ça change, plus c'est la même chose.

(French saying, meaning: The more things change, the more they stay the same.)

Risk management does not operate in a static environment – change occurs constantly.

Some of the change is external in origin, occurring outside the organization, and forces the organization to react. Examples include the rapidly increasing rate of globalization of economies, the ebb and flow of government regulation, government policies, and economic and monetary management measures, the changing nature of the organization's customers, suppliers, and vendors, and even changes in insurance, carriers, policy forms, pricing, and market availability.

Other change is internal in origin, occurring within the organization, and forces the organization to react. At one level of complexity, the organization may undertake acquisitions, mergers, and divestitures or develop new and untested product lines. At another level of complexity, the organization must react to actions meant to control risk (the program reduces risk of one type, but may create a new risk of a different type). For example, the risk manager implements a new safety program. The safety program reduces injuries but also reduces productivity. At another level, it might be something as simple (or as obvious) as the fact that an organization's workforce is constantly changing, one part aging, and another part coming in new and inexperienced.

The understanding of risk is also changing. Not many years ago, the traditional concept of "risk" focused on pure risk only, the chances of loss or no loss and did not encompass the other broader concepts discussed in other chapters. The traditional idea of "risk management" meant focusing on treating insurable risks, and was little more than "insurance management." Over the years, however, the definition has changed both subtly and dramatically to include "enterprise risk management."

Similarly, the role of the risk manager has changed from being little more than the purchaser and manager of insurance policies, taking what the insurance market offered (and complaining about it), to becoming a recognized member of the organization's management team, using time-tested financial management concepts to address risk.

During this time of change, one fact has become increasingly clear: that a fragmented risk treatment approach (one that treats each risk or exposure to loss separately) is less effective than a comprehensive risk treatment approach that does not create or tolerate redundancies in effort and expense.

To understand the changing view of risk, and role of the risk manager, we examine the metamorphosis of risk management over the years.

History

Historically, there was no identifiable discipline of risk management. An organization's risks were handled by insurance, and losses that were not insured were paid by the organization as best as could be managed. Loss control focused on insurable risks from the viewpoint of protecting the insurance carrier, not the insured organization. Similarly, claims management focused on minimizing the expense to the insurance carrier, since insurance was the primary means of handling risk.

The discipline of non-traditional risk management began in the early 1960s, when two professors of finance laid the groundwork for enterprise risk management by moving beyond basic insurance management. They recognized that an organization could purchase insurance or it could systematically "self-insure" its own risk, that the organization could focus loss control efforts and manage claims to minimize the expenses of its own risk.

However, the early focus of traditional risk management was still aimed at what were considered to be insurable risks. Risks were identified and evaluated. Loss control was applied to prevent as many losses as possible, and insurance and other risk transfer methods were applied to address the losses that were not prevented. Claims analysis was used to identify problem areas that could be treated with control or more insurance or risk transfer.

In this atmosphere, the risk management process became an extension of the general management process: identifying issues, identifying possible solutions, evaluating solutions, choosing the solution that promises the optimal result, and monitoring the solution, modifying it if necessary. The risk management methods or techniques were five: avoidance, control, insurance transfers, non-insurance contractual transfers, and retention through well-defined insurance policies, generally retrospectively rated plans. Insurance was considered to be a transfer of risk from the organization to the insurance carrier.

Beginning in the mid 1970s and early 1980s, widespread social unrest and the natural business cycles of the insurance industry suffered several serious glitches or hiccups. Insurance carriers retreated from lines of insurance in a magnitude never seen before. Property underwriters practiced "redlining," or wholesale withdrawal of availability of property insurance on a geographic basis. The practice was called "redlining" because of the red lines drawn on maps around areas that could not be insured. Manufacturers were faced with very expensive premiums for products liability insurance, if such coverage was even available. Consequently, many manufacturers simply stopped producing many important products while others raised the price of their products to cover the additional costs of insurance.

This market failure or dislocation led to governmental action and the creation of social insurance mechanisms and legislation like the Risk Retention Act of 1981. These measures were enacted as a means of assisting insureds in finding an affordable alternative to traditional insurance when the voluntary insurance market would not respond.

Legislation like the Risk Retention Act (RRA) facilitated the actions of smaller organizations to create an insurance mechanism that replaced the traditional insurance market. Social insurance programs such as the Fair Access to Insurance Requirements (FAIR) Plan and the National Flood Insurance Program solved the market problems for those organizations that could not find property insurance in urban areas or in areas subject to flooding. While these solutions closely resembled traditional insurance, the means by which the funds were collected to pay for losses quickly led to the recognition that alternative risk financing was possible (even when the insurance market offered coverage) to minimize the premium outlay.

Prior to this time, the concept of business continuity meant purchasing business interruption coverage for insurable property perils. However, when the product liability insurance market collapsed, with the resulting withdrawal of many products deemed to be high hazard (such as football helmets, where the number of manufacturers dwindled from two dozen to two), the concept of business continuity took on a new meaning. Encouraged by the RRA, the new identity in risk management began to see that alternative risk financing techniques, such as captive insurance companies and risk retention groups, might keep such products in the market, without being subject to the regular impulses of the insurance marketplace.

As these ideas took hold, the traditional insurance marketplace recovered from its periodic cycle and again solicited the lines of coverage it had just recently rejected, but many organizations refused to climb back onto the premium/availability roller coaster. Experts have estimated that 33% of the traditional insurance premium that left the traditional market in the 1960s and 1970s never returned.

At the same time, the concept of the total cost of risk developed. As organizations began to retain more of their own risk through alternative risk financing, the organizations began to recognize that insurance premiums and retained losses were not overhead items, but specific costs associated with their operations, and could be readily included in the pricing of their goods and services, just as raw materials, research and development, and labor were included. Risk managers applied the techniques used by cost accountants to capture the numbers of insurance premiums, retained losses and expenses, and administrative costs of various types and allocate them to specific activities. Thus, the total cost of risk concept grew in value and usage.

Along with these dramatic changes, insurance and risk management disciplines became the focus of education and communication. Interest in insurance and risk management as major courses in universities grew, and insurance professional societies expanded their educational endeavors to include the discipline of risk management.

In the late 1970s and early 1980s, another market disruption occurred. Products liability insurance availability issues returned, along with medical malpractice liability issues. Again, those organizations whose operations were disrupted turned to new alternative risk financing techniques and another substantial portion of the traditional insurance premium volume left the insurance industry, never to return.

At the same time, several other new ideas began to emerge. The exponential growth of technology, including access to high-powered computers by even the smallest organizations (and individuals) and the growth of the Internet revolutionized the insurance and risk management fields. The use of technology aided the development of indexing of risk, or measuring risk against other variables. Lastly, financial managers and risk managers began to realize that risks could be managed strategically, just as an organization strategically plans its growth and development, new products and territories, new marketing and sales approaches, and new clients and supply chains.

From this viewpoint of strategy, it was an easy step to the concept of viewing risks on an enterprise-wide basis.

Risk management has taken on a higher profile within organizations. Executive management and boards of directors are acquiring a deeper understanding of how risk is managed, and how to manage risk to create the greatest reward for their shareholders.

The future of risk management appears to be the holistic approach. The effective risk manager of the future will recognize and adapt to new forms of risk, new methods of risk control and risk financing, new market trends, and other changes in the risk management environment. The old practice of simply reacting to a change in risk with control methods, financing, insurance markets, and environments will be replaced by proactive risk management, managing what does not exist today by methodologies not yet created to solve problems that have not yet occurred.

The Concept

During the late 1980s, when managers began to discuss the concept of enterprise risk management, the innovative thought was to apply risk management principles across the organization or "enterprise" rather than using them as merely a function of a purchasing department, a finance office, or perhaps a risk management department.

As discussion and thought continued, the idea that any risk, insurable or not, had to be treated in a systematic manner. Simply shrugging the shoulders and saying, "That loss wasn't covered; how will we pay for it?" did not solve the problem. At the same time, organizations began to recognize that only a fraction of the identified risks were even insurable. Compliance risks associated with Sarbanes-Oxley became a concern for public and private businesses alike.

Another concept under discussion was the relationship between an organization's risk profile and the ways various risks impact the organization's earnings and stakeholder value. Risk managers began to realize how the long-accepted financial relationship between reward and risk could be applied to risk management decisions. Earnings and value (the reward) could be positively impacted with higher levels of business risk while higher levels of pure risk could negatively impact earnings and value, but risk managers could effectively control the level of pure risk and add to the earnings and value.

Also during the 1980s, the insurance industry underwent a transformation that aided the growth of enterprise risk management. As insurance carriers transitioned to financial services companies with multiple product lines not limited to insurance products, and began seeking executive management not from insurance ranks, but from investment banks, there began an era of greater emphasis on the management of cash flow to increase (or replace) underwriting profit, and cash flow underwriting became essential.

Last, risk managers, aided by financial managers, started to view risk as not being differentiated, thus breaking out of the traditional risk management confines of pure risk and insurable risk, and incorporating speculative risk into new risk management treatments. Out of this came the realization that the pure risk insured by an organization becomes the speculative risk of the insurance carrier. Risk really is risk, regardless of its type, and risk can be treated.

Risk managers and financial managers soon recognized that the approach of managing risks separately is not as efficient and effective as managing risks together, regardless of the type of risk. The nature of risks' impact on the organization changes when two or more disparate risks are managed from the same perspective or platform.

With a coordinated treatment, several elements change. There should be:

- An increase in cost predictability

- Decreased risk-based expenses

- A realignment of risk financing involving a multi-risk, integrated program to eliminate coverage redundancies

- An improvement in financial security as a result of partnering with fewer insurers

- The creation of detailed awareness of risk scenarios and their potential impacts

- Reduced cash flow/earnings volatility

- Improved stock performance (for publicly traded companies)

- Reduced capital costs

- An increase in stockholder and stakeholder confidence that risks are understood and managed

Perhaps most importantly, there should be a comprehensive understanding of all risks, permitting limited corporate resources to be allocated for optimal outcomes.

Thus, the concept of enterprise-wide risk management was borne.

For purposes of this book, we define "enterprise-wide risk management" as a framework for handling all of the risks facing an organization, whether insurable or not. In an enterprise-wide risk management structure, the pure risks and speculative risks and the insurable risks and non-insurable risks are managed from the same perspective or platform.

Enterprise-wide risk management is not, however, a new type of risk management. It is simply a shift in approach that expands the range of tools and methodologies used to identify, analyze, and treat risks, while considering the relationship of risk profile and its impact on earnings and value.

Objectives of Enterprise-Wide Risk Management

While organizations incorporating an enterprise-wide risk management philosophy will have different goals and objectives, most organizations share five common or general goals:

Compliance

Compliance is the process of reacting to external corporate governance guidelines that concern risk identification, disclosure, management, and monitoring. For example, certain provisions of Sarbanes-Oxley and the Securities and Exchange Commission regulations address risk identification, disclosure, management, and monitoring.

Defense

Defense is the anticipation of problems before they threaten the organization's strategic objectives. Sometimes this is referred to as avoiding the land mines, some obvious and others completely hidden.

Coordination/Integration

Coordination and integration involves breaking down internal barriers by coordinating various pockets of risk management activity for the sake of efficiency and effectiveness. For example, if an organization suffers a breach in its customer database, it may suffer a loss of reputation and be the subject of litigation. Through coordination and integration, the organization would combine the traditional functional area responses of increased security, legal action, marketing, and public relations into a single response.

Exploiting Opportunities

Exploiting opportunities means understanding how risks interact across the enterprise and taking advantage of natural opportunities that arise.

Creating Value

The goal of creating value is to increase the net worth (or excess of revenues over expenses for non-taxable entities) and the value of the organization for its shareholders and stakeholders.

What makes an organization's enterprise-wide risk management program unique from this standpoint is the relative priority the company gives to each of these objectives.

The Scope of an Enterprise-Wide Risk Management Program

Since enterprise-wide risk management focuses on all risks that impact the organization, it becomes awkward to discuss these risks without a simplifying framework. To aid in the identification and analysis, the risks can be grouped into four broad categories: strategic, financial, operational, and hazard.

Strategic Risks

Strategic risks are those risks that originate with the decisions coming out of the executive boardroom. These risks are associated with identifying customer demands, industry changes, competitive pressures, merger and acquisition integration, research and development, intellectual capital, marketing, and board composition.

Financial Risks

Financial risks are those risks that originate with the decisions coming out of the finance department of an organization. These are closely associated with interest rates, investments, credit, liquidity, asset market value, equity and commodity market risks, receivables, currency and foreign exchange, and cash flow.

Operational Risks

Operational risks are those whose origins are centered in the principle operations of the organization, the day-to-day affairs. These are associated with regulations and the regulatory environment, community relationships, supply chain, quality control, information systems, accounting controls, and talent management.

Hazard Risks

Hazard risks are those commonly addressed in traditional risk management programs. Typically, these take the form of legal liability, property damage, and natural catastrophes, and arise out of contracts, natural events, vendor and supplier relationships, litigation, public access and interaction, products and services, property, and employees.

Given the broad scope of enterprise-wide risk management, enterprise-wide risk management influences a number of management processes within the organization. For example, enterprise-wide risk management should influence strategic planning, internal audit, capital management, asset allocation, risk financing, merger and acquisition activities, financial and risk modeling, and performance management.

In establishing the scope of the enterprise-wide risk management program, managers need to make certain that the scope of risks and the scope of management processes are aligned and that they are likely to help the company reach the objectives set forth for enterprise-wide risk management.

Who Is Responsible for Enterprise-Wide Risk Management?

In the traditional risk management scenario, the risk manager or risk management department generally reports to a boardroom level executive position, sometimes the chief financial officer, sometimes general counsel, sometimes operations. In the enterprise-wide risk management scenario, risk is risk and its treatment cuts across traditional functional lines on an organization chart. However, it is difficult for the risk manager to cut across those lines because of organizational culture, status, access, and tradition. Consequently, some organizations have made use of the concept of the Chief Risk Officer, a boardroom level position that overcomes the barriers created by culture, status, access, and tradition.

Large financial institutions, particularly banks, originally embraced the Chief Risk Officer concept. Long before enterprise-wide risk management became popular, many large banks understood the enterprise-wide benefits of an enterprise-wide approach to managing risk, especially operational risk.

Other organizations use a team approach, or the enterprise-wide risk management policy committee, as an alternative to the Chief Risk Officer position. The advantage of the team approach is that it engages personnel with various disciplines and high-level thinking skills, and serves as an integrating mechanism within the organization by nature of its cross-functional structure.

Regardless of the approach, the function of the Chief Risk Officer is the focal point of enterprise-wide risk management activities. Those activities or functions include direct activities such as purchasing the proper insurance coverage, executing financial derivatives trades, and buying and selling options, as well as establishing and maintaining a comprehensive and integrated risk management plan, and supportive activities such as coordination of risk treatment options, technical resources, risk assessment capabilities, risk audits, risk modeling, and risk monitoring and reporting.

Goals and Required Skills

The goal of the Chief Risk Officer function is to support the efforts to protect and enhance shareholder (or stakeholder) value as efficiently and effectively as possible, using the enterprise-wide risk management philosophy.

This high-level approach to managing risk requires a number of skills, some of which the typical risk manager will possess, and some that are generally found in higher levels of management. First, the Chief Risk Officer must provide overall leadership in the execution of the organization's enterprise-wide risk management program. In addition, the Chief Risk Officer needs a high level of capability in the traditional management skills of communication, generating organizational buy-in, managing staff and tasks, and seeing the "big picture".

The Chief Risk Officer function must also have specific skills in insurance risk analysis and treatment options, as well as highly developed financial and analytical capabilities. Last, the Chief Risk Officer function must have the ability to synthesize the efforts of the various staff members responsible for component parts of the enterprise-wide risk management program and effectively communicate results in appropriate financial language to other members of the top management team.

Challenges

While the goals of enterprise-wide risk management and the Chief Risk Officer function are valuable, there are very real challenges to implementing enterprise-wide risk management or a Chief Risk Officer function:

- Some top managers express concerns that all risk management functions report to one executive, a consolidation of power into a small focal point.

- Others cite "organizational culture" as a barrier to a successful implementation of enterprise-wide risk management and the Chief Risk Officer function.

- Another impediment to expansion of the Chief Risk Officer function is the belief by many that the Chief Risk Officer is a technical role, a super-risk manager, and therefore not appropriate for a boardroom position.

Benefits

When enterprise-wide risk management programs are in place, a number of benefits accrue to the organization in addition to working to increase shareholder or stakeholder value:

- Improved risk response decision making. The wider scope of enterprise-wide risk management and cross-functional philosophy lends itself to more solutions, not just more problems.

- Less operational disruption, and improved contingency planning and disaster response.

- Increased ability to meet corporate strategic goals due to a focus on strategic, financial, and operational risks

- Increased management and business unit accountability and a better allocation of capital and resources to address risks

APPENDIX

Glossary

–A–

ACRS – Accelerated Cost Recovery System; values taken from the IRS table of allowable depreciation.

ADR – See **Alternative dispute resolution**

ALAE – See **Allocated loss adjustment expense**

AP – Accounts payable

AR – Accounts receivable

A priori – Proceeding from cause to effect

Absolute liability – Liability imposed without regard to negligence, usually applied to manufacturers of products found to be defective.

Accident – an event definite as to time and place that results in injury or damage to a person or property

Accounting system – organized set of accounting methods, procedures, and controls to collect, record, classify, and present accurate and timely financial data for use in management decision making.

Active retention – Planned acceptance of losses to be financed internally through the use of deductibles on insurance policies, loss sensitive insurance plans where some, but not all, risk is consciously retained rather than insured, and deliberate non-insurance. See **Passive retention** for the opposite approach

Actual cash value (ACV) – Replacement cost less "insurance" depreciation

Actuary – Person, often holding a professional designation (e.g., ACAS, FCAS), who computes statistics relating to insurance, typically estimating loss reserves and developing premiums.

Adhesion contract – A contract (usually standardized) offering goods or services on a "take it or leave it" basis. Typically, the weaker party has no real choice as to its terms. The "Doctrine of Adhesion" is a general legal rule stating that any defect or ambiguity in the contract language should necessarily be construed against the drafting (stronger) party.

Admitted assets – Assets whose value is included in the annual statement of an insurance company to insurance regulators

Admitted company or admitted insurer – An insurance company authorized to do business in a state by the state's insurance department. While the procedure may vary from state to state, approval is usually granted when an insurer presents financial information demonstrating its acceptable financial stability.

Agency – An office where insurance is sold. It may be directed towards property and casualty (liability) insurance, life and health insurance, or both. Also, it might be an independent organization placing insurance for a number of insurers or a company subsidiary group known as a direct writer.

Agency captive – A captive owned by an insurance agency, formed to insure the risks of the agency's clients or to participate with the insurance company in providing coverage for a difficult risk.

Agent – A person authorized to act on behalf of another person. In the case of insurance, a person or organization who solicits, negotiates, or instigates insurance contracts on behalf of an insurer. Agents can be independent contractors or employees of the company.

Aggregate limit – The maximum amount of protection for all losses occurring under a particular section of an insurance policy or funding arrangement during the specified term of the contract (usually one year).

Aleatory contract – Contract in which the happening of a fortuitous event is the condition that triggers a promise by one party to perform for another party. Insurance contracts are almost always aleatory contracts.

Allocated loss adjustment expense (ALAE) – Includes all expense (other than actual loss payment) directly assigned to or arising out of a particular claim; any expense assigned and recorded directly to a particular claim. Examples of ALAE include court fees and the expenses outside legal counsel. May also be noted as allocated loss expense.

Alternative dispute resolution – Methods for resolving legal disputes other than full litigation through formal trial. Arbitration proceedings are the most commonly used ADR technique.

Alternative risk financing facilities – Any risk financing mechanism that does not involve a commercial insurance company (e.g., captive insurers, risk retention group, pools, and self-insurance).

Annuity – A stream of periodic payments made over a specified period of time.

Asset – Anything of commercial value, including real or personal, tangible or intangible property

Association captive – Captive insurance company owned jointly by a number of non-insurance companies involved in the same or similar industries or by a trade or professional association

Automatic treaty – Reinsurance treaty under which the ceding company must cede exposures of a defined class that the reinsurer must accept in accordance with the terms of the treaty.

Avoidance – Risk control technique in which an organization attempts to entirely avoid the consequences of a loss by not engaging in activities that create the chance of loss.

–B–

B Value – See **Ballast Value**

Bailee – Person or organization that has possession of the property of others, usually for storage, repair, or servicing (e.g., a dry cleaning operation).

Bailor – Person or organization that owns property that has been entrusted to another (e.g., the owner of a coat who has entrusted it to a dry cleaning operation for cleaning). **Bailment** – Situation in which property of one has been entrusted to another. A bailment can be for the benefit of either party or both parties. The degree of care owed by the bailee to the bailor differs according to whom has the benefit of the bailment.

Ballast Value (B Value) – Used in computing workers compensation experience modifications, a specific value taken from a rating manual table used to limit the effect of a single severe accident, or shock loss, on the modification factor. The B Value has the effect of dampening swings in the experience modification factor.

Basic premium – Used in retrospectively rated plans, the basic premium provides for insurance carrier expenses, including loss control and agent/broker commissions, profit and contingency loadings, and an adjustment for limiting the retrospective premium between the minimum and maximum retrospective premiums. The basic premium is determined by multiplying the standard premium by a negotiated basic premium factor.

Basic premium factor – Used in retrospectively rated plans, a factor based on the Table of Expense Ratios, the Table of Insurance Charges, and the individual loss limitation, if selected

Basic rate – The manual rate that is adjusted to compensate for varying exposure to risk.

Benefit level adjustment factor – Factors calculated for each state by the National Council on Compensation Insurance (NCCI) or other workers compensation rating agencies representing the impact of regulatory changes on workers' compensation costs. Benefit level adjustment factors are used to trend historical losses to current benefit levels.

Bond – Contract that guarantees the performance of a contract, as in surety bonding, or protects against the dishonesty of employees, an in fidelity bonding. Unlike many contracts and all insurance contracts, a surety bond has three, not two, parties: the surety (the guarantor – e.g., the insurance company or surety company), the principal or obligor, (the one to whom the obligation is owed – e.g., the building owner in a construction project), and the obligee (the party who owes the obligation – e.g., the contractor or builder in a construction project).

Book value – 1) Value of an organization's assets as carried on the balance sheet in accordance with Generally Accepted Accounting Principals (GAAP). 2) Historic or acquisition cost. See **Net book value**.

Breach – Failure to live up to the conditions or warranties contained in a contract.

Broker – A solicitor of insurance who does not represent an insurance carrier as its agent, but instead represents the insured.

–C–

CA – See **Current asset**

CF – See **Cash flow**

CGS – See **Cost of goods sold**

CL – See **Current liability**

CS – See **Common stock**

Captive Insurer – 1) Insurance company formed by a non-insurance entity and established for the primary purpose of insuring all or part of the risk of its owners. 2) Legal entity created for the purpose of insuring the loss exposures of its owner(s), reducing or stabilizing costs, providing and arranging specific risk management services, and taking advantage of certain tax situations. 3) A closely held insurance company whose insurance business is primarily supplied by and controlled by its owners, and in which the original insureds are the principal beneficiaries.

Captive pool – Groups of individually owned captives that combine to reinsure one another; risk swapping

Case reserve – Amount the claims adjuster assigns to an individual claim that has not yet been paid; there is no provision for loss development and incurred but not reported (IBNR) losses; also known as claim reserve.

Cash discounting – A method of correcting estimated cash flows to give present values to future amounts, using the appropriate cost of capital, and incorporating judgments of the uncertainty (riskiness) of the future cash flows. This process reflects the fact that the present value of the money is entirely different from the future value.

Cash flow – Measurement of cash flowing through an organization's operations, financing, and investing activities

Cash flow plan – Insurance plans or retention plans that allow the insured, rather than an insurance carrier, to derive benefits from holding unused funds, either in the form of unpaid loss reserves or deferred premiums.

Casualty Actuarial Society (CAS) – Professional society for actuaries in areas of insurance work other than Life Insurance. This society grants the designations of Associate and Fellow of the Casualty Actuarial Society (ACAS and FCAS).

Cede – To transfer to a reinsurer all or part of the risk.

Ceding Company – Direct or primary insurance carrier that contracts with a reinsurer to share all or a certain portion of the losses it has assumed under insurance contracts in return for a stated premium.

Cession – Transaction that transfers liability from the ceding company to the reinsurer.

Claim – Demand or obligation for payment as a result of a loss.

Claim reserve – See **Loss reserve and Case reserve**.

Claims run – See **Loss report**

Combined ratio – Formula used by insurance companies to relate premium income to claims, administration and dividend expenses.

Commission – Stated percentage of premium written that is retained by or paid as compensation to insurance agents and brokers.

Common stock – Share or shares of ownership in a corporation with rights to vote on management and corporate policy but not preferred over other classes of stock in regard to the payment of dividends or distribution of assets. Dividends are not guaranteed, but common stock is usually the only class of stock with voting rights. See **Preferred stock**

Compensatory damages – Money awarded in a civil lawsuit to make an injured person whole, including special damages (specific dollar recompense for damaged property, lost wages or profits, medical expenses, etc.) and general damages (payment for non-monetary losses like pain, suffering, bereavement, etc.)

Contractual liability – Liability of another party assumed under a contract or agreement, either expressed or implied, as opposed to liability incurred directly, as in tort (civil wrongs not arising out of contractual obligations).

Contractual risk transfer – See **Non-insurance risk transfer**

Cost of risk allocation – Contribution of risk management costs from specific sections of an organization or company. These sections can include departments, locations, divisions, profit centers, etc.

Cost of risk allocation system – Process that identifies and attributes the cost of risk among the various sections of an organization or company.

Cost of goods sold – 1) Labor, material, and overhead expenses including inventory shrinkage; 2) the purchasing or production costs and expenses, both direct and indirect, of the merchandise sold during a certain period. These expenses include raw materials, direct and indirect labor costs, plant costs (such as depreciation), electricity, water, and shipping costs, etc.

Cost of risk – All components that are allocated to cover losses and expenses. Usually includes insurance premiums, retained losses, risk management department costs, and outside services (such as consultants). Can also include indirect costs, such as loss of productivity, cost of overtime, and opportunity costs.

Credibility – The relative confidence (statistical reliability) associated with a given body of data (e.g., loss experience for an individual division). Expressed as a number between zero (0%) and 1.0 (100%) with 1.0 representing "full credibility."

Current asset – Cash or other assets that will be (or could be) converted into cash or consumed within an organization's normal operating or accounting cycle (usually the next twelve months). Current assets include marketable securities, notes receivable, accounts receivable, inventory, and prepaid items.

Current liability – Liabilities that must be satisfied within the current operating or accounting cycle (usually the next twelve months). Current liabilities include trade accounts payable, taxes, wage accruals, current installments on long-term debt, and short-term notes payable.

–D–

D-ratio – See **Discount ratio**

DFL – Degree of Financial Leverage

DOL – Degree of Operating Leverage

Deductible – An amount specified in an insurance policy that is subtracted from a loss in determining the amount of insurance recovery.

Deposit premium – The premium paid at the inception of an insurance contract that provides for future premium adjustments. It is based on an estimate of what the final premium will be. Because it can be subject to audit, it is also known as provisional premium.

Detrimental reliance – Legal concept holding that a false statement will be treated as a promise when the listener relied upon the false statement to his/her detriment. The maker of the false statement is barred (estopped) from denying the statement. Also known as "equitable estoppel" or "**promissory estoppel**."

Development factor – Factor designed to correct errors in estimating the reserves for known but unsettled losses and to make an allowance for incurred but not reported (IBNR) losses. See also **Loss development factor**.

Discount Ratio (D-ratio) – Factor used in the workers compensation experience modification plan to separate the expected total losses into primary and excess losses. A D-ratio is the normal ratio of primary expected losses to the total expected losses, and varies by state and by classification code.

Discounted losses – Liability estimates that have been reduced to reflect the potential to earn investment on funds set aside to pay losses that have occurred but not yet been paid.

–E–

EBIT – Earnings before interest and taxes

ELR – See **Expected loss rate**

EPS – See **Earnings per share**

Earned premium – Amount of the premium that has been "used up" during the term of a policy. For example, if a one-year policy has been in effect six months, half of the total premium has been earned.

Earnings per share – Corporation's net profit, minus preferred stock dividends, divided by common shares outstanding.

Economic value – Future income assigned to the property

Estimated premium – Amount of premium charged at the time a policy is issued. The estimated premium based on estimated exposures times the negotiated premium rates. This amount may be subject to adjustment during the policy term in case of changes in coverage or additional underwriting information, or after the policy term in case of changes in exposures (e.g., payroll higher than estimated at inception).

Excess insurance – Insurance protection for limits above those contained in a primary policy or above a self-insured retention. Excess insurance usually does not include a duty to provide a defense, and typically does not provide any loss control or claims services.

Excess loss premium – Used in retrospective rating plans for worker's compensation, a premium that compensates the insurer for the fact that the insured has elected to limit the effects of any one large loss under the retrospective rating formula. For example, the insured might elect a loss limitation of $50,000, which would mean that would be the maximum amount of any one loss that would go into the retrospective calculation to be charged as a retrospective premium due.

Excess premium – Premium that is not a part of a loss sensitive rating formula. For example, in a retrospective rating plan, the non-subject or excess premium usually purchases the excess insurance (over the selected loss limits, not to be confused with insurance in excess of primary coverage or a self-insured retention). The excess premium is a guaranteed cost premium and not adjustable based on losses. In a retrospectively rated premium plan, the excess premium is not subject to the retrospective rating formula. See also **Non-subject premium**.

Expected loss costs – Initial estimate of losses for a given policy period.

Expected loss rate (ELR) – Used in computing workers compensation experience modifications, the factor taken from actuarial tables and used to calculate total expected losses for the specific classification, given the audited exposures

Expected losses – Loss projections (the so-called "loss pics" or "loss picks") based on probability distributions and statistics; frequently developed using actuarial techniques; average frequency × average severity ("average" is the arithmetic mean or any other appropriate measure of central tendency)

Expense constant – Expense factor (usually expressed as a dollar amount) added to the premium charged for a class of policies that would otherwise produce insufficient premium to cover the cost of issuing and servicing them.

Expense ratio – Formula used by insurance carriers to relate premium income to administrative expenses

Experience modifier – Factor developed by measuring the difference between the insured's actual past experience and the expected experience of the class. The factor may be either a debit or credit (greater than or less than 1.0). When applied to the manual premium, the experience modification produces a premium that is more representative of the actual loss experience of an insured.

Experience rating – Describes any plan that uses the past loss experience and exposure levels of the individual risk as a basis of determining premiums.

Exposure – 1) Situation, practice, or condition that might lead to a loss, such as an activity or resource (assets, people); 2) State of being subject to loss because of a hazard or contingency; 3) Units used to measure loss costs (e.g., payroll is the exposure used for workers' compensation, number of vehicles for auto liability, revenue for general liability, and number of units in service or dollar amounts sold for products liability). Forecasts of exposures can be used to forecast future losses.

–F–

FA – See **Fixed asset**

FASB – Financial Accounting Standards Board

FC – See **Fixed cost**

FIFO – First in, first out; an accounting method used to value inventory and the cost of goods sold. Sales are considered to be made against the earliest-purchased or produced merchandise or inventory. During times of increasing prices, the FIFO method tends to overstate profits and understate inventory values.

Facultative reinsurance – Reinsurance of individual risks by offer and acceptance, wherein the reinsurer retains the "faculty" to accept or reject each risk offered. (See **Reinsurance**.)

Fiduciary – 1) Person or organization holding valuables of another in a position of trust; 2) Under the Employee Retirement Income Security Act of 1974 (ERISA), "any person who exercises any discretionary authority or control with respect to the management or administration of the plan or its assets."

Fixed asset – Capital asset, especially a permanent or immovable one, required for use in the operations of a business (e.g., buildings and machinery).

Fixed cost – Costs that do not vary with the level of output, especially fixed financial costs such as mortgage payments, interest, lease payments, and sinking fund payments

Force majeure – In the law of insurance, a superior or irresistible force. Also common to construction contracts to protect parties in the event that a part of the contract cannot be performed due to causes that are outside the control of the parties and could not be avoided by the exercise of due care. Also referred to as "Act of God" or "Vis major."

Fortuitous event – Event subject to chance, without the implication of suddenness.

Frame construction – Exterior walls of wood, brick veneer, wood ironclad, or stucco on wood.

Frequency – 1) The number of claims per unit of exposure; 2) The number of times an incident occurs; 3) The likelihood that a loss will occur; usually expressed as low or high frequency.

Fronting – Use of an insurer or reinsurer to issue "paper" (i.e., an insurance policy) on behalf of a self-insured organization or captive insurer without the issuer's intention of bearing any of the risk. Fronting is typically used for compliance with regulations or conditions in a contract that require an admitted insurance carrier or a minimum financial rating.

Functional Replacement – Cost to repair or replace damaged property with materials that are functionally the equivalent of the damaged or destroyed property (e.g., replacing a mahogany banister with a pine banister).

Funded reserves – Setting aside sufficient sums of money to meet future liabilities.

Future value – Value in the future of a payment or payments made in the present.

–G–

GAAP – See **Generally Accepted Accounting Principles**

Generally Accepted Accounting Principles (GAAP) – Principles in financial accounting that serve to assure consistency in financial reporting. GAAP is a type of self-regulation in which members of the financial accounting profession have agreed that these principles will govern their accounting techniques and interpretations.

Government accounting – Non-commercial accounting system (e.g., government and non-profits) that features accounts for budgets, encumbrances, and restricted-use assets. Government accounting often recognizes revenues in the period when they become available and measurable, and expenses in the period when the liability occurs. Also called "fund accounting," multiple reports that can detail expenditures and revenues for multiple funds.

Group captive – Insurance carrier jointly owned by a number of non-related, non-insurance companies or organizations for the purpose of insuring the risks of those different entities

Guaranteed cost – Premiums charged on a prospective basis. While the cost is not "guaranteed," in the sense that the premium is subject to audit based on exposures that differ from the estimated value, the rate is never adjusted or changed on the basis of loss experience during the policy period. The phrase "guaranteed cost" is really a misnomer; the more appropriate expression would be "guaranteed rate" subject to audit adjustment.

–H–

HIPAA – Health Insurance Portability and Accountability Act of 1996. This Act is meant to amend the Internal Revenue Code of 1986 to improve portability and continuity of health insurance coverage in the group and individual markets, to combat waste, fraud, and abuse in health insurance and health care delivery, to promote the use of medical savings accounts, to improve access to long-term care services and coverage, to simplify the administration of health insurance, and for other purposes. A key provision establishes privacy of an individual's health information and regulates the sharing of that information.

HPR – See **Highly protected risk**

Hazard – A condition or circumstance that increases the likelihood and/or severity of a loss.

Highly protected risk (HPR) – Property that is judged to be subject to a much lower than normal probability of loss by virtue of low hazard occupancy or property type, superior construction, special fire protection equipment and procedures, and management commitment to loss prevention.

Historical cost – Price paid to acquire the property

Hold harmless agreement – Provision in a contract that requires one contracting party to respond to certain legal liabilities of the other party. Sometimes called an "indemnification agreement."

–I–

IBNR – See **Incurred but not reported**

IRR – Internal Rate of Return

IRS – Internal Revenue Service

ISO – Insurance Service Office

Incident – Event that disrupts normal activities and may become a loss or claim.

Increased limit factors – Ratio applied to losses at one retention level (e.g. $1,000,000 per occurrence) to determine expected losses at another retention level (e.g., $5,000,000).

Incurred but not reported (IBNR) – Represents the liability for unpaid claims not reflected in the case reserve estimates for individual losses. The two components of this liability derive from additional development on known cases and the reporting of claims that have occurred but not yet been recorded as of the evaluation date.

Incurred expense –Expenses not yet paid. Can also include paid expenses in some accounting systems.

Incurred loss ratio – Portion of an earned premium dollar that is spent on incurred losses

Incurred losses – 1) The total amount of paid claims and loss reserves associated with a particular period of time, usually an insurance policy year. Generally, incurred losses are the actual losses paid and outstanding, interest on judgments, expenses incurred in obtaining third-party recoveries, and allocated loss adjustment expenses; 2) paid losses, case reserves, and IBNR reserves until ultimate incurred losses are reached, at which time there is no remaining IBNR.

Indemnify – To make compensation to an entity for incurred hurt, loss, or damage; or to restore to original position.

Indemnity – The payment restoring an injured party to the financial position enjoyed prior to a loss; or reimbursing an injured party suffering loss for the amount of the loss.

Independent adjuster – Organization or a person hired by an insurer and paid a fee for settling claims.

Independent contractor – Individual or entity that agrees to perform specific work for another but is not subject to direction or management by, nor is an employee of, the person who contracted for the services.

Indexed ultimate total loss – Incurred losses that have been developed (trended) and indexed (adjusted) for inflation.

Inflation index factor – A premium loading to provide for future increases in claims costs and loss payments resulting from inflation.

Insurance – A formal social device for reducing risk by transferring the risks of several individual entities to an insurer. The insurer agrees, for a consideration, to assume, to a specified extent, the losses suffered by the insured.

Insurance carrier – Insurance company

Insured – The person(s) protected under an insurance contract.

Insurer – Insurance company that assumes risks for insureds and performs other insurance-related operations, such as loss control and claims settlement.

–J–

Joint and several liability – A legal doctrine, applying in some states, that allows an injured person to sue and recover the full amount from any one or more of several wrongdoers at his option, regardless of that wrongdoer's degree of negligence.

Joint venture – Association of two or more individuals or organizations who engage in a specific or limited business transaction; a partnership between two corporations.

Joisted Masonry construction – Exterior walls of masonry material (adobe, brick, concrete, gypsum block, hollow concrete block, stone, tile, or similar materials), with combustible floor and roof.

–K–

–L–

LDF – See **Loss development factor**

LIFO – Last in, first out. An accounting method used to value inventory and the cost of goods sold. Sales are considered to be made using the latest-purchased or produced merchandise or inventory. During times of increasing prices, the LIFO method tends to understate profits and overstate inventory values.

LTD – 1) Long-term debt; 2) Long-term disability

Layering – Building an insurance program in steps, whereby each insurer writes its limits in excess of lower limits accepted by other insurers.

Law of large numbers – Used in probability and statistics. The larger the number of units independently exposed to loss, the more accurate the ability to predict loss results arising from those exposure units.

Liability – Legally enforceable obligation

Liquidity – Ability of an organization to convert assets into cash quickly with little or no cost, (e.g., selling or factoring accounts receivable and selling marketable securities).

Loss – 1) The basis of a claim for damages under the terms of an insurance policy. 2) Loss of assets resulting from risk; a reduction in value.

Loss control – Risk management technique that seeks to reduce the frequency of losses and reduce the severity of those losses that do occur. See also **Risk control**.

Loss conversion factor – Used in retrospective rating, a factor that is designed to cover claim adjustment expenses and the cost of the insurer's or third-party administrator's claim services.

Loss development – Difference between the value of a loss as originally reported to an insurer and its subsequent evaluation at a later date or at the time of its final disposition.

Loss development factor – Ratios that are applied to a current valuation of losses to determine an estimate of ultimate incurred losses. These factors are calculated by comparing the period-to-period changes in values of loss reserves, under the assumption that current losses will be paid according to the same pattern as prior losses at similar states of development. Loss development factors (LDF) are frequently calculated separately for incurred losses, paid losses, and claims counts.

Loss forecasting – Predicting future losses through an analysis of past losses. Depending upon the type of losses being forecast, a minimum number of losses or a minimum number of years must be accumulated before any degree of statistical credibility exists.

Loss limits or limitations – Used in retrospective rating formulas, a limit lower than the policy limit that reduces the effect of catastrophic losses that would otherwise be considered in full in computing any retrospective premium adjustment.

Loss rating – Rating technique that establishes the prospective rate that will be applied to an exposure base to compute the premium based upon historical losses.

Loss ratio – Proportionate relationship of incurred losses to earned premiums expressed as a percentage.

Loss report – Listing of reported claims providing such information as the names of insureds and/or claimants, the date of occurrence, type of claim, amount paid and amount reserved for each as of the report's valuation date.

Loss reserves – Estimation of the liability for unpaid claims that have occurred as of a given date, including those losses incurred but not yet reported, losses due but not yet paid, and amounts not yet due.

Loss retention – See **Retention**

Loss run – See **Loss report**

Loss trending – Adjusting historical losses to account for inflationary trends so that the ultimate value is more current or meaningful. Loss trend factors are multiplied by actual historical losses to trend losses.

Losses incurred – Total losses, paid or unpaid, that are sustained during a given period. See **Incurred losses**

–M–

Management accounting – Accounting system that provides accurate and timely financial information for use by internal managers to make short-term and day-by-day financial decisions.

Manual rates – Rates as promulgated by a rating bureau before application of any credits, discounts, surcharges, or deviations. Such rates are referred to as "manual rates" because they traditionally were published in a rating manual, now mostly available online.

Market value – What a willing buyer would give to a willing seller in exchange for an asset.

Masonry noncombustible construction – Exterior walls of masonry material (adobe, brick, concrete, gypsum block, hollow concrete block, stone, tile, or similar materials) with floor and roof of metal or other noncombustible materials.

Maximum possible loss – The worst possible loss that could occur.

Maximum probable loss – Estimate developed for property insurance underwriters that represents the worst amount of loss that is likely to happen, as opposed to the worst possible result that could happen. Also known as probable maximum loss, PML estimate includes adverse conditions, such as the impairment or failure of a sprinkler system, a delayed fire alarm, insufficient water supply, or delayed firefighting response, if such conditions seem reasonable.

Maximum retrospective premium – Percentage of the standard premium determined by multiplying the maximum retrospective premium factor by the standard premium. The maximum retrospective premium is the greatest amount of premium to be paid by the insured under a retrospective rating plan. It has the effect of placing a maximum dollar amount on the financial responsibility of the insured. Once the maximum retrospective premium has been paid, all additional losses are the responsibility of the insurer, subject to the limit of liability of the applicable insurance policies. The excess loss premium may be included in the maximum or in addition to the maximum, depending on the retrospective rating agreement.

Maximum retrospective premium factor – A factor established by agreement between the insured and the insurance carrier that, when multiplied by the standard premium, determines the maximum retrospective premium.

Mini-tail – Automatic 60-day extended reporting period allowing for the making of claims after expiration of a "claims made" liability policy.

Minimum retrospective premium – Percentage of the standard premium determined by multiplying the minimum retrospective premium factor by the standard premium. The minimum retrospective premium is the least amount of premium to be paid by the insured under a retrospective rating plan.

Minimum retrospective premium factor – Established by agreement between the insured and the insurance carrier that, when multiplied by the standard premium, determines the minimum retrospective premium.

Mitigation of Damages – Rule, "The doctrine of Mitigation of Damages," which requires an injured party to exercise reasonable diligence and ordinary care in attempting to minimize damages after injury or loss, sometimes referred to as the "Doctrine of Avoidable Consequences."

Moral Hazard – Proclivity to cause a loss to effect an insurance recovery (e.g., arson).

Morale Hazard – Indifference to loss, such as poor housekeeping or maintenance.

–N–

NAIC – National Association of Insurance Commissioners

NCCI – See **National Council on Compensation Insurance.**

NI – See **Net Income.**

NP – Net Profit

National Council on Compensation Insurance (NCCI) – Association of insurers selling workers compensation coverage that operates as a rating organization NCCI collects statistics, develops rates and policy forms, and makes state filings for its members. The NCCI operates in most, but not all states.

Negligence – Failure to use that degree of care that is considered to be a reasonable precaution under the given circumstances. Acts of either omission or commission, or both, may constitute negligence.

Net book value – 1) Value of an organization's assets as carried on the balance sheet in accordance with Generally Accepted Accounting Principles (GAAP) less accumulated accounting depreciation. 2) Historic or acquisition cost less accumulated accounting depreciation

Net income – Balance of funds remaining after all of an organization's expenses, including taxes, are subtracted from gross sales; the excess of revenues over expenses; the "bottom line" or net profit. Net income is the amount that can be distributed to an organization's owners or kept as retained earnings.

Net worth – Total value of all assets minus all liabilities.

Non-admitted asset – Assets of an insurer that are not permitted by the state insurance department or other regulatory authority to be taken into account in determining an insurer's financial condition. Non-admitted assets are typically illiquid assets, such as furniture, fixtures, agents' past-due debit balances, receivables, and securities whose value is questionable

Noncombustible construction – Exterior walls, floor, and supports made of metal, gypsum, or other noncombustible materials.

Non-insurance risk transfer – Transfer of risk from one party to another party other than an insurance company. This risk management technique usually involves risk transfers by way of hold harmless or indemnity provisions in contracts and is also called "contractual risk transfer."

Non-ledger assets – Assets that are due and payable but have not yet been entered into the balance sheet

Non-subject premium – Used in loss sensitive plans, a premium that is not a part of the loss sensitive rating formula. For example, in a retrospective rating plan, the non-subject premium usually purchases the excess insurance (over the loss limits, not to be confused with insurance in excess of primary or SIR). The expression "non-subject" refers to the fact that the premium is a guaranteed cost premium and is not adjustable based on losses.

Nuisance value – Amount an insurer will pay to settle a claim that may not be valid or may be of lesser value so as to avoid expensive litigation or the risk of an adverse judicial result or damage to an organization's reputation. Sometimes known as a "solatium" payment, it may also consist of compensation for injured feelings as distinct from financial loss or physical suffering.

–O–

Obligee – Person, firm, or corporation protected by a surety bond; the party to whom the principal under the bond is obligated.

Obligor – Under a surety bond, the party who owes the obligation to the obligee and who must (unlike insurance) pay back the surety if payment is made under the bond, also known as the **principal**.

Occurrence – Accident with the limitation of time removed (an "accident" that is extended over a period of time rather than a single observable happening). Also, continuous or repeated exposure to the same or similar conditions **that results in bodily injury or property damage neither expected nor intended by the insured. See Accident.**

Outstanding losses – In a loss run, the amount calculated by subtracting paid losses from incurred losses and representing the remaining liability to be paid on a loss or group of losses.

–P–

PD – Physical damage (as in damage to the insured automobile) or property damage (damage to other people's property).

P/E – Price/earnings

PIE – See **Paid-in excess**

PML – See **Probable maximum loss**

PS – Preferred Stock

PV – Present Value

Paid loss retrospective rating plan – Retrospectively rated insurance plan that uses only paid losses to determine the retrospective premiums due at each adjustment. A paid loss retrospective rating plan allows the insured to hold loss reserves until they are paid out in claims and gain the cash flow advantage.

Paid losses – Amount actually paid in losses during a specified period of time, not including estimates of amounts (i.e., reserves) that will be paid in the future for losses occurring in the specified period.

Paid-in capital – Capital acquired by a corporation from sources other than business operations. The most common source is the sale of the corporation's own common and preferred stock. The amount of paid-in capital becomes part of the **stockholder's equity** shown on a balance sheet.

Paid-in excess -- Original cost of a newly issued share of common stock less its stated par value. Insurance company common stock (and commercial bank stock) often has a cost per share that includes an additional contribution to surplus that provides a safety cushion for early periods of operation to create a conservative balance sheet.

Parole evidence – Oral or verbal evidence. In contract law, parole evidence relates to the inadmissibility of oral representations that would otherwise alter or defeat the provisions of a written contract. Also referred to as "Extraneous evidence."

Passive retention – Unplanned acceptance of losses because of failure to identify risk, or failure to act or forgetting to act on identified risk.

Payout profile – Schedule illustrating the percentage of loss dollars actually paid in settlement of claims over time.

Peril – Cause of loss, an event that causes a loss (e.g., fire, theft, collision).

Personal property – All tangible property not classified as real property. See **real property**.

Plaintiff – Party bringing a lawsuit against another.

Pool – 1) An organization of insurers or reinsurers through which particular types of risk are underwritten with premiums, losses, and expenses shared in agreed ratios. 2) A group of organizations (generally not large enough to self-insure individually) that form a shared risk pool.

Preferred stock – Class of stock or stocks issued by a corporation that has ownership privileges with respect to payment of dividends and distribution of assets greater than those of common stock owners, but carries no voting rights. The dividend is expressed as a percentage of the stated par value much like interest but is not tax deductible to the organization.

Premium – Amount of money an insurance carrier charges to provide the coverage described in an insurance policy.

Premium discount – 1) A discount allowed on premiums paid in advance of one year based on projected interest to be earned. 2) A discount allowed on certain workers compensation and comprehensive liability policies to allow for the fact that larger premium policies do not require the same percentage of the premium for basic insurer expenses such as policy underwriting and issuance. The discount percentage increases with the size of the premium.

Present value – Value today of a future payment or payments, discounted at the appropriate discount rate, called "**cash discounting.**"

Primary actual losses – Used in computing workers compensation experience modifications, the actual loss amount (each loss equal to or less than $5,000) is included in the calculation at its full value. Each loss over $5,000 is limited to a primary loss value of $5,000, with the excess over $5,000 applied at a lesser rate.

Principal – The entity whose performance is being guaranteed in a surety bond, also known as the **obligor**.

Pro rata – Proportionate or proportionately (e.g., the premium due for a six-month insurance policy would be pro rata of the annual premium or 50%).

Probable maximum loss – See **Maximum probable loss.**

Promissory estoppel – Legal concept holding that a false statement will be treated as a promise when the listener relied upon the false statement to his/her detriment. The maker of the false statement is barred (estopped) from denying the statement. Also known as "**equitable estoppel**" or "**detrimental reliance.**"

Public adjuster – An independent adjuster who represents policyholders in the adjustment of their losses with insurers for a fee.

Punitive damages – Damages, also called exemplary damages, in excess of those required to compensate the plaintiff for the wrong done and imposed to punish the defendant because of the particularly wanton or willful character of the wrongdoing. Damages are designed to deter future similar acts.

Pure risk – Uncertainty as to whether a loss or no loss will occur (break even); a pure risk can only produce loss (not loss or gain as is true of **speculative risk**).

–Q–

Quota share reinsurance – Form of reinsurance whereby the reinsurer accepts a stated percentage of each exposure written by the ceding company on a defined class of business. The insurance carrier and reinsurer share the premiums and losses according to the percentage agreed upon.

Quid pro quo – Latin for "this for that," or "one thing for another." In contract law, it refers to the exchange of a "legal consideration" of values required by both parties as a requirement to establish a valid contract. In insurance, it is the exchange of the premium for a promise to pay a covered loss.

–R–

RAP – Regulatory Accounting Principles; also called Statutory Accounting Principles, or SAP

RE – Retained Earnings

RIMS – Risk and Insurance Management Society

RMIS – See **Risk management information system**

RML –See **Residual Market Load**

ROA – Return on Assets

ROE – Return on Equity

ROI – Return on Investment

RRG – See **Risk Retention Group**

Real property -- Land and most things attached to the land, such as buildings and vegetation.

Reinsurance – Practice whereby one party, the "reinsurer," in consideration of a premium paid to it, agrees to indemnify another party, the "reinsured," for part or all of the liability assumed by the reinsured under a policy or policies of insurance that it has issued; essentially it is insurance on insurance.

Reinsurer – Insurance carrier who accepts all or a portion of the liabilities of the ceding company.

Reinsurance ceded – Portion of the risk that the primary or original insurer transfers to the reinsurer.

Rent-a-captive – 1) Captive that uses the capital of third-party investors in lieu of capital from the insured. 2) Licensed offshore insurers owned by an outside organization (e.g., a broker, reinsurer, insurance company, or other business enterprise). These facilities are available to other eligible organizations for a fee.

Replacement cost – Amount to replace old or destroyed with new property of like kind and quality without deduction for insurance depreciation.

Reserve – Amount of money earmarked for a specific purpose.

Residual Market Load (RML) – Separate charge intended to subsidize an assigned risk or involuntary market.

Retention – 1) Budgeted losses plus the "tolerance corridor." See **Tolerance Corridor**; 2) Assumption of risk of loss as through the use of non-insurance, self-insurance, or deductibles. This retention can be intentional (active retention) or, when exposures are not identified, unintentional (passive retention). 3) In reinsurance, the net amount of risk the ceding company or the reinsurer keeps for its own account or that of specified others; it may be expressed as a percentage, a specific dollar amount, or a combination of both.

Retention level – Amount of loss that is self-insured. It is usually expressed on a per occurrence basis, but can be per claim. It is sometimes referred to as the self-insured retention (SIR).

Retrospective rating – Rating plan that adjusts the premium, subject to a certain minimum and usually a maximum, periodically to reflect the actual loss experience of the insured. Retrospective rating combines actual losses with graded expenses to produce a premium that more accurately reflects the current experience of the insured. An adjustment is performed periodically following policy expiration to recognize the fluctuation in developing losses.

Risk – Common definitions: 1) Chance of loss; 2) Uncertainty concerning loss; 3) A possibility of a variation of outcomes from a given set of circumstances; 4) The difference between expected losses and actual losses.

Risk control – Technique of minimizing the frequency or severity of losses with training, safety, and security measures. See **Loss control.**

Risk financing – Most cost effective risk management techniques to assure post-loss financial resource availability. Risk financing programs can involve insurance plans or captive insurers, as well as an organization's internal financial resources.

Risk management – There are various definitions of risk management, but the basic theme is to protect the company's assets through identification and analysis of exposures, controlling the exposures, financing of losses with external and internal funds, and implementation and monitoring of the risk management process. Further, risk management should be practical and professional; be interdisciplinary and enterprise-wide; consider strategic, operational, and financial risks; utilize the five steps of the risk management process of identification, analysis, control, financing, and administration; and optimize cost of risk to help an enterprise achieve its goals.

Risk management information system – Information system made up of various elements, which supports the user in identifying, measuring, and managing risk in their organization or in the instance of a risk management consultant or insurance agent, the organizations of others.

Risk management process – System for treating pure risk: identification and analysis of exposures, selection of appropriate risk management techniques to handle exposures, implementation of chosen techniques, and monitoring the results.

Risk profiling – Measurement of expected losses for a finite period of time based on historical data including but not limited to, total losses, number of losses, average loss size, and timing of payment

Risk purchasing group – Group formed in compliance with the Risk Retention Act for the purpose of negotiating for and purchasing insurance from a commercial insurer.

Risk quantification – Actual forecasting of loss frequency and severity to determine allocation decisions

Risk retention – Conscious acceptance of losses that the organization or company will bear.

Risk retention group – Group self-insurance plan or group captive insurer operating under the Risk Retention Act of 1986.

Risk volatility – Difference between an anticipated result (loss) and the standard deviation

–S–

SAP – See **Statutory Accounting Principles**

SCF – Statement of cash flows

S/E – Stockholders Equity

SEC – Securities Exchange Commission

SIR – Self-insured retention. See also Retention level and Self insured retention

Savings clause – Contract provision that rescues the balance of a contract if one or more parts are held to be invalid or unenforceable. Also referred to as "Separability" clause or "Severability" clause.

Self-insured retention – Dollar amount specified in an insurance policy that must be paid by the insured before the insurance policy will respond to a loss.

Several liability – Legal doctrine holding that a defendant is liable only to the extent of his or her responsibility for the plaintiff's injury. See **Joint and Several Liability.**

Severity – 1) Measurement of the monetary or financial impact of losses; 2) Average claim size.

Single parent captive – Wholly-owned insurance subsidiary of a non-insurance company, which insures or reinsures all or part of its parent's exposures

Speculative risk – Uncertainty about an event under consideration that could produce either a profit or loss

Standard premium – 1) Calculated by using state rating classifications and rates and applying them to an insured's estimated exposures for the policy period allowing for various adjustments. 2) Used in retrospective rating plans, standard premium is the premium for the insured as determined on the basis of authorized rates modified by any experience rating modification applied to the estimated exposure, plus loss constants, where applicable, and minimum premiums. It specifically excludes premium discounts and expense constants.

Statutory Accounting Principles (SAP) – Those principles required by statute that must be followed by an insurance company when submitting its financial statement to the state insurance department. Typically considered to be stricter, such principles differ from Generally Accepted Accounting Principles (GAAP) in some important respects, particularly in the admissibility or inclusion of certain assets and in the matching of premium income and expenses.

Stockholder's equity – On an organization's balance sheet, the portion that represents the capital received from investors in exchange for stock, donated capital, and retained earnings. Also known as "shareholders' equity" or the book value of the organization, this item comes from the funds originally invested in the company, and any additional investments, and from retained earnings the company has accumulated over time through operations.

Strict liability – Legal doctrine under which one party is liable to another party regardless of the degree of care exercised by the first party. Strict liability is often applied in inherently dangerous activities (e.g. owners of dangerous animals or fireworks manufacturers). **Structured settlement** – Settlement in which the plaintiff agrees to accept a stream of payments, in whole or in part, in lieu of a lump sum. Annuities are usually used as a funding mechanism.

Subject premium – Used in retrospective rating plans, the portion of the premium applied to the retrospective rating formula. It is generally used to help calculate the basic premium, both before and after audit calculations.

Subrogation – 1) The right of a person to assume a legal claim of another; the right of a person who has paid a liability or obligation of another to be indemnified by that person; an insurer's substitution in place of the insured in regard to a claim against a third party for indemnification of a loss paid by the insurer; 2) The substitution of one person in place of another with reference to a lawful claim, demand, or right held or owned by the original party.

Substantial performance – A legal doctrine that protects the party to a contract, who makes an honest endeavor in good faith to perform his/her part of the contract with the results of his/her endeavor being beneficial and retained by another party to the contract, from having the party who received such benefit avoiding performance. The equitable doctrine of substantial performance protects a party from forfeiture under the contract for technical inadvertence or trivial variations or omissions in performance.

Surety – The promisor under a bond; the party that promises to fulfill the obligation of the bonded party or principal; a surety company.

–T–

TIE – Times Interest Earned, a financial ratio that measures how much of the interest obligation of the organization is covered by the net income

TPA – See **Third-party administrator**

Tail factor –Used in calculating loss development factors from historical data, the factor that recognizes that at some point, older data becomes unavailable or is no longer relevant due to changing circumstances. The tail factor is a loss development factor used to take losses from the oldest available valuation period to ultimate. It is generally based upon industry data or an extrapolation of less mature loss development factors.

Tax multiplier – Used in retrospective rating plans, a factor applied to an insurance premium to increase the premium to cover licenses, fees, assessments, and taxes which the insurance carrier must pay on the premium which it collects. It may also include a provision for subsidy of the assigned risk market.

Third-party administrator – Claims administrator or insurance company that processes claims on behalf of a self-insured organization

Tolerance corridor – Marginal retention amount beyond budgeted retention of losses that may also be actively retained.

Tort – Civil or private wrong (not criminal wrong) giving rise to legal liability.

Transfer of risk – Risk management technique whereby risk of loss is transferred to another party through a contract (e.g., a hold harmless agreement, or to a professional risk bearer, (i.e., an insurance company)).

Treaty reinsurance – General reinsurance agreement that requires the reinsurer to assume the agreed amount of reinsurance coverage on all insurance falling within the terms of the agreement between the ceding company and the reinsurer, as contrasted with facultative reinsurance, or individually negotiated reinsurance contracts. (See **Reinsurance**.)

Trend factor – Used to adjust past loss experience to the current cost levels, generally taking into account inflation and other similar forces.

Total incurred losses – Incurred losses that have not been developed nor indexed for inflation.

–U–

ULAE – see **Unallocated loss adjustment expense**

Ultimate losses – Total losses that will have been paid when all claims have reached final settlement (fully developed).

Ultimate total loss – Total of incurred losses that have been developed.

Unallocated loss adjustment expense (ULAE) – Salaries, overhead, and other related adjustment costs not specifically allocated or charged to the expense incurred for a particular claim

Unearned premium – Amount of premium remaining after deducting the earned premium from written premium; the portion of a premium representing the unexpired part of the policy period.

Unfunded reserves – Not having sufficient sums of money or any sum of money to meet future liabilities.

–V–

Valuation date – Cut-off date for adjustments made to paid claims and reserve estimates in a loss report.

–W–

WACC – See **Weighted average cost of capital.**

WIP – Work-in-progress, or inventory that is in the process of being manufactured or worked upon.

Waiver – 1) The surrender of a right or privilege; 2) The intentional or voluntary relinquishment of a known right, claim, privilege, or the opportunity to take advantage of some defect, irregularity, or wrong.

Weighted average cost of capital – After-tax cost to the firm of an average dollar of capital or long-term funds. Capital consists of long-term debt, preferred stock, common stock, and retained earnings (or issued common stock).

Weighting value – Used in workers compensation experience modifications, a percentage value taken from the same actuarial tables used above to determine the percentage of excess losses to be used in the calculations

Working layer – An area of excess insurance or reinsurance in which loss frequency is expected.

Written premium – The total premiums on all policies written by an insurer during a specified period of time, regardless of what portions have been earned.

–X–

–Y–

–Z–

Academy Publications 2009

Discover how insurance publications by The Academy will change the way you do business!

For identifying current trends and getting straight-up information to help meet the challenges of the insurance industry, Academy publications are just the resource you've been searching for.

The Academy features books about improving the agency's sales and marketing efforts, streamlining performance, managing growth, enhancing service, and managing risk. And you'll also find the practical publications about exposures, exclusions, and coverages that belong on the shelves of every practicing insurance professional.

Call or visit our website for the latest information on Academy publications.

800-633-2165

www.TheNationalAlliance.com/publications

Agency Disaster Planning: Get Your Agency Ready

Develop a new disaster plan or improve and existing one with the checklists, forms, and worksheets included on a bonus CD. Take care of your employees, clients, office building and contents, and financial concerns. See how surveyed agencies are planning and read about 15 real agency disaster experiences. 198 pages

The CSR Profile: An In-Depth Look at Customer Service Professionals (3rd Edition)

Use the results of a nationwide survey to compare your compensation, servicing volume, and responsibilities. Read about qualifications, experience, skills, and knowledge for both commercial and personal lines CSRs. Chart a future course with checklists, job descriptions, and career paths. 170 pages

Decoding Executive Liability Insurance: Simplifying the Exposures and Coverages (4th Edition)

Gain a valuable understanding of the exposures and coverages to properly insure your clients, reduce E&O exposures, and gauge market updates. Learn to use risk management techniques and implement the coverage checklists. 111 pages

Dynamics of Selling Audio Series (3rd Edition)

Refresh, review, and reinforce your selling skills. Learn how to super qualify prospects, build rapport, probe for needs, overcome objections, and master the selling sequence. Energize your sales process with this learning and reinforcement tool. 7 CDs

Dynamics of Selling –The Diagnostic Appointment DVD

A valuable sales tool for sales managers to use in sales meetings, producers to hone their selling skills, and company marketing representatives to share with their agencies. It reinforces the first step in the Dynamics of Selling process with three role-play scenarios, followed by critiques. 85 minutes

Growth and Performance Standards (GPS) 2006 Edition (8th Edition)

Compare to income and expense averages, productivity measures, and balance sheet ratios of other agencies. Discover how well the best performing agencies are doing, and gauge the results of agencies which focus on either commercial or personal lines business. Use the companion CD to compare your numbers, compute variances, and improve results. 195 pages

Insurance Essentials Handbook: Property and Casualty Insurance (7th Edition)

Learn the basic insurance terms, concepts, coverages, and exclusions for P&C insurance. Focus on the key aspects of Homeowners, Commercial General Liability, Workers Compensation, and other pertinent topics. Practical examples are provided throughout to aid in the explanation and understanding for insurance professionals. 304 pages

Life & Benefits Essentials

Learn the basic insurance terms and concepts for life insurance, health insurance, and employee benefits. Focus on the key aspects of term and permanent life insurance, major medical health insurance, annuities, retirement planning, long term care, and the Medicare program. CD study guide is included. 191 pages

Managing Human Resources in an Insurance Agency

Protect your agency from HR problems without spending a lot of time and/or money. Improve your systems and procedures with regard to hiring and firing, employment law, job descriptions, an employee manual, and a procedures manual. Tailor the forms and agreements with the bonus CD. 210 pages

Maximizing Agency Value II: A Guide for Buying, Selling, and Perpetuating Insurance Agencies (2nd Edition)

Use the sample letters, checklists, and detailed agreements to assist with buying and selling an agency. Follow steps to analyze other agencies, as well as your own, to maximize current value and future net worth. 235 pages

The Paperless Agency: Transformation through Innovation

Learn how to use front-end scanning to manage information and move towards a paperless office environment. Discover the benefits for your agency and apply the recommended best practices. Use the detailed project management steps and learn from survey results to maximize operational innovation. 106 pages

Producer Profile: Compensation, Production, and Responsibilities (3rd Edition)

Compare survey results on annual compensation, commission rates, benefits, and equity to attract and retain top producers. Examine annual sales production, growth rates, and new business focus. Use checklists, data tables, and job descriptions for both commercial and personal lines producers. 211 pages

Risk Management Essentials

Learn the basic risk management principles, terms and concepts for the various risk management activities: identification, analysis, control, finance, and administration. Focus on the key areas of financial statements, loss data, claims management, information technology, and enterprise risk management. Included is a CD study guide with questions and answers for each chapter.

Street Smart Selling: Beliefs, Strategies, and Management Ideas of Successful Insurance Professionals (2nd Edition)

Improve sales with advanced topics. Establish beliefs to know that you are the product and be known for the problems you solve. Use marketing strategies to position yourself as an insurance expert and define the rules of engagement. Apply management ideals to evaluate sales training and improve your sales culture. 91 pages

Zoom In On Sales: Target Marketing, Prospecting, and Sales Centers

Zero in on your marketing goals with target marketing and prospecting results. Find out how to organize your marketing and sales activities by operating a sales center. Learn how agencies use direct marketing, delegate prospecting duties, and monitor results. 118 pages

The 25 Most Innovative Agents in America

The winners of "The Most Innovative Agents in America" award, sponsored by The National Alliance for Insurance Education & Research and Rough Notes magazine, tell their stories in a collection of visionary examples. This publication will inspire you to be more creative in your own career. 154 pages

CRM Courses - Demonstrate Your Knowledge

Earning the Certified Risk Managers International (CRM) designation demonstrates that you are knowledgeable in all of the areas of managing risks, hazards, and exposures.

The five courses give you in-depth knowledge about some of today's highest priorities: identifying, analyzing, controlling, financing, and administering operational risks – as well as political risks, catastrophic loss exposures, third-party exposures, fiduciary exposures, human resources, juridical, legal, political, social, economic, and physical risks, and more – whether insurable or not. The skills you learn in discovering how risk can affect the flow of earnings, and how to protect against it, will make you more proactive and valuable to your organization.

The five CRM courses are:

- Principles of Risk Management

- Analysis of Risk

- Control of Risk

- Financing of Risk

- Practice of Risk Management

Each course includes 2-½ days of instruction, followed by an optional exam. Any eligible individual may attend any of the classes without taking the examinations or working toward the designation.

CRM courses cover all areas of risk management and feature:

- Highly experienced instructors, skilled at making the most sophisticated subjects interesting and directly applicable

- Curricula developed by leading risk management practitioners and recognized as the most practical in the industry

- Curricula advisory committees made up of risk management professionals and educators, who regularly review the course content to ensure the CRM Program's ongoing integrity and practicality

- Presentations that reflect the most current laws and policy changes.

To Earn the Designation, You Must:

Take all five CRM courses and pass all five CRM exams within five calendar years after you complete your first CRM exam.

Principles of Risk Management Course

We recommend you take this course first because it lays a solid foundation in risk management essentials, and it gives you the tools for identifying exposures – the first step in the risk management process. It also provides the fundamentals to ensure your success in the courses that follow.

Topics covered:

- Risk Management Concepts and Their Effect on the Organization
- Risk Identification: Methods
- Risk Identification: Logical Classifications
- Ethics and the Risk Management Process
- Financial Concepts for Risk Management
- Loss Data Analysis
- Risk-Taking Appetite and Ability

Analysis of Risk Course

In this course, you will acquire rock-solid insights into the analysis and measurement of exposures and the use and projection of loss data that are fundamental to risk management. We recommend that you take Analysis of Risk before embarking on the Financing of Risk course. This will help you build on your growing knowledge in the most effective way possible.

Topics covered:

- Introduction to Analyzing Risk
- Qualitative Analysis
- Quantitative Analysis: Tools
- Quantitative Analysis: Forecasting
- Cash Discounting Concepts
- Risk Analysis Applications (I)
- Risk Analysis Applications (II)

Control of Risk Course

Risk control is a core aspect of risk management. This course will give you added proficiencies in the risk control essentials, such as safety, alternative dispute resolution, employment practices, claims and crisis management, among many others.

Topics covered:

- Introduction to Controlling Risk

- Risk Control Fundamentals

- Risk Control and Mitigation I

- Risk Control and Mitigation II

- Claims Management

- Crisis Management

Financing of Risk Course

Financing of risk can be an intricate and complex task. In this course, you will compare the various financing options presented: insurance and non-insurance transfers, guaranteed cost plans, retro plans, dividend plans, pools, and various types of captives. You will learn how to deliver the cost of risk message to management in present value dollars. We recommend that this course follow Analysis of Risk.

Topics covered:

- Introduction to Financing Risk

- Quantitative Analysis: Tools and Methods

- Simple Transfer Options

- Loss-Sensitive Transfer Options

- Alternative Transfer Options

- Actuarial, Accounting, and Auditing Perspectives

- Case Study

Practice of Risk Management Course

This course consolidates what you have learned. It also helps you tackle the daily managerial and organizational requirements of risk managers and risk consultants.

Topics covered:

- Introduction to Implementing and Monitoring the Risk Management Process

- The Risk Manager

- Building Your Risk Management Team

- Information Technology for Risk Managers

- Allocating the Cost of Risk

- Due Diligence During Organizational Change

- Executive Risk

Emerging Trends
Case Study

A new case study is interwoven throughout each 20-hour course, with exercises throughout to reinforce the information. The same case study/application case will reappear in each CRM course, with content pertinent to subject matter, resulting in exposure to the practical application of a comprehensive risk management program.